*I*f 1995 was a preview of things to come, 1996 should be exceptional on both the PGA TOUR and Senior PGA TOUR.

My first full season as Commissioner produced some truly memorable moments: three victories apiece for Greg Norman and Lee Janzen, including THE PLAYERS Championship for Lee; Billy Mayfair's triumph in THE TOUR Championship after his earlier win at the Motorola Western Open; and first major titles for multiple winners Corey Pavin and Steve Elkington.

There was Ben Crenshaw capturing his second Masters, John Daly winning the British Open for his second major. Peter Jacobsen, Vijay Singh, Mark O'Meara and Fred Funk had two victories each. Peter won the AT&T Pebble Beach National Pro-Am and the Buick Invitational of California back-to-back, Vijay prevailed in playoffs at the Phoenix Open and the Buick Classic, where he also won a playoff in 1993.

Dave Stockton earned over $1 million for a record third consecutive season; Bob Murphy won four tournaments, matching the total for his first two Senior TOUR campaigns. Hale Irwin, still competing on the PGA TOUR, claimed two Senior TOUR titles.

Jim Colbert, Raymond Floyd, J. C. Snead, George Archer and Lee Trevino all were multiple winners; Trevino increased his Senior TOUR victory record total to 26.

Nick Faldo returned to the PGA TOUR and won at Doral, Jack Nicklaus claimed yet another title at The Tradition Presented by Scotts. David Graham joins the Senior TOUR ranks this year.

Speaking of Graham, he and Arnold Palmer will serve as captains for the second Presidents Cup Match, to be played in September at Robert Trent Jones Golf Club near Lake Manassas, VA. The United States has a score to settle after losing the Ryder Cup to Europe last year. The "Rest of the World" had better beware.

Who will be the David Duvals, Justin Leonards and Woody Austins joining the ranks of the world's best golfers in 1996? No matter what happens, fans of the PGA TOUR and Senior PGA TOUR will be treated to some of the finest golf our sport has to offer.

I hope you will be able to see such competition in person. But television offers an alternative.

Not only the PGA TOUR and Senior TOUR, but also the NIKE TOUR will be available right in your living room. More than 1,000 hours of pleasurable golf viewing, featuring the best the game has to offer.

This Viewers Guide will help maximize that pleasure: all the insights and inside information a golf fan can want, right at your fingertips!

I definitely expect that 1996 will be a special year along the PGA TOUR and Senior TOUR. We appreciate your support of all our tournaments and the charitable causes of our various events.

Enjoy the viewing!

Tim Finchem
Commissioner

THE PRESIDENTS CUP MATCH HIGH-LIGHT OF 1996 PGA TOUR SEASON

The United States has something to prove and the second Presidents Cup Match may be just the forum it needs.

In 1995, U.S. teams lost the Ryder Cup, Dunhill Cup and Walker Cup. The first two featured American members of the PGA TOUR, the latter is a biennial competition involving top amateur golfers.

No matter, the United States went 0-for-three of golf's most prominent team competitions.

The second Presidents Cup Match, coming up in September, may be an opportunity for U.S. redemption.

The Presidents Cup was created to give non-European professionals an international team match play competition opportunity. Played in non-Ryder Cup years, it features the best the "Rest of the World" has to offer.

A United States Team captained by Hale Irwin won the inaugural Presidents Cup Match in September, 1994. That event was contested at the Robert Trent Jones Golf Club near Lake Manassas, VA, site of this September's second Presidents Cup Match. The United States won 20-12.

Arnold Palmer succeeds Irwin as captain of the U.S. side, David Graham returns for a return engagement against the Americans. And while former President Gerald R. Ford served as Honorary Chairman for the inaugural, another former Chief Executive and equally avid golfer, George Herbert Walker (as in Walker Cup) Bush, is performing that role this year.

Ten members of the U.S. Team will be selected using a system based on the official PGA TOUR money list. Players receive one point for each dollar earned in 1995 and two points per dollar earned from the 1996 Mercedes Championships through the NEC World Series of Golf. Two others will be captain's choices, as will two members of the International Team. Ten players for the International side will be chosen on the basis on the Sony World Rankings, which go to a two-year point system effective January 1, 1996.

If the teams had been named following the 1995 season, they would have looked like the following (minus captain's choices, but with 15 possibles listed):

U. S. Team		International Team	
1. Billy Mayfair	1,543,192	1. Greg Norman	22.21
2. Lee Janzen	1,378,966	2. Nick Price	15.83
3. Corey Pavin	1,340,079	3. Ernie Els	15.81
4. Davis Love III	1,111,999	4. Steve Elkington	10.72
5. Peter Jacobsen	1,075,057	5. Jumbo Osaki	10.47
6. Jim Gallagher, Jr.	1,057,241	6. Vijay Singh	8.68
7. Mark OíMeara	914,129	7. David Frost	7.64
8. David Duval	881,436	8. Mark McNulty	6.23
9. Payne Stewart	866,219	9. Michael Campbell	5.26
10. Mark Calcavecchia	843,552	10. Frank Nobilo	4.72
11. Tom Lehman	830,231	11. Robert Allenby	4.52
12. Jay Haas	822,259	12. Peter Senior	4.50
13. Scott Simpson	795,798	13. Craig Parry	4.49
14. Scott Hoch	792,643	14. Brett Ogle	4.08
15. Bob Tway	787,348	15. Tommy Nakajima	3.99

The actual competition runs over three days; the 1996 dates will be September 13-15. Ten matches (five foursomes and five four-ball matches) will be played each of the first two days, and each member of the two 12-man squads must play every day.

Twelve singles matches involving all players will be contested the final Sunday. All matches will be played to conclusion.

All matches are worth one point each for a total of 32 points. If a Presidents Cup Match is deadlocked at the end of singles competition, a sudden-death playoff will be held between two players designated in advance by the captains.

Charity was the ultimate winner at the 1994 Presidents Cup Match and will be again in 1996. Net revenues are divided into equal shares, which the captains and players designate for charities or golf-related projects of their choice.

Contributions in their names are made through PGA TOUR Charities, Inc. The inaugural Presidents Cup raised a total of $650,000 for individual charities.

In announcing the charity amount, Commissioner Tim Finchem said: "The first Presidents Cup experience truly was a positive one, made even more so by the charity involvement of the participants. We look forward to the second Presidents Cup in 1996, along with the generation of additional dollars for charities worldwide."

We would like to express or gratitude and thanks to the following for their help in developing this Edition.

ART DIRECTION AND COURSE GRAPHICS
Golf Guide Group, INC.
The Design Company

COVER
Photograph courtesy PGA TOUR INC.

PRINTING
Performance Printing, Inc. Charlotte, NC

We hope you enjoy this expanded Edition of
The Viewers Guide

WinSport Productions,LC
Creative Marketing Solutions
10033 West Sawgrass Drive
Ponte Vedra, Florida 32082
Phone (904)-273-6394
Fax (904)273-9711

ISBN: 09631259-3-1
Library of Congress Cataloging in Publication Card Number: 91-091348
Main Entry Under Title: The 1995 Viewers Guide To The PGA TOUR
1. McClelland, Whitney
Copyright 1995 by GolfGuide Group. All rights reserved.
No part of the contents of this book may be reproduced by any means
without the written permission of the publisher.
Published in 1995 by WinSport,LC, Ponte Vedra, Florida 32082
For distribution and ordering information contact:
WinSport,LC, 1-800-4 PGA TOUR.

TABLE OF CONTENTS

TABLE OF CONTENTS

JANUARY

4-7	**Mercedes Championship**	
	LaCosta Resort & Spa, Carlsbad, California	ABC/ESPN
11-14	**Nortel Open**	
	Tucson National Golf Club, Tucson, Arizona	ESPN
18-21	**Bob Hope Chrysler Classic**	
	Indian Wells/Indian Ridge/Bermuda Dunes/LaQuinta,	
	Indian Wells, California	NBC
25-28	**Phoenix Open**	
	TPC of Scottsdale, Phoenix, Arizona	ESPN

FEBRUARY

1-4	**AT&T Pebble Beach National Pro-Am**	
	Pebble Beach/Spy Glass/Poppey Hills, Pebble Beach, California	CBS/USA
8-11	**Buick Invitational of California**	
	Torrey Pines Golf Courses, LaJolla, California	NBC
15-18	**United Airlines Hawaiian Open**	
	Waialae Country Club, Honolulu, Hawaii	
22-25	**Nissan Open**	
	Riviera Country Club, Pacific Palisades, California	CBS/USA
29-Mar 3	**Doral-Ryder Open**	
	Doral Resort & Country Club, Miami, Florida	CBS

MARCH

7-10	**Honda Classic**	
	TPC at Eagle Trace, Coral Springs, Florida	NBC
14-17	**Bay Hill Classic**	
	Bay Hill Club & Lodge, Orlando, Florida	NBC
21-24	**Freeport-McDermott**	
	English Turn Golf & Country Club, New Orleans, Louisiana	NBC
26-31	**The Players Championship**	
	TPC at Sawgrass, Ponte Vedra, Florida	NBC

APRIL

4-7	**BellSouth Classic**	
	Atlanta Country Club, Marietta, Georgia	CBS/ESPN
11-14	**The Masters**	
	Augusta National Golf Club, Augusta, Georgia	CBS/USA
18-21	**MCI Classic**	
	Harbour Town Golf Links, Hilton Head Island, South Carolina	CBS
25-28	**Kmart Greater Greensboro Open**	
	Forest Oaks Country Club, Greensboro, North Carolina	CBS/USA

MAY

2-5	**Shell Houston Open**	
	TPC at The Woodlands, The Woodlands, Texas	ABC
9-12	**Bryon Nelson Classic**	
	TPC at Four Seasons-Las Colinas, Irving, Texas	ABC
16-19	**MasterCard Colonial**	
	Colonial Country Club, Fort Worth, Texas	CBS/USA
23-26	**Kemper Open**	
	TPC at Avenel, Potomac, Maryland	CBS
30-Jun 2	**Memorial Tournament**	
	Muirfield Village Golf Club, Dublin, Ohio	ABC

JUNE

J6-9	**Buick Classic**	
	Westchester Country Club, Rye, New York	CBS/USA
13-16	**96th Mens U.S. Open Championship**	
	Oakland Hills Country Club, Birmingham, Michigan	NBC/ESPN
20-23	**Federal Express St. Jude Classic**	
	TPC at Southwind, Memphis, Tennessee	CBS
27-30	**Canon Greater Hartford Open**	
	TPC at River Highlands, Cromwell, Connecticut	CBS

JULY

J4-7	**Motorola Western Open**	
	Cog Hill Golf Club, Lemont, Illinois	CBS/USA
11-14	**Michelob Golf Classic**	
	The River Course at Kingsmill Golf Club, Williamsburg, Virginia	ESPN
18-21	**British Open**	
	Royal Lytham & St. Anne's, Blackpool, England	ABC
18-21	**Deposit Guaranty Classic**	
	Annandale Golf Club, Madison, Mississippi	
25-28	**New England Classic**	
	Pleasant Valley Country Club, Sutton, Massachusettes	

AUGUST

A1-4	**Buick Open**	
	Warwick Hills Golf & Country Club, Grand Blanc, Michigan	CBS
8-11	**PGA Championship**	
	Vahalla Golf Club, Louisville, Kentucky	CBS/TBS
15-18	**Sprint International**	
	Castle Pines Golf Club, Castle Rock, Colorado	CBS/ESPN
22-25	**NEC World Series of Golf**	
	Firestone Country Club, Akron, Ohio	CBS/USA
29-Sept1	**Greater Milwaukee Open**	
	Brown Deer Park, Milwaukee, Wisconsin	ABC

SEPTEMBER

S5-8	**Bell Canadian Open**	
	Glen Abbey Golf Club, Oakville, Ontario, Canada	ESPN
12-15	**Quad Cities Open**	
	Oakwood Country Club, Moline, Illinois	GOLF CHNL
12-15	**President's Cup**	
	Robert Trent Jones Golf Club, Lake Manassas, Virginia	ESPN
19-22	**B.C. Open**	
	En-Joie Golf Club, Endicott, New York	
26-29	**Buick Challenge**	
	Callaway Gardens Resort, Pine Mountain, Georgia	ESPN

OCTOBER

O3-6	**Las Vegas Invitational**	
	TPC Summerlin, Las Vegas, Nevada	ESPN
10-13	**LaCantera Texas Open**	
	LaCantera Golf Club, San Antonio, Texas	TBA
17-20	**Walt Disney World/ Oldsmobile Classic**	
	Four Courses, Lake Buena Vista, Florida	TBA
24-27	**PGA TOUR Championship**	
	Southern Hills Country Club, Tulsa, Oklahoma	ABC/ESPN

NOVEMBER

n7-10	**Lincoln-Mercury Kapalua International**	
	The Plantation Course, Kapalua Resort, Maui, Hawaii	ABC/ESPN
14-17	**Franklin Templeton Shark Shoot-out**	
	Sherwood Country Club, Thousand Oaks, California	CBS/ESPN
21-24	**The World Cup of Golf**	
	TBA	TBA
30-Dec 1	**The Skins Game**	
	Rancho LaQuinta Golf Club, LaQuinta, California	ABC

DECEMBER

D5-8	**J.C. Penney Classic**	
	Copperhead Course at Innisbrook Hilton Resort, Tarpon Springs, Florida	ABC/ESPN
12-15	**Diners Club Matches**	
	Jack Nicklaus Resort Course at PGA West, LaQuinta, California	ABC/ESPN
Jan 3-5	**Andersen Consulting World Championship of Golf**	
	Grayhawk Golf Club, Scottsdale, Arizona	ESPN

JANUARY

5-7	Open	ESPN
12-14	Open	
19-21	Senior Tournament of Champions	
	Dorado Beach Golf Club, Dorado Beach, Puerto Rico	
27-28	Senior Skins Game	
	Mauna Lani Resort, Kohala Coast, Hawaii	ABC

FEBRUARY

2-4	Royal Caribbean Classic	
	The Links at Key Biscayne, Key Biscayne, Florida	ESPN
9-11	The Greater Naples Challenge	
	Lely Resort & Golf Club, Naples, Florida	ESPN
16-18	The GTE Suncoast Classic	
	TPC of Tampa Bay, Tampa Bay, Florida	ESPN
23-25	Senior Golf Classic Presented by Business Week	
	Sarasota, Florida	TBA

MARCH

1-3	FHP Healthcare Classic	
	Ojai Valley Inn & Country Club, Ojai, California	ESPN
4-5	Senior Slam	
	TBA TBA	TBS
15-17	Toshiba Senior Classic	
	Newport Beach Country Club, Costa Mesa, California	ESPN
'22-24	Liberty Mutual Legends of Golf	
	TPC Stadium at PGA WEST, LaQuinta, California	ABC
28-31	SBC Presents the Dominion Seniors	
	San Antonio, Texas	TBA

APRIL

4-7	The Traditions	
	Presented by Scotts Cochise Course, The Golf Course at Desert Mountain, Scottsdale, Arizona	ESPN
11-14	Open	
18-21	PGA Senior Championship	
	The Champion Course, PGA National Resort & Spa Palm Beach Gardens, Florida	NBC/USA
26-28	Las Vegas Senior Classic	
	TPC at Summerlin, Las Vegas, Nevada	ESPN

MAY

3-5	World Senior Invitational	
	TPC at Piper Glen, Charlotte, North Carolina	ESPN
10-12	Nationwide Championship Golf Club of Georgia	
	Alpharetta, Georgia	ESPN
17-19	Cadillac NFL Classic	
	Upper Montclair Country Club, Clifton, New Jersey	ESPN
24-26	BellSouth Senior Classic at Opryland	
	Springhouse Golf Club at Opryland Hotel, Nashville, Tennessee	NBC
31-Jun 2	Bruno's Memorial Classic	
	Greystone Golf Club, Birmingham, Alabama	

JUNE

7-9	Dallas Reunion Pro-Am	
	Oak Cliff Country Club, Dallas, Texas	
14-16	Quicksilver Classic	
	Quicksilver Country Club, Pittsburg, Pennslyvania	
21-23	Bell Atlantic Classic	
	Chester Valley Golf Club, Malvern, Pennsylvania	ESPN
28-30	Kroger Senior Classic	
	The Golf Center at Kings Island, Mason, Ohio	ESPN

JULY

4-7	**U.S. Senior Open** Canterbury Golf Club, Cleveland, Ohio	NBC/ESPN
11-14	**Ford Senior Players Championship** TPC of Michigan, Dearborn, Michigan	ABC/ESPN
19-21	**Burnet Senior Classic** Bunker Hill Golf Club, Coon Rapids, Minnesota	
26-28	**Ameritech Senior Open** Kemper Lakes Country Club, Long Grove, Illinois	CBS

AUGUST

2-4	**VFW Senior Open** Loch Lloyd Country Club, Belton, Missouri	ESPN
9-11	**First of America Classic** Egypt Valley Country Club Ada. Michigan	
16-18	**Northville Long Island Classic** Meadow Brook Country Club, Jericho, New York	ESPN
23-25	**Bank of Boston Senior Classic** Nashawtuc Country Club, Concord, Massachusetts	ESPN
29-Sept1	**Franklin Quest Championship** Park Meadows Country Club, Park City, Utah	

SEPTEMBER

6-8	**Northwest Classic** Inglewood Country Club, Seattle, Washington	
13-15	**Bank One Senior Classic** Kearney Hill Links, Lexington, Kentucky	
20-22	**Brickyard Crossing Championship** Brickyard Crossing Golf Club, Indianapolis, Indiana	
27-29	**Vantage Championship** Tanglewood Park, Clemmons, North Carolina	ESPN

OCTOBER

4-6	**Ralphs Senior Classic** Rancho Park Golf Course Los Angeles. California	
11-13	**The Transamerica** Silverado Country Club, Napa, California	
18-20	**Raley's Senior Gold Rush** Rancho Murieta Country Club, Sacramento, California	
25-27	**Hyatt Regency Maui Kaanapali Classic** Royal Kaanapali Golf Course, Maui, Hawaii	ESPN

NOVEMBER

1-3	**Emerald Coast Classic** The Moors, Pensacola, Florida	
7-10	**Energizer Senior TOUR Championship** The Dunes Golf and Beach Club, Myrtle Beach, South Carolina	ESPN
17	**Open**	
24	**Open**	

DECEMBER

6-8	**Open**	
9-15	**Diners Club Matches** PGA West Jack Nicklaus Resort Course, LaQuinta, California	ABC
9-15	**Lexus Challenges** PGA West Jack Nicklaus Resort Course, LaQuinta, California	NBC

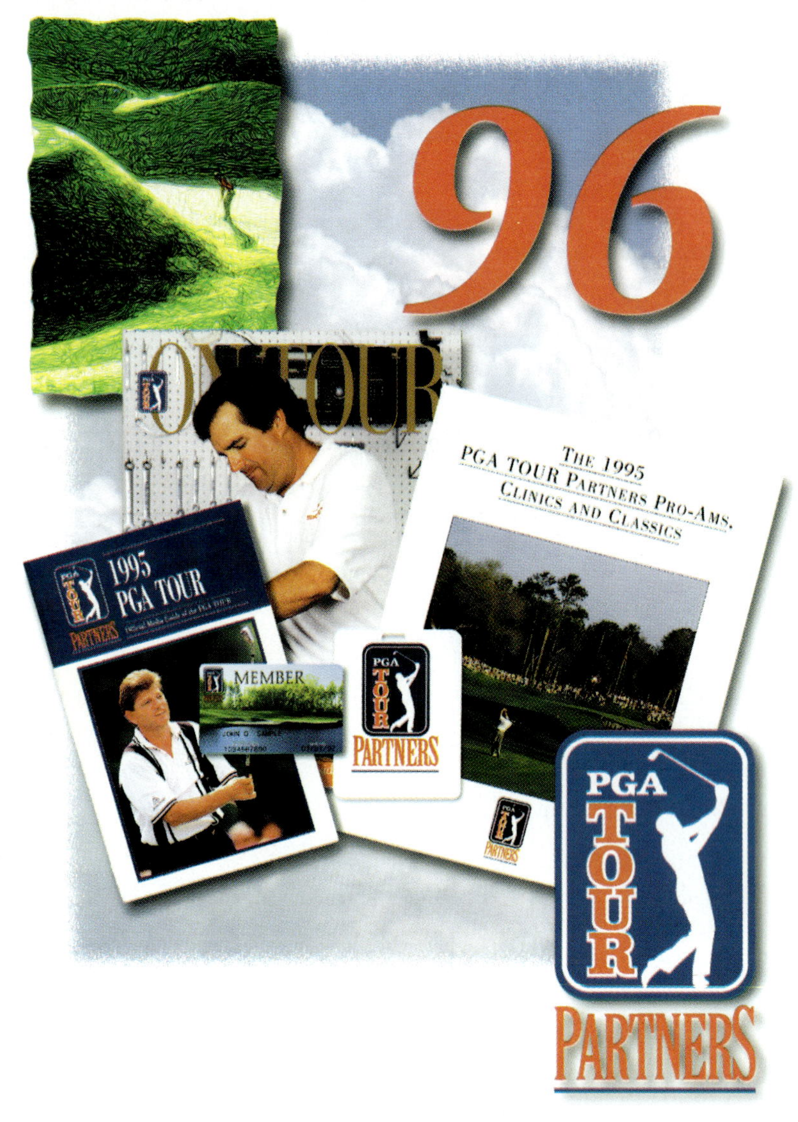

PGA TOUR Partners '96

PGA TOUR Partners Puts You Closer To The Action!

While TOUR Professionals fight for years to earn their spot on the TOUR, you can become part of the PGA TOUR with just one phone call. When you become a PGA TOUR Partner you become a member of the most exclusive club in golf -- a chance to access information about the players, play tournament-style golf on TOUR courses, and attend a TOUR event free. If you love playing or watching golf, you'll love PGA TOUR Partners. With your exclusive annual membership, you'll receive:

- **A VIP Tournament Pass to a PGA TOUR event**
- **A full year of ON TOUR -- the magazine the pros read while they're on TOUR**
- **A personalized Partners bag tag to show your special clout**
- **A personalized membership card giving you access to special Partners events throughout the year**
- **Invitations to play in Partners Classics golf tournaments and Access Days on courses TOUR players play**

This exclusive Partners membership can be yours only by calling **1-800-PGA-TOUR** and joining today! A full year membership is $29.95 (plus $4.95 shipping and handling).

Special offer: *Call today and mention the Viewers Guide and receive the 1996 PGA TOUR Media Guide absolutely free!*

THE PGA TOUR SHOP.

MAKE IT YOUR BEST DRIVE.

PGA TOUR SHOPS FEATURE EXCLUSIVE MERCHANDISE FROM 26 PGA TOUR EVENTS.

PGA TOUR Shop, Dallas/Ft. Worth International Airport

PGA TOUR Tournament Merchandise Available:

- B.C. Open
- Bell Canadian Open
- BellSouth Classic
- Buick Challenge
- Buick Classic
- Buick Invitational of California
- Buick Open
- GTE Byron Nelson Classic
- Canon Greater Hartford Open
- Deposit Guaranty Golf Classic
- Federal Express St. Jude Classic
- Freeport-McMoRan Classic
- K Mart Greater Greensboro Open
- Kemper Open
- LaCantera Texas Open
- Las Vegas Invitational
- Motorola Western Open
- NEC World Series of Golf
- New England Classic
- Nissan Open
- Northern Telecom Open
- Presidents Cup
- Quad Cities Open
- Shell Houston Open
- THE PLAYERS Championship
- THE TOUR Championship

PGA TOUR SHOPS

Owned and Operated by The Paradies Shops, an Exclusive Licensee of the PGA TOUR.

Located in these International Airports:
Burbank - Glendale - Pasadena, Dallas/Ft. Worth, Detroit Metropolitan, Indianapolis, Jacksonville, Nashville, Pittsburgh, Sarasota, Savannah, St. Louis, Toronto, and coming soon...West Palm Beach, Reno/Tahoe, Tucson, and Vancouver

Located at these Select Shopping Malls:
Tyson's Corner - McClean, Va., Union Station - Washington, D.C., Perimeter Mall - Atlanta, GA

THE COURSE: LA COSTA RESORT AND SPA, CARLSBAD, CALIFORNIA

*T*he Mercedes Championship is an event that includes only the winners of the previous year's PGA TOUR® events. The field is thus small and elite. Each eligible player who enters the event is not only guaranteed a substantial check, but is also insured first-class treatment at La Costa Resort and Spa. This prestigious event starts the golf year off with an exciting competition of champions.

The tournament was inaugurated in 1953 in Las Vegas with a first prize of $10,000. In 1969, the tournament was moved to its present location of La Costa Resort and Spa in Carlsbad, California. The composite course designed by Dick Wilson features challenging rough, narrow fairways and well-bunkered greens, making La Costa one of the tougher challenges on the PGA TOUR®.

Dates:	January 4-7, 1996
Network:	ABC & ESPN
Times:	ESPN
	Fri 4:00-6:00 EST
	ABC
	Sat/Sun 3:00-6:00 EST
Yardage:	7,022
Par:	72
Slope:	142
Rating:	75.4
Total Purse:	$1,000,000
1st Prize:	$180,000
1995 Winner:	Steve Elkington
1995 Winning Score:	278 (69-71-71-67)
Principal Charitable Beneficiary:	Various
Charitable Benefits to Date:	$1.9 million in last 10 years
Ticket Information:	1-800-918-4653
Resort Information:	1-619-438-9111

1

Par 4
412 yards

A tough opening hole that can catch players off-guard. A left to right wind helps push drives towards the right rough. Three bunkers surround the small, round green.

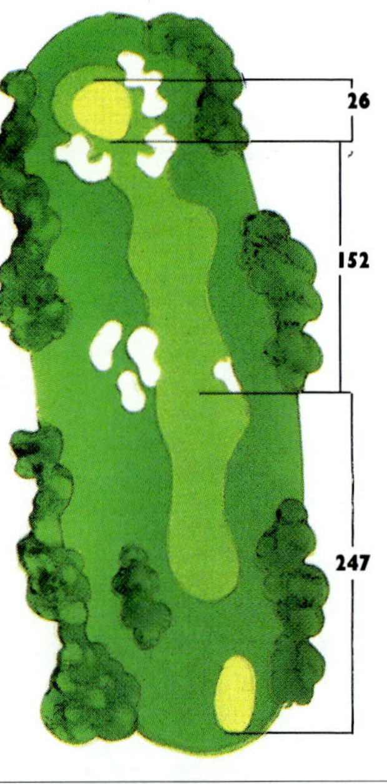

2

Par 5
526 yards

The longer hitters will play down the right middle of the fairway in an effort to shorten the second shot to the green. The gently sloping putting surface will yield many birdies.

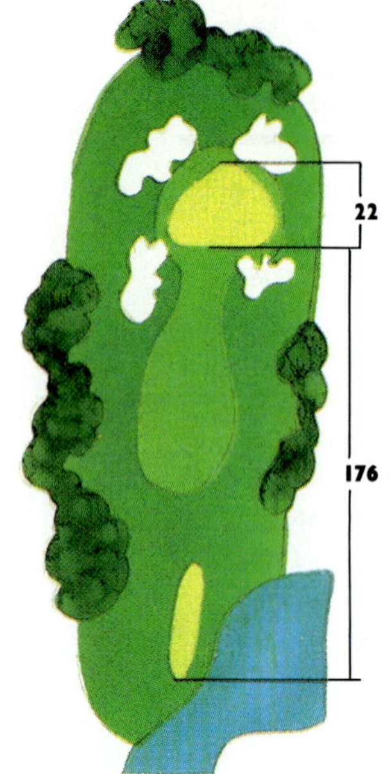

3

Par 3
187 yards

The green slopes back to front making it more desirable to be short of the pin. Birdies will be frequent on this hole.

4

Par 4
386 yards

The two bunkers on the outside corner of the dogleg provide the target from the tee. A fading drive will place the ball in prime position for the approach to the long green.

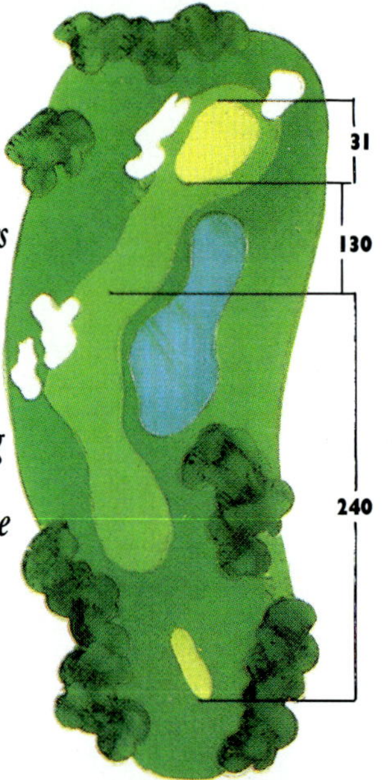

5

Par 4
446 yards

The drive must be hit long and accurate down the right side. The second shot will be with a fairway wood or long iron into the smallest green on the course.

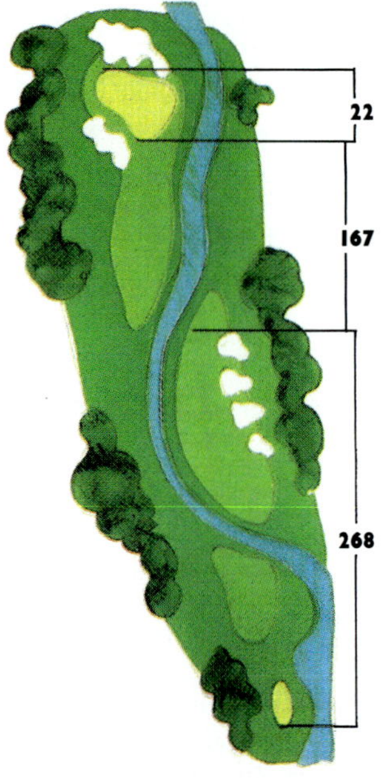

6

Par 4
365 yards

Birdies are as common as "others" on this short hole. An iron from the tee will leave an approach of about 150 yards into the long, well-bunkered green.

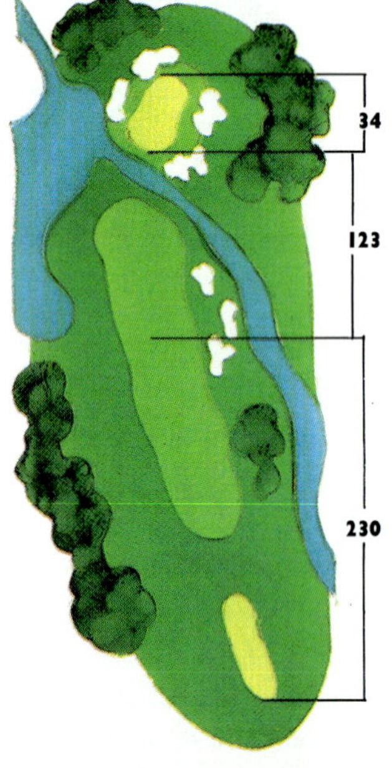

7

Par 3
188 yards

Water, sand and wind are the main ingredients on this hole. The short, wide green demands an accurate approach shot.

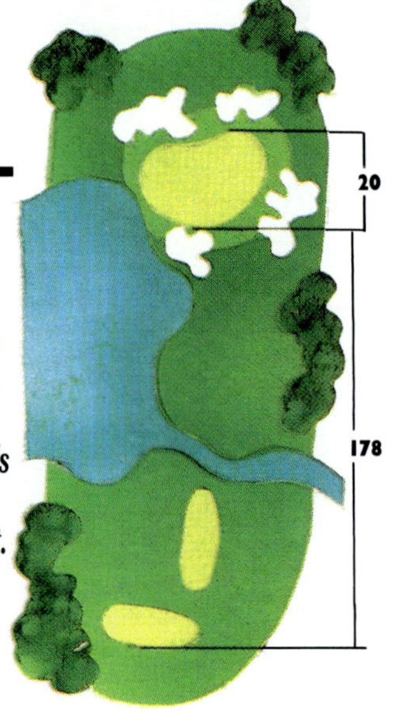

8

Par 4
398 yards

A narrow fairway dictates a straight drive. The kidney-shaped green invites the approach and allows for many birdies.

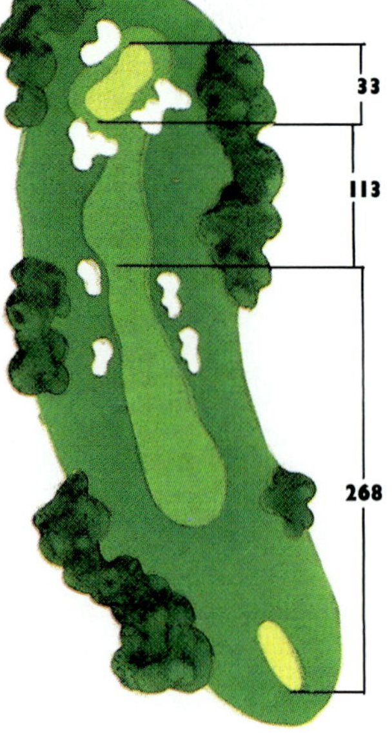

9

Par 5
538 yards

A long hole, especially into the wind. Three well hit shots are required to hit the long narrow green. Large bunkers encircle the putting surface.

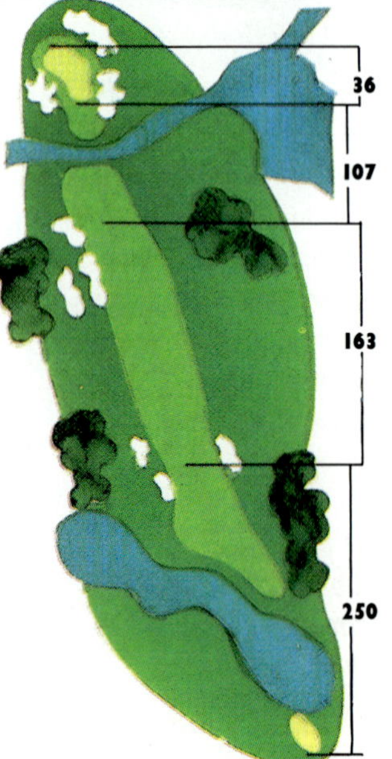

10

Par 4
450 yards

Three bunkers on the left and trees along the right define the edges of the narrow fairway. A large lake guards the path to the green — a tough hole.

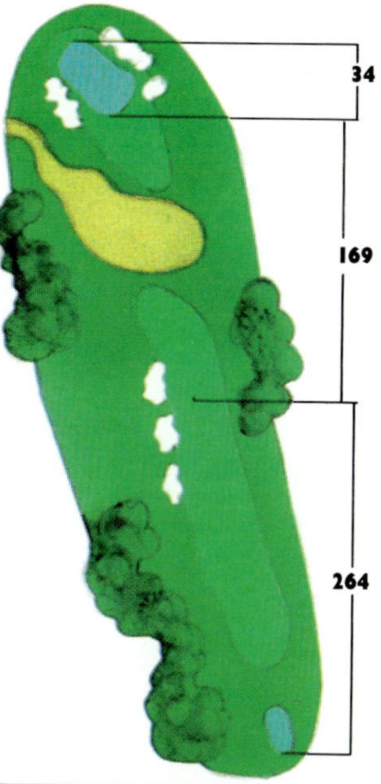

11

Par 3
180 yards

Club selection can be difficult on this par 3. The long narrow green can be deceiving from the tee. Four large bunkers surround the putting surface.

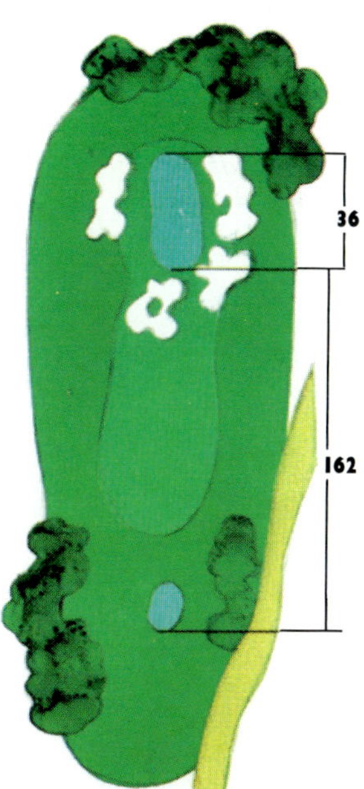

12

Par 5
541 yards

A long fading drive off the tee will set up for a second shot that may be able to reach the green. The putting surface slopes gently — most close putts are makeable.

13

Par 4
410 yards

The trees on both sides of the fairway can make this a difficult hole. The kidney-shaped green is set tightly among the bunkers and trees.

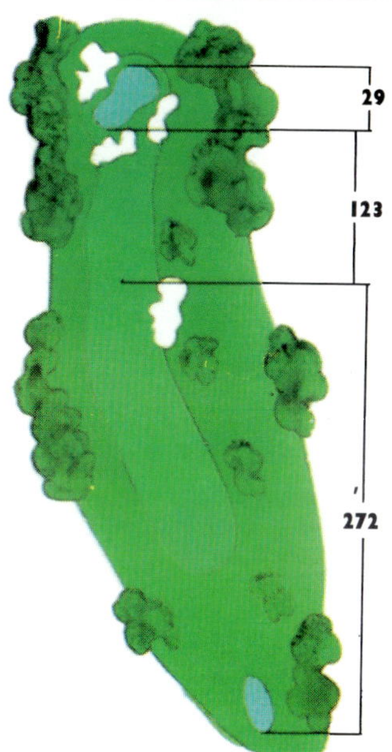

14

Par 3
204 yards

A prevailing breeze from the left will make tee shots difficult. The flat green will allow putts to drop if the ball is hit true.

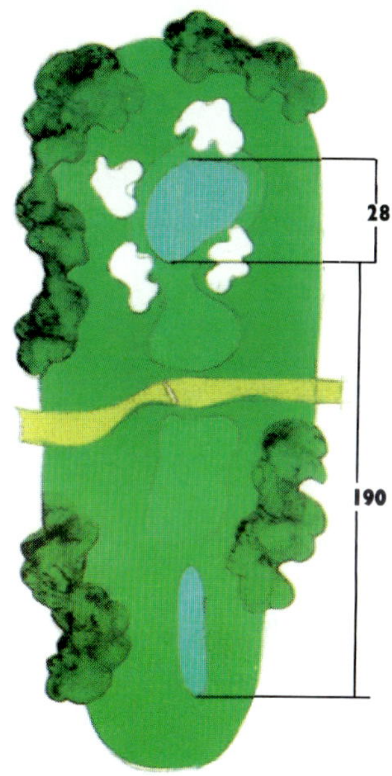

15

Par 4
378 yards

Only a mile to go to reach the clubhouse — but the mile is long. Fairway wood or long-iron off the tee will be follow-ed with a short-iron to the green — the last good chance for birdie.

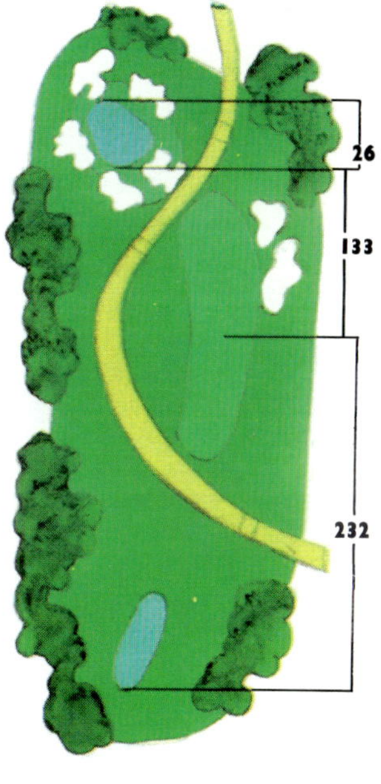

16

Par 4
423 yards

First fairway without a bunker along the side. The length is amplified with the prevailing wind against the players. A club or two extra on the approach is advised.

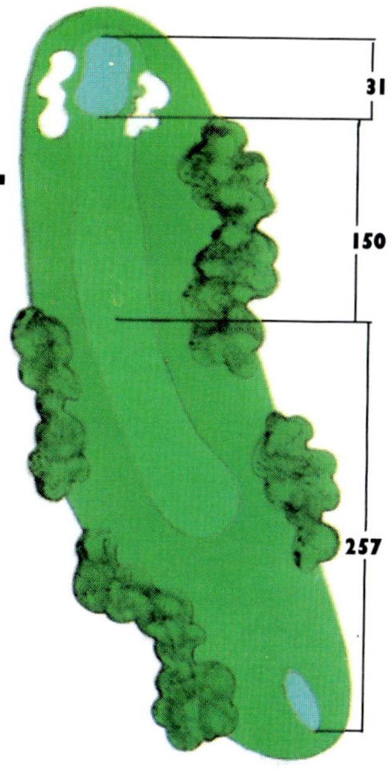

17

Par 5
569 yards

The wind does not help on this hole — three long shots are re-quired to reach the putting surface. Players will be playing this hole conser-vatively for the par 5.

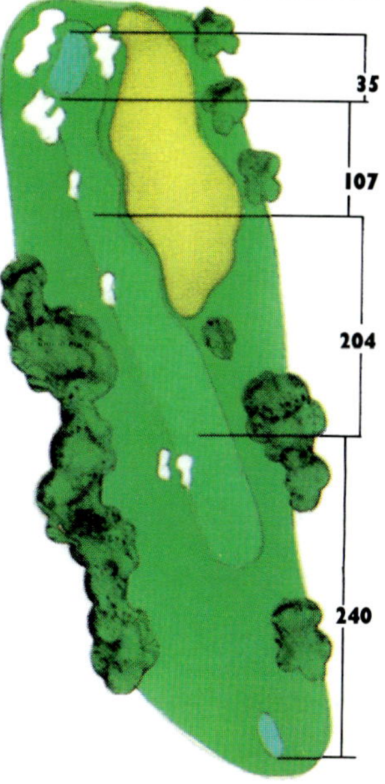

18

Par 4
421 yards

As the championship comes down to the last hole, watch for the players playing safely to the heart of the elevated, shallow green. Birdies can clinch the title.

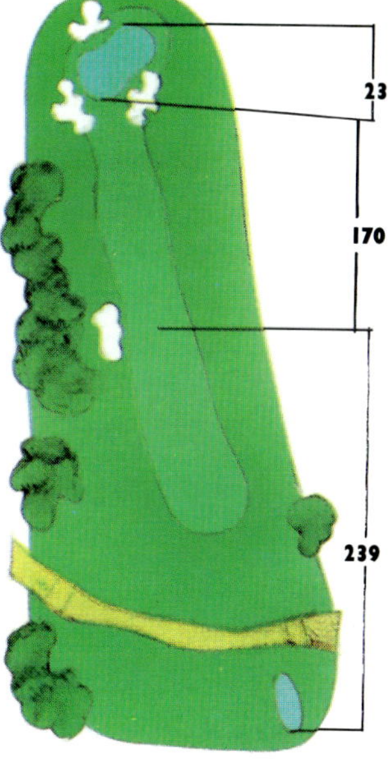

THE COURSE: TUCSON NATIONAL GOLF AND CONFERENCE RESORT, TUCSON, ARIZONIA

*T*he theme for the 1996 Nortel Open is "Links to the Future" and it marks the eighth year that Nortel, a telecommunications manufacturer and the world's leading supplier of fully digital communications systems, has served as the event's title sponsor. This year marks the fifth purse increase to $1,250,000.

The tournament, that began in 1945, is the ninth oldest on the PGA TOUR®. The event has earned a reputation as the "Futurity Open", a launching pad for careers of young PGA TOUR® entrants and the resurgence of veterans.

Tucson continues to be a favorite stop for many PGA TOUR® professionals. Several have played in Tucson for more than 20 years and have witnessed the tournament's evolution to one of the most beautiful and exciting PGA TOUR® events.

Dates:	January 11-14, 1996
Network:	ESPN
Times:	Thur 4:00-6:00 EST
	Fri 3:30-5:30 EST
	Sat 7:30-9:30 EST
	Sun 5:00-7:00 EST
Yardage:	7,148
Par:	72
Slope:	136
Rating:	71.1
Total Purse:	$ 1,250,000
1st Prize:	$225,000
1995 Winner:	Phil Mickelson
1995 Winning Score:	269 (65-66-70-68)
Principal Charitable Beneficiary:	Youth Athletic Programs of Southern Arizona
Ticket Information:	1-800-882-7660 or 1-520-571-0400

1

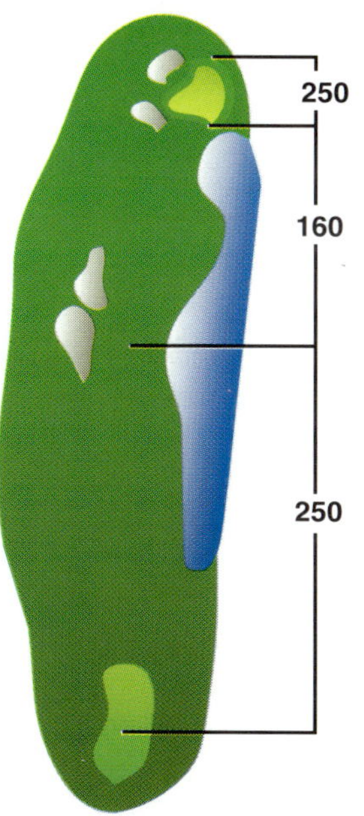

Par 4
410 yards

This is a rather mild opening to the round; medium length slight dogleg right par 4. This hole will undoubtedly yield many birdies, and set the stage for the front nine.

2

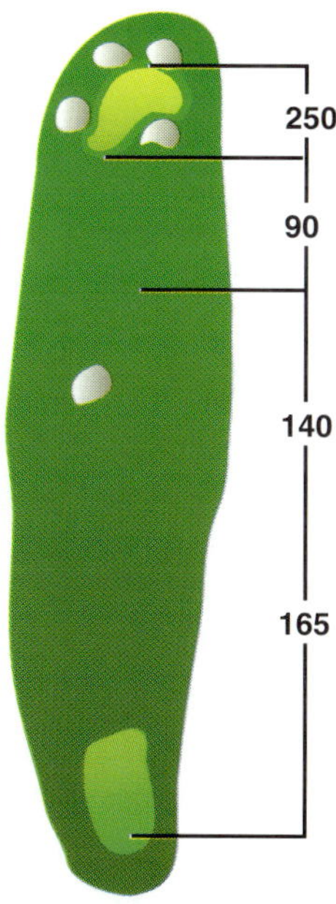

Par 5
495 yards

Par 5 will be reached in two by almost everyone. If players miss this green, however there are some difficult pitch shots.

3

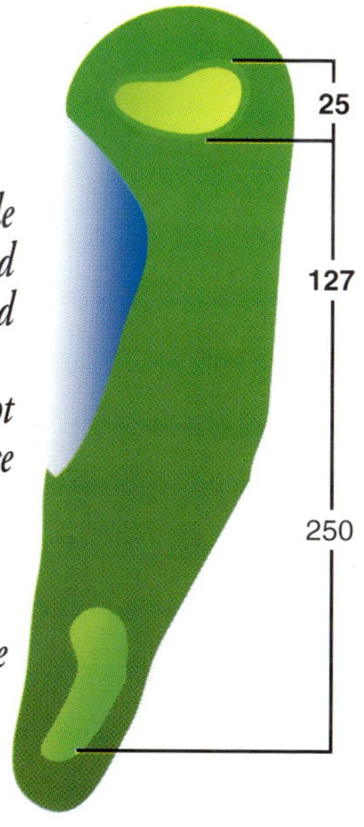

Par 4
377 yards

Shot par 4. This hole will usually be played with a fairway wood or long iron off the tee. An errant tee shot to the left can produce a great deal of tree trouble, and will make players think twice about the lake short of the green.

4

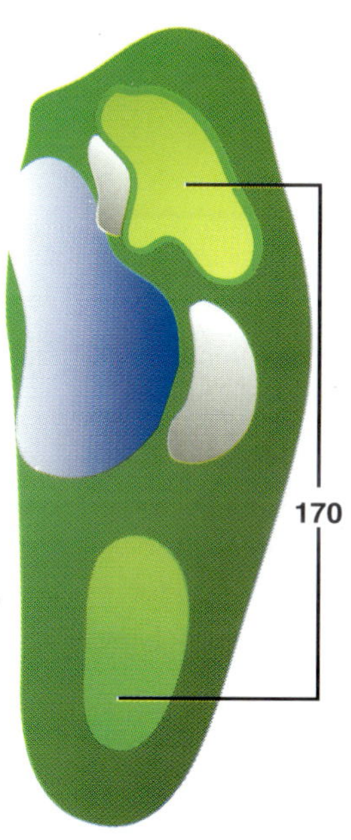

Par 3
170 yards

This hole is of only average length, but mounding behind and water short can cause problems for only an average tee shot. One rule of thumb on this hole: "Don't miss it left."

5

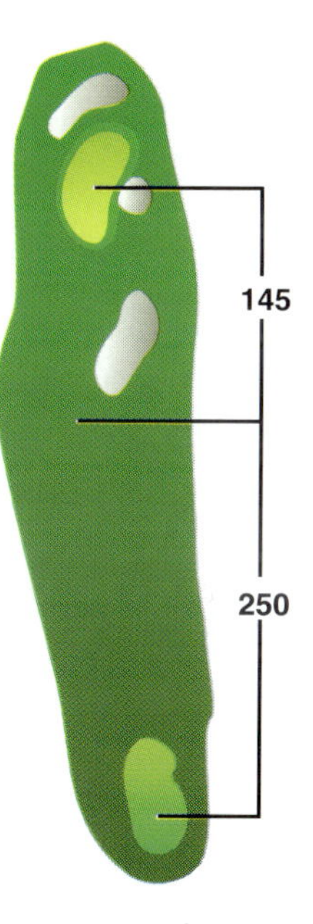

Par 4
395 yards

Dogleg right. Any tee shot to the right will present a great deal of difficulty. Bunkers guard both the front and back of this green, and club selection is extremely important on the second shot.

6

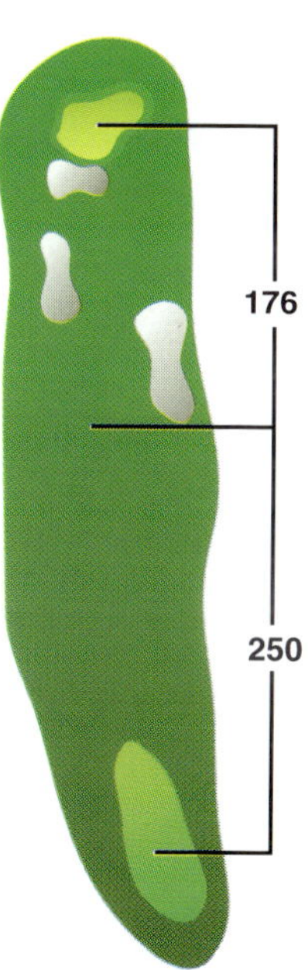

Par 4
426 yards

Longish par 4. Fairway bunkers protect the right side against an errant tee shot. The elevated green is well-protected with mounds and grass bunkers. A pin placement on the right side will produce a difficulty rating over par.

7

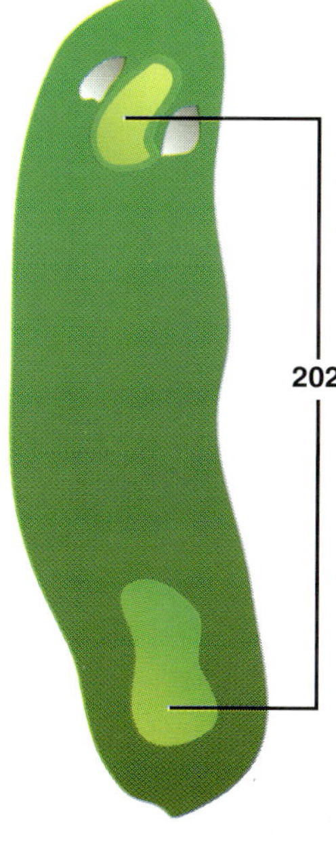

Par 3
202 yards

This hole can be treacherous if there is even a hint of wind. This is another elevated green which offers some very interesting pitch and lob shots if missed.

8

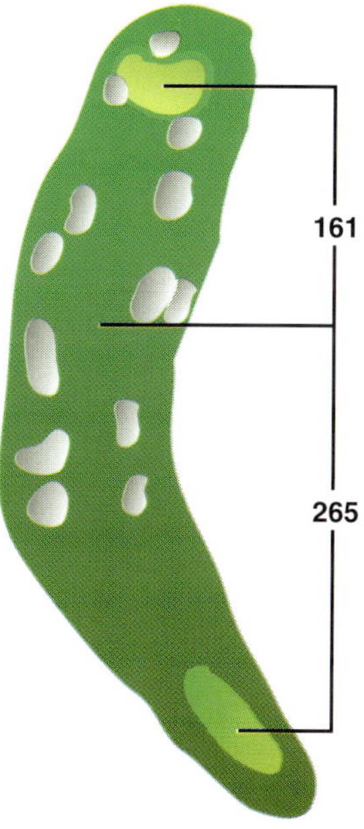

Par 5
528 yards

This dogleg right par 5 is reachable in two by the longer hitters. Risks must be taken to do so however, as the boundary cuts close to the right side of the fairway and the green is will-bunkered.

9

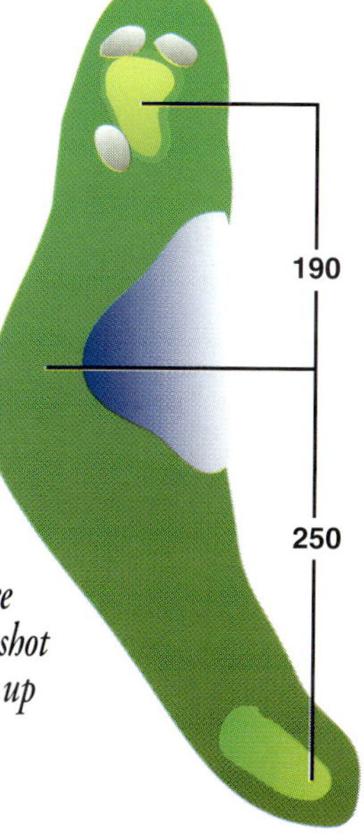

Par 4
440 yards

This is an outstanding finishing hole. A lake along the right side of the fairway cuts down your chances of getting away with anything but a well-placed tee shot. Players will lay up with a long iron, but are then faced with a second shot of more than 180 yards up the hill.

10

Par 4
364 yards

This par 5 hole will be difficult. It calls for an accurate draw off the tee with a large lake left and trees right. The green is once again elevated and a pin placement on the right side will call for a very accurate second shot.

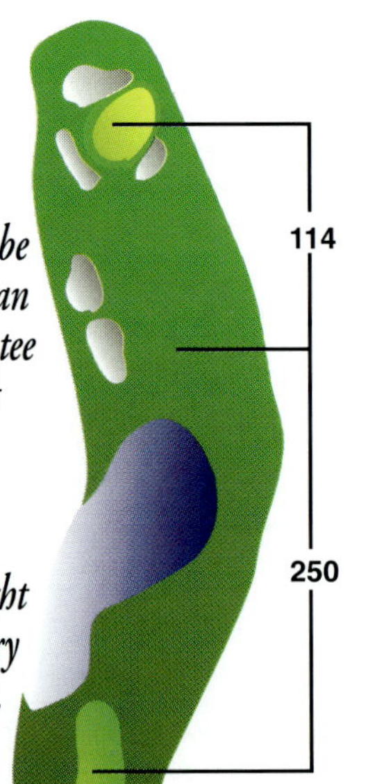

11

Par 5
525 yards

This hole is reachable in two, if a player chooses to challenge the lake and hit a driver down the left side of the fairway. The second shot must be played either short of the bunkers and left of the trees or over the trees. Regardless of a player's choice to lay up or go for it, the second shot will make or break this hole.

12

Par 3
182 yards

On this uphill par 3, the real trouble lies in the slope of the green. Any putt from behind the hole will be treacherously fast, so positioning the ball below the hole will be of paramount importance.

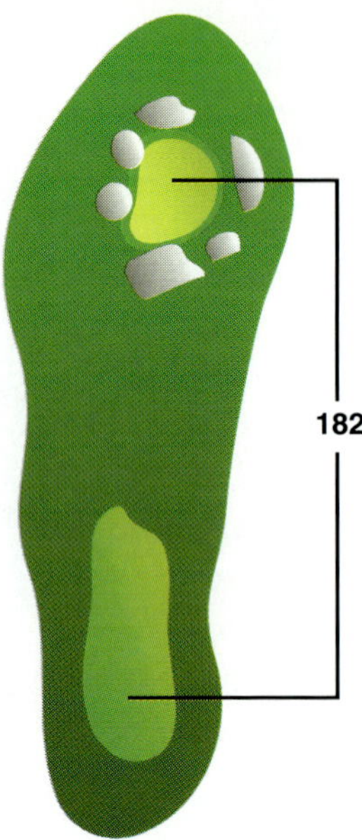

13

Par 4
417 yards

Downhill dogleg left. This hole should prove to be incredibly difficult for the professionals. A large tree strategically placed short of the green on the right side can come into play with a front right pin placement.

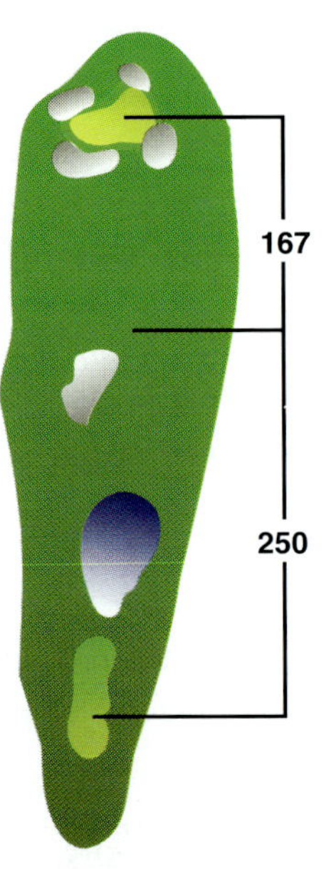

14

Par 4
435 yards

This 405-yard, par 4 requires two solid shots and a couple of putts for par. Nothing difficult or exciting, but don't let this one get away.

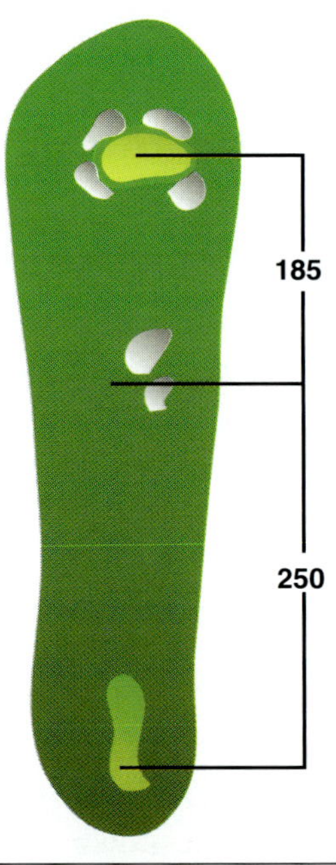

15

Par 5
561 yards

Only the longest of the PGA Tour professionals will even think of trying to reach this 600-plus par 5 in two. We will see a lot of birdies, with the benefits gained by the longer hitters.

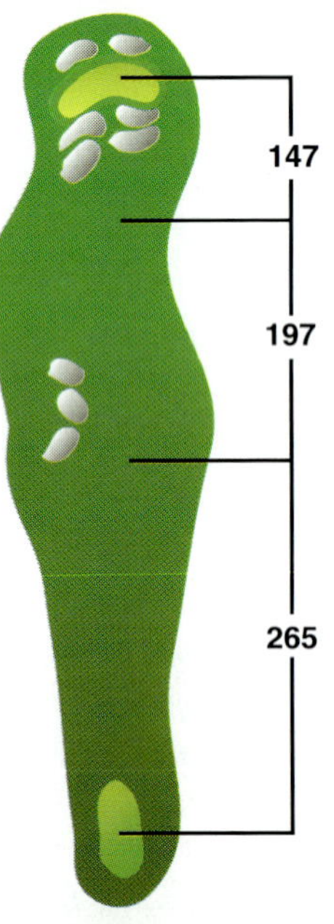

16

Par 4
436 yards

This dogleg right is protected by a tangled mess of bunkers along the right side. Most players will play their tee shots left center to open up this uphill green. With a bit of wind, this will test decision-making in club and shot selection.

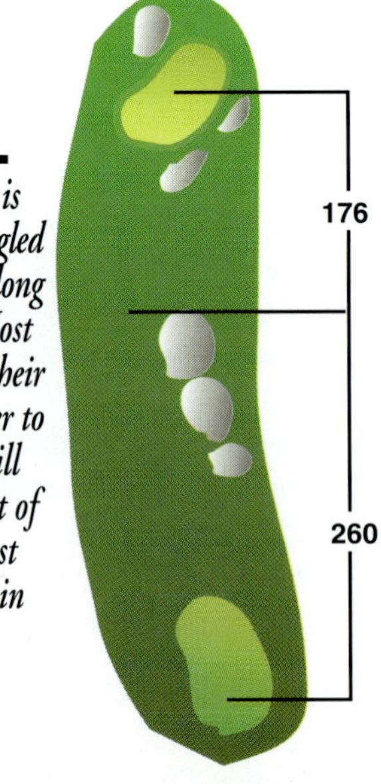

17

Par 3
210 yards

With the largest green on the course, This par 3 can play up to a four club difference from front to back. A missed shot to the left can be trouble and end up in the long greenside bunker, but a shot missed to the right can teach the boundary or the wash and prove disastrous.

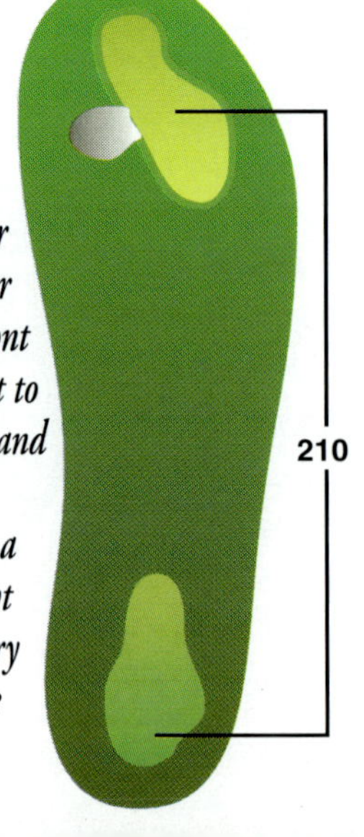

18

Par 4
458 yards

This hole has been characterized as one of the toughest finishing holes on the PGA Tour. The tee shot must be played long and left of the first lake but short of the water beyond. A well-placed tee shot will leave a long iron to a well-bunkered, and sloping green.

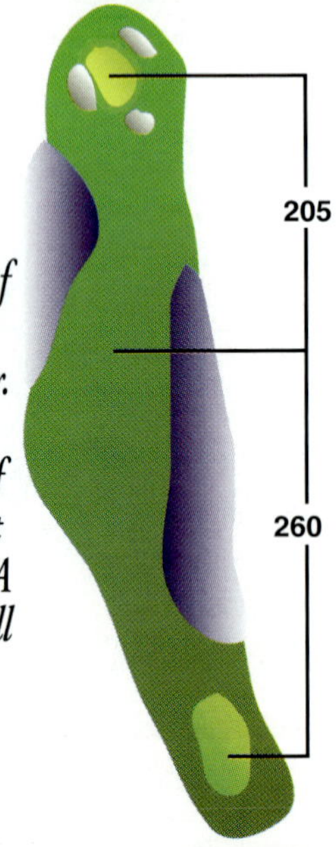

THE COURSE: INDIAN RIDGE COUNTRY CLUB,
PALM DESERT, CALIFORNIA

Bob Hope is the host of the desert classic that has been the most elegant golf outing for 31 years. The 90-hole format has golf professionals paired with amateurs for four rounds and a fifth round is played by professionals only, on the host course. The four courses that will be used for the 1996 Bob Hope Chrysler Classic include Tamarisk Country Club, Indian Wells Country Club, Bermuda Dunes Country Club and the host course, Indian Ridge Country Club.

Throughout its history, the event has been known for many exciting finishes decided by playoffs. Arnold Palmer was declared the first "King of the Desert" for playing in every Classic and winning 5 of them. The reigning champ is crowned "King" at the end of each year.

This year's host course has rolling fairways with sensational mountain views which beckon golf enthusiasts. It is one of Arnold Palmer's best, it is one of his most beautiful. Lush fairways and smooth bentgrass greens are accented by stately groves of citrus and palm trees and stunning water features on 11 holes.

Dates:	January 17-21
Network:	NBC
Times:	Sat 3:30 - 6:00 pm EST
	Sun 4:00 - 6:00 pm EST
Yardage:	7,037
Par:	72
Slope:	126
Rating:	71.0
Total Purse:	$1,200,000
1st Prize:	$234,000
1995 Winner:	Kenny Perry
1995 Winning Score:	335 (63,71,64,67,70)
Principal Charitable Beneficiary:	Eisenhoeer Medical Center
Charitable Benefits to Date:	Over $26 million in 35 years
Ticket Information:	619-346-8184

1

Par 4
418 yards

This formidable Par 4 will have players aiming down the left side to allow hillside to position their ball in the middle of the fairway. Good drives will leave short irons and wedges to this deep sloping green. Birdie is a real possibility.

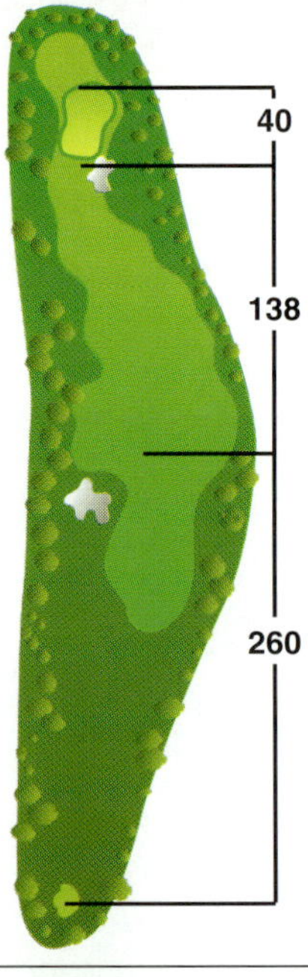

2

Par 4
408 yards

This dogleg right Par 4 will host many birdie chances. Players will have a variety of wedges for their second shot. This tricky and undulating green will play havoc with those approaches finishing above the hole.

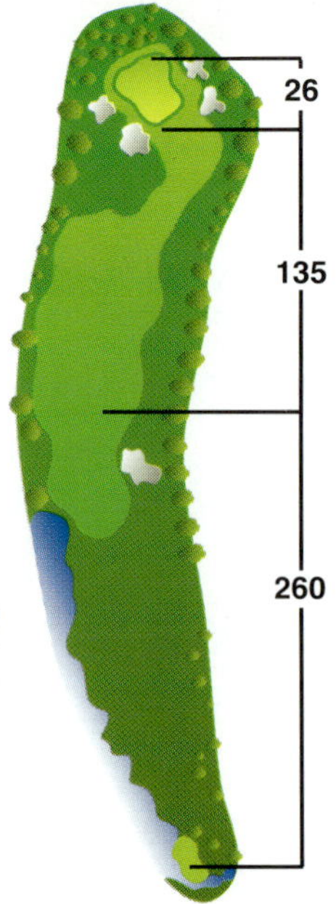

3

Par 5
609 yards

A blistering drive down the left side will allow the player a chance for the green. The usual play will be a driver, fairway wood or long iron and a short wedge to this well bunkered green.

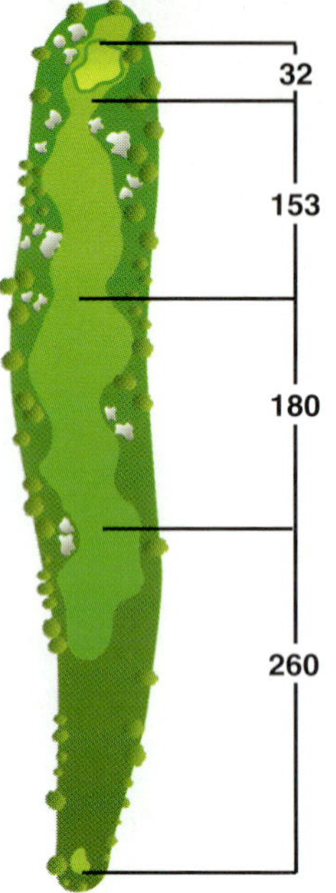

4

Par 4
427 yards

This #1 handicap hole requires a right to left shaped drive to avoid the fairway bunker on the leftside. Second shots short and right will require the skills of a magician to get up and down for par. A successful passage of Indian Ridges "Amen Corner" begins with a four here.

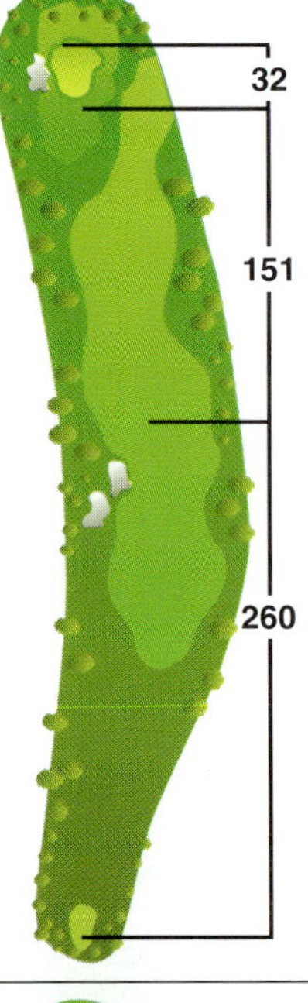

5

Par 3
209 yards

While this hole was named "Treasure Island" by the members, it's bounty is seldom realized. Usually playing into a prevailing wind this long par three will gobble up tee shots drifting the least bit to the right. With no lifeguard on duty the left portion of the green will see plenty of action.

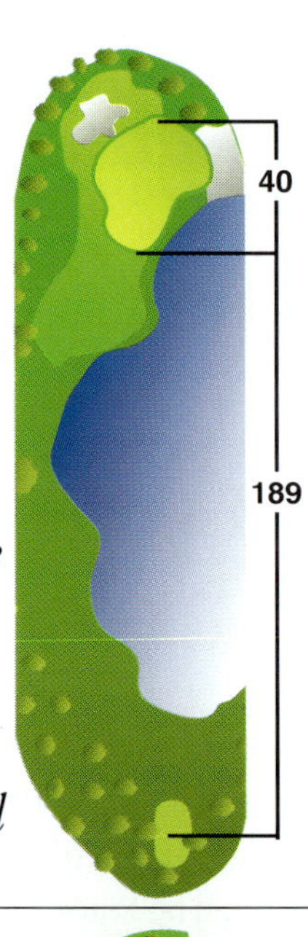

6

Par 4
430 yards

Local knowledge is a must here for drive placement. With a lake fronting the green and water down the left side even the bold and courageous will throw up the caution flag here. The two tiered beach front green yields very few birdies but plenty of "other".

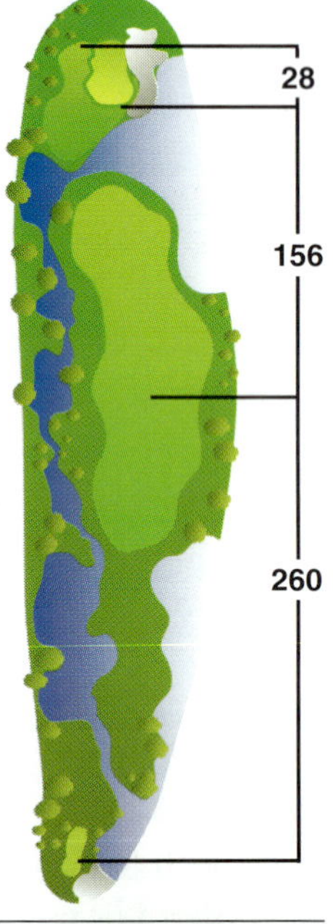

7

Par 5
524 yards

Bombs away. This reachable in two par five should see more shelling than Sarejevo. Par here will lose a shot to most of the field, however eagles are still on the endangered species list. A nice hole to regroup and make up some shots to par.

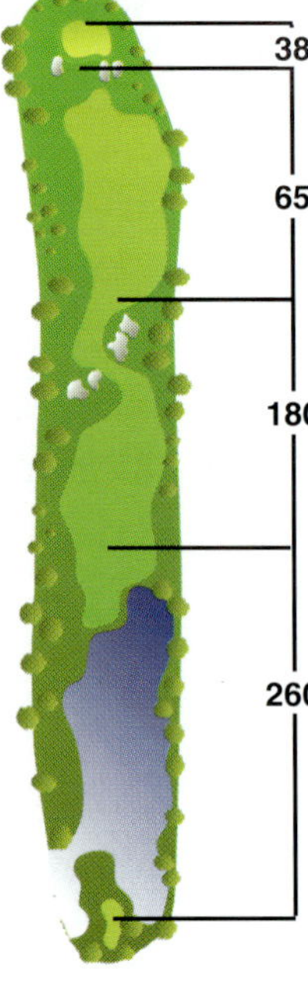

8

Par 3
231 yards

The 12,000 square feet of green becomes a smallish target on this "Palmer" signature hole. Guarded by water, a fairway wood or well struck long iron is the play to reach the dance floor. Though very picturesque, this hole provides endless entertainment for its residents and par here will set you up for a good outward half.

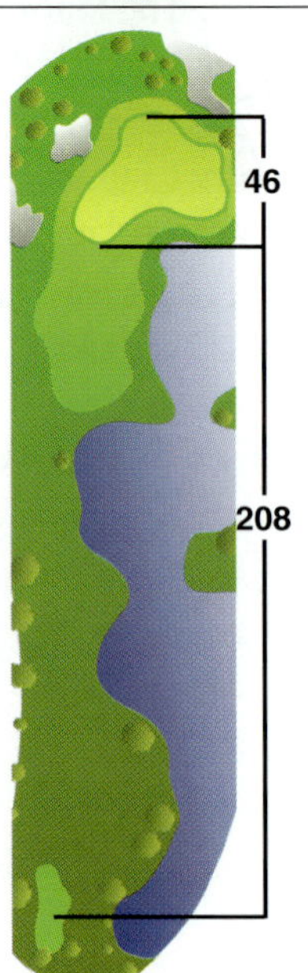

9

Par 4
368 yards

A fairway wood or long iron up the right side will give the player the best angle to the green for this short finishing hole. The green slopes dramatically from back to front, so approaches below the hole will give best birdie putts. Anywhere else and a three putt could pay you a visit.

10

Par 5
507 yards

This is a gorgeous Par 5. Reachable in two, the player must flirt with the lake fronting the green. Traps on the right and out-of-bounds left makes a long straight drive a premium. The lie in the fairway will dictate the second shot decision.

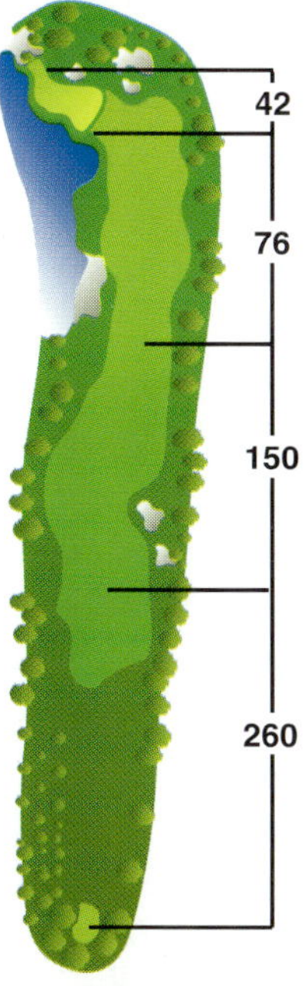

11

Par 3
165 yards

A slightly elevated tee gives you an unobstructed view of this demanding Par 3. A lake that fronts and wraps around the left of the green make club selection paramount. Well bunkered behind the green makes bailing out not an option. The slope in the middle will feed everything left.

12

Par 4
459 yards

Like #4, a long right to left shaped drive will set you up for a middle to long iron into a green that is well protected in front and on the left side with sand. This hole usually plays into the wind and provides an illusion of narrowness off the tee. The right fairway trap will see lots of racking.

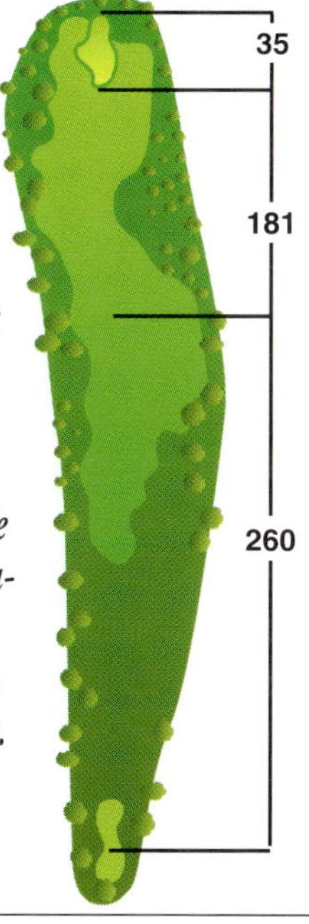

13

Par 4
335 yards

Arnie left no directions on how to play this apparently benign little Par 4. A good drive can get you on or near the green where you are faced with something resembling a slide. Playing to the middle of the green never seemed more prudent than now.

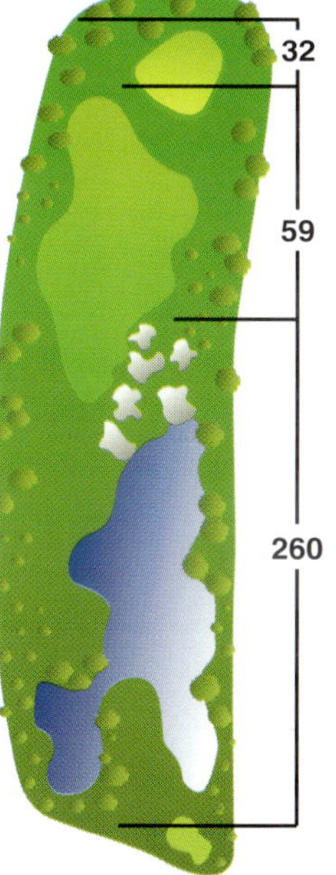

14

Par 4
424 yards

The fairway bunkers rarely come into play and make for a nice outline outline for this straight away Par 4. Two good shots will provide decent birdie opportunities on this relatively flat putting serface. The players oun imagination might be the only trouble encountered

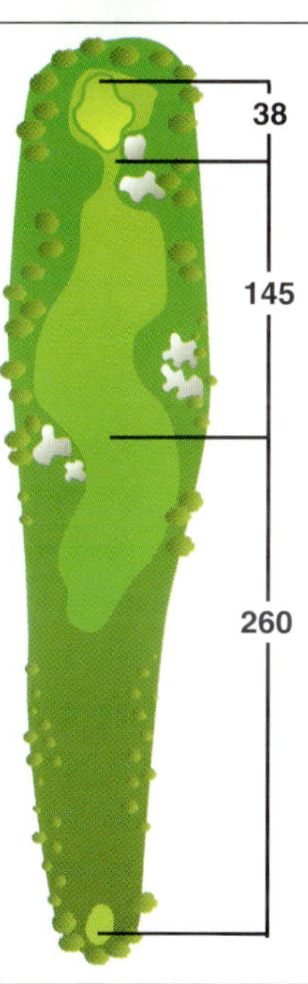

15

Par 5
530 yards

A dogleg right, this hole can be shortened by the player willing to risk the out of bounds on the right. The second shot must be high and soft or short and running. This green will not accept anything else. Water down the entire left side will force many layups and bunkers in front and behind the green will help remind the player that risk is not always rewarded.

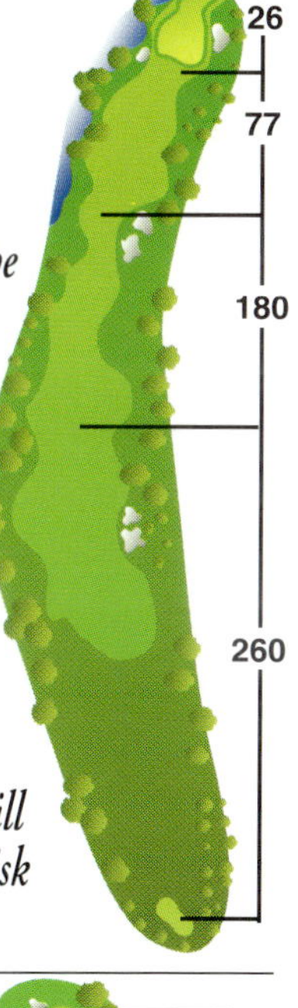

16

Par 4
452 yards

Lenght is a big requirement on this hole. The drive finding the middle of the fairway will leave a middle to short iron remaining to a green narrow in depth but generous in width. With the pin tucked left this makes for one of the most difficult holes played. Options here are many, though the right side of the green is very popular.

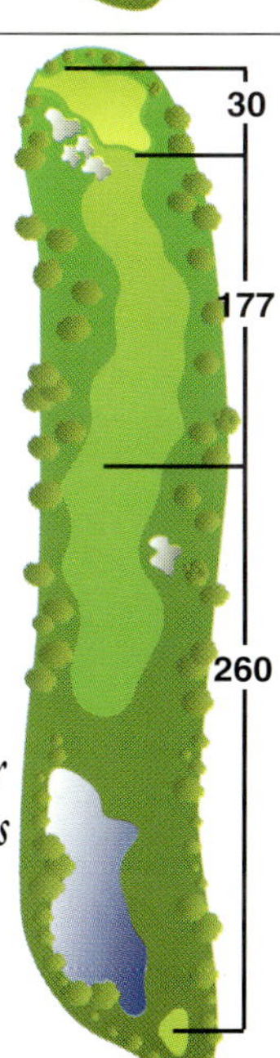

17

Par 3
159 yards

Three clubs can be the difference in getting close here. This green is gigantic. Appropriate club selection will lead to possible birdies. Tee shots hit short or to the right, into the deep bunkers, could make you work for your par.

18

Par 4
423 yards

This finishing hole will reward those favoring the right side off the tee. Water protects the left side and sand bunkers the right. Middle to short irons will be played to a green that will feed shots down towards the water. Definitly a hole where it can be won or lost in one swing.

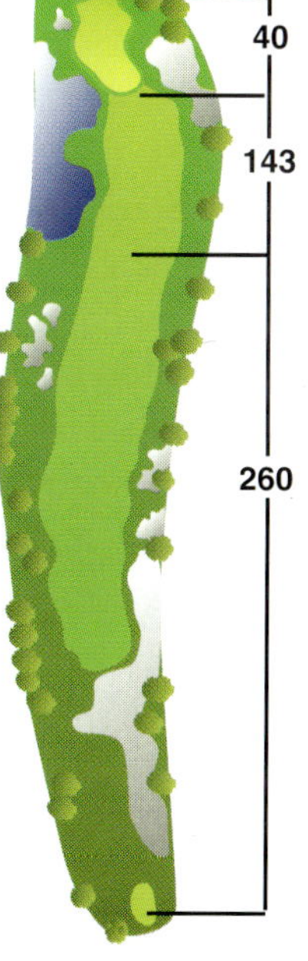

THE COURSE: HYATT DORADO BEACH RESORT AND CASINO, DORADO, PUERTO RICO

The Hyatt Senior Tournament of Champions is an event that includes only winners of the previous year's SENIOR PGA TOUR® events. The field is small but brings those who have excelled during the previous year. Each eligible player who enters the event is guaranteed a substantial check and a week of excitement at the famous Hyatt Dorado Beach Resort and Casino. This prestigious event is the beginning of the SENIOR PGA TOUR® schedule.

The Hyatt Senior Tournament of Champions was first played in California in 1984 and moved to the island of Puerto Rico in 1995 for its inaugural outside the United States. The Robert Trent Jones, Sr. course will again test the Seniors with narrow fairways, well-bunkered greens and fairways, and strategically placed water hazards.

Dates:	January 19-21, 1996
Network:	ESPN
Yardage:	6,985
Par:	72
Rating:	72.3
Total Purse:	$825,000
1st Prize:	$148,000
1995 Winner:	Jim Colbert
1995 Winning Score:	209 (72-66-71)
Principal Charitable Beneficiary:	Various
Ticket Information:	1-800-796-1234

1

**Par 4
360 yards**

A gentle dogleg right. The key shot is the drive which should be kept left to assure an open approach shot. The daring can cut the corner a little, but watch out for the lemon and lime trees.

2

**Par 5
520 yards**

A gradual curve right. After two woods, the key shot is an approach to a well-bunkered green. On this hole the golfer can loosen up and at the same time maybe catch a birdie.

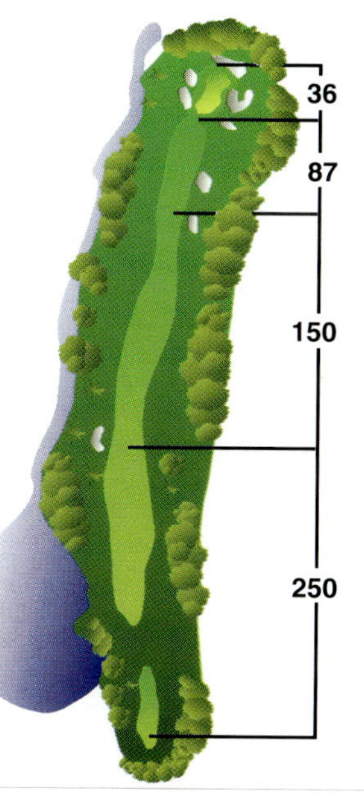

3

**Par 3
175 yards**

A straight-away hole in which club selection is the key.

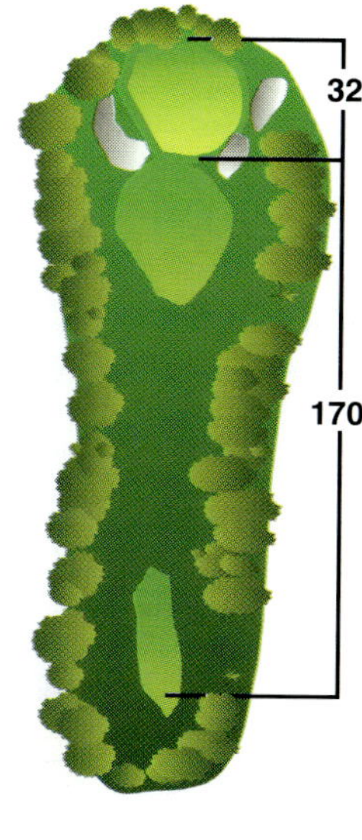

4

**Par 4
380 yards**

Short, but challenging, this hole demands a well-placed drive. The fairway is well bunkered and slopes right to left with a gradual incline. If you get this far, the approach shot is to a well-bunkered green.

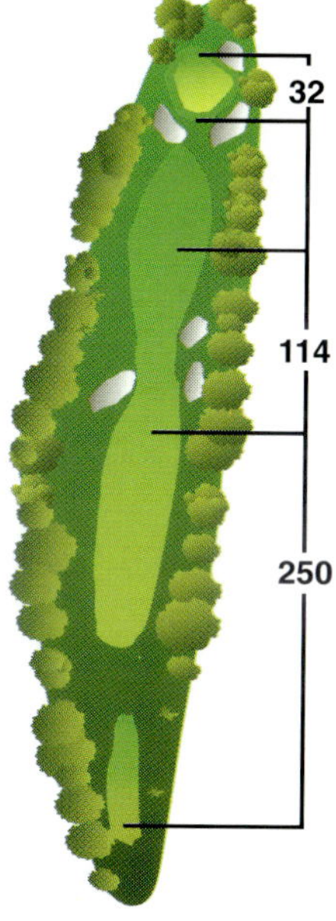

5

**Par 5
565 yards**

The name of the game here is to keep the ball in play. The fairway slopes right to left with dense foliage on both sides through the green. Play for five, and hope for the best.

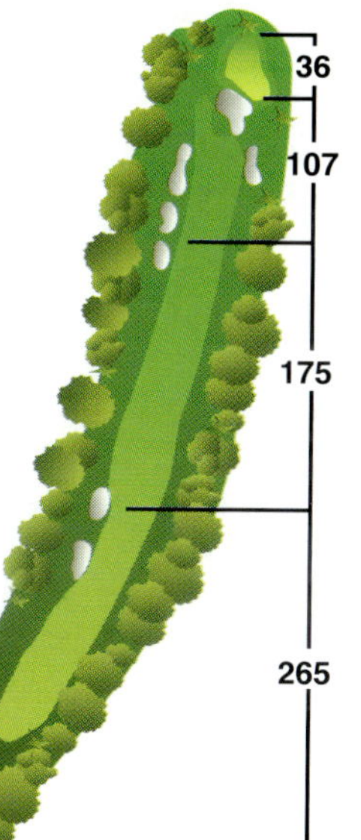

6

**Par 4
355 yards**

Since the hole is a downhill, slight dogleg left with water 280 yards out, you should lay it up thus assuring you a dry second shot. The green has a bunker in front and water on the right. Be careful!

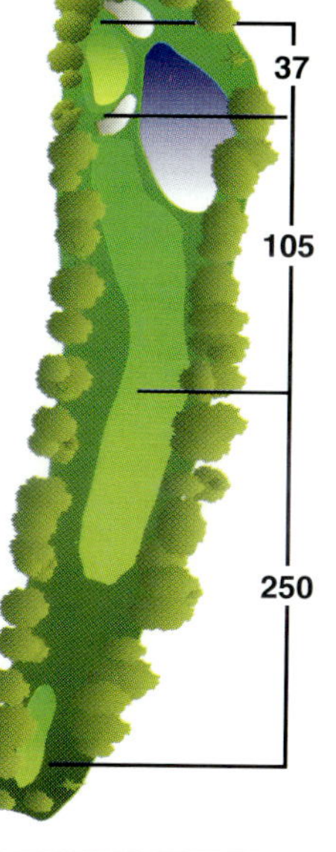

7

**Par 4
400 yards**

Trouble on the left! Keep your drive on the right center. The green is narrow and long front to back. The pin placement will vary club selection considerably.

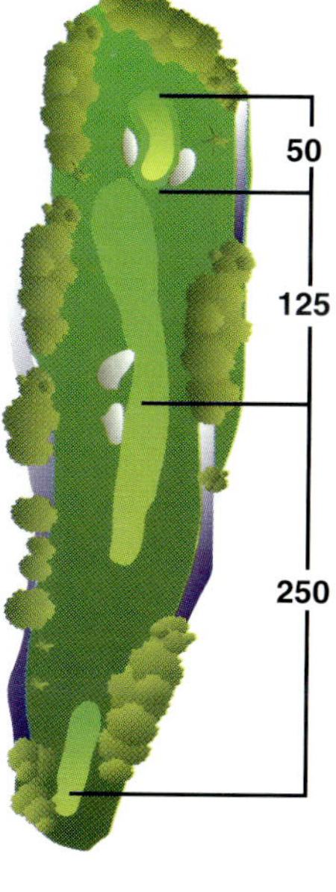

8

**Par 3
180 yards**

Water seems lateral to the fairway and cuts in slightly before the green. There is a bunker on the right for those who have hydrophobia. Make sure you have enough club and play for three.

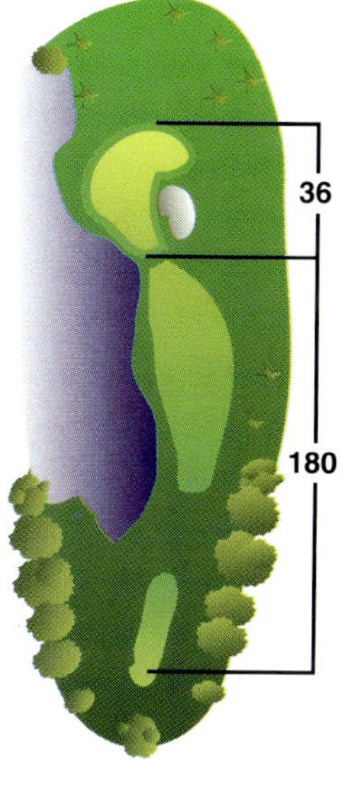

9

**Par 4
440 yards**

A dogleg left with well-bunkered fairway and running along the ocean between the palms. A long, narrow green with bunkers either side make you come to attention and obey its calling.

10

Par 5
510 yards

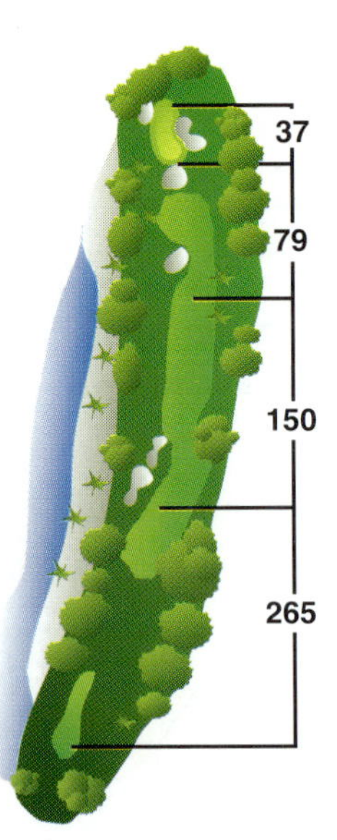

The hole runs parallel to the Atlantic Ocean on the left making wind a factor. It doglegs left narrowing into a well bunkered green. It can be reached in two, but don't blink your eyes. Most will settle for a placement second

11

Par 3
225yards

Shot from a cannon your balls better fly like a' frozen rope. The fairway is bordered by water as is a well-bunkered green. Hope for par!

12

Par 4
380 yards

A nice breather after the 11th. Keep your drive left center, setting up for a possible birdie.

13

Par 5
500 yards

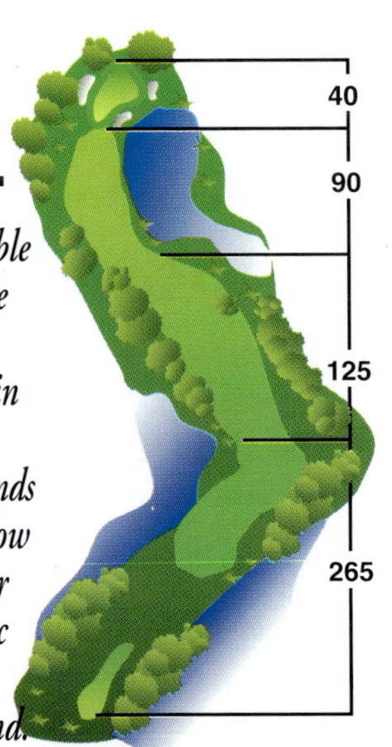

The famous double dogleg affords the strong player a reachable green in two. You must tranverse two ponds or otherwise follow the Z fairway for par. The Atlantic Ocean forms a scenic background.

14

Par 3
205 yards

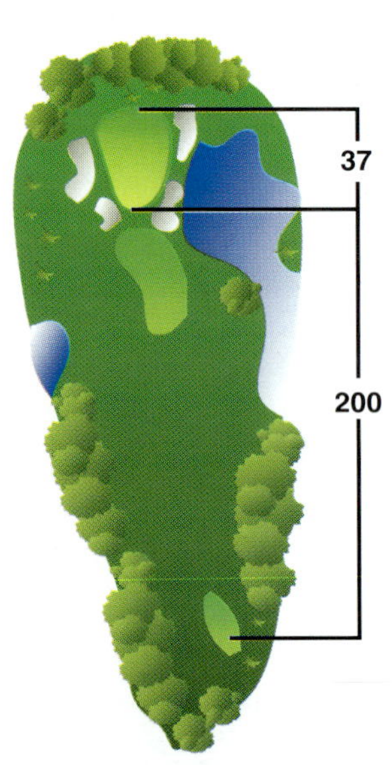

Watch the pin placement for proper club selection. The green is will bunkered with water on the right.

15

Par 4
415 yards

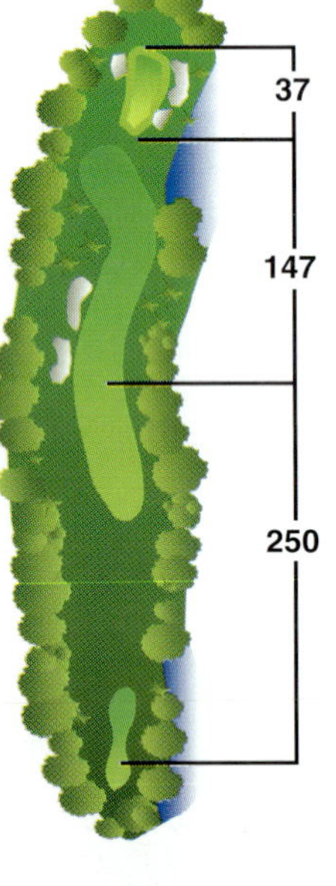

The drive is the important shot here. The hole doglegs to the right to an elevated green; therefore, it demands an approach from the left center of the fairway. Tall tress line the right side.

16

Par 4
460 yards

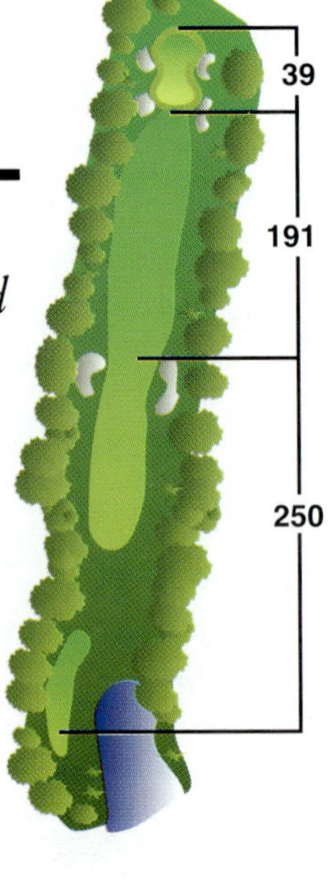

A nice quiet hole which is long and straight.

17

Par 4
400 yards

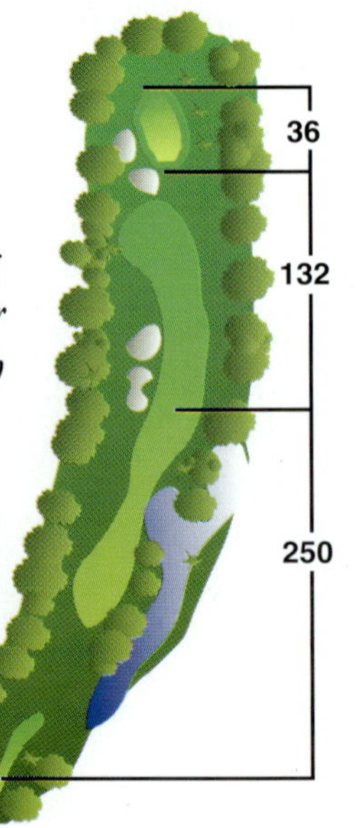

Dogleg left requiring the drive right center for the best approach shot. If you cut the corner which necessitates a strong drive, the approach becomes shorter but trickier due to greenside bunker

18

Par 4
405 yards

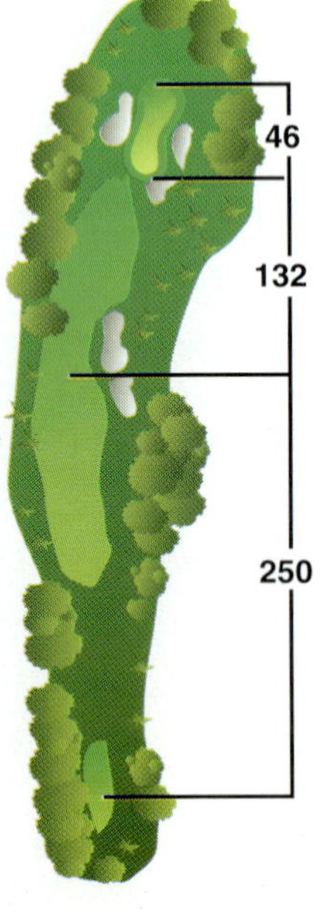

A slight bend to the right with a crosswind right to left makes this hole interesting. Keep the drive in the fairway, but be careful on your approach. The green is well bunkered and a lazy L in shape.

THE COURSE: TOURNAMENT PLAYERS CLUB OF SCOTTSDALE,
PHOENIX, ARIZONA

The beautiful Tournament Players Club of Scottsdale will once again play host to the 61st Phoenix Open. With the picturesque McDowell Mountains as its backdrop, the TPC, adorned with its grassy knolls and amphitheater-style seating, offers fans of the Valley's top sporting event an unobstructed view of one of the country's finest golf courses.

Since moving to the Tournament Players Club of Scottsdale in 1987, the Thunderbirds and the Open have enjoyed unparalleled success. Record crowds flock to the TPC every January, and the tournament has earned the distinction of being the world's top spectator golf event with over 360,000 fans for the week-long festival.

Dates:	January 25-28, 1996
Network:	ESPN
Times:	Thur - 2:00 - 4:00 pm
	Fri - 5:00 - 7:00 pm
	Sat - 4:30 - 6:30 pm
	Sun - 4:30 - 7:00 pm
Yardage:	6,992
Par:	71
Slope:	130.7
Rating:	73.9
Total Purse:	$1,300,000
1st Prize:	$234,000
1995 Winner:	Vijay Singh
1995 Winning Score:	269 (70-67-66-66)
Principal Charitable Beneficiary:	Arizona Special Olympics, United Way, Valley Boys and Girls Club and The Make-A-Wish Foundation
Ticket Information:	1-602-870-0163

1

Par 4
410 yards

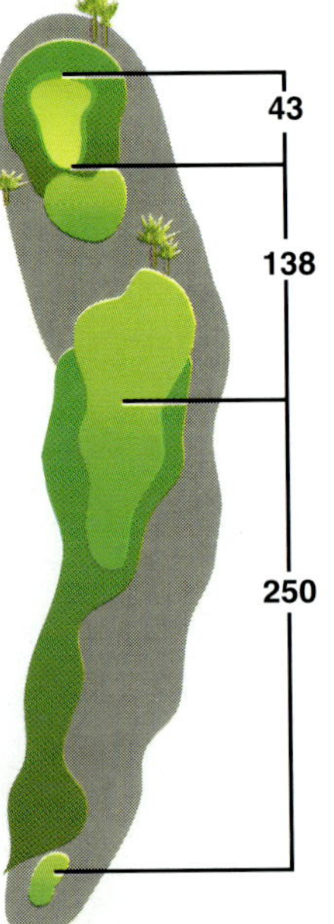

A medium length par 4, with most players using a fairway wood or long iron to avoid driving through the fairway. The green is protected on the right side by a large, deep bunker. Best approach to green is from the left side of the fairway.

2

Par 4
416 yards

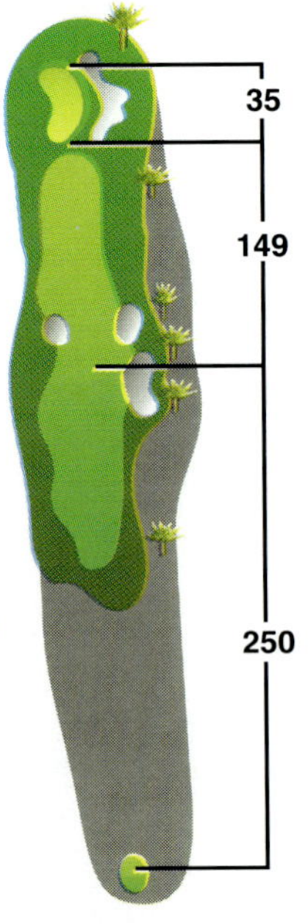

A slight downhill par 4 of medium length with players using a driver to avoid three right side fairway bunkers and one small, deep pot buker on the left side. Second shot is palyed to the small green, well protected by a right-side bunker.

3

Par 5
554 yards

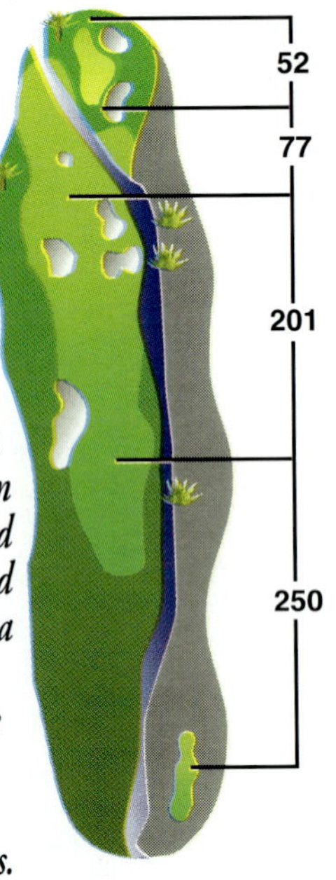

A long par 5 reached in two by only the longest hitters. A player's tee shot must avoid a huge bunker on the left and a small stream on the right. The second shot must avoid five sand traps in the landing area and water hazard fronting the green. The green is split level, protected in front and rear by two deep bunkers.

4

Par 3
150 yards

The shortest of the par 3's. This green has three distinct levels, well protected by surrounding bunkers. Putting can be a challenge.

5

Par 4
453 yards

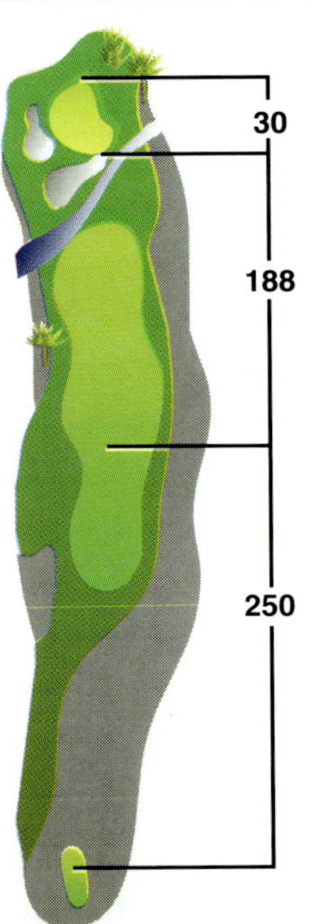

Long, straight par 4 with out-of-bounds down the entire right side. Enormous green guarded on the left by a lone bunker. This hole is extremely difficult if a strong prevailing wind is present.

6

Par 4
389 yards

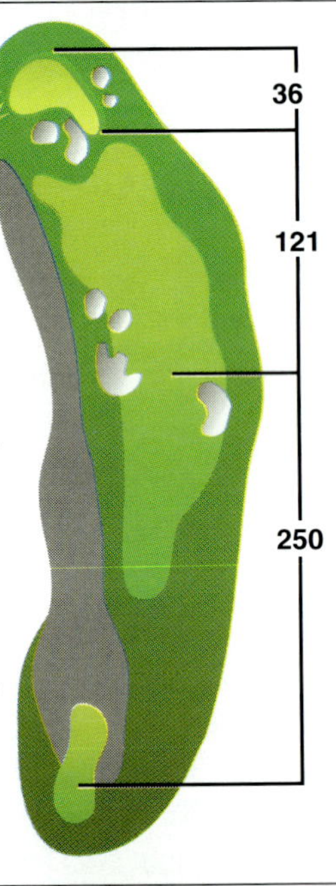

Depending on wind, this hole can be very difficult or very easy. The tee shot sets the tone where the player must avoid the left and right fairway cross bunkers. Bunkers exist right and left of green with birdies a common score.

7

Par 3
212 yards

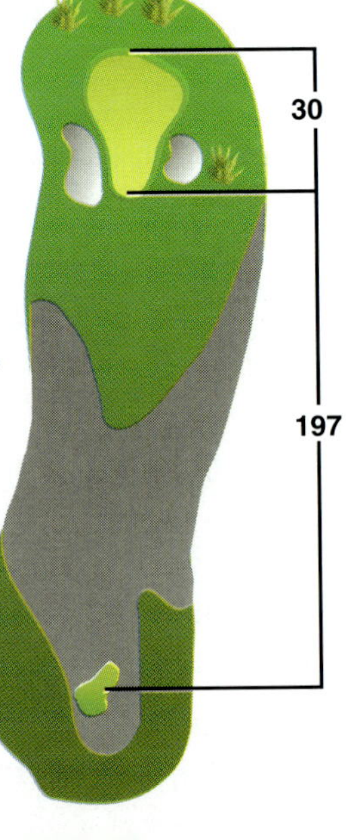

The longest of the par 3's, requiring fairway wood to long iron from the tee. Bunkers located on both sides of the green with an abrupt slope protecting the opening to this green.

8

Par 4
470 yards

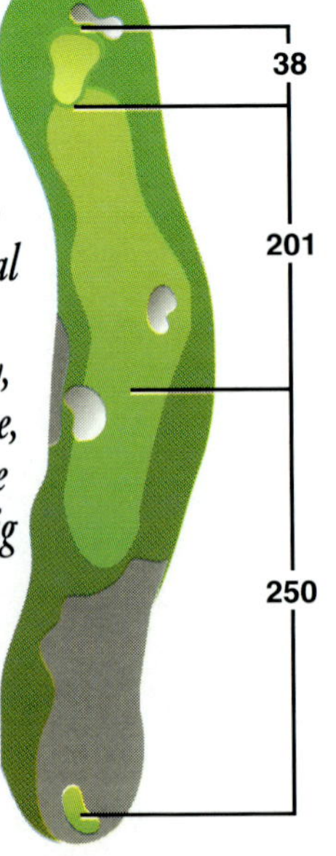

Long par 4 dogleg to the left. A directional bunker in the right center of the fairway, 300 yards from the tee, providing players the line off the tee. A big grass swale exists on the right side of the green with par a good score.

9

Par 4
415 yards

On this hole, players must avoid deep bunker on the right side of fairway. The green is wide but short in depth, protected by front pot bunker, grassy hollow back left and a deep bunker to the right. A significant ridge

10

Par 4
403 yards

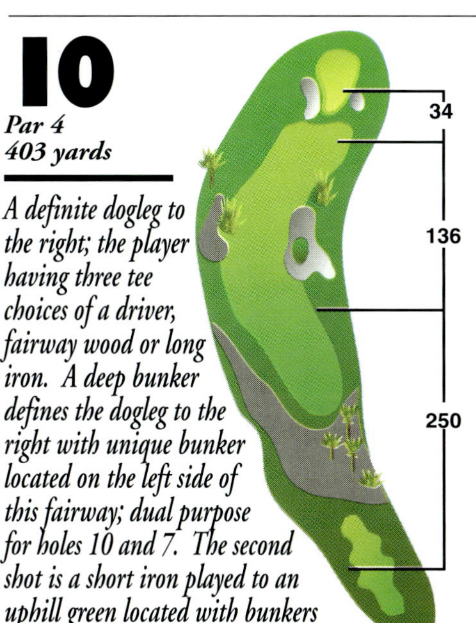

A definite dogleg to the right; the player having three tee choices of a driver, fairway wood or long iron. A deep bunker defines the dogleg to the right with unique bunker located on the left side of this fairway; dual purpose for holes 10 and 7. The second shot is a short iron played to an uphill green located with bunkers right and left.

11

Par 4
469 yards

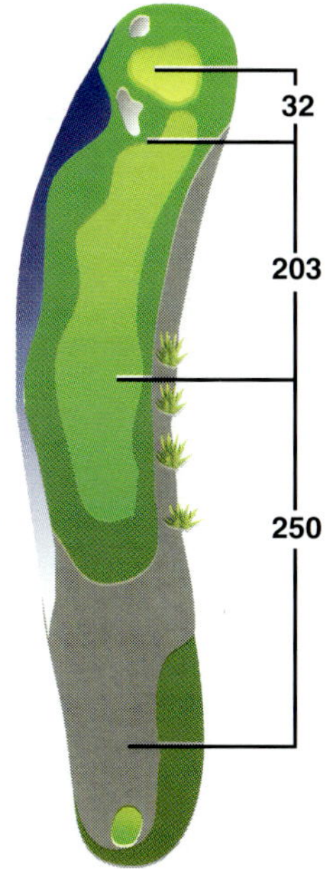

A demanding and dangerous hole. The lake along the entire left side is the player's biggest concern. A beach bunker protects the left front of this green with a hidden bunker behind the green. A good, strong par 4 hole with par always a good score.

12

Par 3
195 yards

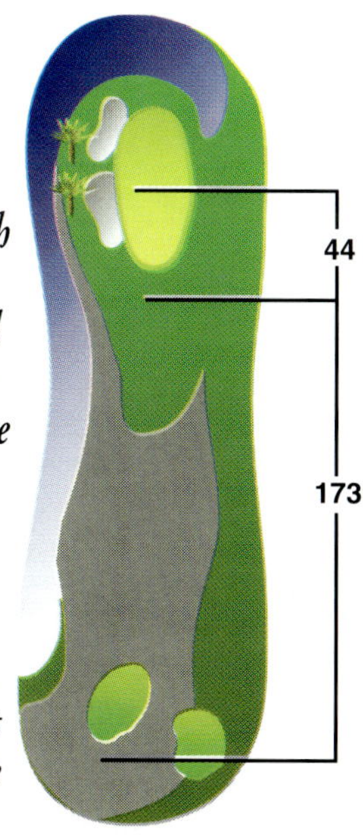

A difficult par 3 with water guarding the entire right side and sand bunkers to the left and behind. The green is long and narrow with a two club difference between front and back pin placement. This hole is the most over-par-played hole

13

Par 5
576 yards

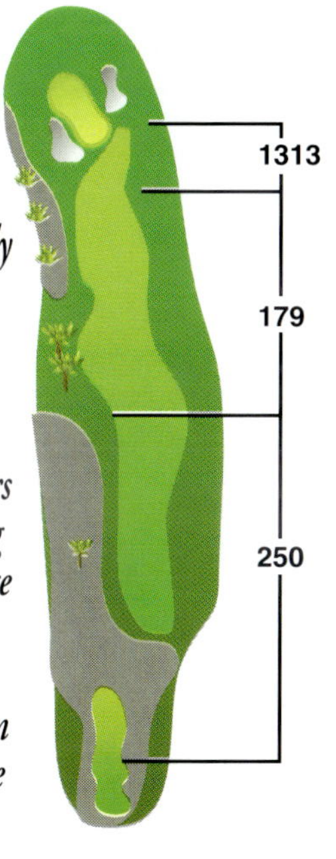

Par 5 with a split fairway. Played downwind, the shot is probably the right fairway, driving between the water and island desert. The conservative player plays the left providing the player a wider driving area. The second landing area is wide, protected by an large

14

Par 4
444 yards

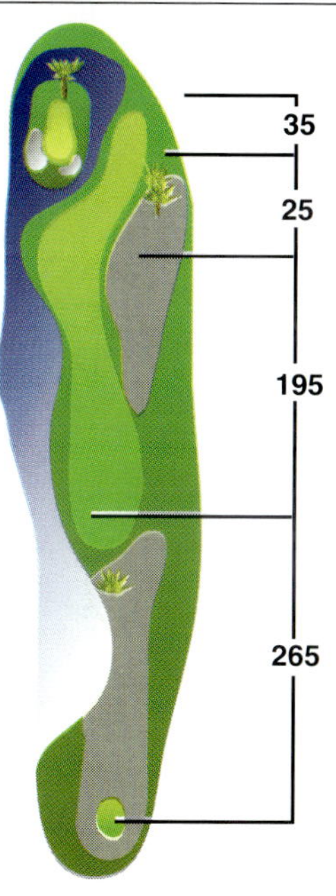

A par 4 hole, slightly uphill with mounding on both sides of the driving area. The proper placed tee shot favors the right side giving the player advantage and visibility in playing his second shot to a small green with bunkers on the

15

Par 5
501 yards

A reachable par 5 for the players. Water in play on the tee shot, second shot and pitch to island green. Water totally surrounds the green with bunkers left and right. Scores range from 3-7 making it a very pivotal hole and exciting for the

16

Par 3
162 yards

Tom Weiskopf's favorite par 3 on the Stadium Course. The green is an elusive target, requiring accuracy. Scores vary from 2-4, offering the player a good birdie opportunity.

17

Par 4
332 yards

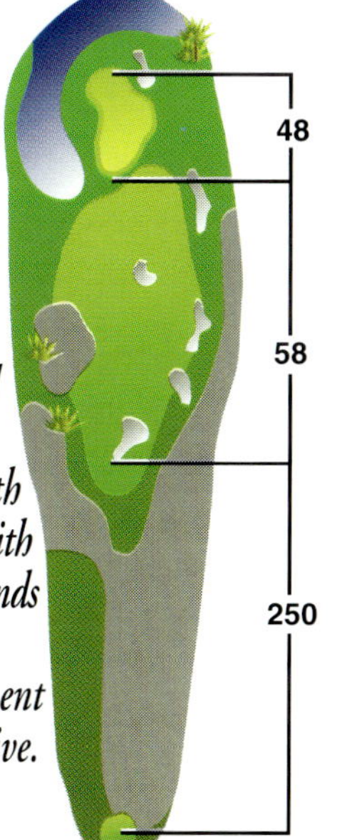

A very exciting par 4. This hole can be driven from the tee. Danger lurks around the green with water and sand, and on both sides of the fairway with sand. This hole demands accuracy and finesse, rewarding the placement of a long, straight drive.

18

Par 4
438 yards

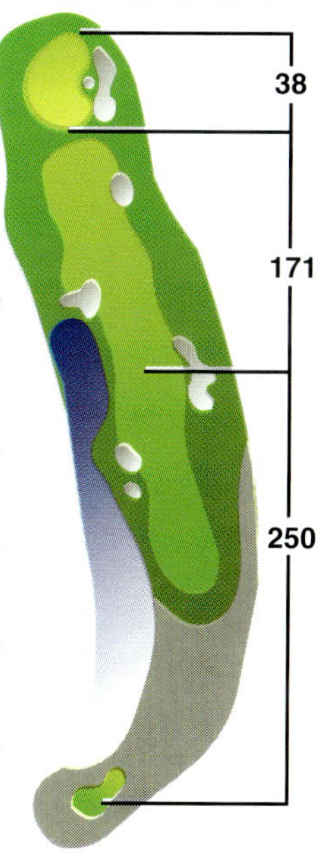

This par 4 on the left and sand evident on the right. Two directional bunkers give proper direction for playing tee shot. The tee shot is demanding, so too is the second shot into a green with a very deep bunker right of the green and a difficult slope protecting the left side and front.

THE COURSE: MAUNA LANI RESORT, KOHALA COAST, HAWAII

The 1996 Senior Skins Game brings together the legends of the links. The Skins competition format is another brainchild of television sports genius Don Ohlmeyer whose other successes include "Monday Night Football" and "SPORTSWORLD". With head-to-head competition by golf greats the likes of Nicklaus, Palmer, Trevino and others, the Senior Skins has become a highly anticipated annual match-up and an unsurpassed success.

The legends compete for "skins" on each hole, at values of at least $15,000 for each hole won. For holes that result in a tie, the skin is carried over to the next, enabling a player back into the thick of competition with the win of just one hole. Big money winning highlights the tournament.

The I'I Brown Golf Course-South was new for the 1992 Senior Skins Game. Built on the prehistoric Kaniku flow, the layout features rolling fairways defined by hardened lava beds and spectacular Pacific views.

Dates:	January 27-28, 1996
Network:	ABC
Times:	Sat - 2:30-5:00 pm
	Sun - 1:30-4:00 pm
Yardage:	6,763
Par:	72
Total Purse:	$540,000
1st Prize:	$420,000
1995 Winner:	Raymond Floyd
1995 Winning Score:	14 Skins
Ticket Information:	1-808-885-6655
Resort Information:	1-808-885-6677

1

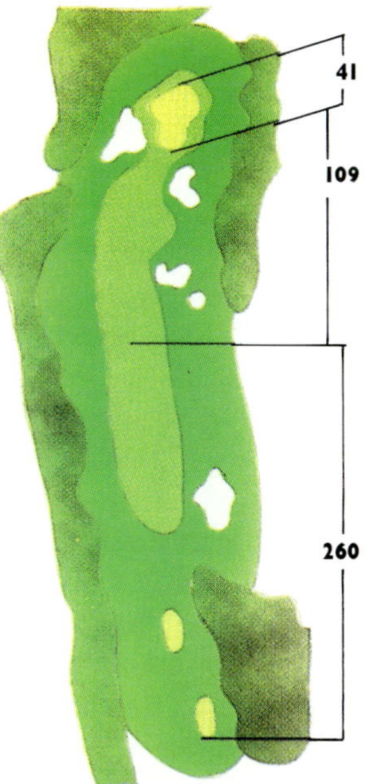

Par 4
390 yards

The Skins Game begins Saturday with a 390 yard, slight dogleg right. The left side of the fairway is favored — a large grass swale on the right will blind the second shot.

2

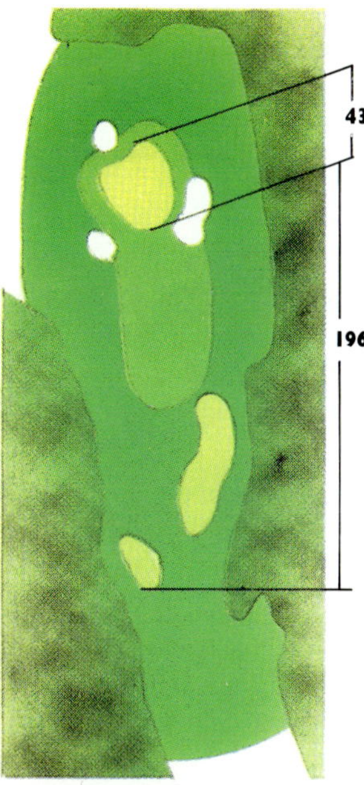

Par 3
218 yards

A lava outcropping lies between tee and green. The back to front, two-tiered sloping green can play very long into the kona winds. Bunkers await beyond the green.

3

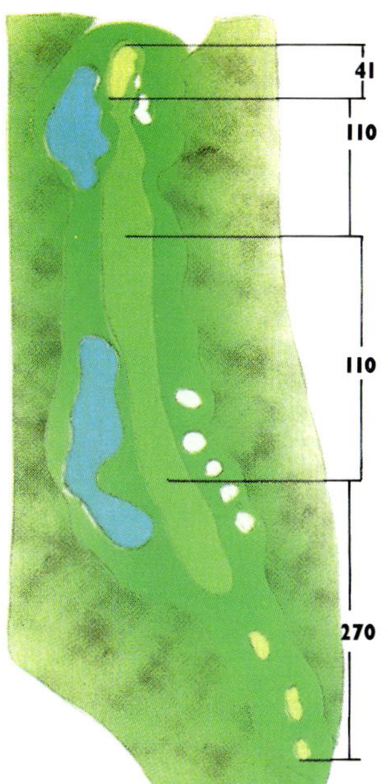

Par 5
601 yards

The shot off the tee must safely navigate between the water on the left and sand and lava to the right. The fairway tightens toward the long narrow green.

4

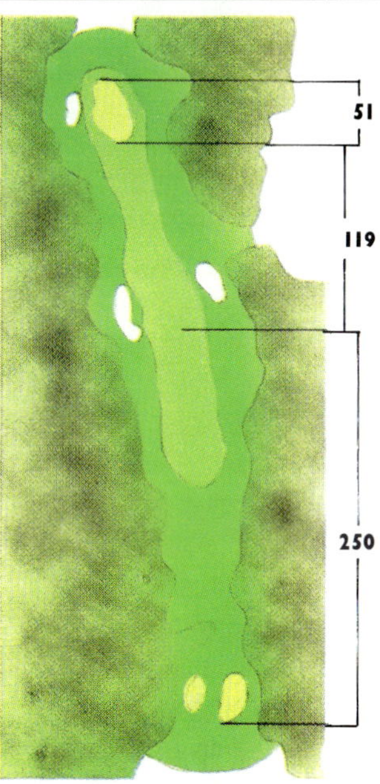

Par 4
395 yards

A lava gully crosses the path to the fairway. The flat fairway is well defined by sand on the left and lava to the right. The oval green is encircled by deep, penalizing bunkers.

5

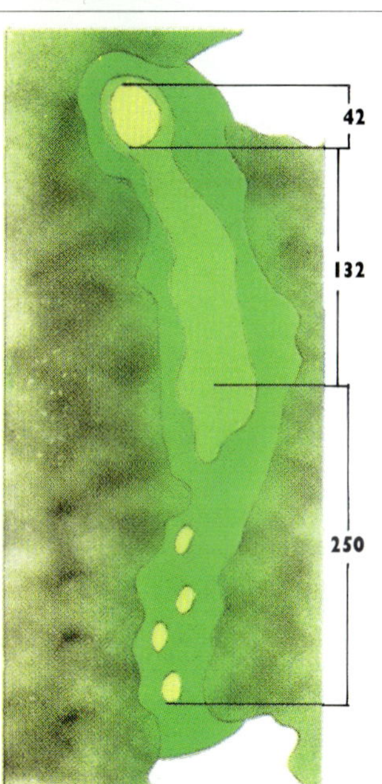

Par 4
403 yards

The tee shot must be long and accurate to find the plateau fairway. Lava on both sides can ruin hopes of birdies. The approach is straight out to an ocean-side green.

6

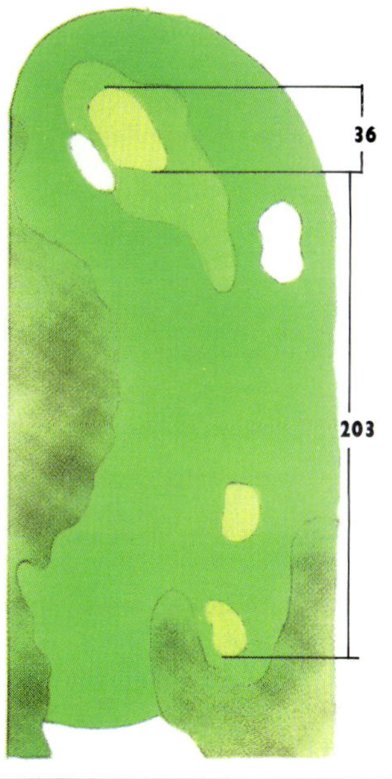

Par 3
221 yards

Parallel to the menacing Pacific, this sixth plays downhill to a severely undulating putting surface. Accuracy is key to avoid the many hazards that lie between tee and green.

7

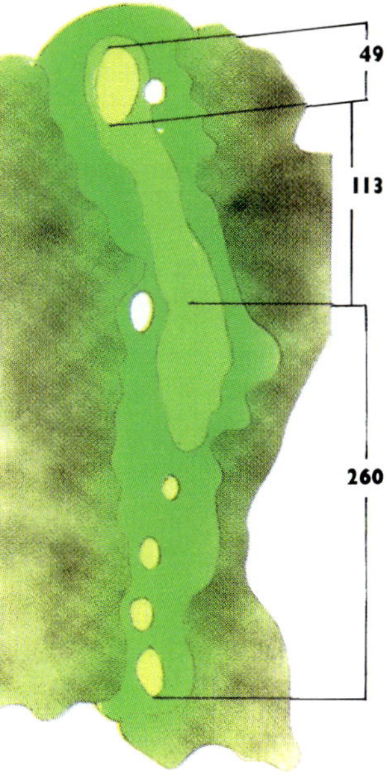

Par 4
398 yards

The seventh bends slightly to the left. Heading back inland, this hole presents the possibility for birdie. An approach left just short of the hole will leave an easier uphill putt.

8

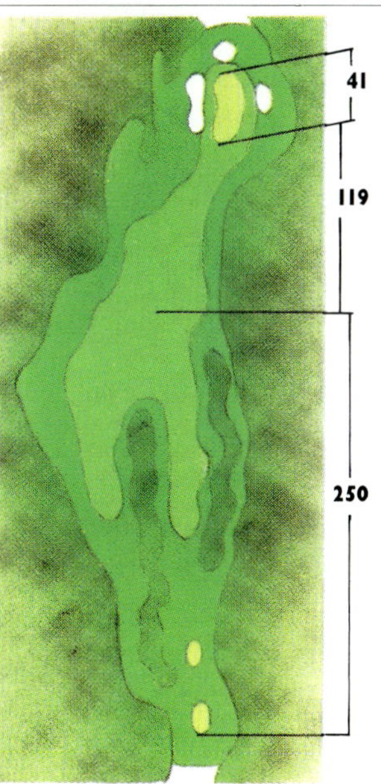

Par 4
390 yards

Two routes are available to the putting surface. Players will most likely favor the upper right side of the fairway for an approach to the long narrow flat green

9

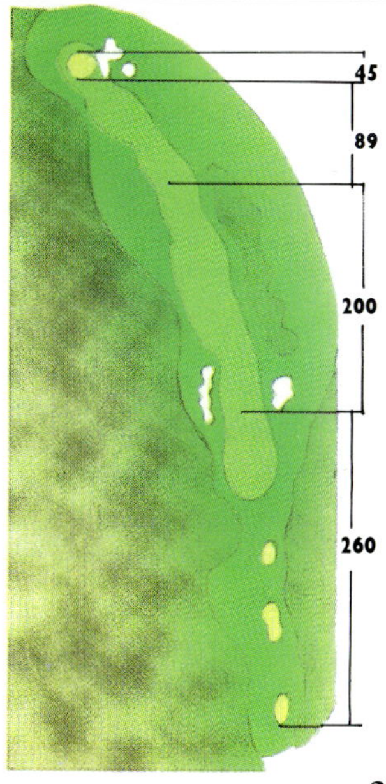

Par 5
572 yards

This long par 5 is out of reach for all but the longest hitters. A drive down the right side will set up for a second down the middle. The approach is played between lava right and left.

10

Par 5
535 yards

For Sunday, the back nine opens with a short par 5. The wide fairway is bordered by lava right and an old herding trail along the left. A birdie 4 will be the score to beat.

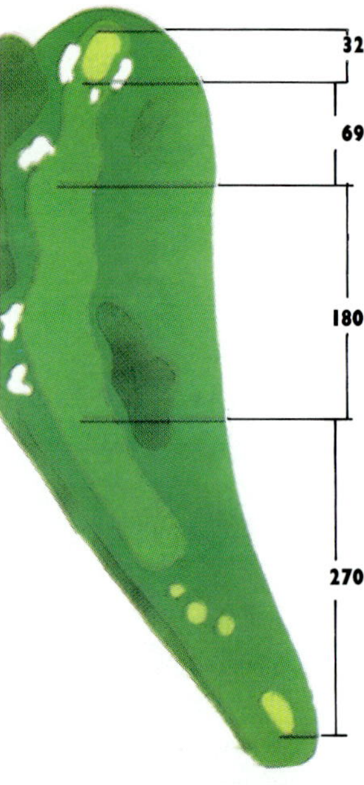

11

Par 4
408 yards

The sharp dogleg left allows players to cut the corner. The green is cut in beyond the sand on the right — a pin placement to the back right corner can be difficult to hit.

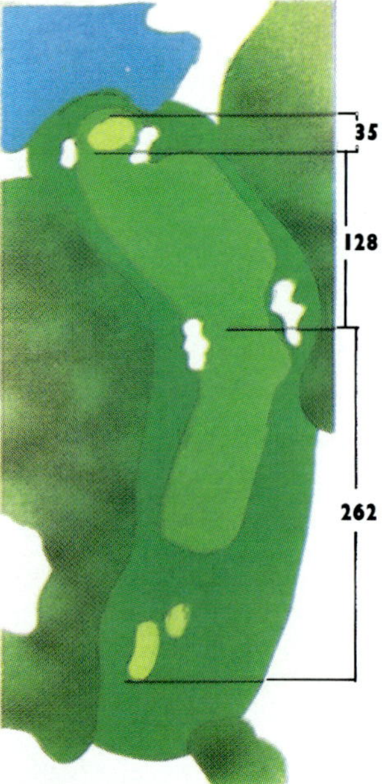

12

Par 3
202 yards

The tee shot must carry the water the entire way to the green. Players will be using up to 3 clubs more if the wind is against them. Pars will tie — birdies will most definitely win!

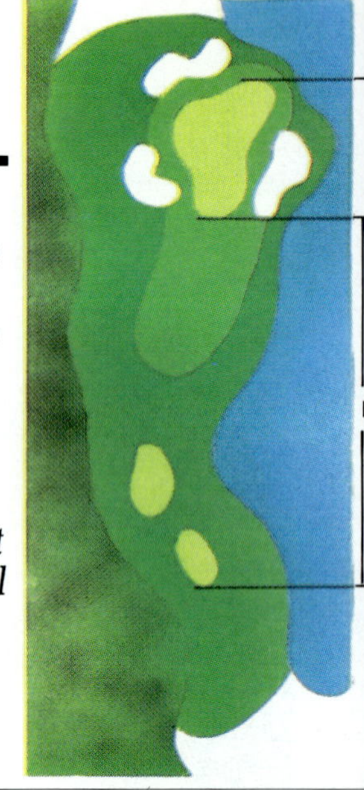

13

Par 4
387 yards

Straight at the ocean for this 13th! Care must be taken to place this drive in position for the approach. Out-of-bounds is to the right and the green slopes away towards the ocean.

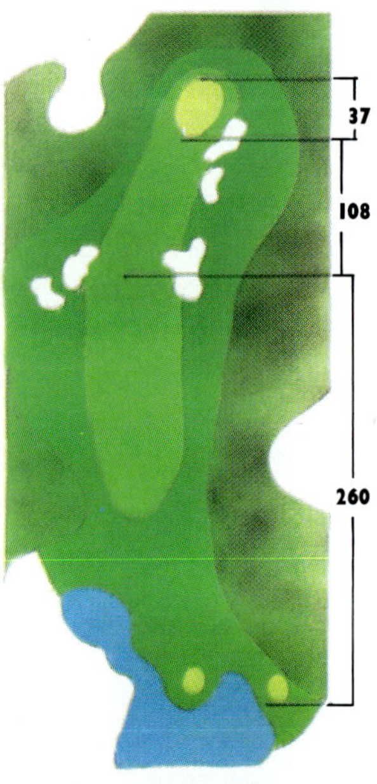

14

Par 4
413 yards

Lava is the biggest obstacle on this dogleg left 14th. The drive should be played just along the right side to open up the angle on the wide, shallow green.

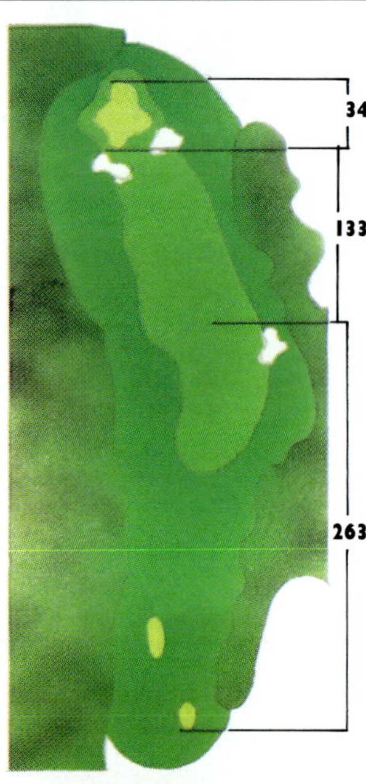

15

Par 3
202 yards

The tee shot must carry 202 yards over crashing surf to a large, well bunkered green. Wow! Players may get a glimpse of whales cavorting majestically in the deep waters.

16

Par 4
368 yards

Players will favor the left side of this dogleg-right par 4. The approach is to a narrow, undulating green. Accuracy is a must to avoid the several bunkers surrounding the putting surface.

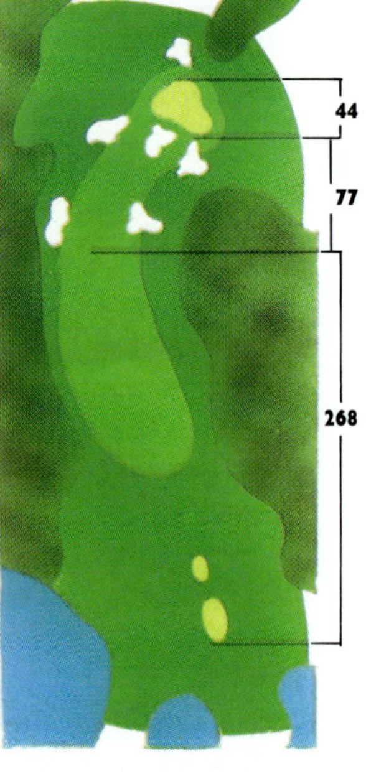

17

Par 4
411 yards

The tee shot will roll right to left on this sloping fairway. Consequently, the approach is from a sidehill lie into a green that is guarded by lava on the left. The putting surface is flat.

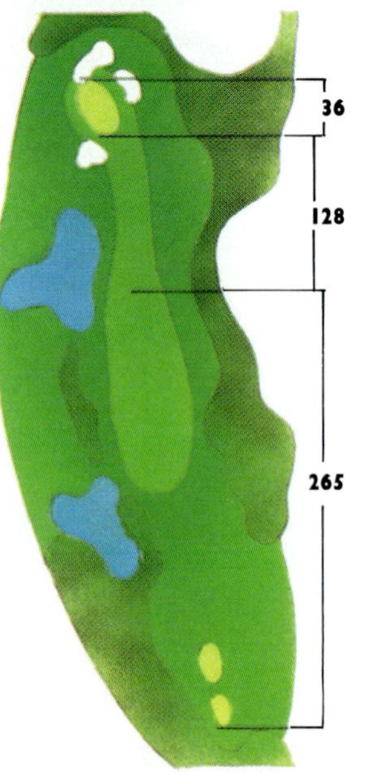

18

Par 5
515 yards

A short but difficult hole. The wide fairway is kind to most drives. However, into the kona wind, this finishing hole can be a monster.

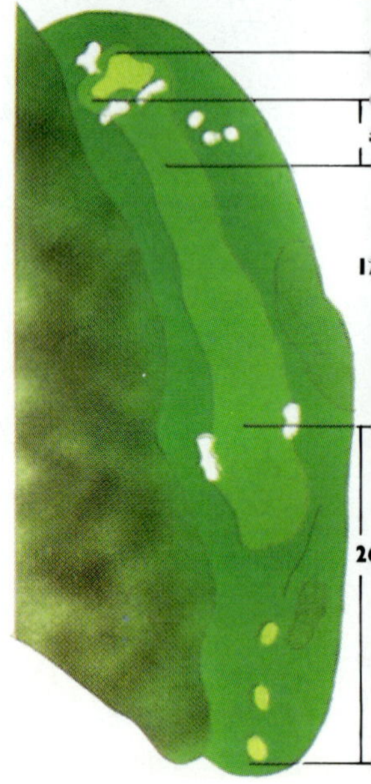

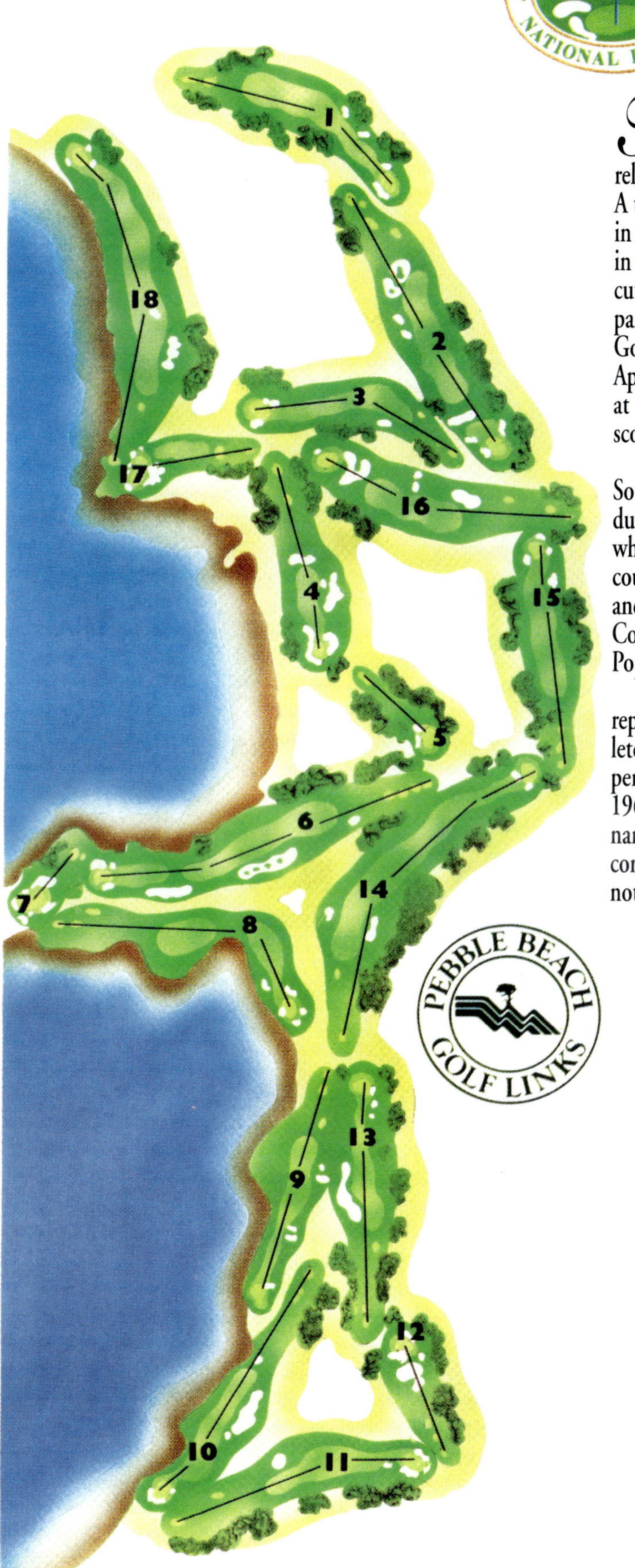

THE COURSE: PEBBLE BEACH GOLF LINKS, PEBBLE BEACH, CALIFORNIA

The AT&T Pebble Beach National Pro-Am is possibly one of the most relaxed and enjoyable event of the year with all the celebrities and professionals. A total of 180 professionals and 180 amateurs team up for a 72-hole tournament in which the teams play all four days. It is the only event on the PGA TOUR® in which the amateurs finish with the pros on Sunday - provided they make the cut. Three courses are used for the event. For Thursday, Friday and Saturday, the participants will play one round each at Pebble Beach Golf Links, Poppy Hills Golf Course and Spyglass Hill Golf Course, playing a different course each day. Approximately 25 low teams and the 60 low professionals will conclude the event at Pebble Beach Golf Links for the final 18 holes on Sunday. The pro-am team scores are based on a best-ball format, calculated with the amateurs' handicaps.

The pro-am event was first played in 1937 at Rancho Santa Fe in Southern California and hosted by Bing Crosby. The "Clambake", as it was dubbed after the first tournament, eventually moved to the Monterey Peninsula where it became the first PGA TOUR® event to be played on more than one golf course. Initially, Monterey Peninsula Country Club, Pebble Beach Golf Links and Cypress Point Golf Club hosted the event. However, Spyglass Hill Golf Course replaced Monterey in 1967 as the third course of the trio and in 1991 Poppy Hill replaced Cypress Point.

As the tournament has progressed through the years it has gained the reputation as a very entertaining event. Well-known movie starts, musicians, athletes and prominent business leaders have been among the list of amateurs. A perennial crowd favorite is Jack Lemmon who has tried, unsuccessfully since 1969, to make the final cut to be able to play on Sunday. But all in all, the tournament is an anticipated event each year. The entertaining and humorous play combined with the fantastic golf of the professionals provides a show that cannot be missed.

Dates:	February 1-4, 1996
Network:	CBS and USA
Times:	USA - Thur/Fri 1:00-3:00 EST
	CBS - Sat 1:00-3:00 EST
	Sun 12:30-3:00 EST
Yardage:	6,799
Par:	72
Slope:	144
Rating:	75
Total Purse:	$1,400,000
1st Prize:	$252,000
1995 Winner:	Peter Jacobsen
1995 Winning Score:	271 (67-73-66-65)
Principal Charitable Beneficiary:	AT&T Pebble Beach Golf Foundation
Charitable Benefits to Date:	$16.5 million since 1947
Ticket Information:	1-408-541-9091
Resort Information:	1-800-654-9300

1

Par 4
373 yards

Players will be using a fairway wood or long-iron to place their drives at the corner of the dogleg. A short approach shot is all that remains to the slightly elevated green.

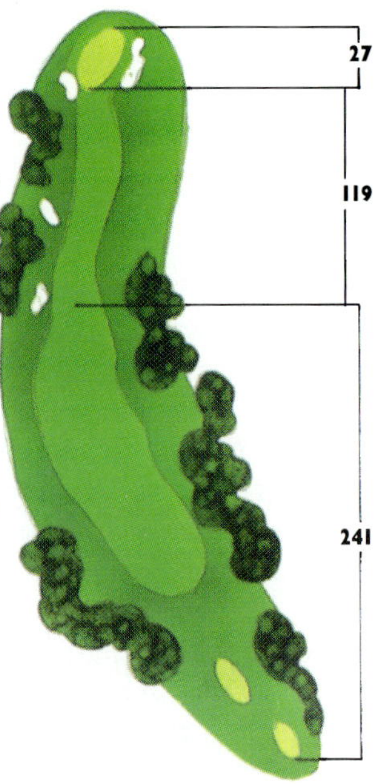

2

Par 5
502 yards

Two well hit shots can reach this green in two but the odds favor the safe play. The drive must carry some 240 yards to even reach the fairway.

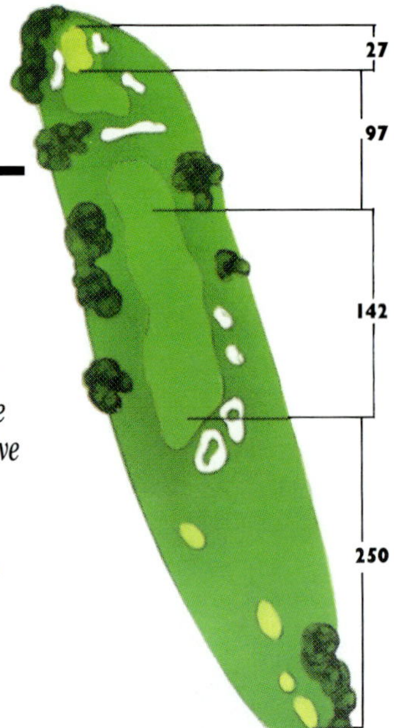

3

Par 4
388 yards

The longer hitters will cut the corner. Barranca on the left will grab drives left short. The approach must find a firm grip on the green that slopes away from the fairway.

4

Par 4
327 yards

The ocean to the right persuades players to play for the left. Care must be taken to avoid bunkers along the left. Bunkers surround the small, flat green.

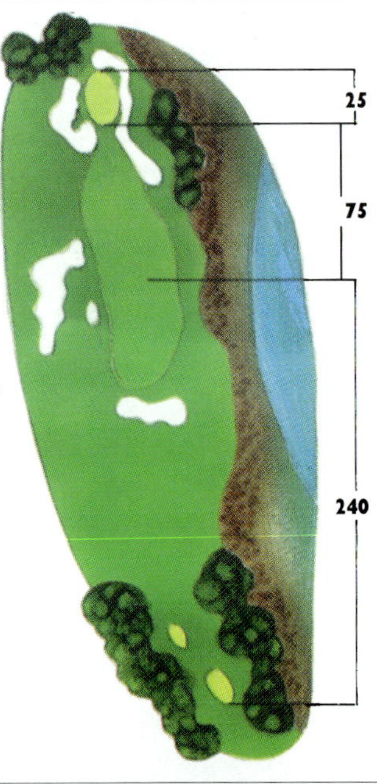

5

Par 3
166 yards

A right-quartering headwind from the Pacific adds difficulty to this somewhat short par 3. The tee angled to the right gives the illusion of a "dogleg par 3".

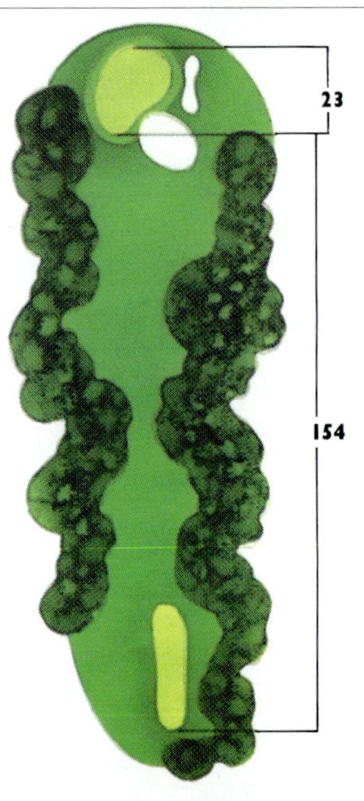

6

Par 5
516 yards

The fairway rises up near the second fairway bunker on the left. A blind second shot must clear the ridge in order to set up for a short approach.

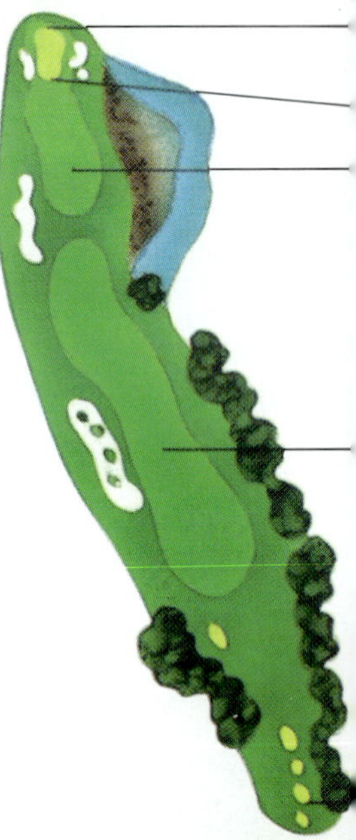

7

Par 3
107 yards

If length meant difficulty, this hole would be easy. However, this 100 yard shot can be the most difficult on the golf course. The tee is elevated, the green is small and surrounded by bunkers.

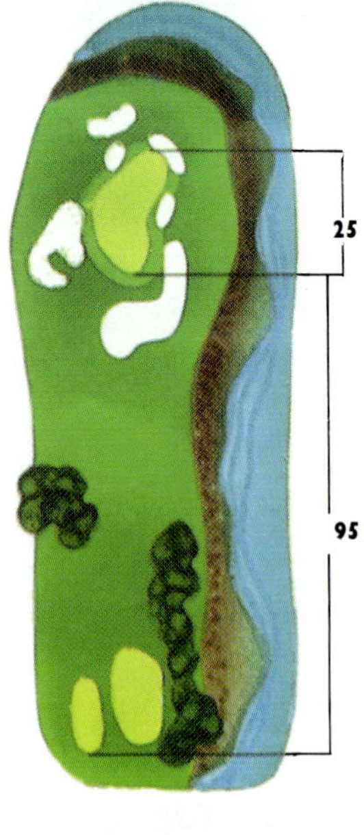

8

Par 4
431 yards

A well hit drive should leave the player a mid-iron to the putting surface. However, the approach must be played over an open gorge that drops off drastically to the ocean.

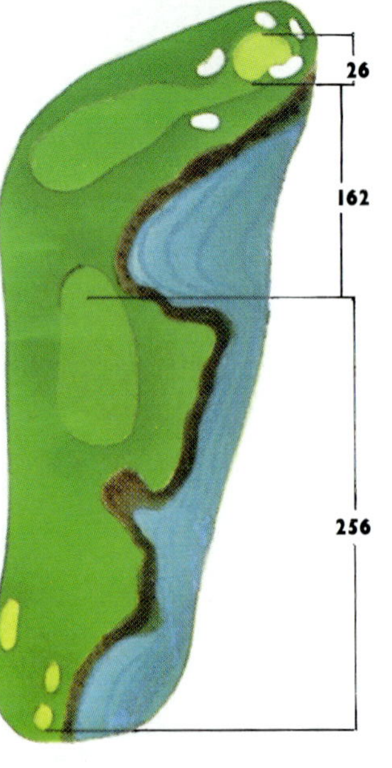

9

Par 4
464 yards

Strategically placed fairway bunkers require a well planned route down the fairway. The approach, from the rolling fairway, must clear a small valley to reach the green.

10

Par 4
426 yards

The curving cliff line defines the extent of the fairway. A careful tee-shot should be placed in the middle for a mid-iron to the ocean-side green.

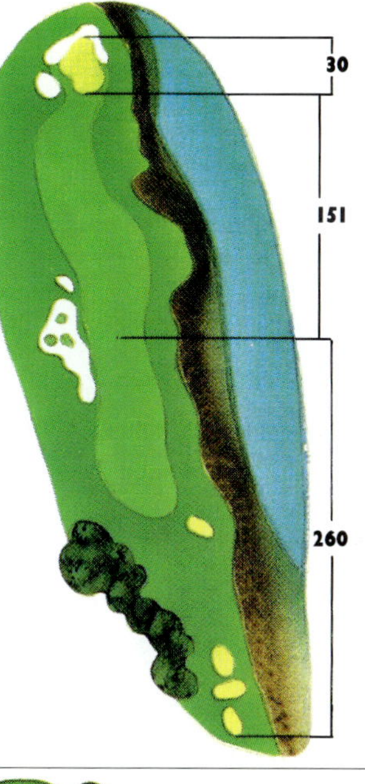

11

Par 4
384 yards

The eleventh turns the course back towards the mountains. An uphill drive should be placed to the left side of the fairway for players to get an optimal angle on the approach.

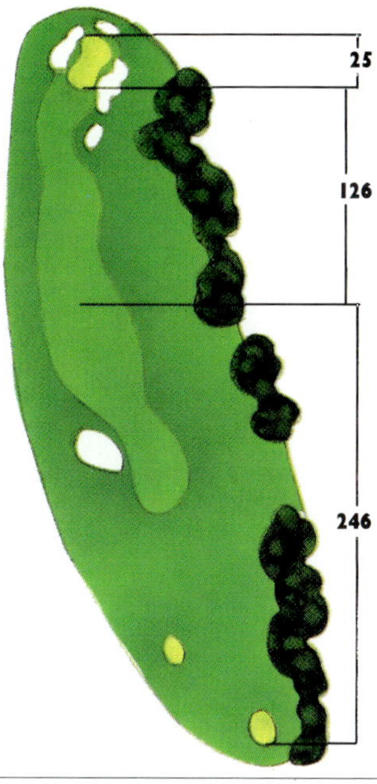

12

Par 3
202 yards

Out-of bounds to the right and a large bunker on the left. Players will play a tee shot right to left to keep the ball away from trouble right and into the wind from the left.

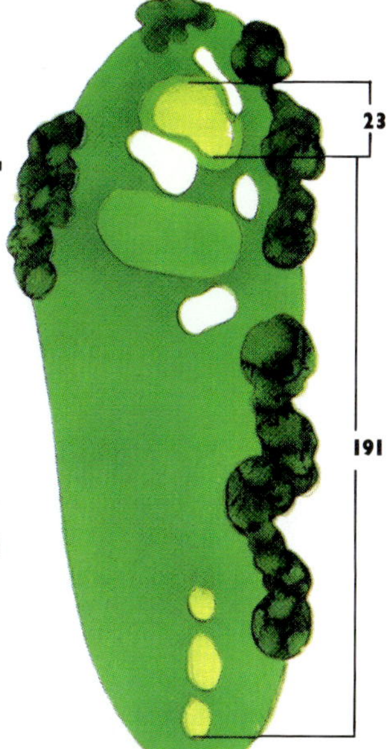

13

Par 4
392 yards

The large bunker along the left protects that side as out-of-bounds does the right. However, the fairway is wide and the green is open. Many birdies can be had on this hole.

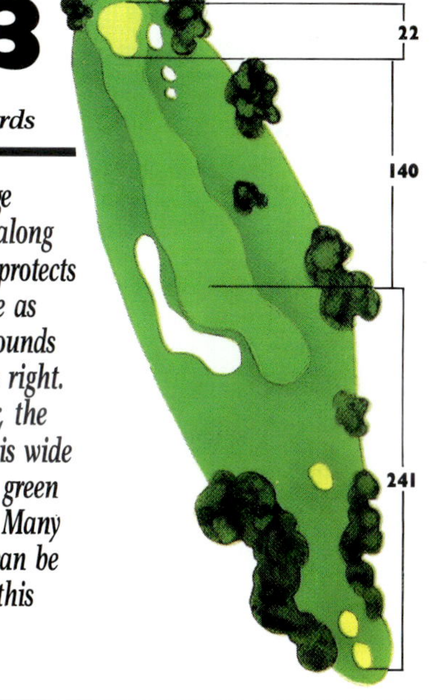

14

Par 5
565 yards

This long dog-leg right par 5 demands three well planned shots. The players may favor the right middle of the fairway to shorten the hole.

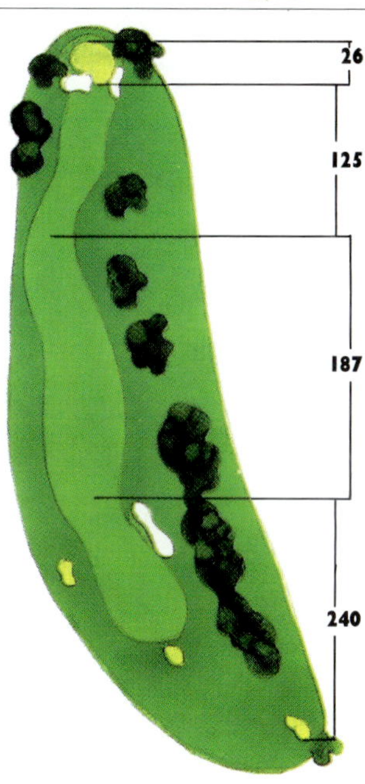

15

Par 4
397 yards

The tee shots must clear a deep, overgrown ravine before disappearing from sight into the fairway. The large flat green is susceptible to easy putts. Birdies are common.

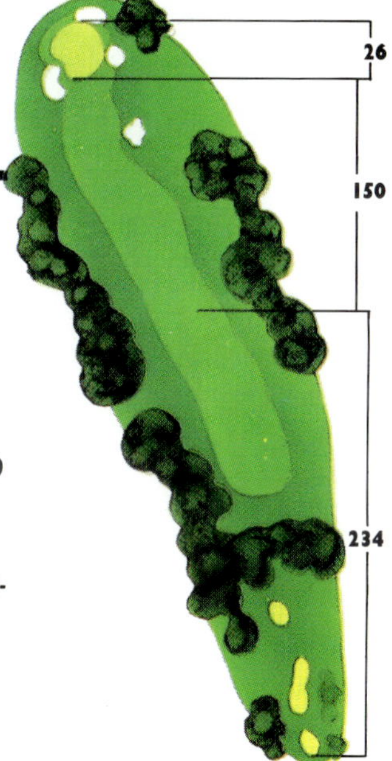

16

Par 4
402 yards

The final three starts with this tricky sixteenth. The large bunker in the center of the fairway demands a well hit drive. The green is tucked in among more bunkers and trees.

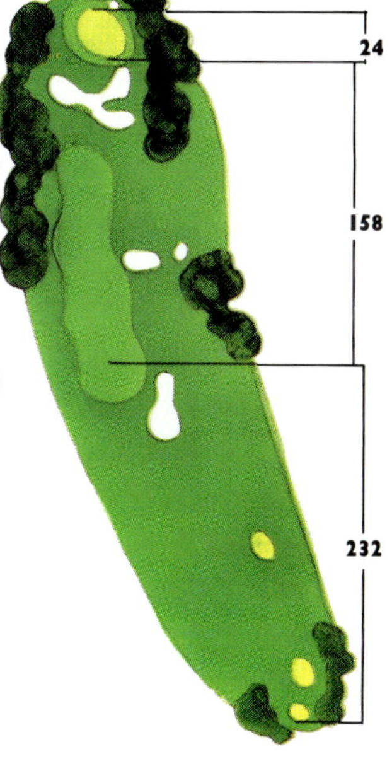

17

Par 3
209 yards

Tournaments can be won on this second to last hole. At 209 yards and sometimes into a strong ocean breeze, the tee shot can be long.

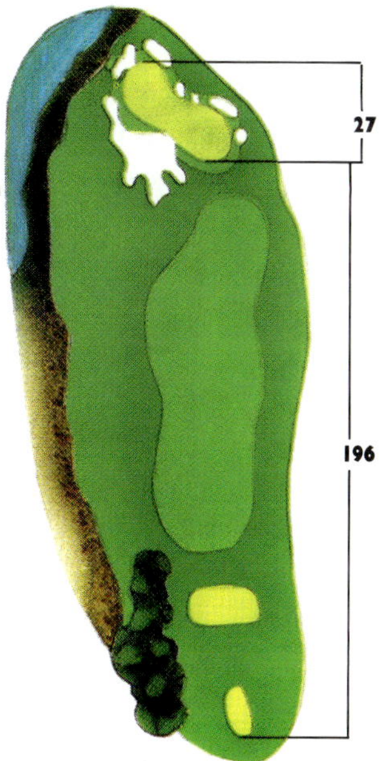

18

Par 5
548 yards

As if the rocky shoreline did not add enough difficulty, a couple of trees in the fairway dictate for the drive to be played over the ocean.

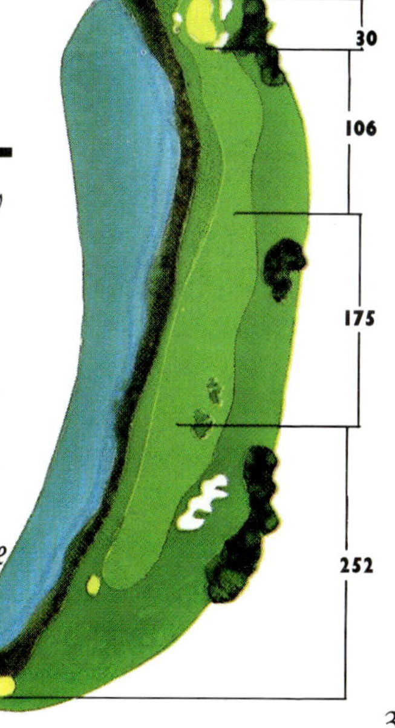

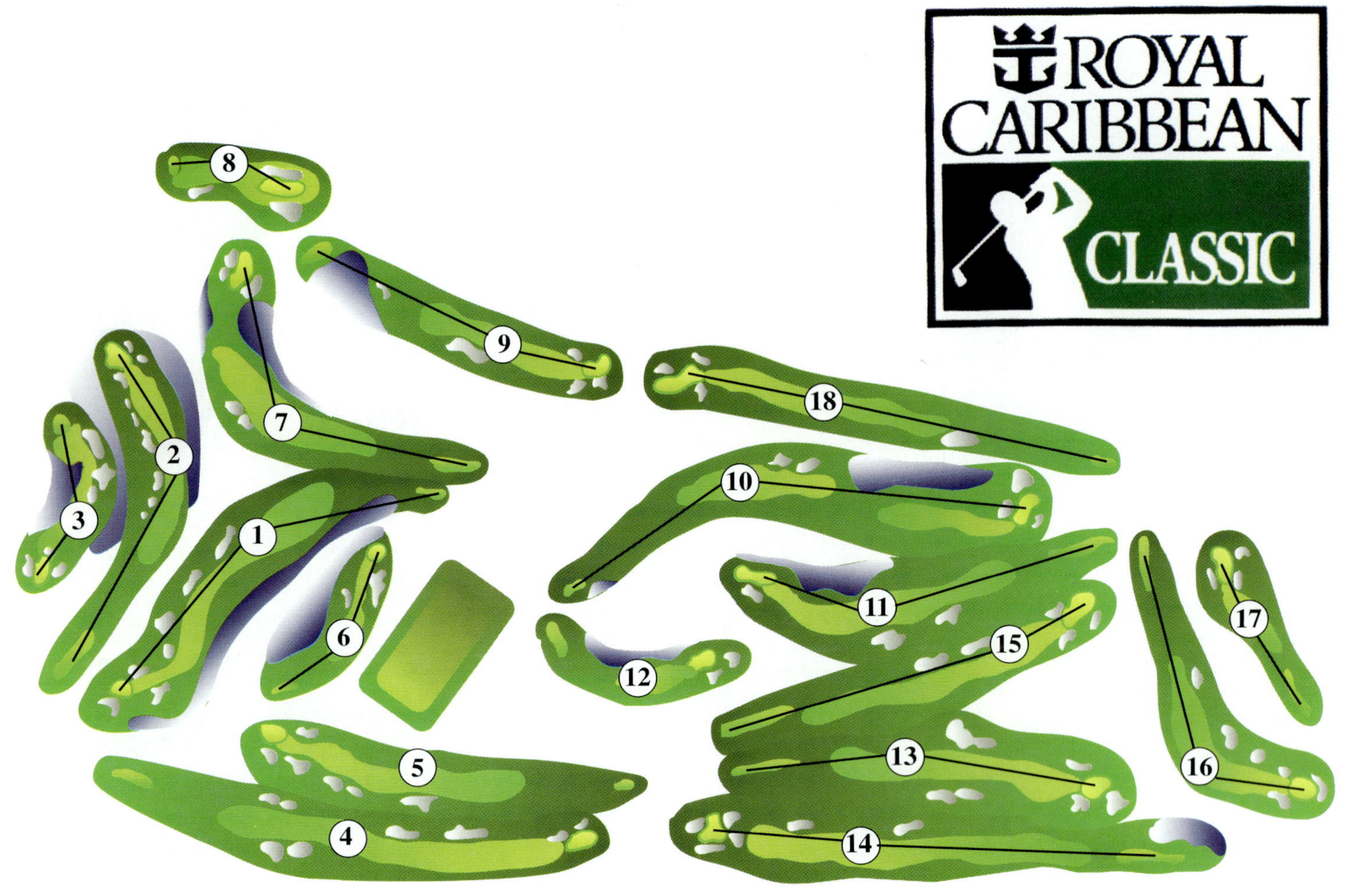

THE COURSE: THE LINKS, KEY BISCAYNE, FLORIDA

The 7th Annual Royal Caribbean Classic takes place at The Links at Key Biscayne. As the first full-field Senior PGA TOUR® event of the year, the tournament attracts golf legends like Raymond Floyd, Chi Chi Rodriguez, Gary Player, Arnold Palmer, Jim Colbert, Don Massengale, Mike Hill, Lee Trevino, and defending champion J. C. Snead.

The Links at Key Biscayne offers beautiful weather, one of the best public golf courses in the country and panoramic views of scenic Biscayne Bay and the Miami skyline. The Royal Caribbean Classic is broadcast on ESPN and receives coverage from the local, national and international press. An estimated 70,000 golfing enthusiasts attend the tournament each year.

Dates:	February 2-4, 1996
Network:	ESPN
Times:	Fri - 3:30-5:30 EST
	Sat - 5:30-7:00 EST
	Sun-5:30-7:30
Yardage:	6,754
Par:	71
Total Purse:	$725,000
1st Prize:	$127,500
1995 Winner:	J. C. Snead
1995 Winning Score:	209 (69-75-65)
Principal Charitable Beneficiary:	Selection of South Florida Charities
Ticket Information:	1-305-365-1090

1

*Par 5
538 yards*

An accurate drive between water and sand is required to have any chance of getting home in two. A narrow landing area places a premium on the approach shot.

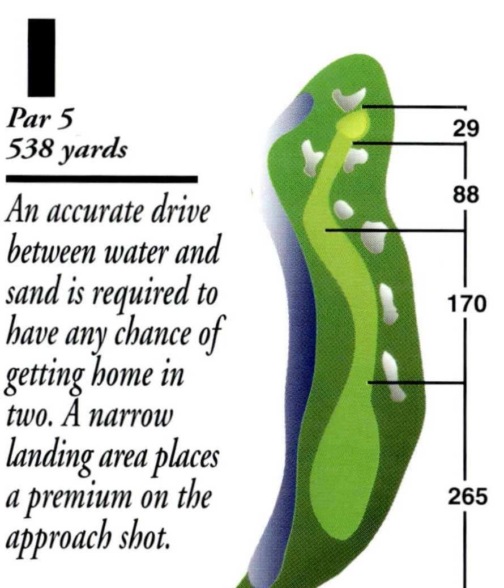

2

*Par 4
451 yards*

Par will be a good score on this difficult dogleg left. The tee shot must find the fairway in order to leave a reasonable approach shot made with a mid to long-iorn.

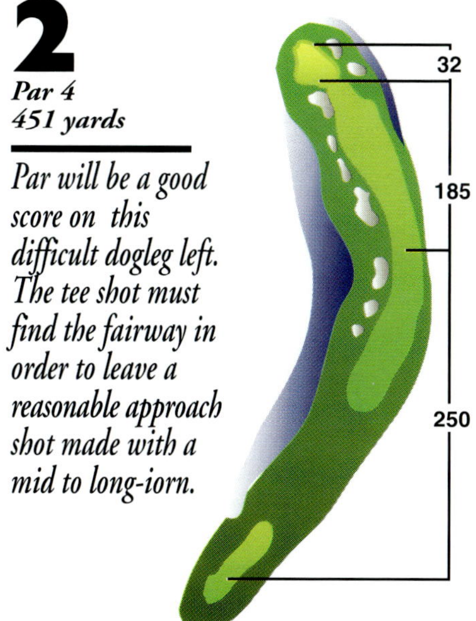

3

*Par 3
187 yards*

Concentration is the key as mangroves, water and sand unite to form a picturesque setting. Wind will factor as players through a mangrove chute across water to a well-bunkered green.

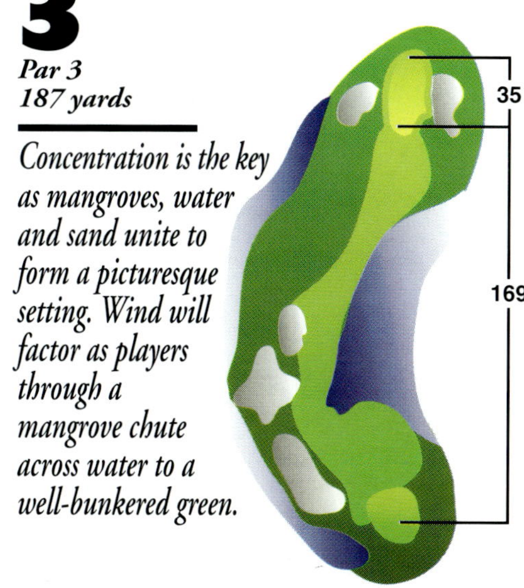

4

*Par 5
593 yards*

A lengthy track of land, which can be extended to 642 yards, is further complicated by the prevailing headwinds. Three solid shots will be required for a birdie try on the longest hole on the course.

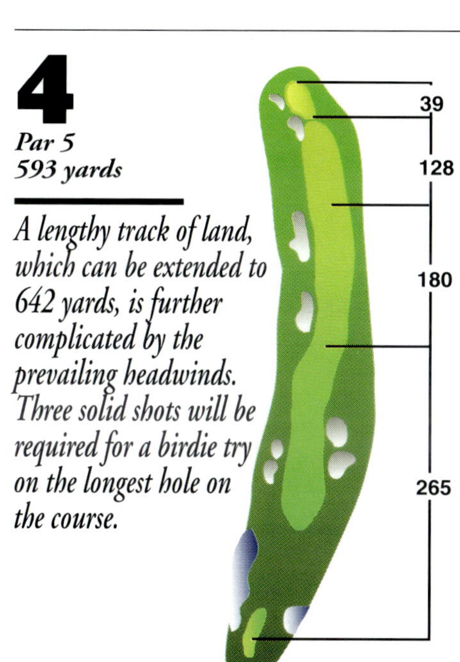

5

*Par 4
423 yards*

A well-hit drive leaves a mid-iron shot to an elevated putting surface. Protecting the well-mounted green are three deep bunkers which must be avoided.

6

*Par 3
182 yards*

Pin placement and club seletion are key factors as the players hit over mangroves to a green 140-feet long.

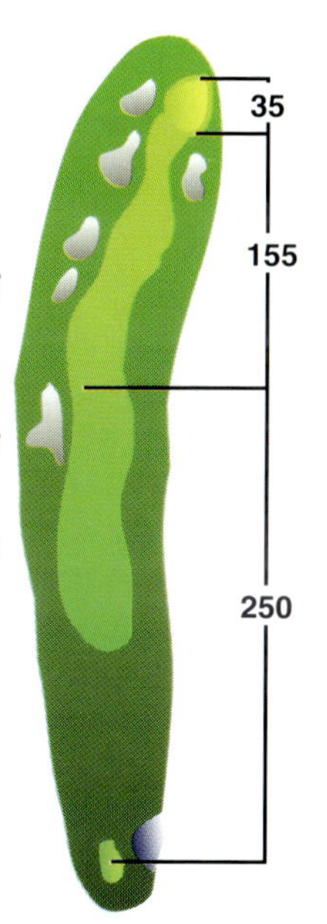

7

*Par 4
434 yards*

The most difficult hole on the course and one of the most difficult on the PGA Tour requires both precision and length off the tee. Approach shots will range from 150-200 yards over a salt water lagoon to a green well guarded by sand.

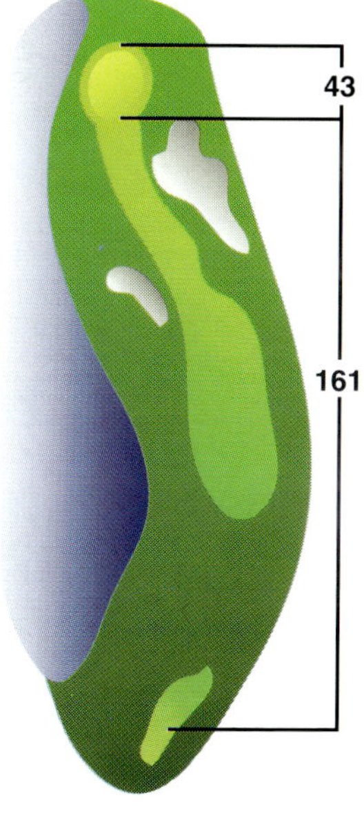

8

*Par 3
141 yards*

This is a relatively short hole surrounded by trees which mask the wind. But the gusts above the tree line play a crucial role in determining club selection.

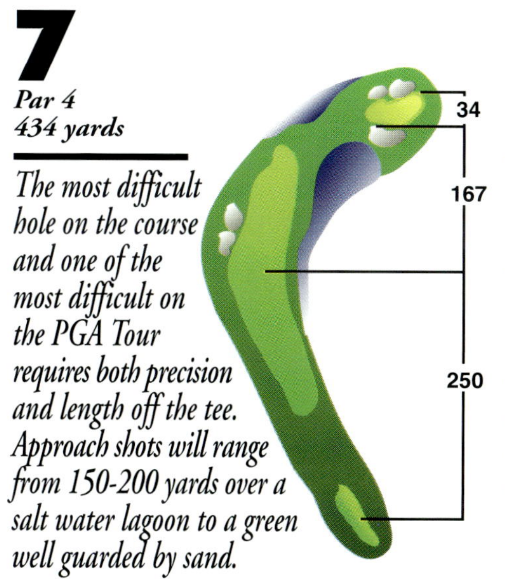

9

*Par 4
380 yards*

An iron or fairway wood may be the popular choice off the tee to keep the ball in play. The crowned fairway is the only safe landing area, with water to the left and sand to the right.

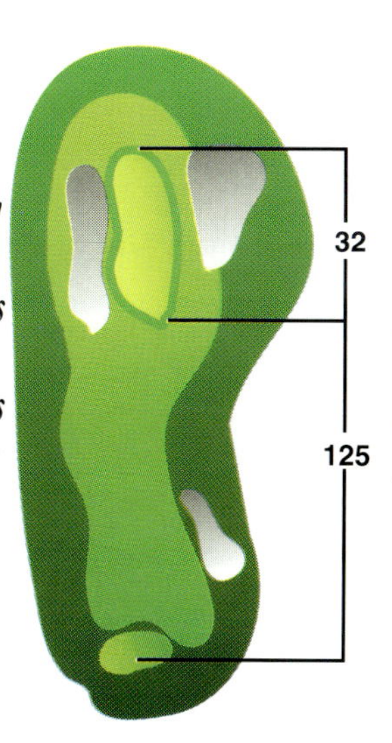

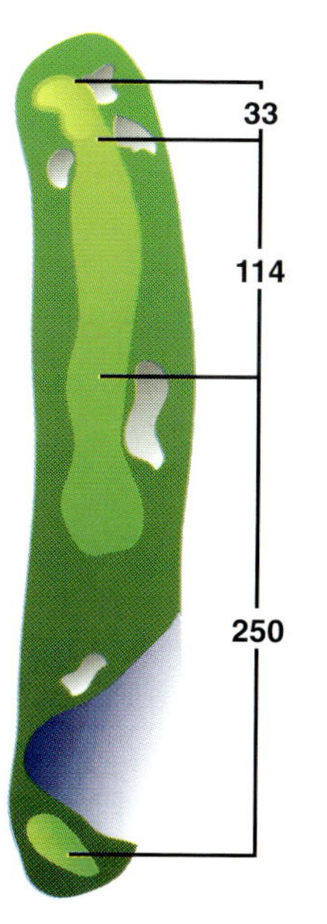

10

Par 5
533 yards

Destined to be a pivotal hole, the keys here are patience and strategy. Birdie is a distinct possibility if the third shot is set properly

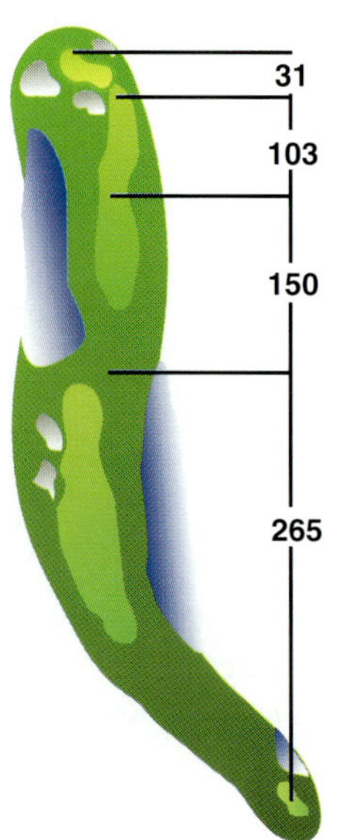

11

Par 4
384 yards

This hole presents a challenging approach shot over water and between two deep-faced bunkers to an elevated undulating green.

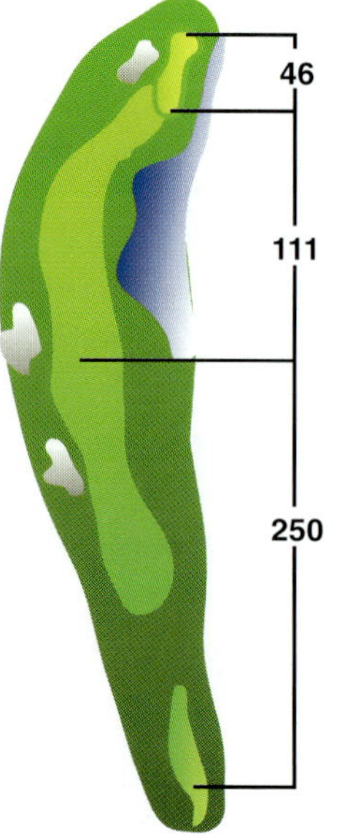

12

Par 3
168 yards

Water comes into play when the wind kicks up, so care must be taken in club selction. A back-left pin position will challenge even the best shotmakers. High mounding makes this hole a great spectator spot.

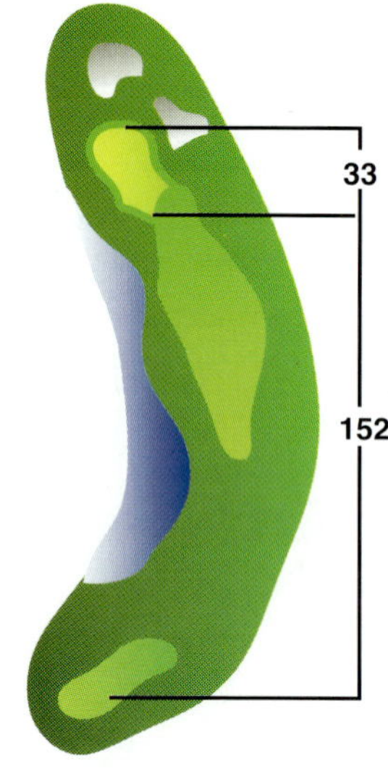

13

Par 4
390 yards

Wide open and straight forward, this hole normally plays into a headwind. Players will be left with mid to long-iron shots into a large green.

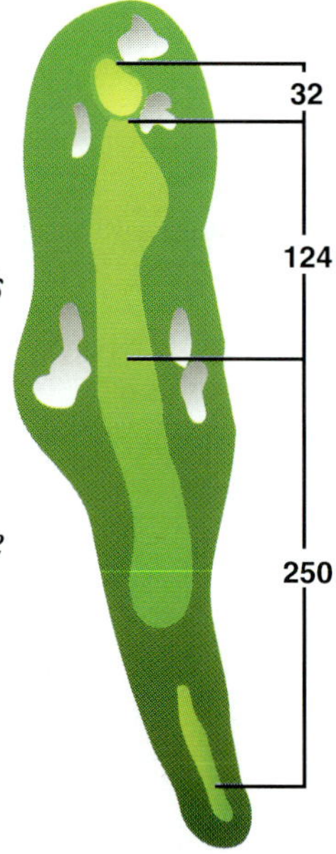

14

Par 5
521 yards

A great driving hole that benefits the long hitter. If conditions are right, players can get home in two and be rewarded with at least a birdie, or possibly an eagle.

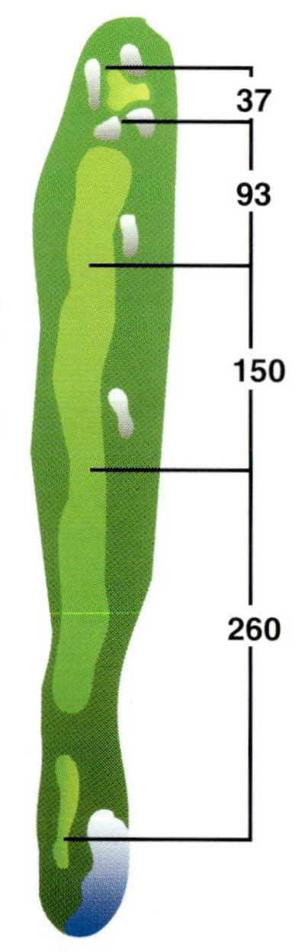

15

Par 4
424 yards

Flanked on both sides by tall trees, players must split the middle of the fairway to avoid trouble. A narrow green adds a degree of difficulty to an approach shot of 150-175 yards.

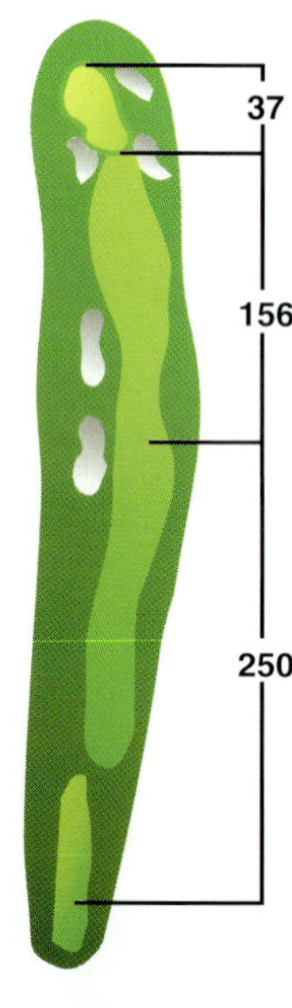

16

Par 4
389 yards

With sand left and water right, the best tee shot placement is left center of the fairway on this sharp dogleg left. A mid to short-iron shot will remain to this heavily bunkered green.

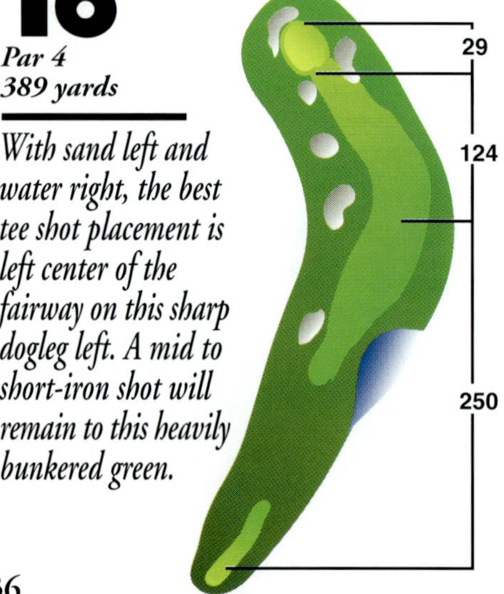

17

Par 3
187 yards

This hole is completely sur-rounded by trees. A deceiving wind, which blows off the bay and over the tree line, makes club selection difficult as shots must carry pass a deep bunker that guards the front.

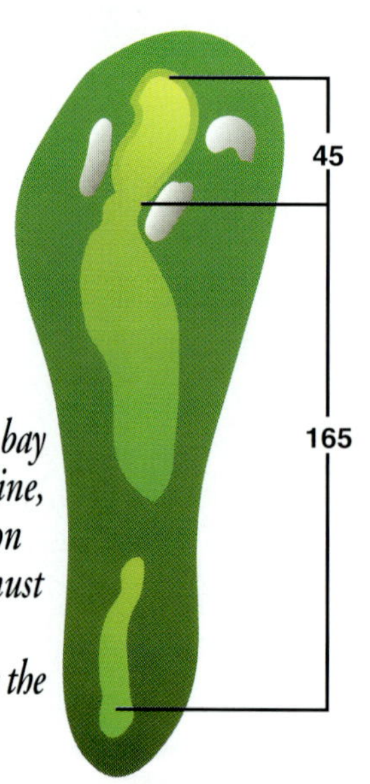

18

Par 4
419 yards

A great finishing hole, converted from a short par 5, that requires a perfect drive to avoid water on both sides of the fairway. Most players will be left with about 150-165 yards to a tight green that completes this magnificent hole.

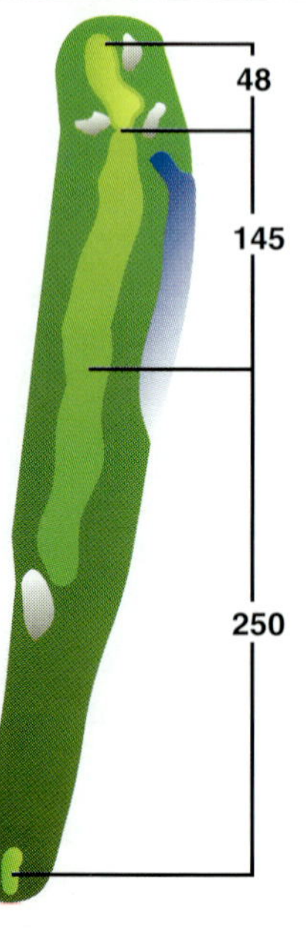

THE COURSE: TORREY PINES MUNICIPAL GOLF COURSE, SAN
DIEGO, CALIFORNIA

*T*orrey Pines is situated on the rugged Pacific coastline and offers a challenge for players that is not found at other courses throughout the year. Strong winds rip in off the ocean to increase the difficulty of the many canyons and barrancas. The dangerously quick greens have frustrated many players vying for the championship title.

The municipal layout, designed by William P. Bell and finished by his son, William F. Bell, provides a very formidable challenge for the pros during this San Diego tournament, especially during the unpredictable February weather.

The 1996 San Diego PGA TOUR® event will mark the fifth year for Buick Motor Division as the title sponsor, continuing Buick's distinction as the first corporation to sponsor four PGA TOUR® events. Other events sponsored by Buick include the Buick Classic, the Buick Open and the Buick Challenge.

The inaugural San Diego Open at Torrey Pines was played in 1968 and won by Tom Weiskopf. J. C. Snead won the tournament in 1975 and successfully defended the title the following year. Other two-time winners at Torrey Pines have been Tom Watson (1977 & 1980) and Steve Pate (1988 & 1992). George Burns beat the course by scoring a record 22 under par 266 in 1987.

Dates:	February 8-11, 1996
Network:	NBC and ESPN
Times:	ESPN
	Thurs/Fri 1:00-3:00 EST
	NBC
	Sat 4:30-6:00 EST
	Sun 4:00-6:00 EST
Yardage:	7,021
Par:	72
Slope:	131
Rating:	74
Total Purse:	$1,200,000
1st Prize:	$216,000
1995 Winner:	Peter Jacobsen
1995 Winning Score:	269 (68-65-68-68)
Charitable Beneficiary:	San Diego County Junior Golf Association and Boys and Girls Clubs of San Diego
Benefits to Date:	$2 million
Ticket Information:	1-800-888-BUICK

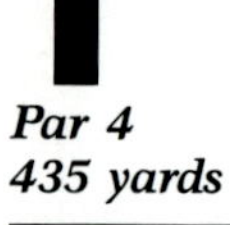

1

Par 4
435 yards

This first hole starts off long. The left side of the fairway is favored to open the view to the green. A mid to long iron must be hit short of the hole to leave an uphill putt.

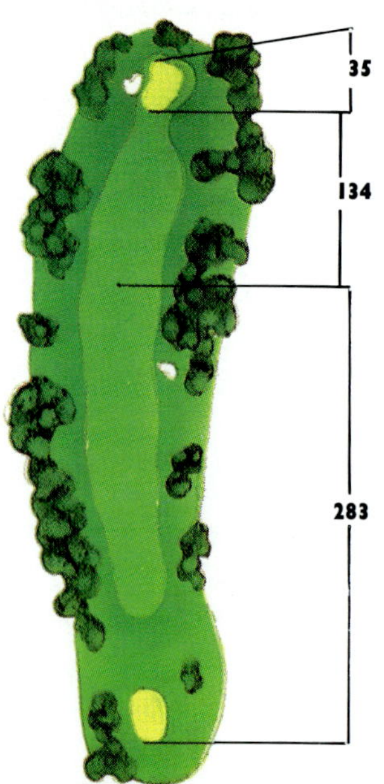

2

Par 4
350 yards

A driver, again down the left side, will set up for a good chance at birdie. The narrow green is protected by a bunker on the left and many trees on the right.

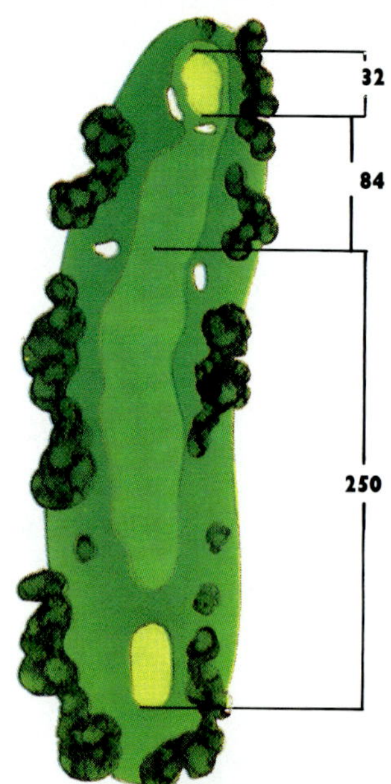

3

Par 3
174 yards

The short wide green is guarded by bunkers front and back. The undulating putting surface can make three putts an unfortunate possibility.

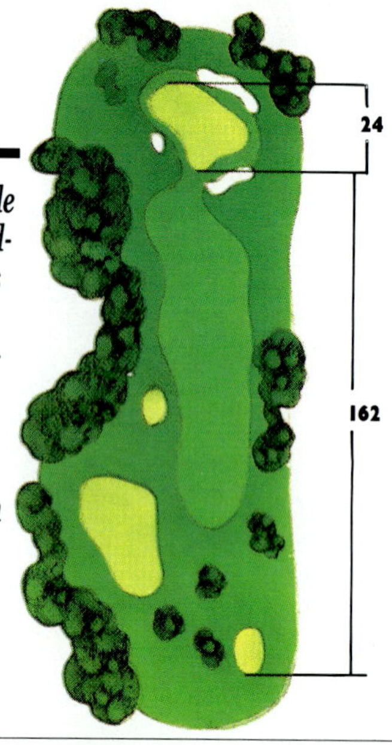

4

Par 4
447 yards

Long and straight down the middle — the drive should be followed by a high lofted shot into the green. Two bunkers protect the putting surface left and right.

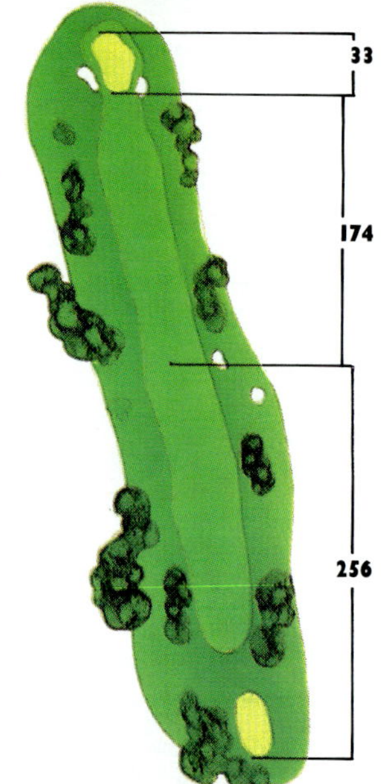

5

Par 4
404 yards

Players will favor the left side of the fairway to avoid the fairway bunker and trees on the right. The small, round green is receptive to one-putts.

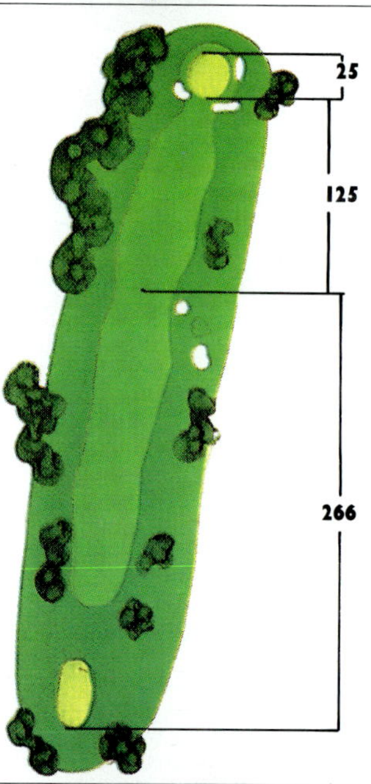

6

Par 5
537 yards

A fade that follows the curve of the hole will allow some players to get home in two. Pin placements on the back left or right can be difficult to hit.

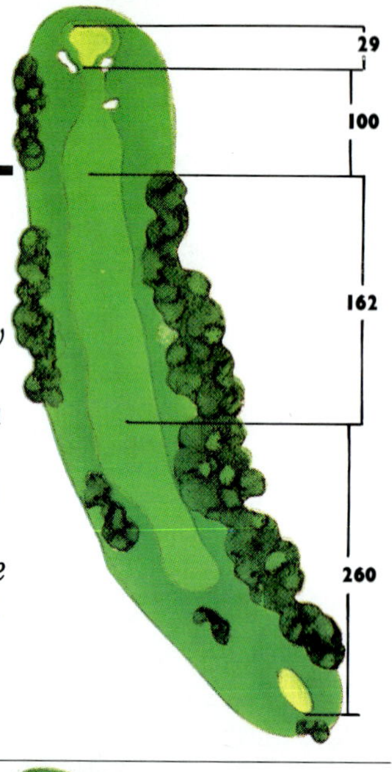

7

Par 4
454 yards

Usually into the wind and always long, this seventh is a good par 4. The green is cut into the hillside with a bunker on the lower right side.

8

Par 3
171 yards

The long green provides many difficult pin positions. Swirling winds above the treeline can cause problems for tee shots. The green slopes from back to front.

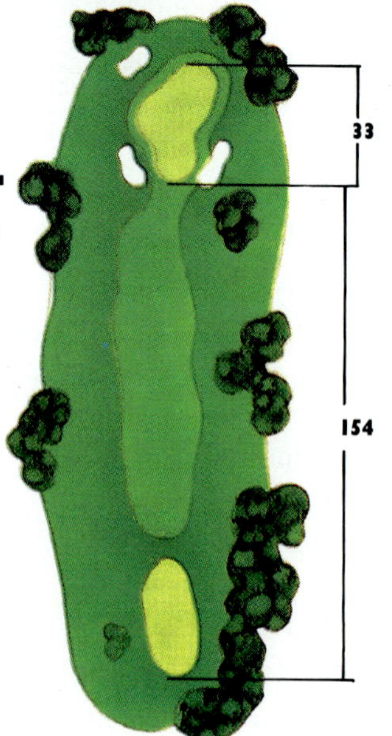

9

Par 5
537 yards

Players tear up this final hole on the front nine. Birdies are plentiful and eagles are not uncommon.

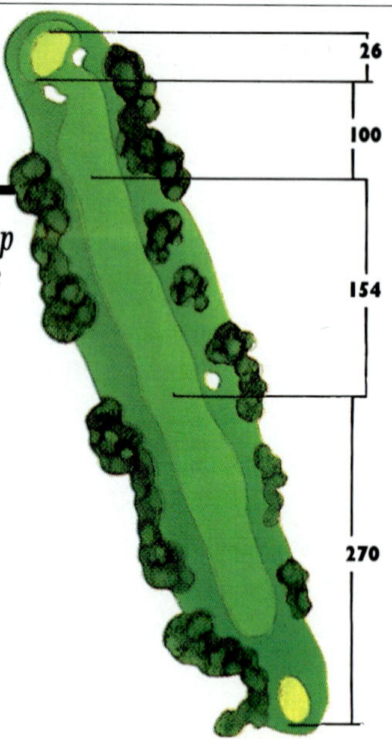

10

Par 4
373 yards

The momentum gained from the ninth hole should carry into this tenth for another birdie. The bunker short left comes into play when the pin is placed on the back left corner.

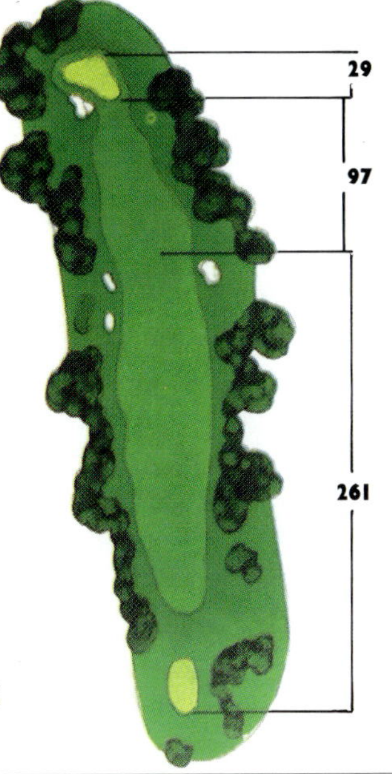

11

Par 3
206 yards

A mid to long iron will be used from the tee. The small green can be tricky — players will be satisfied with a 3 on this hole.

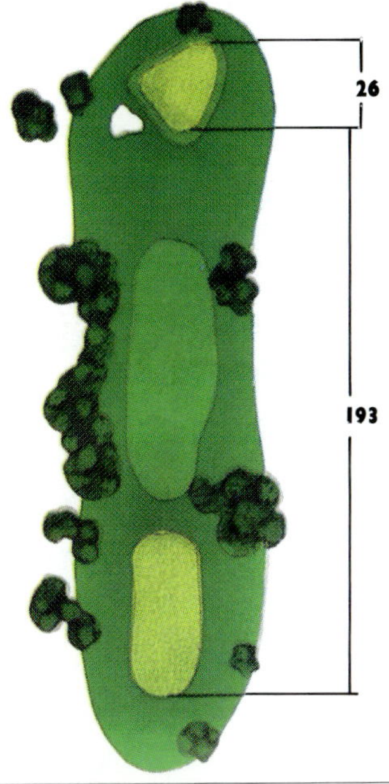

12

Par 4
469 yards

Into the wind, this par 4 can be tough. Two well hit shots are required to get to the putting surface. The long narrow green is guarded by bunkers left and right.

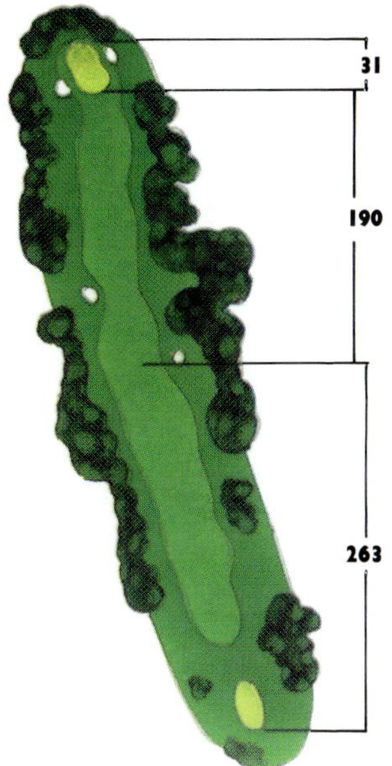

13

Par 5
533 yards

A level drive should end up just beyond the bunker on the right. Two perfect shots are a necessity to get home in two. Birdies are common but eagles will be rare.

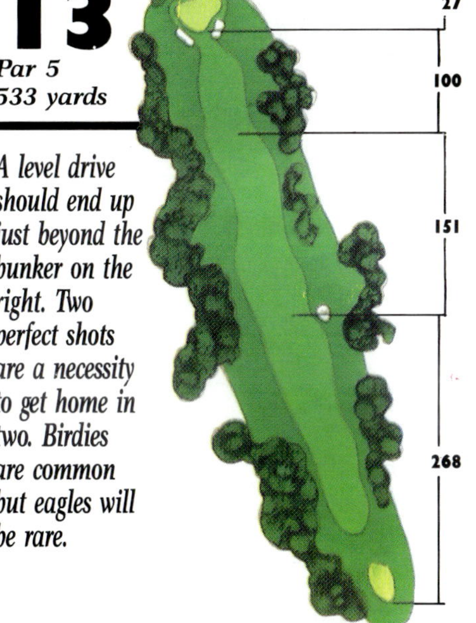

14

Par 4
396 yards

Players will favor the right side of the fairway on their drives. An accurate mid-iron to the green will allow for chance at birdie.

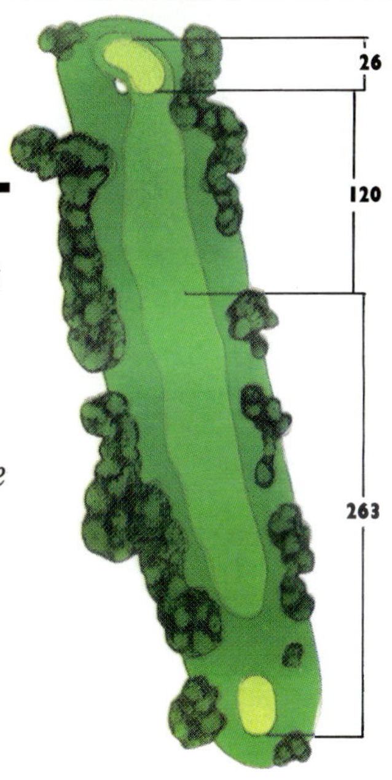

15

Par 4
390 yards

A drive down the left middle of the fairway should avoid the trees to the right and also set up for a short approach. The elevated green is fronted by two deep bunkers.

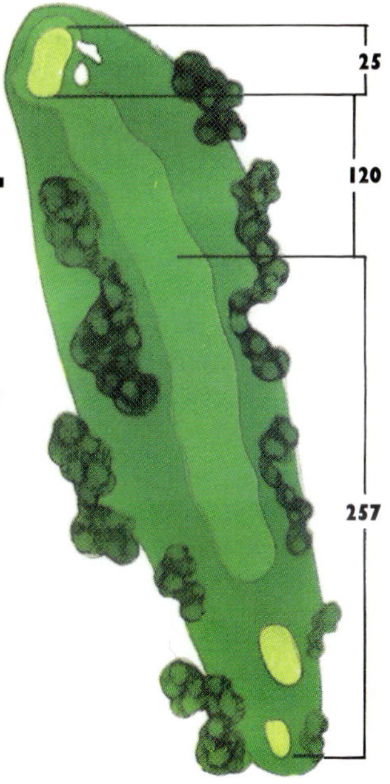

16

Par 3
201 yards

The winds can make this par 3 even more difficult. With the tournament on the line, players will be playing for the heart of the green.

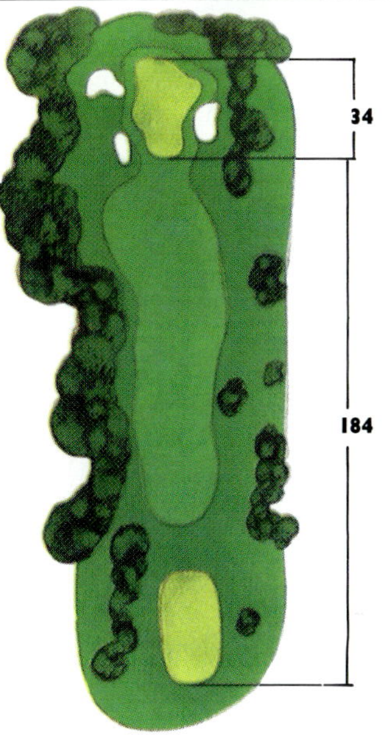

17

Par 4
426 yards

A canyon threatens from the left side. A long drive down the right middle will leave a mid iron to the putting surface. A birdie on this hole would get the competition concerned.

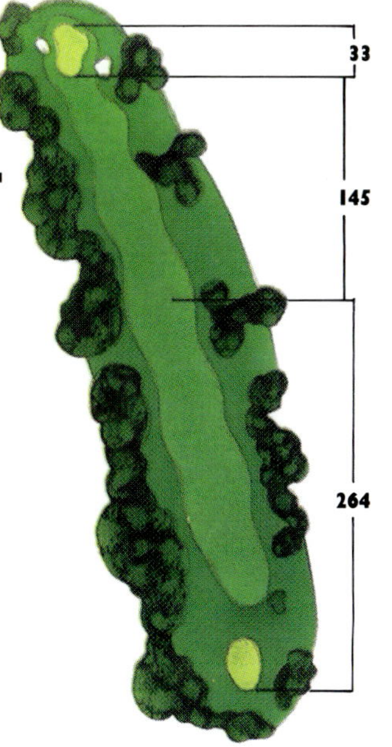

18

Par 5
499 yards

Players have a chance to come from behind on this short par 5. "Devlin's Billabong" protects the front left of the green. Birdies and eagles finish the tournament in style.

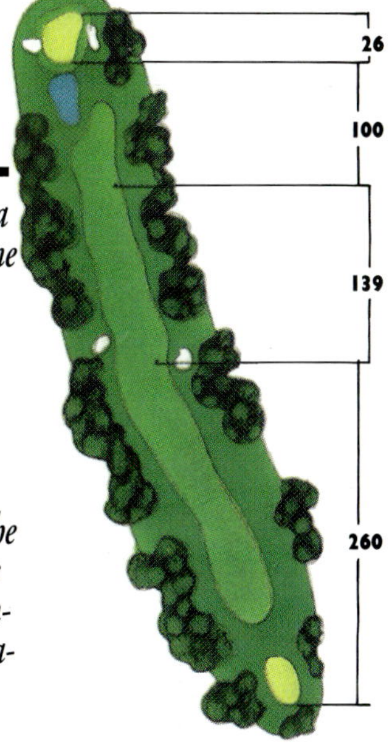

THE COURSE: THE CLASSICS COURSE AT LELY RESORT & C.C., NAPLES, FL.

*P*almer, Nicklaus, Trevino, Floyd, Player, Rodriguez, Littler, Barber, January, Weiskopf, Murphy... these are the names that thrust professional golf to the forefront in the 1960's. And many of these golfing greats helped establish the SENIOR PGA TOUR® in 1980. From just two tournaments and $250,000 in prize money in 1980, SENIOR PGA TOUR® professionals will vie for almost $30 million in 42 events in 1996.

    Defending champion Bob Murphy's quest to be a two-time winner here will not be an easy one. The expected world-class field with past champions Gary Player, Gene Littler, Jimmy Powell and the field's other two-time champions, Lee Trevino and Mike Hill, will do its best to make sure someone other than Murphy picks up this year's winner's check. Make your plans now to be a part of Southwest Florida's most exciting and visible event. Remember, while some great golfer will be leaving Naples with $90,000 more than he came with, the real winner will be the local charities.

Dates:	February 9-11, 1996
Network:	ESPN
Times:	Fri - 5:00 - 7:00 EST
	Sat - 4:30 - 6:30 EST
	Sun - 4:30 - 7:00 EST
Yardage:	6,722
Par:	72
Slope:	128
Rating:	71.1
Total Purse:	$500,000
1st Prize:	$90,000
1995 Winner:	Bob Murphy
1995 Winning Score:	137 (67-70)
Principal Charitable Beneficiary:	The Boy Scouts of America Southwest Florida Chapter
Ticket Information:	1-800-457-PROS

1

Par 4
387 yards

A well struck tee shot leaves a short iron to this generous green.

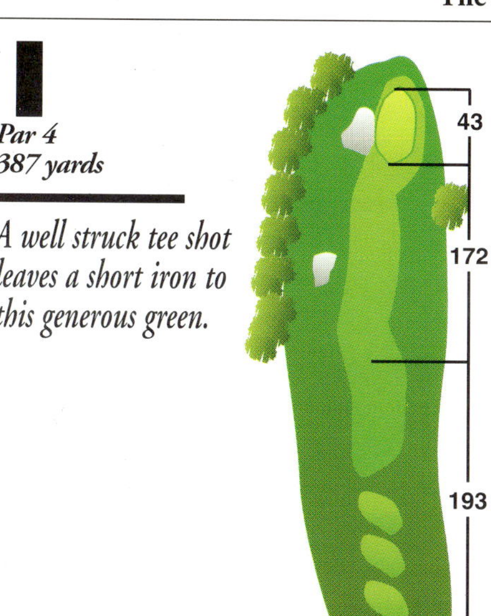
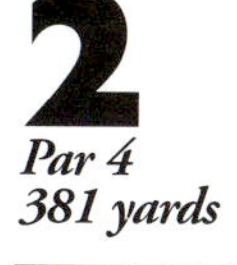

2

Par 4
381 yards

Water along the right side forces players to favor the left side off the tee. A front right bunker makes this green open up form the left side of fairway.

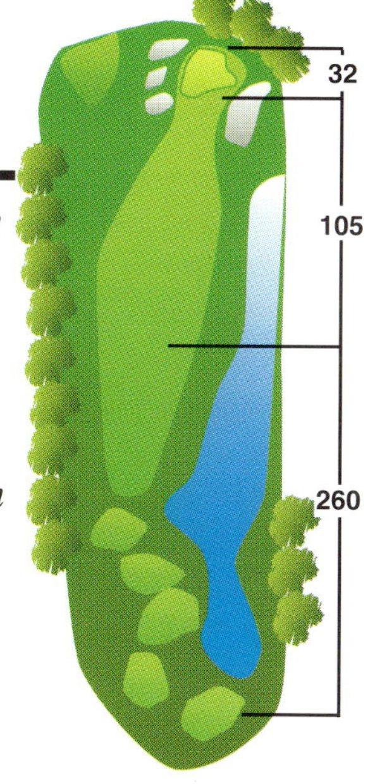

3

Par 5
581 yards

The longest hole on the course requires two solid shots to get into short iron range of this well -bunkered green.

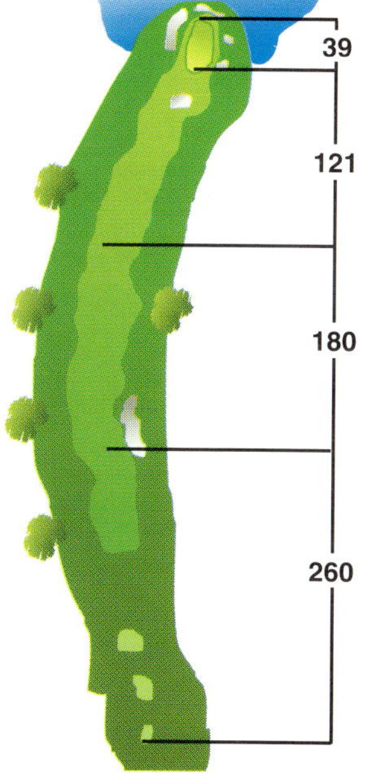

4

Par 3
185 yards

A well-struck middle to long iron is required on this Par 3. The water guarding this kidney-shaped green should not come into play as much as the sand..

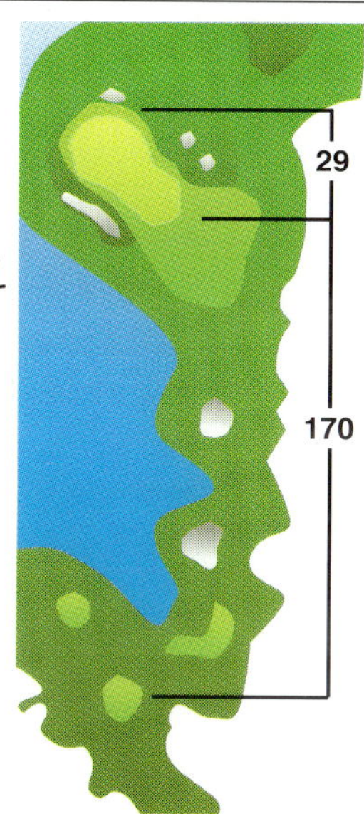

5

Par 4
375 yards

Accuracy off the tee is the key on this tight dogleg left Par 4. A three wood into the right side of the fairway opens up the green for a short iron approach.

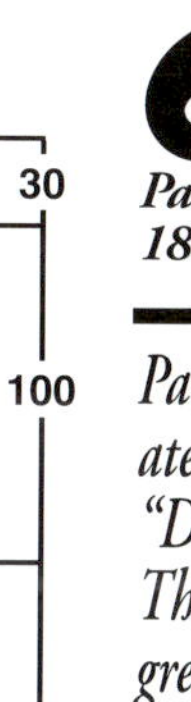

6

Par 3
181 yards

Par 3 appropriately named "Desert Storm." This island green is surrounded by waste area. Proper club selection is imperative.

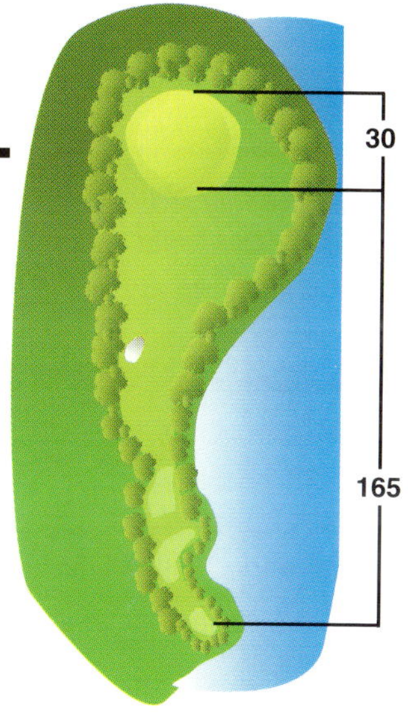

7

Par 5
512 yards

A good drive down the right side allows the longer hitters to go for this green in two. Long, two-tiered green makes tow putting a difficult task.

8

Par 4
407 yards

Depending on which tee used, players can have anything from wedge to 3 iron into this green. Keeping the ball below the hole is important as this green slopes sharply from back to front.

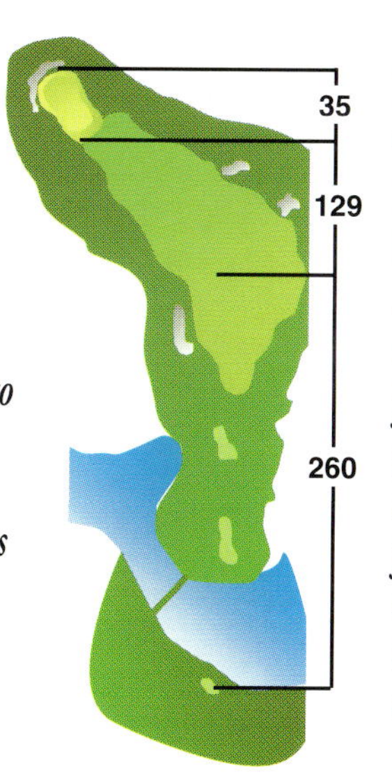

9

Par 4
426 yards

This sharp dogleg right places a premium on the tee shot. The fairway is very generous, but the player must favor the left side to avoid being blocked out by trees.

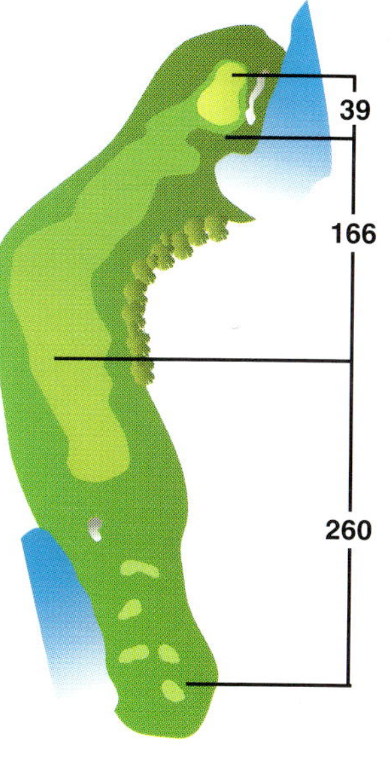

10

Par 4
427 yards

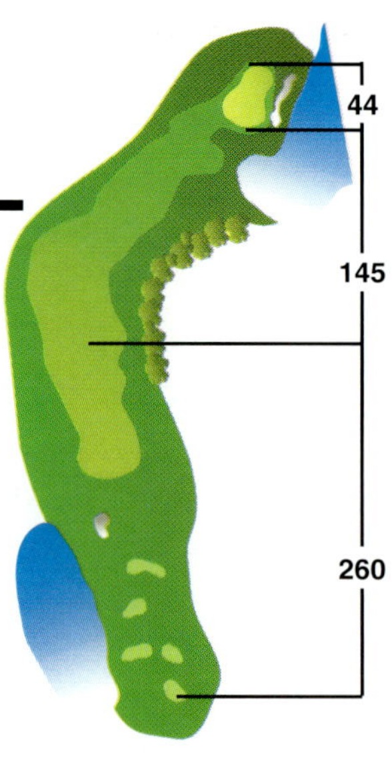

The ideal drive is down the left center of the fairway. The green is well-bunkered and slopes toward the tee. One of the best par 4's on the course.

11

Par 5
523 yards

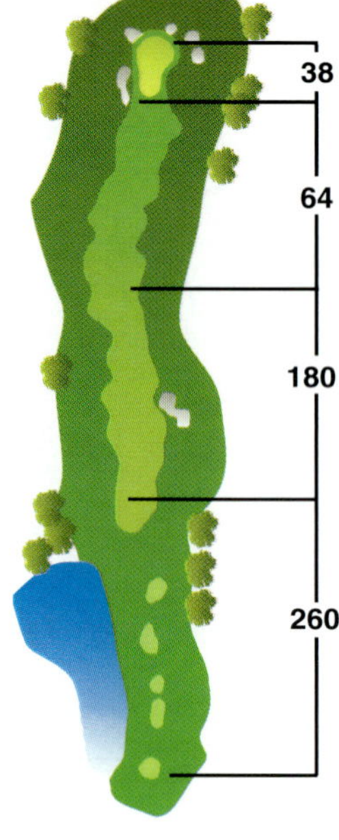

This elevated green is the most severely sloping green on the course. Players hitting wedge in for their third shot must keep the ball below the hole for a reasonable chance at birdie.

12

Par 3
162 yards

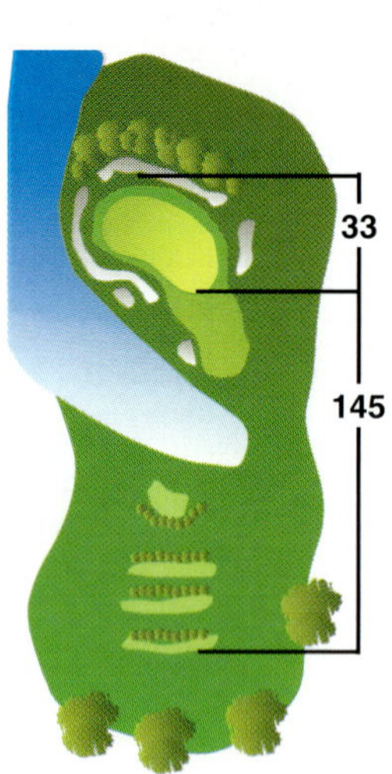

A middle iron shot from an elevated tee over water to this flat well-bunkered green. Proper club selection is a must.

13

Par 4
352 yards

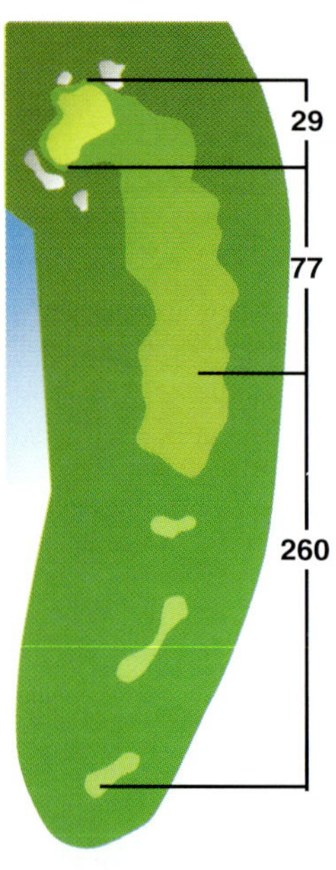

The club of choice off the tee should be a long iron or 3 wool. Players must avoid deep pot bunker in front of green with their short iron approach.

14

Par 4
417 yards

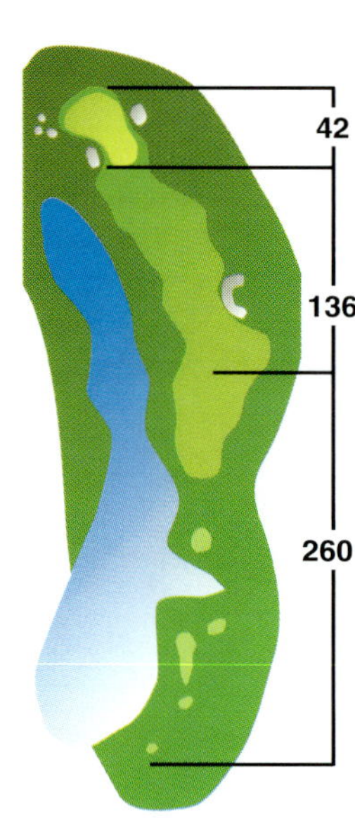

Water along the left side of the fairway makes this arguably the toughest tee shot on the course. Anywhere in this fairway is good. This very deep green makes proper club selection a must.

15

Par 4
365 yards

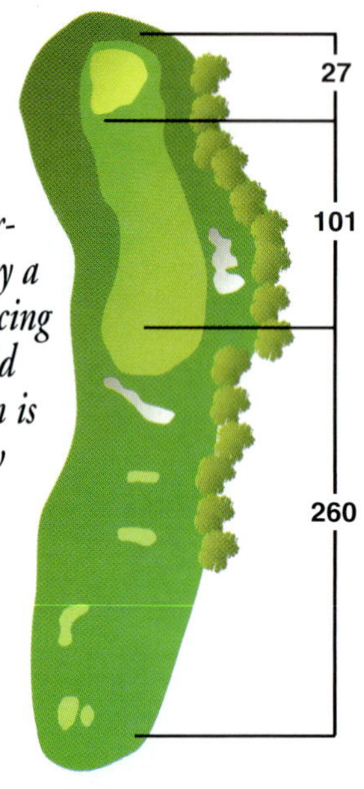

Target golf! This fairway is surrounded by a natural wetland placing a premium on a solid tee shot. A short iron is left to a very shallow green.

16

Par 3
190 yards

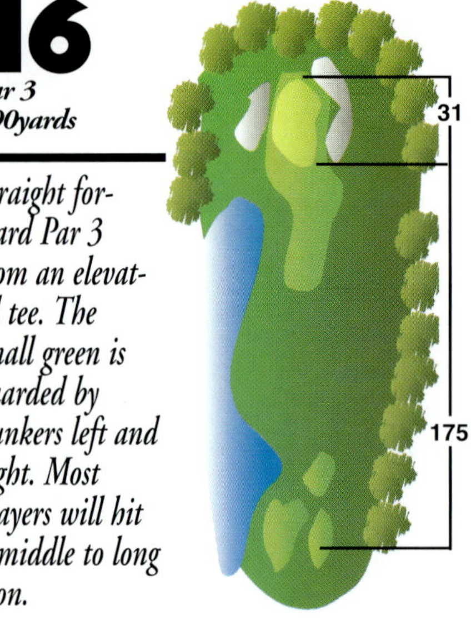

Straight forward Par 3 from an elevated tee. The small green is guarded by bunkers left and right. Most players will hit a middle to long iron.

17

Par 5
507 yards

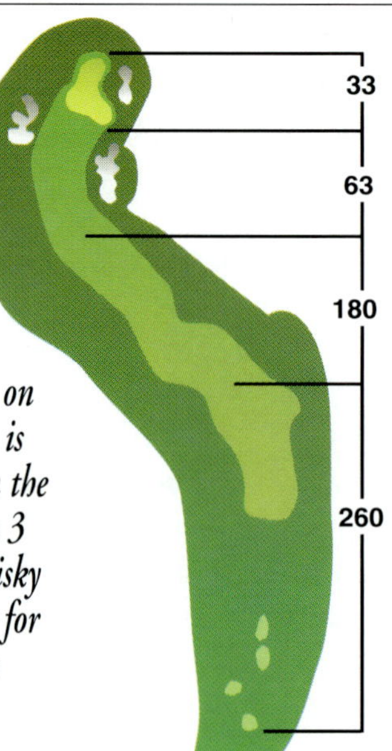

Tee shot must be right center to avoid oak tree on left. The green is tucked back in the trees making a 3 wood second risky business. Look for a lot of birdies here.

18

Par 4
427 yards

What a finishing hole! The tee shot requires a solid driver to a fairway flanked with water left and waste area right. The green is elevated and very shallow from front to back making it hard to hold. Advantage long hitters! It is much easier to hold this green with a short iron.

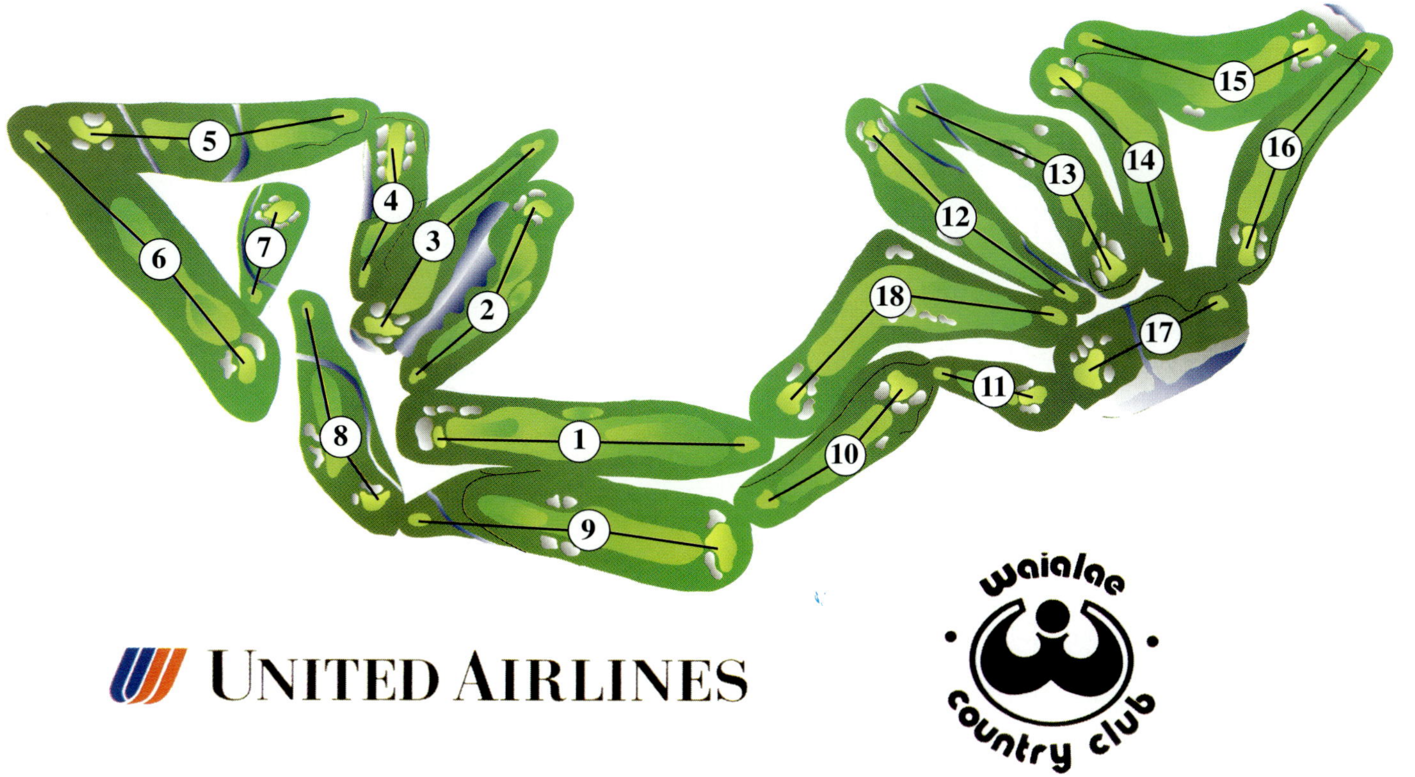

THE COURSE: WAIALAE COUNTRY CLUB, HONOLULU, HAWAII

*J*ohn Morse won his first PGA Tour championship with his 19 under par 269 at the 1995 United Airlines Hawaiian Open winning $216,000.

The 30th Anniversary Hawaiian Open saw Morse garner 18 of his 19 winning strokes on the Waialae Golf Course par 5's. He had 3 eagles, 12 birdies and one par over the 16 par 5's.

Duffy Waldorf and Tom Lehman finished 3 strokes back at 272 for a tie at second place earning $105,600 each while Paul Azinger, Bill Glasson and Dan Pohl finished at third placeworth $49,600 each.

The 31st Anniversary United Airlines Hawaiian Open should be as memorable since the dates are back to mid February a traditional position not used in the past five years under the PGA Tour schedule.

Opened in 1927 the Waialae Golf Course designed by Seth Raynor is located just minutes from Waikiki and is a private member only course. Course play is reversed during the tournament with the par 5 9th becoming the 18th finishing hole and providing the sun spotlight from the West. It will be remembered for the dramatic 1983 one shot bounce directly into the cup 128 yard eagle shot by Isao Aoki to win the Open.

Dates:	Febuary 12-18
Network:	ABC
Times:	TBA
Yardage:	7024
Par:	72
Slope:	133
Rating:	73.2
Total Purse:	$1,200,000
1st Prize:	$216,000
1995 Winner:	John Morse
1995 Winning Score:	269 (71, 65, 65, 68)
Principal Charitable Beneficiary:	Bobby Benson Foundation
Charitable Benefits to Date:	$1,000,000
Ticket Information:	808.-526-1232

1

Par 5
539 yards

Great opening hole. Down-wind par five that's reachable in two. O.B. left and right, however, on the tee shot. A large bunker guards the left front of the green and a series of three bunkers on the right. Good birdie opportunity to start the round.

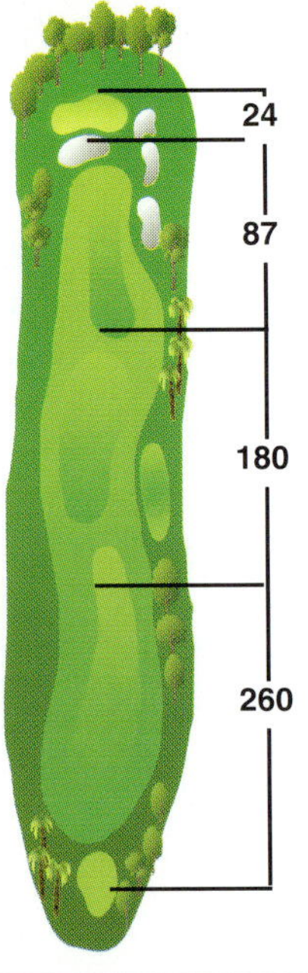

2

Par 4
362 yards

Be careful on the drive. A hoooked drive is in the lake and the trees on the right come into play for drives played too safe. Toughest pin position is on the far right of the green behind the bunker.

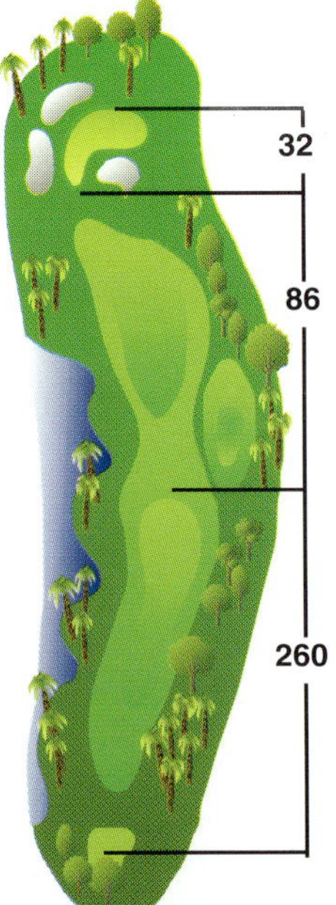

3

Par 4
419 yards

Named after "Mr. Golf" in Hawaii, Waialae founding member Francis I"I Brown once drove this green. The green has been redesignrd and brings the lake more into play on the second shot. A long accurate drive off the tee will reward the player with a short iron left, for this dangerous second shot.

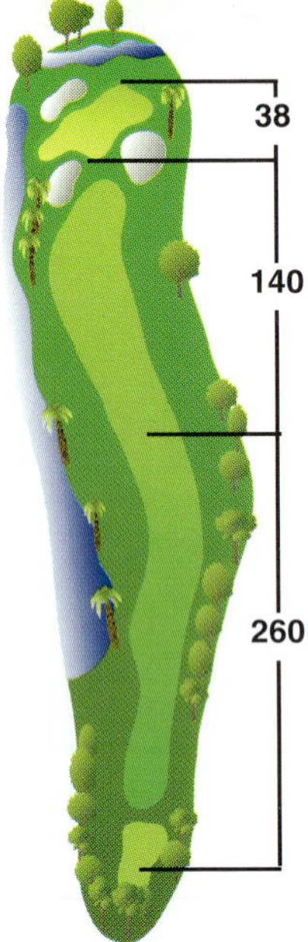

4

Par 3
196 yards

A very difficult par three played into the wind. Classic Seth Raynor-designed green over 55 yards long with a deep swale running across the middle. Par is a welcome score here.

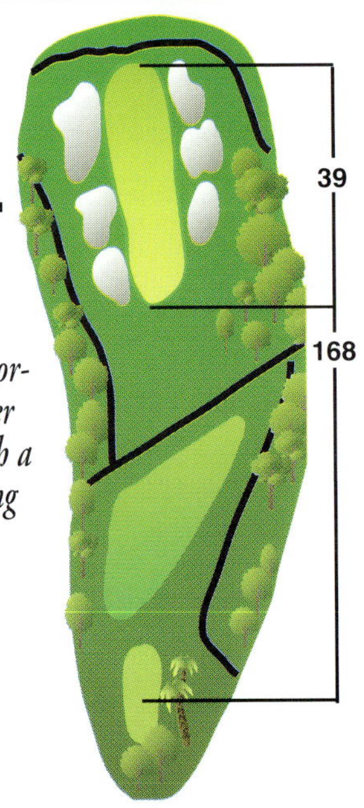

5

Par 4
460 yards

A tough driving hole with two ditches running across the tree lined fairway. A good drive leaves a short iron to the most heavily contoured green on the golf course. Putting is very tricky and birdies will be rare on this hole.

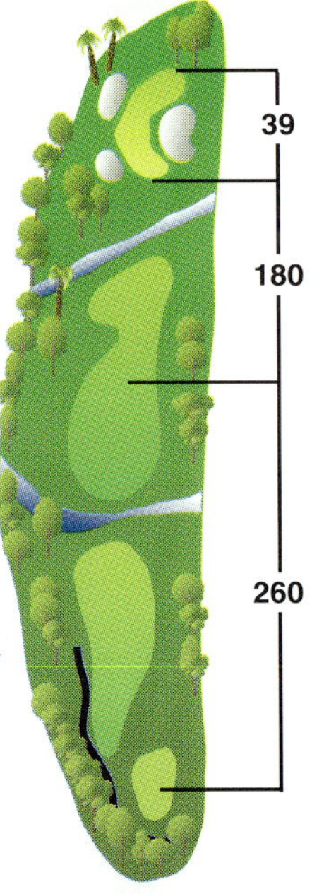

6

Par 4
463 yards

A prevailing left-to-right wind blows straight towards O.B. on the right. Drives have been known to "go astray" here. Large mounds and trees protect the corner of the dog-leg so a well placed drive must be kept left. The second shot is a middle iron to a green bunkered on bothsides.

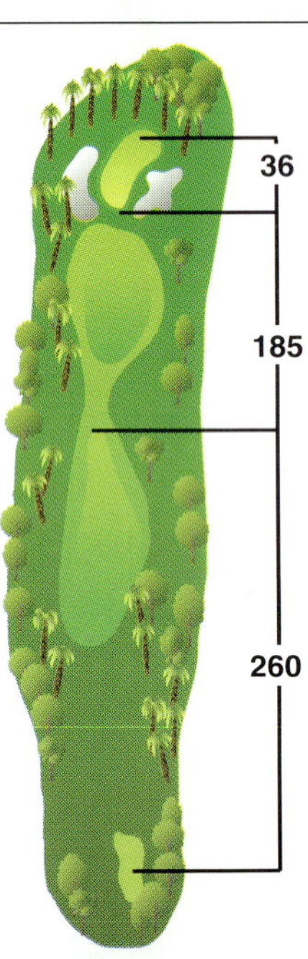

7

Par 3
182 yards

The second of the par threes on the front. This green is as wide as the par three #4 green was long. Originally this green was completely surrounded by sand giving the hole its name. Bunkers still wrap-around the entire front green runs laterally front to back.

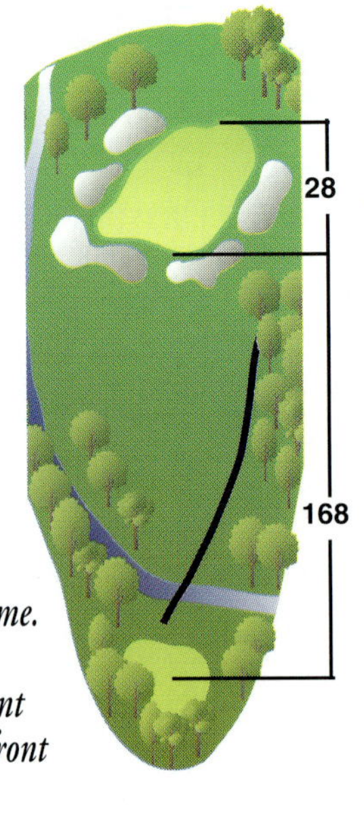

8

Par 4
419 yards

The tee shot is the "hairy shot" on this dog-leg left par four. Played from an elevated tee, the drive must carry a creek 220 yards out and avoid two fairway bunkers on the right. Once that is accomplished, a short iron is left to the green. Definite birdie hole.

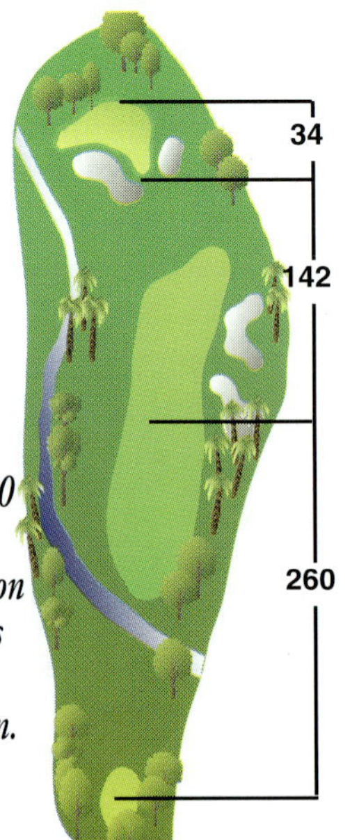

9

Par 5
513 yards

Normally played as #18 by the members, this par-five requires accuracy on both the drive and second shots. O.B. runs down the entire hole on both sides. A strong left-to-right wind against the player makes things even tougher. This hole is reach-able in two however, and this hole will give up lots of birdies.

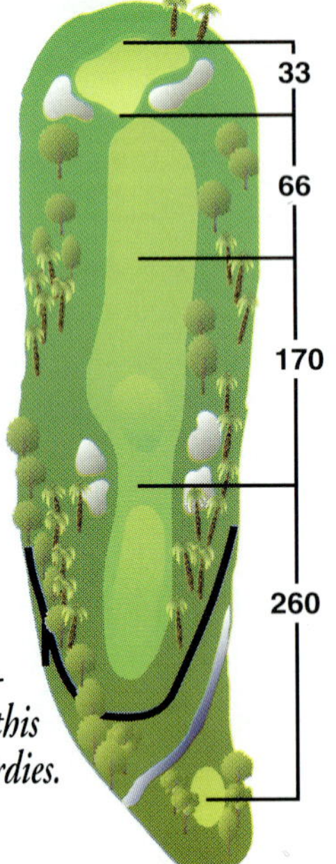

10

Par 4
349 yards

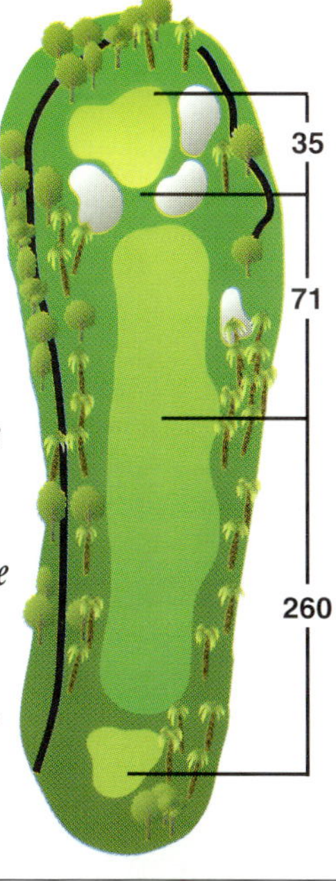

At 349 yards, this is the shortest par four on the course. Best place for the drive is on the right side of the fairway. The green is protected by several deep bunkers and three towering palm trees standing sentry on the left. Good birdies hole.

11

Par 3
181 yards

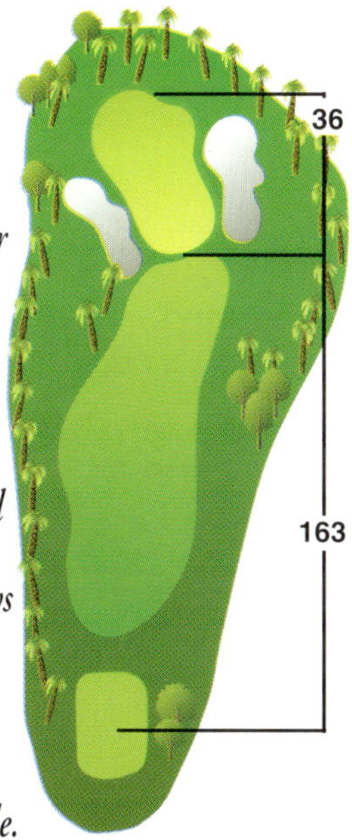

The real challenge for the players on their tee shot is not to be distracted by the magnificent sweeping view of the Pacific Ocean behind the green. The prevailing wind blows left to right so the large bunker on the right will see lots of action. This is an excellent one shot hole.

12

Par 4
446 yards

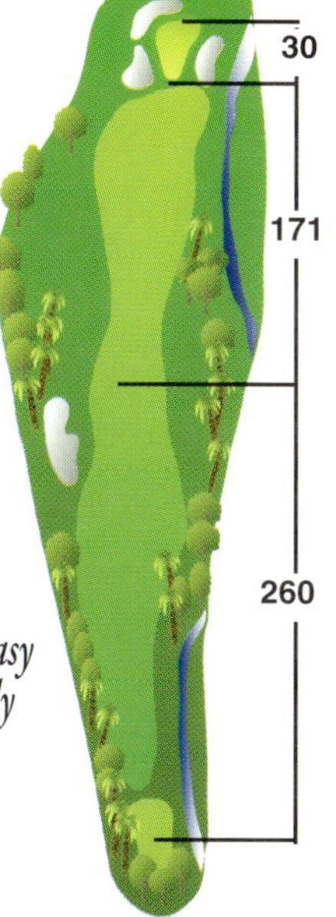

A long hole requiring both length and accuracy off the tee. The drive must be placed between the fairway bunker on the left and a series of mounds on the right. A middle iron sets up an easy birdie putt on a relatively flat putting surface.

13

Par 5
508 yards

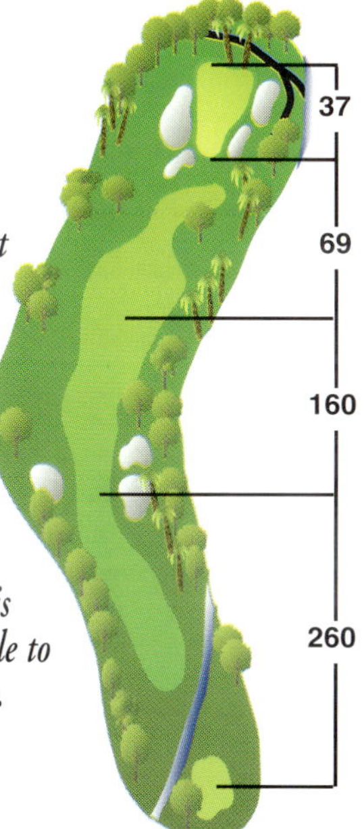

A short dog-leg right par five easily reachable in two. The fairway bunkers and the series of mounds and trees on the right tighten the driving area but this is still the easiest hole to birdie on the course.

14

Par 4
412 yards

A dog-leg left par four played back towards the mountains. A well placed drive to the right side of the fairway leaves a short iron shot to a green that is sloped steeply from back to front. Players will try to stay below the pin for the ideal birdie putt.

15

Par 4
398 yards

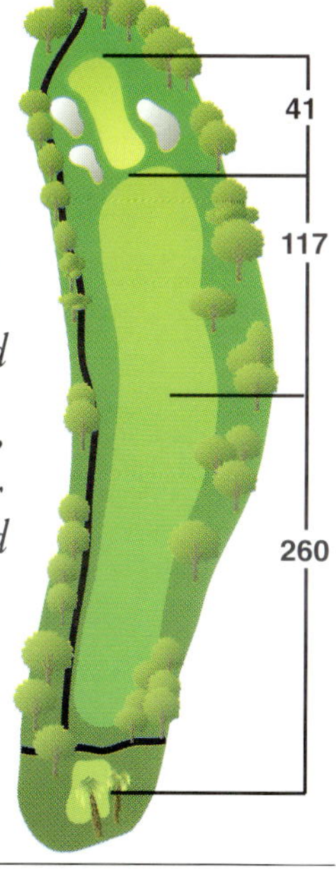

This hole can certainly be trouble. O.B. runs up the entire left side and both the drive and second shots are played into the wind. Tee shots out to the right are blocked on their second shot by a huge, old Kiawe tree which dominates the right side of the fairway about 100 yards from the hole.

16

Par 4
434 yards

Tee it high and let it fly. The players head for the finish with the wind at their back. The best place for the drive is on the right side of the fairway just inside the fairway bunker. The second shot is a short iron played to a green framed by the Pacific Ocean and several large palm trees. Most scenic spot on the golf course.

17

Par 3
191 yards

A very difficult par three requiring a long or middle iron. The green is a classic Redan-style green with a large bunker on the left and a series of four deep and hidden bunkers guarding the right. Par three is a good score, especially in the final round.

18

Par 5
552 yards

Great, exciting finishing hole. Isao Aoki proved this in 1983 with a spectacular eagle for his victory. Aoki knocked it in from 126 yards out but this hole is reachable in two. The tee shot must avoid the series of bunkers on the left and the pot bunker on the right. The second shot is played straight down-wind to the green. Look for another dramatic finish this year.

THE COURSE: TPC OF TAMPA BAY, TAMPA FLORIDA

*T*his will be the fifth consecutive year that the tournament will be held at TPC of Tampa Bay and all the big names on the SENIOR PGA TOUR® are expected to compete for a purse of $625,000. The winner's check will be $112,500.

Expect to see former champions Rocky Thompson, Bob Charles, Mike Hill, Dale Douglass, and of course, crowd favorites Arnold Palmer and Chi Chi Rodriguez.

Dates:	February 16-18, 1996
Network:	ESPN
Times:	TBA
Yardage:	6,638
Par:	71
Total Purse:	$625,000
1st Prize:	$112,500
1995 Winner:	Dave Stockton
1995 Winning Score:	204 (70-66-68)
Principal Charitable Beneficiary:	Various local charities
Ticket Information:	1-813-265-GOLF

1

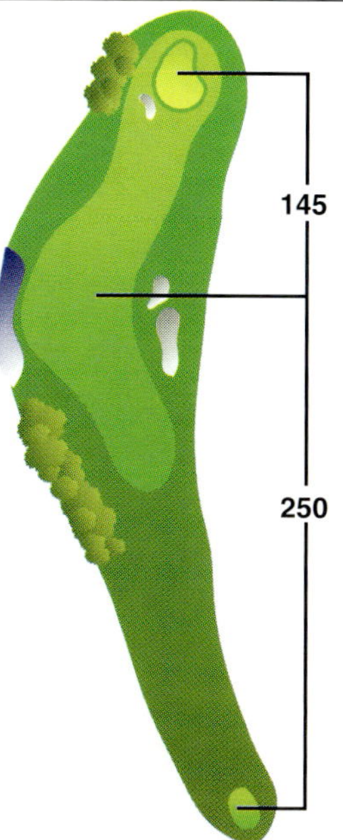

Par 4
395 yards

This dogleg right requires a drive to the left center to open up a green protected in the left front by a bunker. A drop off beyond the green will require a deft return pitch for shots that go long.

2

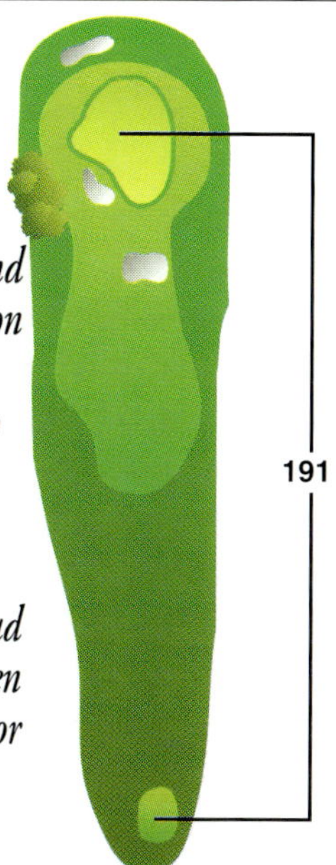

Par 3
191 yards

Depending on wind conditions, a six iron to fairway wood could be needed to hit this large undulating two-tiered green. An isolated cypress head to the left of the green may become a factor on windy days.

3

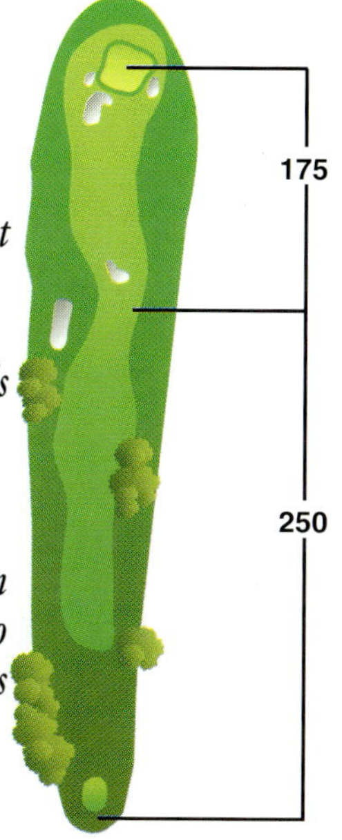

Par 4
425 yards

A drive to the right center of the fairway will leave a mid-iron into this well bunkered green. A cypress head at the drive zone will require an accurate tee shot to be successful on this hole.

4

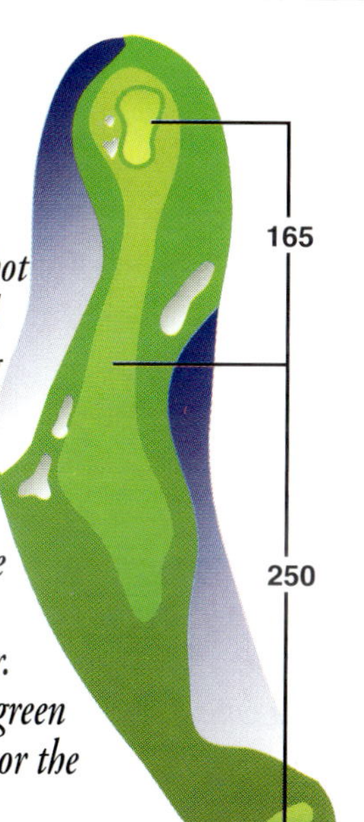

Par 4
415 yards

An accurate tee shot is needed to avoid the lake bordering the right side and well placed fairway bunkers to the left. The large green drops off severely at the rear. Shots missing the green certainly must favor the right side.

5

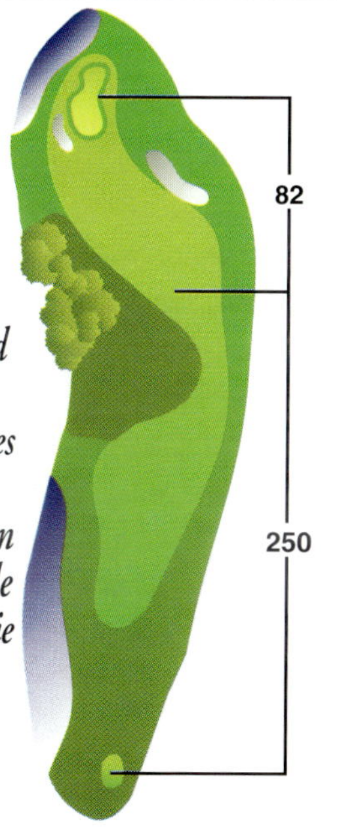

Par 4
332 yards

A drive to the right center short of the fairway bunkers and avoiding the cypress head on the left leaves an approach shot requiring a short iron to a narrow but wide green. A definite birdie hole.

6

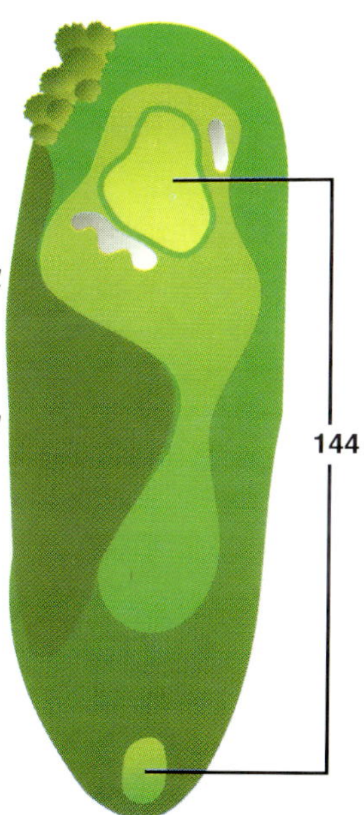

Par 3
144 yards

Swirling winds are prevalent in this area of the course. Club selection will be critical for this carry over wetland marsh to an elevated green protected by a large greenside bunker on the left.

7

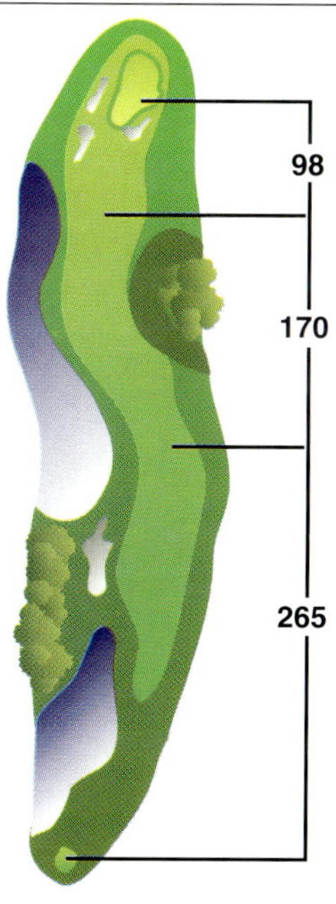

Par 5
533 yards

A lagoon running down the left side, then a carry over a wetland area face those attempting to reach the green in two. Putting the ball on the right tier of the green will be essential for birdie opportunities.

8

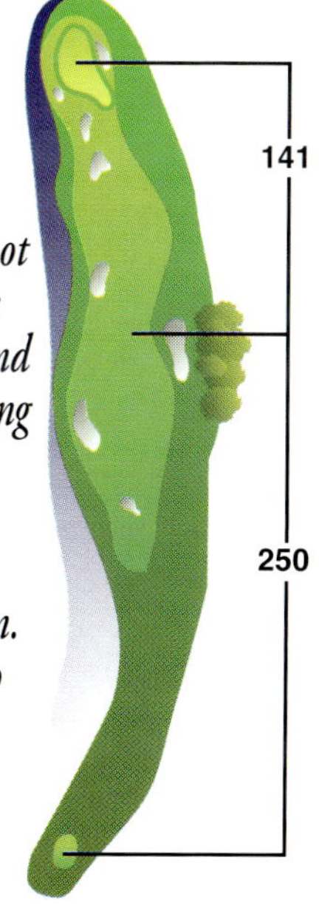

Par 4
391 yards

A demanding tee shot avoiding the cypress head on the right and the water hazard along the entire left side leaves a long to medium iron to the course's largest green. Players will want to avoid missing this green.

9

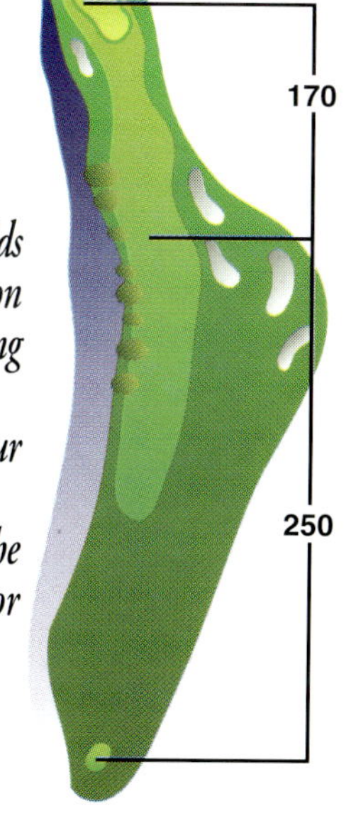

Par 4
420 yards

A drive to the right center of this hole avoids the well placed pines on the left and leaves a long to medium iron shot into the two-tiered hour glass green. A water hazard to the left of the green could be a factor in the wind.

10

Par 4
395 yards

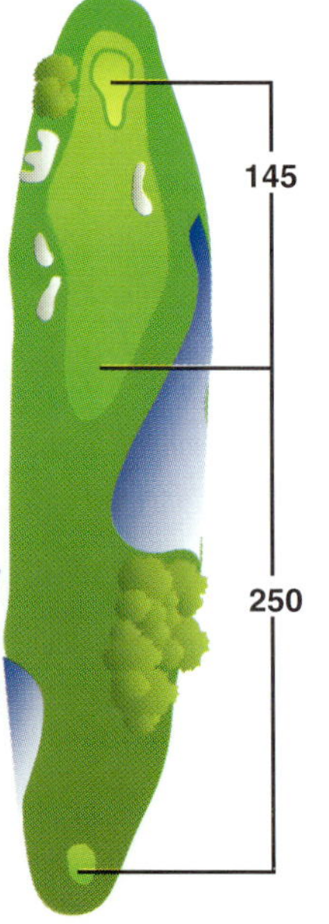

Water down the entire right side and out of bounds and bunkers to the left require an accurate tee shot. The green is guarded by water on the right and a cypress mitigation area left. Steep run offs behind and left of the green will require a

11

Par 3
179 yards

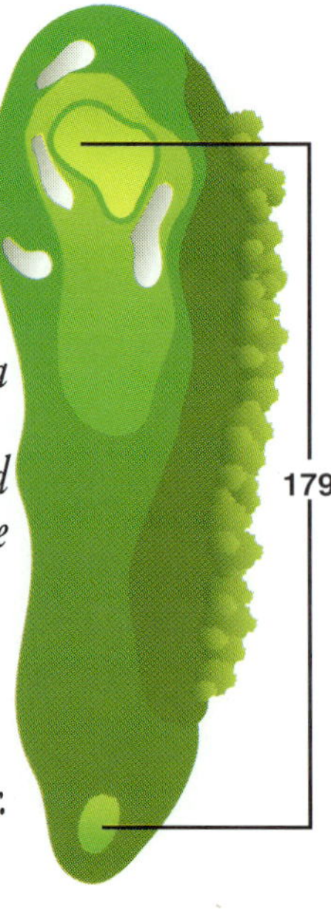

Mid-iron accuracy is essential to avoid the cypress mitigation area on the right. Players will also want to avoid the left hand greenside bunker due to its unique bunker face design. Some skillful sand shots could be seen from this bunker.

12

Par 5
495 yards

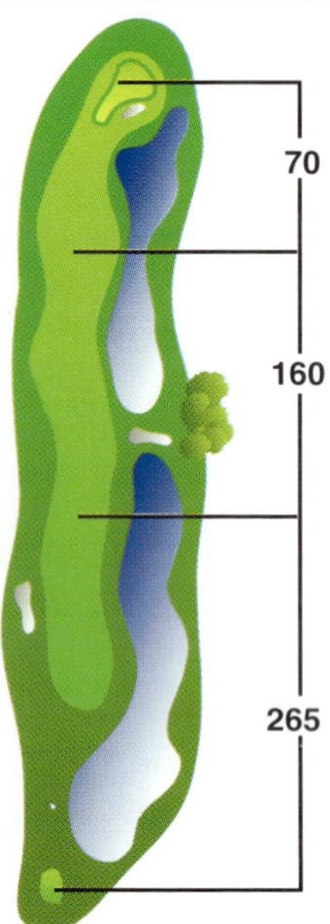

A fairway bunker placed between two lakes guard the entire right side of the hole. A left center drive leaves a fairway wood to long iron into this reachable par five. The green is nestled beside a lagoon, requiring accuracy for any player trying to get

13

Par 4
345 yards

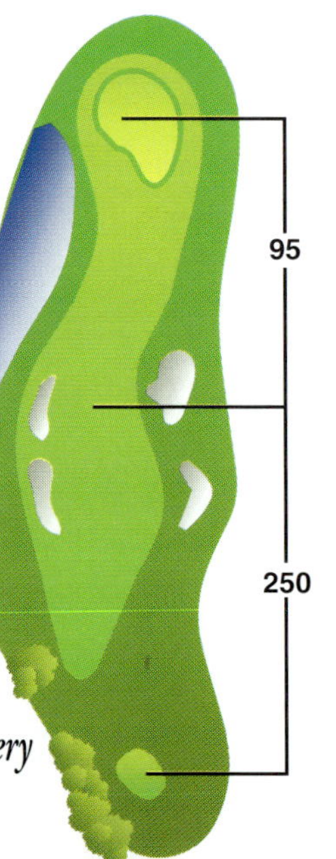

The most elevated green on the golf course requires an extremely accurate short iron to the correct tier. Missing the green will leave the player a prcarious recovery shot. Pin placement could make this hole very interesting.

14

Par 5
528 yards

The second shot must avoid strategically placed bunkers. An undulating green, water left and bunkers right require an accurate third shot. Balls landing at the back of the green are likely to roll of the back due to the unique mowing pattern.

15

Par 4
425 yards

One of the most difficult holes, with a combination of lagoon and wetlands protecting the entire left side. The green is nestled against the lagoon with a beautiful cypress backdrop. Crisp, accurate, long iron second shots must avoid the water left and bunkers on both sides of the green.

16

Par 4
413 yards

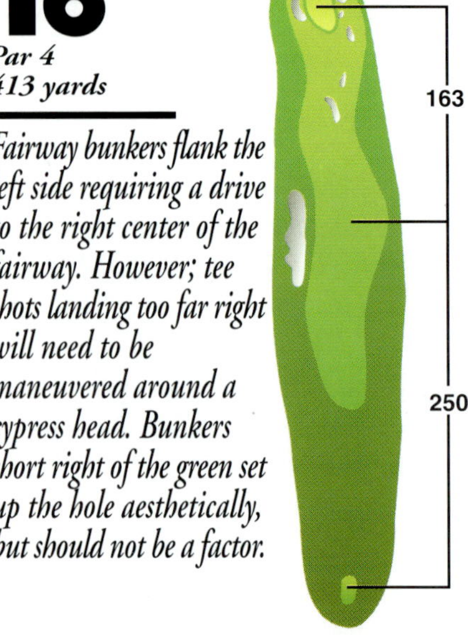

Fairway bunkers flank the left side requiring a drive to the right center of the fairway. However; tee shots landing too far right will need to be maneuvered around a cypress head. Bunkers short right of the green set up the hole aesthetically, but should not be a factor.

17

Par 3
197 yards

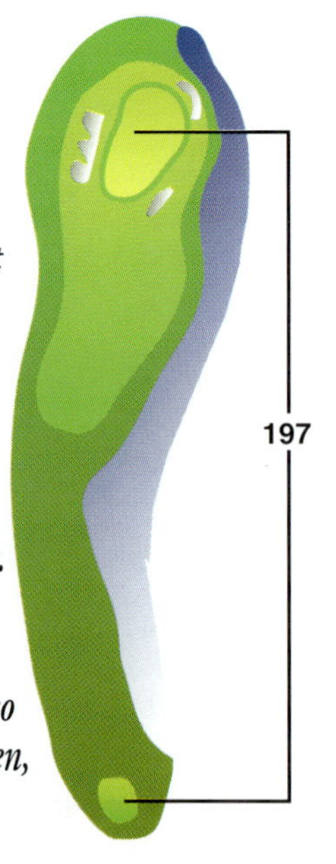

The long tee shot that gets close will be rewarded on this 11,000 sq. ft. green. Subtle undulations throughout the green will make birdies rare. Spectators will thoroughly enjoy this area as action can also be viewed at #10 green, #11 tee, and #18 tee.

18

Par 4
415 yards

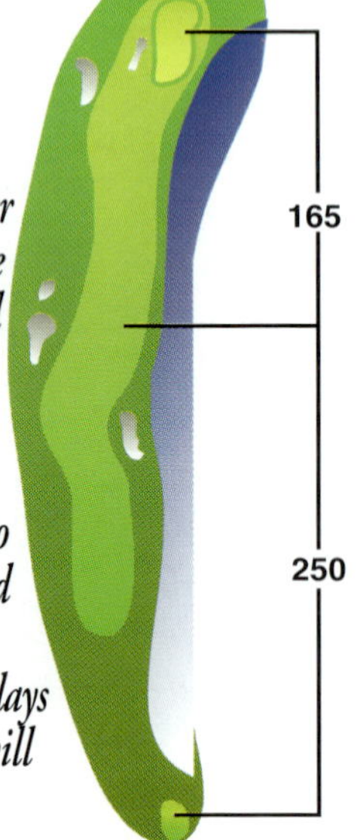

Driving to the left center of the fairway avoids the fairway bunkering and water down the right side. An accurate fairway wood to mid-iron will be required to avoid the water hazard at the right side of the green. When this hole plays into the wind, a par will gain on the field.

*I*t was the simple idea of the Los Angeles Junior Chamber of Commerce to promote Los Angeles with a professional golf tournament. This took place in 1926 and the tournament has become the longest running, civic-sponsored professional golf tournament.

The tournament has had many winners over it 67 years of competition play. Harry "Lighthorse" Cooper won the inaugural event playing at such a fast pace that a local writer dubbed him "Lighthorse". Cooper managed to take over the lead on the 15th hole of the final round, finishing with an eagle on the 18th and a three-stroke margin. In 1937, Cooper won again with 274.

Four-time winners include Mac Smith (winning in 1928, '29, '32 and '34) and Lloyd Mangrum (winning in 1949, '51, '53 and '56). Lanny Wadkins holds the 72-hole record of 264 which was good enough to win by a margin of 7 strokes in 1985.

The Riviera Country Club was designed and built for the Los Angeles Athletic Club by architects George C. Thomas and William P. Bell in 1925. Dense foliage lined the riverbed at the bottom of the Santa Monica Canyon where the course was to be constructed. Creative thinking and planning produced a golf course that has become world renowned as a very formidable layout. In addition to hosting the Los Angeles Open for 32 years, the course has hosted other great championships such as the 1948 U.S. Open, and the 1983 and 1995 PGA Championships.

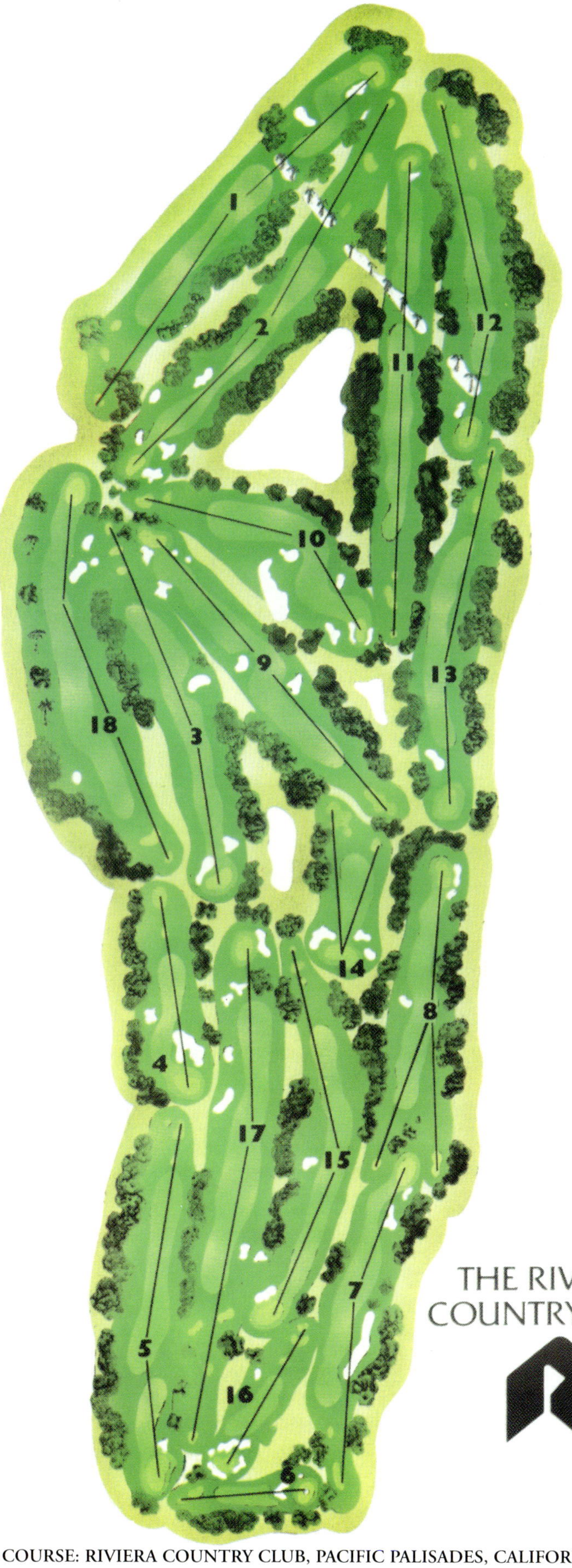

Dates:	February 22-25, 1996
Network:	CBS and USA
Times:	USA
	Thur/Fri 4:00-6:00 EST
	CBS
	Sat/Sun 4:00-6:00 EST
Yardage:	6,946
Par:	71
Slope:	142
Rating:	75.7
Total Purse:	$1,200,000
1st Prize:	$216,000
1995 Winner:	Corey Pavin
1995 Winning Score:	268 (67-66-68-67)
Principal Charitable Beneficiary:	LA Junior Chamber of Commerce
Ticket Information:	1-213-482-1311 or 1-800-752-OPEN

THE RIVIERA COUNTRY CLUB

THE COURSE: RIVIERA COUNTRY CLUB, PACIFIC PALISADES, CALIFORNIA

1

Par 5
501 yards

The players get a chance to look down on the course that lays before them from the elevated tee. A great opportunity for an opening birdie.

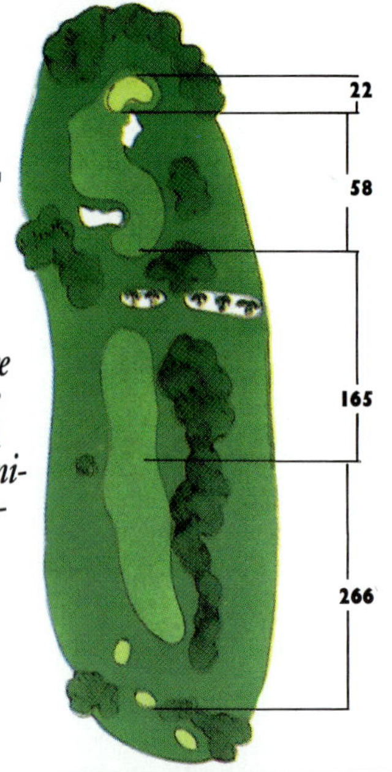

2

Par 4
460 yards

A very narrow fairway is viewed from the tee box. Players will keep their drives down the right to set up for the long approach to the tightly guarded green.

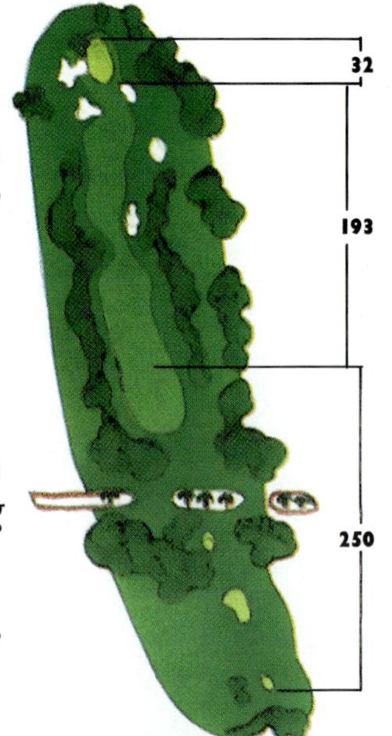

3

Par 4
434 yards

Long and into the wind — this dogleg right par 4 is tough. The second shot is played long and into a shallow green that slopes away from the fairway.

4

Par 3
238 yards

The green slopes severely from right to left and a massive bunker guards the front. Fairway-woods and long-irons are the clubs of necessity to reach the putting surface.

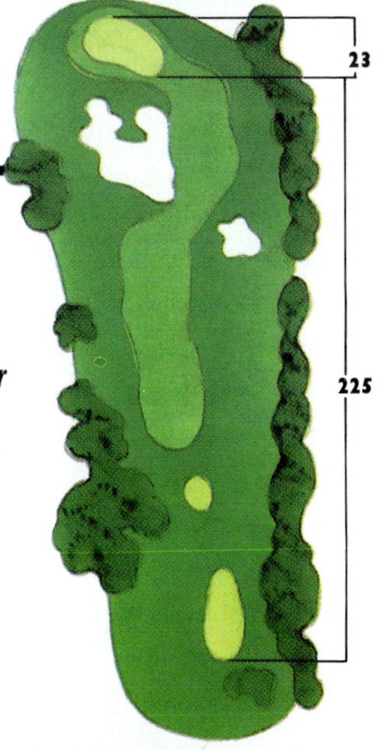

5

Par 4
426 yards

The right-to-left sloping requires good placement from the tee — out-of-bounds to the right and trees are along the left. The green sits 60 feet below the level of the fairway.

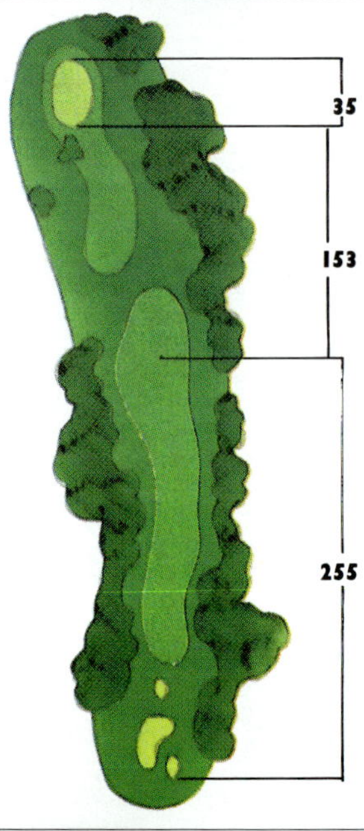

6

Par 3
170 yards

The length is not an issue — however, the two tiered green with a bunker built right in the center can cause havoc.

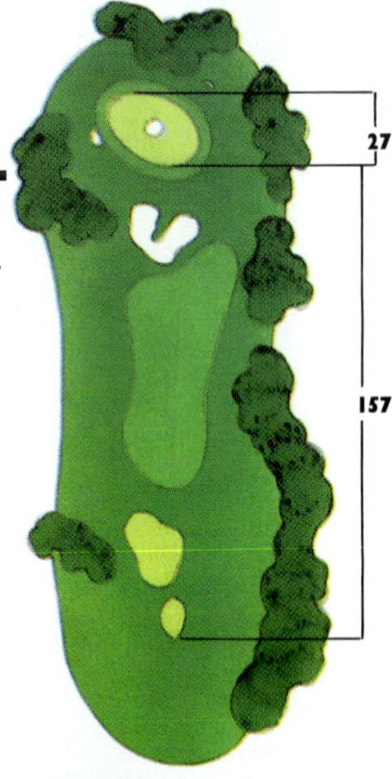

7

Par 4
406 yards

A fade off the tee is favored to set up for the approach shot. Eucalyptus trees and out-of-bounds define the right side of the fairway. The green is long and narrow.

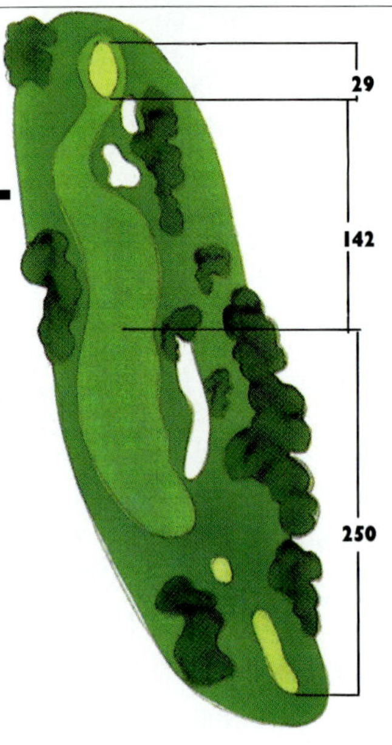

8

Par 4
468 yards

Birdie opportunities are never more possible than on this eighth. A tee shot hit just right of the fairway bunker will leave a short approach to the generous sized green.

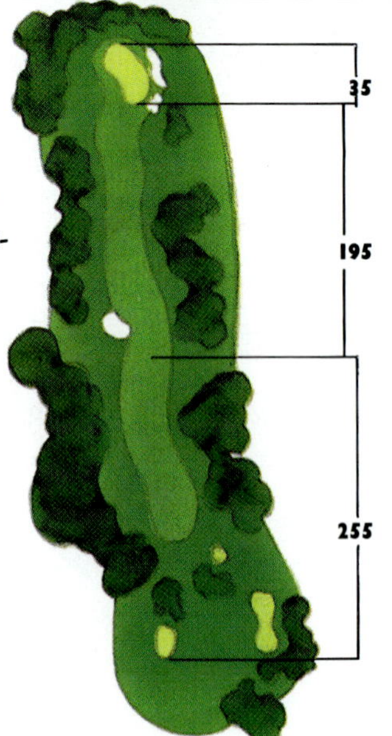

9

Par 4
418 yards

The narrow landing area is defined by fairway bunkers to both the left and right. A mid-iron to the green must be accurate to avoid long putts.

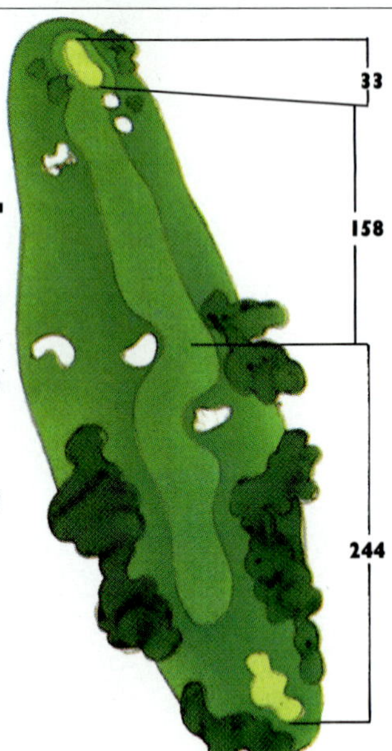

10

Par 4
311 yards

The long hitters will be able to reach this green from the tee. The rest of the players will place their drives just beyond the fairway bunkers on the right. Birdies are abundant.

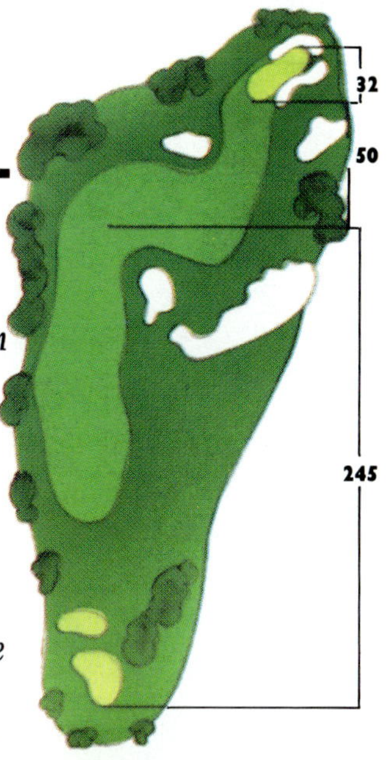

11

Par 5
561 yards

The second shot should clear the deep, crossing bunker. Three shots are normally used to get home to this small green. One lone bunker guards the front right.

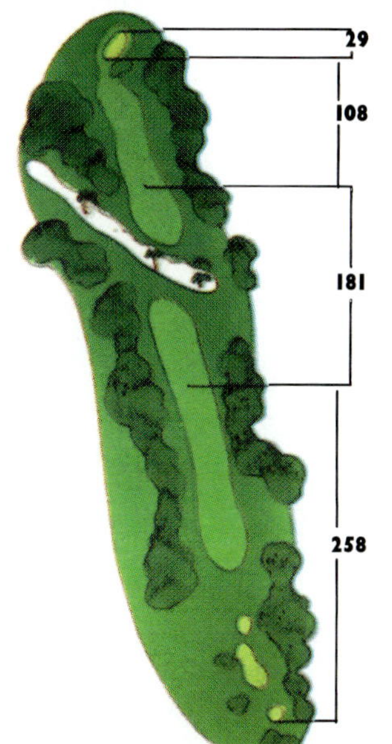

12

Par 4
413 yards

Accuracy as well as length are required to put the ball in good position for the approach. A deep hazard crosses the fairway just short of the green.

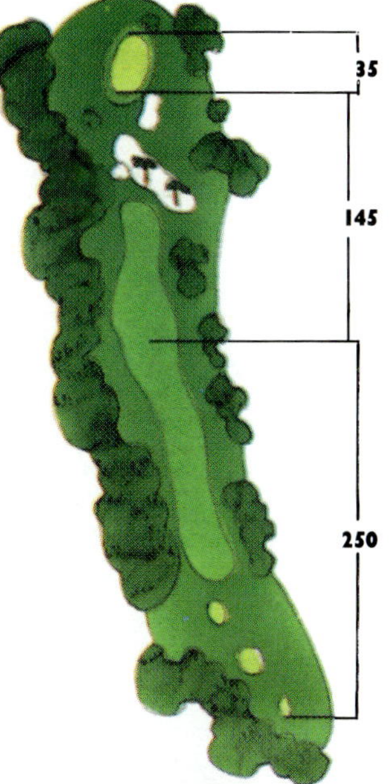

13

Par 4
420 yards

The dogleg wraps around to the left. A slight slope in the fairway also goes from right to left. The flat level green is bordered by out-of-bounds just 15 feet on the left.

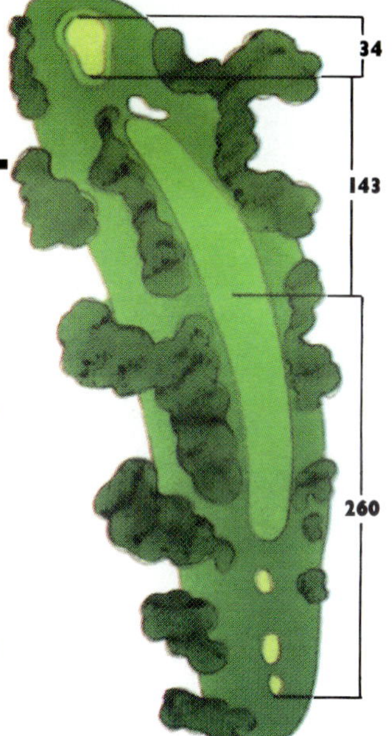

14

Par 3
180 yards

The green is short and very wide. The elevated putting surface is slightly hidden by the three bunkers in the front.

15

Par 4
447 yards

Tied with the 18th as the longest par 4 on the course, this 15th can be a big turning point on Sunday. The left and right side of the green are joined by a gentle valley.

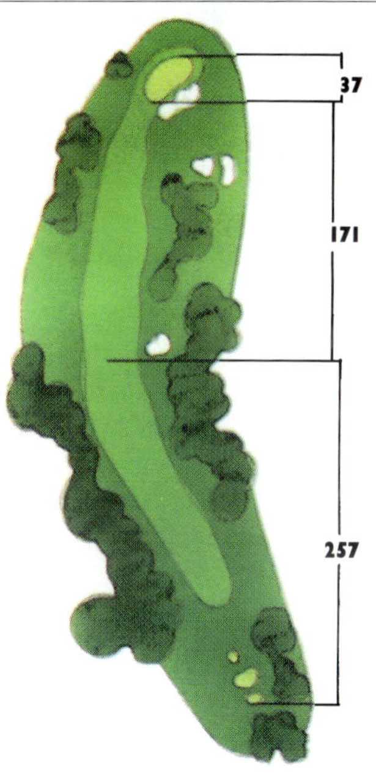

16

Par 3
168 yards

The putting surface is hidden from view by the surrounding bunkers. All putts are makeable on the small green.

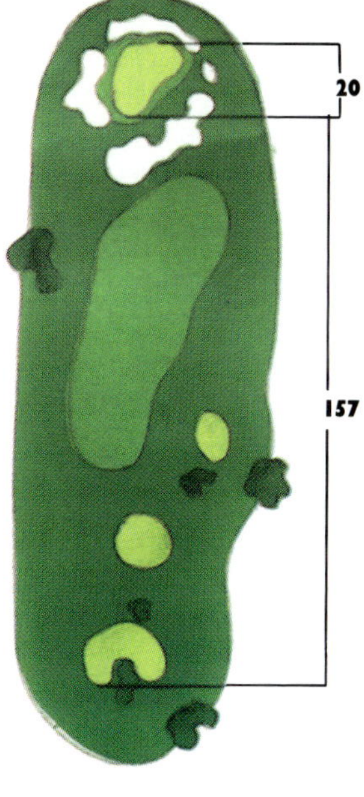

17

Par 5
578 yards

The open fairway allows for the big drive. All three shots are needed to reach the green. The approach is best left short and below the hole to avoid treacherous downhill putts.

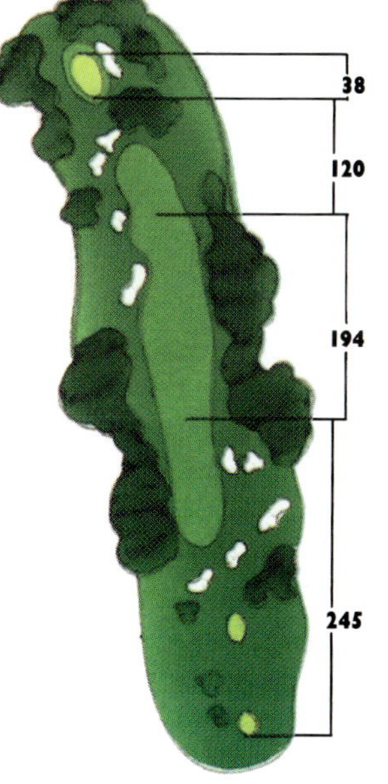

18

Par 4
447 yards

A very tough finishing hole—the blind shot must safely find the fairway that slopes left to right. The clubhouse sits auspiciously above and beyond the green.

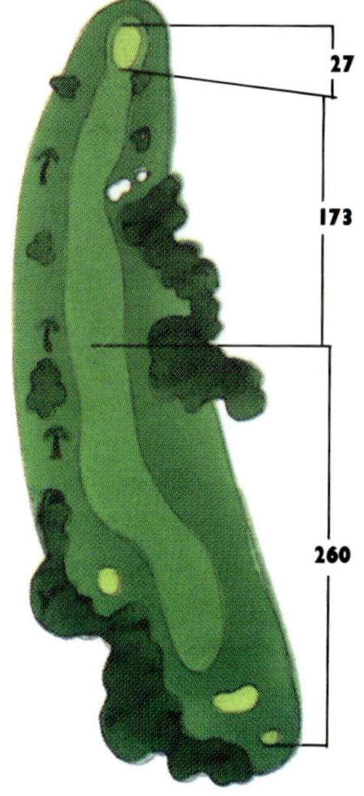

THE COURSE: DORAL RESORT & COUNTRY CLUB, MIAMI FLORIDA

For more than thirty years, the greatest names in golf have gone head-to-head with the "Blue Monster", the nick-name given to the wind-whipped greens and fairways of Doral. Billy Casper took the first trophy in 1962, and saw his name again on the leader board, at age 57, in 1989. His love of Doral's challenge is not at all singular among his peers. Jack Nicklaus has played the Open more often than any other tournament, other than majors, winning in 1972 and 1975. Tom Kite won it in 1984 and finished second the next three years.

Since Ryder's participation in 1987, the tournament has become one of the highest paid purses on the PGA TOUR® - a long way from Doris and Alfred Kaskal's dream of 2,400 acres of south Florida swamp in the late 1950s. The Doral-Ryder Open is the American Cancer Society's largest sports fund-raiser and has donated more than $5 million since 1969.

Dates:	February 29-March 3
Network:	CBS
Times:	Sat/Sun - 4:00-6:00 EST
Yardage:	6,939
Par:	72
Slope:	127
Rating:	72.0
Total Purse:	$1,500,000
1st Prize:	$270,000
1995 Winner:	Nick Faldo
1995 Winning Score:	273 (67-71-66-69)
Principal Charitable Beneficiary:	American Cancer Society
Charitable Benefits to Date:	Over $5 million
Ticket Information:	1-305-477-4653

1

Par 5
533 yards

Bunkers lie waiting along the right side of the fairway. Players will most likely go for the green in two — this first hole is a definite birdie opportunity.

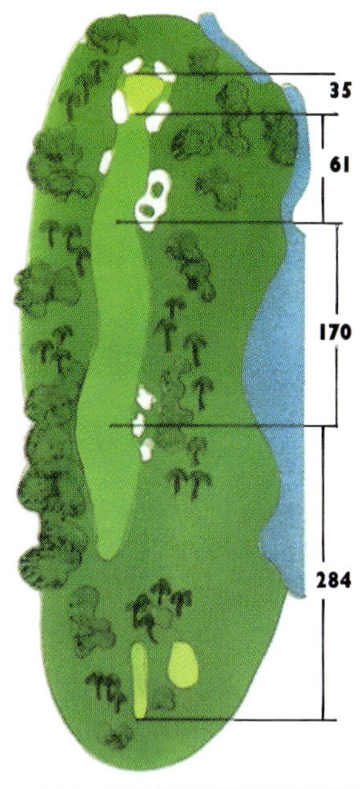

2

Par 4
366 yards

A second shot must be played from the fairway if the player wants any chance of holding the shallow green. Driving accuracy is a priority.

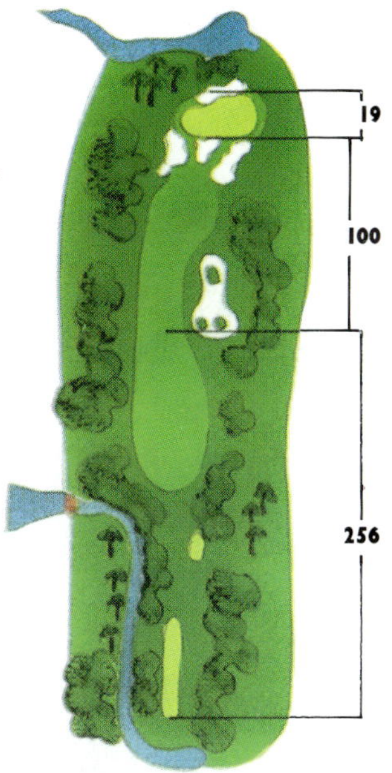

3

Par 4
402 yards

As driving accuracy was stressed on the last hole, this hole demands the best from the players. Water can come into play on both sides of the fairway.

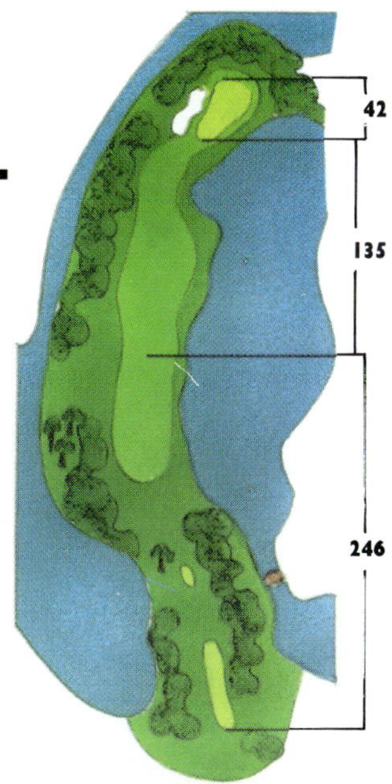

4

Par 3
225 yards

The most difficult of the par threes. The long narrow fairway has bunkers to the left and water to the right. The putting surface slopes severely from back to front.

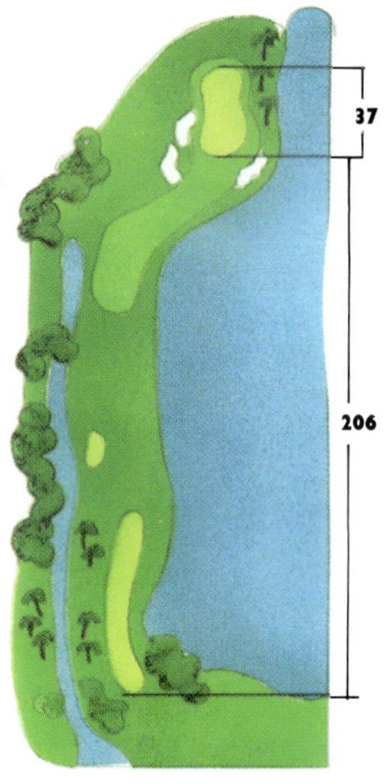

5

Par 4
374 yards

Bunkers abound on the path to the green. Positioning off the tee is key. Players will be hitting a fairway wood or long iron for the drive followed by a short iron to the shallow green.

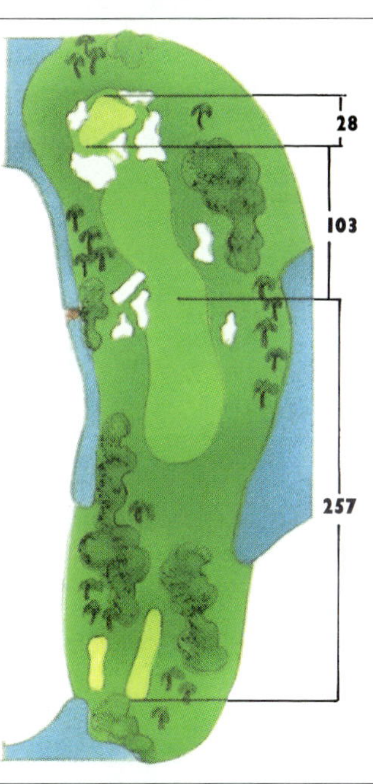

6

Par 4
437 yards

The right side of the fairway is favored to reach the small green. Three bunkers on the left side will deter the players who try to cut the corner.

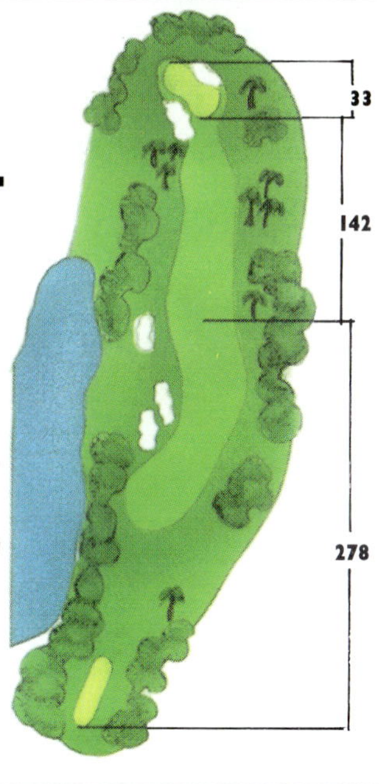

7

Par 4
427 yards

As the easiest hole on the front nine, this seventh requires a good drive to reach the large green. Players will be looking for the birdie on this hole.

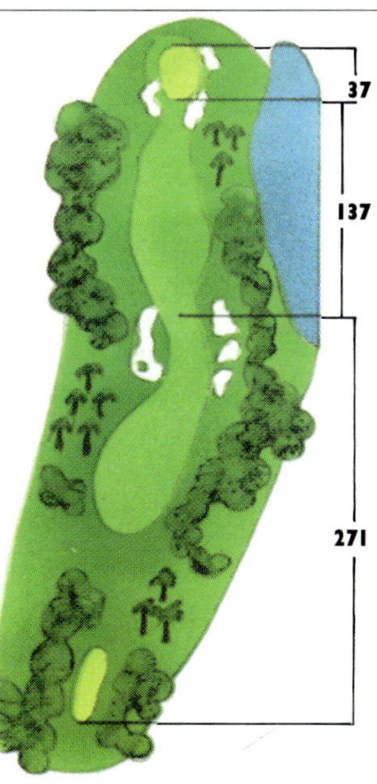

8

Par 5
528 yards

A little, double-dogleg. Players can reach the green in two if they don't mind the risk. The putting surface slopes back to front and right to left.

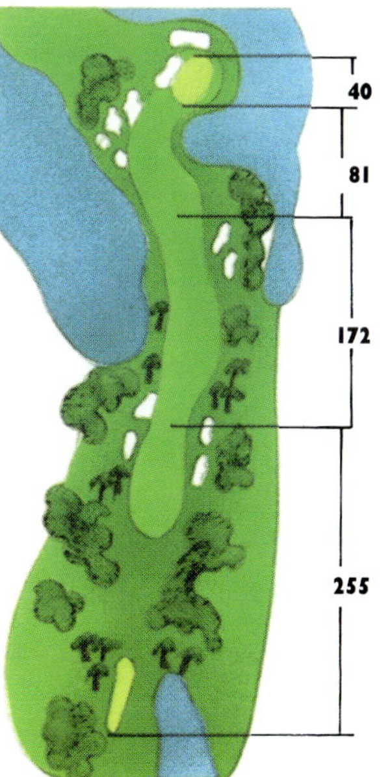

9

Par 3
181 yards

Club selection is vital for hitting the ball close to the pin. The very large green is a generous target from the tee but the wind can cause some problems.

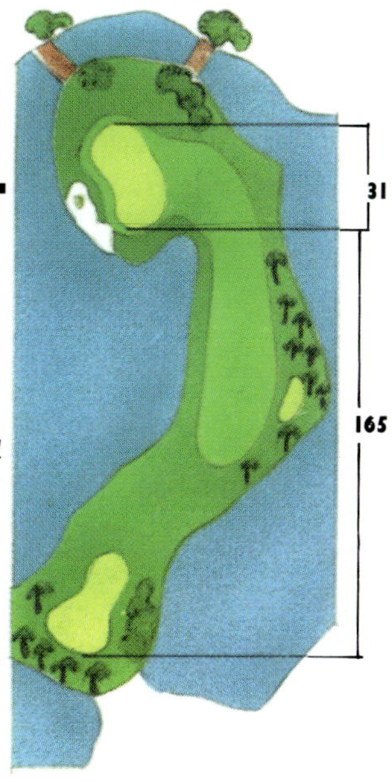

10

Par 5
543 yards

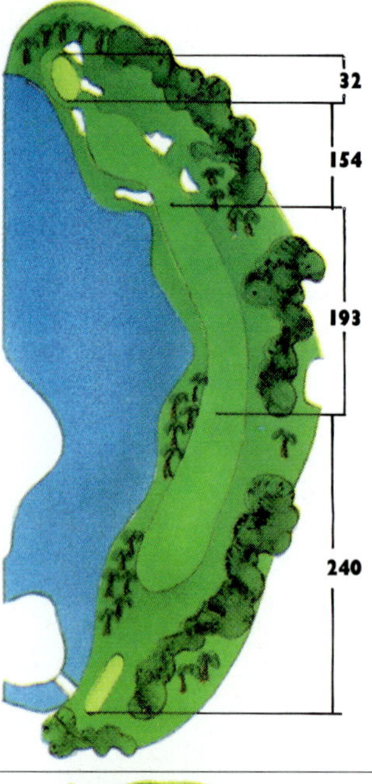

The green is in sight the entire way from the tee. However, water along the left will make the hole seem much longer than it is — the safe play is to hit all three shots to the green.

11

Par 4
351 yards

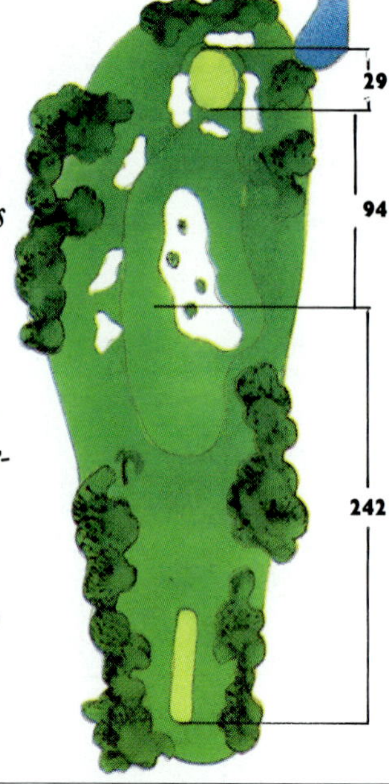

A bunker splits the fairway into two sides. Players have the option of playing left or right. By favoring the left, a player will have a long approach onto the elevated green.

12

Par 5
608 yards

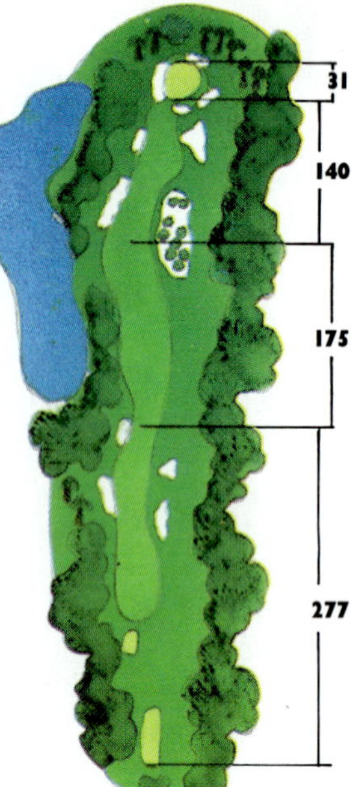

The most difficult hole on the course, and it's not all yardage. Dense trees along the right and bunkers on both sides of the fairway make the path to the green very narrow.

13

Par 3
246 yards

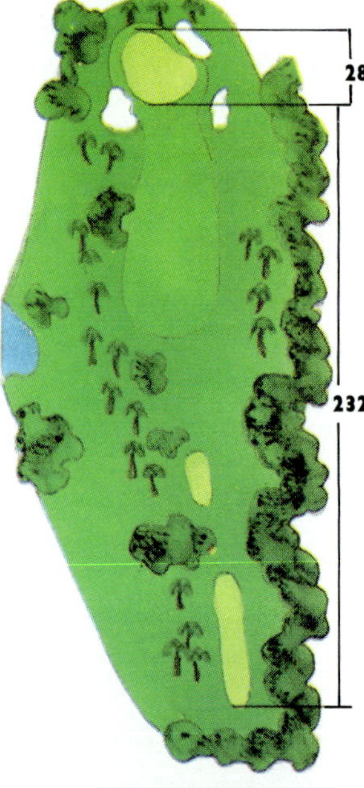

Some players will be using woods to reach this long par 3. The significantly raised green is difficult to hold — thus the bunker beyond will see a lot of play.

14

Par 4
419 yards

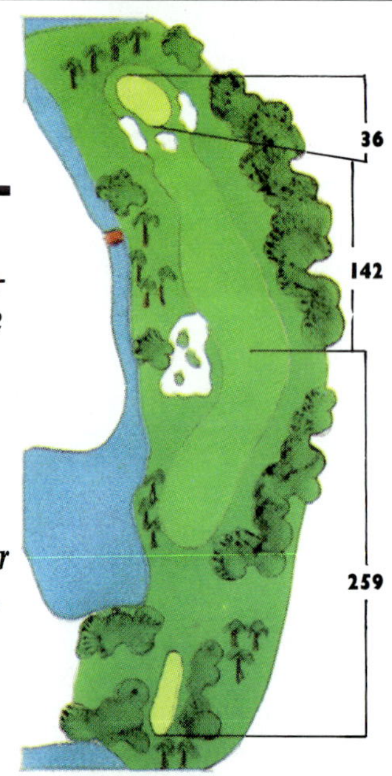

The sharp dogleg is defined by the large bunker at the corner. The well-trapped green is an easy target from the center of the fairway.

15

Par 3
183 yards

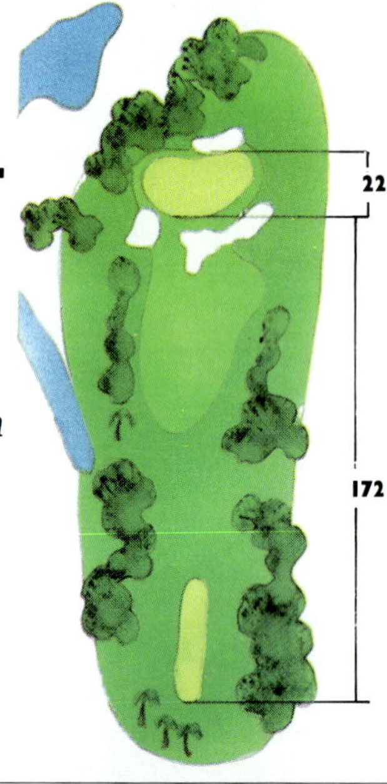

The prevailing winds are either against or across the players tee shot. The green is very shallow and well protected by bunkers.

16

Par 4
379 yards

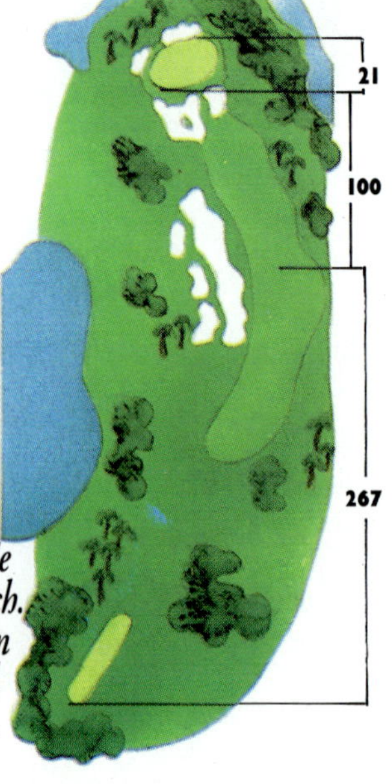

Players will be staying to the right side of the fairway to avoid the bunker at the corner of the dogleg and to get a good angle for the approach. The small green is elevated and well-bunkered.

17

Par 4
406 yards

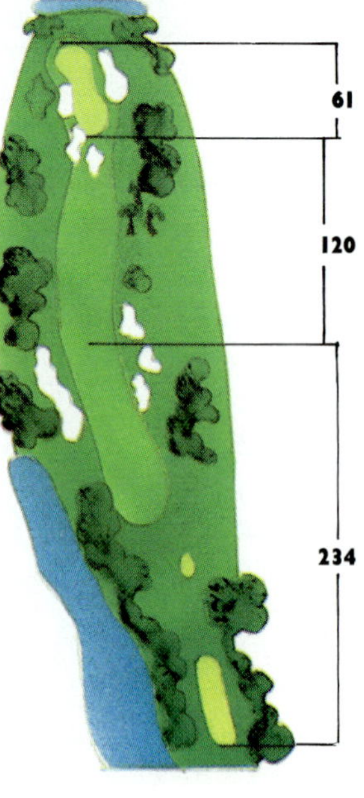

A good, long drive is a necessity off the tee. The second shot is to a 60-yard long green. The putting surface has three levels from front to back.

18

Par 4
437 yards

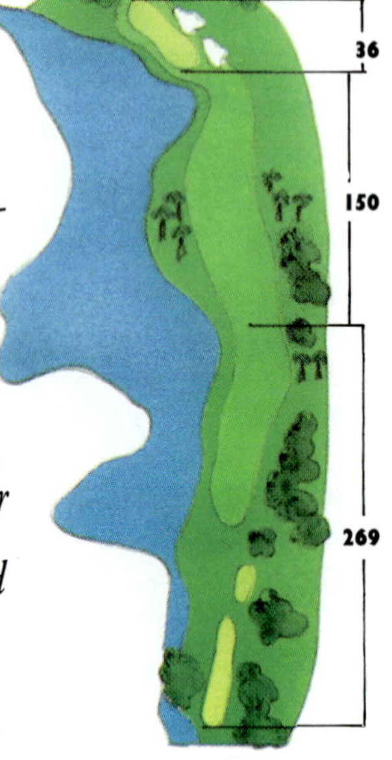

The "Blue Monster" is a great finishing hole. The rolling fairway is bordered by water and trees. Players going for the championship will need to hit two perfect shots to the narrow green.

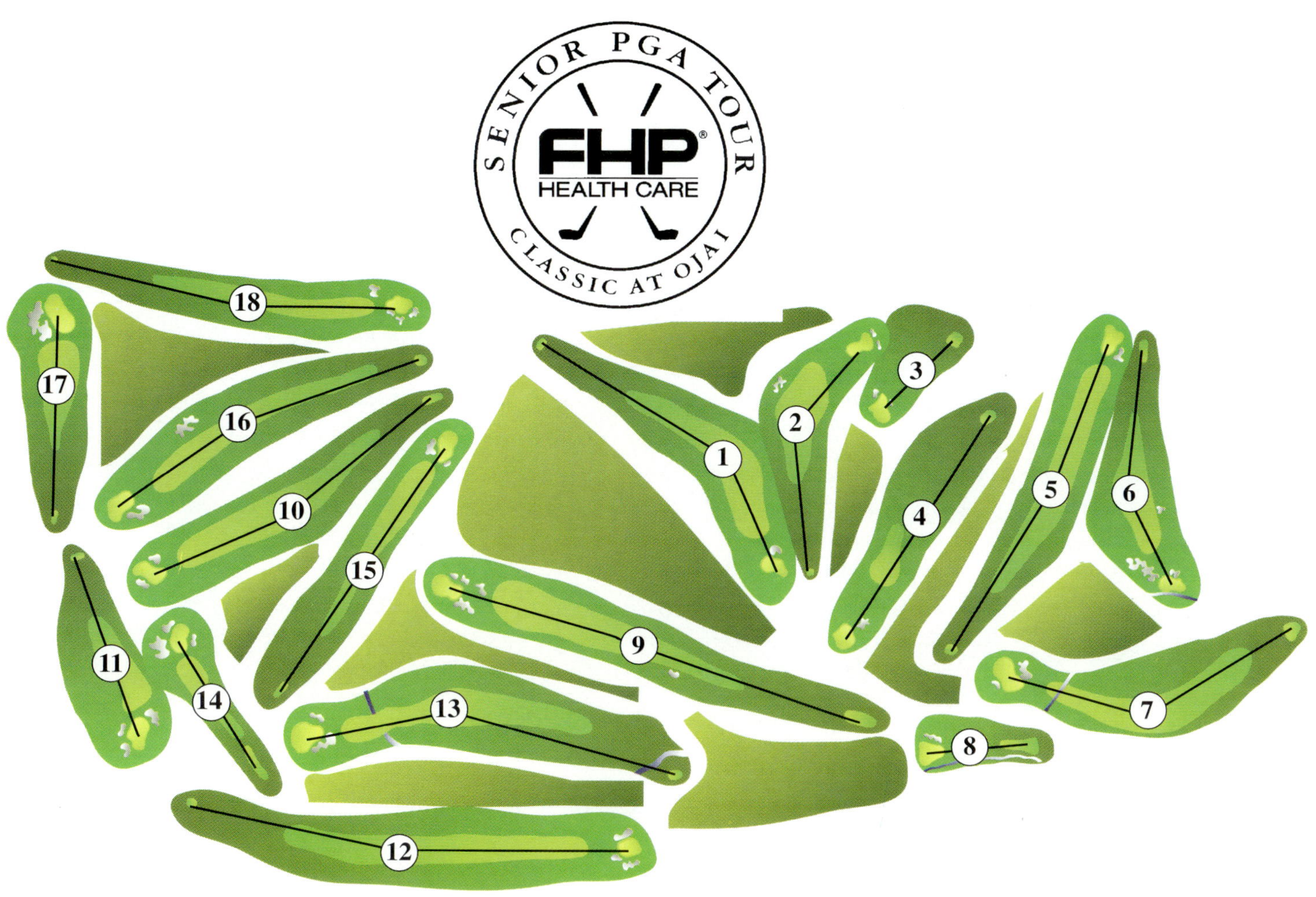

THE COURSE:OJAI VALLEY INN & COUNTRY CLUB, OJAI, CALIFORNIA

The FHP Health Care Classic, played at the picturesque Ojai Valley Inn & Country Club, has long been regarded as one of the most prestigious events on the SENIOR PGA TOUR®.

Annually attracting the most outstanding senior golfers in the world, the FHP Health Care Classic Champions honor roll features some of the greatest legends in golf: Bob Charles in 1987, Harold Henning in 1988, Walter Zembriski in 1989, Chi Chi Rodriguez in 1991, Bruce Crampton in 1992, Al Geiberger in 1993, Jay Siegel in 1994 and last year's winner Bruce Devlin.

Dates:	March 1-3, 1996
Network:	ESPN
Times:	Fri - 4:00-6:00 EST
	Sat - 5:00-7:00 EST
	Sun -6:00-7:30 EST
Yardage:	6,752
Par:	70
Slope:	121
Rating:	70.6
Total Purse:	$625,000
1st Prize:	$112,500
1995 Winner:	Bruce Devlin
1995 Winning Score:	130 (64,66)
Principal Charitable Beneficiary:	Local Charities
Ticket Information:	1-805-646-5511

1

Par 4
412 yards

Big hitters will try to drive over the trees on the corner leaving a short iron, others will play safely into the left side of the fairway. The second shot is uphill to one of the largest greens on the course.

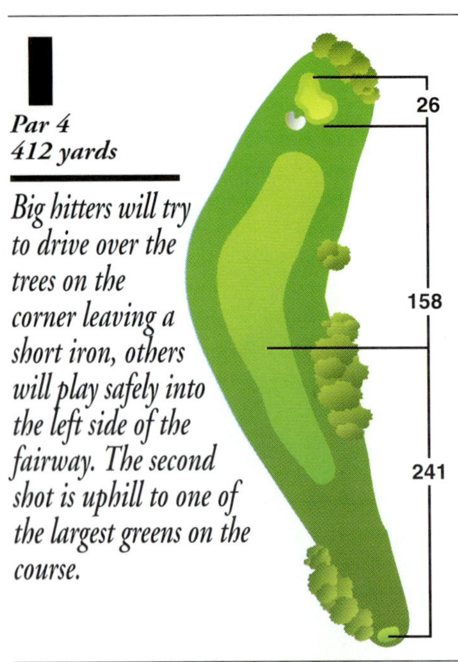

2

Par 4
358 yards

Competitors will take a conservative approach off the tee and hit a long iron or fairway wood into the fat part of the fairway. Second shot plays back over a deep barranca to a green framed by large oaks.

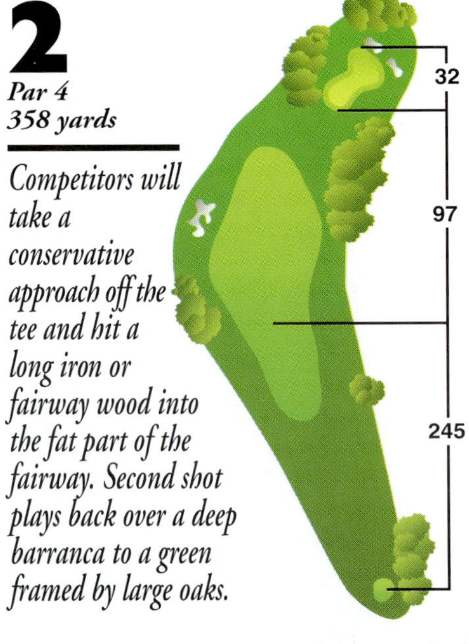

3

Par 3
115 yards

Just a wedge at only 115 yards but the penalty is severe if you miss the green. Players must keep the ball below the hole on a green that slopes from back to front.

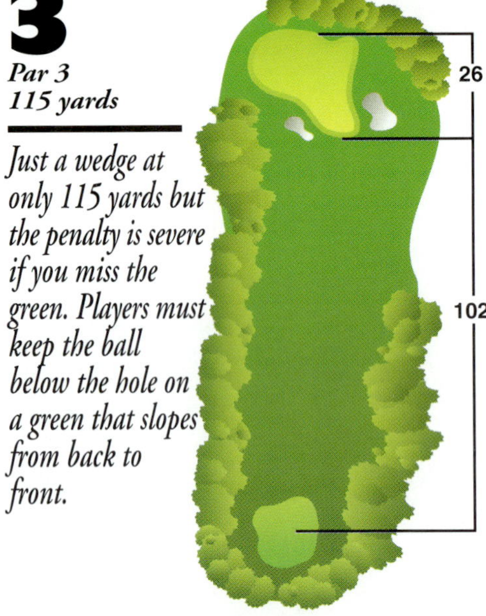

4

Par 4
297 yards

At only 297 yards, this par 4 is almost reachable from the tee. Most will play safe with a long iron over a deep ravine. Second shot is uphill through a narrow opening in the oaks. A large bunker protects one of the smallest greens on the course.

5

Par 4
440 yards

Players tee of nearly one hundred feet above a fairway with trouble on the left side. Second shot is a mid-iron to a severley sloping green.

6

Par 4
312 yards

A short par 4 that will temp some of the long drivers. Most will lay up even with the fairway bunker on the left to allow a full shot into a small green. Any shot short will catch the bunkers, long will find a creek behind the green.

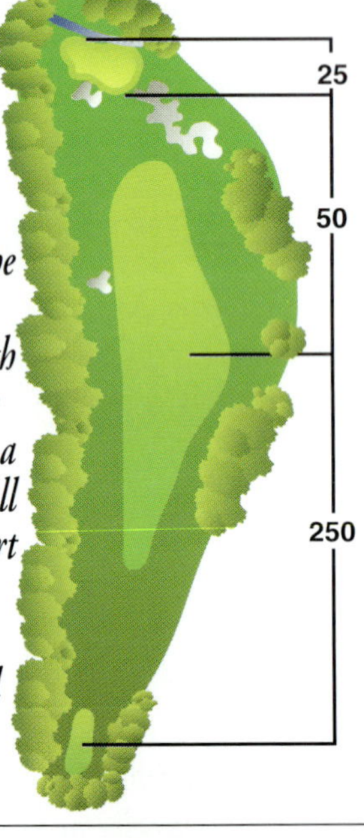

7

Par 4
392 yards

A long tough par four requiring a well played drive down the left center of the fairway. Anything right will be blocked by large eucalyptus and pine trees, demanding a second shot to an elevated green protected by a huge front bunker.

8

Par 3
128 yards

Only a short iron but a shot left will find a deep creek bed only a few feet from the green. Club selection can be tough as winds may swirl in this tight little canyon.

9

Par 5
517 yards

Straightaway par five that can be reached with a strong tee shot and fairway wood. O.B. left and right to a two tiered green that demands an accuate shot. Expect to see lots of birdies and a few eagles here.

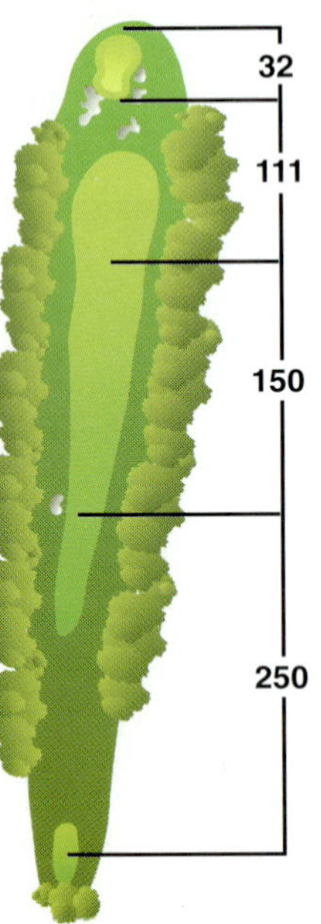

10

Par 4
405 yards

Wide driving area flanked by fairway bunkers on both sides. Uphill second shot to tiered green can be deceiving. Hole plays longer than it appears from the fairway. Players will want to land ball on proper side of tier.

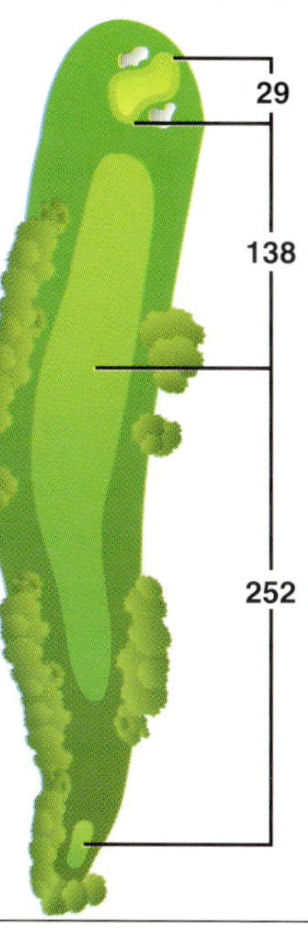

11

Par 3
203 yards

A solid long iron that usually plas into the preailing wind. Balls missing left or right can leave some very tricky recovery shots.

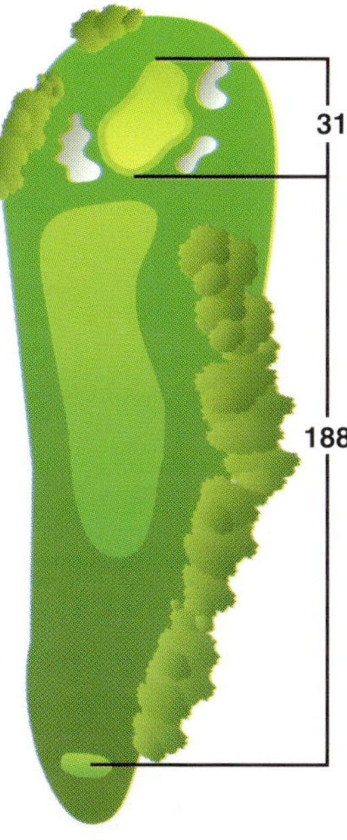

12

Par 5
562 yards

At 562 yards the longest hole on the course, usually playing into the wind. Tee shot must be played into the right side of a sloping fairway. Fairway narrows in landing area of second shot, again sloping left to a wooded hazard area.

13

Par 4
442 yards

The tee shot must be positioned in the opening that leaves the player a clear shot to one of the most heavily protected greens on the course. Second shot is uphill over a ravine to a very deep green.

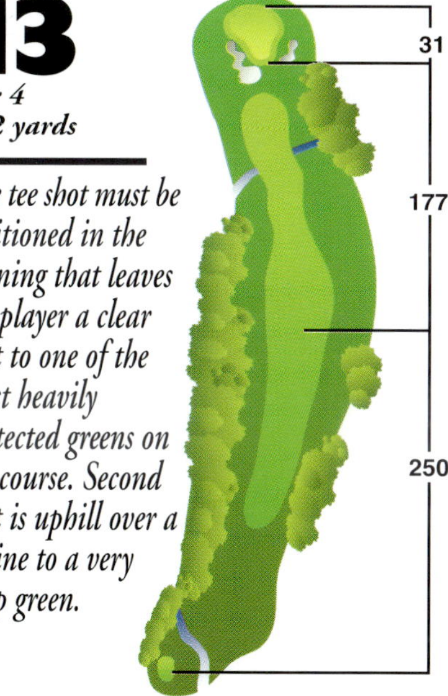

14

Par 3
177 yards

A straight foward par three with deep bunkers left, right and behind. Back right pin placement can be especially tough.

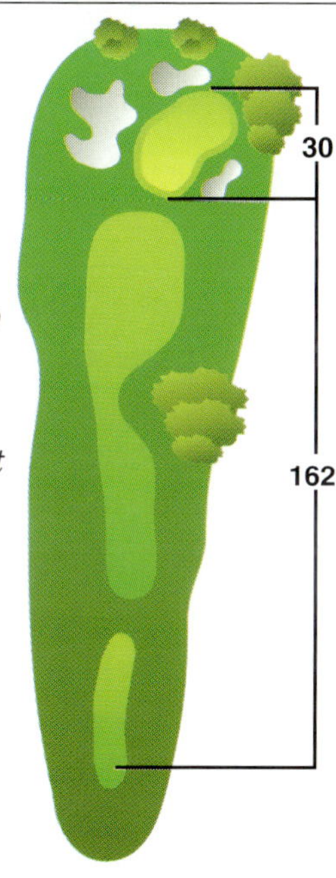

15

Par 4
359 yards

The toughest short par four on the course. Tight driving area with O.B. right and trees left. Second shot is uphill to a multilevel green. Balls landing short will find the toughest bunker shot on the course.

16

Par 4
402 yards

A good driving hole that favors a rigtht to left shot. Middle iron to a severely undulating green. Club selection is critical on second shot. False tongue on left front of green can cause some problems.

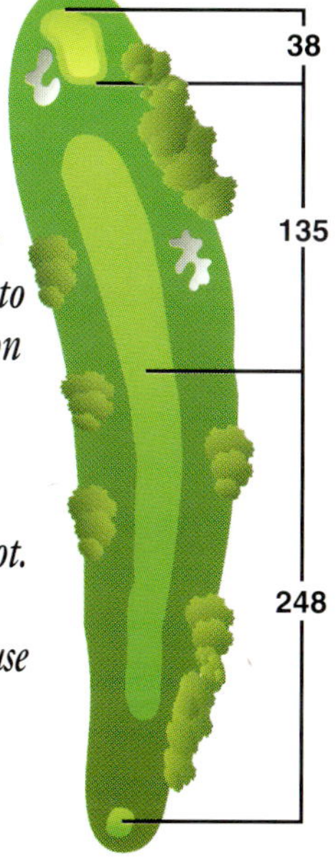

17

Par 3
181 yards

A good par three that can play from 181-227 yards. Huge bunker on left will attract some shots when pin is cut left. One of the deepest greens on the course.

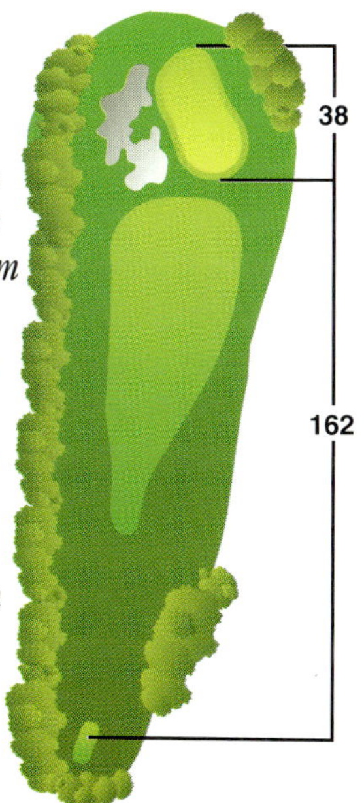

18

Par 5
487 yards

Gamblers can reach this green in two so you will see some good chances for eagles. However, those missing the green might face some of the toughest pitches to one of the subtly difficult greens at Ojai.

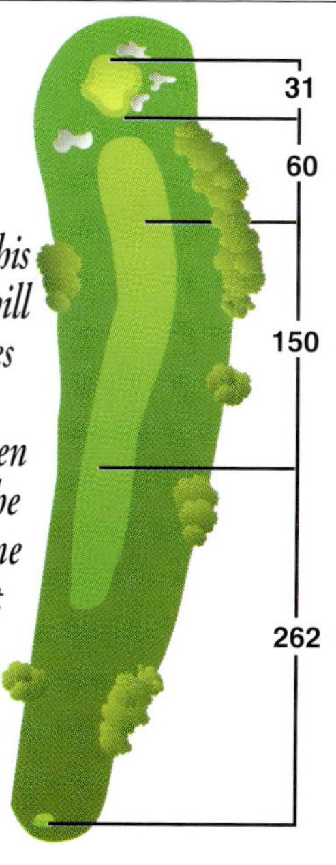

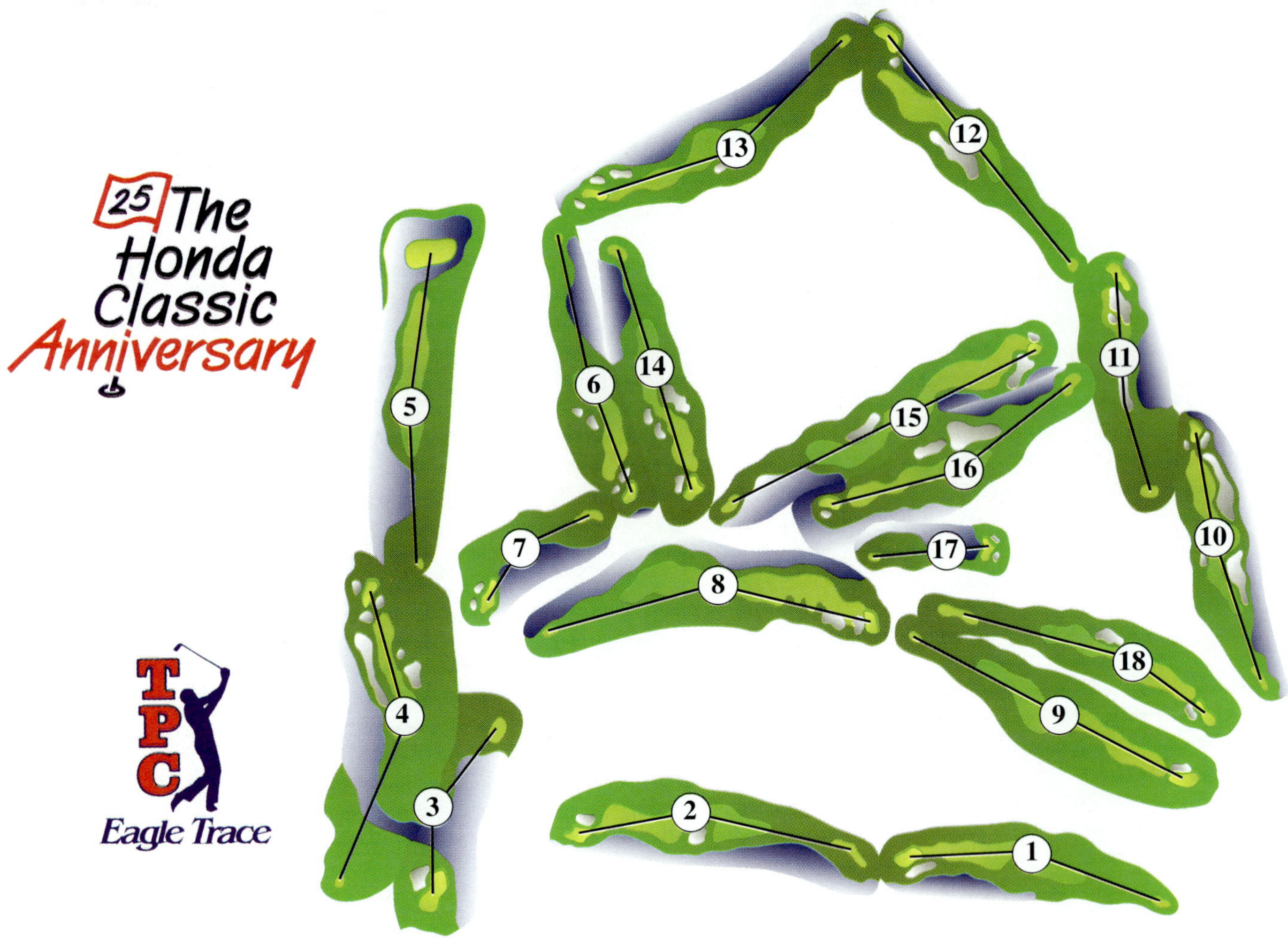

THE COURSE: TPC AT EAGLE TRACE, CORAL SPRINGS, FLORIDA

The Honda Classic will celebrate its 25th Anniversary on familiar ground March 3-10, 1996 when it returns to The Tournament Players Club at Eagle Trace following a four-year absence.

Tom Weiskopf won the Inaugural event in 1972 at Inverrary Country Club in Lauderhill, Florida when the tournament was called the Jackie Gleason Inverrary (1972-1980). Bruce Lietzke won the first Classic at Eagle Trace in 1984 with 280. The tournament's history minus Honda's involvement extends back to 1972 on a variety of Florida's toughest courses. Jack Nicklaus has won the tournament three times, consecutively in 1976, '77 and '78. Johnny Miller has won twice, in 1980 and 1983. Hale Irwin holds the record for the lowest winning score of 269 in 1982.

Eagle Trace played host to The Honda Classic from 1984-91. It provided a wide range of scoring, which was directly related to weather conditions. In 1986, when chilly winds reached 45 miles per hour during the third round, Kenny Knox eventually won with a score of 1-under-par 287. Three years later under warm, calm conditions, Blaine McCallister won at 22-under-par. For the last four years the Honda has been played at Weston Hills Country Club. The winner last year was Mark O'Meara.

Dates:	March 3-10
Network:	NBC & USA
Times:	Thur 4:00-6:00 EST
	Fri 4:00-6:00 EST
	Sat 4:00-6:00 EST
	Sun 4:00-6:00 EST
Yardage:	7,040
Par:	72
Slope:	134
Rating:	74.0
Total Purse:	$1,200,000
1st Prize:	$234,000
1995 Winner:	Mark O'Meara
1995 Winning Score: Principal	275 (68,65,71,71)
Charitable Beneficiary:	South Florida Children's Charities
Ticket Information:	954-346-4000

1

Par 4
396 yards

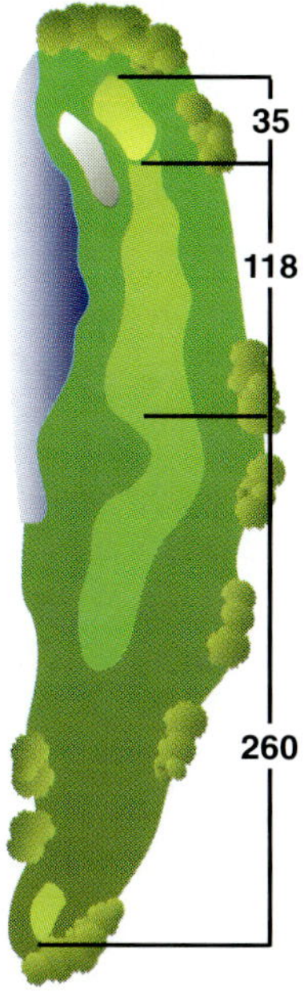

This starting hole is disarmingly open and appears almost easy. There can be many birdies made here, putting players into an upbeat frame of mind. The hole is open off the tee, with only two small grass hunkers on the right and a grassy hill on the left of the dogleg. The water on the left is almost out of play, seldom creating a penalty. The player may leave this hole with the feeling that today's the day to score low.

2

Par 4
442 yards

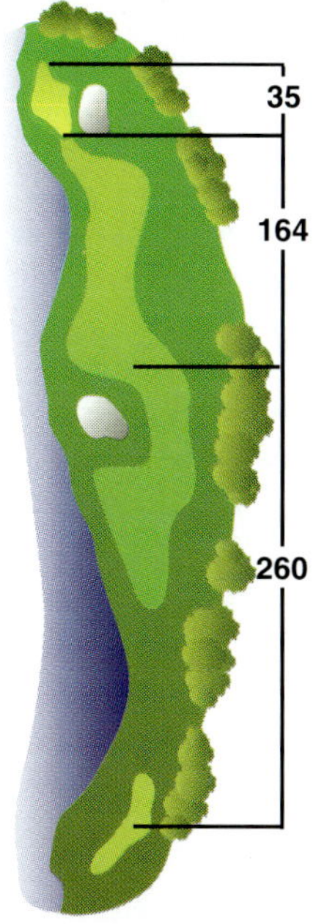

One of four long Par 4s, this hole demands two excellent shots. The dogleg bunker was made smaller to widen the landing area and enable the hole to be played at full length except when a strong north wind kicks up.

3

Par 3
179 yards

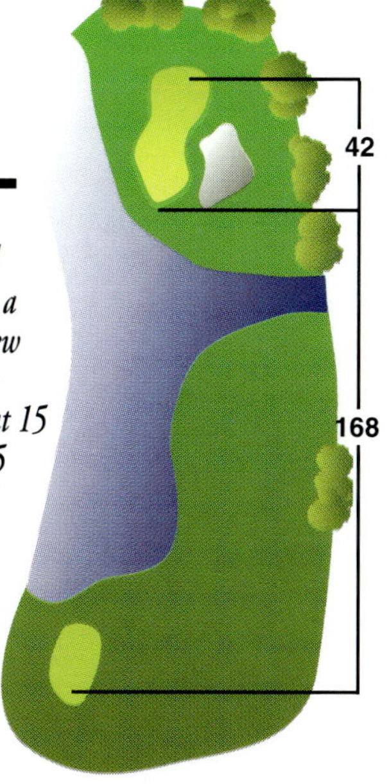

This is a very fair and well-balanced hole that promises a lot of birdies. A new tee further left has lengthened it about 15 yards (as of the '85 tournament), and the angle into the green is now away from the water.

4

Par 4
367 yards

This beauty proves that a golf hole can be tough and challenging without great length. A drive across the lake and the large waste area can cut off some distance—as much as ability will allow. An overly ambitious shot, though, can end up in the water for a quick seven. The two-level, undulating green sits right on the lake "shoreline." This hole makes for exciting viewing for the gallery.

5

Par 5
521 yards

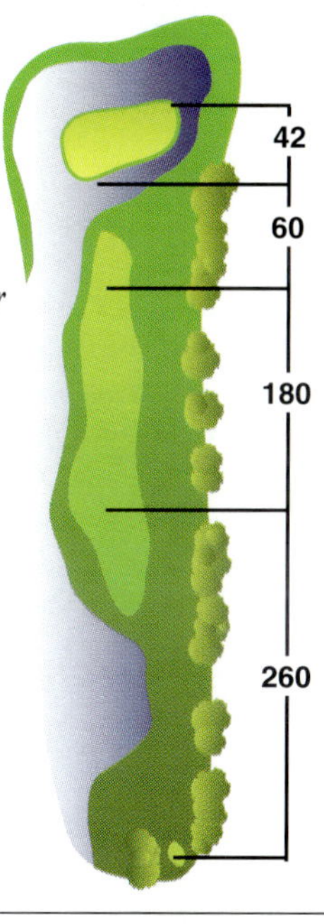

This huge island green can be made in two under the right conditions, and sometimes is dismissed as an easy target because of its size. But a deep swale through the green means that the pros must hit their shots dead on line if they are to have a reasonable putt for three.

6

Par 4
369 yards

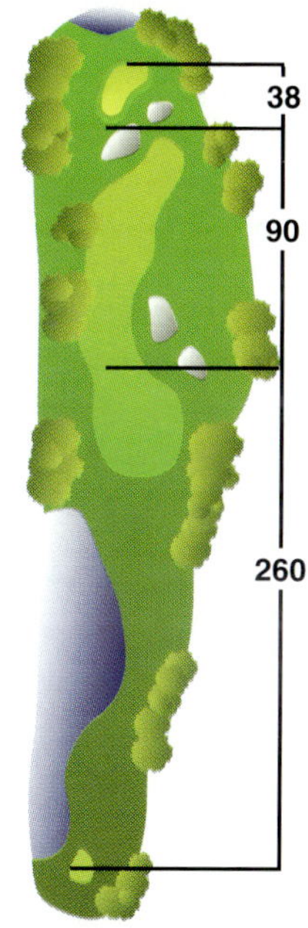

This is an unusual Par4 for South Florida in that it's uphill all the way. The landing area has been tightened with the addition of two large mounds inset with two treacherous pot bunkers at the right dogleg. This is a finesse hole from start to finish.

7

Par 3
193 yards

This hole is completely over water to a green fronted by railroad ties. From the tee, the putting surface looks like a ledge, and in the wind this hole will present problems. Club selection and tee shot accuracy are critical, because to fly the green will result in a delicate bunker or pitch shot looking right down the barrel of a gun—the lake. A variety of angles and teeing areas make this a new hole virtually every time it's played. Each year of the tournament, it is consistently one of the tougher holes.

8

Par 5
548 yards

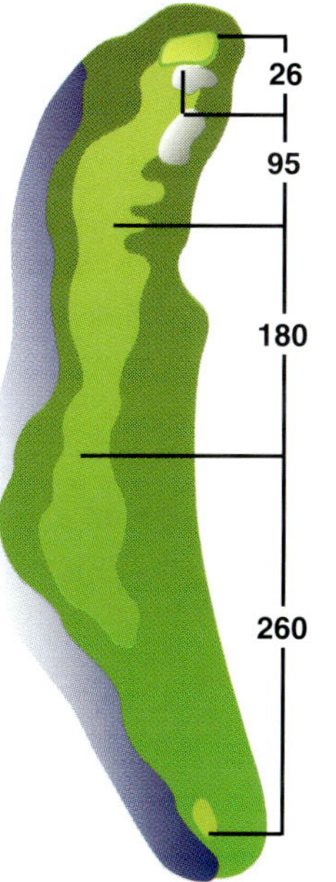

As the longest of the Par 5s, this hole calls for a strong left-to-right tee shot to set up any chance to hit the green in two. Out-of-bounds comes into play to the right of the green, and shifting winds can make this an eagle opportunity or a tough, tough bird.

9

Par 4
460 yards

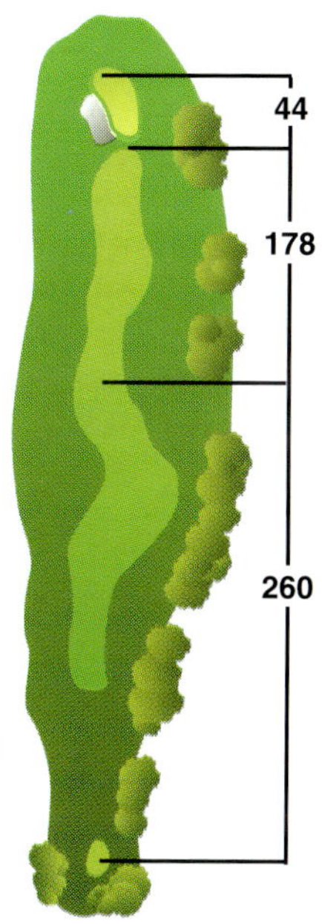

Another long Par-4, this hole calls for skill with the long irons on the second shot. Just in front of the green it is wide and open, and the green shelf is large and long. But beware the back left that's guarded by a large bunker. This is another of those great viewing holes that Stadium Golf was invented for.

10

Par 5
526 yards

Making the turn, two great shots are demanded right off the bat on this "spectator hole." The trick is to thread the narrow green entrance, because the green is contoured in such a way as to require the utmost precision to make a birdie. For added anxiety, there are the sandy wastes lining the right side of the hole.

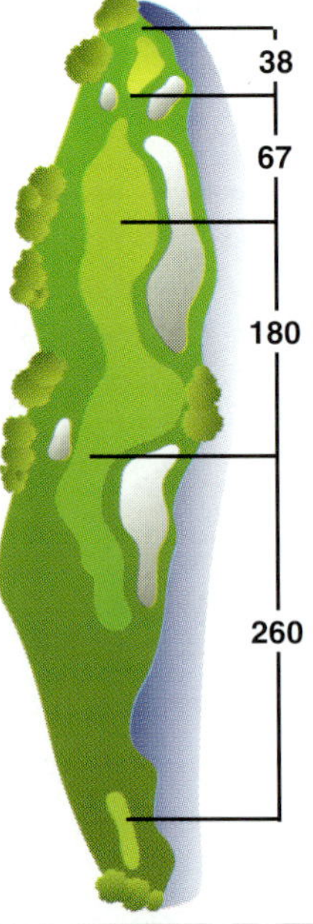

11

Par 3
214 yards

Tee shot needed here? Long and strong. There is a "bail-out" area provided at the back left of the green, but the pitch shot back is a delicate one. Some might hit a slightly right-to-left shot into the green, but a blocked shot is sure to find the water. A safer shot, depending on wind conditions, may be to cut off the left side. A new tournament tee has improved the line of play into the green.

12

Par 4
391 yards

Here the bold tee-shot maker will be rewarded with a shortened second shot that's best played from the right side of the fairway. For added interest, the green has been designed with three distinct levels, each receptive in its own way to a well-struck shot. This tournament hole has been made easier since '84 when it proved to be the toughest in relation to par.

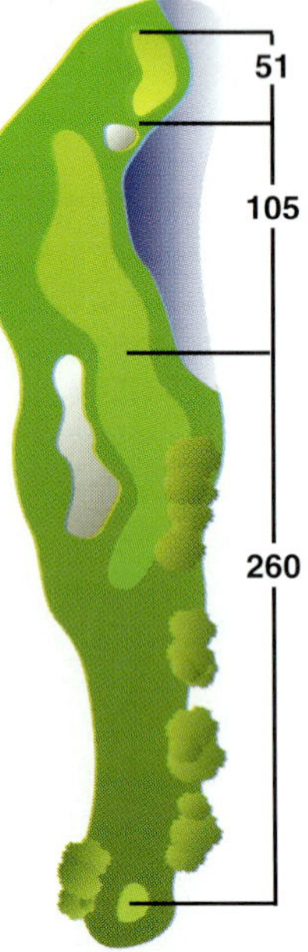

13

Par 4
452 yards

Another example of a "stretch hole," this Par-4 is an example of the course's tremendous balance. Wind factors can mean a long iron or wood or a medium-short iron. The best shot to the green is intended as left-to-right.

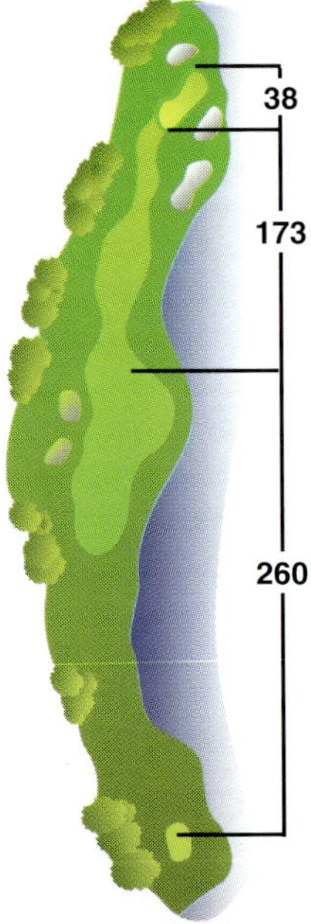

14

Par 4
376 yards

The medium-length hole is relatively easy. A slight draw up the right side will run between fairway bunkers up to the green's opening. However, a back right pin placement and a crisp following wind will test even the best players. Nonetheless there's plenty of birdie potential here.

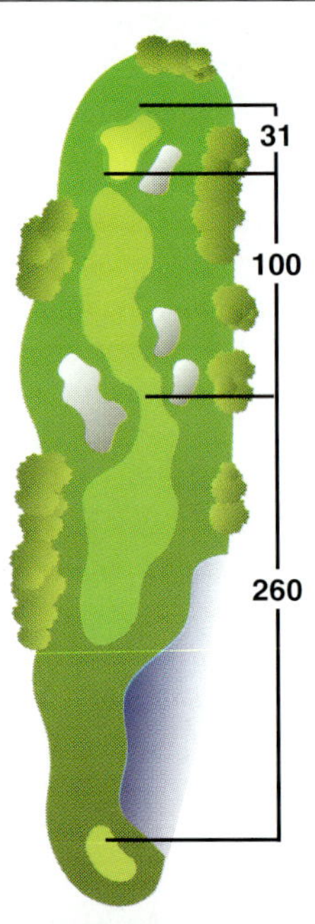

15

Par 5
540 yards

Another slight draw shot and a fairway run will set up many players to be on in two. The second shot, ideally, should be high and soft in order to hold the green. There's a big bonus in store for the perfectly made tee shot.

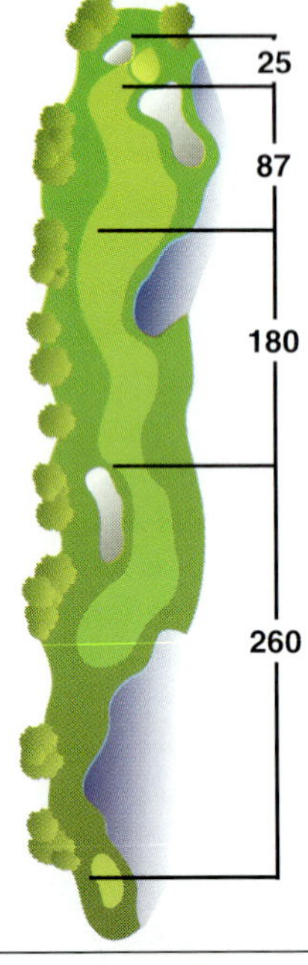

16

Par 4
406 yards

A honey of a medium length Par-4, the rule here is: if the tee shot's long, it's gotta be straight. The fairway to the green is shaped like a funnel, and from the back tee this hole will challenge the world's golfing greats. It's also a great hole to watch from the stadium mounding that lines it. As for the green, it sits on a promontory right out of the water.

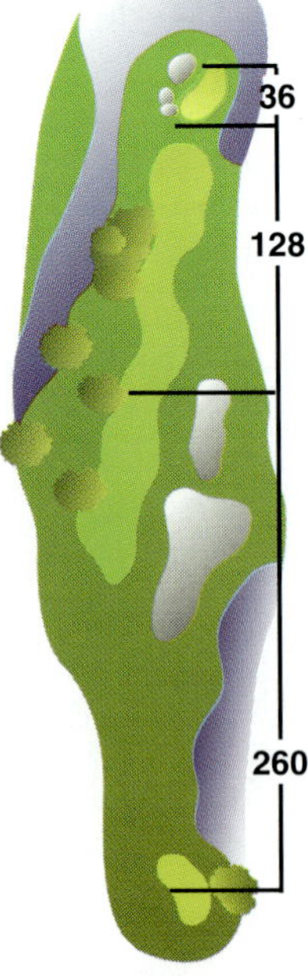

17

Par 3
180 yards

No matter which tee is being played, this hole requires a super shot. There's just no margin for error, with the water having been cut in closer to the front of the green. Spectators are promised a death-defying show here.

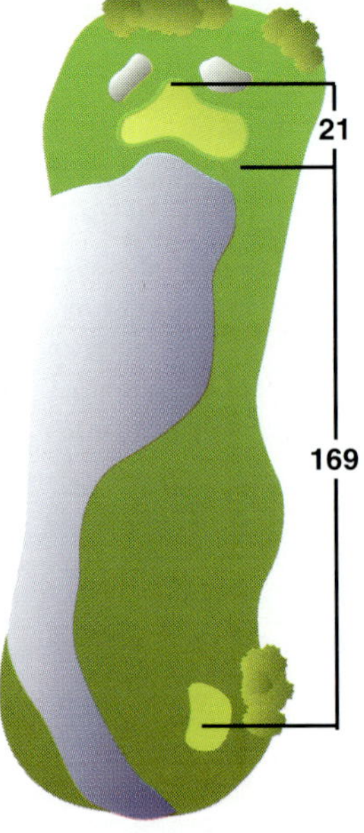

18

Par 4
470 yards

A long grand finale, this hole rewards the perfect tee shot down the left, skirting the bunker. The second shot: long but open if Shot No. 1 is pretty. There's some room for error on the right. Birdies here are distinctly of the rare variety, but when made, all the more dramatic for the finisher.

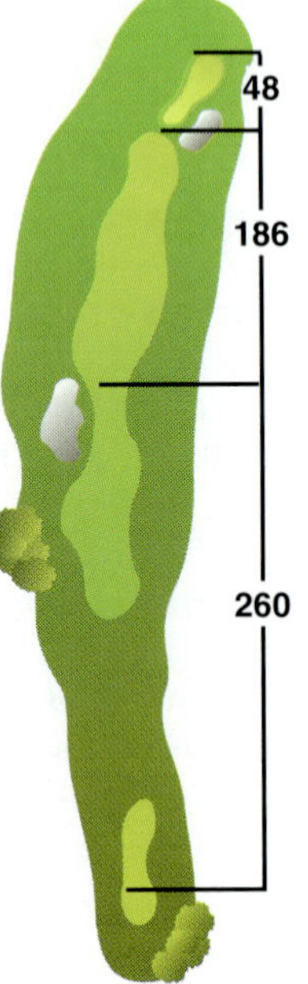

As designer and host, Arnold Palmer again welcomes the Bay Hill Classic to his signature Bay Hill Club in Orlando, Florida. This will be the seventh year of sponsorship by Office Depot and the seventeenth consecutive year that Palmer has held his PGA TOUR® at Bay Hill Club.

In 1994, Loren Roberts made par at 17 and 18 to post a 13 under par score of 275. Fuzzy Zoeller and Vijay Singh each played the last two holes two over par to finish tied with Nick Price at 276, one shot behind Roberts. Roberts won again in 1995.

Dates:	March 14-17, 1996
Network:	NBC
Times:	Sat/Sun - 4:00-6:00 EST
Yardage:	7,114
Par:	72
Slope:	141
Rating:	74.6
Total Purse:	$1,200,000
1st Prize:	$216,000
1995 Winner:	Loren Roberts
1995 Winning Score:	272 (68,65,68,71)
Principal Charitable Beneficiary:	Arnold Palmer Hospital for Children & Women
Ticket Information:	1-407-876-2888

THE COURSE: THE CHAMPIONSHIP COURSE AT BAY HILL CLUB,
ORLANDO, FLORIDA

1

**Par 4
401 yards**

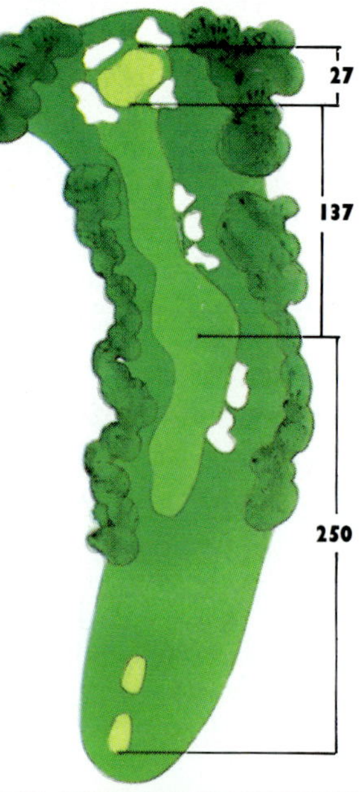

Bunkers along the right side direct the drive down the left middle. Gentle rolling fairway leads up to the contoured green. Four bunkers encircle the putting surface.

2

**Par 3
218 yards**

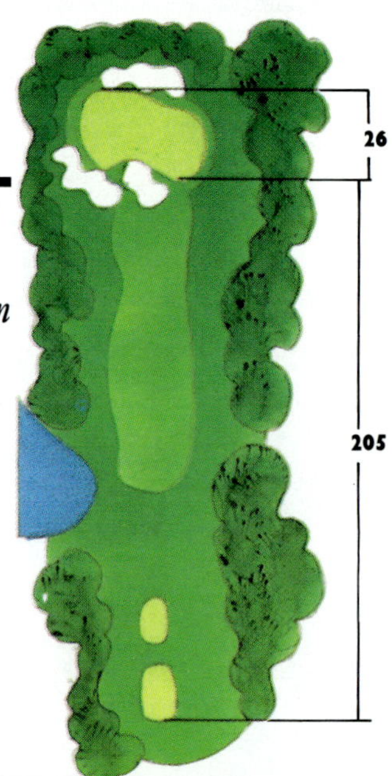

The elevated teeing area looks down on the small upside-down U-shaped green. The two-tiered green makes putting difficult.

3

**Par 4
395 yards**

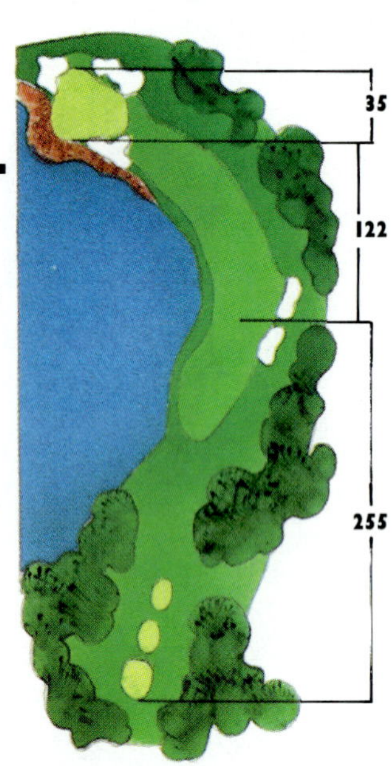

Sharp dogleg left. Players will be playing their drives just over the corner, shortening the hole. The long green is sided by rocks and water left and bunkers right.

4

**Par 5
530 yards**

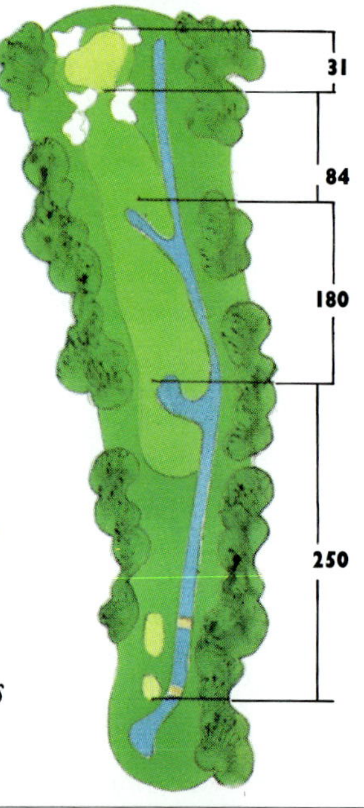

Water and bunkers lie within the landing area for the tee shot. Careful planning is a must for the players to hit three good shots to the hole. Well-bunkered green discourages the eagle-seeker.

5

**Par 4
365 yards**

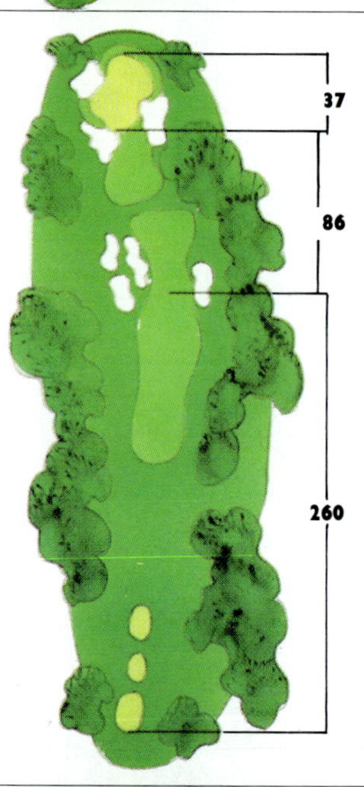

Players will be using irons off the tee to place their drives in position for the approach. A large mound on the right side of the green adds significantly to the putting surface.

6

**Par 5
543 yards**

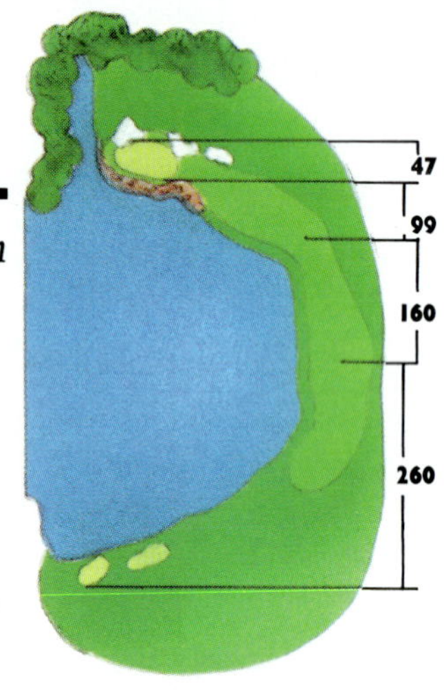

The sharp turn to the left allows players to cut the corner and get home in two. Caution must be taken to avoid the ever-present water along the left.

7

**Par 3
197 yards**

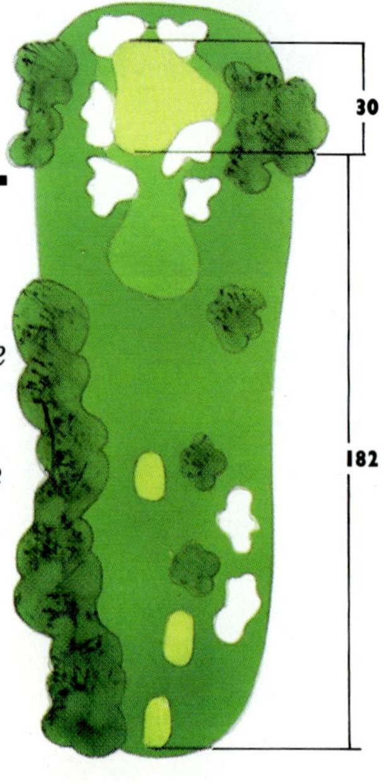

Slightly uphill, this par three can be difficult. The hole is just out of sight and the contours of the green provide rolling putts.

8

**Par 4
424 yards**

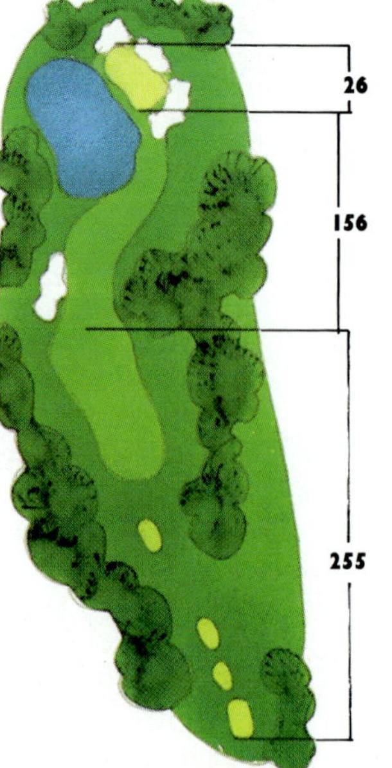

The drive is persuaded to the left by the trees on the right. Players must play their shots to the narrow green with enough club to keep the ball from backing into the water.

9

**Par 4
467 yards**

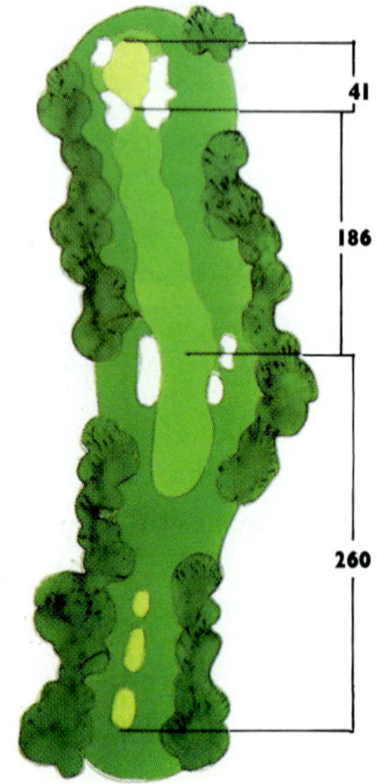

Before making the turn, players must get past this long ninth hole. Fairway bunkers left and right are within driving range. Mounds and bunkers encircle the green.

10

Par 4
400 yards

This is the first dogleg to the right. A drive along the right side of the fairway will put the ball in excellent position for the second shot.

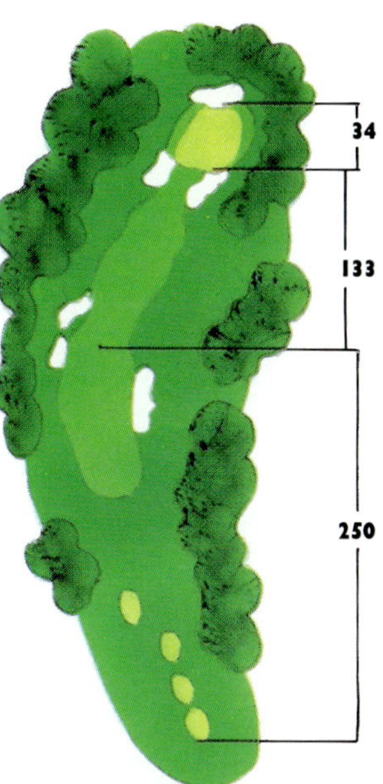

11

Par 4
428 yards

The players will be hitting their drives down the right side of the fairway to open up the angle for the approach. Long narrow green sits tightly within bunkers right and water left.

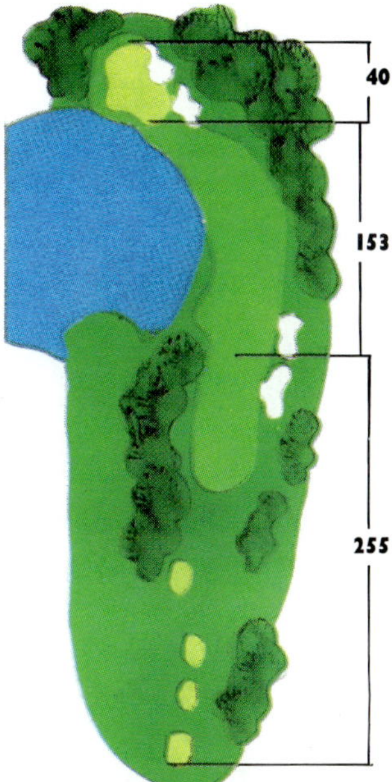

12

Par 5
570 yards

The slight dogleg hides the landing area for drives behind the right fairway bunker. The second shot is a lay-up to allow a full approach onto the green.

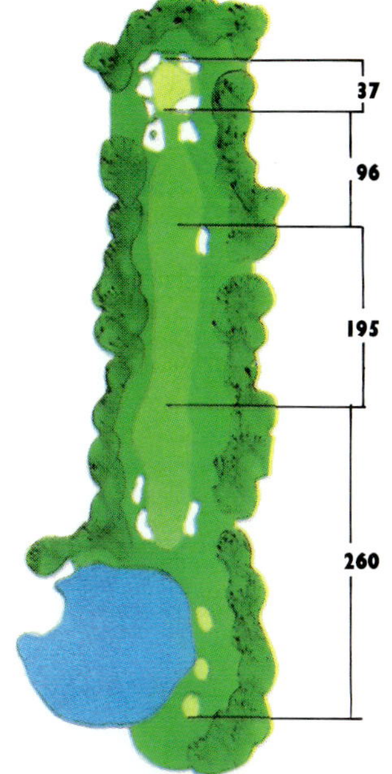

13

Par 4
364 yards

A long iron or fairway wood is used to place the drive in perfect position for the approach. The rock-lined edge of the water borders the tight, contoured green.

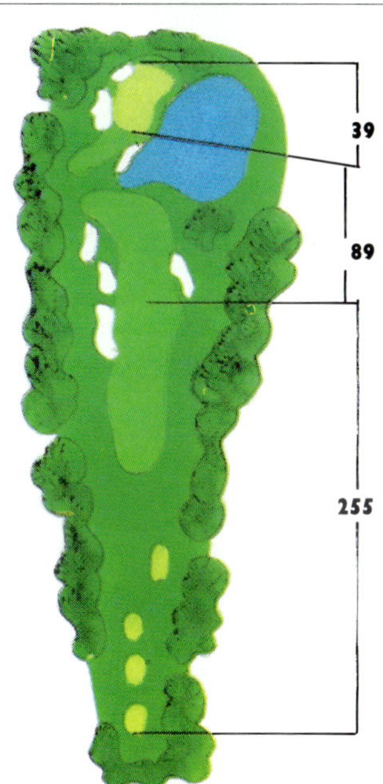

14

Par 3
206 yards

Similar to the seventh hole, this fourteenth is also uphill but slightly longer. Palm trees and bunkers surround the long undulating putting surface.

15

Par 4
425 yards

Flat, but somewhat long. Nothing short of hitting right down the middle is necessary to get the ball in good position for the approach. Large, spacious green creates some long putts.

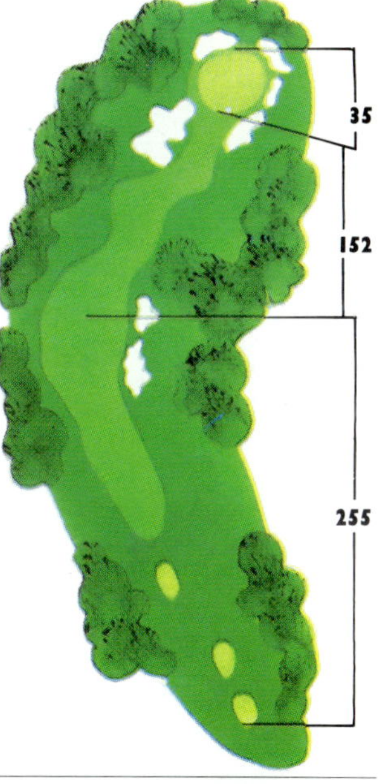

16

Par 5
481 yards

At only 481 yards it would appear that this hole should be easily reached in two. But the pond in front of the tight, two-tiered green challenges second shots.

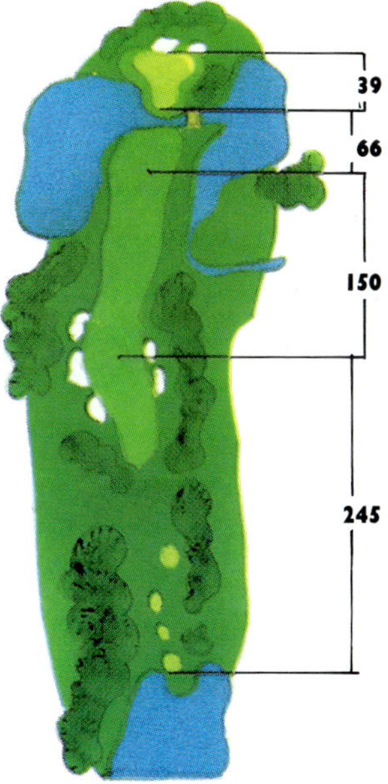

17

Par 3
219 yards

A gusting wind will tighten the nerves of the players. Water almost completely surrounds the green. Pars are welcomed on this 219 yard hole.

18

Par 4
441 yards

The tee shot disappears over a ridge setting up a long approach to the green bordered by bunkers on the left and water to the right. Pin placements in back corner are difficult.

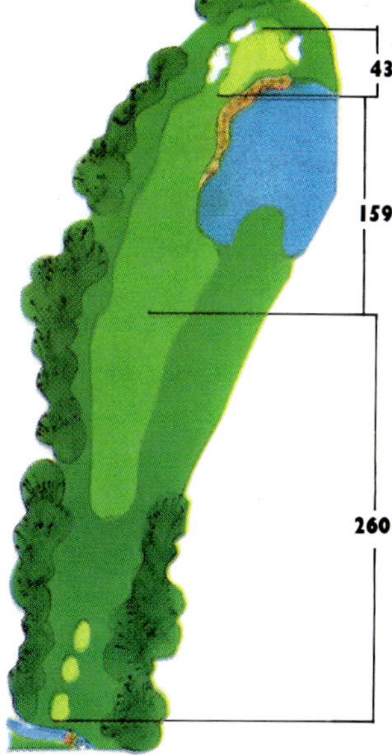

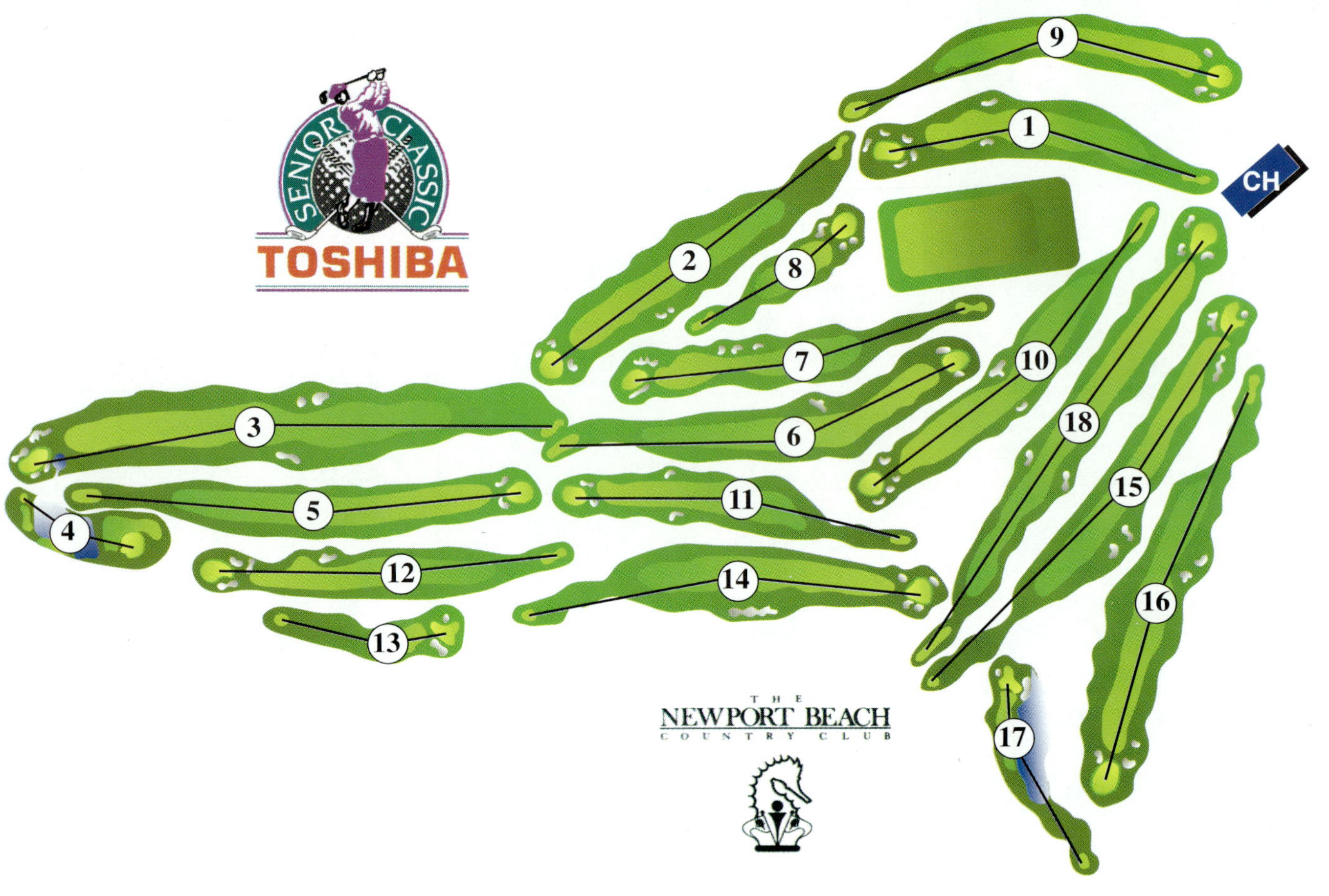

THE COURSE: NEWPORT BEACH COUNTRY CLUB, NEWPORT BEACH, CALIFORNIA

The Toshiba Senior Classic moves to the Newport Beach Country Club for its second run in 1996, featuring a traditional layout of soft rolling hills, cooling ocean breezes and a scenic location less than a half mile from the Southern California coastline. Situated less than an hour from Los Angeles in the heart of one Orange County's most famous recreational communities, the Newport Beach Country Club features a par-71 layout with a rich history of hosting local and regional tournaments.

Defending champion George Archer will lead a strong field for this million dollar event, one of the richest on the senior tour with a winner's share of $150,000, that marks only the second time in the past 28 years that a PGA event has been held in Orange County.

Dates:	March 15-17
Network:	ESPN
Times:	TBA
Yardage:	6,598
Par:	71
Slope:	126
Rating:	71.5
Total Purse:	$825,000
1st Prize:	$120,000
1995 Winner:	George Archer
1995 Winning Score:	(199) 67, 68, 64
Principal Charitable Beneficiary:	Make-A-Wish Foundation National Dyslexia Foundation Amyotrophic Lateral Sclerosis Association
Ticket Information:	714-646-9007 $25 Daily ---- $60 weekly

1

Par 4
339 yards

A slight dogleg to the left, the first hole puts the premium on the location of the drive. The long hitter may elect to use the long iron to better position his second shot to a deceptive green. There are large trees on both sides of the fairway. The second shot demands hitting to a small two-tier green where you want to avoid being above the hole.

2

Par 4
390 yards

A slightly uphill hole that requires the tee shot be worked from left to right. A drive hit to the right side of the fairway sets up the opening of the green. A large bunker fronts the left side of the green.

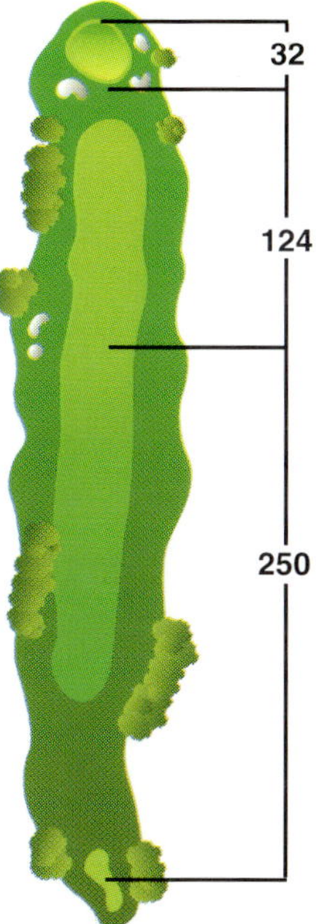

3

Par 5
549 yards

After teeing off of an elevated tee, the longer hitters are confronted with the choice of trying to reach the green with a fairway wood or a long iron. There is a small pond in front of the green and a lake to the left of the green. The green is also protected by bunkers on the left and the right side.

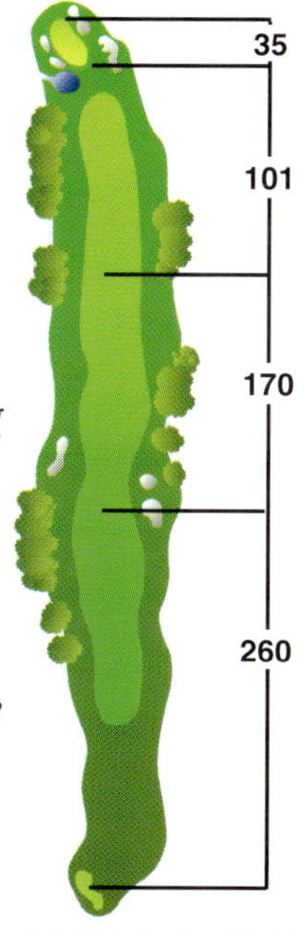

4

Par 3
143 yards

A short but tricky hole which is normally played up wind with a lake covering the front and left sides of the green. The green has a large undulation which adds to the challenge.

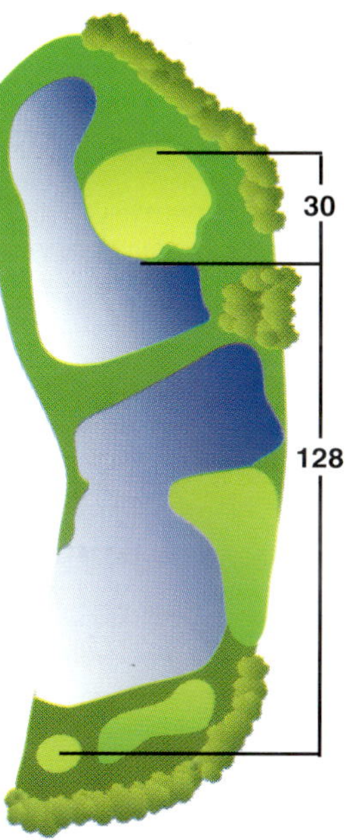

5

Par 4
455 yards

A straightaway uphill hole which is usually played upwind. A wide fairway lets you open up on the tee shot but the second shot is played to a well-bunkered green.

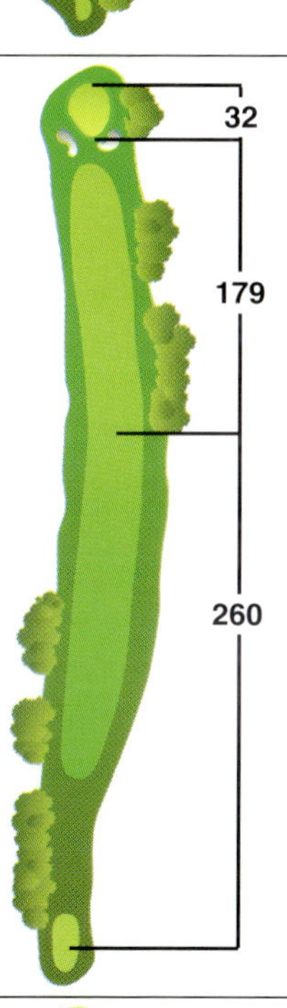

6

Par 4
418 yards

A dogleg left with large trees on both sides of the fairway. A drive down the right center of the fairway will give you an unblocked shot to a well guarded subtle rolling green.

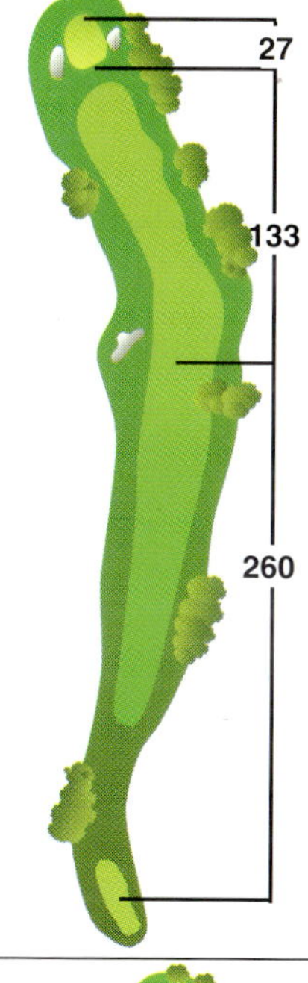

7

Par 4
360 yards

This hole can be played with the driver or a mid-iron from the tee. If you elect the driver and can hit it over the large tree on the right side of the fairway, you then have a very short shot to the green. Many players will select an iron off the tee leaving a short shot to the green. This is one of the larger greens on the course and has a huge undulation. Good judgement will tell you not to hit the ball above the pin.

8

Par 3
203 yards

A very strong Par 3 that normally plays upwind. The bank to the right of the green slopes down and away making a difficult pitch to get the ball up and down for par.

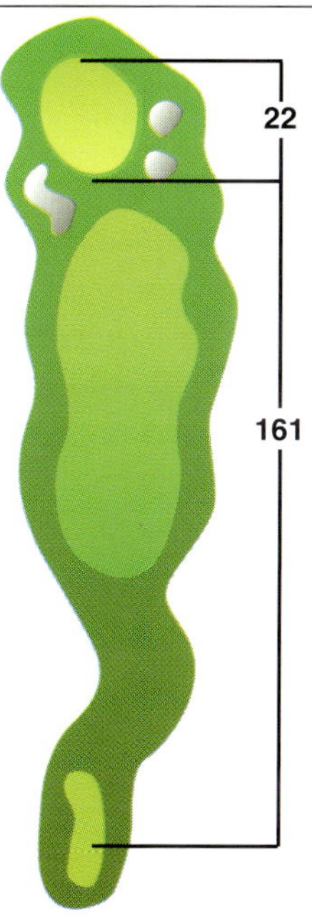

9

Par 4
407 yards

A really fine driving hole. Large trees left and right of the fairway demands a well positioned tee shot. A dogleg right but the hole sets up from the left center of the fairway. The second shot is uphill and rather deceptive. Out of bounds guards the left and rear of the green

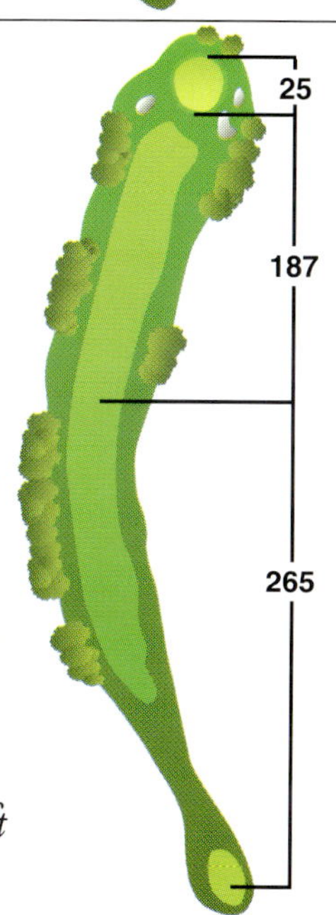

10
Par 4
429 yards

A straightaway hole that has two bunkers looking at you as you tee off. The tee shot between them leaves you with a mid-iron to a small, tightly-bunkered green.

11
Par 4
344 yards

Plenty of driving room off the tee. The second shot into a small elevated green with bunkers located both left and right makes the hole a little tougher than it looks.

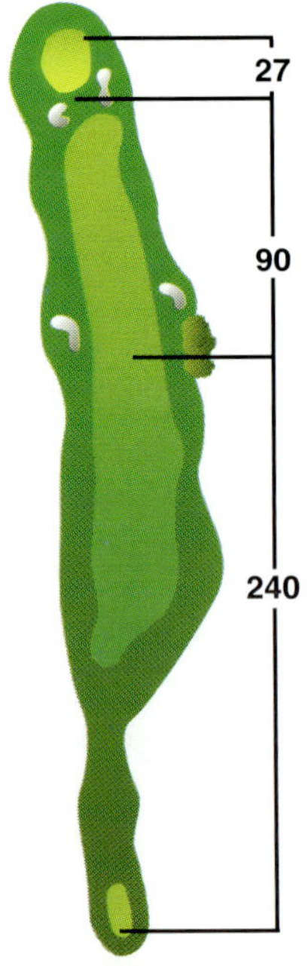

12
Par 4
370 yards

This hole has two important characteristics the player must overcome. The landing area for your tee shot is narrow and there is a large eucalyptus tree in front of the green on the right side. The left side of the green is well guarded by bunkers.

13
Par 3
170 yards

A beautiful par 3 into a slightly tilted green which is sur rounded by trees. Out of bounds runs along the entire right side of the fairway and generally plays into the wind.

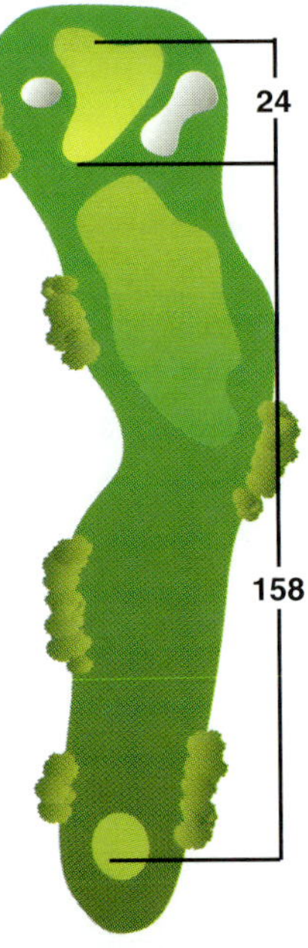

14
Par 4
397 yards

This is one of the tougher holes on the course. It has length, and you need a well placed tee shot. Large trees on the left side of the fairway and large deep bunkers on the right side. The green is lower than the fairway and is very small and well bunkered.

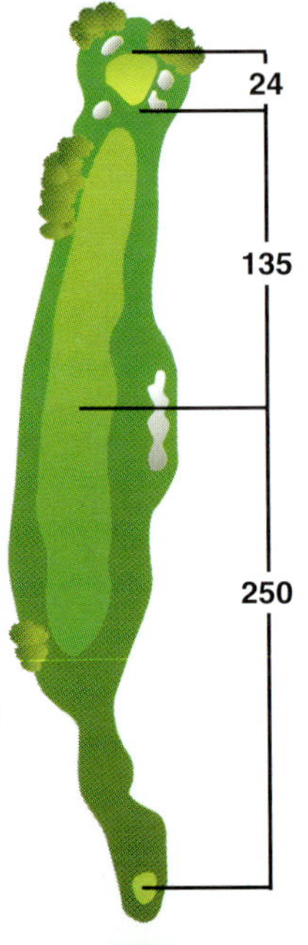

15
Par 5
492 yards

A challenging hole that rewards and will make you pay the penalty if you make a mistake. A good drive sets you up to see the green and all the trouble that surrounds it. Bunkers surround the left side of the green and a pot bunker positioned on the right side of the green. The green is two-tiered with mounds and swales around the outer side. Some thirty palm trees around the green will offer challenge if you tend to stray just a little.

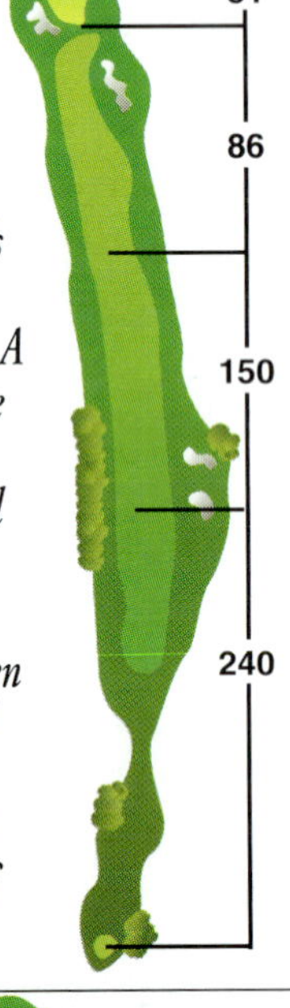

16
Par 4
437 yards

Perhaps the best par four on the course. It requires a long tee shot avoiding out of bounds left and trees right, leaving a long iron to a large rolling green that has well placed bunkers guarding the front of the green.

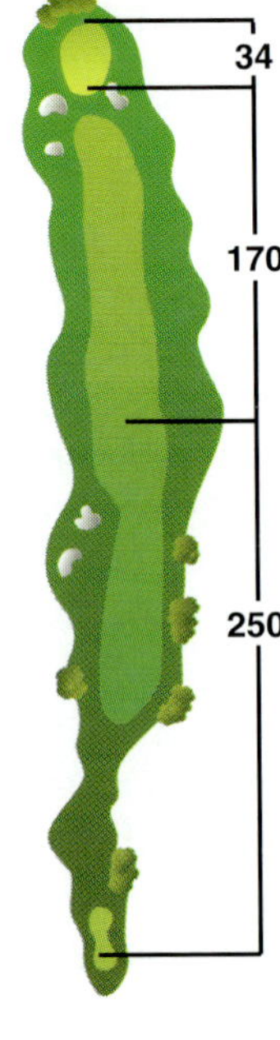

17
Par 3
185 yards

A beautiful hole with a large lake in front of the tee and to the green's edge. A two-tiered rolling green with a large trap guarding the front and a pot bunker behind the green. Mounds and swales will present a challenge if you miss the green.

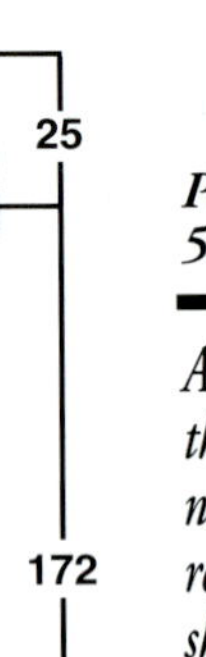

18
Par 5
510 yards

An uphill finishing hole that presents an opportunity for the long hitter to reach this green in two shots. A wide fairway with large trees both right and left and a bunker covering the green's front right side. The green is slightly elevated from the fairway and is deceptive to pitch to.

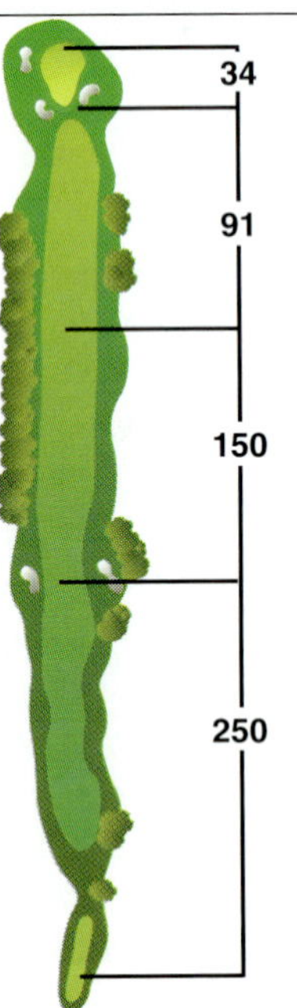

McDermott

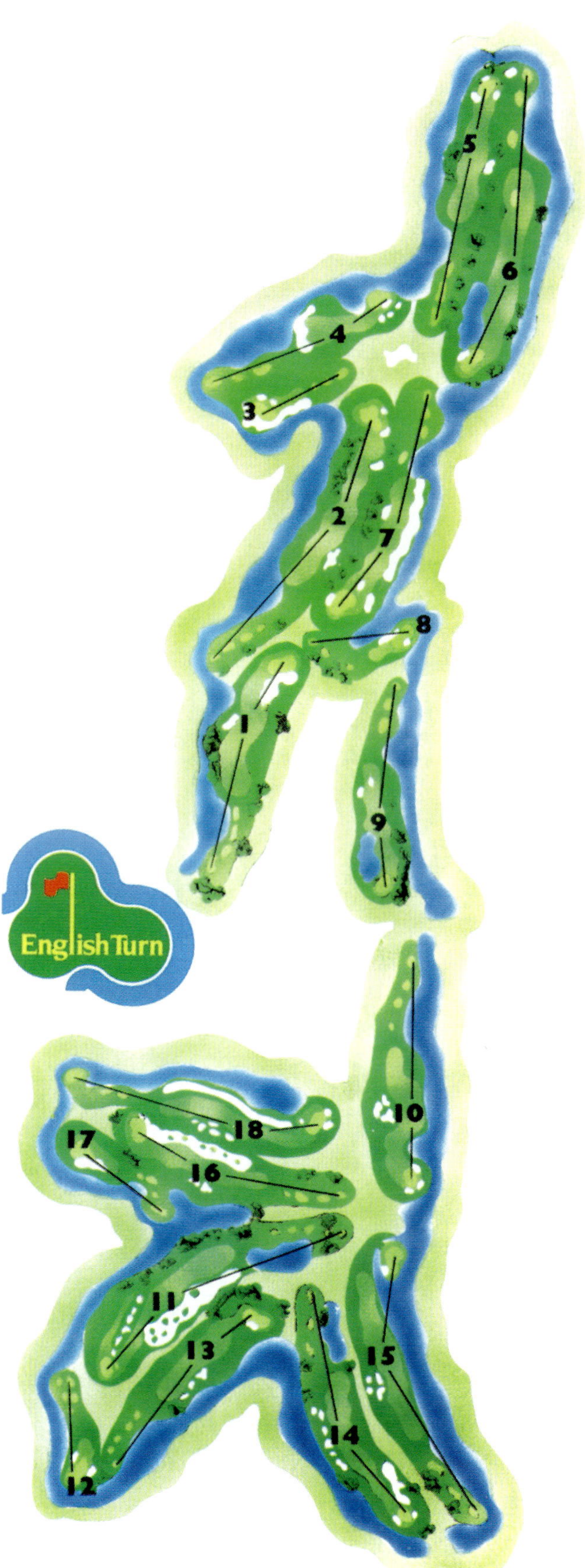

*E*nglish Turn is actually a bend in the Mississippi River where, in 1699, five badly out-numbered French explorers, in two canoes, bluffed a heavily armed English ship into reversing its course and fleeing down river. The name English Turn, or "Detour Des Anglais", has endured for almost three hundred years at this bend in the river where this colorful incident took place.

The English Turn Golf Club, designed by Jack Nicklaus and home of the Freeport McDermott Classic, hosted its first tournament in 1989. Players were impressed with the new course and looked forward to subsequent tournaments at the club. Greg Norman said after the final round, "Jack did his usual good job on layout. He used what nature had provided and added to it. There are some super holes here." Water comes into play on every single hole and a plethora of mounding and deep bunkers reveal the overwhelming character of the challenging course.

The first Classic in 1938 was won by Harry Cooper with a 285 total at City Park Course. Chip Beck currently holds the 72-hole tournament record of 262, which he scored at the Lakewood Country Club a year before the event moved to English Turn. Other winners at the new course include: Tim Simpson in 1989 with a 14-under 274, David Frost in 1990 with 276, Ian Woosnam in 1991 with 275, Chip Beck in 1992 with 276, Mike Standly in 1993 with 281, Ben Creshaw in 1994 with 273 and Davis Love III in 1995.

Dates:	March 21-24
Network:	NBC
Times:	Sat/Sun - 4:00-6:00 EST
Yardage:	7,108
Par:	72
Slope:	141
Rating:	74.1
Total Purse:	$1,200,000
1st Prize:	$216,000
1995 Winner:	Davis Love III
1995 Winning Score:	274 (68,69,66,71)
Principal Charitable Beneficiary:	Children's Hospital
Ticket Information:	1-504-831-4653

THE COURSE: THE ENGLISH TURN GOLF CLUB, NEW ORLEANS, LOUISIANA

1

**Par 4
398 yards**

Nicklaus requires accuracy right from the beginning on this layout. Water along the left and mounding amidst the high rough on the right can intimidate the drive.

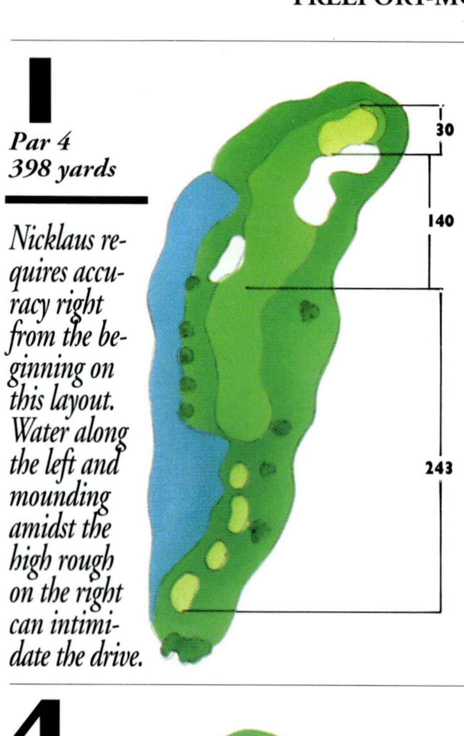

2

**Par 5
519 yards**

The four bunkers on the right provide the target line from the tee. Mounding partially hides the green from view. The large putting surface can leave some very long putts.

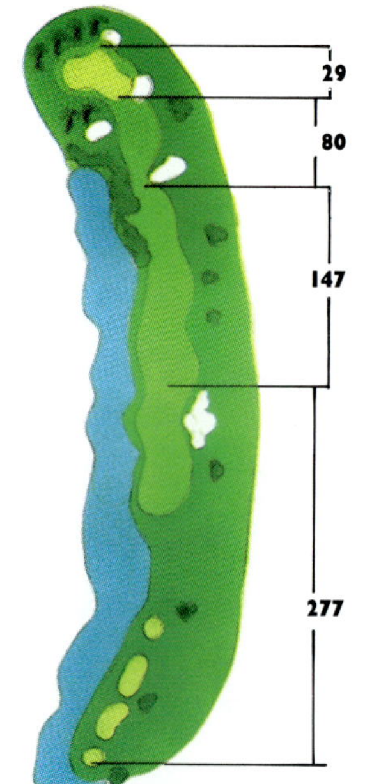

3

**Par 3
200 yards**

Length and accuracy are a must on this third hole. The severe undulating green truly tests the player's putting skills.

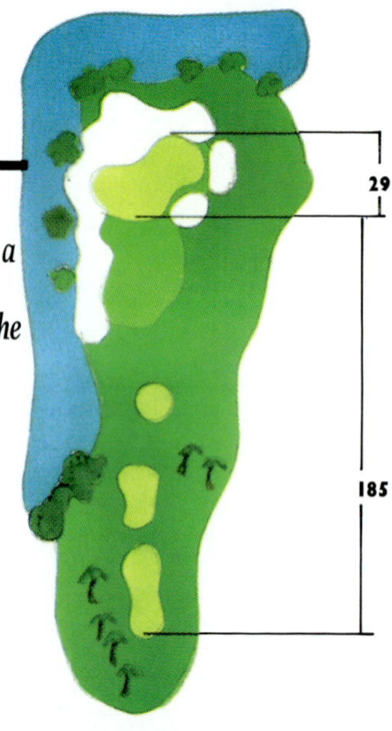

4

**Par 4
349 yards**

Now the screws get tightened just a bit more. A large bunker crosses the path to the palm-lined fairway. The approach will be played with a short-iron to the two-tiered green.

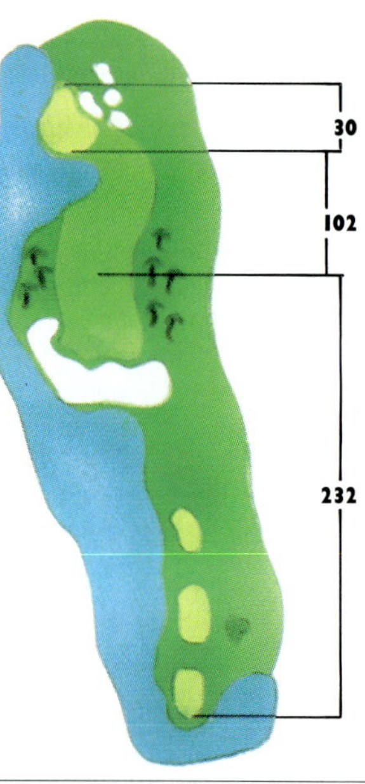

5

**Par 4
463 yards**

A good par 4 — straight and long. A big drive will help get home to the green in regulation. The putting surface is two-tiered with the division just about halfway back.

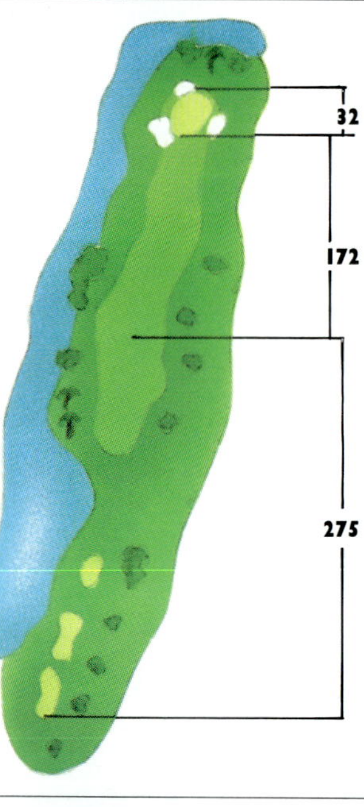

6

**Par 5
557 yards**

The bunker in the fairway should be carried with no problem. Some may try for the green in two, however the safer play is along the left side. The putting surface rolls from front to back.

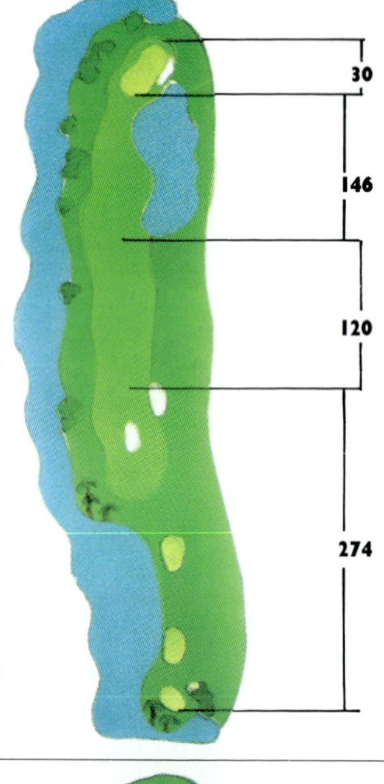

7

**Par 4
445 yards**

Players may be cutting the corner just slightly on this dogleg right. Two ominous bunkers make the flag look closer than it actually is — correct club selection is vital.

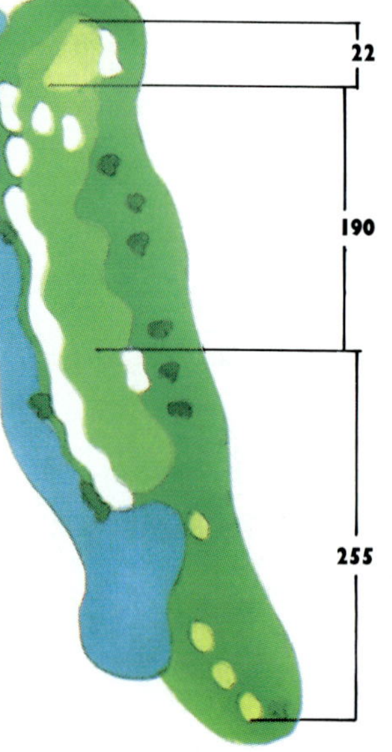

8

**Par 3
176 yards**

A gusting wind will make for a tough tee shot. Players will be hitting right to left to keep well clear of the hazards. A depression in the middle of the green can cause a few tricky putts.

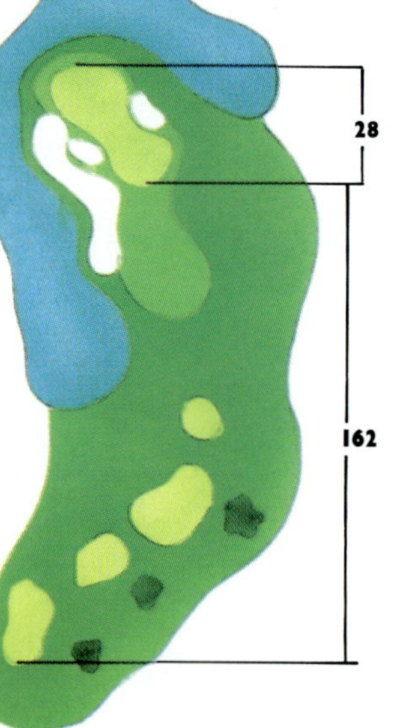

9

**Par 4
370 yards**

A birdie hole. Players will be hitting their tee shots along the left side of the fairway to shorten the approach and get a good angle to the green.

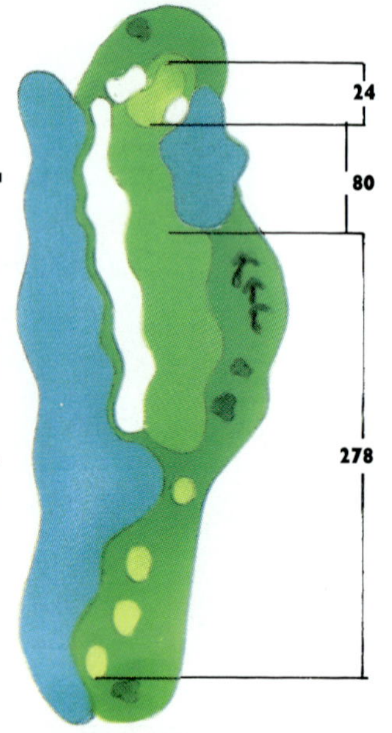

10

Par 4
420 yards

The second shot should be played from the middle of the fairway just left of the bunkers on the right. The putting surface is fairly flat except for a depression on the right side.

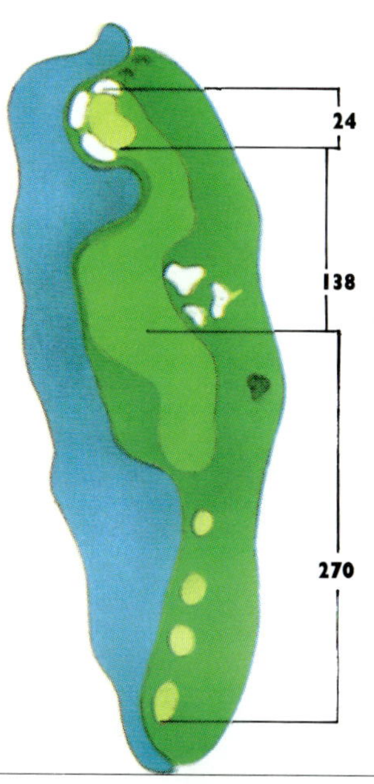

11

Par 5
550 yards

A par 5 that requires some planning. The easiest approach shot is from the elevated right side of the fairway — beyond the crossing bunkers.

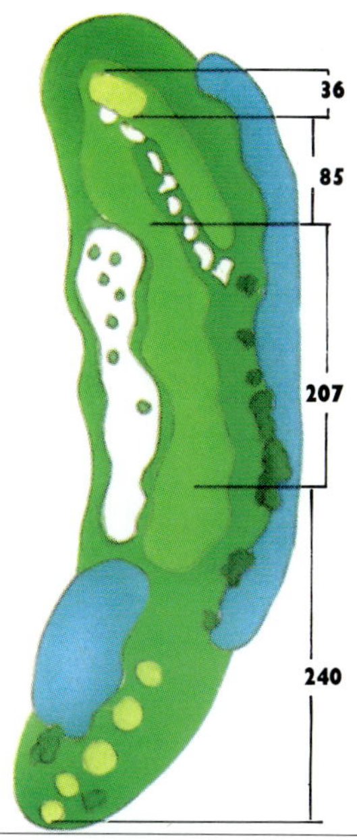

12

Par 3
158 yards

The green is long and has a second level about halfway back. Pin placements on the upper level of the green are difficult to reach.

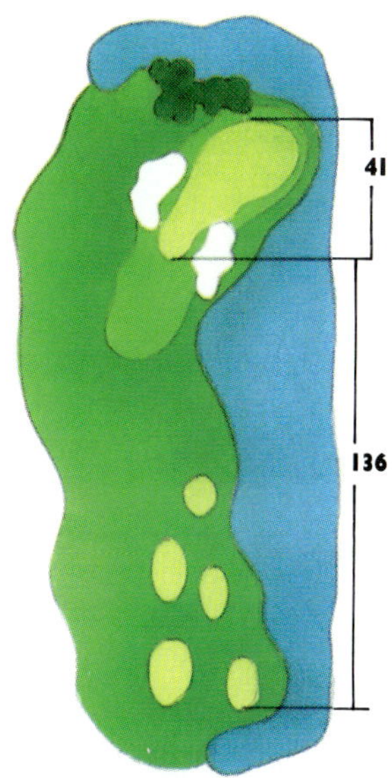

13

Par 4
380 yards

Players will be hitting either a fairway wood or long iron from the tee. The second shot must be played with sufficient spin to hold the undulating putting surface.

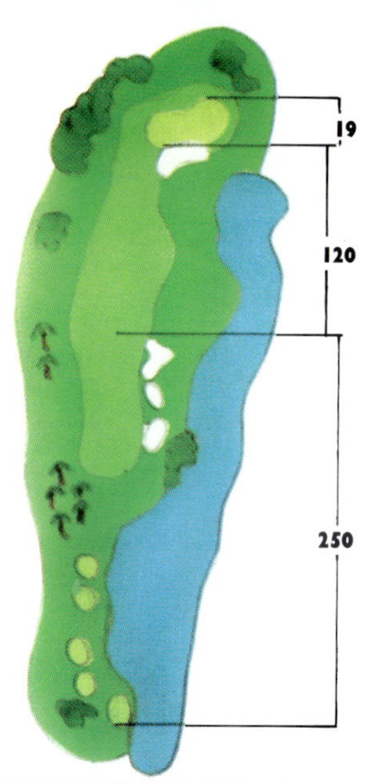

14

Par 4
469 yards

Considered the most difficult hole on the course, this fourteenth requires two excellent shots to reach the green. A ridge runs across the putting surface halfway back.

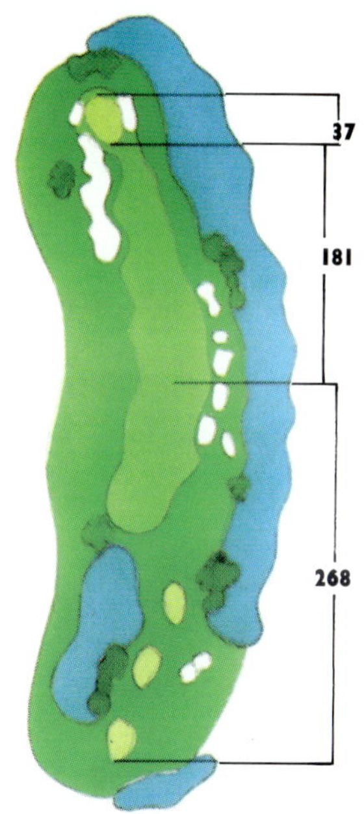

15

Par 5
542 yards

An island green is the goal. Two thoughtful shots should place the ball in perfect position for the approach. Going for this in two would be insane!

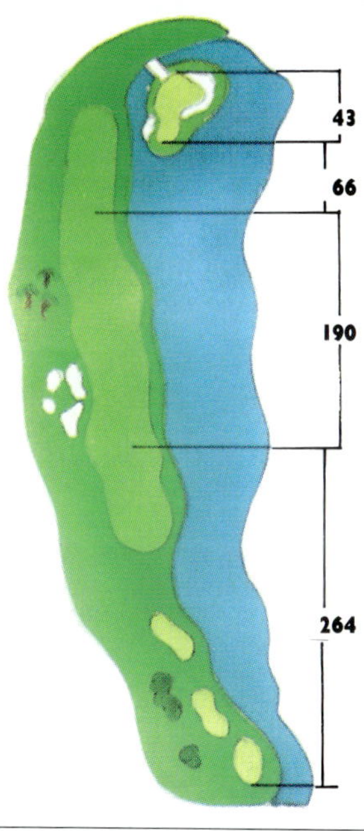

16

Par 4
442 yards

The bunkers along the left side of the fairway provide the target line from the tee. Bunkers on the right and around the green dictate that a long approach is more desirable than being short.

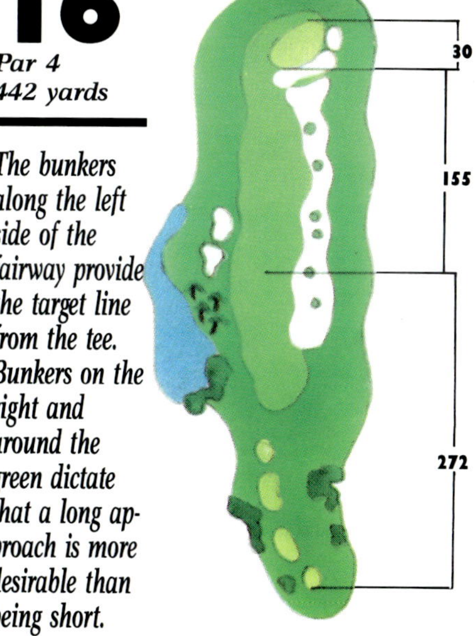

17

Par 3
207 yards

The bunkers and water will be relentless to miscalculated tee shots. The tournament can be won and lost on this hole — lengthy putts can more likely turn into three putts on the spacious green.

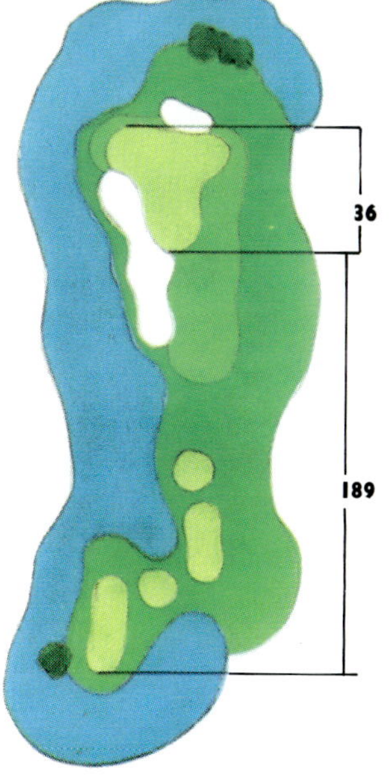

18

Par 4
471 yards

A big drive down the left middle will set up for a shorter approach over the water. Bunkers surround the green making it imperative that the second shot is accurate!

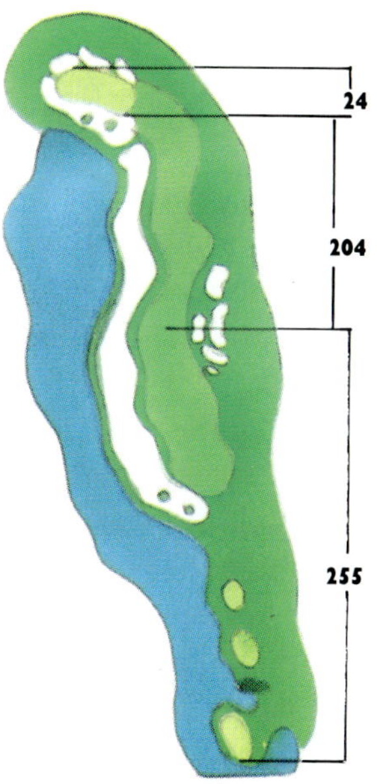

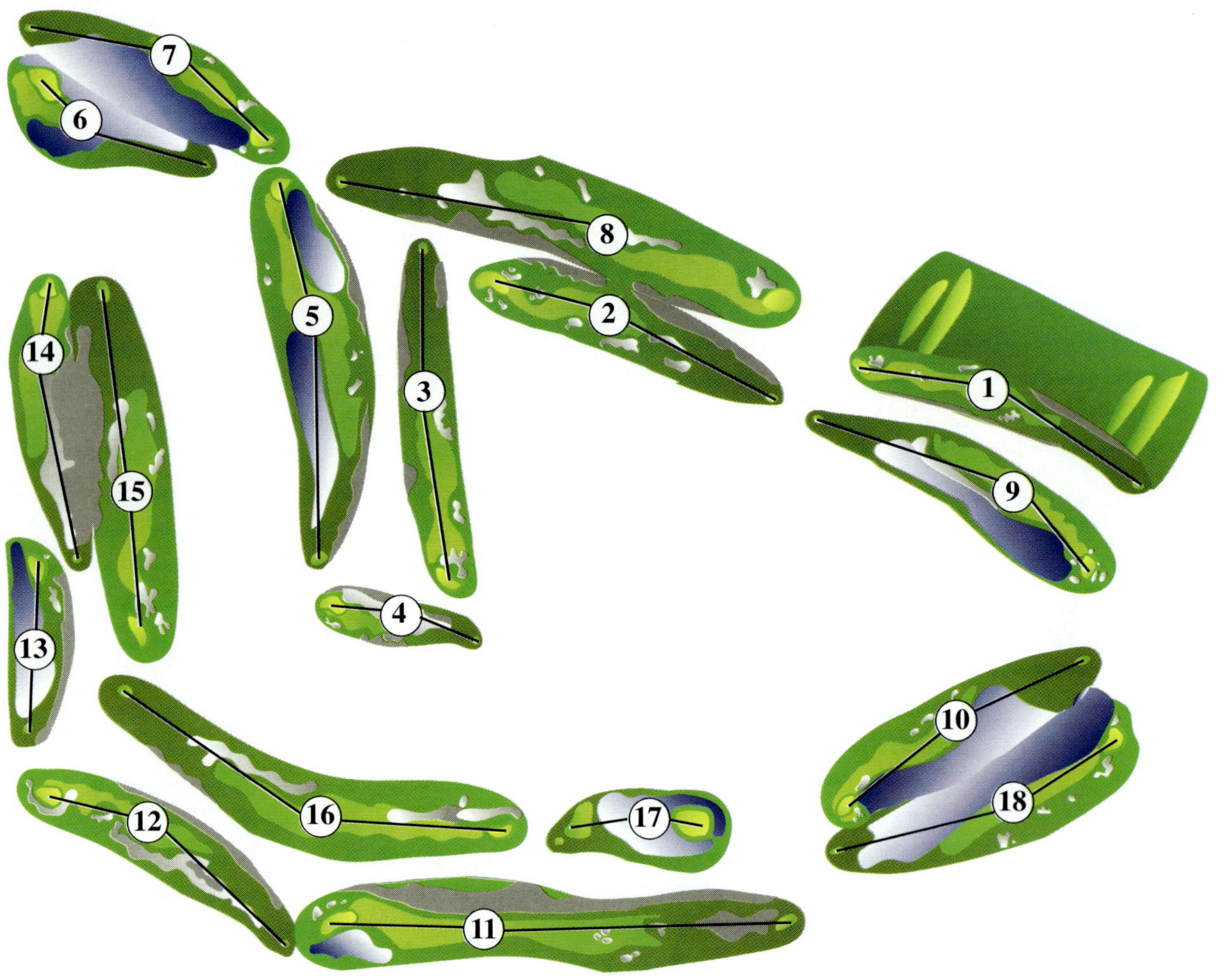

THE COURSE: TPC STADIUM AT PGA WEST, LAQUINTA, CALIFON

*T*he Liberty Mutual Legends of Golf will again play host to the finest names in Senior Golf at PGA West in La Quinta California. Now in its 19th season, our unique best-ball team format will continue to be played on Pete Dye's TPC Stadium Golf Course.

The Legends of Golf originated in 1978 as the first event dedicated solely for senior golfers. The timing was perfect and founder Fred Raphael utilized the perfect format for players such as Sam Snead, Tommy Bolt, Jimmy Demaret, Julius Boros, and others. After the famous 6-hole play-off in 1979, featuring Tommy Bolt/Art Wall vs. Julius Boros/Roberto DeVicenzo, senior golf was well on its way as one of the most remarkable growth stories in the entire world of sports.

In 1996, 64 of the greatest names in golf will once again play for a purse in excess of $1 million dollars. Joining in the fun will be 14 very special golfers invited to play in the Demaret Division - a separate division for golfing greats over 70.

Dates:	March 22-24, 1996
Network:	ABC
Times:	Sat 1:00-3:00 EST
	Sun 2:00-4:00 EST
Yardage:	6,854
Par:	72
Slope:	139
Rating:	74.4
Total Purse:	$1,000,000+
1st Prize:	$200,000 each
1995 Winner:	Mike Hill/Lee Trevino
1995 Winning Score:	195 (64,66,65)
Principal Charitable Beneficiary:	The Viva Foundation
Ticket Information:	1-612-777-1150

1

Par 4
440 yards

This hole is a combination of length and a small green introducing the difficulty of what lies ahead. A player wants to avoid the sand bunkers on the left which would leave a long to middle iron to the green.

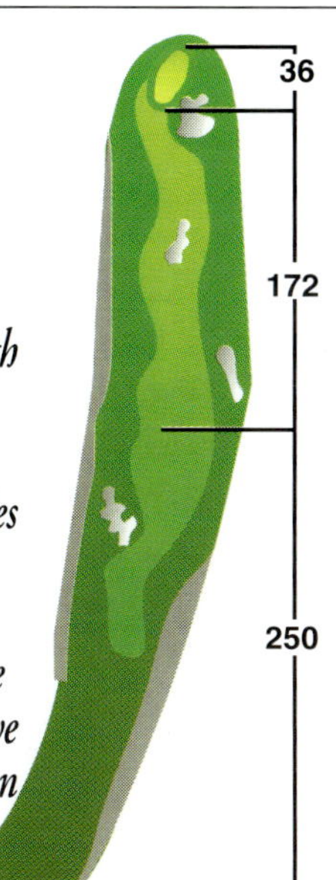

2

Par 4
373 yards

This hole requires an accurate tee shot, possibly using a 3 wood or long iron, leaving a short iron to a very deep green. Emphasis on staying to the right avoiding the "craters".

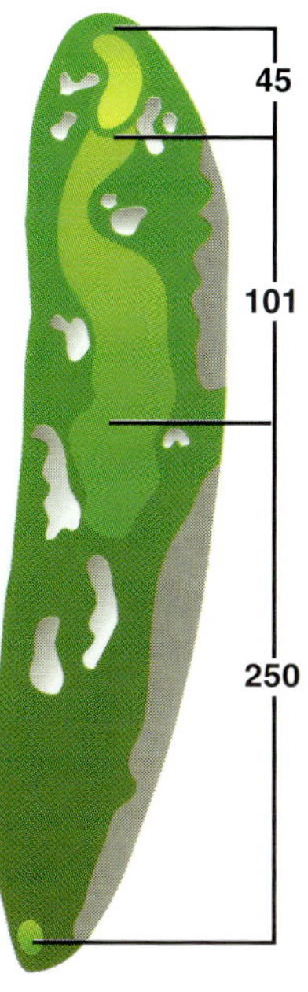

3

Par 4
470 yards

On this straight away hole, length is very important off the tee. Equally important is the long second shot demanding all carry to a well bunkered green. Keep the drive to the right side avoiding the "crescent" bunkers on the left side.

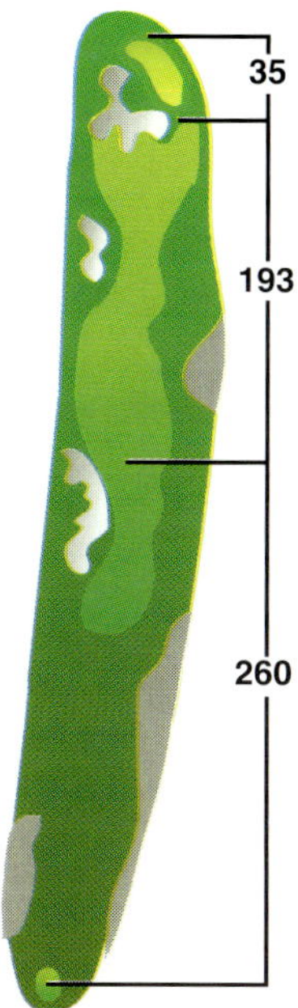

4

Par 3
184 yards

This hole calls for a middle to long iron shot. Do not let the "sand pit" on the right lead you to believe that left of the green is safe. Shoot for the center of the green.

5

Par 5
533 yards

Strategy is your best chance with water off the tee on the left and then again on the right for your second shot. Placement, not distance, is the key.

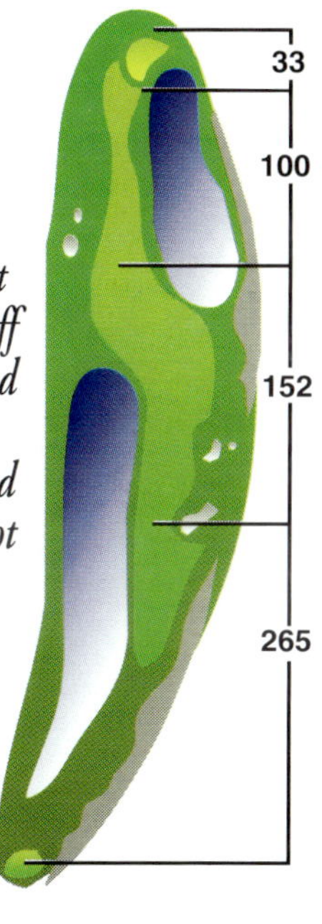

6

Par 3
255 yards

This is a tough and tremendously long hole but the size of the green should help. Try to keep your tee shot left. The carry becomes greater the more you let your shot leak to the right. If you hit this green, say "AMEN"!

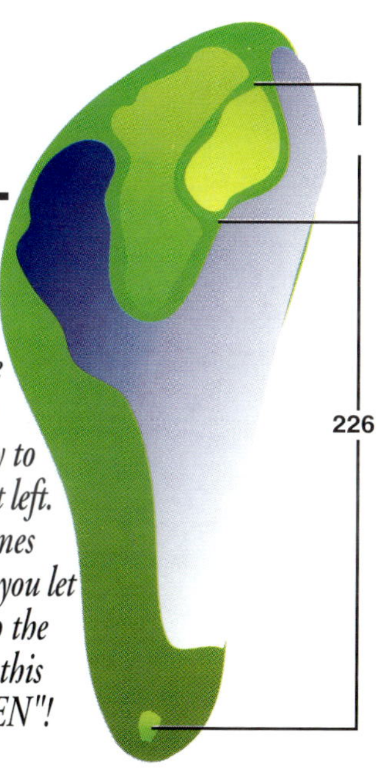

7

Par 4
350 yards

This has to be the most picturesque hole on the course using the mountains as a back drop. Avoiding the "black hole" and the sand bunker on the left side is half the battle.

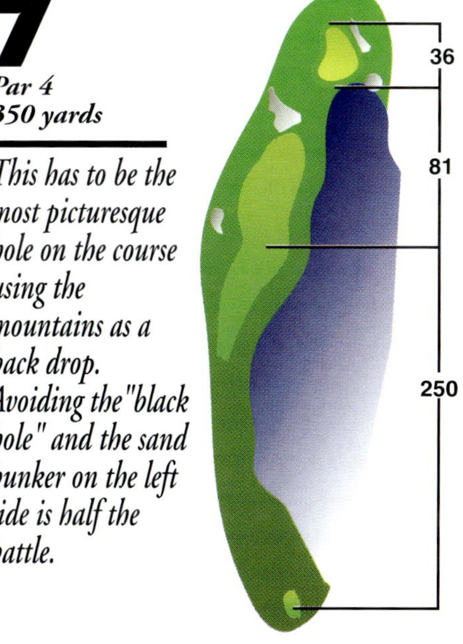

8

Par 5
557 yards

This hole tempts a long hitter to go for it in two. It is very deceiving because a player does not realize how difficult a shot pulled to the left can become for their third shot.

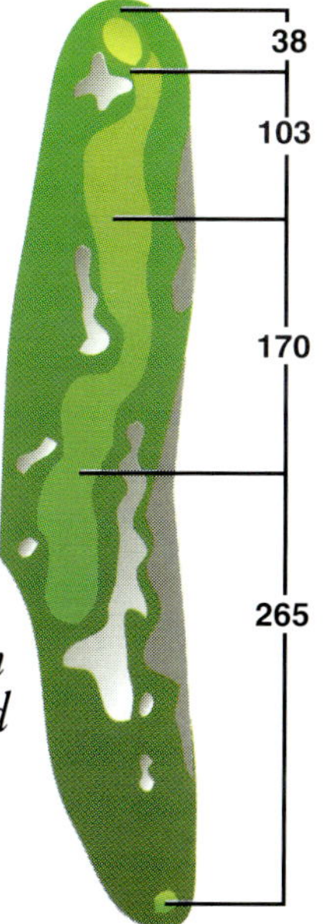

9

Par 4
450 yards

A tee shot down the left side is imperative. The hole is both long and very tight. A good tee shot will still leave a player with a long iron over both water and sand.

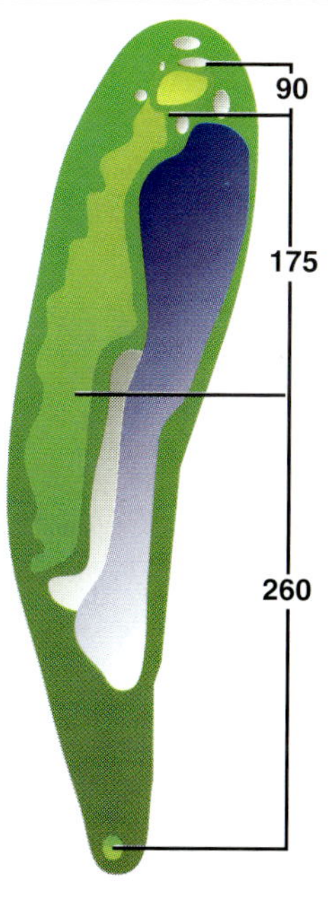

10

*Par 4
414 yards*

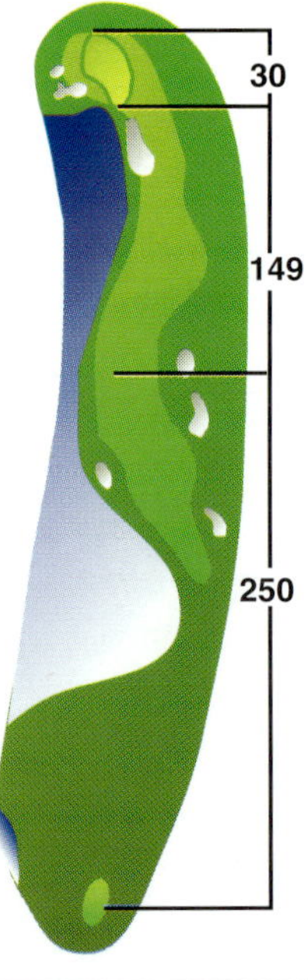

This hole has great definition with the water running the length of the hole down the left and bunkers on the right. It is very clear that a good tee shot is a must to avoid the rock "quarry"!

11

*Par 5
618 yards*

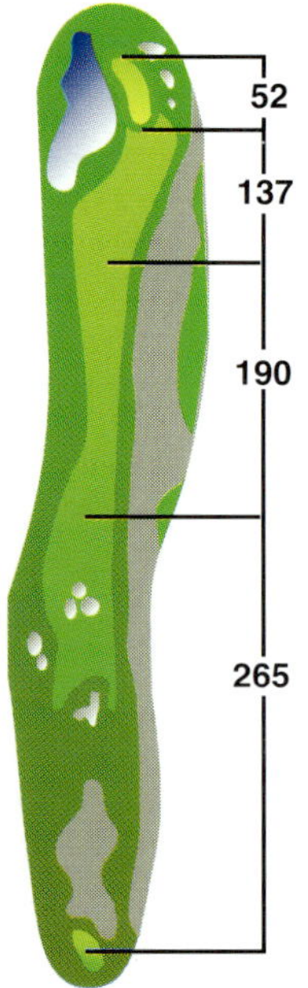

This hole is most deserving of its name. The longest hole on the golf course with its right to left sloping fairway, large fairway bunker, and water left of the green.

12

*Par 4
360 yards*

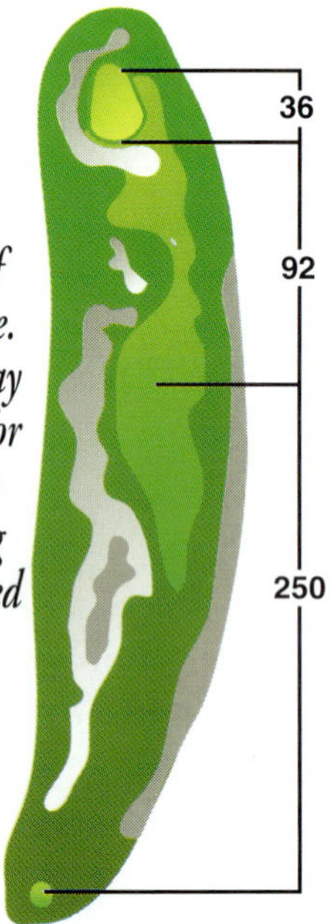

Do not let the lack of distance fool you here. Your tee shot must stay to the right in order for a player to be able to see the green and flag position. A well played second shot must be accurate or a player will end up in the "moat" surrounding the green.

13

*Par 3
220 yards*

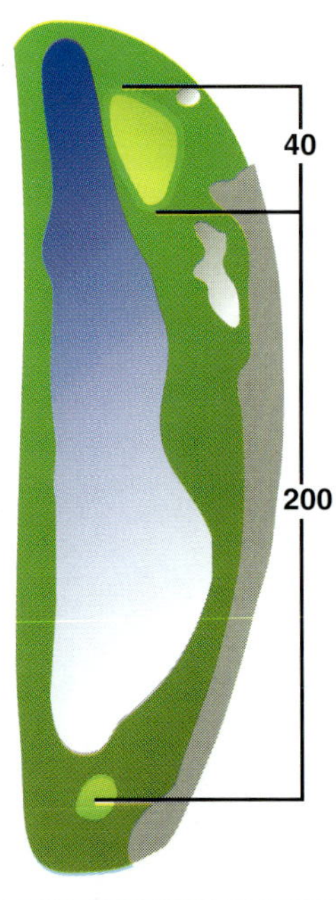

Getting close to this hole is asking a lot . A very difficult shot and a player really will have "second thoughts" about going for the pin here. Favor the right side of the green.

14

*Par 4
390 yards*

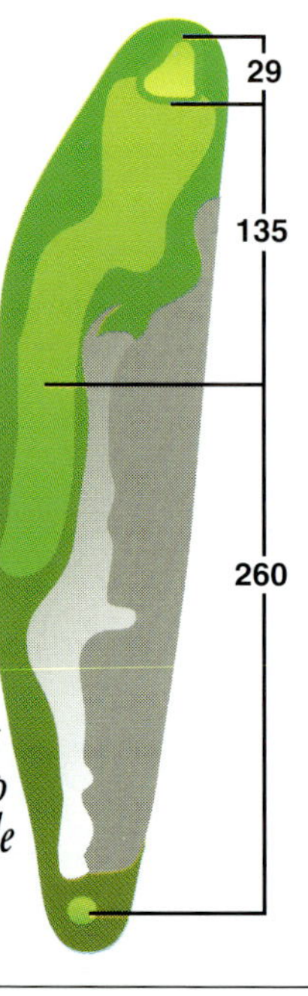

This is a very underrated hole. It requires a straight tee shot avoiding a huge bunker down the right side and leaving a second shot to the smallest green on the course. Be careful of both the bunker in front of the green and the deep "cavern" on the left side of the green.

15

*Par 4
470 yards*

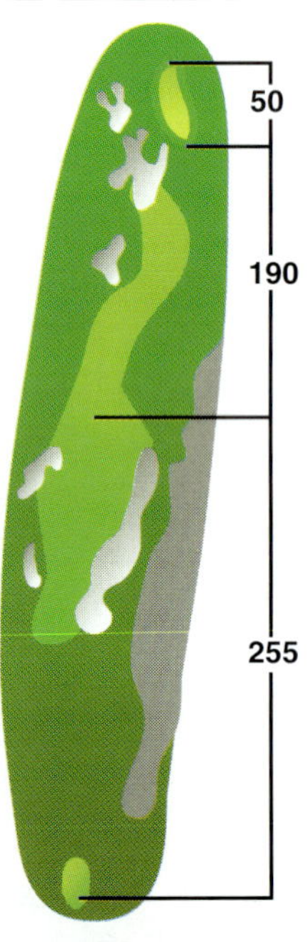

What makes this hole great is the presence of fairway bunkers guarding both the left and right side of the fairway. Your drive must be precise and your second shot must be all carry with a long iron or possibly a fairway wood.

16

*Par 4
470 yards*

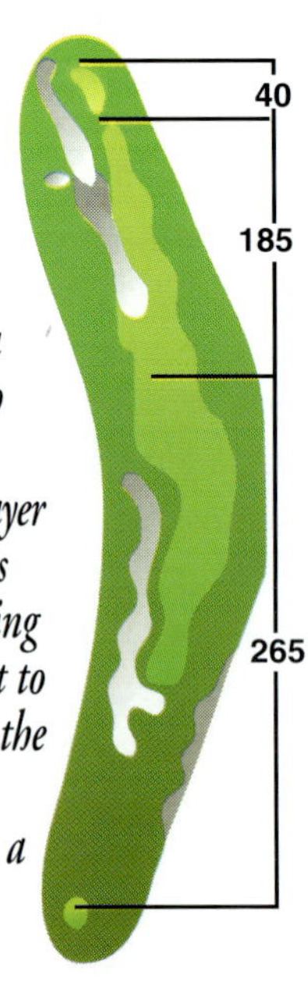

The teeing area is elevated and requires a slight fade off the tee to avoid the long "fault" down the left side. A player must be cautious on his second shot either leaving it short or again keep it to the right side avoiding the 19' "fault" bunker. A player could really lose a good round quick!

17

*Par 3
166 yards*

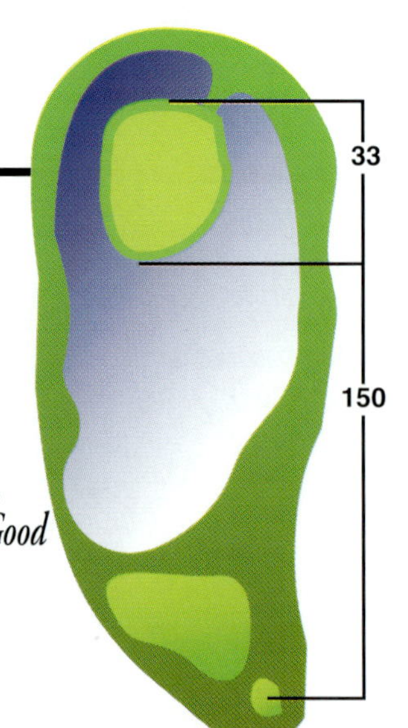

This hole is simple, either you're on or you're not. Exactly yardage is a must. Birdie, Par, or "X"- Good Luck!

18

*Par 4
440 yards*

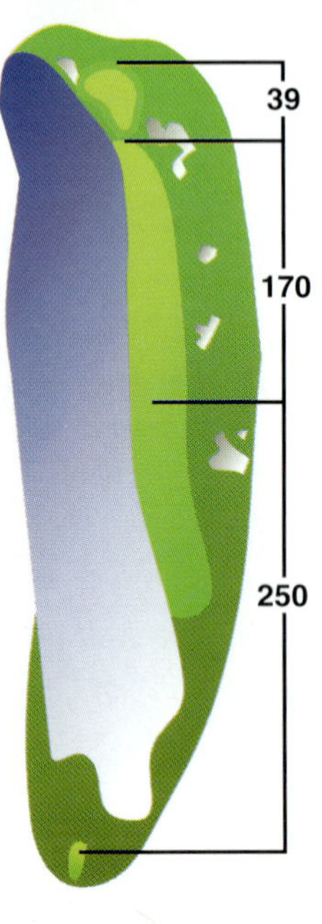

A beautiful finishing hole. Playing this par 4 anything could happen and it is not over until it is over. Avoid the water off the tee and again on your second shot and be sure and use plenty of clubs.

THE PLAYERS
CHAMPIONSHIP

THE COURSE: STADIUM COURSE, TPC AT SAWGRASS, PONTE VEDRA BEACH, FLORIDA

*T*HE PLAYERS Championship was established in 1974 as an event to honor the Men's TOUR events. In 1982, Commissioner Deane Beman introduced the TPC at Sawgrass - a course that was designed by Pete Dye and built for the purpose of providing a permanent location for THE PLAYERS Championship and also the headquarters for the PGA TOUR®. The tournament is one of the most spectacular of the year and, since it is regarded as having the strongest field, accorded expanded coverage.

Pete Dye combines a challenging layout for the players with a course that has been designed with the spectator in mind. Bleacher-like mounding affords spectators unrestricted views of their favorite players battling Dye's creation. The term "target golf" has been coined as a phrase that best describes the course. The 17th hole exemplifies this characteristic with its island green which has eluded many players.

Dates:	March 25-31, 1996
Network:	ESPN and NBC
Times:	USA
	Thur/Fri - 10:00-1:00 EST
	3:00-6:00EST
	(repeat) ESPN
	Sat/Sun - 2:00-6:00 EST NBC
Yardage:	6,857
Par:	72
Slope:	135
Rating:	74.0
Total Purse:	$3,000,000
1st Prize:	$540,000
1995 Winner:	Lee Janzen
1995 Winning Score:	283 (69,74,69,71)
Principal Charitable Beneficiary:	PLAYERS Championship Charities
Charitable Benefits to Date:	Over $17 million since 1977
Ticket Information:	1-904-285-7888 & 1-800-741-3161

1

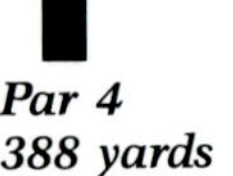

Par 4
388 yards

This first hole quickly reveals to the player that pin-point accuracy is a must. The narrow landing area leaves little margin for error on the drive and the small green is well guarded by bunkers.

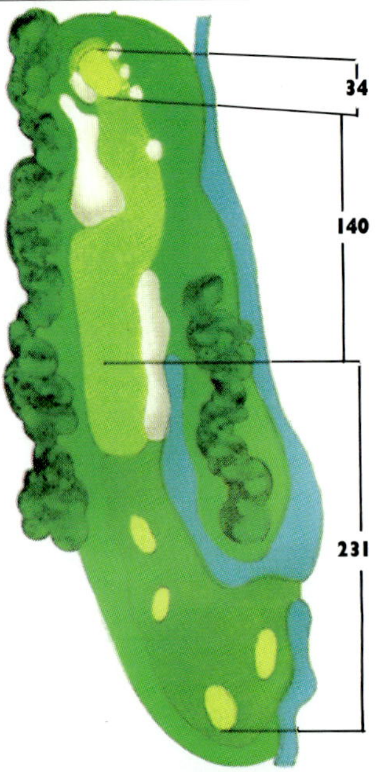

2

Par 5
511 yards

It is just under 200 yards to the fairway from the tee. A mighty drive down the right side could allow a reach in two. The percentages are for the three shot path to the green for easy birdie.

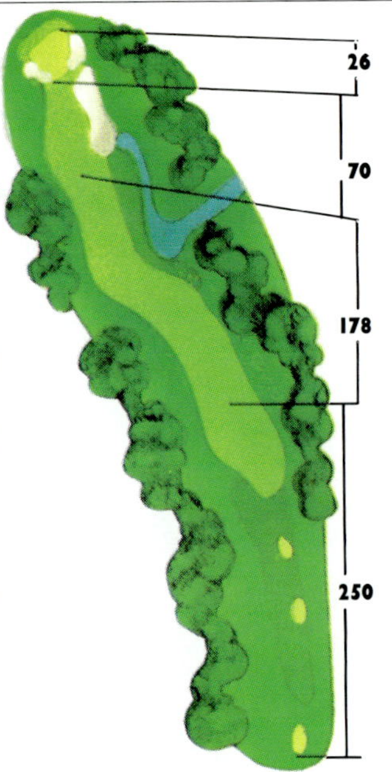

3

Par 3
162 yards

The green has two levels, front and back. Obviously, club selection can be critical when trying to keep the ball on the same level as the pin.

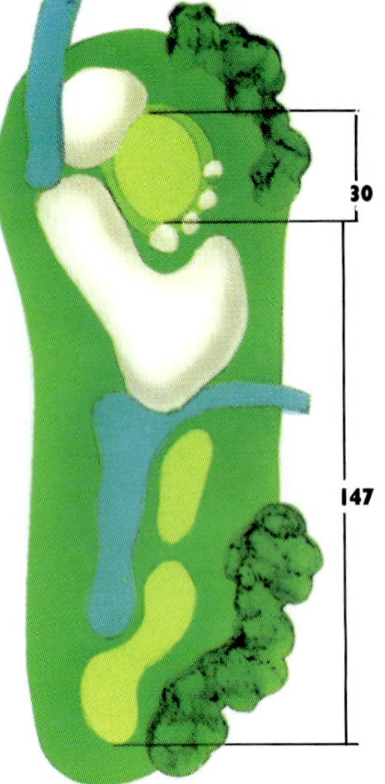

4

Par 4
360 yards

Water is a big ingredient on this fourth hole. Although scenic, this short par 4 can also be very treacherous. It is a good hole to make up some ground on the rest of the field. A fairway wood to the left side for a good angle on the approach. Water protects the front and bunkers cover the back.

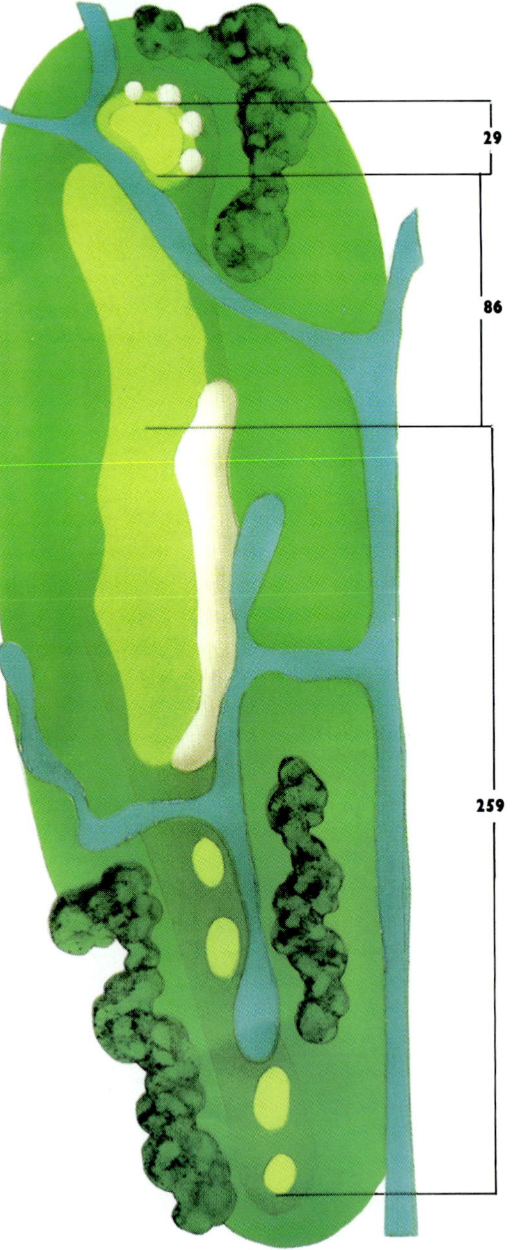

5

Par 4
454 yards

A generous landing area allows for the big drive—which is needed to set up for a somewhat easier approach on this long par 4. Waste bunkers line the short grass making for larger penalties for veering off course. At a hole average of just above par, players will be more than pleased with 4.

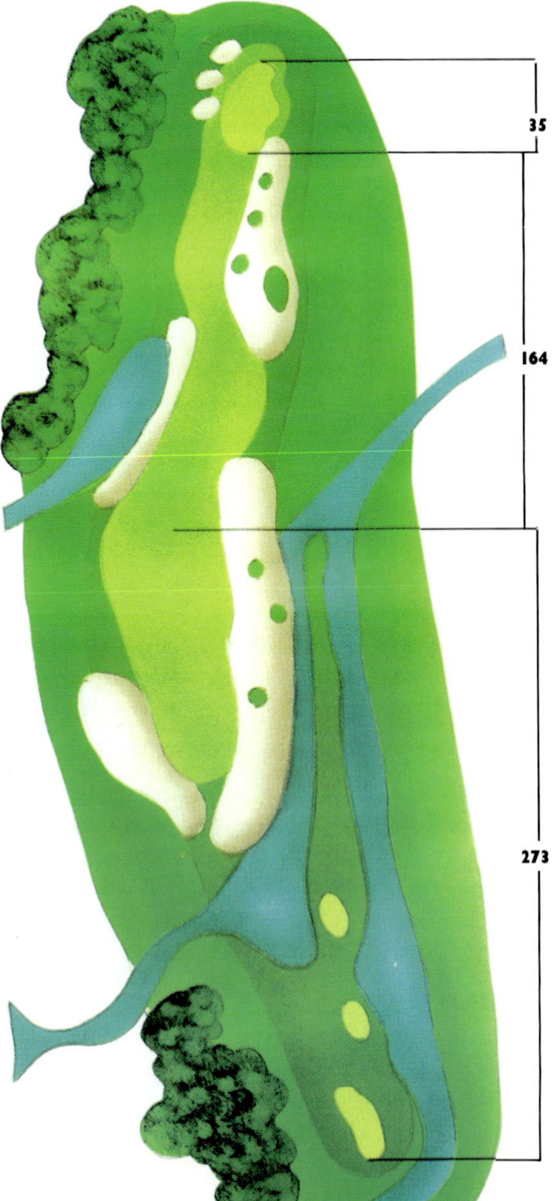

6

Par 4
381 yards

The rolling fairway makes for difficult lies. Hazards on both sides do not help to alleviate the situation. The green fiercely slopes down to the water on the left.

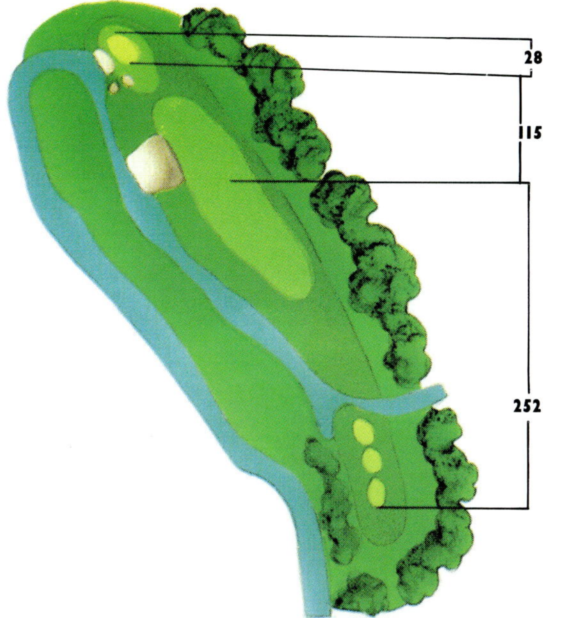

7

Par 4
439 yards

The fairway bunkers along the right side dictate a drive down the left. Sand and water guard the putting surface. Into the wind, this can be a very tough hole to par.

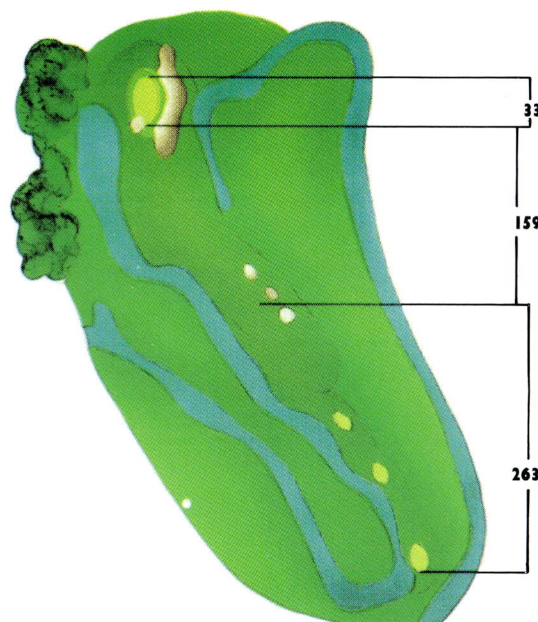

8

Par 3
215 yards

Slightly downhill but quite a distance! Once reached, the rolling putting surface will make all putts challenging. Although the seventeenth gets the glamour, this eighth is considered more difficult.

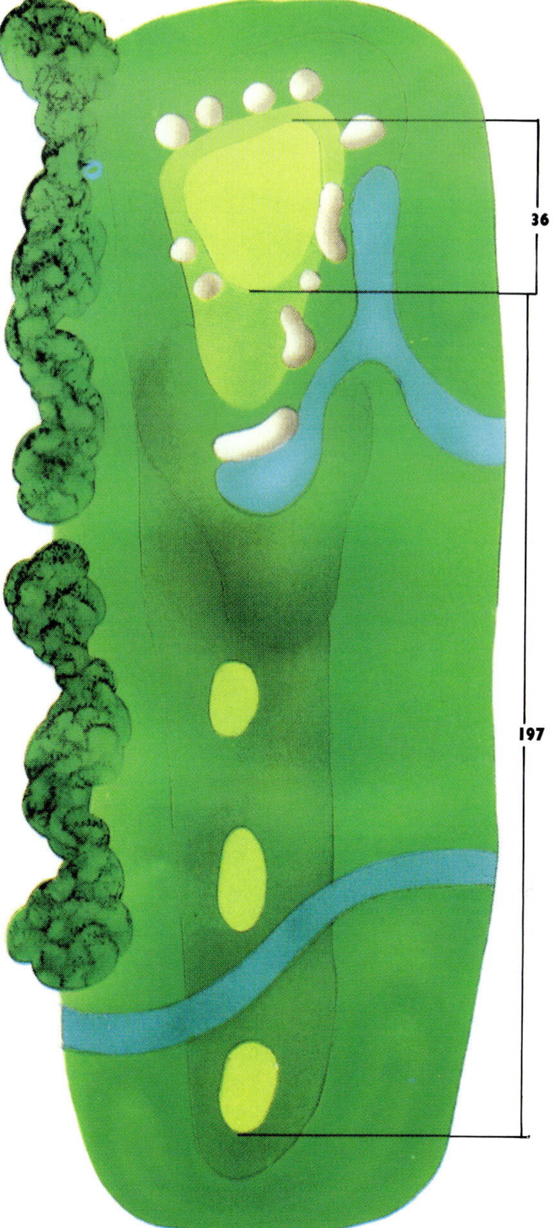

9

Par 5
582 yards

Can be the most difficult par 5 on the Tour. A hefty 582 yards lie between tee shot and the hole. That will keep the players playing all three shots to the green. Drive left, second shot crosses over the water to the right and finally, the approach is to the smallest green on the course. Bunkers and mounds make the green appear even smaller.

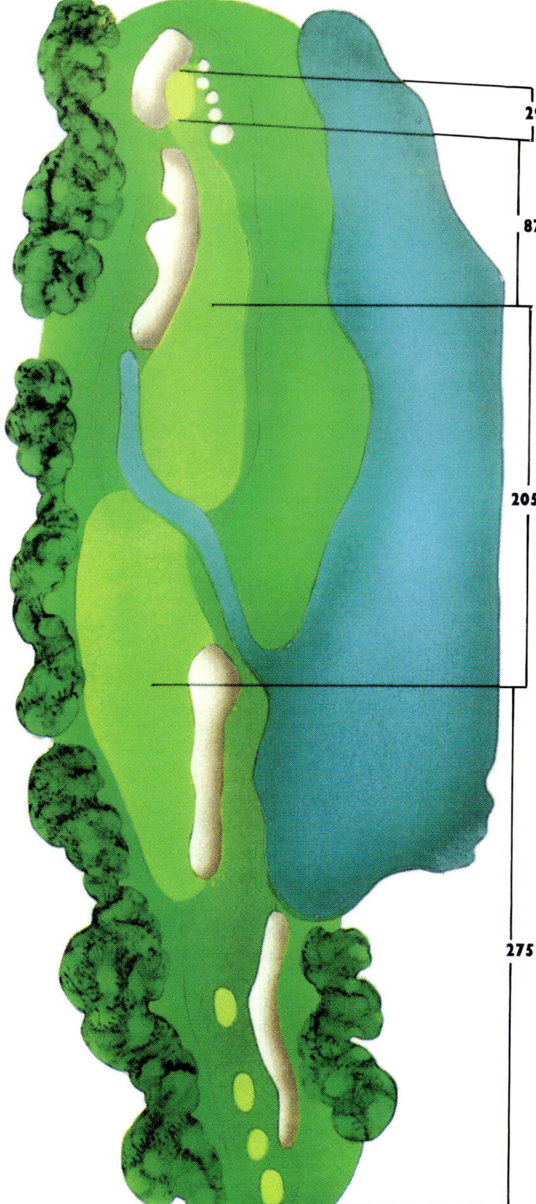

10

Par 4
395 yards

The tenth is very similar to the first only that it bends a different direction — to the left. Players will be using a fairway wood or long-iron to place their drives at the corner of the dogleg. An approach of about 140 yards remains to the forward sloping green.

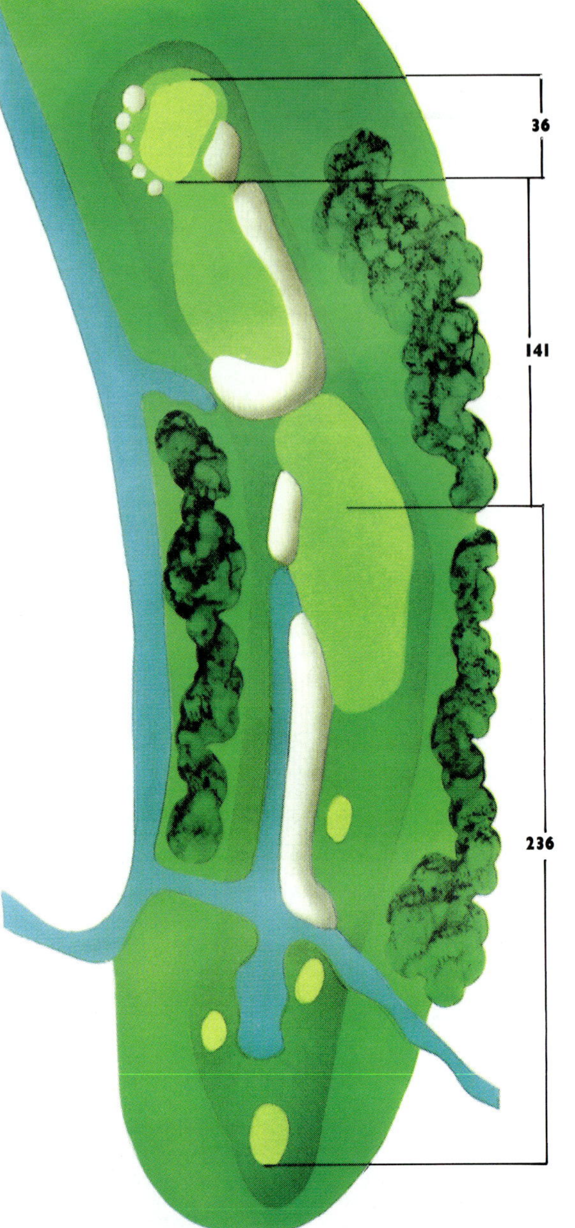

11

Par 5
529 yards

At 529 yards, this hole is not out of reach for the players. However, by playing down the left, the second shot can be placed easily in prime position for a short chip to the putting surface. The more ex- uberant player will hit a big drive down the right side and then follow with a second that must carry water, sand and waste bunker to find a small, well protected green. A good caddy would advise the first route.

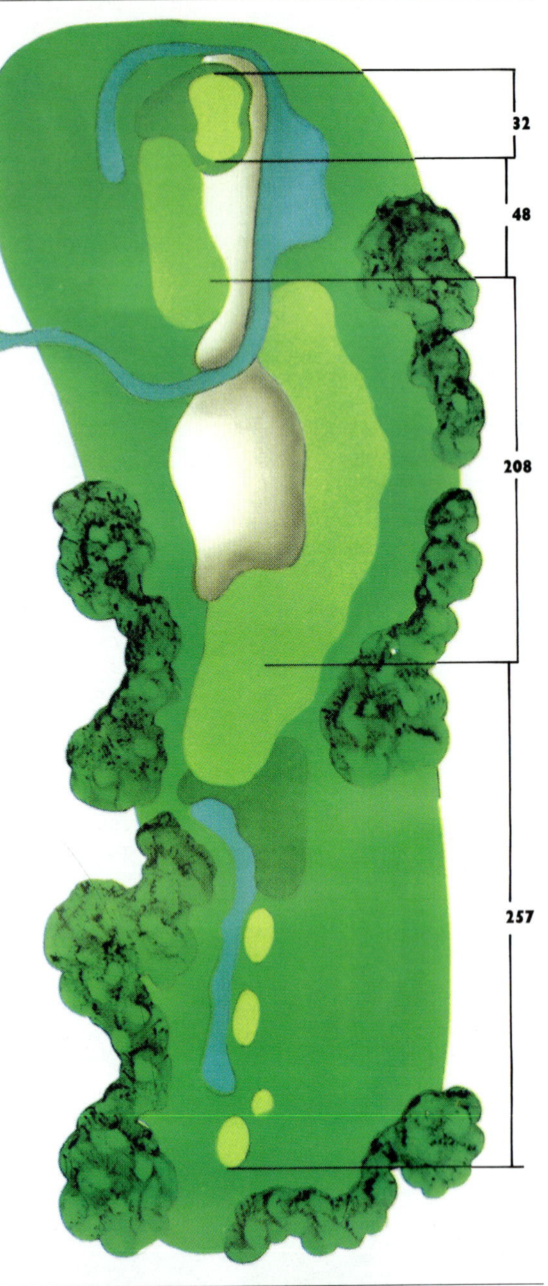

12

Par 4
336 yards

The possibility for birdie is high. Average score for this twelfth is under par. As long as the players can keep it in the fairway and hit the green, the putts should drop.

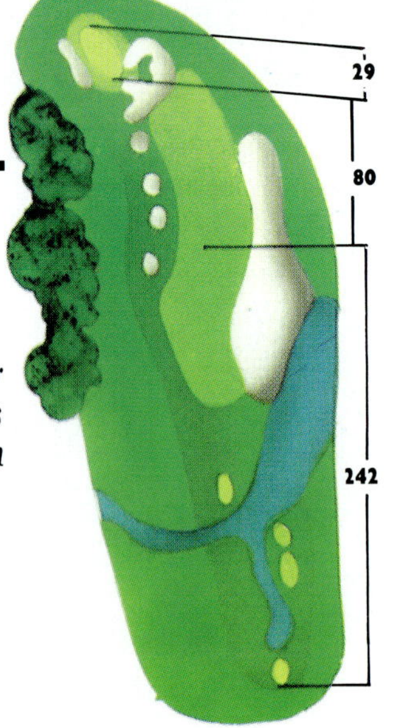

13

Par 3
172 yards

Two bunkers protect the green. The challenge here is not the distance but the ability to get the ball close to the hole. The large putting surface may yield a three putt.

14

Par 4
438 yards

This fourteenth is ranked as the second toughest hole on the course. A spectator mound along the right and a waste bunker left demand a drive long and straight.

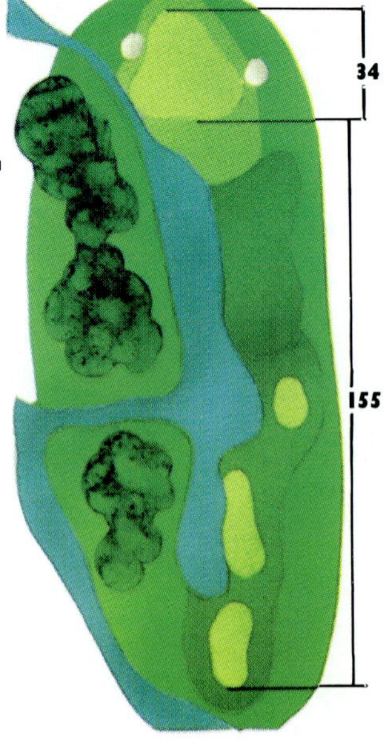

15

Par 4
426 yards

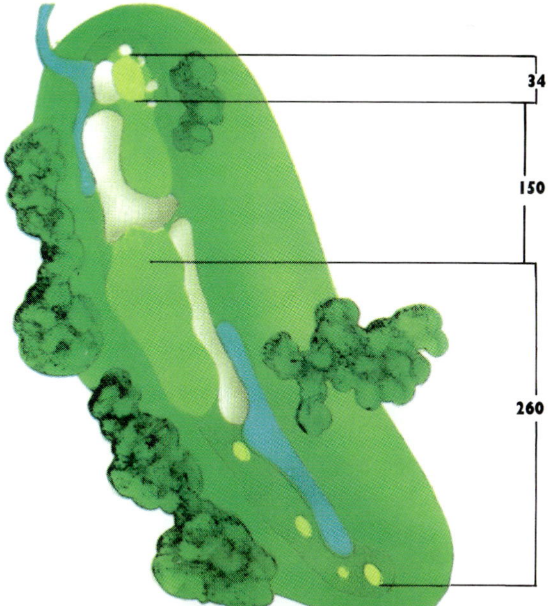

By now the players will be used to having to hit long accurate drives. The larger landing area allows for easier approaches to the big round green.

16

Par 5
497 yards

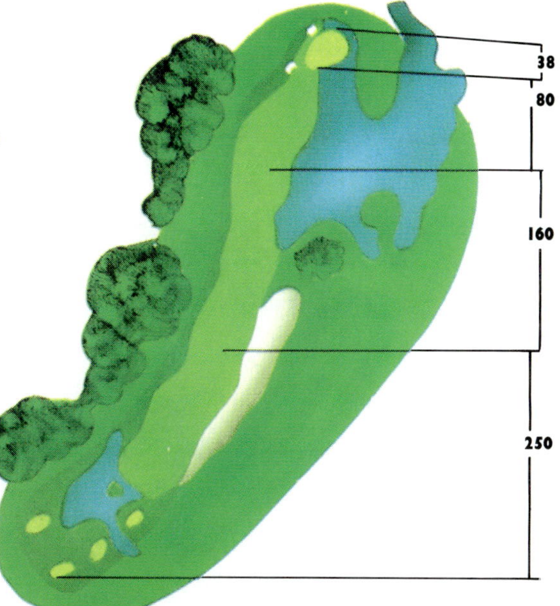

The length is not a problem. However, the long narrow green that is wedged in between trees and water will give second thoughts to those who may try for the green in two.

17

Par 3
132 yards

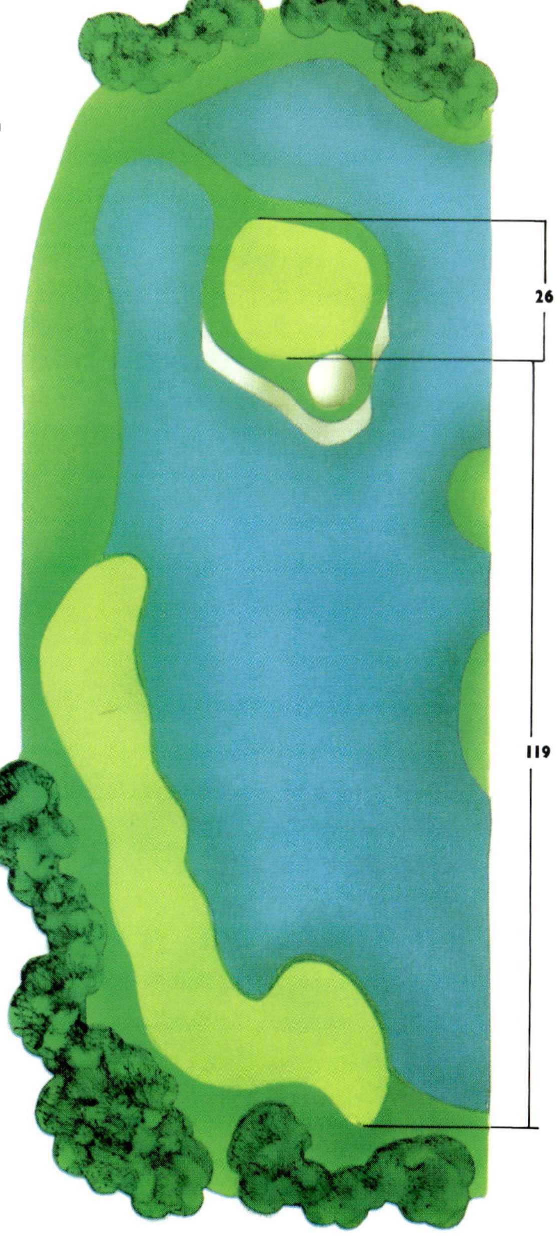

Target golf does not get any more demanding than on this 17th. The slightest miscalculation will most likely require the third shot to be played from the drop area. The putting surface slopes with just enough break that pars are not guaranteed for hitting the green in one shot.

18

Par 4
440 yards

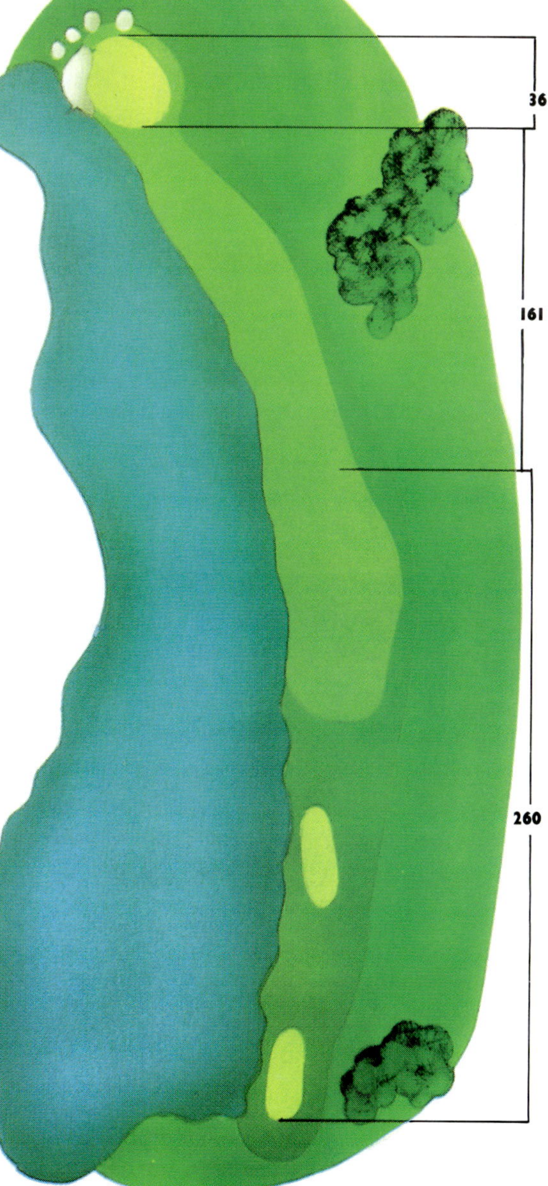

The long bending fairway follows the edge of the water from tee to green. A big drive is required to leave a medium iron to the green. However, the encroaching water from the left and the thousands of spectators along the right, can make for a very difficult drive. The approach is somewhat simpler into a spacious green. This eighteenth hole ranks among the top few that are considered to be the most difficult finishing holes in golf.

THE COURSE: ATLANTA COUNTRY CLUB, MARIETTA, GEORGIA

Atlanta Country Club has been the site of the BellSouth Classic since the event began in 1967. The course was cut out of rolling forest land and stretches 7,018 yards. The BellSouth Classic site is saturated with history and money. Sope Creek, which meanders through the course, was home to a Civil War-era paper mill which printed confederate currency. Its ruins are visible from the 13th tee.

Originally designed by Willard Byrd, the course opened for play in 1965. Jack Nicklaus redesigned the golf course in 1980, making changes to the tee and green positions and adding more undulation to the greens.

The picturesque and challenging layout has hosted two USGA Championships and was the site of the first PLAYERS CHAMPIONSHIP in 1974.

Dates:	April 4-7
Network:	CBS/ESPN
Times:	ESPN
	Thur 4:00-6:00 EST
	Fri 3:00-5:00 EST
	CBS
	Sat 4:00-6:00 EST
Yardage:	7,018
Par:	72
Slope:	138
Rating:	73.9
Total Purse:	$1,300,000
1st Prize:	$234,000
1995 Winner:	Mark Calcavecchia
1995 Winning Score:	271 (67,69,69,66)
Principal Charitable Beneficiary:	Egleston Children's Hospital at Emory University
Charitable Benefits to Date:	$4 million in last 11 years
Ticket Information:	1-404-951-8777

1

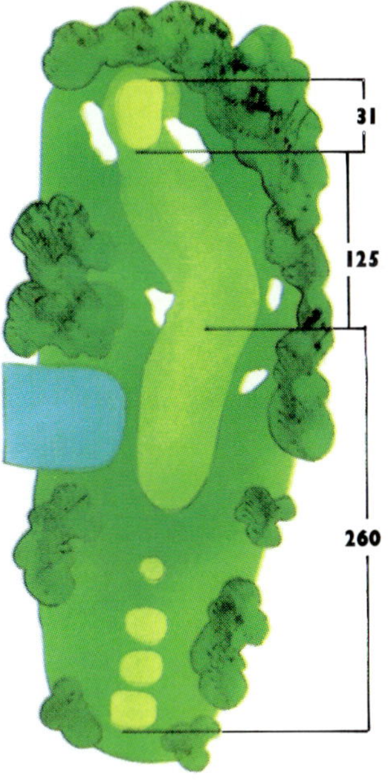

Par 4
401 yards

An elevated tee greets the players to a wide upsloping fairway. The right side of the fairway opens up the angle for the approach. The green slopes back to front.

2

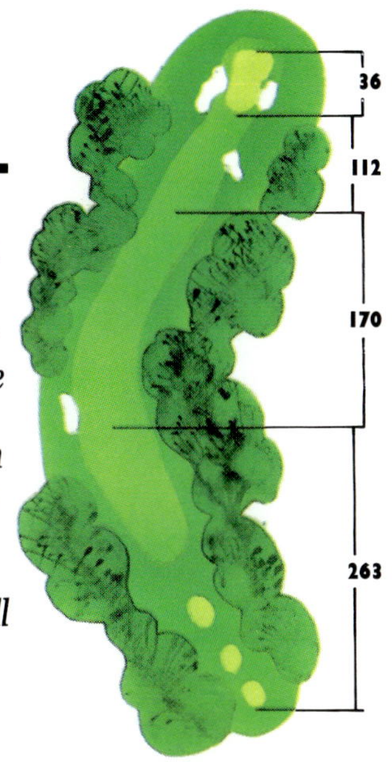

Par 5
563 yards

A big drive down the middle will allow for the chance of reaching the green in two. The long green slopes towards the front — keeping short of the hole will allow for easier uphill putts.

3

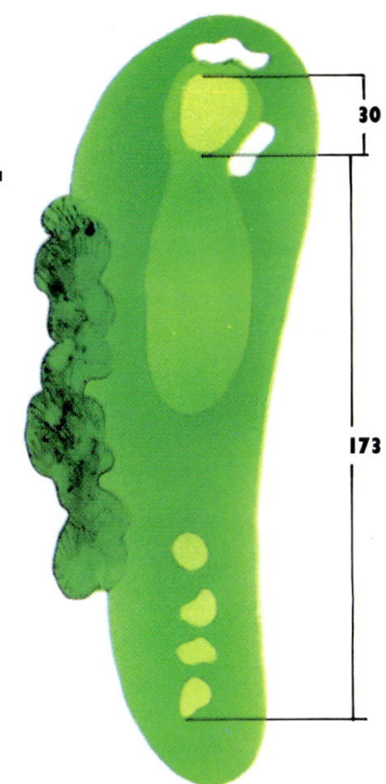

Par 3
188 yards

The green sits below the tee — the hole plays shorter than published. Severe drop-off beyond the green can be a costly destination.

4

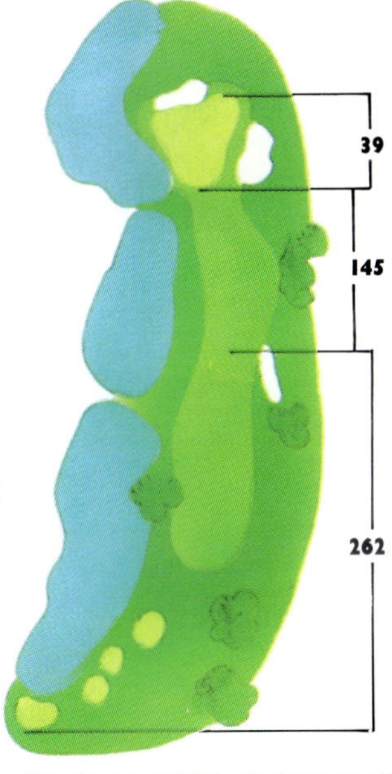

Par 4
427 yards

The right side of the fairway is favored — also the safest. A big drive down the right middle of the fairway will set up for the medium approach to the green.

5

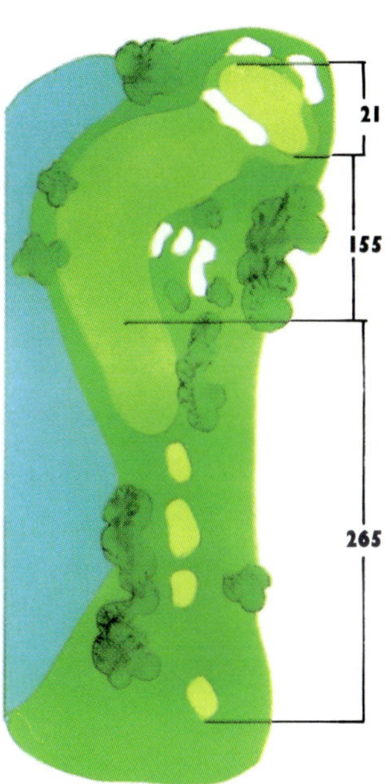

Par 4
432 yards

The hole is almost a 90° dogleg right, but the short-cut over the corner is not advised. A drive down the middle will allow for an easy approach to the shallow green.

6

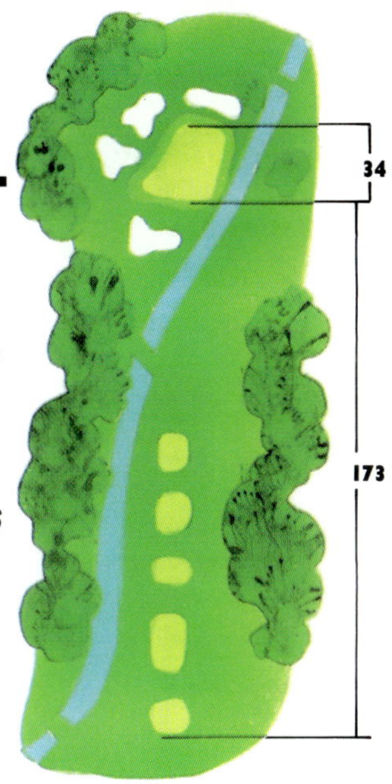

Par 3
190 yards

The wind above the tree-tops can give the players the biggest challenge on this hole. The large green has three levels, making for difficult putts.

7

Par 4
340 yards

Long irons will be the clubs of choice to set the drive in premium position for the approach. From the left side of the fairway, the second shot is played to a two level green.

8

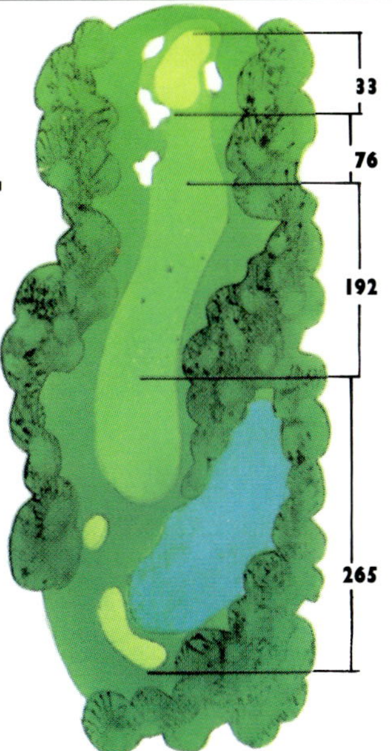

Par 5
550 yards

This eighth has a slight double-dogleg. A big drive down the left side may allow for the possiblity of hitting the green in two. Three bunkers guard the front.

9

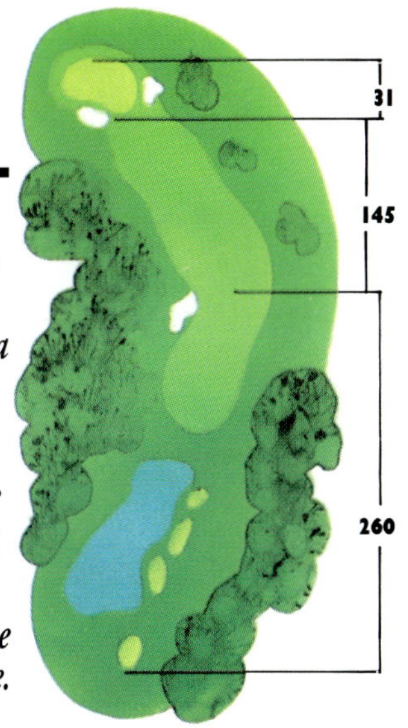

Par 4
421 yards

A difficult finishing hole —uphill, dogleg left to a two-tiered green. A ball hit to the wrong side of the green will be difficult to putt due to the rolling surface.

10

Par 4
457 yards

A big drive down the left side will carry the bunker along the left to a downhill slope in the fairway. The approach must carry a creek to a two-tiered green.

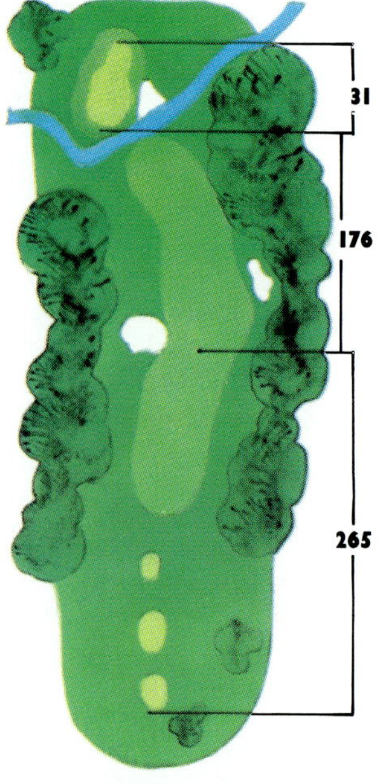

11

Par 5
548 yards

The fairway is tightly defined by trees on either side. The birdie is a necessity for the players to keep up with the rest of the field. Some will be able to reach the green in two shots.

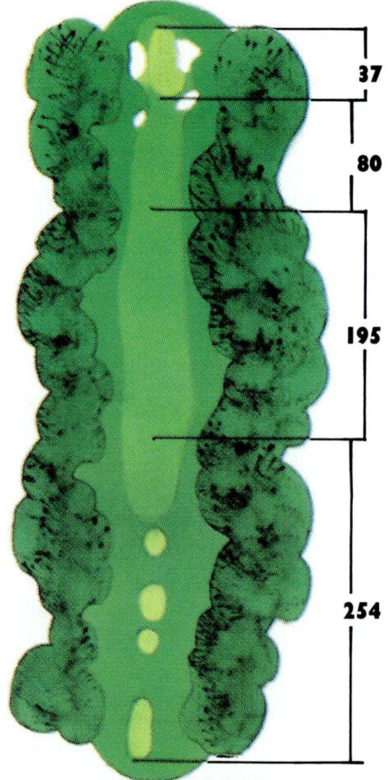

12

Par 4
426 yards

Accuracy is a must off the tee. The hole bends around a large hill to the left. Two well hit shots may yield the birdie.

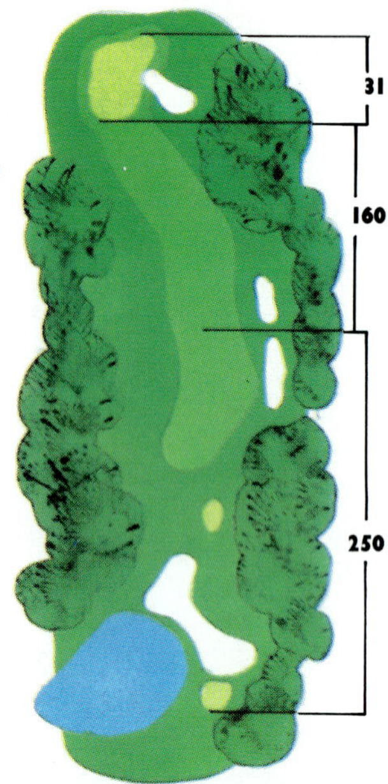

13

Par 3
156 yards

The elevated tee looks down on the hour-glass-shaped green and waterfall. Pinpoint accuracy is key in getting the ball close to the hole.

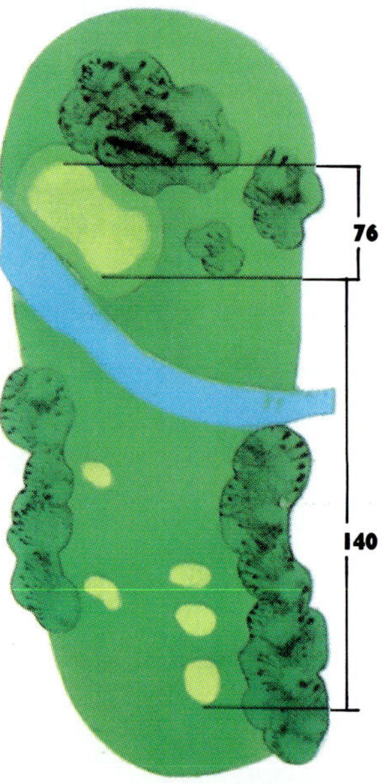

14

Par 4
335 yards

A gentle draw from the tee will place the ball in excellent position for the approach. The sloping green is narrow and produces some difficult putting.

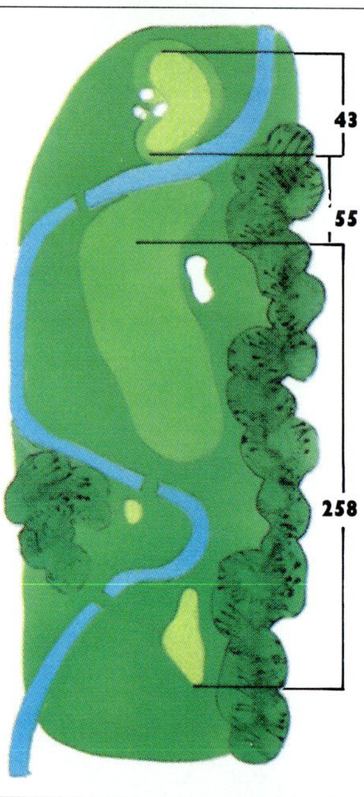

15

Par 4
452 yards

The creek twists its way up the right side of the fairway, then crosses just in front of the green. Surface slopes from back to front with subtle undulations.

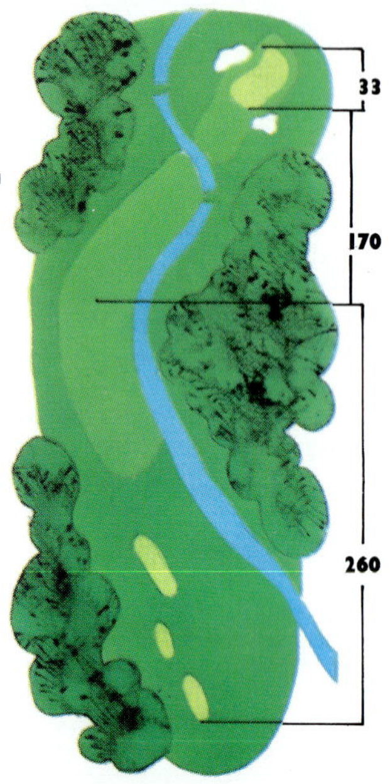

16

Par 3
206 yards

Green slopes back to front — except for the back end which drops off rapidly. The uphill tee shot must avoid the bunkers left and right.

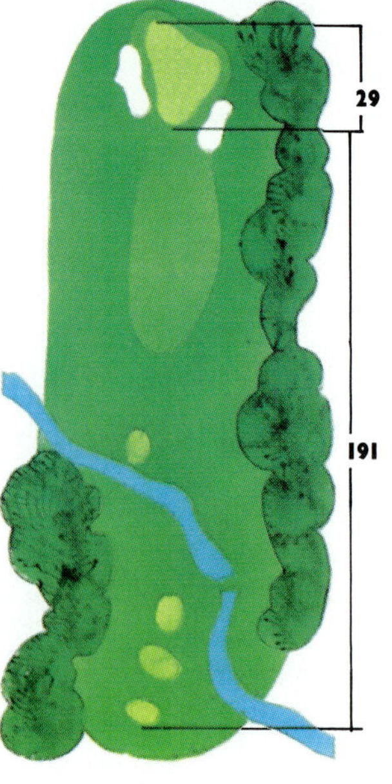

17

Par 4
421 yards

A drive down the middle sets up for a short approach to the low green. Three bunkers are placed in a triangle around the severely undulating green.

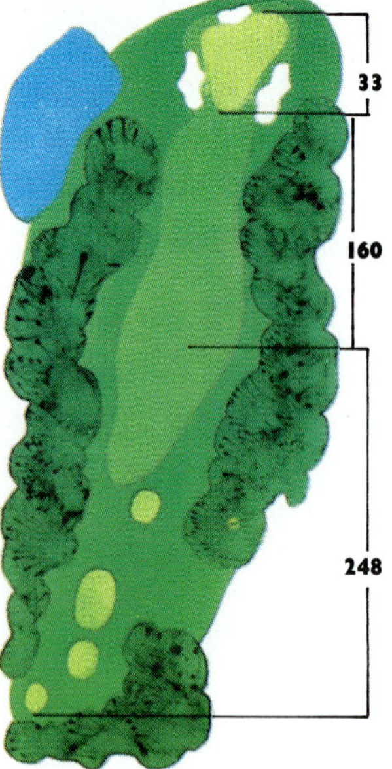

18

Par 5
499 yards

The big chance to make up some ground — two well-hit shots may reach the green but the water in front will grab all missed shots. Birdies and eagles are plentiful.

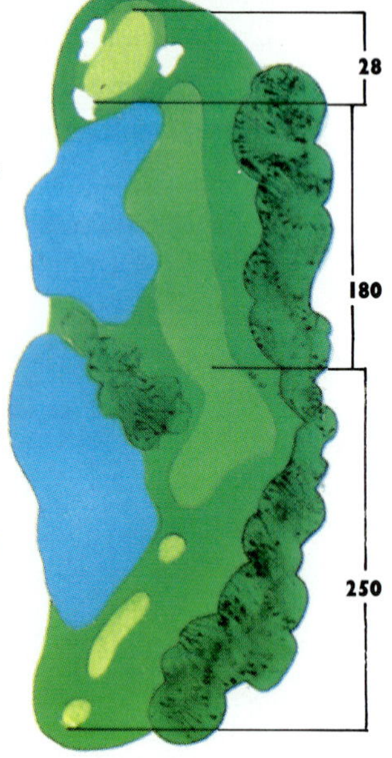

THE COURSE: COCHISE COURSE, THE GOLF CLUB AT DESERT MOUNTAIN,
SCOTTSDALE, ARIZONIA

*T*he Tradition at Desert Mountain, presented by Scotts, is one of the four major championships on the SENIOR PGA TOUR® and is played at one of the top courses in America, the Cochise Course at The Golf Club at Desert Mountain.

The 1995 Tradition attracted the strongest field in Senior golf and was as exciting as had been promised. With golf's greats going head-to-head for four days, it came down to two players, Jack Nicklaus and Isao Ioki, in a three hole playoff. Nicklaus, whose second shot rolled off the green, pitched to four feet and sank his winning birdie. Nicklaus, who designed the course, also won The Tradition in 1990 and 1991. Nicklaus declared, "The Tradition is the Masters of the SENIOR PGA TOUR®. Basically, it's what (Bobby Jones and Cliff Roberts tried to do at Augusta".

Look for another exciting championship that will bring all of golfs greats together for the first leg of the Senior Slam of Golf.

Dates:	April 4-7, 1996
Network:	ESPN
Times:	TBA
Yardage:	6,869
Par:	72
Slope:	128
Rating:	71.2
Total Purse:	$825,000
1st Prize:	$150,000
1995 Winner:	Jack Nicklaus
1995 Winning Score:	267 (69,71,69,67)
Principal Charitable Beneficiary:	Scottsdale Memorial Hospital, Telephone Pioneers of America
Ticket Information:	1-602-443-1597

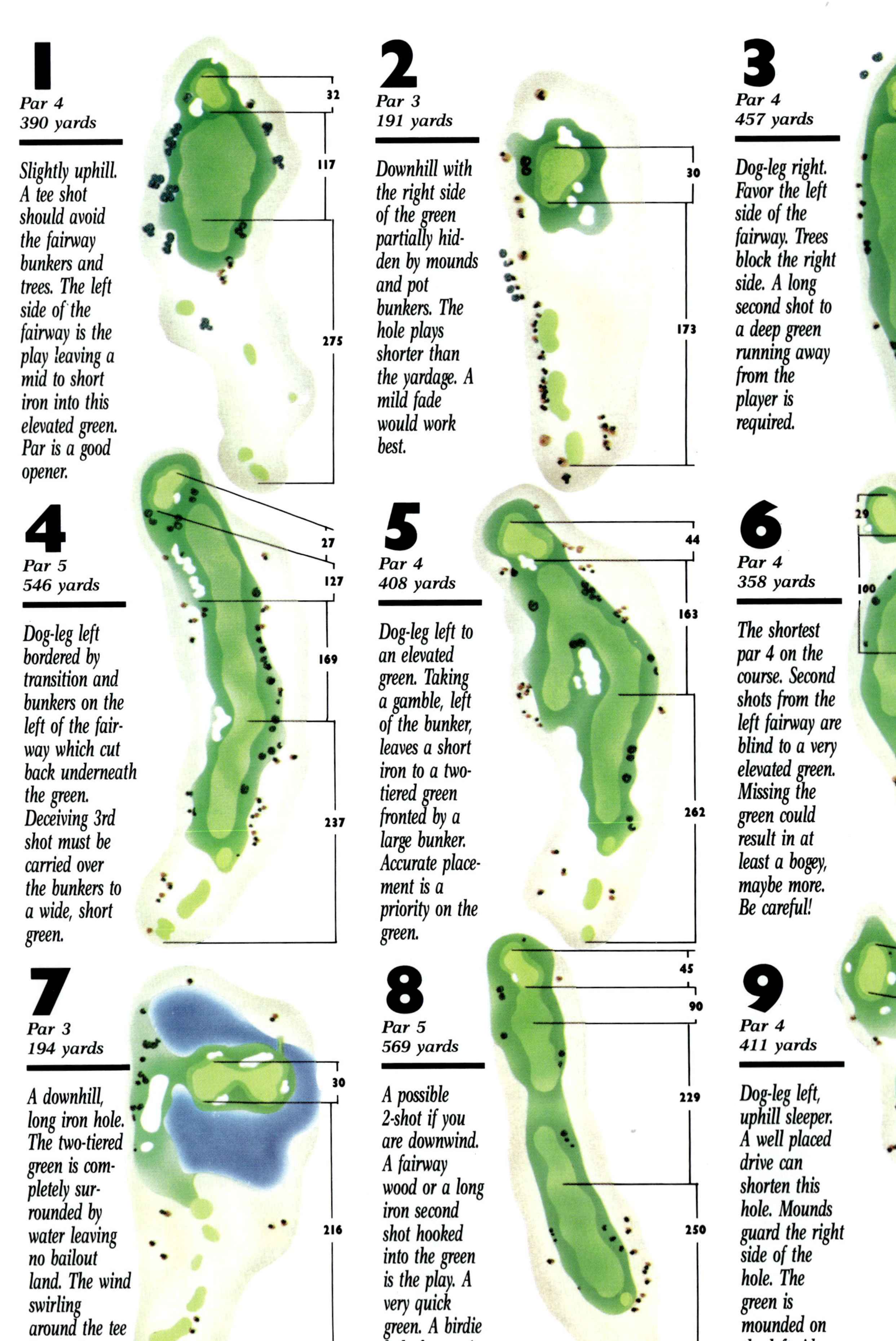

1

Par 4
390 yards

Slightly uphill. A tee shot should avoid the fairway bunkers and trees. The left side of the fairway is the play leaving a mid to short iron into this elevated green. Par is a good opener.

2

Par 3
191 yards

Downhill with the right side of the green partially hidden by mounds and pot bunkers. The hole plays shorter than the yardage. A mild fade would work best.

3

Par 4
457 yards

Dog-leg right. Favor the left side of the fairway. Trees block the right side. A long second shot to a deep green running away from the player is required.

4

Par 5
546 yards

Dog-leg left bordered by transition and bunkers on the left of the fairway which cut back underneath the green. Deceiving 3rd shot must be carried over the bunkers to a wide, short green.

5

Par 4
408 yards

Dog-leg left to an elevated green. Taking a gamble, left of the bunker, leaves a short iron to a two-tiered green fronted by a large bunker. Accurate placement is a priority on the green.

6

Par 4
358 yards

The shortest par 4 on the course. Second shots from the left fairway are blind to a very elevated green. Missing the green could result in at least a bogey, maybe more. Be careful!

7

Par 3
194 yards

A downhill, long iron hole. The two-tiered green is completely surrounded by water leaving no bailout land. The wind swirling around the tee box makes club selection critical.

8

Par 5
569 yards

A possible 2-shot if you are downwind. A fairway wood or a long iron second shot hooked into the green is the play. A very quick green. A birdie hole for sure!

9

Par 4
411 yards

Dog-leg left, uphill sleeper. A well placed drive can shorten this hole. Mounds guard the right side of the hole. The green is mounded on the left side.

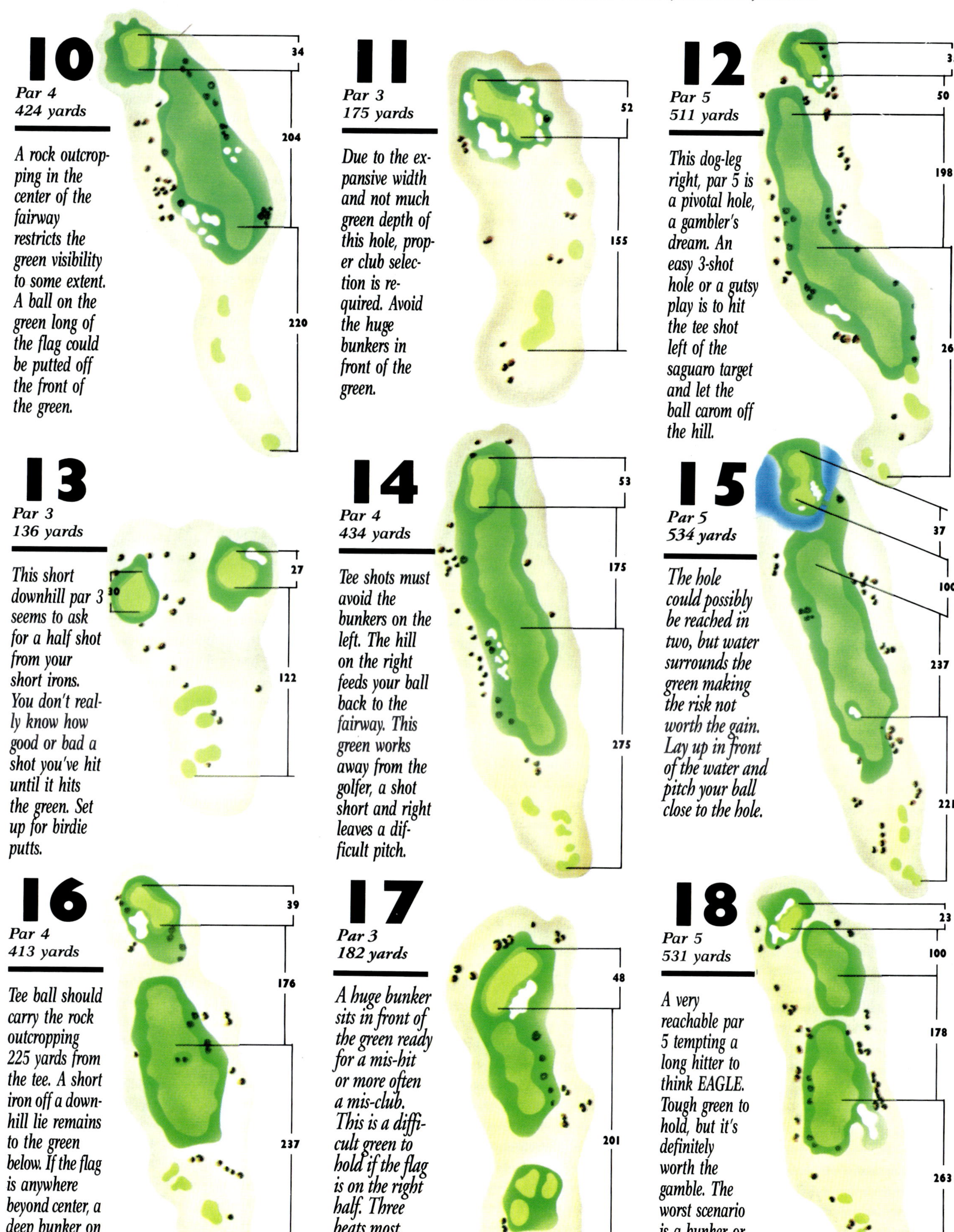

10

Par 4
424 yards

A rock outcropping in the center of the fairway restricts the green visibility to some extent. A ball on the green long of the flag could be putted off the front of the green.

11

Par 3
175 yards

Due to the expansive width and not much green depth of this hole, proper club selection is required. Avoid the huge bunkers in front of the green.

12

Par 5
511 yards

This dog-leg right, par 5 is a pivotal hole, a gambler's dream. An easy 3-shot hole or a gutsy play is to hit the tee shot left of the saguaro target and let the ball carom off the hill.

13

Par 3
136 yards

This short downhill par 3 seems to ask for a half shot from your short irons. You don't really know how good or bad a shot you've hit until it hits the green. Set up for birdie putts.

14

Par 4
434 yards

Tee shots must avoid the bunkers on the left. The hill on the right feeds your ball back to the fairway. This green works away from the golfer, a shot short and right leaves a difficult pitch.

15

Par 5
534 yards

The hole could possibly be reached in two, but water surrounds the green making the risk not worth the gain. Lay up in front of the water and pitch your ball close to the hole.

16

Par 4
413 yards

Tee ball should carry the rock outcropping 225 yards from the tee. A short iron off a downhill lie remains to the green below. If the flag is anywhere beyond center, a deep bunker on the left needs to be carried.

17

Par 3
182 yards

A huge bunker sits in front of the green ready for a mis-hit or more often a mis-club. This is a difficult green to hold if the flag is on the right half. Three beats most competitors.

18

Par 5
531 yards

A very reachable par 5 tempting a long hitter to think EAGLE. Tough green to hold, but it's definitely worth the gamble. The worst scenario is a bunker or a pitch shot.

THE COURSE: AUGUSTA NATIONAL GOLF CLUB

$\mathcal{T}$his is it, Augusta National. For amateur or professional and everyone in between-this is the Masters! Beginning from a "small get-together" of Robert Tyre "Bobby" Jones, Jr. and a few amateur and professional friends, the first Masters, The Augusta National Invitation Tournament, was won by Horton Smith in 1934. At the time, Clifford Roberts offered the idea of naming the event the 'Masters' but Jones humbly declined. Eventually, the press got wind of the idea and instituted it in the headlines. Thus, the title "Masters" was officially adopted in 1938.

Jones and Scottish golf course architect Dr. Alister MacKenzie designed Augusta national as the "perfect course"-blending with the features of the land and revealing its beauty and difficulty subtly throughout. He envisioned a course that could be enjoyable with friends but also provide a challenge when in tournament dress. The rolling fairways are accentuated with pines, magnolias, dogwoods and azalea. The greens are spacious, but very firm snd very fast. Pin placement during the tournament requires the hole to be played from certain locations in the fairway. It is undeniably a masterpiece.

Jack Nicklaus has won the championship a record six times-most recently in 1986 in one of golf's most inspiring come-from-behind victories. Augusta national is relentless to all who compete for the coveted green jackets.

Dates:	April 11-14, 1996
Network:	CBS and USA
Times:	USA
	Thur-Fri 4:00-6:30 EST
	Replay 9:00-11:30 EST
	CBS
	Thur/Fri 11:30-11:45 EST
	Sat 3:30-6:00 EST
	Sun 4:00-7:00 EST
Yardage:	6,925
Par:	72
Total Purse:	$2,050,000
1st Prize:	$396,000
1995 Winner:	Ben Crenshaw
1995 Winning Score:	274 (70,67,69,68)
Ticket Information:	Sold in Advance (Thur-Sun Sold Out)

* An Augusta National Sponsored event.

1

Par 4
400 yards

A large, steep-faced bunker lies guarding the right side of the hole. Tension mounts as the first drive must be hit to an elevated fairway followed with a second shot to a firm green.

2

Par 5
555 yards

As the longest hole on the course, the second hole will actually play shorter than indicated due to the descending fairway. A draw from the tee should be played just left of the fairway bunker allowing for no less than a fairway wood into the green. Some players will be conservative and keep well short of the green on the approach shot — any shots hit over the green will leave the players with a difficult recovery on the sloping green.

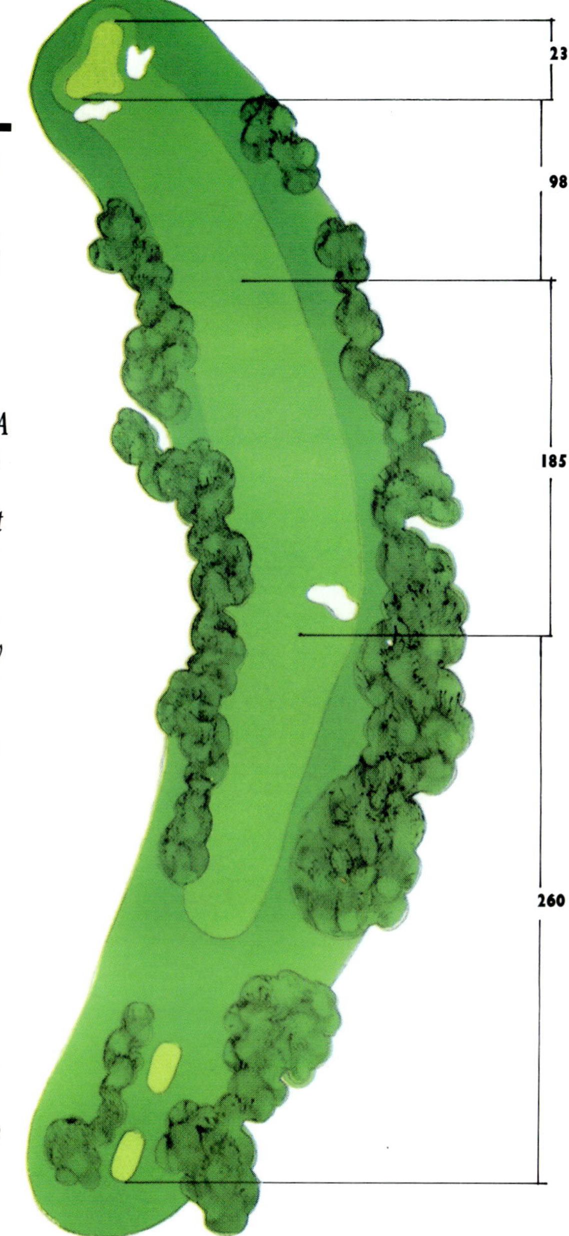

3

Par 4
360 yards

A seemingly short, simple hole. Looking closely, it becomes clear the key to this hole is a well placed drive, followed by a very accurate approach shot. The fairway slopes up from the tee and narrows with four intimidating bunkers. The approach is considered by some players as one of the most difficult of the year due to the putting surface that is firm and fast. Tricky undulations are found short and a steep bank is beyond.

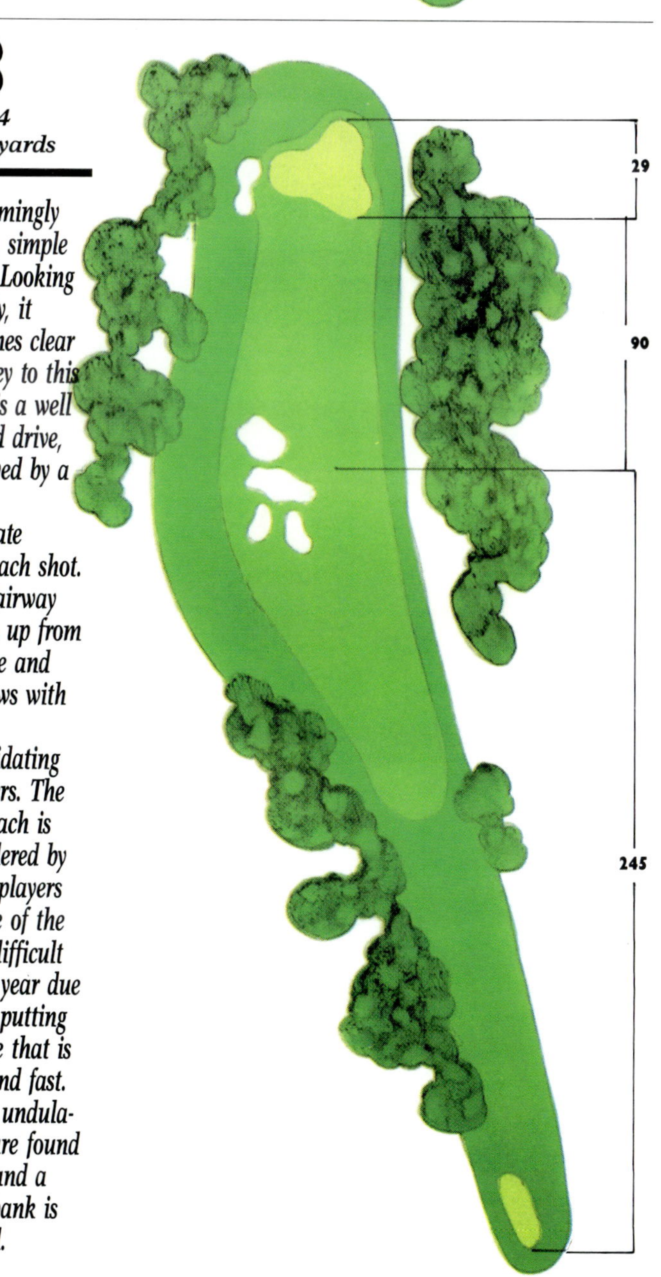

4

Par 3
205 yards

Into a prevailing wind, this hole plays as the longest par 3 at Augusta National. Bunkers lie short of the green while out-of-bounds is just beyond — a strong sure shot is a must.

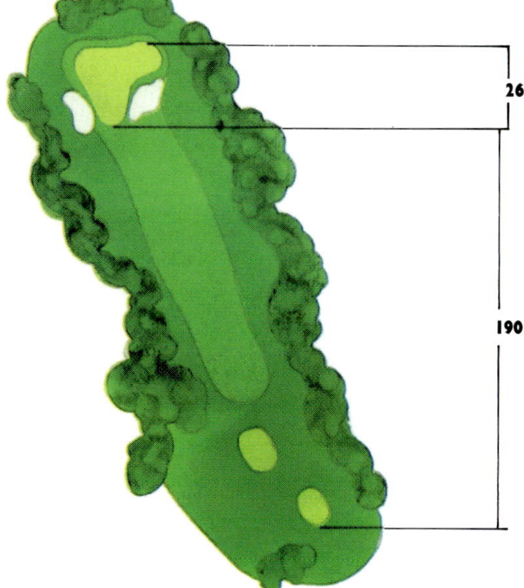

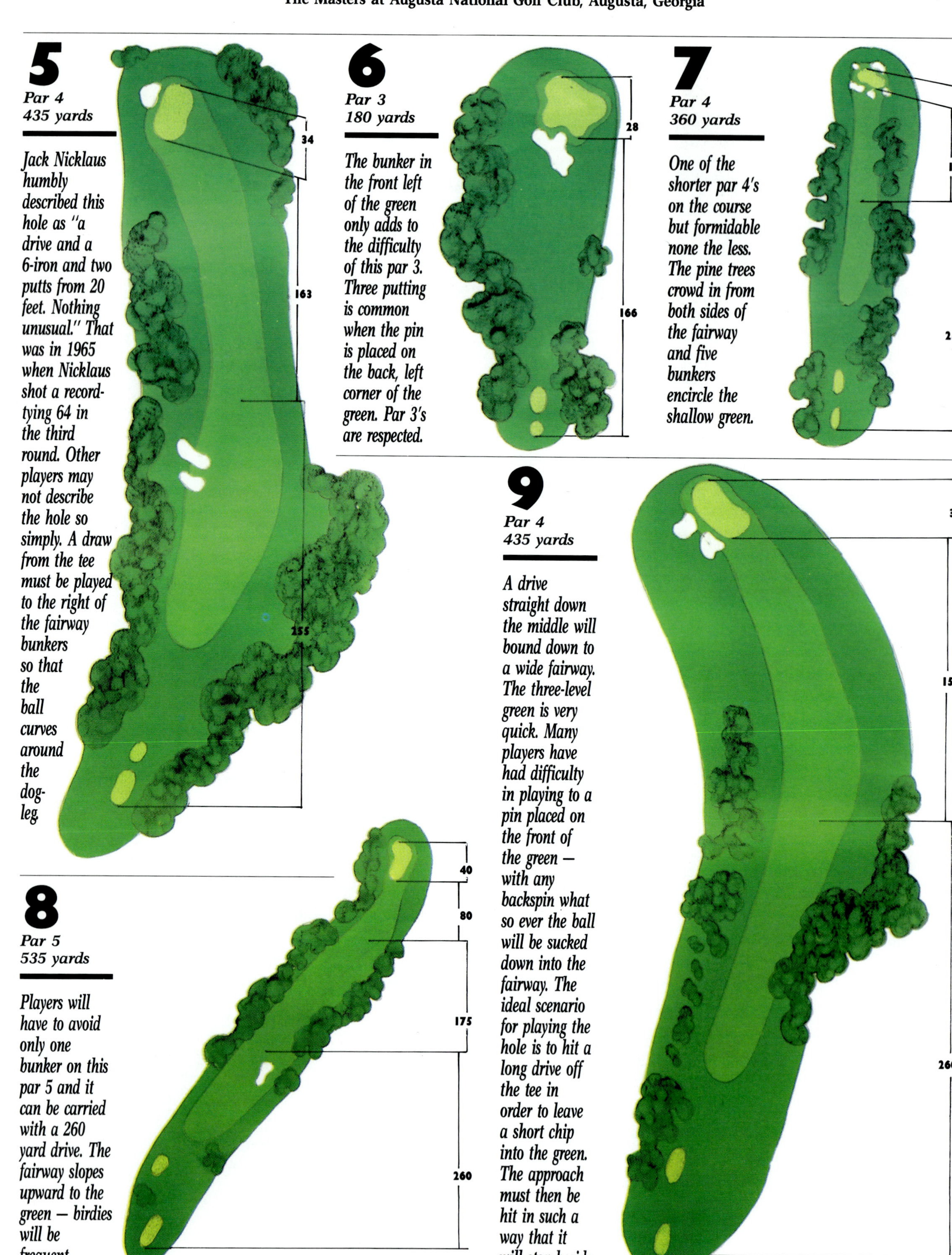

5
Par 4
435 yards

Jack Nicklaus humbly described this hole as "a drive and a 6-iron and two putts from 20 feet. Nothing unusual." That was in 1965 when Nicklaus shot a record-tying 64 in the third round. Other players may not describe the hole so simply. A draw from the tee must be played to the right of the fairway bunkers so that the ball curves around the dog-leg

6
Par 3
180 yards

The bunker in the front left of the green only adds to the difficulty of this par 3. Three putting is common when the pin is placed on the back, left corner of the green. Par 3's are respected.

7
Par 4
360 yards

One of the shorter par 4's on the course but formidable none the less. The pine trees crowd in from both sides of the fairway and five bunkers encircle the shallow green.

8
Par 5
535 yards

Players will have to avoid only one bunker on this par 5 and it can be carried with a 260 yard drive. The fairway slopes upward to the green — birdies will be frequent.

9
Par 4
435 yards

A drive straight down the middle will bound down to a wide fairway. The three-level green is very quick. Many players have had difficulty in playing to a pin placed on the front of the green — with any backspin what so ever the ball will be sucked down into the fairway. The ideal scenario for playing the hole is to hit a long drive off the tee in order to leave a short chip into the green. The approach must then be hit in such a way that it will stop beside the pin.

10

Par 4
485 yards

The fairway drops off from the tee almost 90 feet on its way to the green. Sloping from right to left, the landing area is tightly defined by large pine trees on either side. A large bunker lying short of the green can give the illusion that the putting surface is closer than it actually is. Ben Crenshaw made one of the longest putts in tournament history in 1984 when he rolled in a 70-footer for birdie on his way to victory.

11

Par 4
455 yards

This hole has decided four of five Masters playoffs. The descending fairway slopes right to left. The right side is favored to keep a good angle for the approach. Water, left, can be trouble.

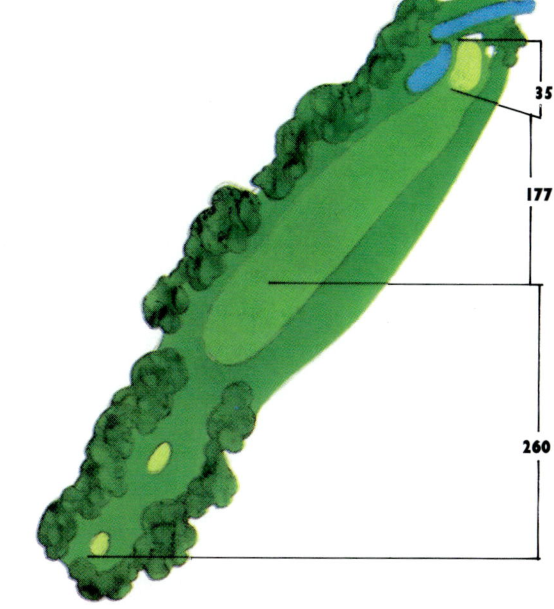

12

Par 3
155 yards

Players will all testify as this being the toughest hole of the course. Swirling winds combined with a shallow putting green will punish any shot that is just a bit off line.

13

Par 5
485 yards

Going for the green in two will present a risk having a very difficult third shot. Many players will give second thought to trying to reach this green — most will play safe and lay up short of the creek. The hole will surely yield a birdie, if played smartly, but for those who try for the eagle they risk the chance of having to contend with the steep bunkers beyond, or falling short into Rae's Creek.

14

Par 4
405 yards

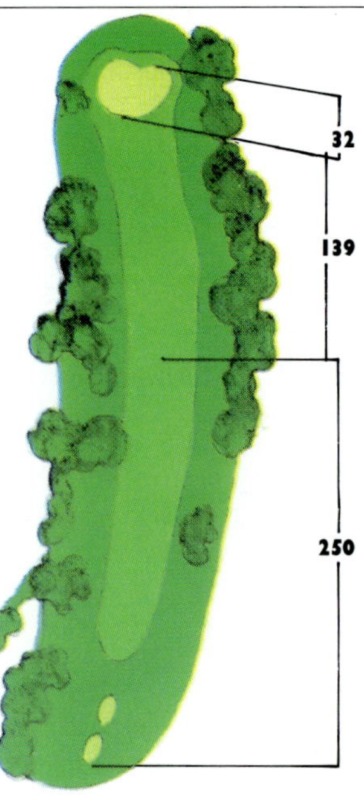

Difficult is an understatement. The fairway bends left but slopes right. The green undulates and slopes with such severity that birdies are very infrequent.

15

Par 5
500 yards

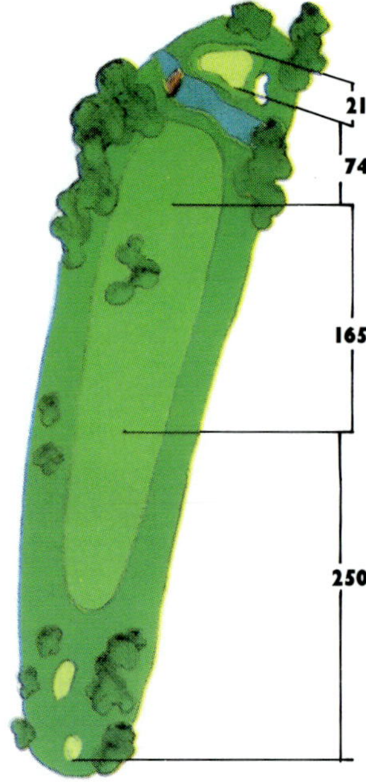

Downhill all the way with a narrow green placed beyond a water hazard. Eagles are fairly common with most players going for the green in two.

16

Par 3
170 yards

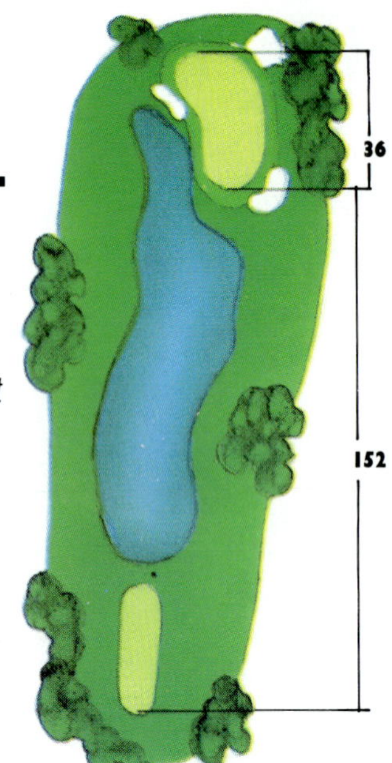

A beautiful but very difficult hole. Redesigned in 1948 by Robert Trent Jones, this 16th will keep the competition heavy going into the last two holes.

17

Par 4
400 yards

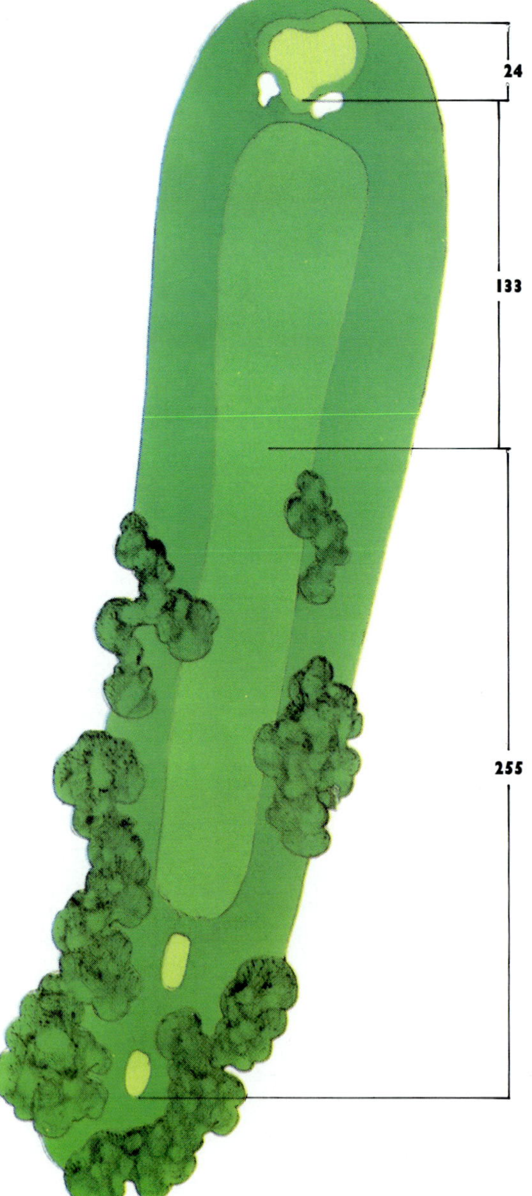

The ascending fairway requires a big drive in order to keep the approach shot short. "Ike's Tree" although President Eisenhower wanted to take a chainsaw to it, remains as an obstacle 180 yards on the left side of the fairway. Jack Nicklaus capped his victory in 1986 with a birdie on this tough hole. The uphill approach must stop quickly and surely to avoid having the ball spin back off the front or run off the back.

18

Par 4
405 yards

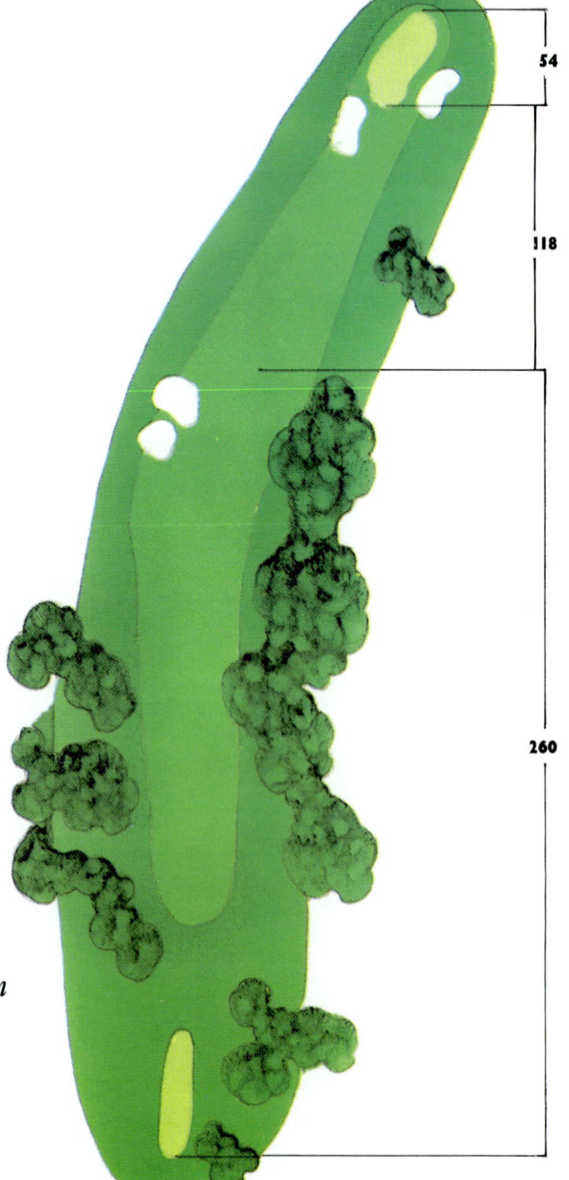

Possibly the best finishing hole in golf—definitely one of the most historical. The uphill stretch to the green requires a fading tee-shot and a very accurate approach. Players that hit past the hole on their second shot will have to contend with a putt downhill on the lightening fast, two-tiered green. Victory can only be assured when the "Green Jacket" has been donned.

THE COURSE: HARBOUR TOWN GOLF LINKS, HILTON HEAD,
SOUTH CAROLINA

*H*arbour Town Golf Links... beautiful Sea Pines Resort... site of South Carolina's only major PGA TOUR® event returns this spring... it's the MCI Classic. In its twenty-seventh year, an outstanding field of TOUR professionals will challenge the famed Harbour Town Golf Links and defending champion Bob Tway for the top prize.

Since its inception in 1969, the tournament has boasted the greatest names in golf including past champions Palmer, Nicklaus, Watson, Zoeller, Norman, Stewart, Faldo and Irwin.

From the parade and opening ceremonies to the tournament itself, the MCI Classic is truly a Classic in the making.

Sponsored by MCI Communications and operated by the non-profit Heritage Classic Foundation, the tournament continues to be recognized as one of the most prestigious stops on the PGA TOUR®.

Dates:	April 18-21, 1996
Network:	CBS
Times:	Sat 4:00-6:30 EST
	Sun 3:00-6:00 EST
Yardage:	6,912
Par:	71
Slope:	134
Rating:	74.0
Total Purse:	$1,300,000
1st Prize:	$234,000
1995 Winner:	Bob Tway
1995 Winning Score:	275 (67,69,72,67)
Principal Charitable Beneficiary:	Hilton Head Hospital
Charitable Benefits to Date:	$3.5 million in last 8 years
Ticket Information:	1-803-671-2448
Resort Information:	1-803-785-3333

1

*Par 4
414 yards*

Harbour Town opens with a tight par 4. The right side of the fairway is favored to allow for an unrestricted approach to the small elevated green.

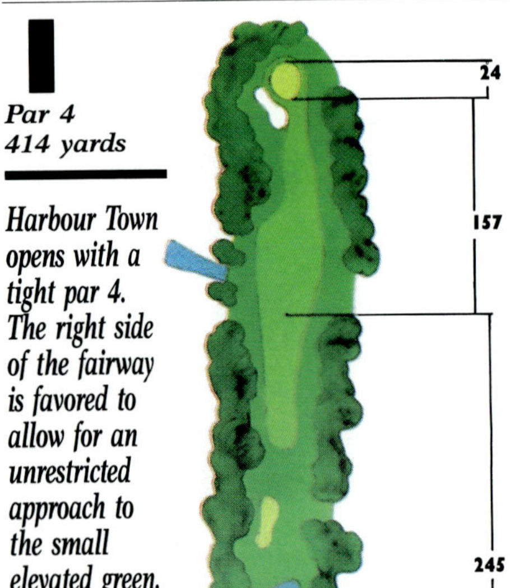

2

*Par 5
505 yards*

Longer hitters should reach the green in two. A drive down the left side will allow for a clear view to the putting sur-face. Birdies are a must for players to keep up with the field.

3

*Par 4
411 yards*

The trees along the left side can be troublesome. Players will keep their drives right of center. The small green placed among the bunkers can be hard to hold.

4

*Par 3
198 yards*

Pete Dye does not ask much in the way of distance. Accuracy, however, is a must. Players will tend to keep the ball to the right side of the green to avoid the water left.

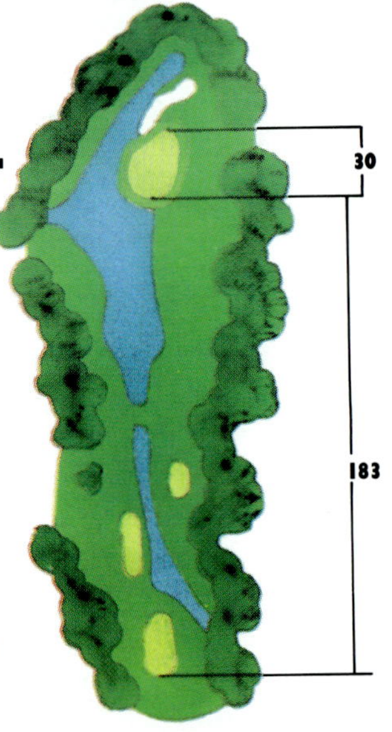

5

*Par 5
535 yards*

Getting home in two is possi-ble. However the bunkers and tightness of the hole make it a good three-shot par 5. The green slopes rapidly left to right, making for tough putting.

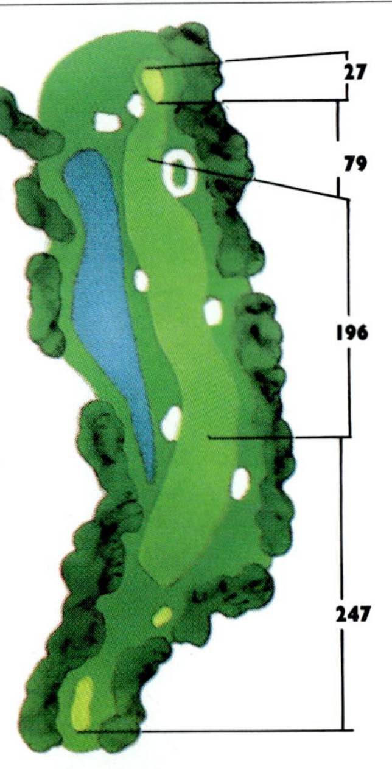

6

*Par 4
419 yards*

The waste bunker along the right will keep players to the left. The long narrow green slopes gradually towards the front. Birdies are frequent.

7

*Par 3
180 yards*

The large un-dulated green is guarded well by the trees and an encircling bunker. Players will have to get their tee shots close to the hole for a chance at birdie.

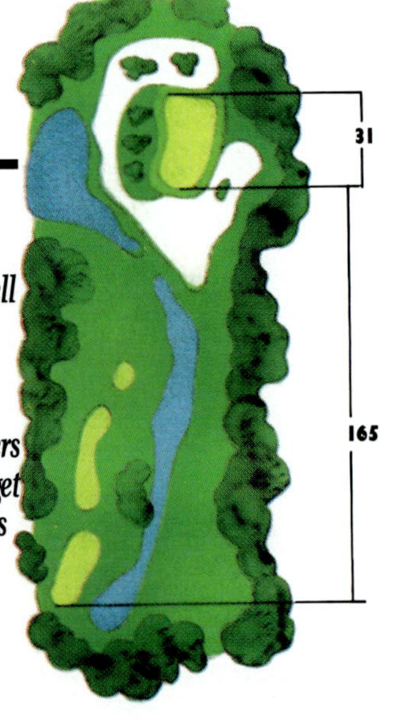

8

*Par 4
462 yards*

This eighth hole is con-sidered one of the most difficult on the course. A long drive is re-quired to get the ball in position for a clear shot to the green.

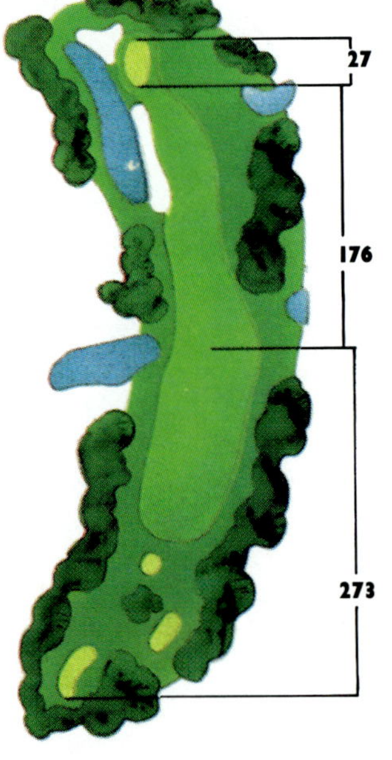

9

*Par 4
337 yards*

Position off the tee is of the ut-most impor-tance for this ninth hole. Players will be trying to keep their drives short in order to leave a full shot into the short, hazard-ous green.

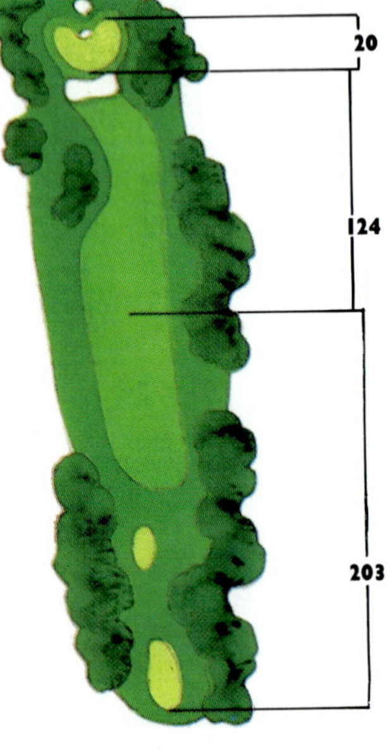

10

Par 4
436 yards

The tenth fairway opens up for the big drive. The green is nestled in among the pines, requiring an accurate approach.

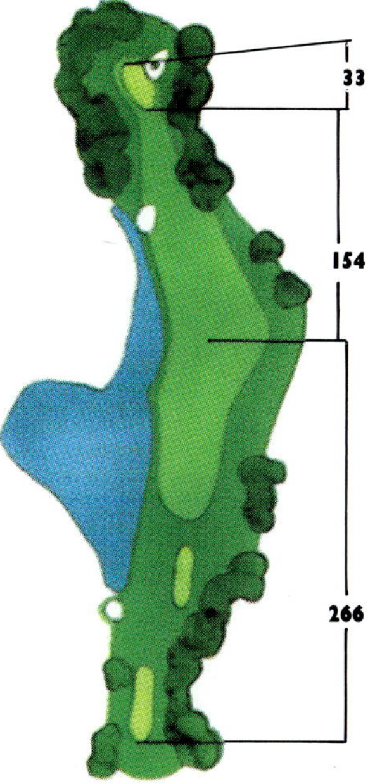

11

Par 4
438 yards

The trees close in on the fairway on this eleventh. The landing area is large, but a drive down the center of the fairway is a must to leave a clear shot to the putting surface.

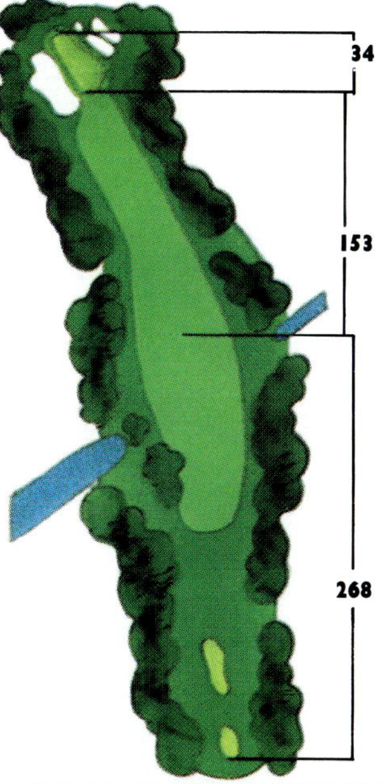

12

Par 4
413 yards

The tree-line along the right side will most likely block any shot to the green if the drive is not kept to the left. The S-shaped green presents tricky pin placements.

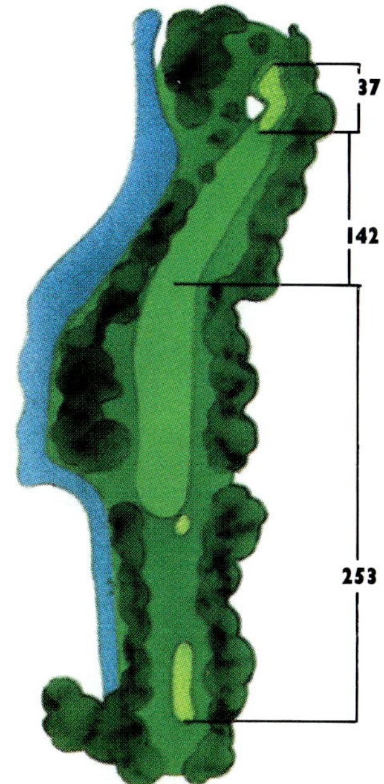

13

Par 4
378 yards

Accurate shot-making is a must on this hole. The drive, as well as the approach, must be hit very well in order to achieve a par.

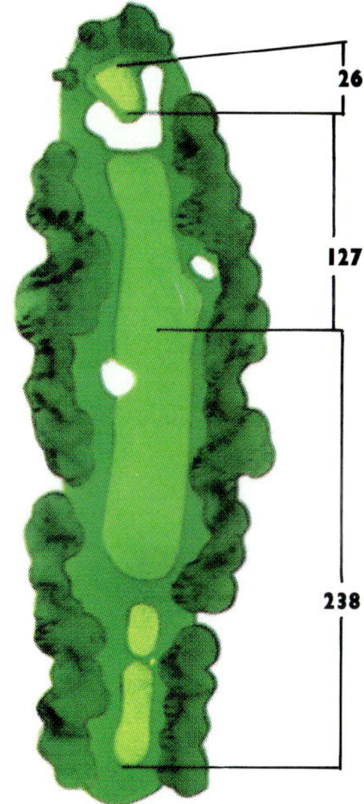

14

Par 3
165 yards

Simply the most beautiful hole during tournament time! With flowers in full bloom, it is difficult to remember the task at hand. Not a long par 3, but unrelenting just the same.

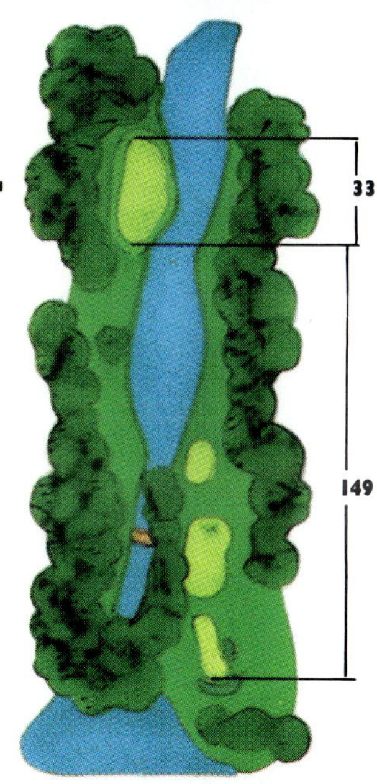

15

Par 5
575 yards

Described as the best par 5 in golf, this fifteenth will gain the player's respect. The drive must be hit down a narrow path. The putting surface has two tiers, left and right.

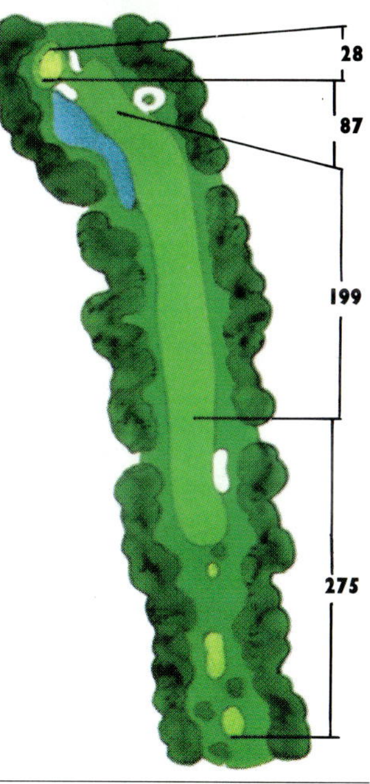

16

Par 4
376 yards

The players will be aiming their drives just left of the second tree located in the fairway. The wind from Calibogue Sound can increase club selection for the approach.

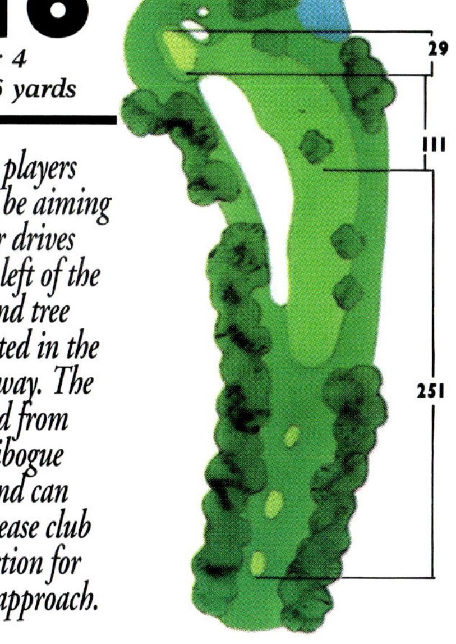

17

Par 3
192 yards

The long narrow green can be difficult to hit into the strong winds off the water. Club selection is vital for those who are in contention for the title.

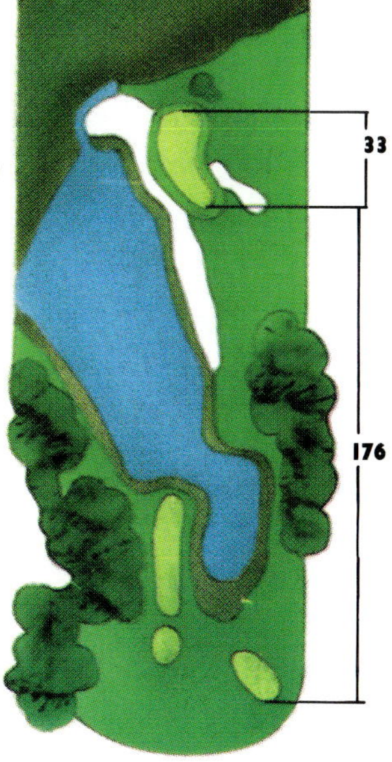

18

Par 4
478 yards

Like all great finishing holes, this eighteenth requires the best from the players. The tee shot and the approach must both carry the marsh.

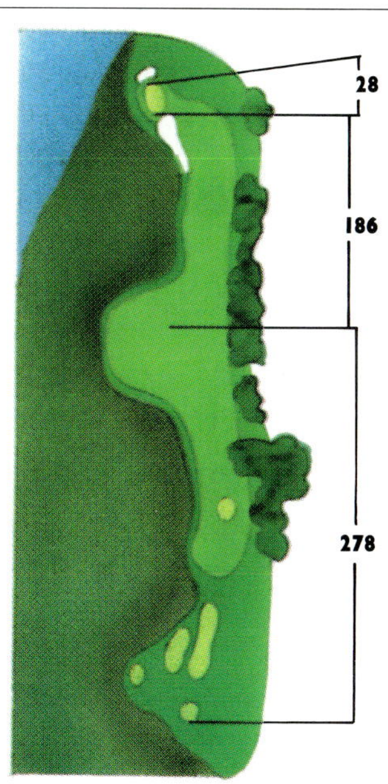

THE COURSE: THE CHAMPION COURSE, PGA NATIONAL RESORT AND SPA, PALM BEACH GARDENS, FLORIDA

*I*ts history dates back to 1937 with Jock Hutchison winning the first tournament at Augusta National. Sam Snead has won the event a record six times. Arnold Palmer won in his first year out on the SENIOUR PGA TOUR®.

The Champion Course at PGA National Golf Club is one of the tougher layouts on the SENIOR PGA TOUR®. Length and accuracy are not only favorable but also a requirement. The original layout was designed by Tom Fazio in 1981 and the course has since undergone redesigning by Jack Nicklaus in 1990. Changes included reworking and sculpting this championship layout, thus modifying both the slope and course ratings.

Dates:	April 18-21, 1996
Network:	NBC and USA
Times:	USA
	Thur/Fri 4:00-6:00 EST
	NBC
	Sat 1:00-3:00 EST
	Sun 12:00-3:00 EST
Yardage:	6,718
Par:	72
Slope:	142
Rating:	72.9
Total Purse:	$1,000,000
1st Prize:	$180,000
1995 Winner:	Ray Floyd
1995 Winning Score:	277 (70,70,67,70)
Principal Charitable Beneficiary:	PGA/Pathfinders Scholarship Fund
Ticket Information:	1-407-622-4653

1

Par 4
362 yards

The elevated tee looks down to an open fairway. The dogleg left requires a drive to the right middle. The green is flat and an easy target. A good starting hole.

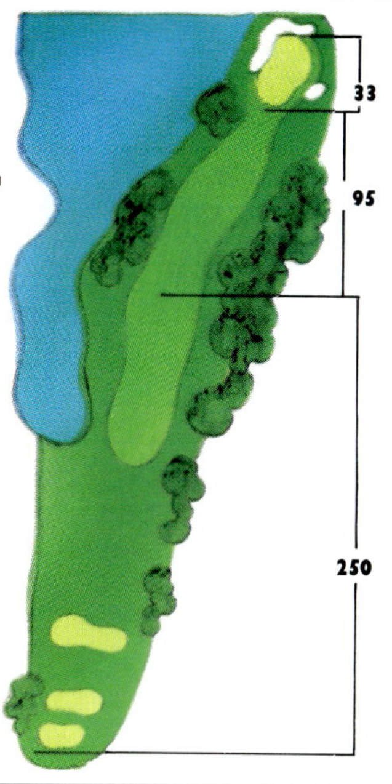

2

Par 4
419 yards

Straight-away and towards the left. The kidney shaped green is well guarded by bunkers.

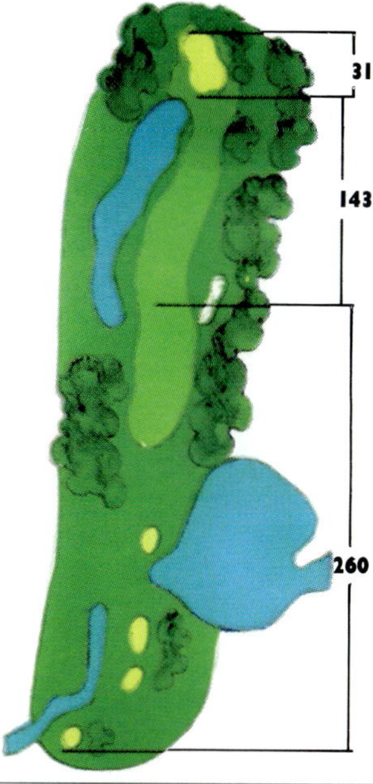

3

Par 5
513 yards

The longer hitters will be able to reach this green in two. Fairway bunkers are placed strategically to catch any drives off-line. Rolling green makes for difficult putts.

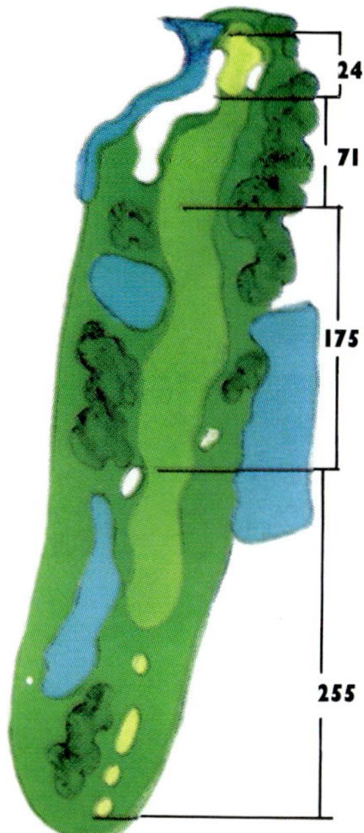

4

Par 4
355 yards

Elevated teeing ground to a low fairway. Bunkers on the left side require a drive directed to the right. The approach is to an elevated green, dropping off to the right.

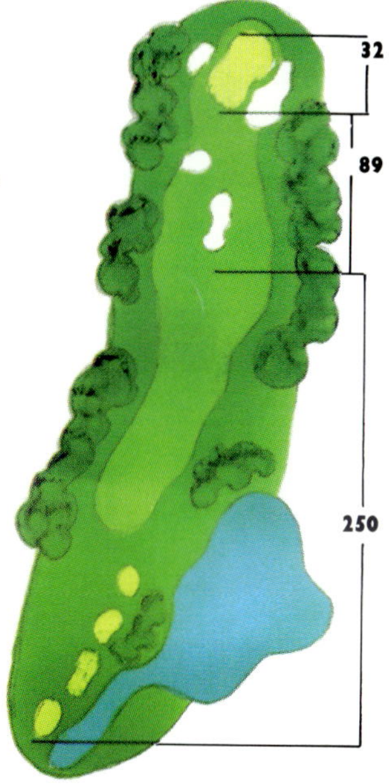

5

Par 3
171 yards

This hole has been reconfigured from a par 4 to a par 3. A stone-lined shore fronts the putting surface, while bunkers lie waiting behind.

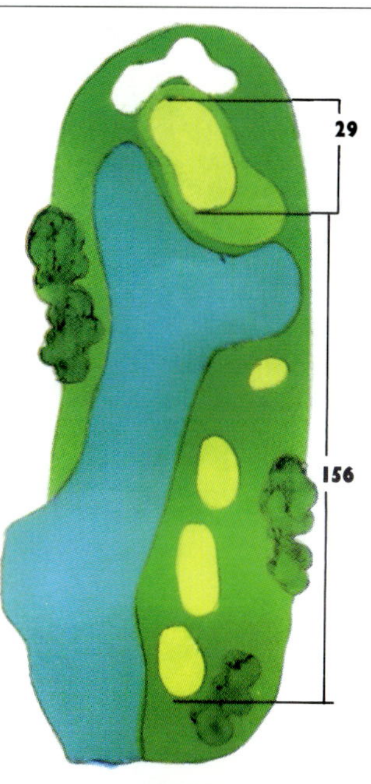

6

Par 5
478 yards

Bunkers along the right side of the fairway increase the importance of an accurate drive. The bolder players will play a big drive down the middle, followed by a second to the putting surface.

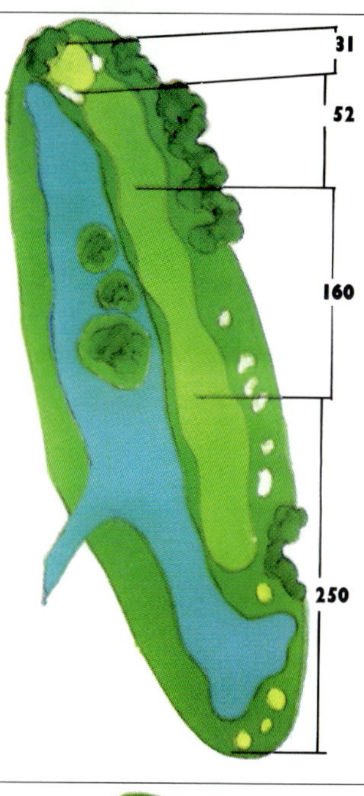

7

Par 3
185 yards

The large, rolling green allows for many different pin-placements. The putting surface is elevated and bunkered on the right.

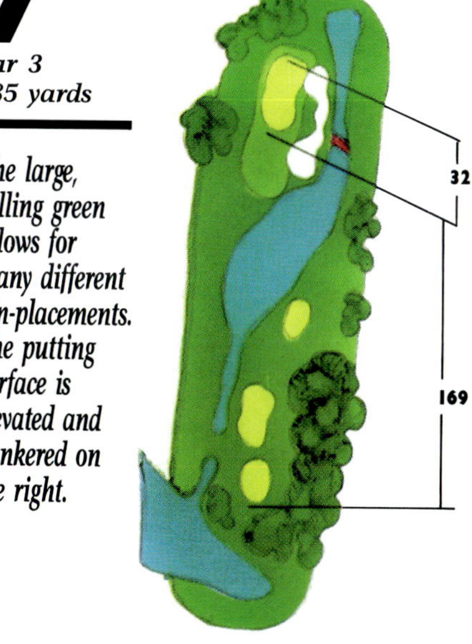

8

Par 4
387 yards

The wide fairway is receptive to all drives. The approach is played to a large, spacious green. Bunkers left and right are best avoided.

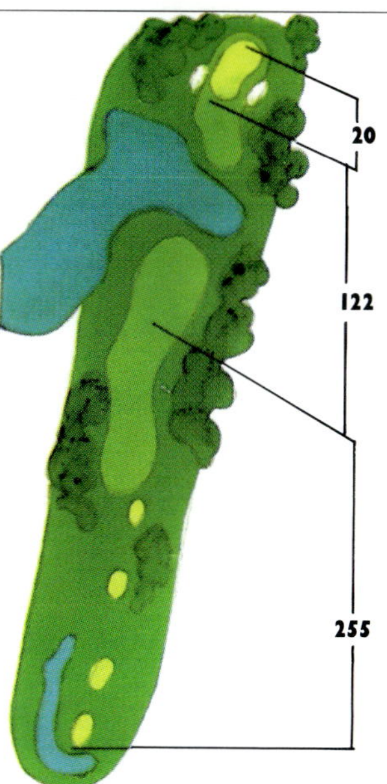

9

Par 4
371 yards

The tee has been moved back from the original design. A long carry over the lake for those who play down the left. A bail-out to the right allows for the safer approach.

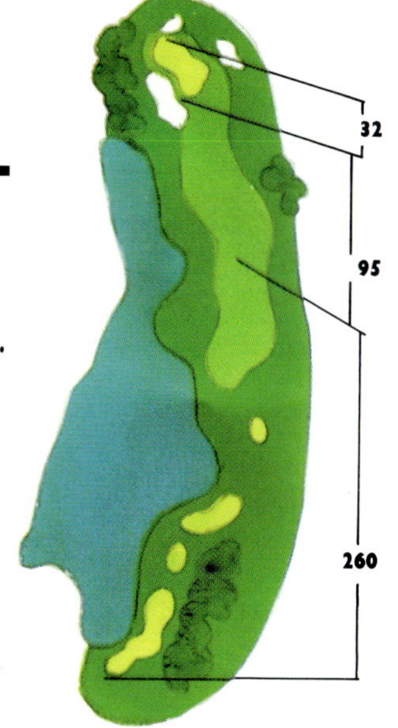

10

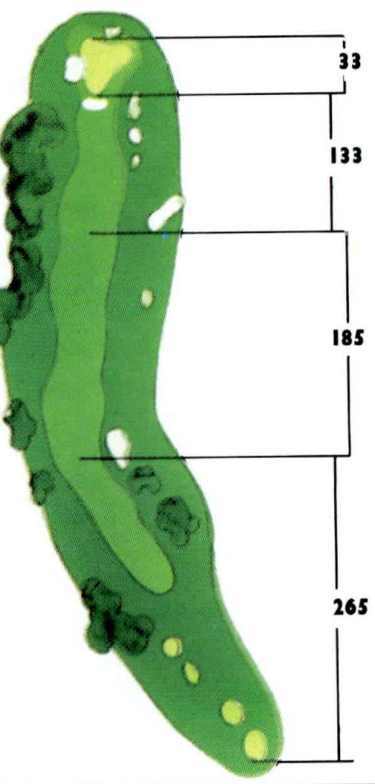

**Par 5
600 yards**

600 yards! Definitely a three shot hole. Jack says its a birdie hole, so we're assuming that those are three very well hit shots. Slight dogleg right to a large green.

11

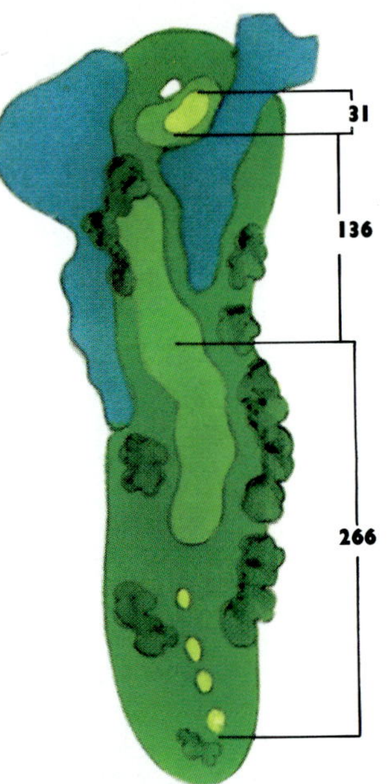

**Par 4
412 yards**

The players will be playing their drives right up to the edge of the lake. The approach must carry the water and find the small green.

12

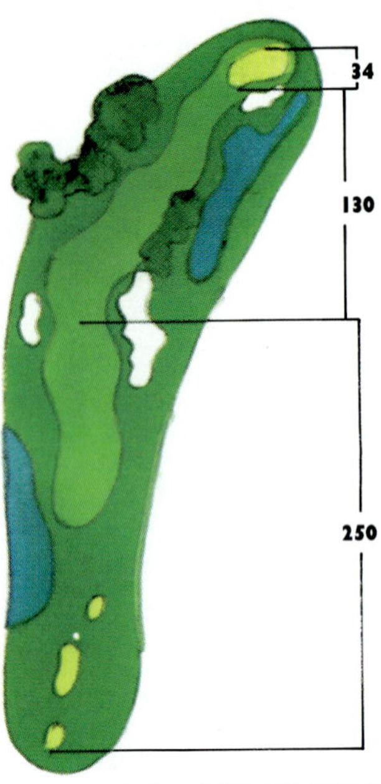

**Par 4
397 yards**

A good dogleg to the right. The drive needs to be placed down the middle, avoiding the bunker along the right and opening up the green. The putting surface has been enlarged.

13

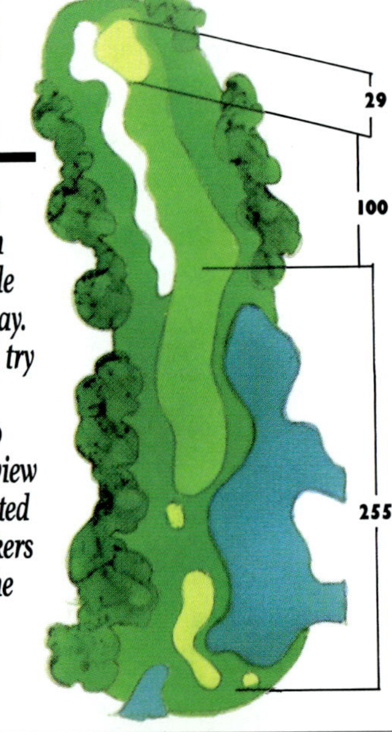

**Par 4
370 yards**

The drive is played down the right side of the fairway. Players will try to keep the ball right to get a good view of the elevated green. Bunkers surround the putting surface.

14

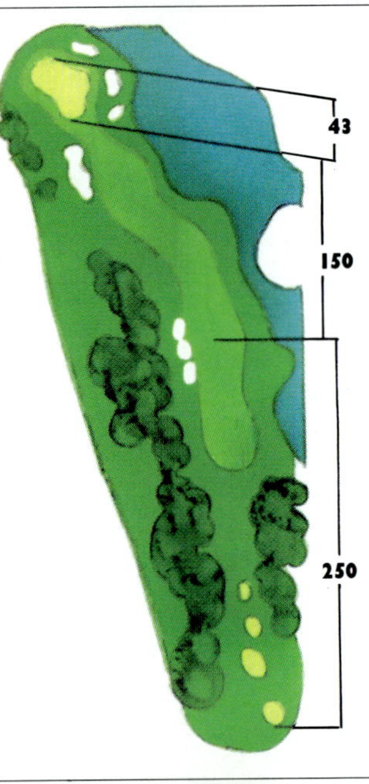

**Par 4
422 yards**

A long hole with a large green. A mighty drive down the left middle is ideal for good positioning on the approach. The green is guarded by both sand and grass bunkers, left and right.

15

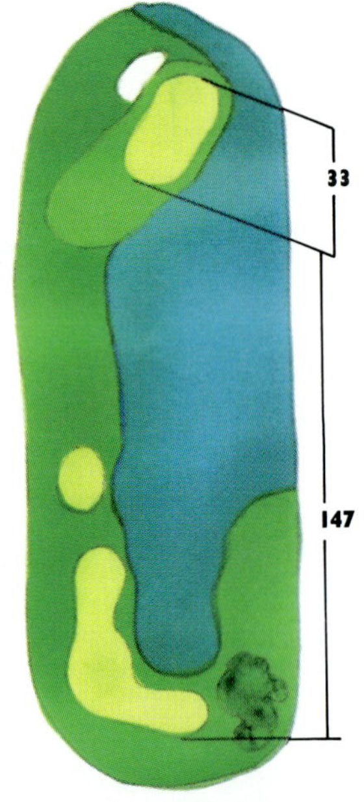

**Par 3
164 yards**

The tee shot must be accurate, otherwise the ball will be wet. The level green is backed by one bunker beyond.

16

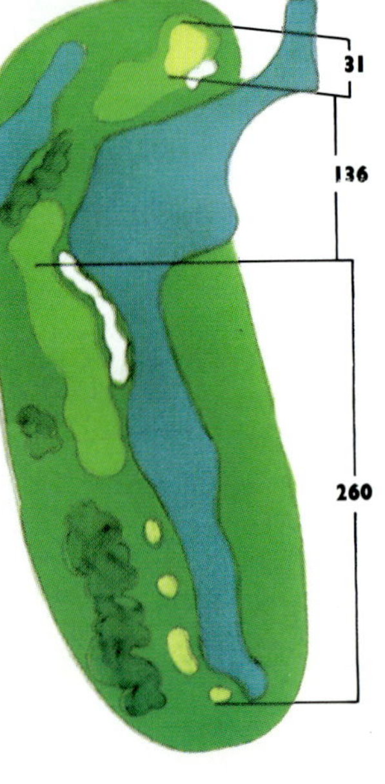

**Par 4
412 yards**

A new fairway bunker along the right side helps to define the tee shot placement. Water on both sides tightens the nerves for the approach. Pin placements to the right side can be difficult.

17

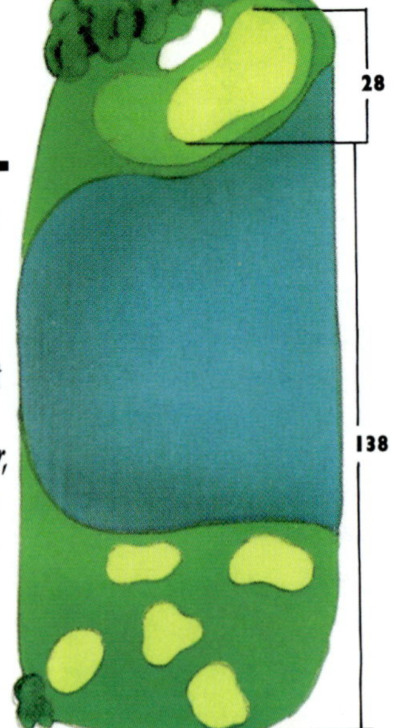

**Par 3
152 yards**

The green has been moved closer to the water. An accurate tee shot is the requirement for a par, and especially for the birdie.

18

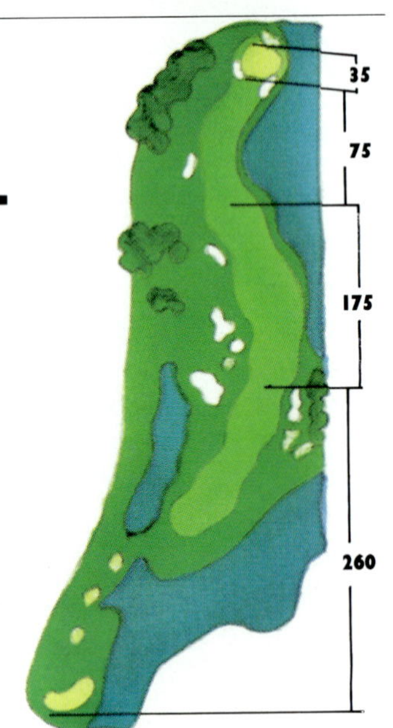

**Par 5
528 yards**

The double dogleg demands accuracy as well as length for those hoping of getting home in two. A good finishing hole.

THE COURSE: FOREST OAK COUNTRY CLUB, GREENSBORO, NORTH CAROLINA

*T*he Kmart Greater Greensboro Open is one of the oldest tournaments on the PGA TOUR®. Beginning in 1938 with a victory by Sam Snead, the tournament celebrates its 58th Championship event this year. Former Champions read like a Who's Who of golf including, Nelson, Hogan, Casper, Rodriquez, Trevino, Floyd, Wadkins, Lyle, Elkington, and Love. Sneads' eight victories at the GCO remain a PGA TOUR® record.

Forest Oaks is well respected by Touring professionals as a course that is tough but fair. New greens were constructed in 1995. High rough and tight fairways provide a considerable challenge and plenty of Sunday excitement. Reigning Champion Jim Gallagher Jr. came from seven shots behind for the biggest comeback on the PGA TOUR® since 1980.

Dates:	April 25-28, 1996
Network:	CBS and USA
Times:	USA
	Thur/Fri 4:00-6:00 EST
	CBS
	Sat 4:00-6:00 EST
	Sun 3:30-6:00 EST
Yardage:	6,958
Par:	72
Slope:	129
Rating:	73.9
Total Purse:	$1,500,000
1st Prize:	$270,000
1995 Winner:	Jim Gallagher, Jr.
1995 Winning Score:	274 (69,70,69,66)
Principal Charitable Beneficiary:	Greensboro Jaycees
Ticket Information:	1-800-999-KGGO

1

Par 4
407 yards

The open fairway invites the first drive of the day. Players will keep their tee shots down the right side of the fairway for a good angle on the approach. Birdies can start the day right.

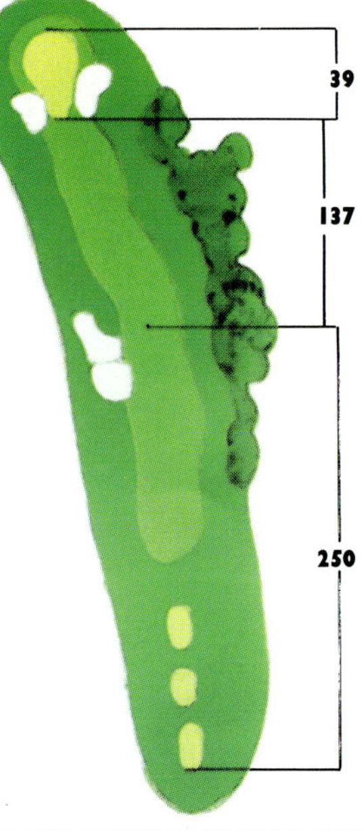

2

Par 5
511 yards

The fairway slopes down to the green on the approach. Getting home in two is not uncommon. The right-to-left sloping fairway will encourage drives to the left.

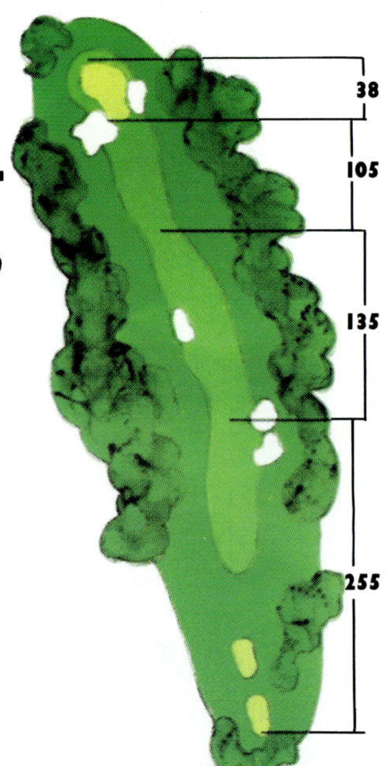

3

Par 4
409 yards

Driving accuracy is a must on this difficult par 4. Water right and trees left can pose problems for the approach. The putting surface is two-tiered, sloping back to front.

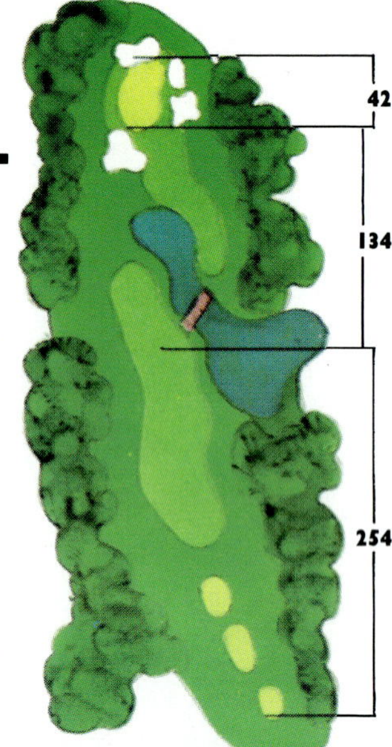

4

Par 3
190 yards

The elevated tee offers a clear view of the green. The flat putting surface may relinquish a birdie if the tee shot is close enough.

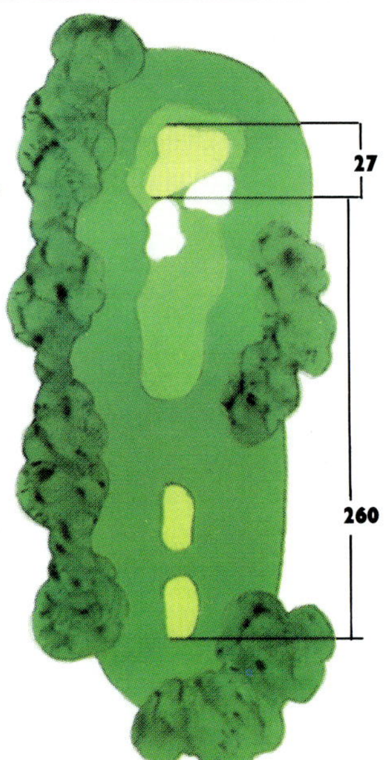

5

Par 4
415 yards

The best drive would be to cut the ball around the corner, leaving a short iron to the right-to-left sloping green. Birdies will be plentiful.

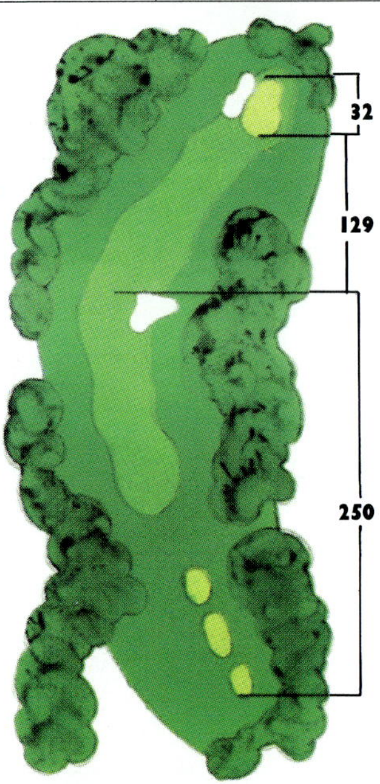

6

Par 4
386 yards

Players will be using either a fairway wood or long iron off the tee. The right side of the fairway is favored to keep away from the bunker and OB left. Getting the approach close to the pin is key.

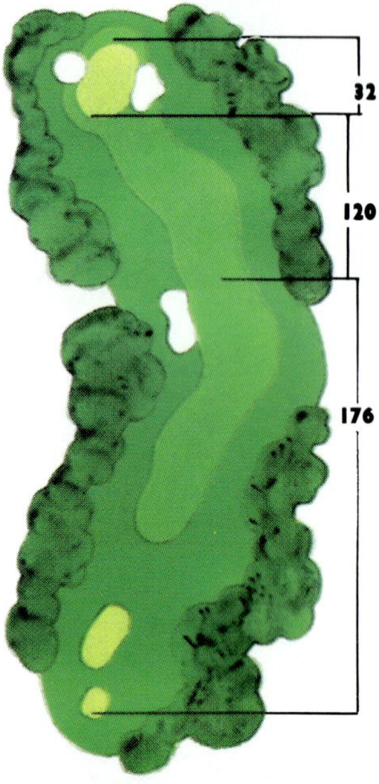

7

Par 4
372 yards

The fairway slopes sharply from right to left. Players will have to keep balls on the right to leave a clear approach. Keeping the ball short of the hole is necessary for the uphill putt.

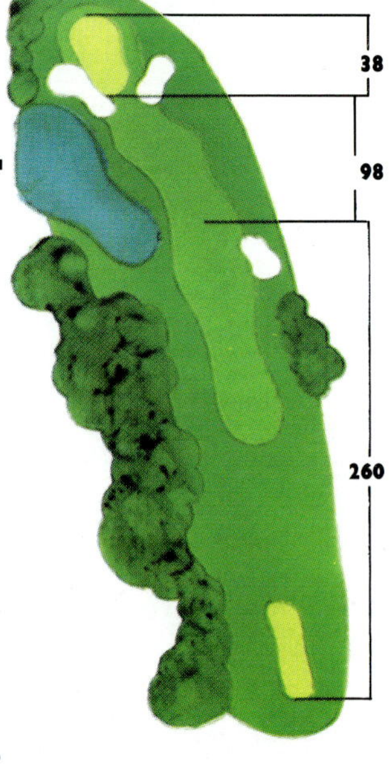

8

Par 3
215 yards

The large flat green is surrounded by three bunkers. As the longest par 3 on the course, this hole can be difficult. Average score is above par.

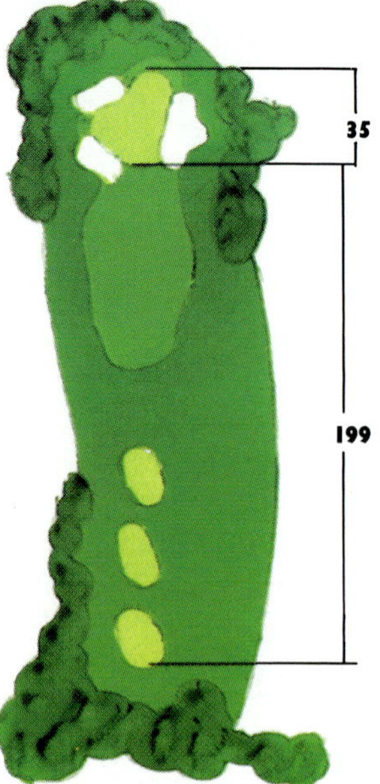

9

Par 5
574 yards

Three well-planned shots should set up for the birdie. The rolling fairway leads up to an elevated green. Birdies proliferate. Anticipate the occasional eagle.

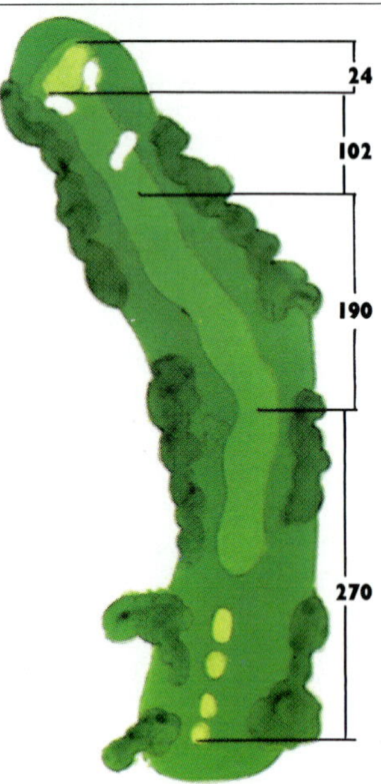

10

Par 4
393 yards

The fairway slopes toward a bunker on the right. Trees nearer the green wait to foil the approach. The averages indicate that this is a good hole to par.

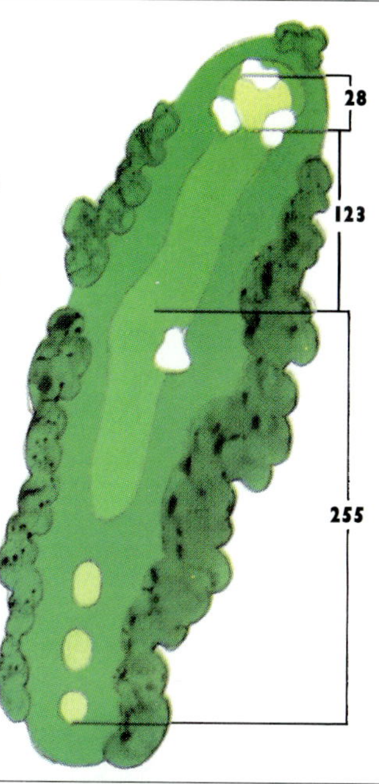

11

Par 4
438 yards

The flat fairway is edged by bunkers and out-of-bounds on the right. The approach is to a spacious green that drops off severely beyond.

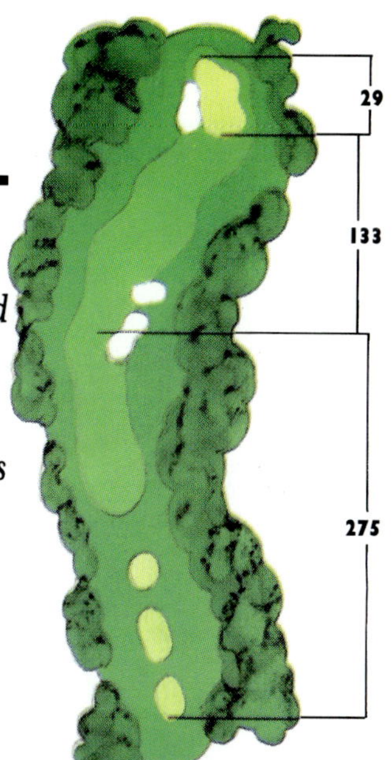

12

Par 3
186 yards

Short of the hole is the key. Beyond the hole are downhill putts, and the green drops off in back. Average score during the tournament is just above par.

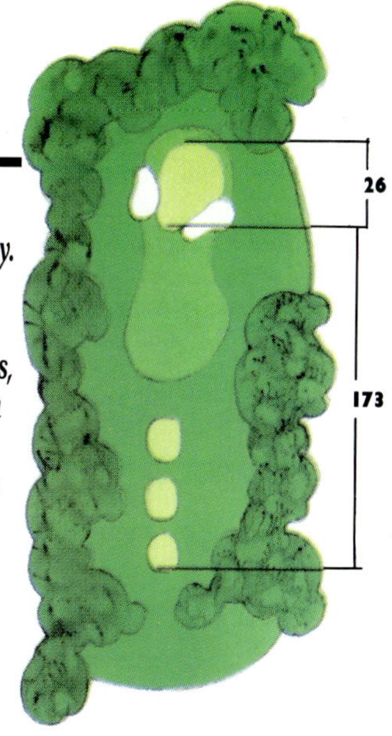

13

Par 5
503 yards

The longer hitters may want to back off their drives a bit to stay short of the water. A long second shot can reach the putting surface. Birdies are a must to keep up with the field.

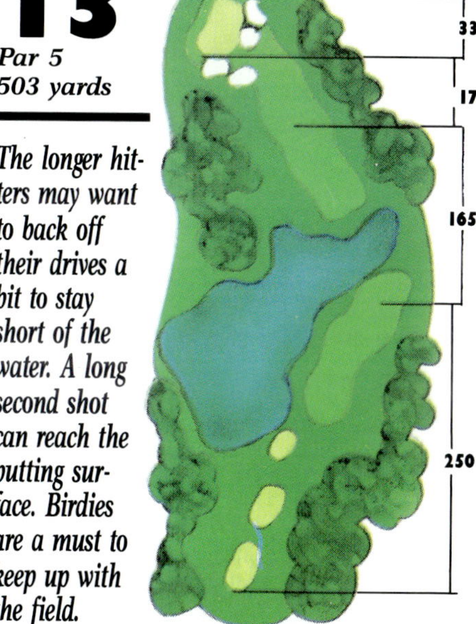

14

Par 4
438 yards

The longest par 4 also possesses one of the largest greens at Forest Oaks. Left fairway is favored from the tee to open the green for the approach.

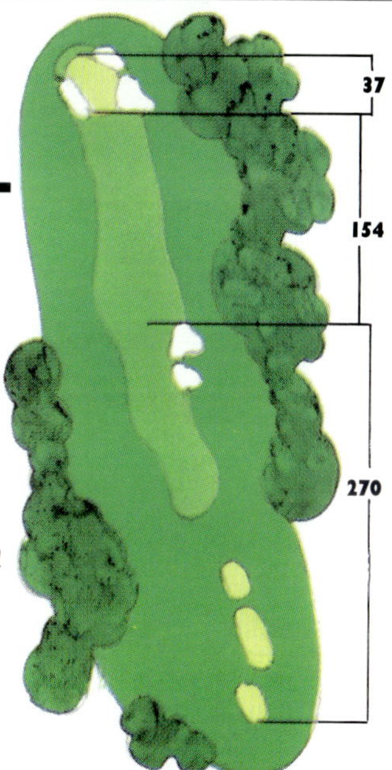

15

Par 5
554 yards

An uphill drive should keep clear of the sand and water to the right. Good positioning on the second shot will leave an easy yet another shot to the large green. Par is a good score here.

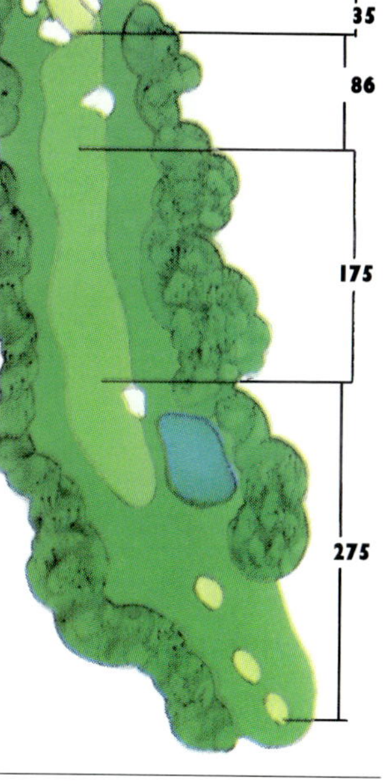

16

Par 4
408 yards

The drive will disappear out of sight over the ridge in the fairway. Accuracy on the approach is a necessity to ensure the par. Bogeys are an unwelcome but likely possibility.

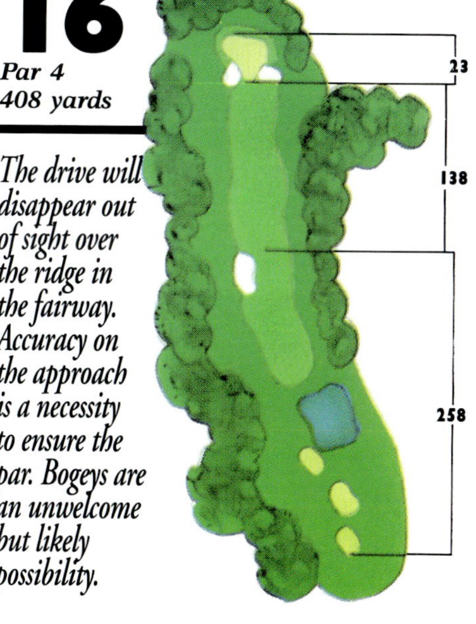

17

Par 3
188 yards

This is where the tournament can get interesting. Club selection must be perfect to keep the ball just below the hole and establish an easier uphill putt.

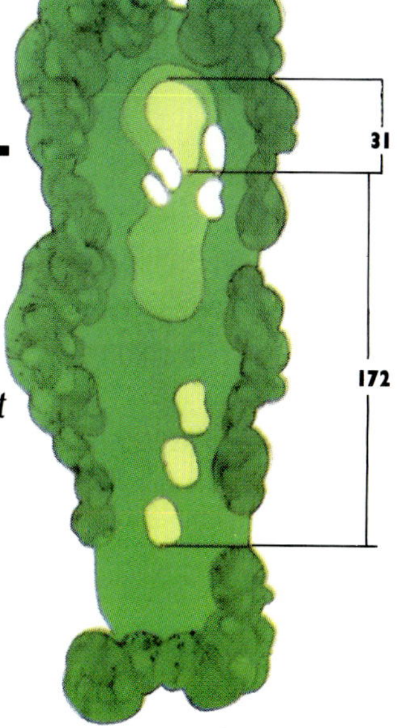

18

Par 4
426 yards

A long finishing hole that can bust a one-stroke lead. Care must be taken to get the ball on the green in regulation. The match is not over until the last putt drops.

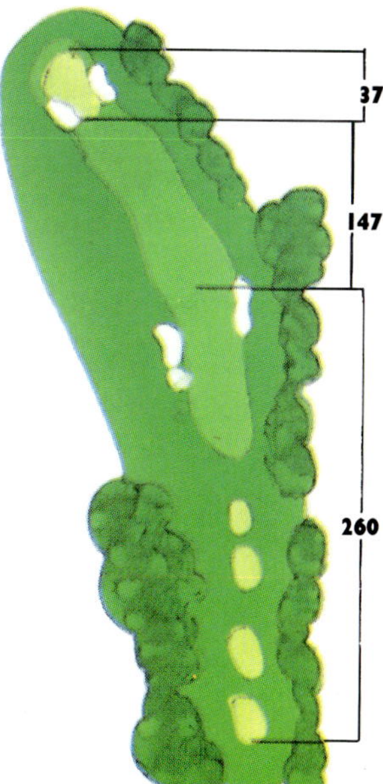

LAS VEGAS SENIOR CLASSIC

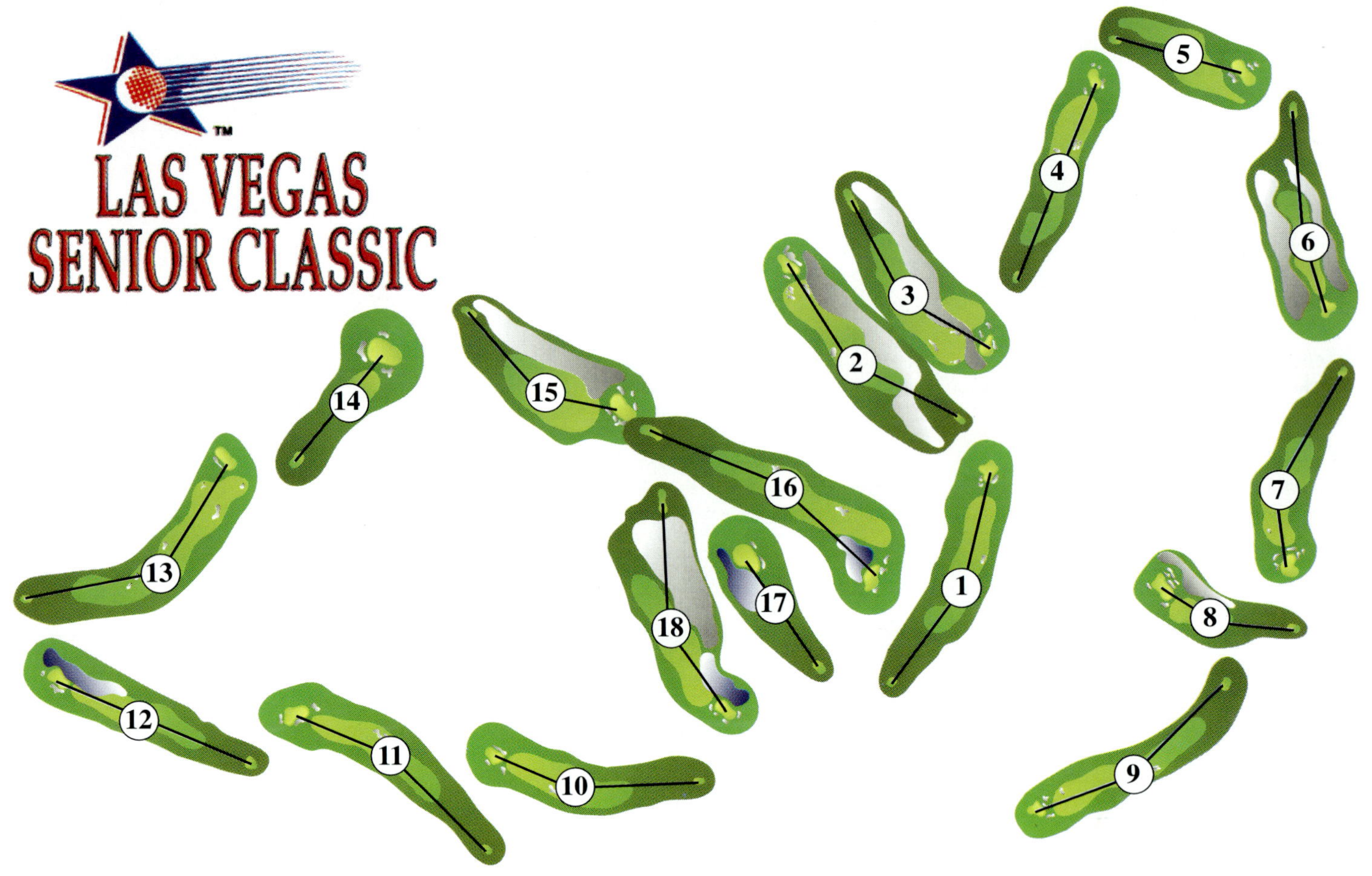

THE COURSE: TPC SUMMERLIN, LAS VEGAS, NEVADA

*A*t the heart of Summerlin's Hills South Village is the Tournament Players Club at Summerlin, Nevada's only stadium course and member of the PGA TOUR's prestigious network of TPC courses. Designed to accommodate spectators with nature amphitheaters and vantage points for unrestricted viewing, the TPC at Summerlin is operated by the PGA TOUR® and began hosting the Las Vegas Invitational in 1992.

An 18-hole championship course designed by architect Bobby Weed and PGA TOUR® professional Fuzzy Zoeller, the TPC at Summerlin has become Nevada's premier private course and was recently ranked by GolfWeek as one of the two top courses in the state.

Dates:	April 26-28, 1996
Network:	ESPN
Times:	Fri 12:00-2:00 / 4:00-6:00 EST
	Sat 3:30-6:00 EST
	Sun 3:30-6:00 EST
Yardage:	6963
Par:	72
Slope:	128
Rating:	71.9
Total Purse:	$1,000,000
1st Prize:	$180,000
1995 Winner:	Jim Colbert
1994 Winning Score:	250
Principal Charitable Beneficiary:	Las Vegas Founders Golf Foundation
Ticket Information:	1-702-382-6616

1

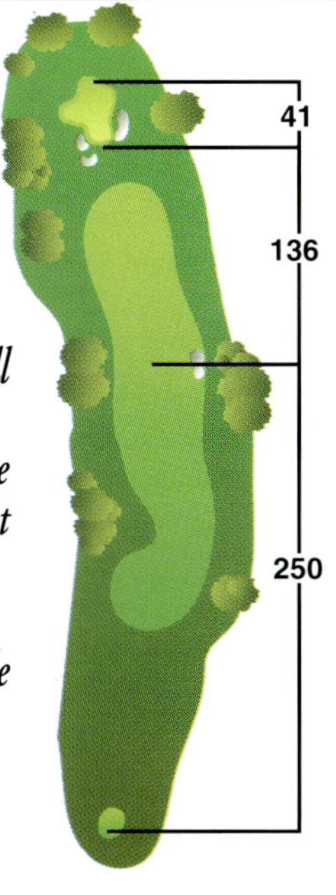

Par 4
408 yards

The opening hole plays straight away to a slightly downhill landing area and green. Positioning the tee shot near the right fairway bunker opens up the green, especially the left side pin placements.

2

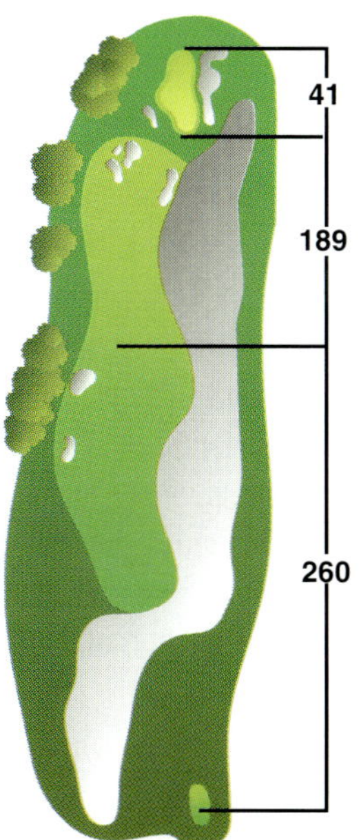

Par 4
469 yards

A long, tough, downhill par 4, along an existing wash. The tee shot angle must be figured in ralation to the diagonal wash carry, with bunkers left. The sloping green is large with a bunker bordering the right

3

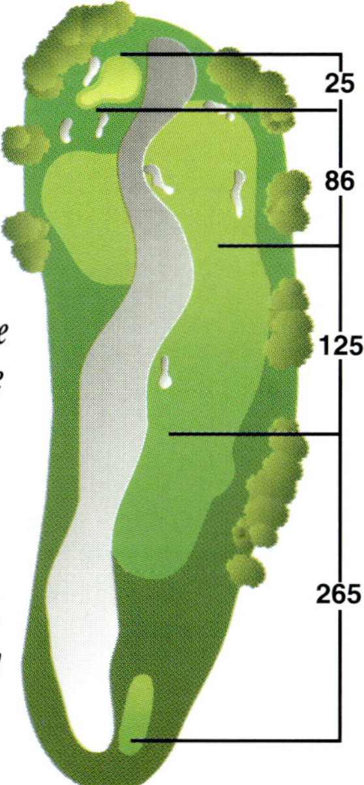

Par 5
492 yards

A short reachable par 5 with a double fairway approach. The green is perched above an existng wash, presenting alternate routes for the second shot. Eventually, the wash must be carried. The hole plays slightly buphill and into the prevailing wind.

4

Par 4
450 yards

A slightly downhill hole with fairway bunkers left and right. The green sets up slightly right to left with a deep bunker front right

5

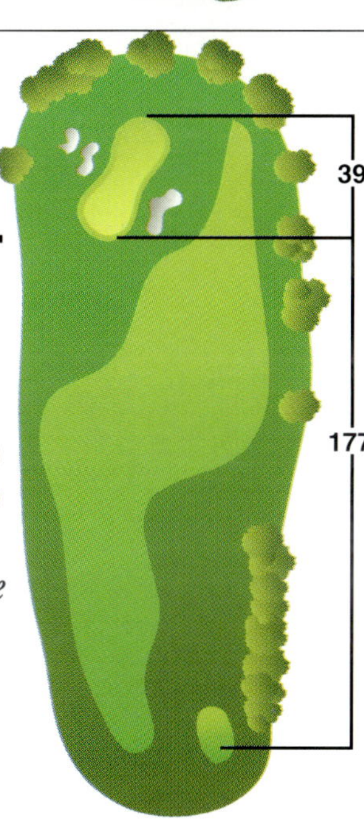

Par 3
197 yards

A scenic, demanding downhill par 3 crossing a wash. The green sets in left to right with challenging pin placements to the rear.

6

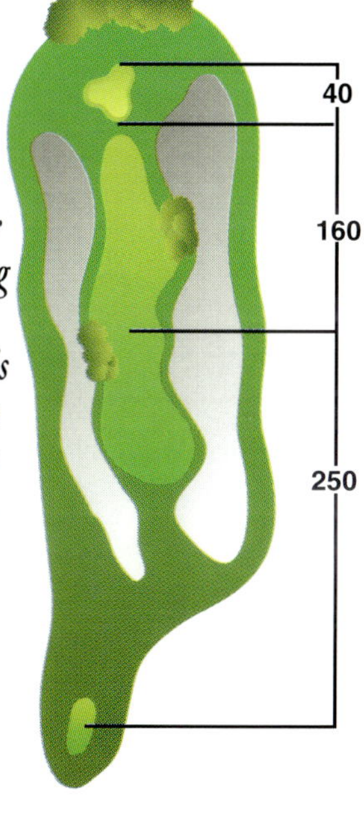

Par 4
430 yards

A slightly uphil par 4 with desert flanking each side of the fairway. The green is elevated, and sets in left to right with no bunkers. Choose an extra club for the approach shot.

7

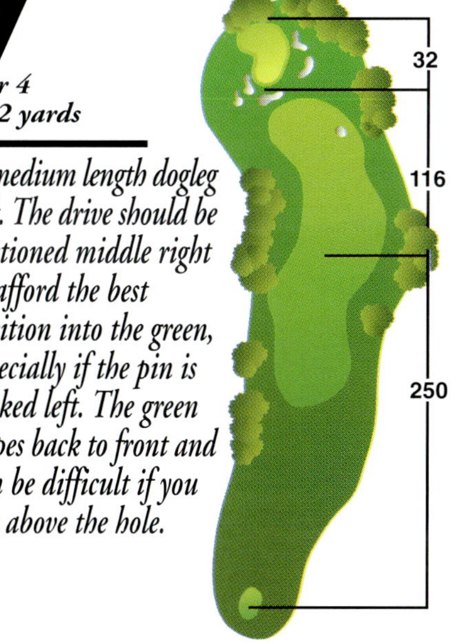

Par 4
382 yards

A medium length dogleg left. The drive should be postioned middle right to afford the best position into the green, especially if the pin is tucked left. The green slopes back to front and can be difficult if you are above the hole.

8

Par 3
239 yards

The longest par 3, playing left to right with a wash running down the right side. A large green with bail-out left awaits the tee shot. A good spectator hole with mounds affording views of #8,3,2

9

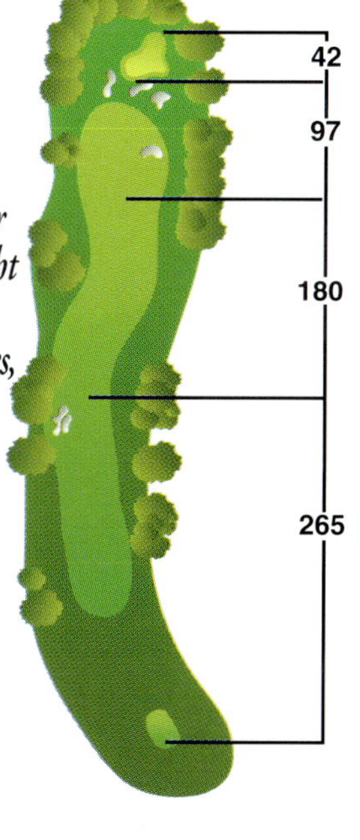

Par 5
563 yards

A long downhill par 5, slightly left to right hole. The green is protected by bunkers, both front and left.

10

Par 4
460 yards

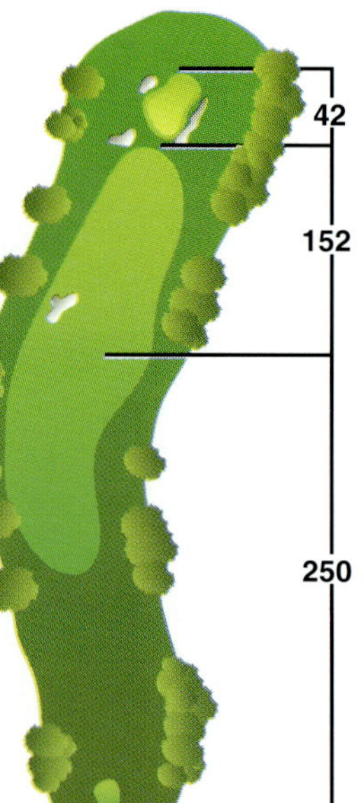

A slightly downhill par 4 playing left-to-right with fairway bunkers left. A large deep bunker is positioned front right with the back of the green falling away slightly.

11

Par 4
448 yards

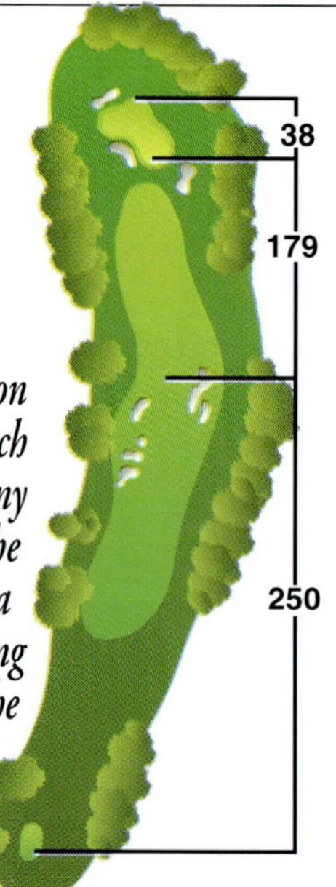

A right-to-left tee shot with fairway bunkers challenging the player on the left side. The approach is to a green making any pin placement along the right side of the green a challenge. Good viewing from the mounds on the right

12

Par 3
182 yards

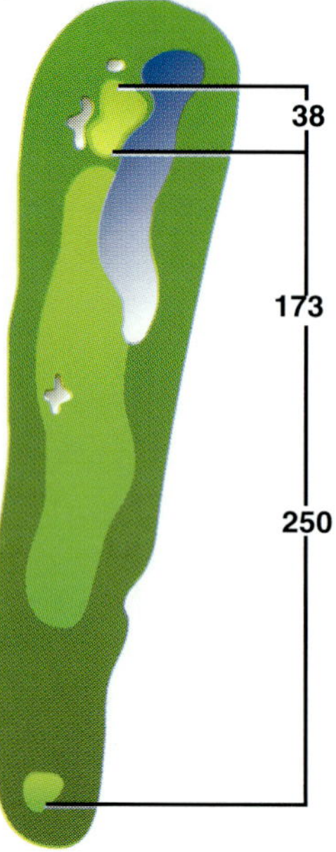

This slightly down hill hole has a lake just beyond the landing area in the right, which extends along side the green making and pin placement along the right side of the green a challenge. Good viewing from the mounds on the right.

13

Par 5
606 yards

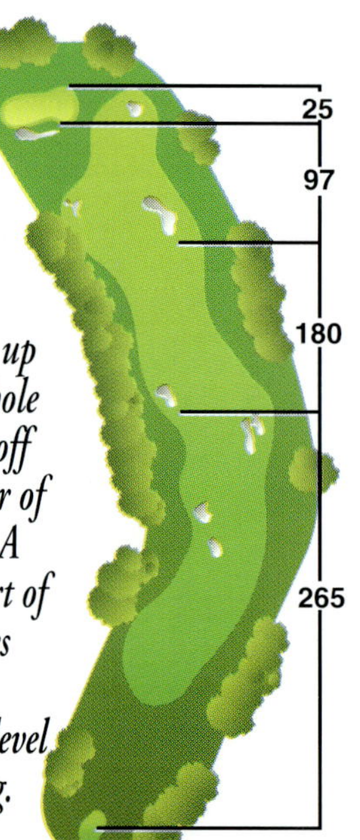

Typically, a 3-shot hole demanding 2 strategic shots to set up the approach. The hole sets up right-to-left off the tee with a cluster of bunkers on the left. A fairway bunker short of the green emphasizes placement for the approach to the split level green. Don't be long.

14

Par 3
156 yards

The shortest par 3 with a right-to-left orientation. The green is wide, but somewaht shallow in depth with bunkers left and right.

15

Par 4
341 yards

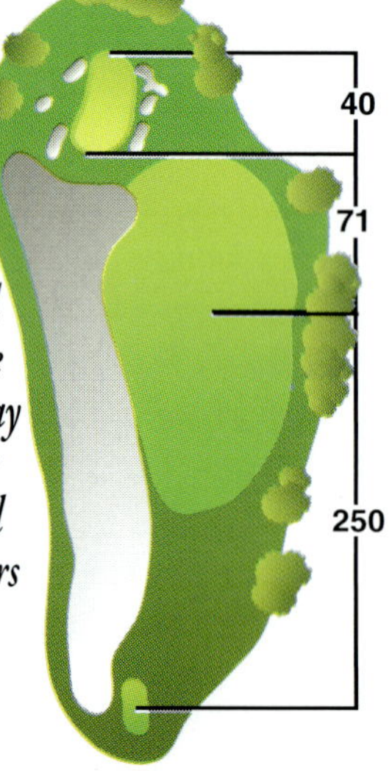

The desert runs the length of the hole on the left with bunkers separating the 2-level fairway. Golfers have alternate routes to play the hole. The green is long and narrow and elevated, with bunkers surrounding it.

16

Par 5
560 yards

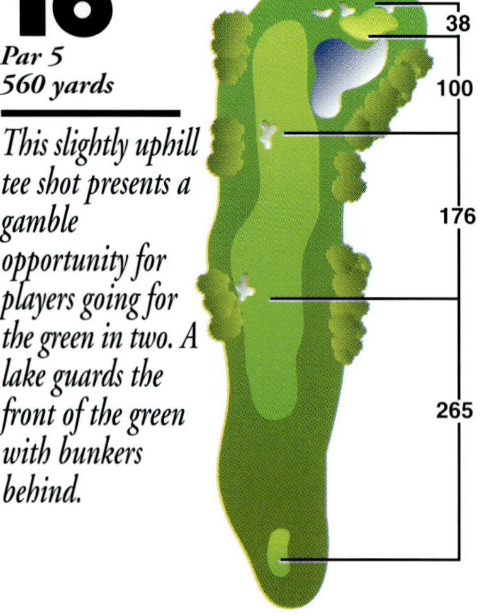

This slightly uphill tee shot presents a gamble opportunity for players going for the green in two. A lake guards the front of the green with bunkers behind.

17

Par 3
196 yards

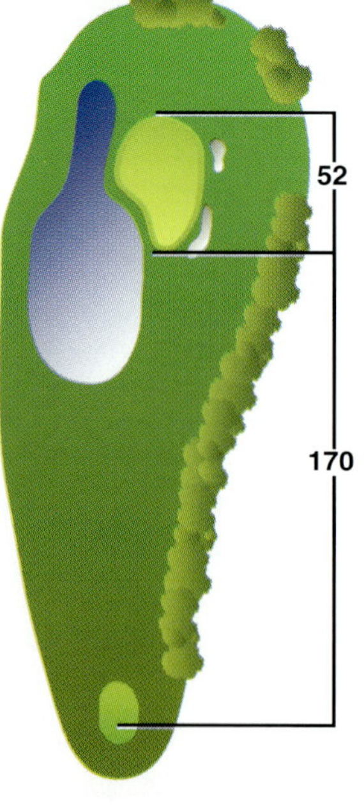

A medium length downhill hole with water protecting the left side. A long green with bunkers on the right to catch the bail-out shot. A great spectaator hole.

18

Par 4
444 yards

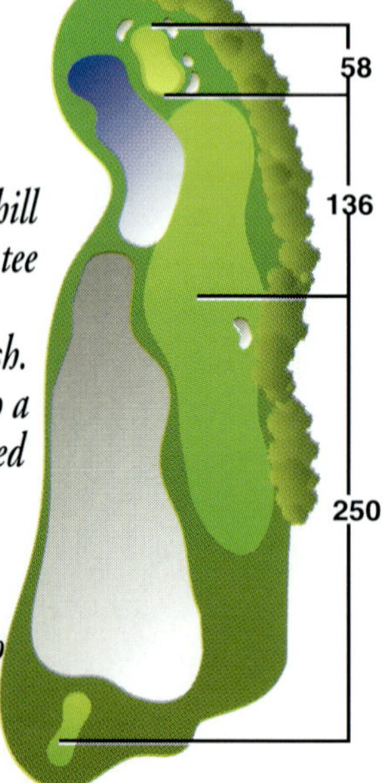

A long, slightly uphill hole requiring the tee shot to diagonally across a desert wash. The approach is to a deep green protected by a small lake on the left. A challenging finish with great spectato viewing.

THE COURSE: TPC AT THE WOODLANDS, THE WOOD-
LANDS, TEXAS

The Shell Houston Open is the 10th-oldest professional golf event in the United States. With the organization of the Houston Golf Association, the city was able to attract the top players of the era to play in the inaugural event. The first tournament in 1946 saw the great Byron Nelson win by two strokes over equally legendary Ben Hogan. For his efforts, Nelson took home a first-place winner's check of $2,000. Today the total purse is over $1,400,000 and the winner will take home $252,000..

The East Course at The Woodlands was chosen as the present site of the Houston Open in 1985. In 1984, the course was redesigned within TPC stadium facility specifications. Carlton Gipson modified the work of architects Bruce Devlin and Bob von Hagge by adding bunkers, mounding and spectator mounds to toughen the character of the course and also afford the galleries better vantage points during the tournament.

Dates:	May 2-5
Network:	ABC
Times:	Sat 2:30-4:30 EST
	Sun 4:00-6:00 EST
Yardage:	7,045
Par:	72
Slope:	135
Rating:	73.6
Total Purse:	$1,400,000
1st Prize:	$252,000
1995 Winner:	Payne Stewart
1995 Winning Score:	276 (73,65,70,68)
Principal Charitable Beneficiary:	Houston Golf Association Charities
Charitable Benefits to Date:	Over $3.85 million in 18 years
Ticket Information:	1-713-367-7999

1

Par 5
515 yards

The tournament opens with a short par 5. The players may go for the big play early and attempt reaching the green in two. If missed, good bunker play will ensure a birdie.

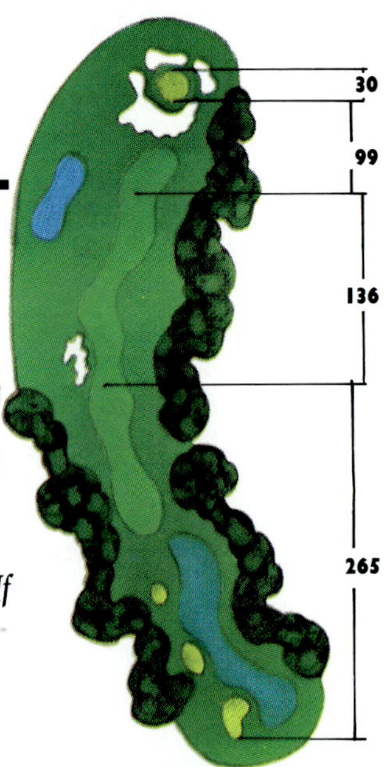

2

Par 4
365 yards

Players will be playing a fairway wood or long iron towards the left bunker. A short approach remains to a right to left sloping green.

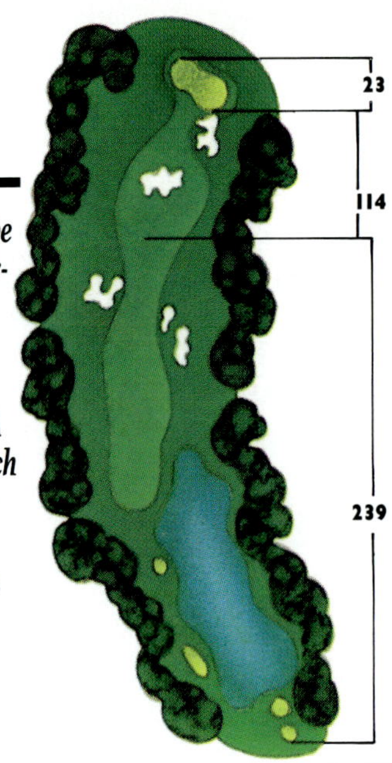

3

Par 3
165 yards

Water presents the biggest hazard — club selection is vital. The green stretches from right to left and slopes from back to front. Strong winds can challenge the tee shot.

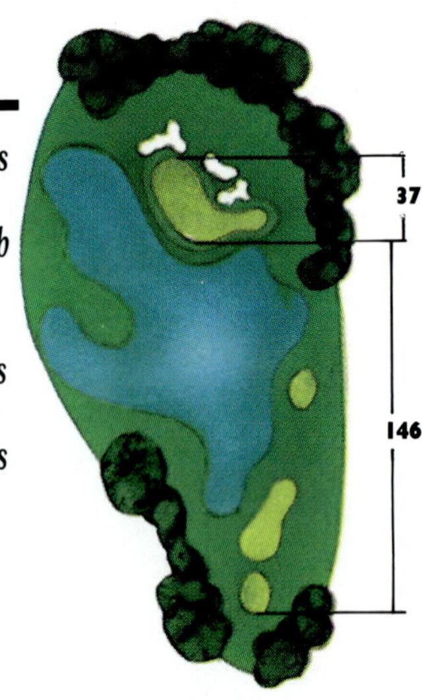

4

Par 4
418 yards

The tee shot should follow the right edge of the fairway. A mid-iron to the green must carry a small bunker just short of the putting surface. The large green provides many long putts.

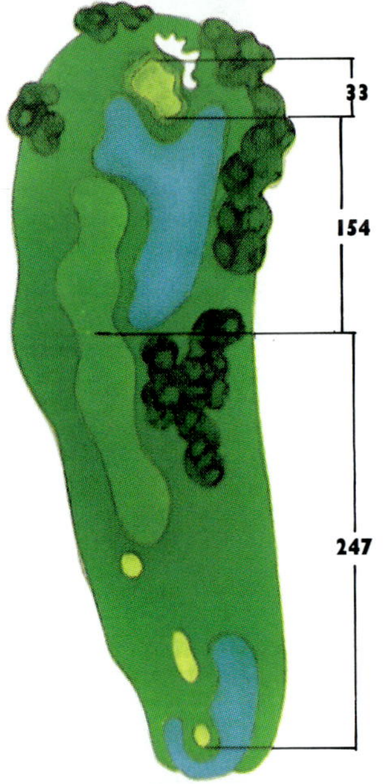

5

Par 4
457 yards

There are no bunkers to be found on this hole–the length and narrowness provide the challenge. Care should be taken on the approach to assure accuracy to this long green.

6

Par 5
557 yards

The favored drive is down the left side of the long, narrow fairway. The second shot is played over the fairway bunker encroaching from the left. The approach should find the pin.

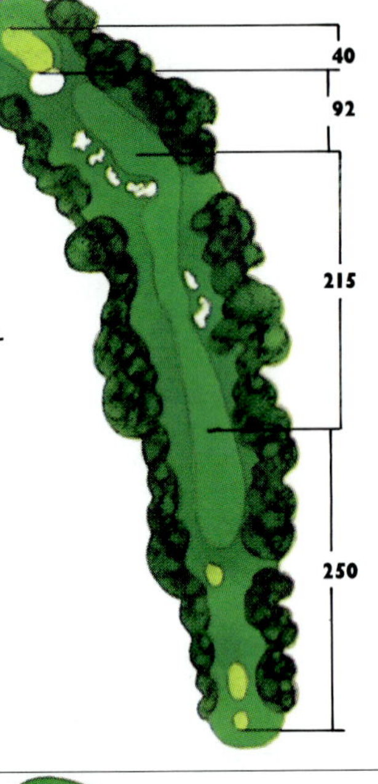

7

Par 4
413 yards

The drive is best played down the right. A 7-9 iron into the green must be accurate to avoid the water to the left and mounding to the right. A difficult approach!

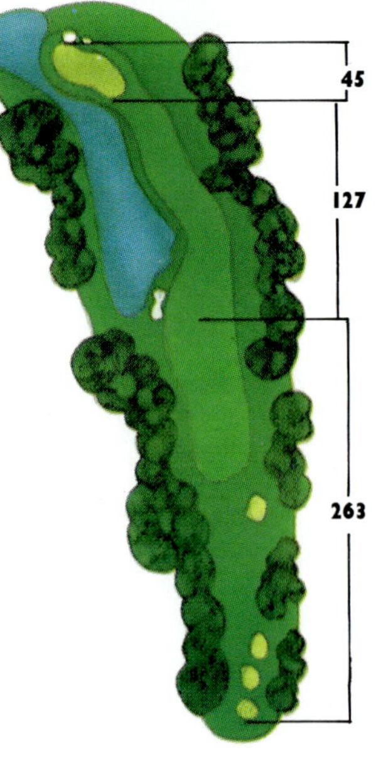

8

Par 3
218 yards

Straight-away seems simple enough. However, the strong winds above the tree line can play havoc with the tee shot. The flat putting surface allows for all putts to be makeable.

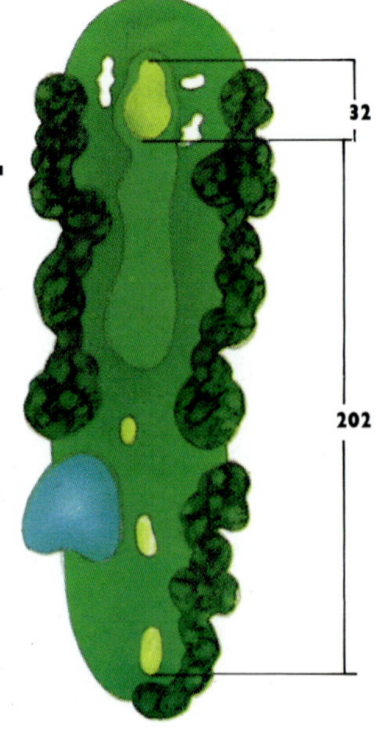

9

Par 4
427 yards

The best angle to the green is from the left side of the fairway. The approach is from an elevated fairway to a lower green. Pin placements left and right rear can cause difficulty.

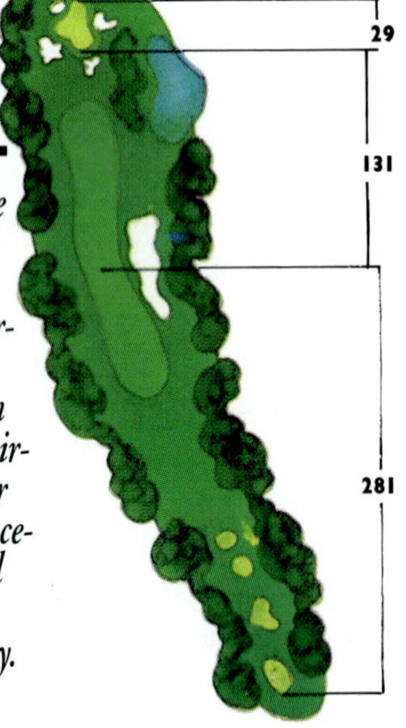

10

Par 4
430 yards

Driving accuracy is put to the test! Four bunkers await the errant tee shot. The kidney shaped green is flat and an easy target.

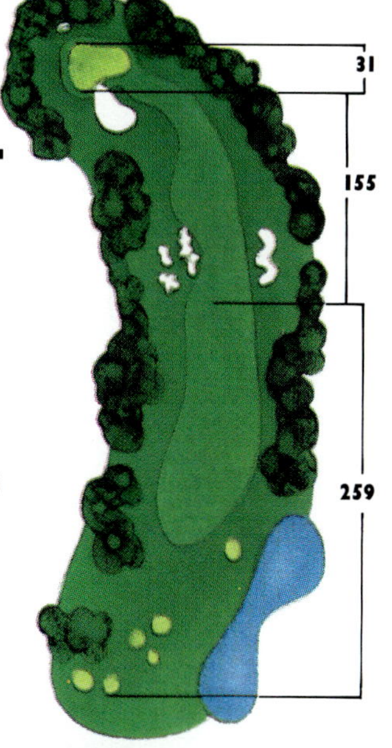

11

Par 4
421 yards

This long straight par 4 has a wide fairway, open for the big drives. A small pot-bunker in front of the green hides the putting surface from view.

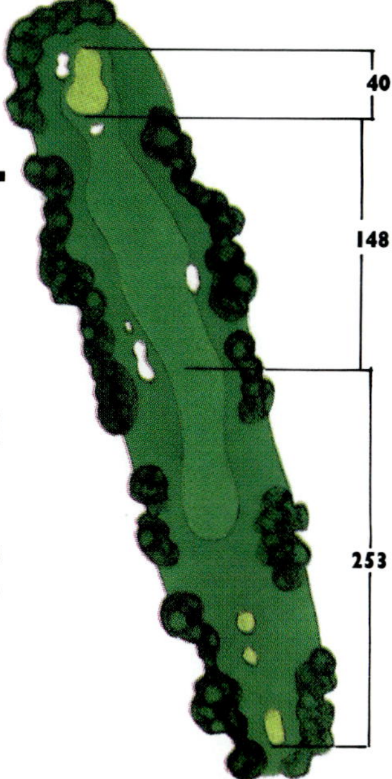

12

Par 4
388 yards

Position is the key on this twelfth. A big drive can carry trees and bunkers on the right but the route is risky. The long twisting green slopes from back to front.

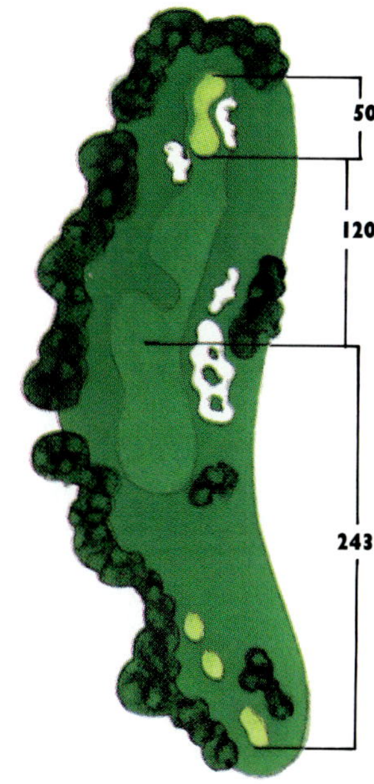

13

Par 5
530 yards

The difficulty level has been turned up a notch. Three shots are recommended to reach this island-like green. Although there is no sand, the water provides a worthy hazard.

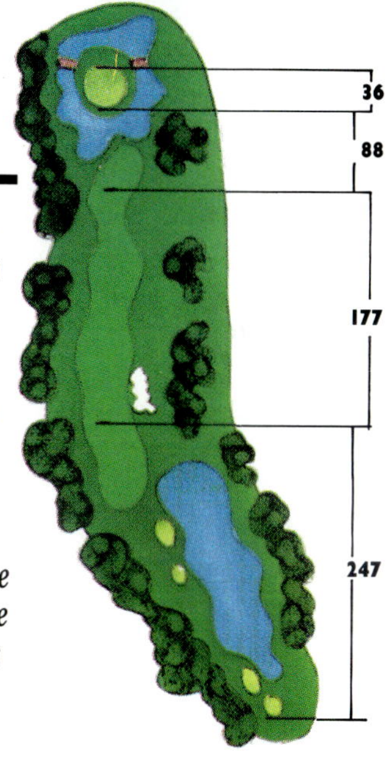

14

Par 3
195 yards

The green is very short and very wide. Length is everything as players will be attempting to hit the ball to the putting surface. The deep bunkers make recovery difficult.

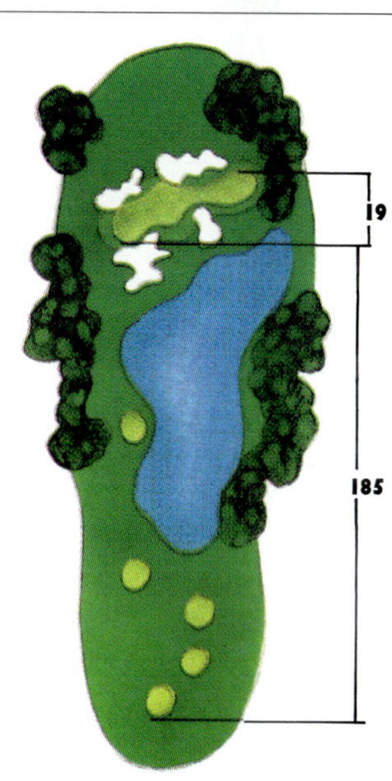

15

Par 5
525 yards

A fading drive down the right side will set up an excellent chance to reach the green in two. The small round green is guarded only by bunkers short and mounding long — look for eagles!

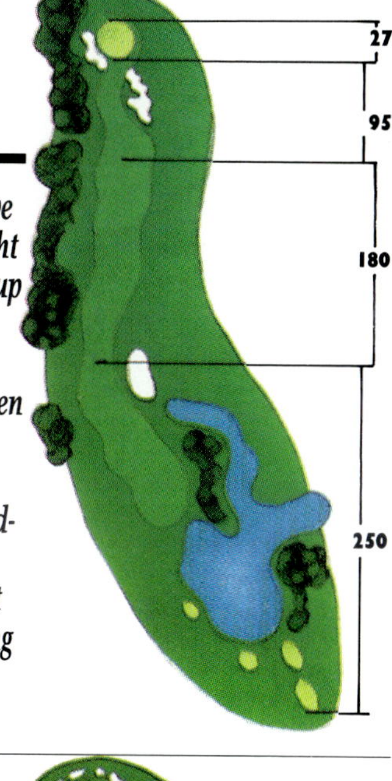

16

Par 3
177 yards

Again, the wind above the tree-line may be the biggest factor on this par 3. The putting surface is settled in between bunkers right and left. Club selection is important to get the ball near the hole.

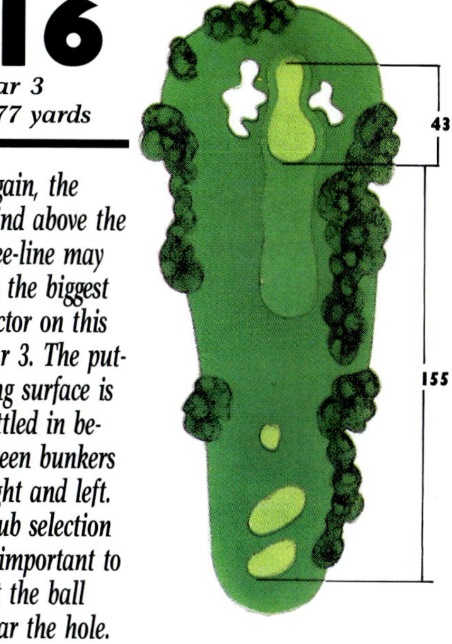

17

Par 4
383 yards

The second shot will most likely have to carry the water here. The short approach is to a short, wide green. Birdies are a must, however bogeys are an unpleasant possibility.

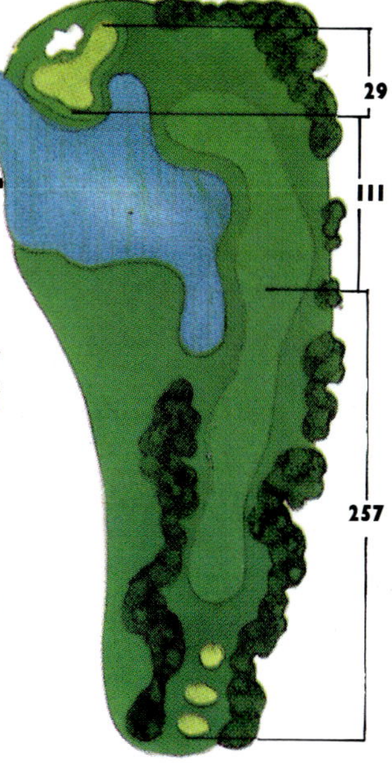

18

Par 4
445 yards

The eighteenth is similar to the 17th only reversed and longer. A fantastic finishing hole that requires length and accuracy to reach the large, stadium-backed putting surface.

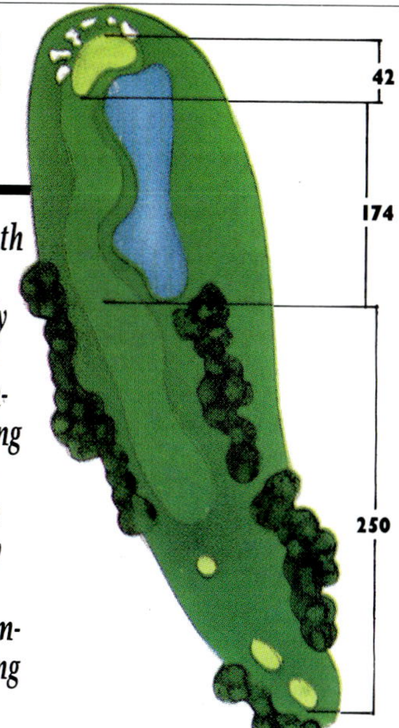

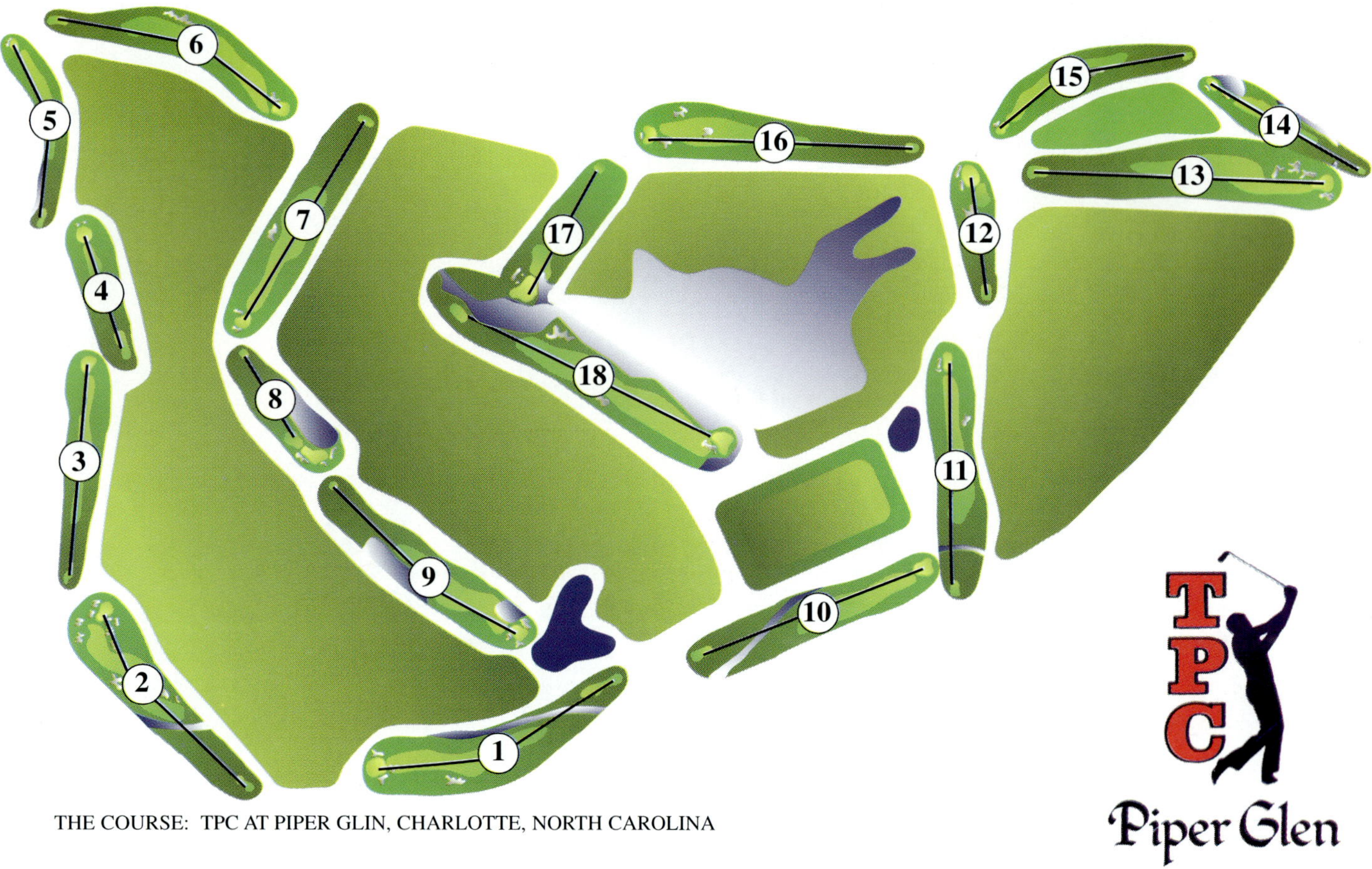

THE COURSE: TPC AT PIPER GLIN, CHARLOTTE, NORTH CAROLINA

*T*he World Senior Invitational created in the early 1980s, was one of the premier events on the SENIOR PGA TOUR. Since its debut it has been held at two different venues. From 1980 to 1989, Charlotte's Quail Hollow Country Club hosted the PaineWebber Invitational. In 1990 the tournament's new venue became the Tournament Players Club at Piper Glen, an Arnold Palmer designed course.

This 6,774 yard, 72 par championship course has since lived up to its concept of "Stadium Golf" with lush Caroline landscape including a spectators choice vantage point on a verdant mound or sweeping amphitheater. All of this providing the ultimate in unrestricted views of the championship competition.

Palmer will compete against the best Senior professional golfers in the world, including defending champion Bob Murphy for the $120,000 first prize at the Palmer-designed TPC course at Piper Glen.

Dates:	May 3-5
Network:	ESPN
Times:	Fri 4:00-6:00 EST
	Sat 4:00-6:00 EST
	Sun 4:00-6:00 EST
Yardage:	6,774
Slope:	72
Rating:	130
Par:	73.2
Total Purse:	$650,000
1st Prize:	$120,000
1995 Winner:	Bob Murphy
1995 Winning Score:	203 (68,66,69)
Principal Charitable Beneficiary:	Various local charities
Ticket Information:	1-704-846-4699

1

Par 4
378 yards

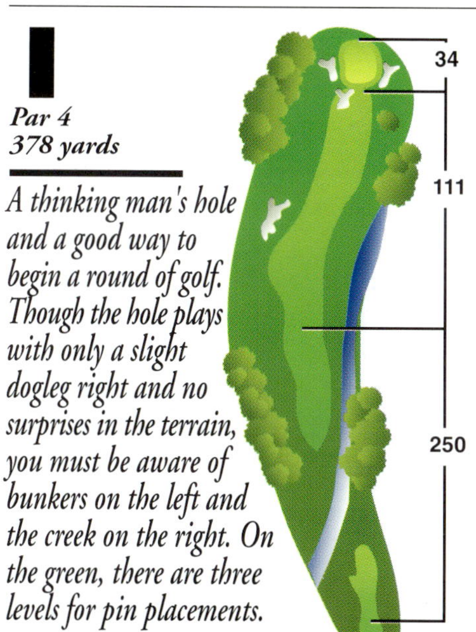

A thinking man's hole and a good way to begin a round of golf. Though the hole plays with only a slight dogleg right and no surprises in the terrain, you must be aware of bunkers on the left and the creek on the right. On the green, there are three levels for pin placements.

2

Par 5
481 yards

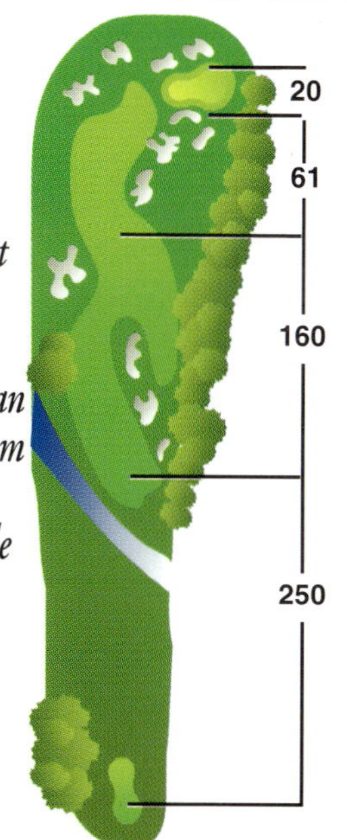

Play it up the right side for a shorter angle to the green, although you also can get there in two from the other landing area on the left side of the fairway.

3

Par 4
415 yards

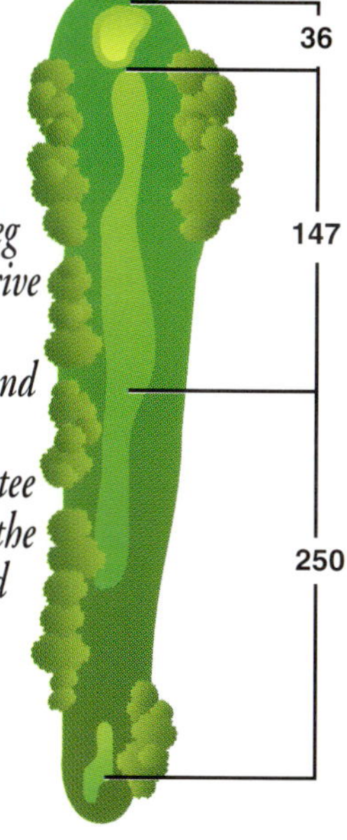

Beware of the dogleg left, because your drive could kick sharply toward the rough and woods. Of you are successful from the tee to the right side of the fairway, the reward will be a downhill second shot to the green.

4

Par 3
189 yards

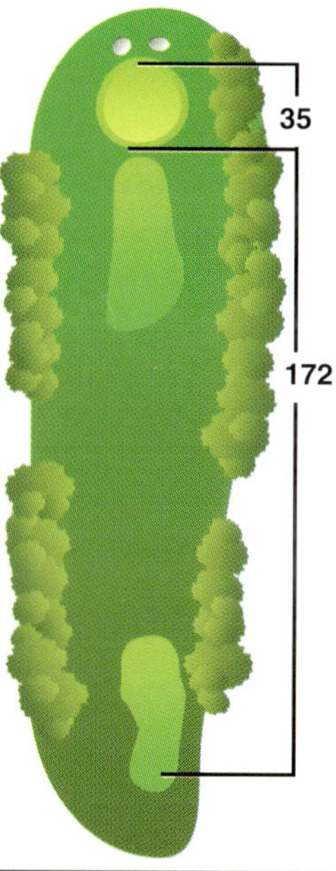

This hole is all pin placement, because of the severely sloping green. The downhill factor makes this one of those devilish par threes that finds most players coming up a half-club off. Adding to that, the bunkers are in the back of the green.

5

Par 4
419 yards

A strong drive and second shot are required on this hole, which bends to the left and sends everything rolling that way. The green sets nicely into the side of the hill.

6

Par 5
529 yards

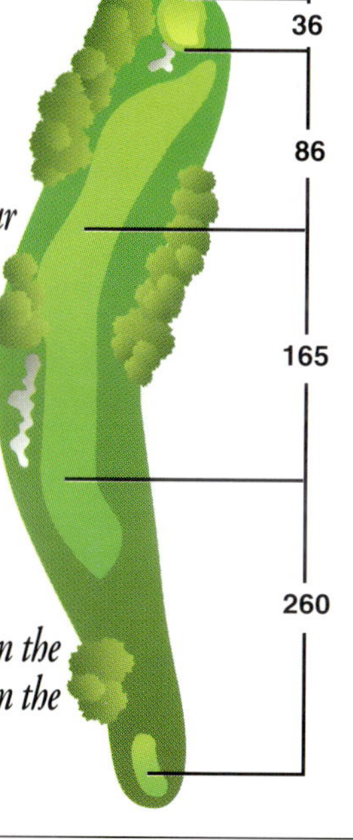

The seniors like the par 5 at Piper Glen, because they're reachable in two. This one can be eagled, but you have to hit long down the narrow fairway. A bonus is that solid contact can put you on the green in two even from the right rough.

7

Par 4
374 yards

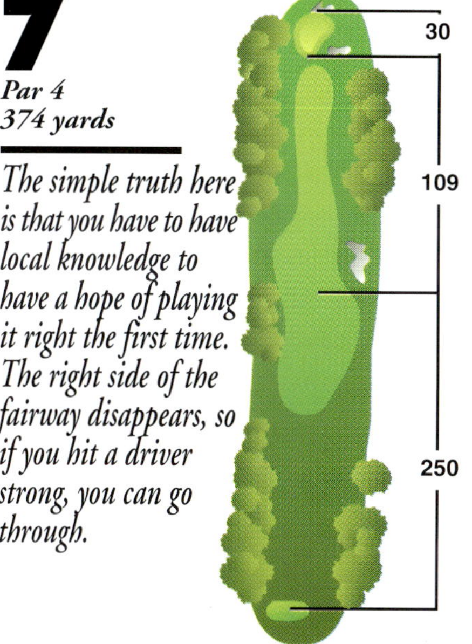

The simple truth here is that you have to have local knowledge to have a hope of playing it right the first time. The right side of the fairway disappears, so if you hit a driver strong, you can go through.

8

Par 3
189 yards

The farther left the pin placement, the more water you must clear, making this a scary hole. But there's nothing over the green, and there's actually more room at the green than it appears from the tee, The hole plays every bit of 189 yards.

9

Par 4
416 yards

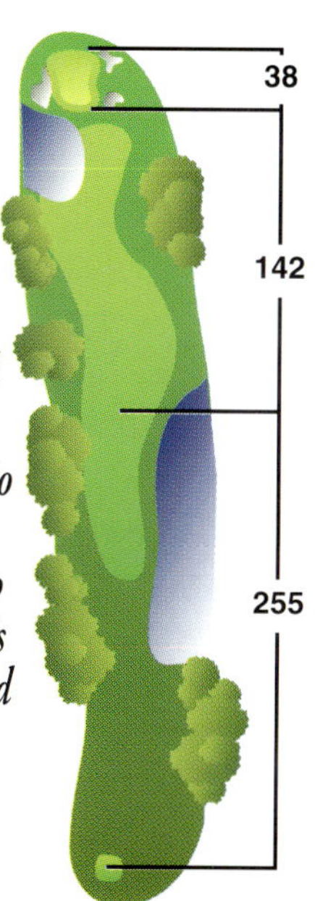

A tough hole to finish the front side. The fairway is narrow, and from the seniors' tee it takes a 240-yard drive to get past the lake on the right. Then you look up and see that the green is three-fourths surrounded by water.

10

Par 4
384 yards

The premium here is the second shot. There's a little bit of an angle as you shoot up the fairway, so you can draw or cut your tee shot. Another diagonally sloped green makes it difficult to get your approach close.

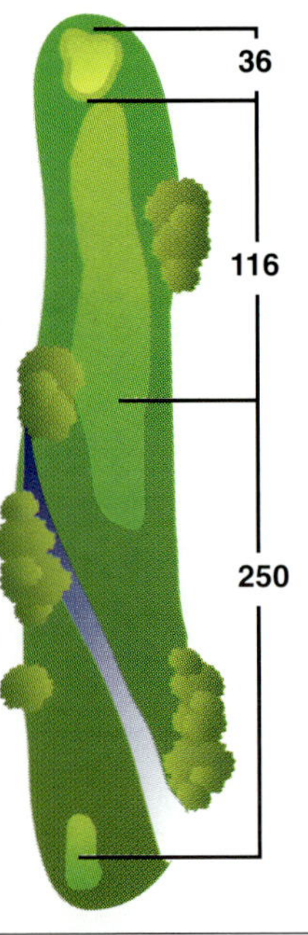

11

Par 4
425 yards

Off the tee, take into consideration the tree to the right of the green. Favor the left-center of the fairway so you're not blocked from the green on your second shot. You have to know exact yardage because of the extreme two-tier elivation on the green.

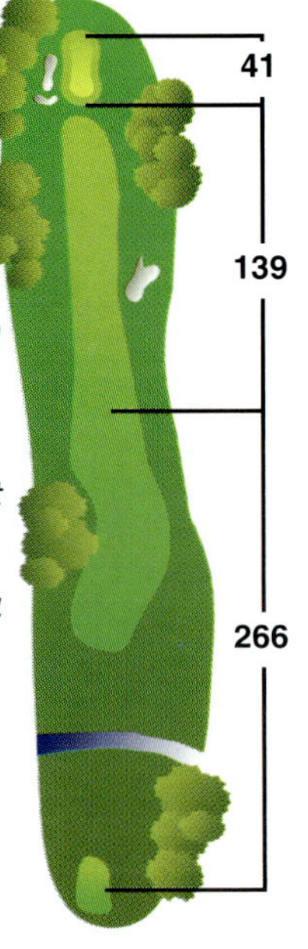

12

Par 3
183 yards

Figure to take about a club less for your tee shot because the hole is downhill on another diagonally sloped green. A neat little par 3 that Arnold Palmer aced during the 1990 PaineWebber Invitational.

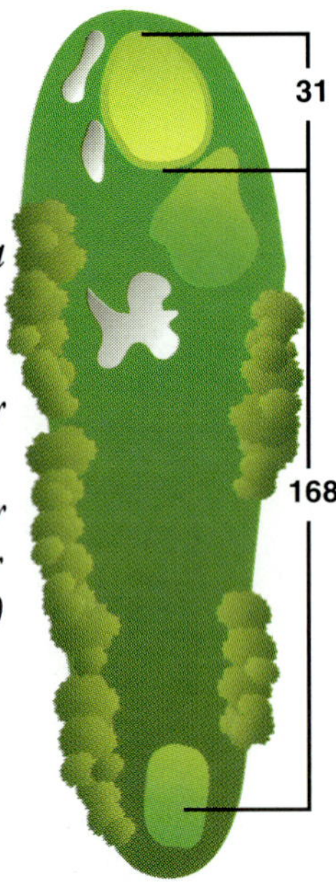

13

Par 4
436 yards

The temptation off the tee is to go right, but you must stay much further left than it looks to avoid some heavy rough. Don't be put off by the four bunkers to the left; only one comes into play. This green also has a diagonal cut.

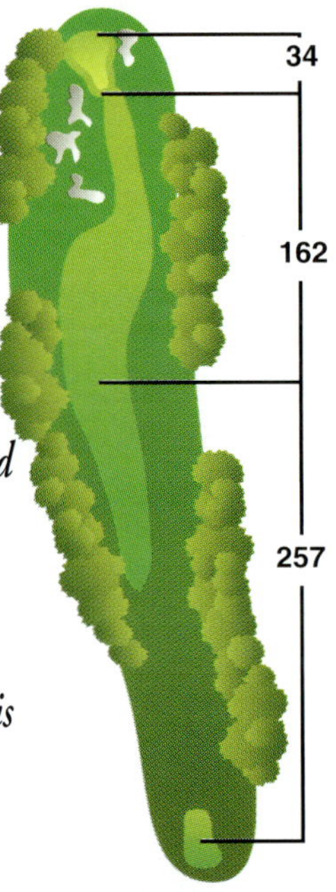

14

Par 4
389 yards

This is the most exacting hole on the course. Everything that lands in the right half of the fairway will kick toward the creek. Then, the small green with water on the right requires a delicate approach.

15

Par 4
410 yards

This hole plays just as it looks-until you get to the green, which has some real subtleties. Try to drive as close to the left-hand bunkers as possible to cut off some of the dogleg. The longer seniors will be able to fly the bunkers.

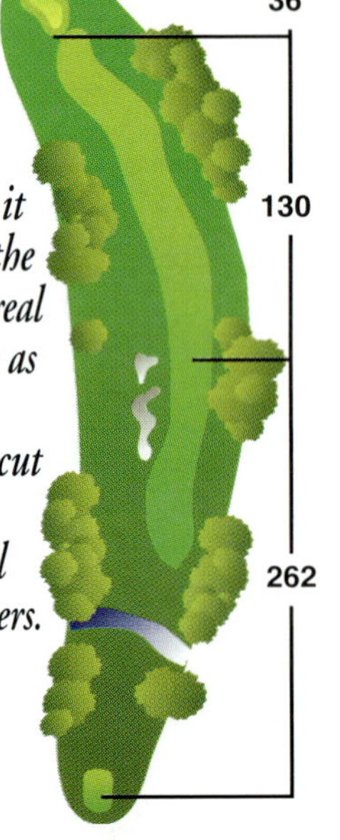

16

Par 5
501 yards

Another par 5 that can be reached in two, and, like No. 18, it favors a player who draws the ball. There's a menacing bunker on the left of the fairway that is about 20 feet below the level of the green. Stay out-you can't even see the pin down there.

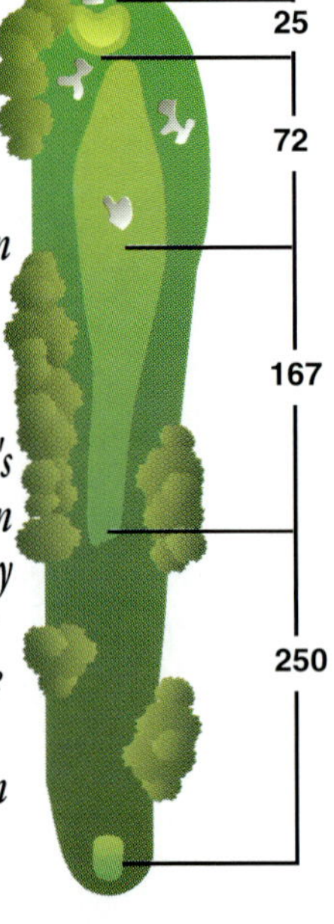

17

Par 3
142 yards

All three sets of back tees might be used. The right-side tee brings the bunker on the right into play more than the lake on the left, behind the green. The tendency is to come up short, but the seniors will play the hole one time and figure it out.

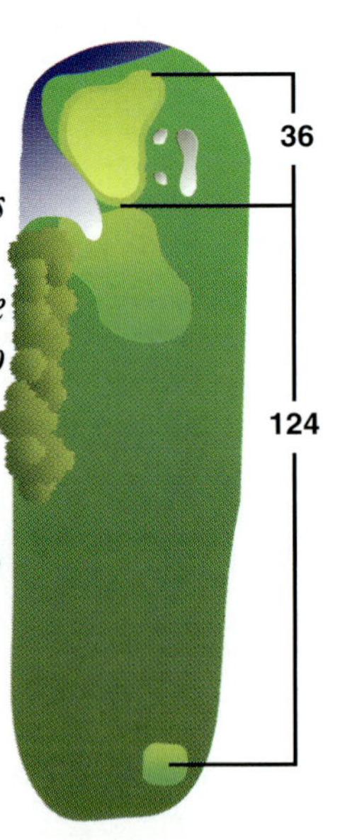

18

Par 5
514 yards

Don't be fooled: it's not as far across the water as it looks. There's also no need to try to cut the corner from the tee. Hit your second shot as far down the right side as you can. The tournament likely will be won at No. 16, 17 and 18.

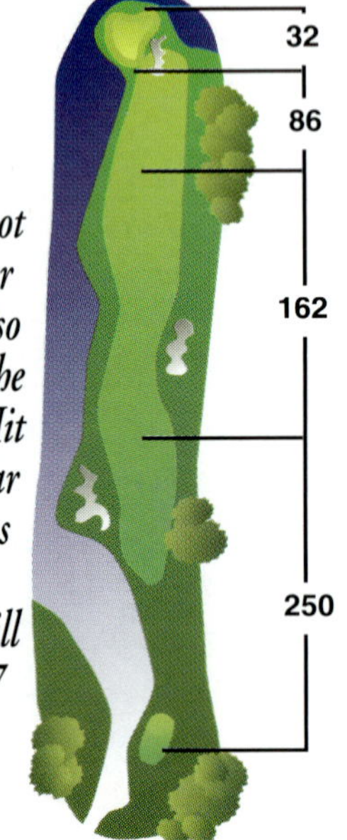

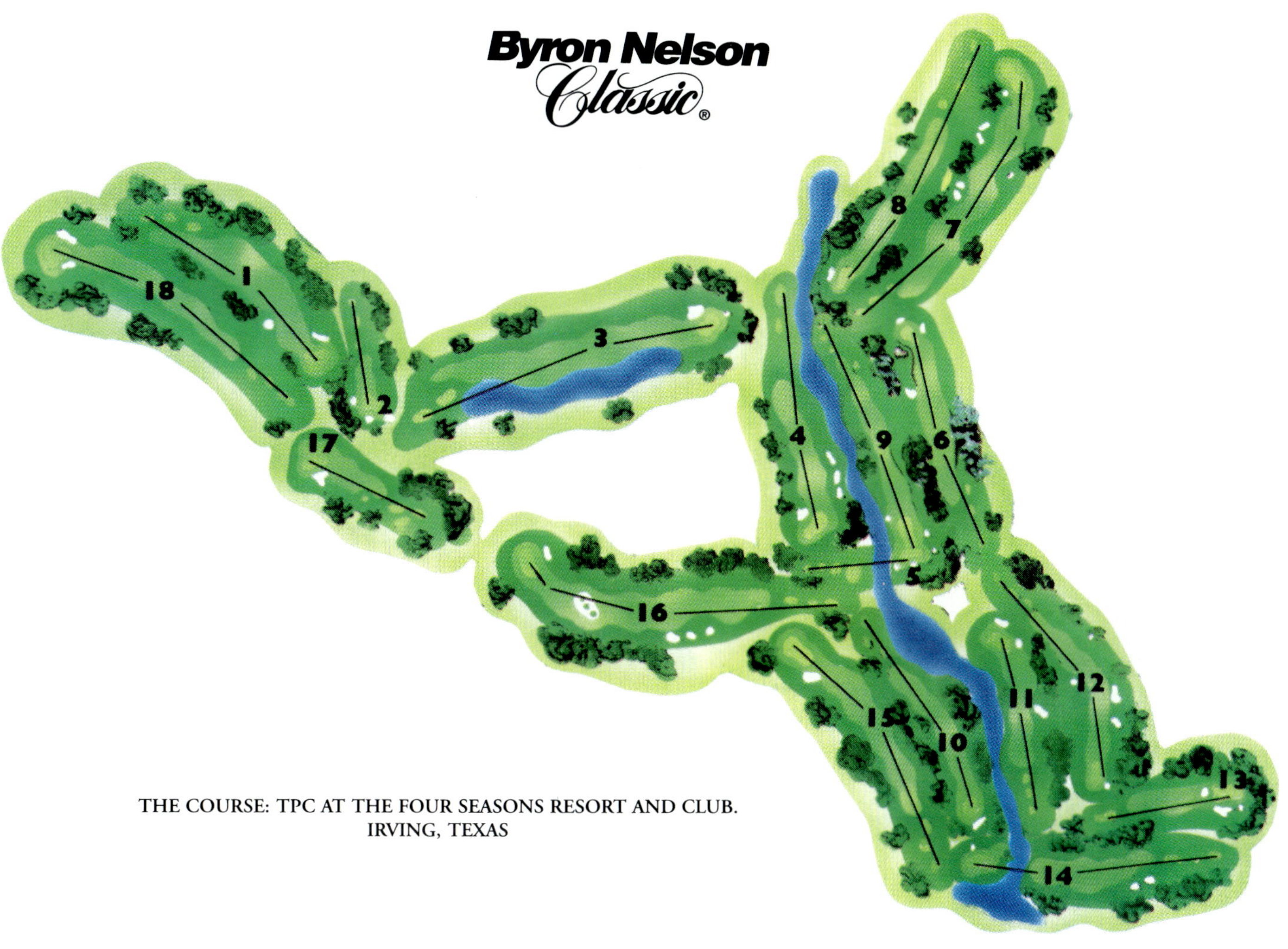

THE COURSE: TPC AT THE FOUR SEASONS RESORT AND CLUB.
IRVING, TEXAS

*L*ord Byron, as he is distinctly recognized, holds claim to a record that no one else has come close to matching - winning a total of eleven consecutive tournaments in 1945. In 1940, Nelson won his first PGA Championship in an extraordinary fashion. At one point in the playoff against Slammin' Sam Snead, Nelson was faced with a stymie that completely blocked his putt to the cup. His solution was to pull out his wedge and bounce the ball perfectly over Snead's and into the hole!. The Byron Nelson Classic is a tribute paid in honor of Nelson's successes on the TOUR and his many contributions to the game of golf.

The Tournament Players Course at the Four Seasons Resort and Club at Las Colinas has been the site of the Classic since 1983. In 1984, the Las Colinas course was resculptured into the seventh TPC by architect Jay Morrish. Morrish was aided with the help and consultation of Ben Crenshaw and Byron Nelson.

Dates:	May 9-12, 1996
Network:	ABC
Times:	Sat 2:30-4:30 EST
	Sun 4:00-6:00 EST
Yardage:	6,826
Par:	70
Slope:	133
Rating:	73.6
Total Purse:	$1,300,000
1st Prize:	$234,000
1995 Winner:	Ernie Els
1995 Winning Score:	263 (69,61,65,68)
Principal Charitable Beneficiary:	Salesmanship Club of Dallas
Charitable Benefits to Date:	Over $30.2 million since 1973
Ticket Information:	1-214-742-3896

1

Par 4
385 yards

A fairway wood or long-iron is the choice of the players to place the drive in perfect position for the approach. The opening birdie is there to be had on this short par 4.

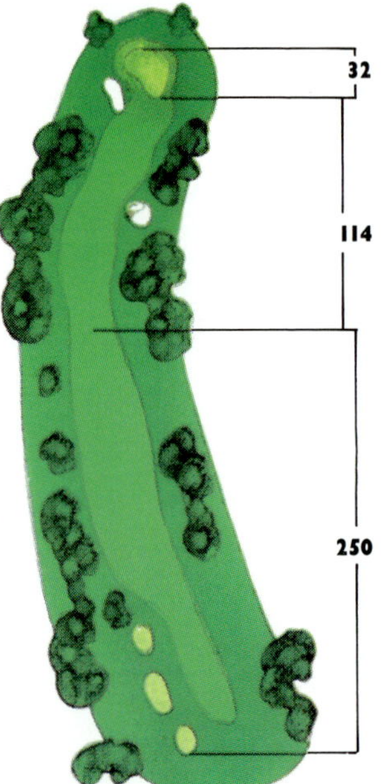

2

Par 3
176 yards

The rolling undulating putting surface will make 3's difficult. Players will be using mid-irons from the tee. The back left pin placement is tough to get to.

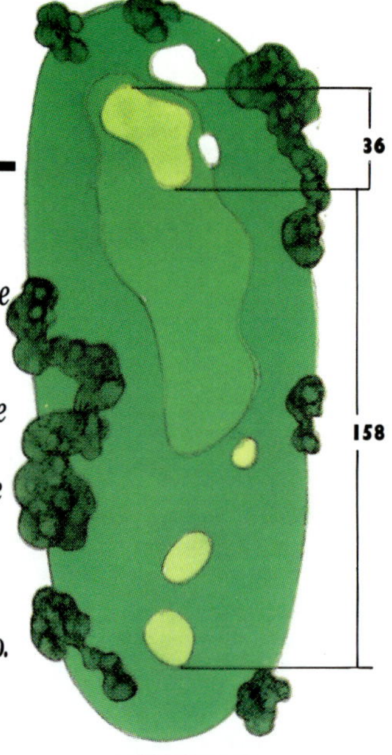

3

Par 4
474 yards

Usually down-wind, this par 4 requires control from the tee. The approach is to a two-tiered green — pars are a welcome score on this hole.

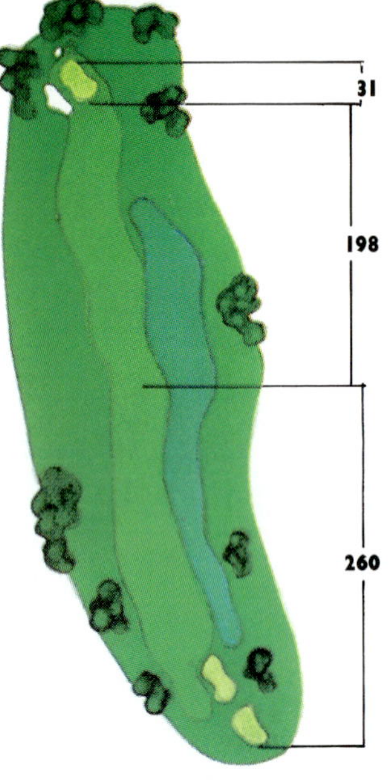

4

Par 4
423 yards

The demands of the tee shot are getting tougher — water left and out-of-bounds to the right make this a very narrow driving hole. Winds right to left can add to the difficulty.

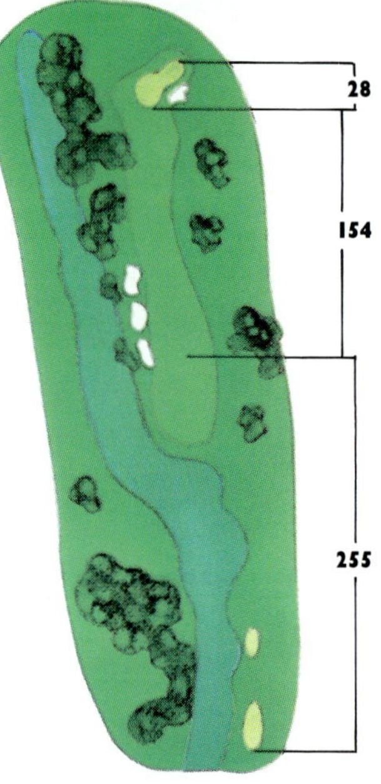

5

Par 3
174 yards

With the wind at their backs, the players should have no problem getting the ball to the green. The only problem is to stop it on the short putting surface.

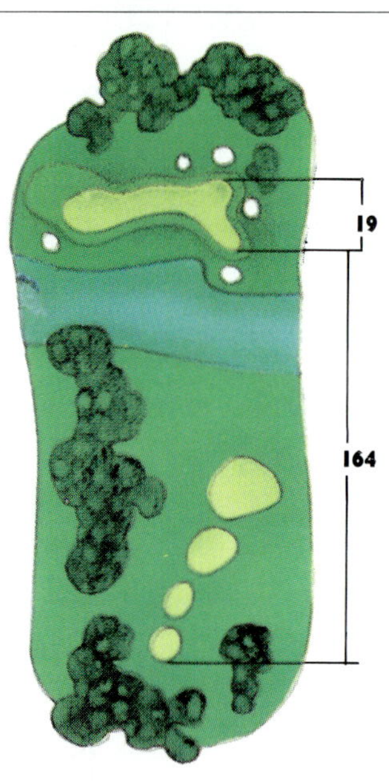

6

Par 4
396 yards

From the tee, the view to the fairway is through a narrow chute of trees — a tough driving hole. The small green is hard and fast.

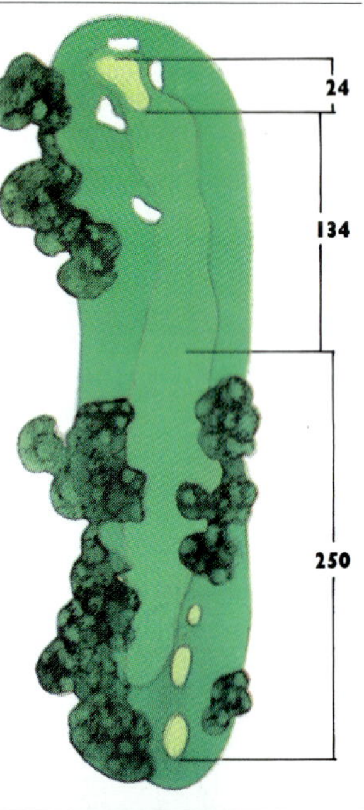

7

Par 5
533 yards

Bunkers define the landing area for the driver. Very few will reach this green in two — three shots is the norm. The green slopes quickly from back to front. Below the hole is a must for a makeable putt.

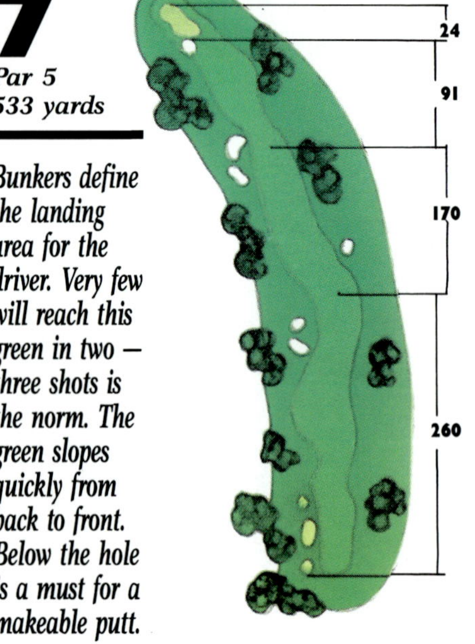

8

Par 4
451 yards

The slight dogleg may cause problems for those who leave their drive off to the right. The contoured green can also be tricky — players must simply hit their second shot accurately.

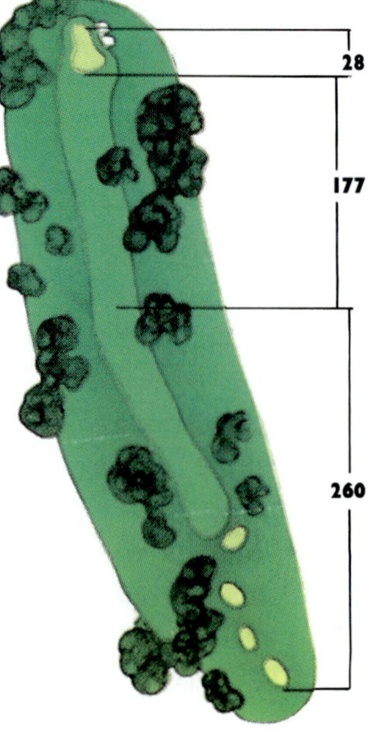

9

Par 4
447 yards

Clearly, the water along the right may present a bit of intimidation. A fairway wood or long-iron will be the safe play in order to achieve an honest par 4.

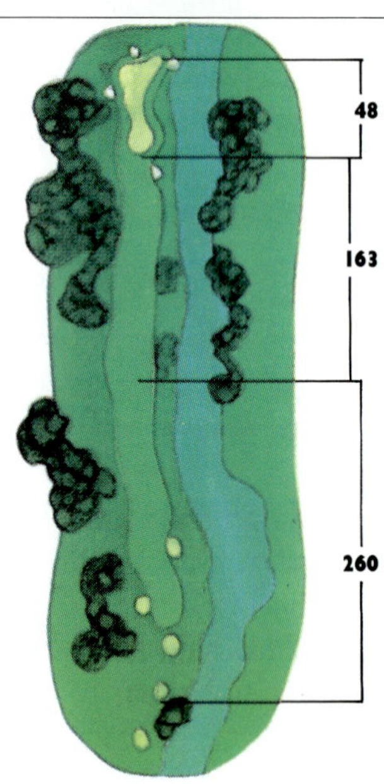

10
Par 4
447 yards

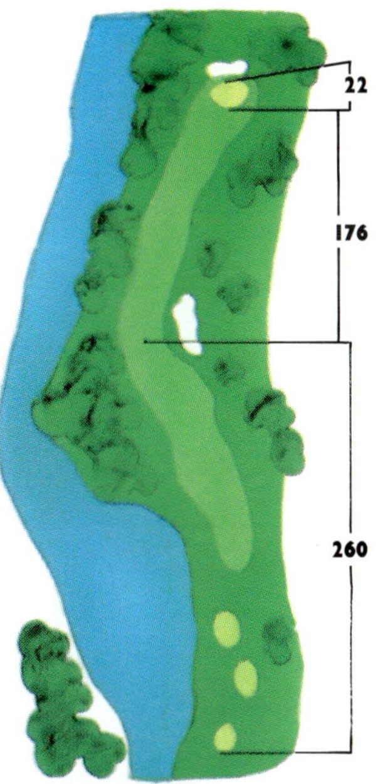

A long drive must pass the corner and leave a short iron into the green in order for a biting approach that will be able to stop on the shallow putting surface.

11
Par 4
331 yards

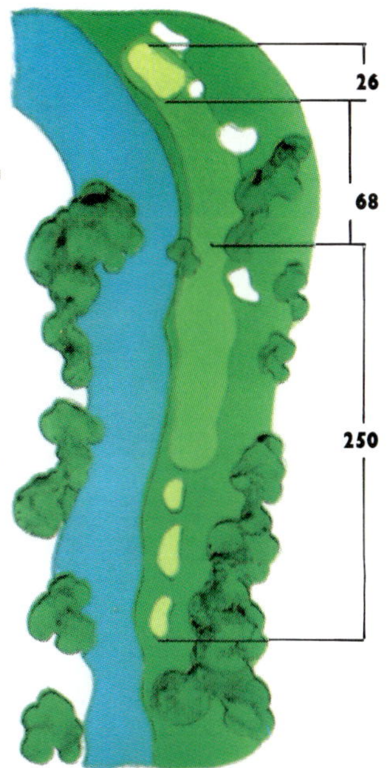

Birdies are there for the taking but the bogeys and "others" loom about. A 2 or 3-iron from the tee should place the ball about 100 yards from the pin.

12
Par 4
426 yards

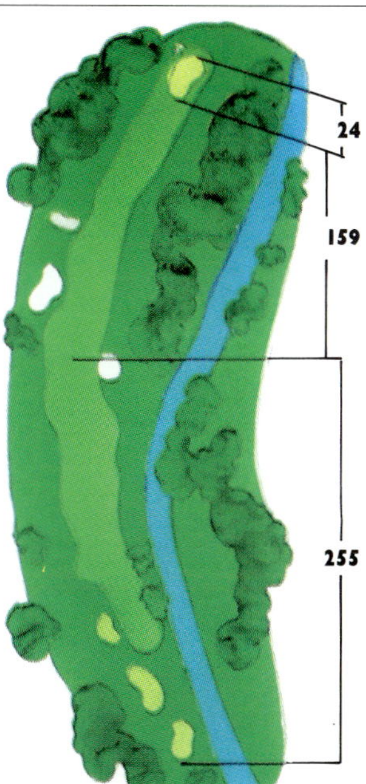

The first bunker along the left side of the fairway is the target from the tee. An approach to the green should remain short of the hole, leaving an uphill putt to the cup.

13
Par 3
183 yards

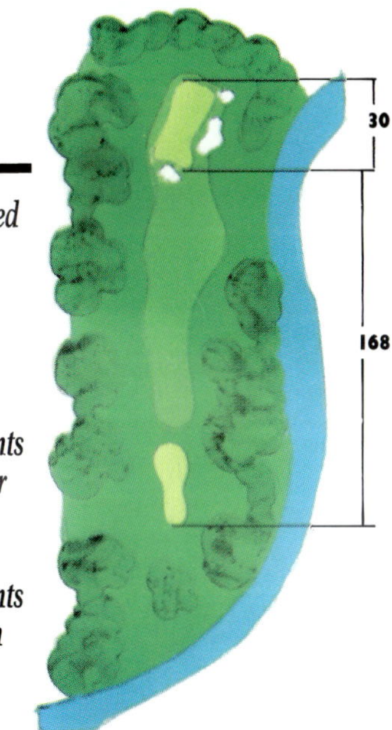

The two-tiered green has a lower level front and upper level back. Front pin-placements will be easier while the upper back pin-placements can be tough to negotiate.

14
Par 4
410 yards

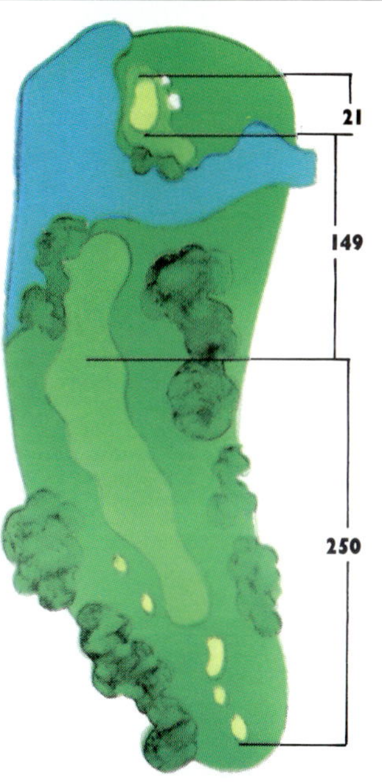

A large mound in the middle of the fairway can direct a good drive into the rough. The approach over the water is to a very small green — players will be happy with the par.

15
Par 4
445 yards

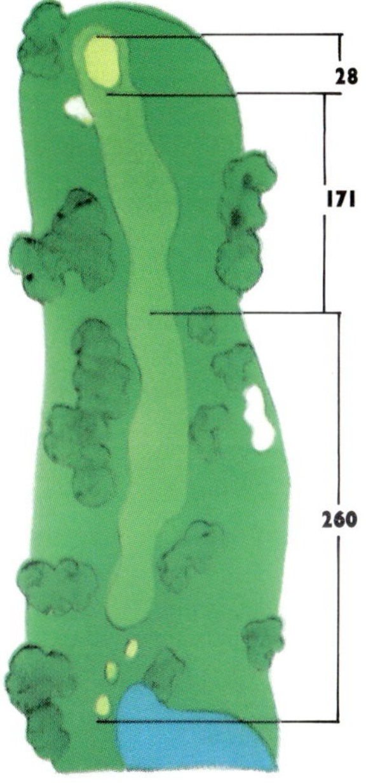

A long hole! A powerful drive down the center will still leave a long-iron to the green. Note that there are no bunkers around the putting surface.

16
Par 5
554 yards

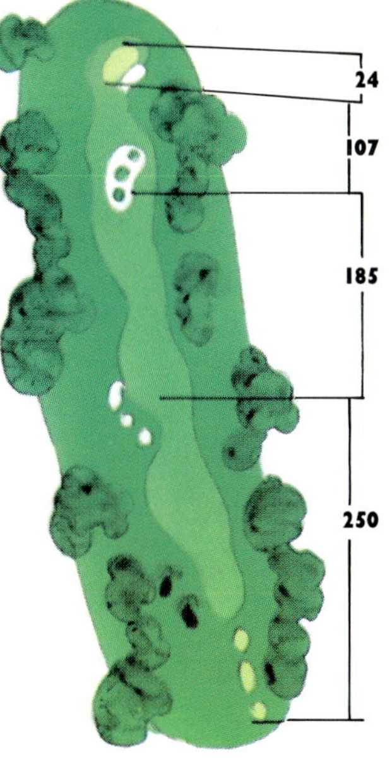

Bunkers along the right dictate for the right side of the fairway to be favored. Second shot must avoid bunkers that are placed in the center of the short grass.

17
Par 3
217 yards

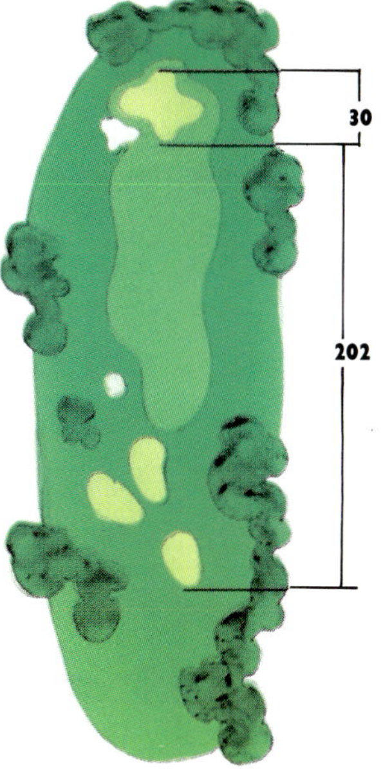

Into the wind, this seventeenth can play very long — especially if a birdie is needed! Clover-leaf shaped green provides for difficult putting.

18
Par 4
415 yards

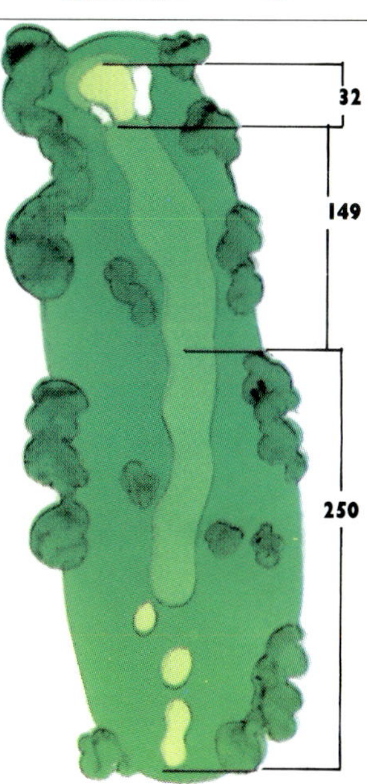

Down to the last hole! With the championship on the line, players will be going after their drives on the open fairway. Birdies will finish the day with style.

The 1996 Nationwide Championship moves to the Lakeside Course at The Golf Club of Georgia. The Lakeside Course features traditional design elements in a manicured, park-like setting. The Lakeside Course was honored as the Best New Private Course in the United States for 1991 by Golf Digest magazine. The 1991-1994 events were held at The Country Club of the South in Alpharetta, GA. As the 1995 champion, Bob Murphy won the first prize winnings of $180,000 and his place among an elite group of champions: Mike Hill, Isao Aoki, and Lee Trevino.

Dates:	May10-12, 1996	
Network:	ESPN	
Times:	Fri	5:00-7:00 EST
	Sat	4:30-6:30 EST
	Sun	4:30-7:00 EST
Yardage:	6660	
Par:	72	
Slope:	137	
Rating:	71.9	
Total Purse:	$1,000,000	
1st Prize:	$180,000	
1995 Winner:	Bob Murphy	
1995 Winning Score:	203 (71,64,68)	
Principle Charitable Beneficiary:	Various Local Charities	

1

*Par 5
528 yards*

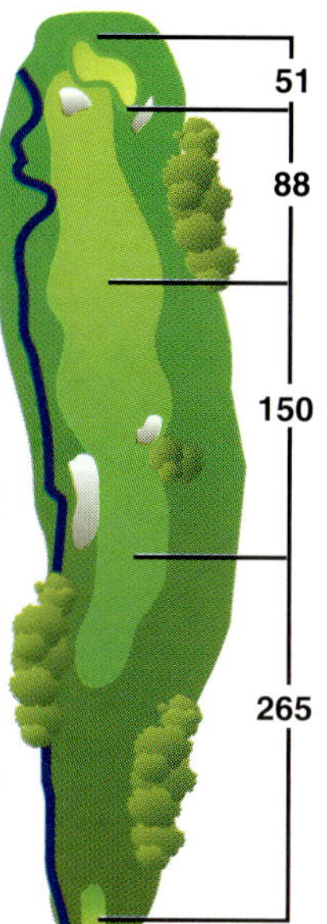

On this par 5, play your drive toward the left edge of the right fairway bunker. Avoid going too far left because the fairway quickly slopes toward the creek. Your second shot should be a fairway wood or a long iron that sets up a wedge shot into this dramatically sloped, two-level green.

2

*Par 4
328 yards*

That fairway sand bunker you see from the tee is a signature Arthur Hills feature of both Golf Club of Georgia courses. The best tee shot is one that lands in front of the immediate sand bunker or to the right of the bunker. This smart strategy leaves a short iron to a round, moderately flat green.

3

*Par 3
167 yards*

Focus on placing your tee shot as close to the pin as possible. The curved portion of the front edge of the green slopes off severely. The rest of the green, however, is fairly flat, but fast and tricky, too.

4

*Par 4
342 yards*

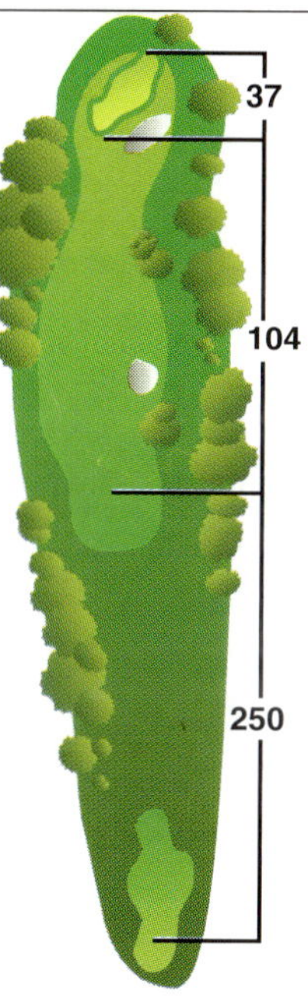

Play your tee shot to the left of the sand bunker or just short of the bunker. From there it's a short iron to the green. And just like the majority of Lakeside greens, it's important here to place your approach shot as close to the pin as possible. This green is large, but very often presents some tremendously challenging putts.

5

*Par 4
383 yards*

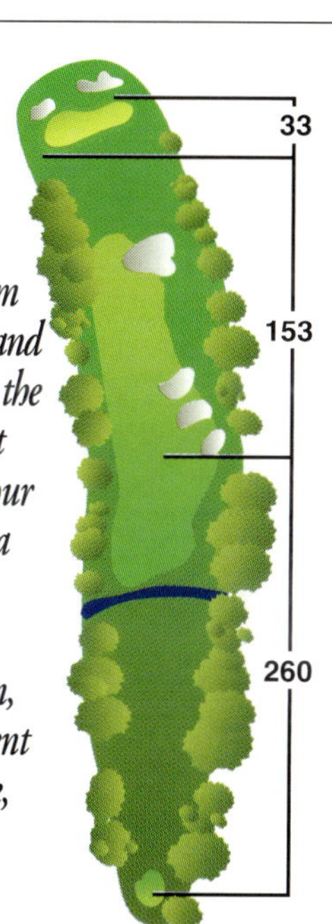

A big driving hole. Aim your tee shot at the far sand bunker and away from the bunkering on the right edge of the fairway. Your approach shot will be a short to mid iron depending on the pin placement. Once again, approach shot placement is critical on this quick, two-level green.

6

*Par 3
198 yards*

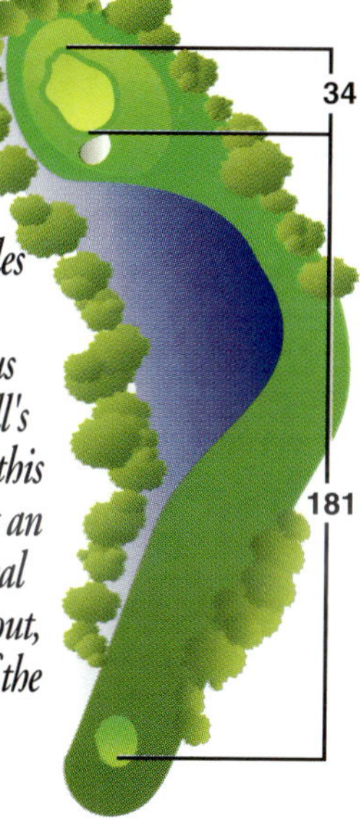

This is one of the prettiest par three holes in the world. The beautiful but ominous pond and Arthur Hill's minimalist design of this hole, however, present an enormous psychological challenge. If you bail out, bail out to the right of the small sand bunker.

7

*Par 4
399 yards*

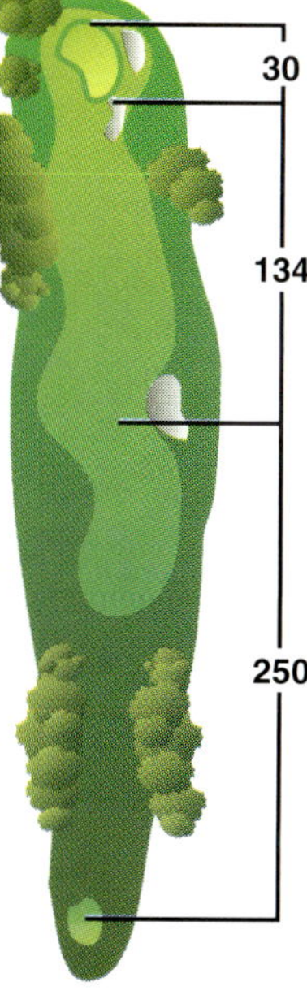

A driving hole, aim your shot right over the right edge of the zoysia grass rough. An accurate approach shot is important because this is one of the smallest greens on the course and it contains some especially tricky spots, particularly on the back side of the green.

8

*Par 4
342 yards*

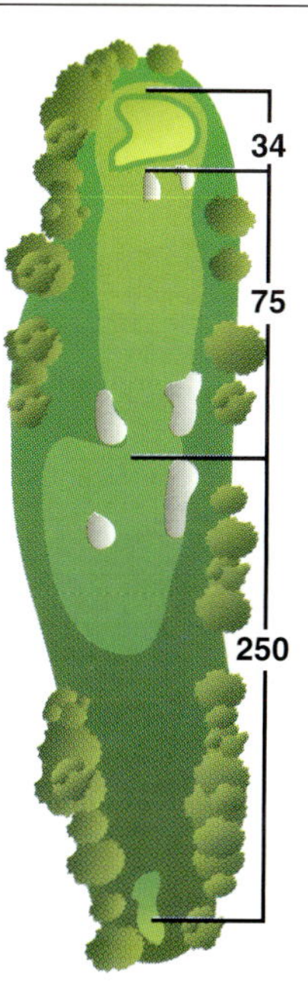

On this hole, take the bunkers out of play by choosing a fairway wood or long iron and aiming up the right-center of the fairway. A high, softly landing approach shot to the green is recommended. Keep in mind, from the fairway the green is slightly farther away than it looks.

9

*Par 5
517 yards*

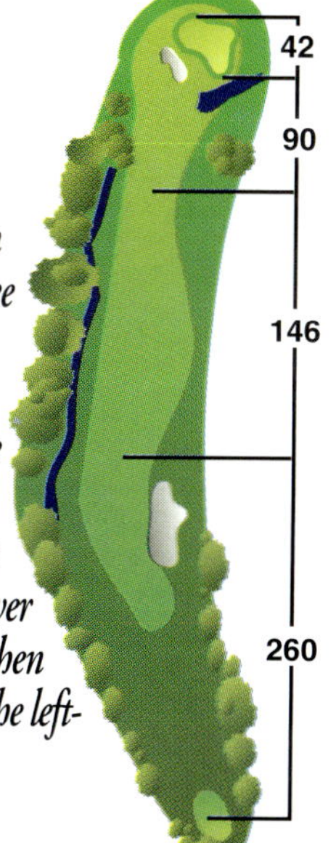

It's tempting here to shorten the hole by playing a long tee shot over the sand bunker. However, get caught in the sand bunker or down in the rough on the right side and your second shot is suddenly blind-and-long. Drive just over the left edge of the bunker, then play your second shot down the left-center of the fairway.

10

Par 4
427 yards

This is a hefty par four that requires a long, left-to-right drive. The two long sand bunkers on the right easily capture weak shots. From the hill, strike a fairway wood or a long iron to a fast green that slopes from the back down to the front.

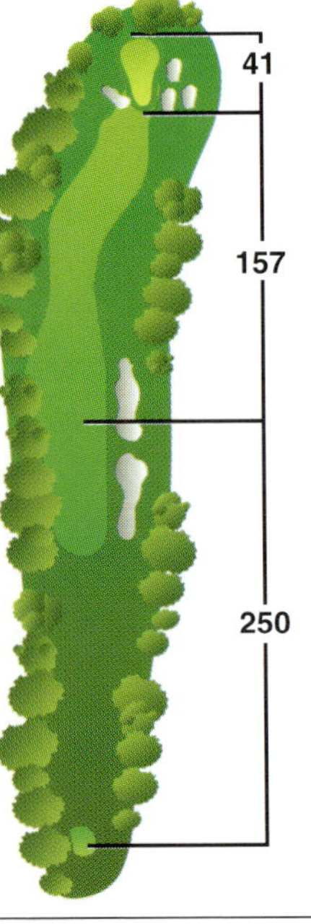

11

Par 5
587 yards

Par or better on this hole requires three strategic shots. Avoid the deep, rough-filled slopes on the left by driving your tee shot far down the right side of the fairway toward the lone box elder. Using a fairway wood or a long iron, place a long set-up shot down the right side of the fairway just to the left of the three sand bunkers. From there, it's a short iron into a big, round, two-level green.

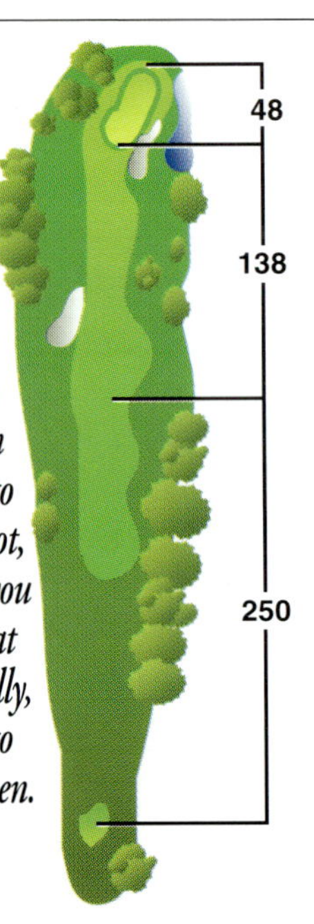

12

Par 4
345 yards

This is a short par 4. A driver, fairway wood, or even a long iron off the tee to the left-center portion of the fairway sets up a wedge or short iron approach. Every inch of this two-level green is quick, so appproach shots placed near the pin are certainly recommended.

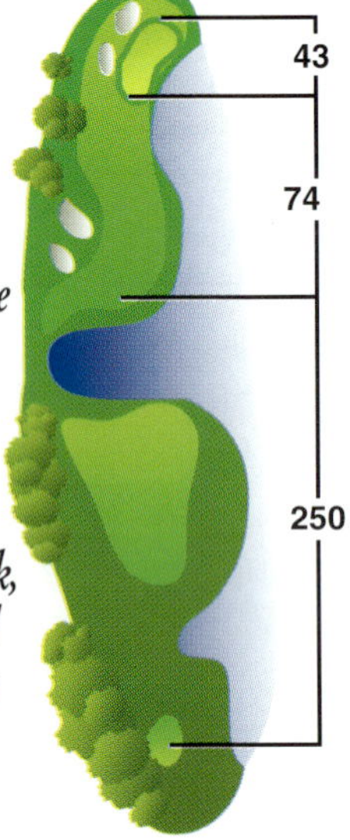

13

Par 3
174 yards

This par 3 rewards accurate tee shots. The green features a mound in the back, middle portion of the landing pad-unseen from the tee-which quickly redirects putts made across it. Confidently fire your shot right to the pin.

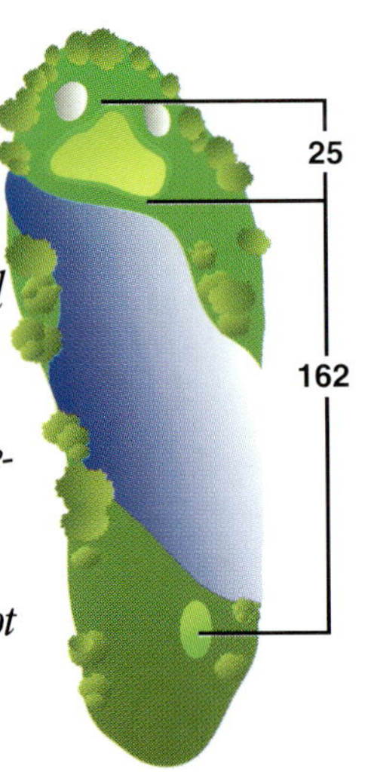

14

Par 4
407 yards

The oak tree at the far, left edge of the fairway requires you to drive to the right-center portion of the fairway. A mid to short iron approach shot, depending on whether you challenge a fairway that slopes away dramatically, should be struck solid to reach this two-level green.

15

Par 4
376 yards

This hole sets up a mid to short iron approach. The flattest green on the Lakeside course is bordered on the left by a small sand bunker that, despite its size, performs an efficient job of seizing high, drifting approach shots.

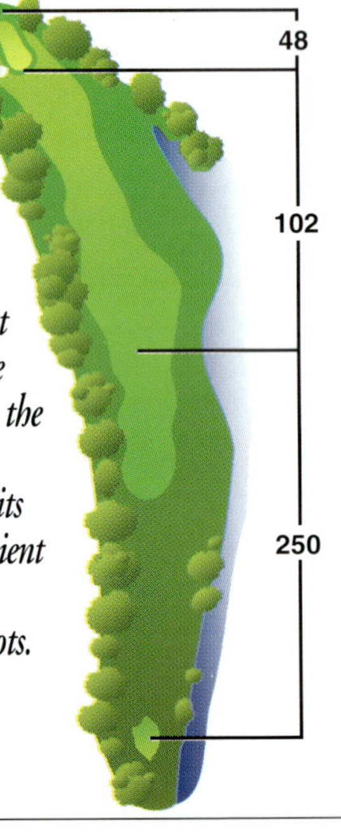

16

Par 4
408 yards

This long, uphill par 4 requires the same strategy required on hole number 11: brute distance. Driver is recommended off the tee and a fairway wood or long iron for the uphill attack. This is a two-level green, but the two portions are relatively flat. A large flat bail out area is provided to the right of the green.

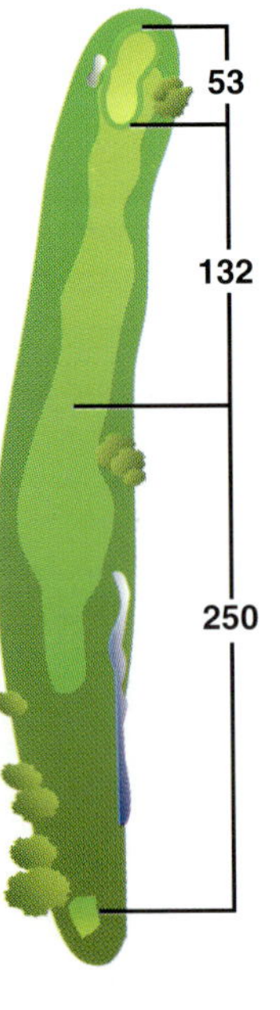

17

Par 3
199 yards

A back, left pin placement requires a accurate long iron or fairway wood shot over the pond. A pin placement at the front of the green simplifies the hole significantly. This green is also heavily undulated, fast, and contains a number of tricky spots.

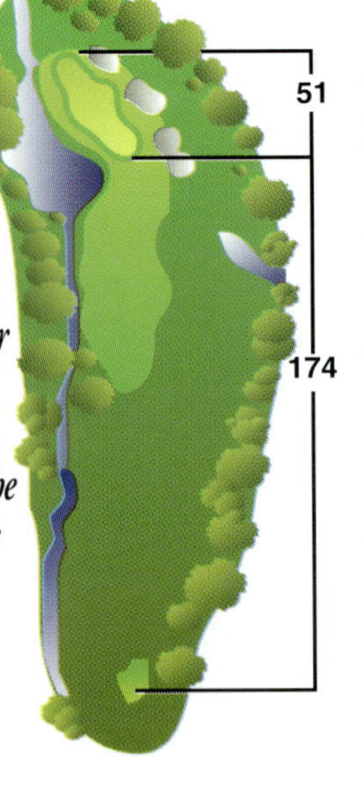

18

Par 5
533 yards

This big hole requires a booming drive from the wooded chute. With a long or mid iron, place your second shot in front of the greenside pond, then a wedge or short iron is needed for the small, hilly green. Attempt to place your approach shot as close to the pin as possible. More often than not, weak shots that bounce around in the rough roll into the pond.

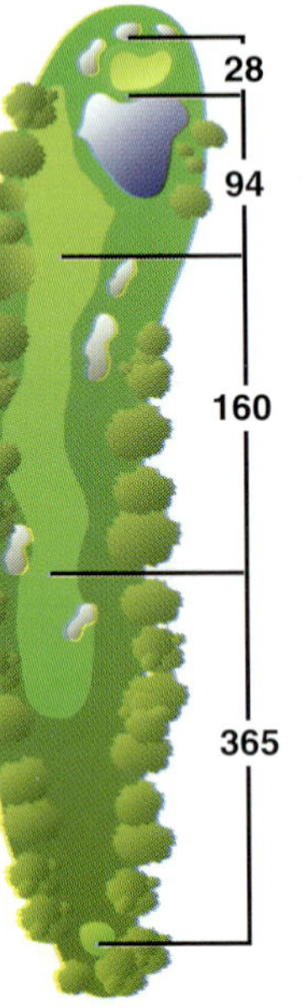

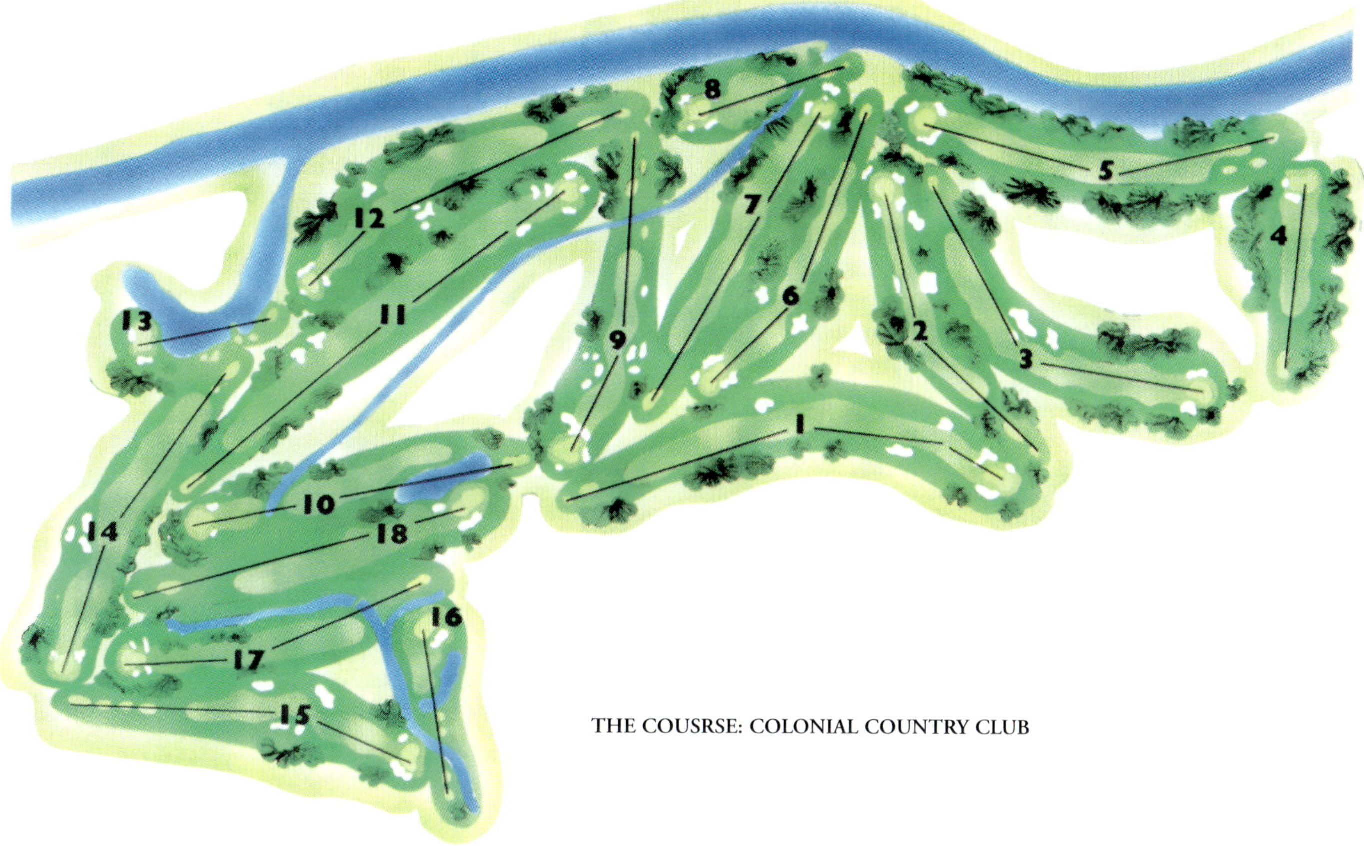

THE COUSRSE: COLONIAL COUNTRY CLUB

*I*n 1941, Colonial Country Club founder Marvin Leonard attracted the U.S. Open Championship to this beautiful Fort Worth, Texas site. Since then, the Colonial has hosted the 1975 Tournament Players Championship; the 1991 U.S. Women's Open Championship, and the longest continuously held PGA TOUR® tournament on the same golf course. No other club in America boasts the same impressive record. Colonial is consistently recognized as one of the top 50 golf courses in the world; in America's top 30 and the No. 1 course in Texas.

Home of the great Ben Hogan (who won the tournament in 1946, '47, '52, '53, and '59), the course itself has earned the nickname " Hogan's Alley", its clubhouse displays the golf legend's multitude of trophies and honors. Other Colonial Champions include Sam Snead (1950), Roberto DeVicenzo (1957), Julius Boros (1960 & '63), Arnold Palmer (1962), Billy Casper (1964 & '68), Al Geiberger (1975 & '79) and Lee Trevino (1976 & '78). Last year's champion was Tom Lehman.

Dates:	May 16-19, 1996
Network:	USA & CBS
Times:	USA
	Thurs /Fri 4:00-6:00 EST
	CBS
	Sat 4:30-6:00 EST
	Sun 3:30-6:00 EST
Yardage:	7010
Par:	70
Slope:	132
Rating:	73.7
Total Purse:	$1,400,000
1sy Prize:	$252,000
1995 Winner:	Tom Lehman
1995 Winning Score:	271 (67,68,68,68)
Principal Charitable Beneficiary:	Community Charities
Ticket Information:	1-817-927-4280

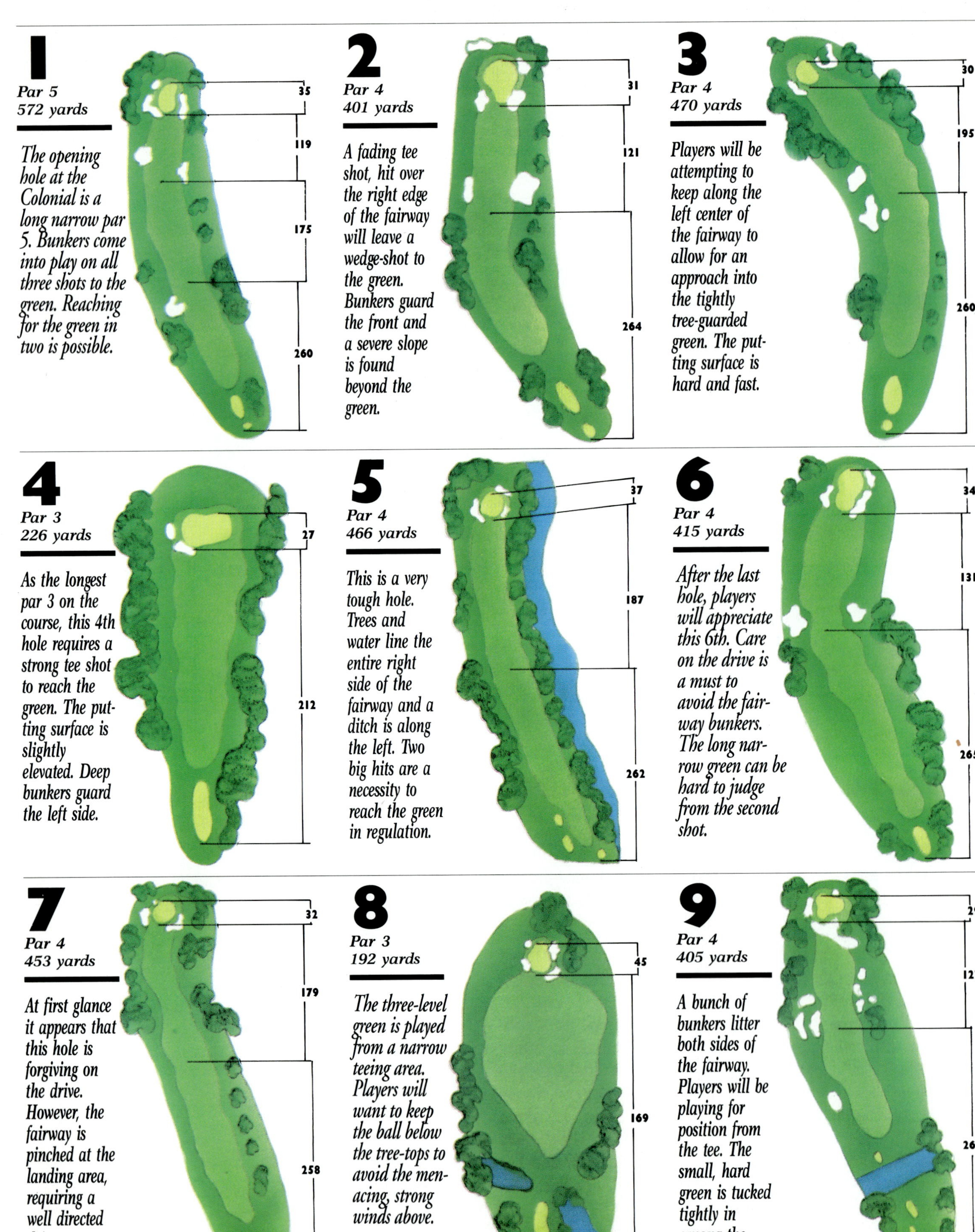

1
Par 5
572 yards

The opening hole at the Colonial is a long narrow par 5. Bunkers come into play on all three shots to the green. Reaching for the green in two is possible.

2
Par 4
401 yards

A fading tee shot, hit over the right edge of the fairway will leave a wedge-shot to the green. Bunkers guard the front and a severe slope is found beyond the green.

3
Par 4
470 yards

Players will be attempting to keep along the left center of the fairway to allow for an approach into the tightly tree-guarded green. The putting surface is hard and fast.

4
Par 3
226 yards

As the longest par 3 on the course, this 4th hole requires a strong tee shot to reach the green. The putting surface is slightly elevated. Deep bunkers guard the left side.

5
Par 4
466 yards

This is a very tough hole. Trees and water line the entire right side of the fairway and a ditch is along the left. Two big hits are a necessity to reach the green in regulation.

6
Par 4
415 yards

After the last hole, players will appreciate this 6th. Care on the drive is a must to avoid the fairway bunkers. The long narrow green can be hard to judge from the second shot.

7
Par 4
453 yards

At first glance it appears that this hole is forgiving on the drive. However, the fairway is pinched at the landing area, requiring a well directed drive.

8
Par 3
192 yards

The three-level green is played from a narrow teeing area. Players will want to keep the ball below the tree-tops to avoid the menacing, strong winds above.

9
Par 4
405 yards

A bunch of bunkers litter both sides of the fairway. Players will be playing for position from the tee. The small, hard green is tucked tightly in among the trees, and behind water.

*I*ntroduction

One of the most exciting projects in the rich history of the game of golf is under construction in America's oldest and most historical city, St Augustine: The World Golf Village

The World Golf Village will contain among other elements, the new World Golf Hall of Fame, a 75,000 square foot interactive museum and shrine to the game's great players. Add to that the golf facilities, golf' library and resource center hotel and conference center and other significant components of the project the World Golf Village is destined to become the international home that the game of golf has need for so long.

*H*istory

In 1987 the PGA TOUR staff began investigating the possibility of establishing a PGA TOUR Hall of fame in northeast Florida in proximity to the TOUR's Headquarters in Ponte Vedra but easily accessible from heavily trafficked Interstate95. In 1991, after unsuccessfully trying to secure a potential site in Duval County, just south of Jacksonville, the owner of property in St John's Country offered 4()() acres to the TOUR on which to build its Hall of fame. The site was located directly adjacent to I-95, about 22 miles south of Jacksonville and eight miles northeast of downtown St Augustine, the nation's oldest city.

At that point PGA TOUR Commissioner Deane Beman invited LPGA Commissioner Charlie Mechem to locate its Hall of Fame within the same facility After receiving approval from his players and Board Commissioner Mechem agreed. Within the next two weeks the TOUR had received letters of confirmation from the Unites States Golf Association Royal & Ancient Golf Club of St Andrews National Golf Founda tion and Augusta National Golf Club all of which agreed to participate by assigning a representative to the World Golf Hall of Fame Advisory Board and by coordinating the development exhibits relevant to their areas of involvement in the game.

The same offer of course, had been made to the PGA of America and some ten months later after determin ing that it would close the PGA World Golf Hall of Fame in Pinehurst N C, the PGA agreed to participate in the project as well. The Advisory Board was solidified with representatives of every major American golf organization as well as the international professional Tours, and the process of developing the new World Golf Hall of fame began at its first meeting in December 1993.

*W*orld Golf Hall of Fame

The new World Golf Hall of Fame building will be approximately 75,000 square feet including a 14,000 square foot wide-screen theater and about 36,000 square feet of exhibits. The building was designed by E. Verner Johnson and Associate of Boston, a company known worldwide for its expertise in designing museums, aquariums and Halls of Fame.

The building was designed to reflect not only some of the traditional architectural styles inherent in older golf clubhouses and hotels, but also the natural environment of the game. High ceilings and large windows will help bring the feeling of the outdoors into the World Hall of Fame. Expansive porches on the

second floor give visitors a chance to look out over the World Golf Village Golf Course. Iron railings on the porches are designed to represent golf balls sitting on tees, above blades of grass, an effect that will he accentuated by the late afternoon shadows on the porch.

The design of the building, then, will in every way mirror the essence of golf.

Exhibits

After an extensive process involving research and personal interviews, Ralph Appelbaum Associates of New York was retained by the World Golf Village to design the exhibits for the World Golf Hall of Fame. Appelbaum has become recognized as perhaps the leader in the field of museum exhibit design; it is currently redesigning the exhibits at the American Museum of Natural History in New York, for example, and achieved worldwide acclaim for its work at the National Holocaust Museum in Washington.

From the outset the Advisory Board has recognized the principal challenge in the exhibit design area: treat the history and traditions of golf with the dignity they deserve while at the same time using technology and various forms of interactivity to make the exhibit experience fun. The goal is to appeal to the avid golfer as well as the novice, the senior golfer as well as youngsters who may not be that familiar with the game.

The preliminary design plan is complete, and includes a number of media experiences, an interactive rules theater, a scale model of St. Andrews and the Old Course made by Scottish artisans, a Command Center with up-to-date information on events around the world, the Ultimate Swing Analyzer, an architect's studio, a shrine to the Hall of Fame members in the 170-foot tower, several outdoor exhibits, and 60 other exhibits concepts dealing with both the history of golf and the contemporary game.

Other Village Components

Other components planned at this point for the World Golf Village include:

- An 18-hole golf course and clubhouse within the Village with 36 holes, more planned within the Saint Johns development at a later date.
- A major resort hotel and convention center.
- As y as 400 two- and three- bedroom villas.
- An l 8-hole natural grass putting course.
- Headquarters for PGA TOUR Productions' television studio, post production facilities and video library.
- An international golf library and resource center.
- Upscale shopping and restaurant surrounding the World Golf Village lake.

- A sports medicine and executive physical facility operated by the Mayo Clinic.

World Golf Village Foundation

All proceeds from the World Golf Hall of Fame and its ancillary activities will benefit the World Golf Village Foundation, which will fund golf-related educational and vocational opportunities for needy youngsters.

10

Par 4
416 yards

The 10th starts the back nine with strong demands. The tee shot must be hit over the water and in position for a clear shot over a gully and to the tree-crowded green.

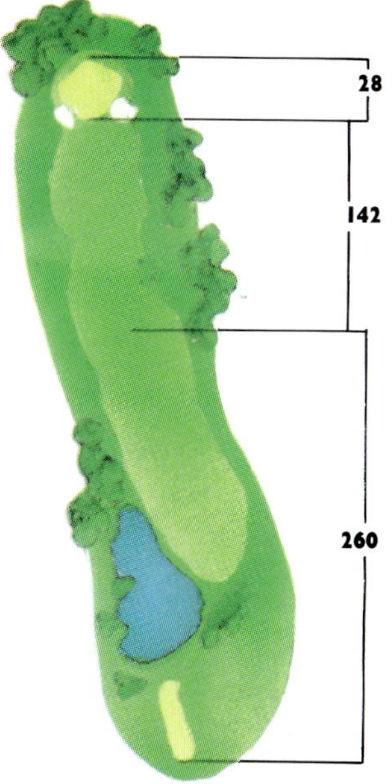

11

Par 5
609 yards

Three shots will be used to reach the large U-shaped green. It's a bit long to hit in two, but birdies are not out of the question.

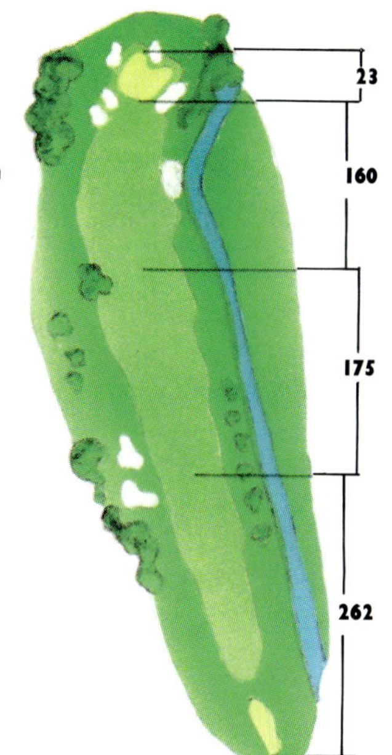

12

Par 4
435 yards

A well-hit drive should easily bound down the slope that starts 260 yards from the tee. The approach is to a medium sized green that is fronted by high-lipped bunkers.

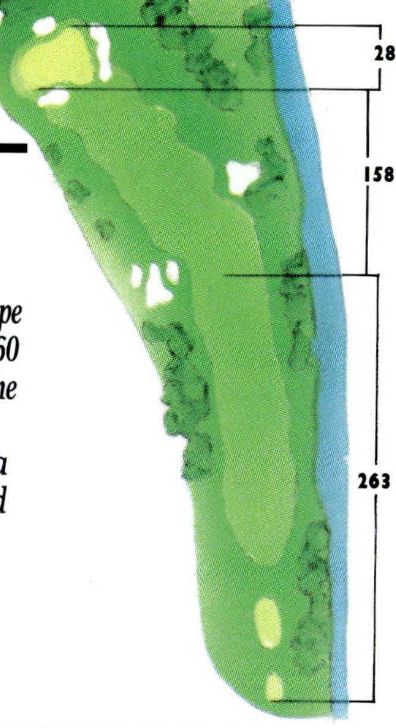

13

Par 3
176 yards

It is all carry to the putting surface. A bail-out area to the left includes a bunker. The short, wide green slopes gradually from left to right. Pars are a welcome score on this hole.

14

Par 4
431 yards

The three fairway bunkers provide a target from the tee. Players will favor the left-middle of the fairway for a good angle to the flat green.

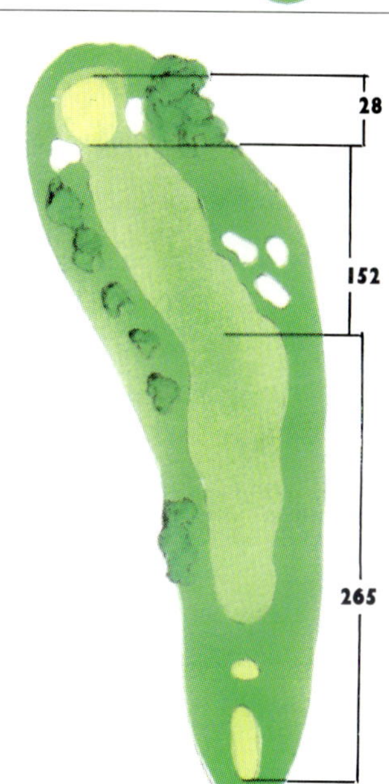

15

Par 4
436 yards

Decisions are the most difficult part of this hole. Either lay up on the drive or go for it and play over the right corner bunkers. The approach is over a deep gully to a shallow green.

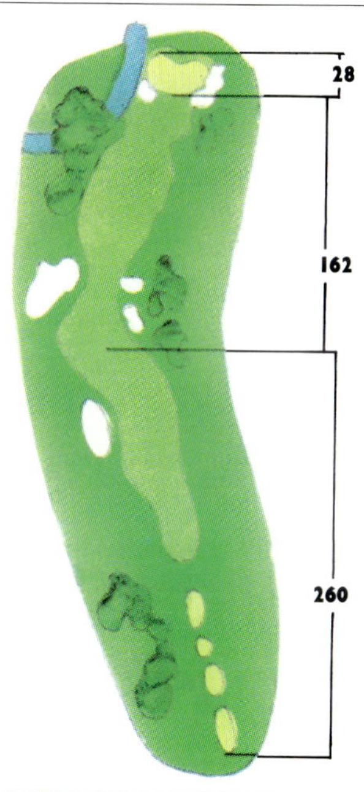

16

Par 3
188 yards

The two-tiered green slopes toward the front allowing the surface to be highly visible. A birdie on this 16th will start a strong charge to the finish.

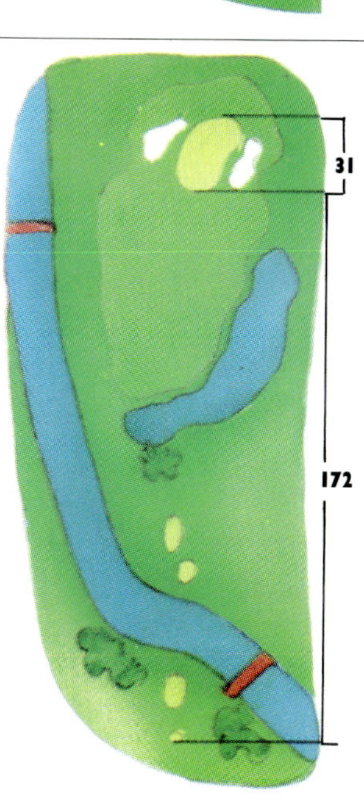

17

Par 4
387 yards

This short 17th hole should be birdied. However, approach shots must be accurate and precise to find the green buried in among the trees and bunkers.

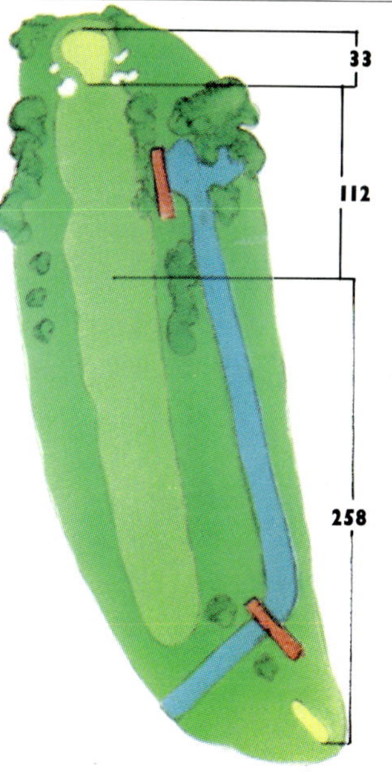

18

Par 4
434 yards

A great finishing hole. Nowhere else but the center of the fairway will allow an open approach to the narrow green. Water will catch any shot that strays left or long

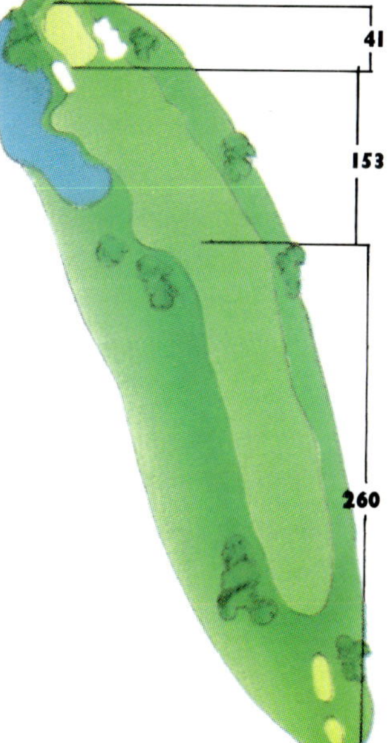

THE COURSE: TPC AT AVENEL, POTOMAC, MARYLAD

The Kemper Open is the longest-running continuous corporate-sponsored event in the United States. The very first tournament was won by Arnold Palmer in 1968 at the Pleasant Valley Country Club in Sutton, Massachusetts. The event has moved a few times since its beginning. Its locations have included Quail Hollow Country Club in Charlotte, North Carolina (1969-1979); Congressional Country Club in Bethesda, Maryland (1980-1986); and its present site of the Tournament Players Club at Avenel in Potomac, Maryland.

Designers Ed Ault and Tom Clark worked together on producing the new course with TOUR player-consultant Ed Sneed. The project brought together the TPC concept with the characteristics of the greater courses of the old country. The result is a masterpiece of Scottish character and rolling Maryland geography making for a truly unique layout.

Dates:	May 23-26, 1996
Network:	CBS
Times:	Sat 4:00-6:00 EST
	Sun 4:00-6:00 EST
Yardage:	7005
Par:	71
Slope:	133
Rating:	74.0
Total Purse:	$1,400,000
1st Prize:	$252,000
1995 Winner:	Lee Janzen
1995 Winning Score:	272 (68,69,68,67)
Principle Charitable Beneficiary:	Boy's Club of America
Ticket Information:	1-301-469-3737

1

*Par 4
393 yards*

A tough beginning hole. The bunker along the right is troublesome. Smart play will keep the drive down the left-middle, leaving a medium iron to the green.

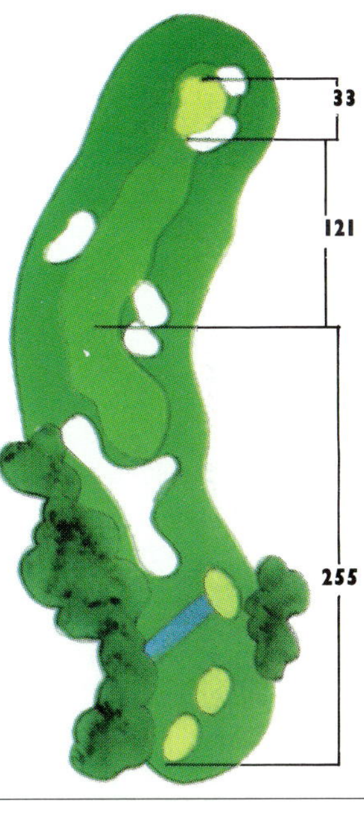

2

*Par 5
622 yards*

Three well placed shots are required to reach the green. Birdies are not out of the question, though care must be taken on the downhill approach to the tight green.

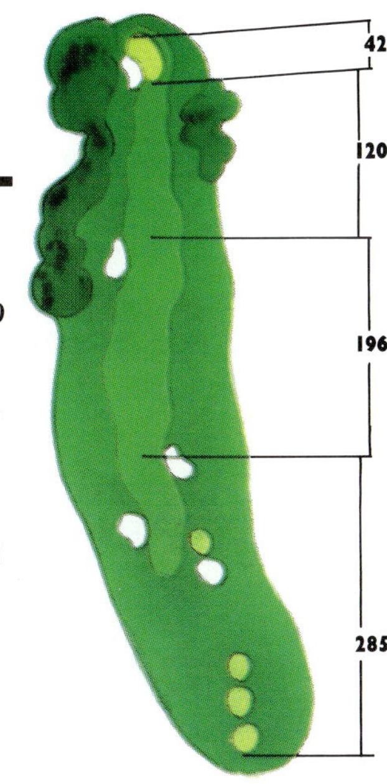

3

*Par 3
239 yards*

This may be one of Arnold Palmer's favorite holes — he had two consecutive holes-in-one during a 1986 Senior PGA TOUR event. Slightly downhill, this par 3 can play long.

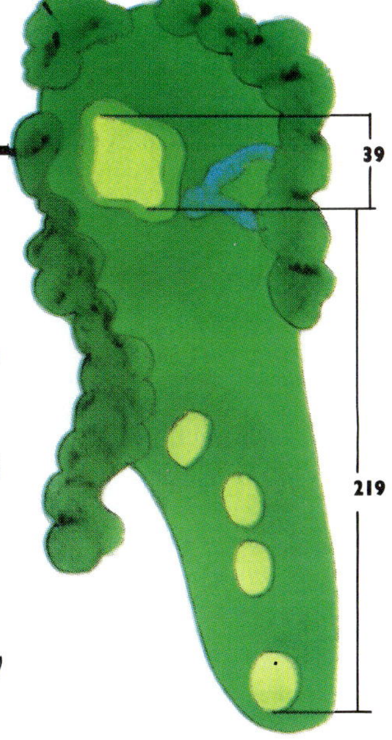

4

*Par 4
435 yards*

The left side of the fairway is favored for the best angle on the approach. The water intimidates the drive and second shot. Deep grass bunker, right of the green, is trouble.

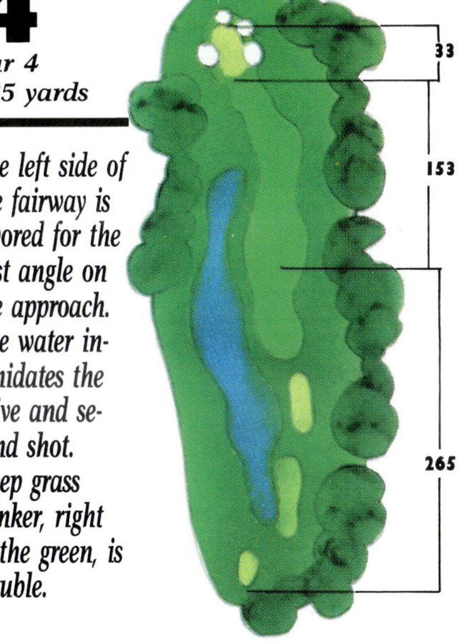

5

*Par 4
359 yards*

Second shortest par 4 on the course. Fairway wood or long-iron will be used to place the drive in position. Deep sand bunkers guard the green — expect many birdies.

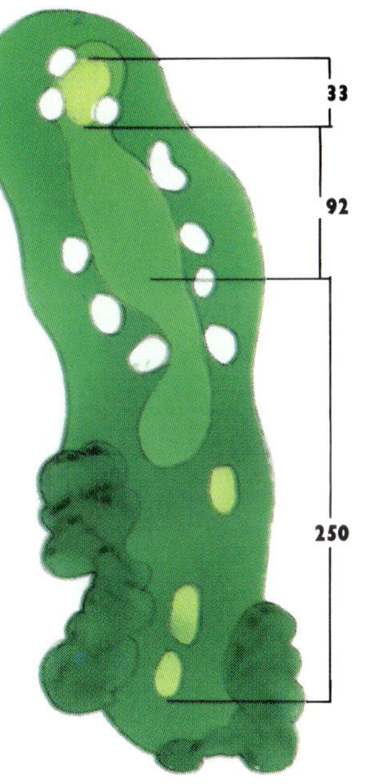

6

*Par 5
520 yards*

A long drive is necessary to have the green in view for the second but the crossing creek will grab all shots short of the putting surface. A high number of eagles will be scored here.

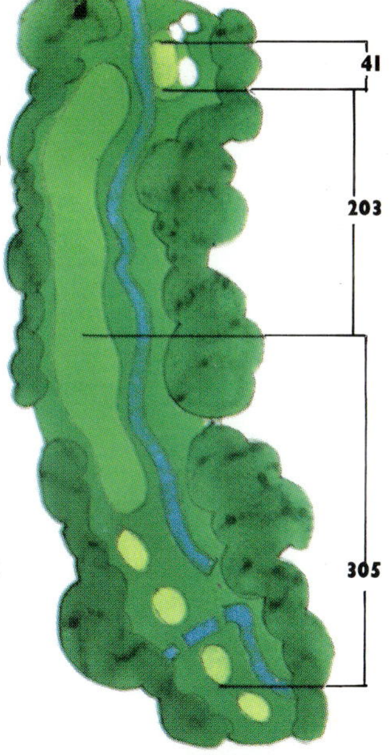

7

*Par 4
461 yards*

The length is again a factor on this par 4. A drive down the left side will present a long approach to a green sloping left to right. Putting surface is long and narrow.

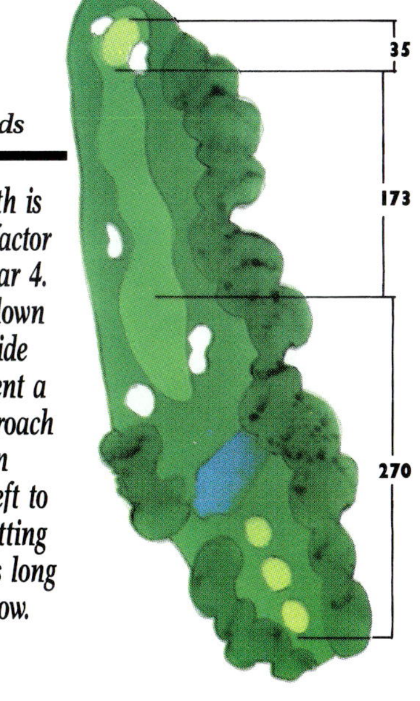

8

*Par 4
453 yards*

The fairway drops down a level just past the landing area. A driver can be used to hit the tee shot to the right center of the fairway. A deep bunker intimidates the second shot.

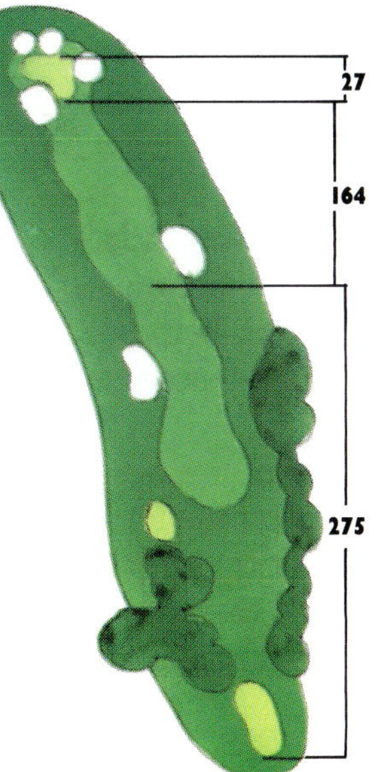

9

*Par 3
166 yards*

A rocky edged pond borders the green front and right. The elevated tee gives a clear view of the putting surface. Average score will be just above par.

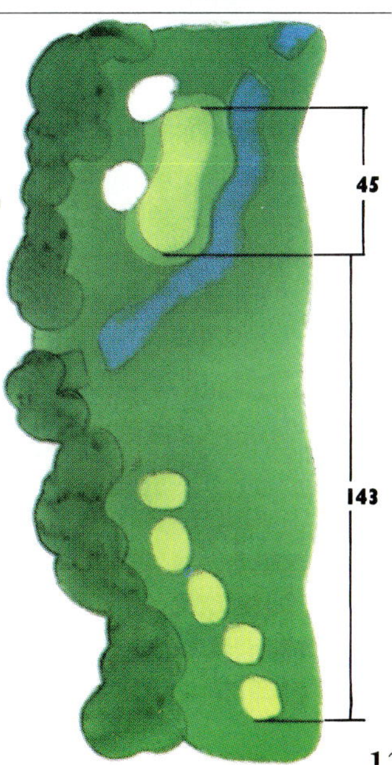

10

Par 4
374 yards

Rock Run Creek crosses the fairway and continues up the left side and comes back into play at the green. Fairway woods and long-irons will put the ball in prime position for the approach.

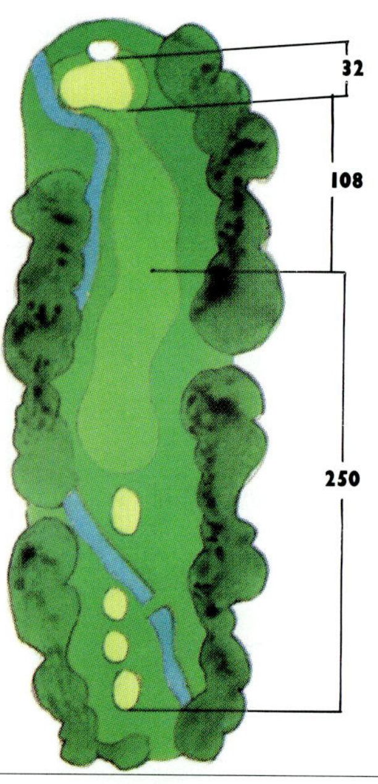

11

Par 3
165 yards

Wind above the tree line can make the tee shot that much more difficult. The deep bunkers and creek make it imperative to reach the putting surface from the tee.

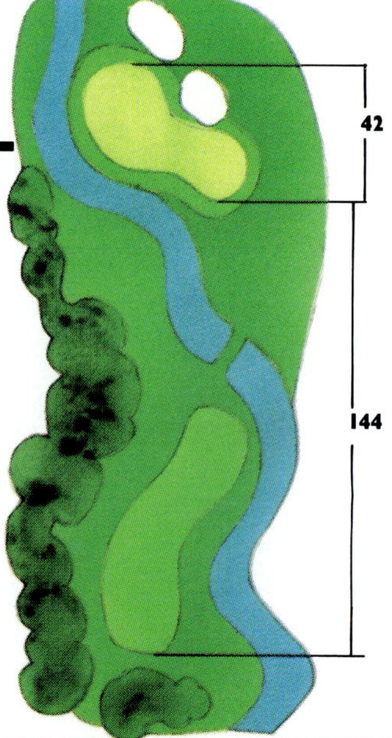

12

Par 4
472 yards

At 472 yards, this par 4 can be difficult to hit with accuracy. Players will be using long-irons into the small green. Pars are almost as good as birdies here.

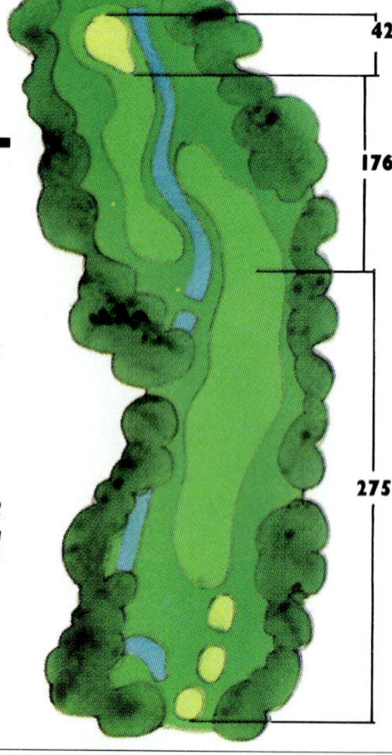

13

Par 5
524 yards

The fairway slopes up away from the tee and then slopes down to the green. A big drive will reach the top of the hill leaving a downhill second to the green.

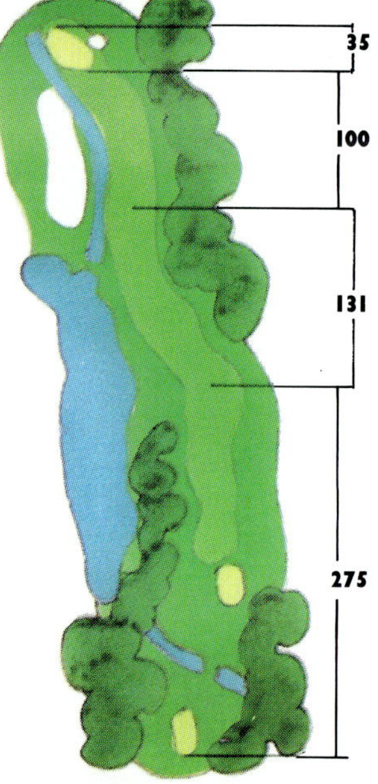

14

Par 4
301 yards

Some players may surprise the crowd with a drive that reaches the green on this hole. The percentage shot is down the left with an iron and a short chip to the putting surface.

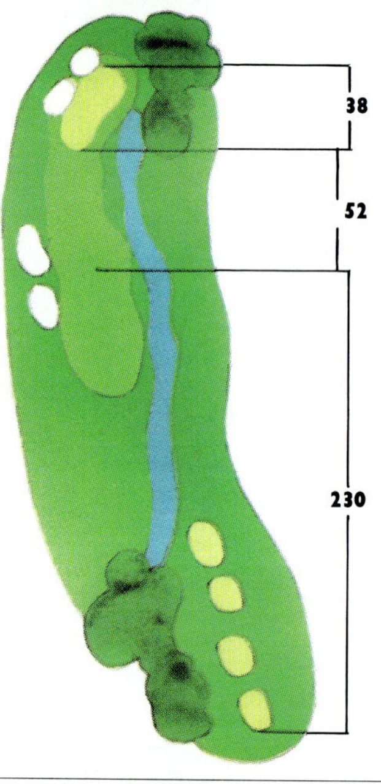

15

Par 4
467 yards

Again, the drive must climb a small grade. Beyond the ridge the fairway slopes back down to a two-tiered green that has levels left and right. Par is excellent on this long hole.

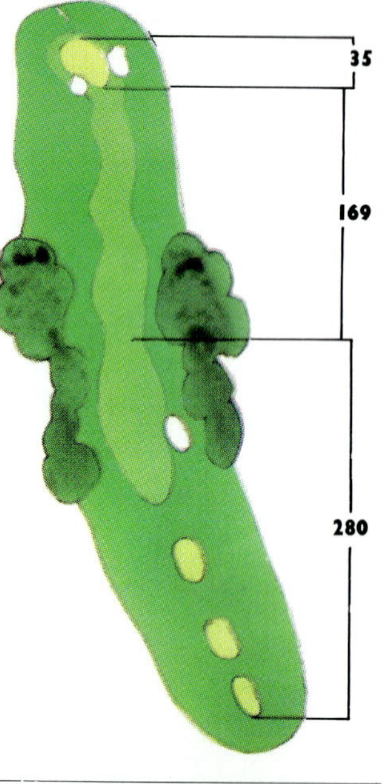

16

Par 4
415 yards

This 16th will keep the competition tight. Open fairway funnels down to a narrow approach. Deepest bunker on the course is found left front.

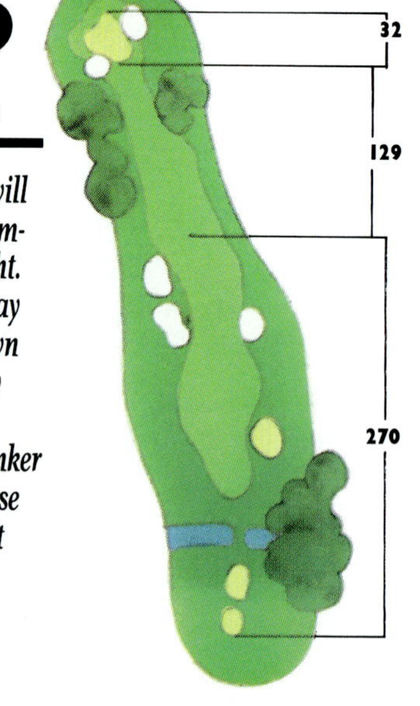

17

Par 3
195 yards

The rolling green may be difficult to hit in a strong breeze. Water and sand hazards can deflate a leader's margin.

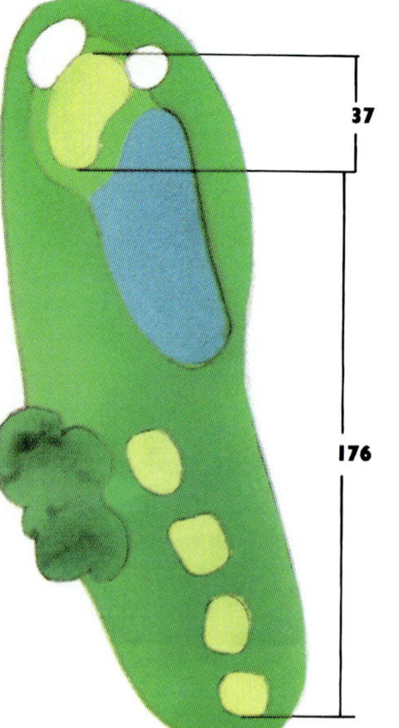

18

Par 4
444 yards

More than 50,000 spectators will be able to see the finish with an unrestricted view. The right side of the fairway opens up the green for the final approach.

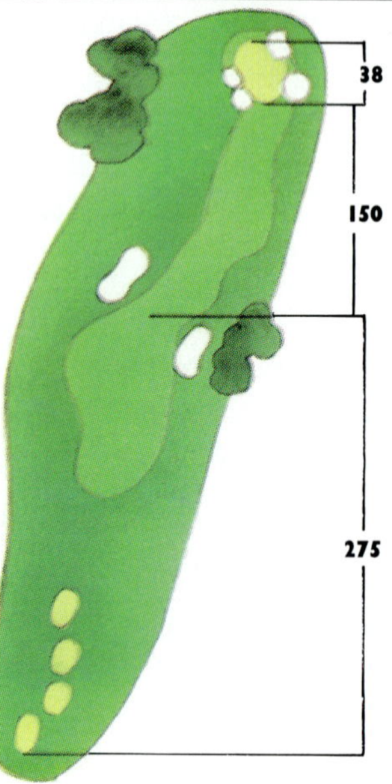

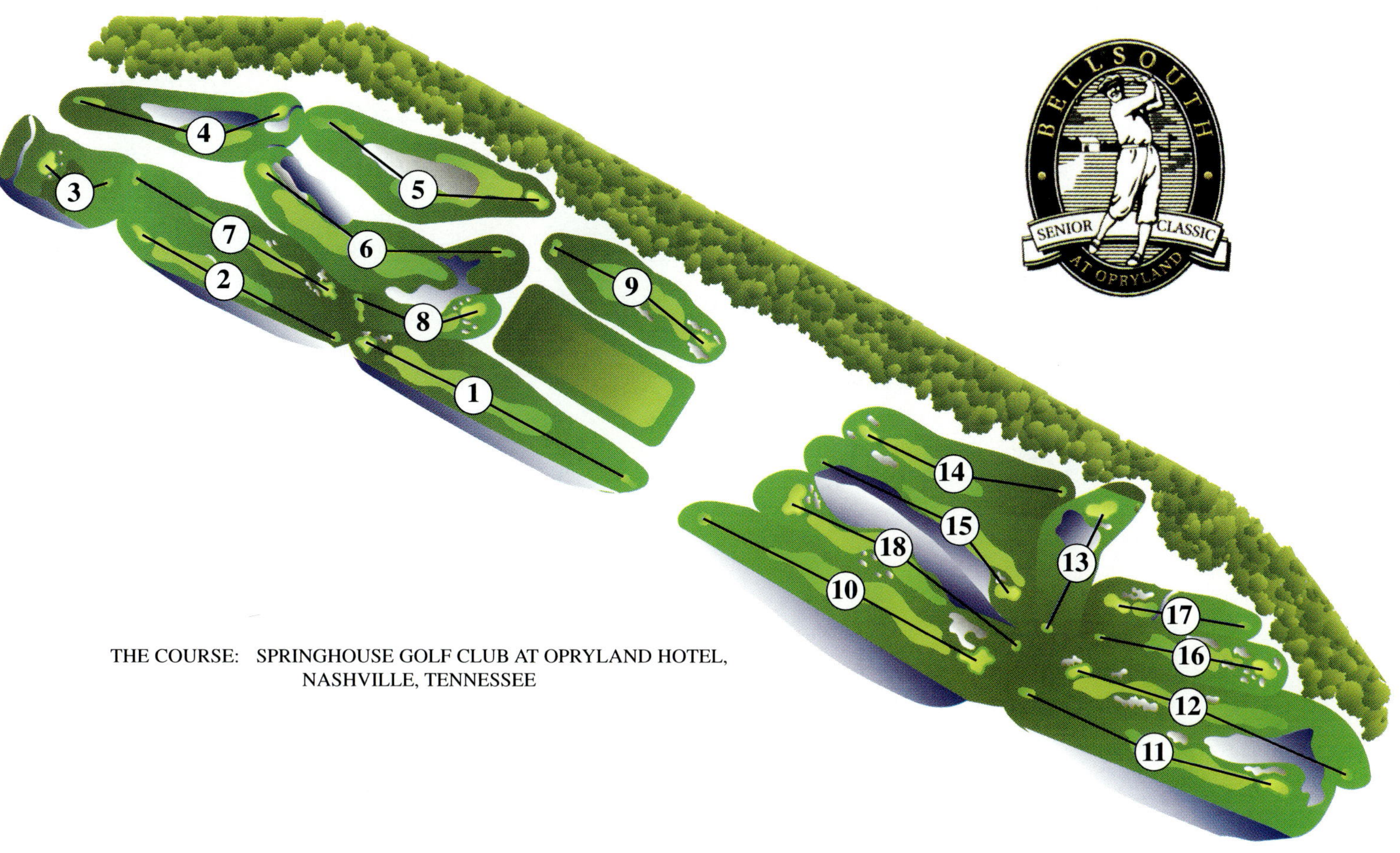

THE COURSE: SPRINGHOUSE GOLF CLUB AT OPRYLAND HOTEL,
NASHVILLE, TENNESSEE

*B*ell South Corporation joined forces with Gaylord Entertainment to bring to Music City USA two favorite forms of entertainment, "The Legends of golf" and country music. Both have emerged to become favored leisure activities of choice among Americans.

The inaugural BellSouth Senior Classic at Opryland earned national attention when Lee Trevino walked away with the 1994 championship. Played at the Springhouse Golf Club at Opryland Hotel, this par 72 layout was designed by PGA TOUR professional Larry Nelson. It is stretched over two-hundred twenty acres and plays about 6,500 yards. Trevino finished one stroke ahead of Jim Albus at 199, seventeen under par in what was one of the most dramatic finishes on tour for 1994. In 1995, Jim Dent claimed his first Senior PGA TOUR victory of the year. Dent finishes the tournament at 13 under, only 1 stroke over Bob Murphy.

In addition to great golf, there are hospitality opportunities including the historic 300 foot, four story musical General Jackson showboat. Docked between the 1st and 10th tee at the Springhouse Golf Club, this is the ultimate in hospitality. Also, you'll find our corporate hospitality in Opry Village and the 18th green skybox very attractive.

Dates:	May 24-26
Network:	NBC
Times:	Sat 1:00 - 3:00 pm EST
	Sun 2:00- 4:00 pm EST
Yardage:	6,783
Par:	72
Rating:	72.0
Total Purse:	$916,000
1st Prize:	$165,000
1995 Winner:	Jim Dent
1995 Winning Score:	(203) (66,69,68)
Principal Charitable	
Beneficiary:	Minnie Pearl Cancer Foundation
	Boys& Girls Clubs of Middle TN
	TN Golf Foundation
Ticket Information:	Success by Six
	Weekly guest passes sell for $30

1

**Par 5
530 yards**

Normally plays into prevailing southerly breeze. Front of green is open, bunkers on right act as a target from the tee. Green is long and narrow to accept a run-on shot or for the player coming in two shots. Eagle opportunity for longer

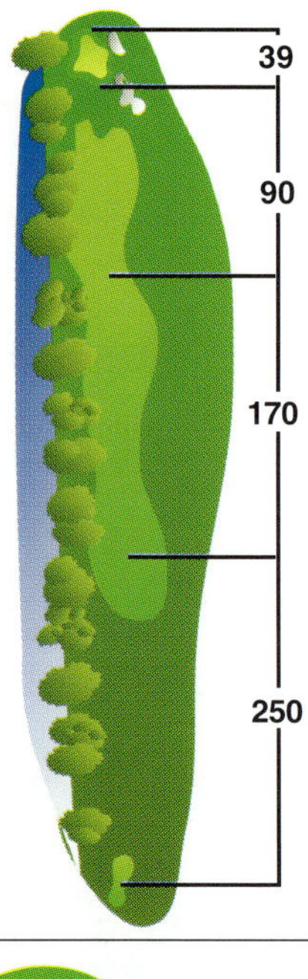

2

**Par 4
420 yards**

First of two long par 4s on the front side and will play longer than yardage indicates due to breeze. Large fairway bunker comes into play at 220 yards out. Second shot requires a high fade to the longest green on the front nine which is guarded by steep grass bunkers and mounds.

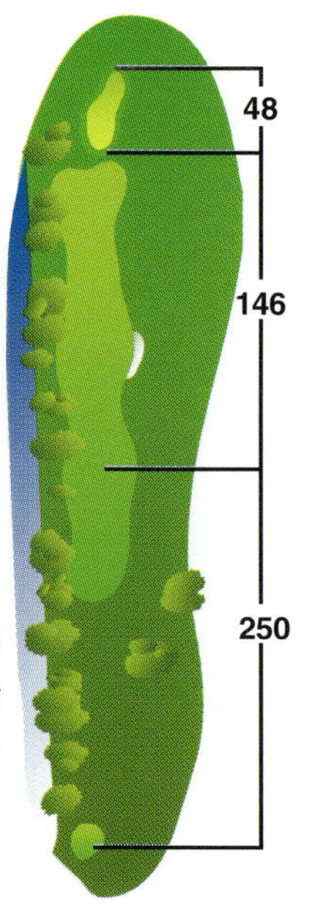

3

**Par 3
162 yards**

Island green surrounded by grass and sand bunkers with pin placement dictating how aggressive players will be. Missing the green on this, the shortest par 3 on the course, will make scrambling for par a chore.

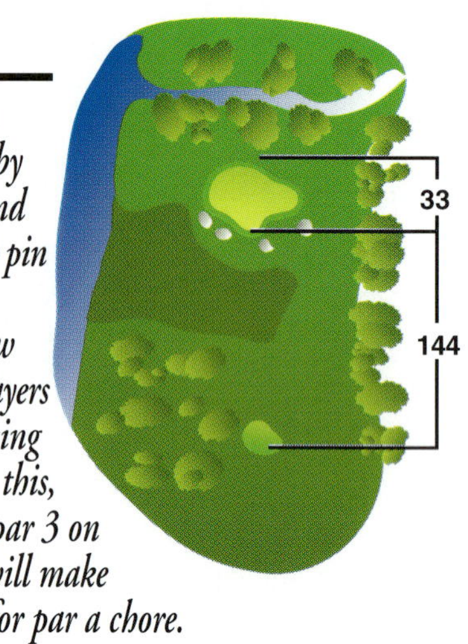

4

**Par 4
391 yards**

Tee shot is played from a narrow chute of trees and golfer will aim at three mounds straight ahead through fairway. Signature hole with actual Springhouse in backdrop of green which is protected by water.

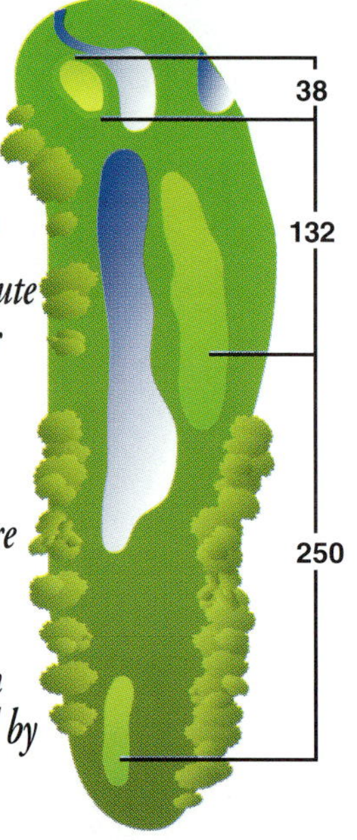

5

**Par 4
435 yards**

Tree lined bluff along entire left side of the hole. Large waste bunker separates fairway giving player a choice off the tee. Being right of the waste bunker commands a high fade with a mid to long iron into sloping right green.

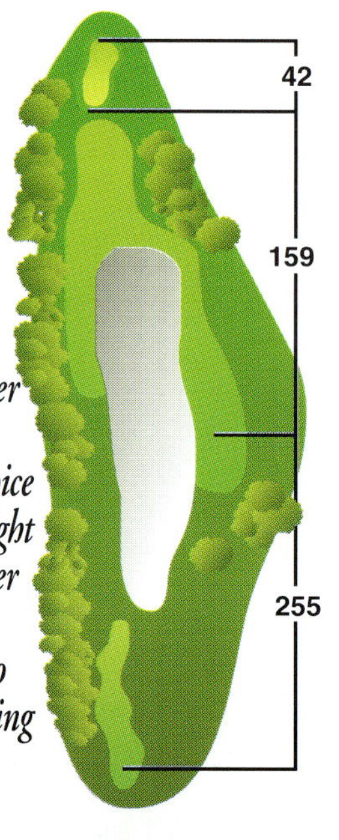

6

**Par 5
535 yards**

Second par 5 on front nine, reachable in two by most professionals. Pond on the right comes into play off the tee. Green is guarded by large bunker on the right and mounds in back. Area in front of green allows for run up shot.

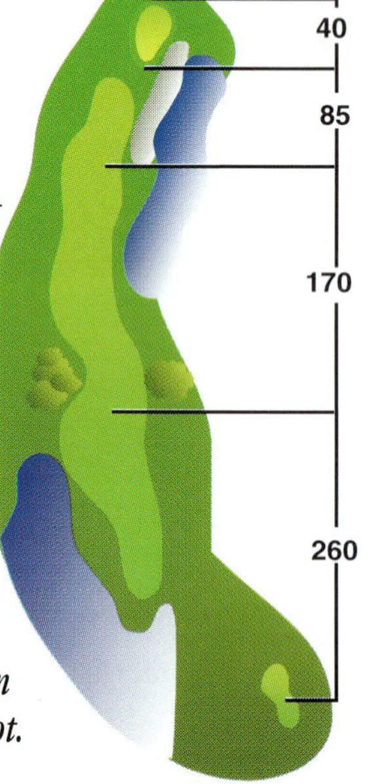

7

**Par 4
415 yards**

Longest par 4 on front nine allows player to RIP IT! Second shot will require mid iron to a heavily bunkered green. Mounds catch stray balls behind green while bunkers are strategically placed among the right and front left of the green.

8

**Par 3
175 yards**

Most heavily bunkered green on the front nine with water along the left side of the hole. Tee placement can command a shot over the water. This could be a pivotal hole.

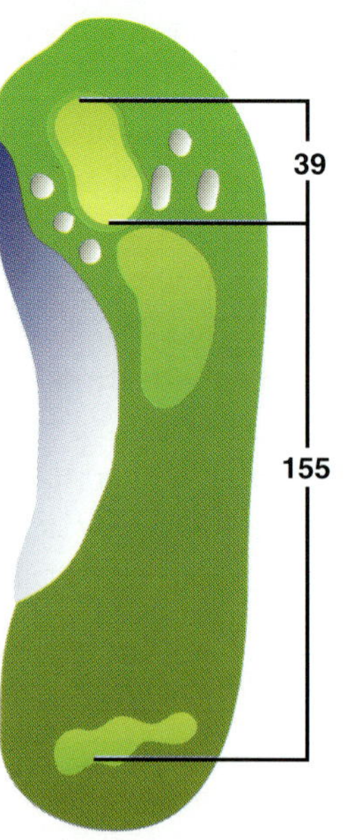

9

**Par 4
360 yards**

Elevated tee gives golfer excellent view of this short hole. Position is vital. Right side off fairway is mounded with long fairway bunker stretching 75 yards. Left side is tree lined within the wetland. Green is gaurded with sand and grass bunkers.

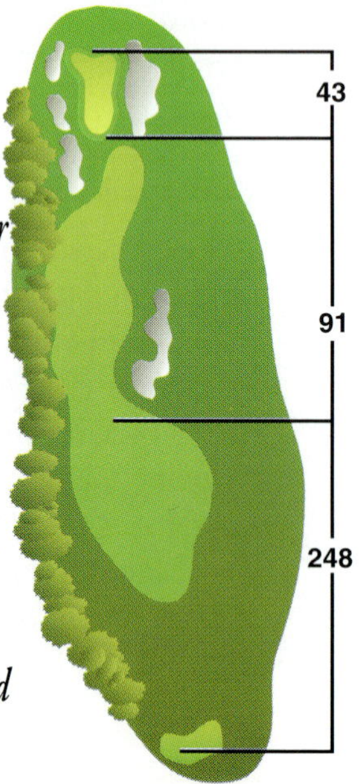

10

Par 5
520 yards

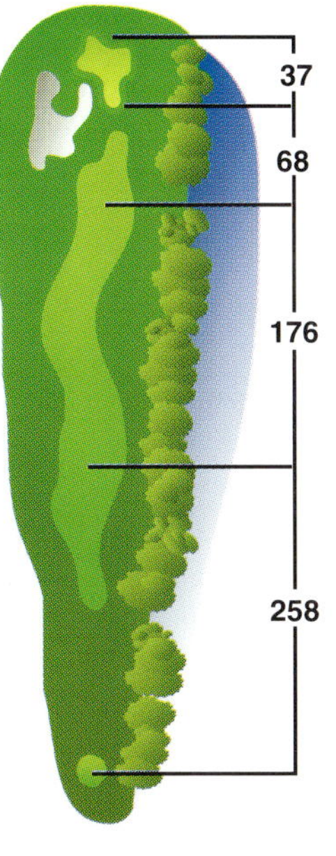

A chance to make up ground or pull ahead from the field with an eagle opportunity. Good par 5 with a row of mounds along left side and Cumberland River on the right. Open green allows for run up shot.

11

Par 4
435 yards

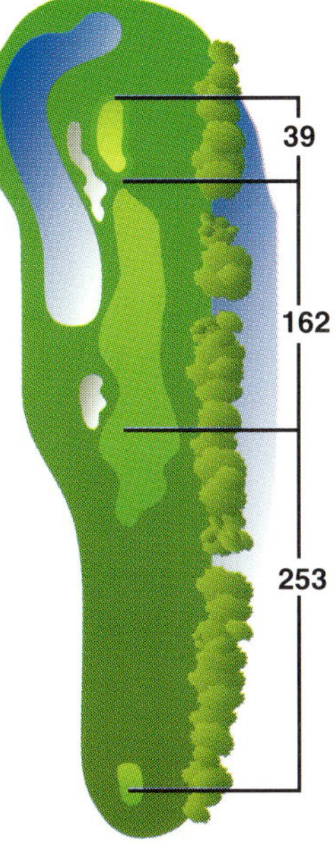

Fairway bunker on the left directs the player to the right. Water comes into play on the left side of fairway at 155 yards out. Long narrow green is guarded by a long bunker on the left.

12

Par 5
531 yards

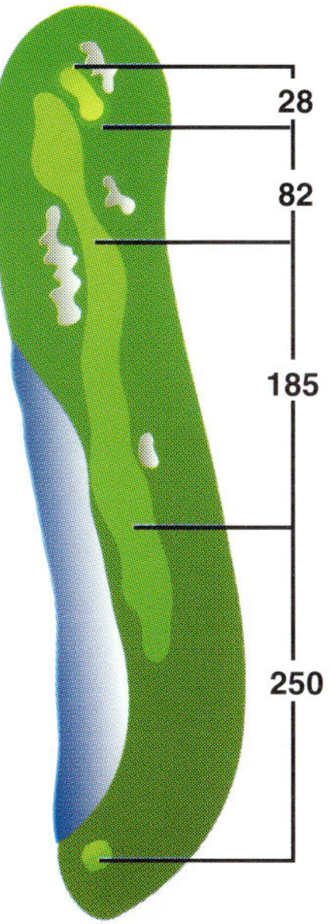

Last par 5 of the round. Narrow landing area between lake on left and fairway bunker to the right. Green is difficult to reach in two due to persistent breeze and elevation. Possible eagle hole.

13

Par 3
170 yards

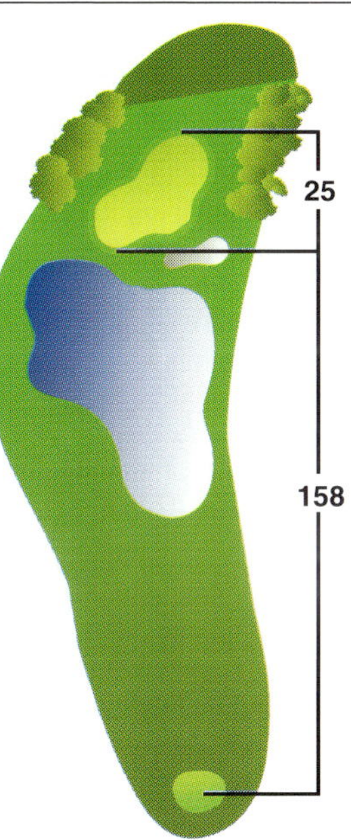

Great par 3 with bluff as backdrop. Large green, but shallow water in front of green and large sand bunker to the right. Green slopes from right to left.

14

Par 4
340 yards

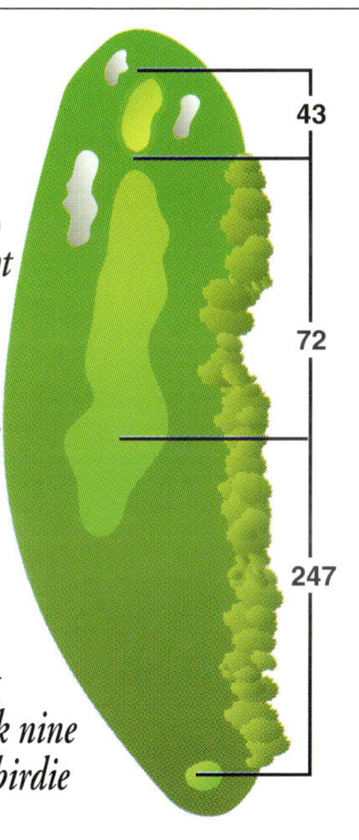

Short dogleg right with placement off the tee the primary objective. Second shot is hit to an elevated green well guarded by sand and grass bunkers. Longest green on the back nine provides a good birdie

15

Par 4
398 yards

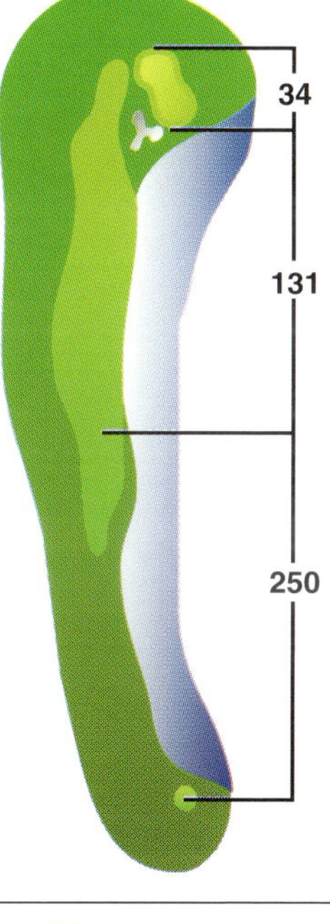

Great par 4 with water running down the entire right side. Second shot will require a mid to short iron be hit to an elevated green that is shallow. Right of the green is a disaster!

16

Par 4
323 yards

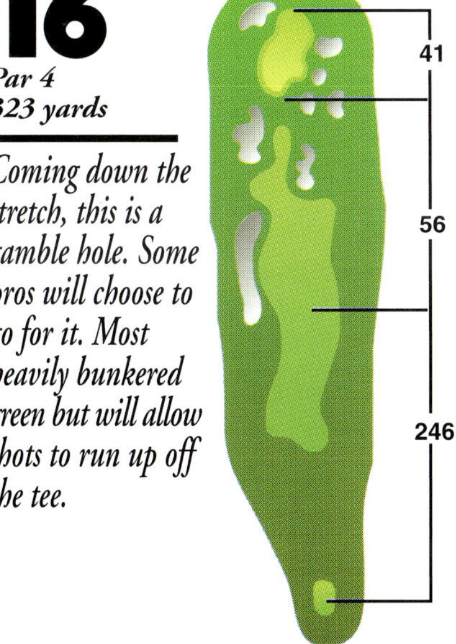

Coming down the stretch, this is a gamble hole. Some pros will choose to go for it. Most heavily bunkered green but will allow shots to run up off the tee.

17

Par 3
212 yards

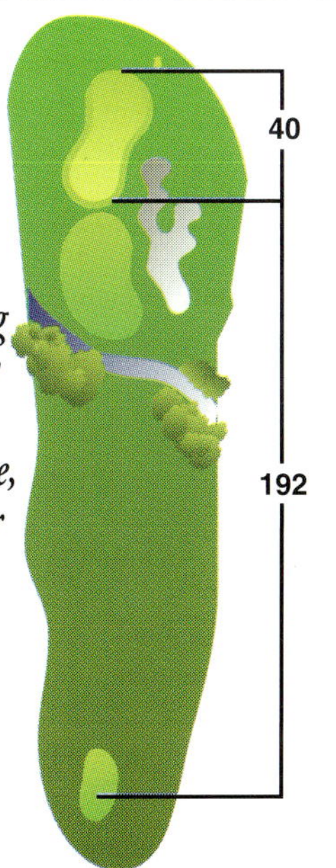

Longest par 3 on the course playing into the southerly breeze. Green is guarded by a large, deep sand bunker on the right side. Long green will hold shots well.

18

Par 4
431 yards

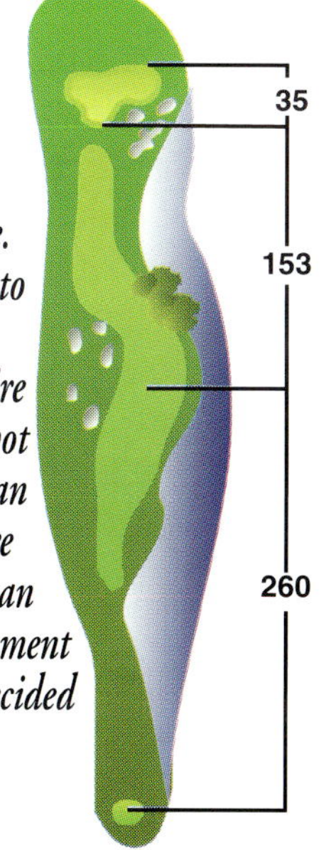

No. 1 handicap hole. Elevated tee hitting to a fairway lined by water down the entire right side. Second shot will be mid iron to an elevated green, where distance and wind can be deceiving. Tournament champion will be decided here!

THE COURSE: MUIRFIELD VILLAGE GOLF CLUB, DUBLIN, OHIO

Conceived in tribute to the venerable Scottish links where he achieved his initial international milestone, and dedicated to the memory of golf's indisputable luminaries, The Memorial at Muirfield Village Golf Club today has emerges as a monument to creator Jack William Nicklaus.

The Captains Club of The Memorial Tournament annually is charged with the selection of the "Honoree", an historic giant or legendary figure whose impact on the game is etched in history.

It is singularly significant then that Robert Tyre "Bobby" Jones would be selected as the "Honoree", for the 1976 inaugural tournament. It also is hardly a secret that club and tournament founder Jack Nicklaus, an avowed Jones disciple from infancy, would design a course that not only would challenge Jones, but would excite and delight him.

It , in fact, serves a dual purpose- a marvelously manicured layout that truly tests the power and precision of all golfers and all shots and, at the same time, providing a maximum number of spectators the most comfortable facility for total enjoyable viewing.

Muirfield Village's hallmark as one of the game's most difficult up-and-down courses is as chronicled as its acclaim for its immaculate conditioning.

Dates:	May 30-June 2
Network:	ABC
Times:	TBA
Yardage:	7104
Par:	72
Rating:	75.5
Total Purse:	$1,700,000
1st Prize:	$306,000
1995 Winner:	Greg Norman
1995 Winning Score:	269 (66,70,67,66)
Principal Charitable Beneficiary:	Children's Hospital of Columbus and Columbus Dispatch Charities
Ticket Information:	1-614-889-6700

1

Par 4
446 yards

The fairway descends away from the tee to a wide landing area. Players will aim their drives just down the right side of the fairway. The large green sits within a cluster of bunkers.

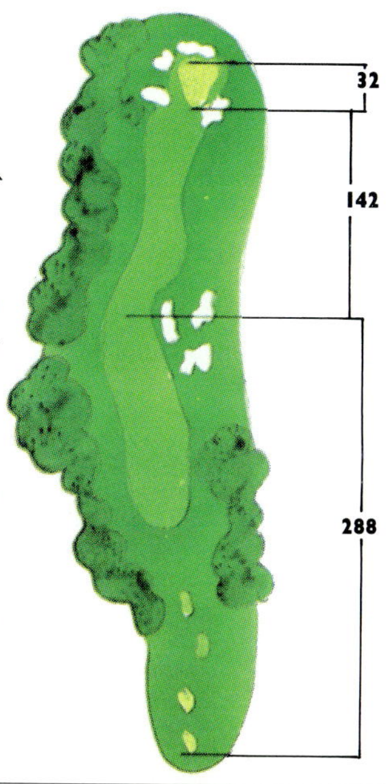

2

Par 4
452 yards

The first taste of water is introduced here. The drive should be along the right side of the fairway to set up for an approach into a green bordered by bunkers and the water.

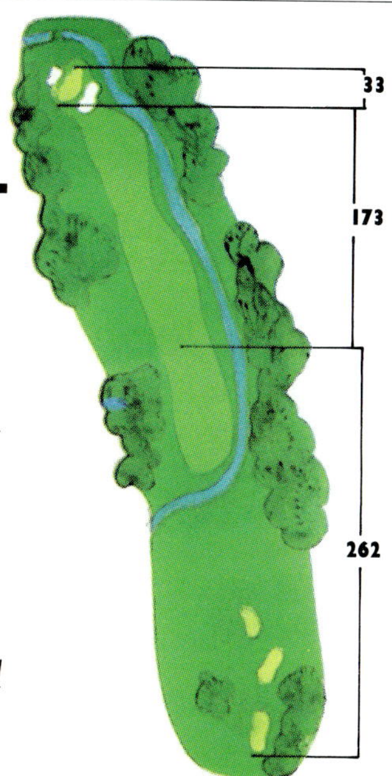

3

Par 4
392 yards

The elevated tee looks down onto an open fairway. A drive to the right middle of the fairway will open up the green for a clear shot on the approach.

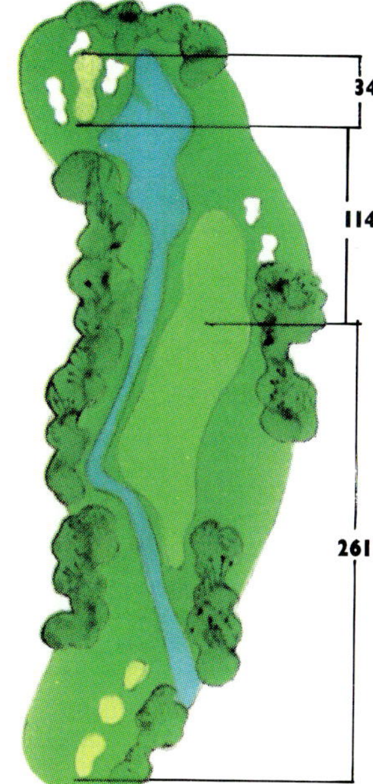

4

Par 3
204 yards

The long narrow green is guarded by surrounding bunkers and trees to the left. The hole is downhill from the tee to the green.

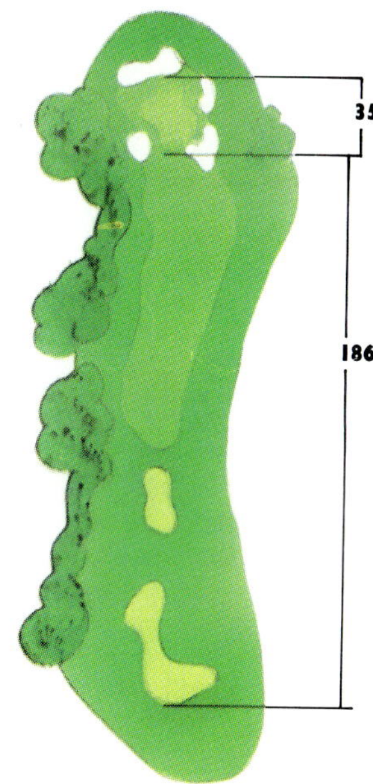

5

Par 5
531 yards

Birdies are a must on this fifth hole. Although it is ranked as 17th in difficulty, the drive is tight and the second shot must avoid the creek that runs through the fairway.

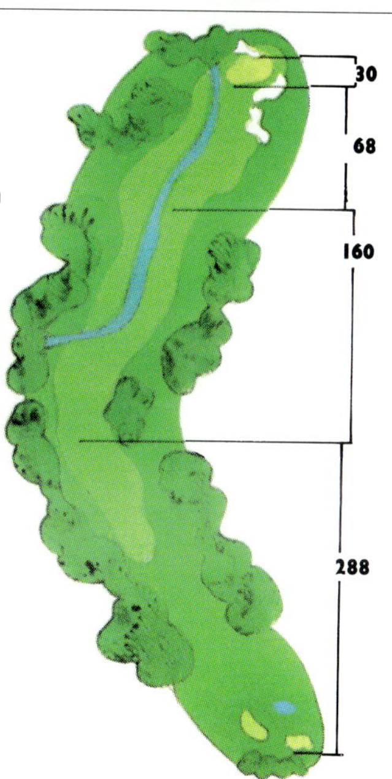

6

Par 4
430 yards

The fairway slopes slightly from left to right. A drive down the left middle of the fairway will allow the players to avoid the oak on the right.

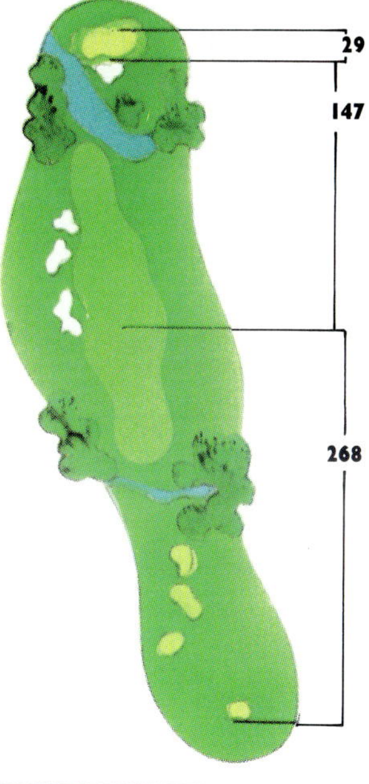

7

Par 5
549 yards

The tee shot is from out of a chute formed by trees along both sides. Fairway bunkers are scattered through the green which slopes slightly to the left.

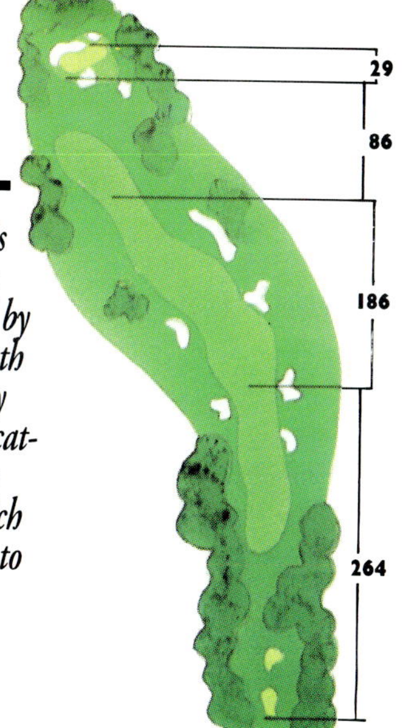

8

Par 3
189 yards

The green is almost completely surrounded by sand. The tee is slightly elevated, making club selection rather difficult.

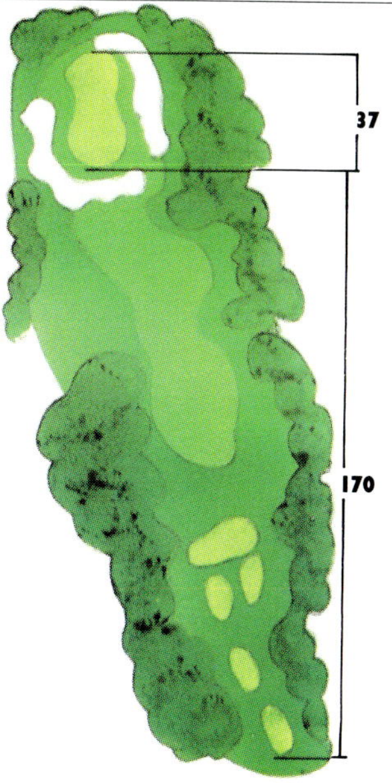

9

Par 4
410 yards

The tee sits low. The fairway rises up in the middle and slopes back down to the green. Players will be aiming their drives along the left side of the fairway for a good angle on the green.

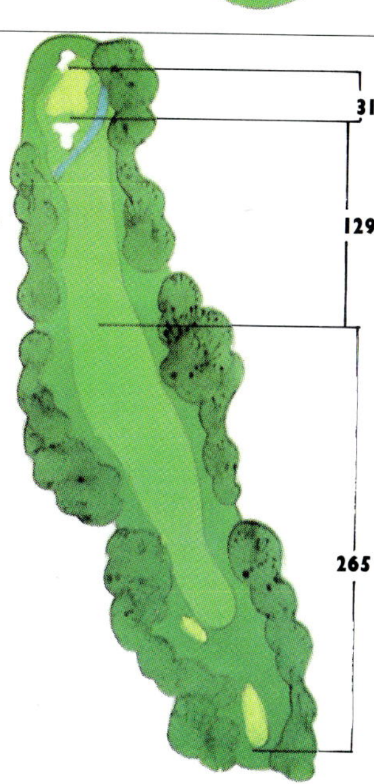

10

Par 4
441 yards

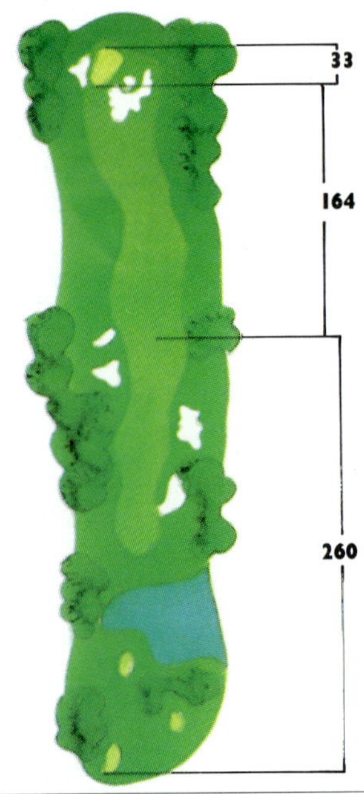

Into the wind, this hole can be a 'bear'. The wide, uphill fairway demands a long drive. The approach must zero in on the large green that's guarded by bunkers front right and left.

11

Par 5
538 yards

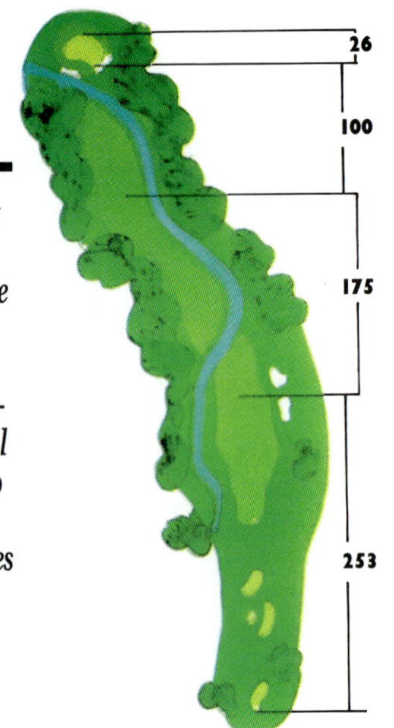

Double dogleg with fairway bunkers on the right. Water zig-zags down the fairway requiring careful shotmaking to the putting surface. Birdies are frequent.

12

Par 3
156 yards

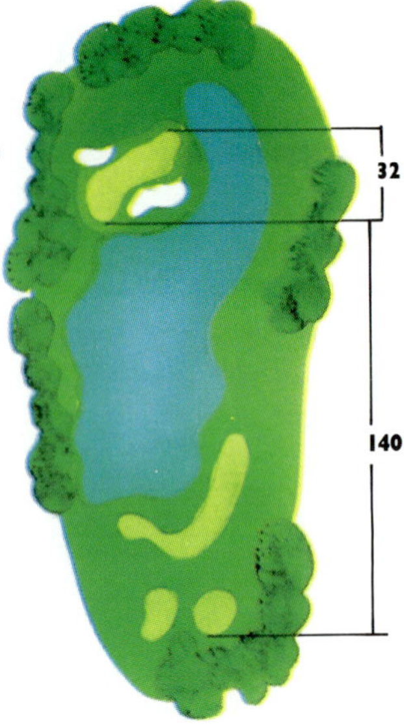

The most photographed hole on the course. The narrow, wide green can be hard to hit when winds are gusting.

13

Par 4
442 yards

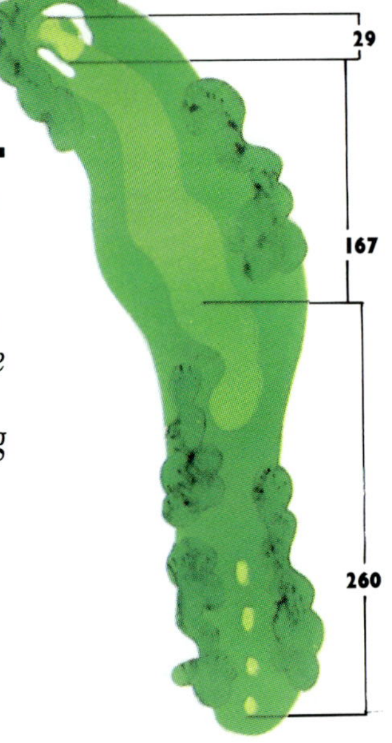

The tee shot is from an elevated green and through a tree-lined chute to a generous fairway. A long second shot is to a large green that slopes from right front to left rear.

14

Par 4
363 yards

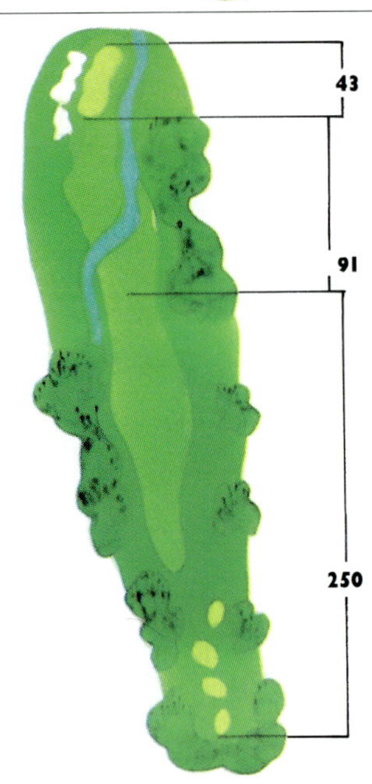

The fairway slopes off to the left, where trouble awaits. Players must be careful to back off on their drives to keep from getting into the water. The green is large and tightly guarded.

15

Par 5
490 yards

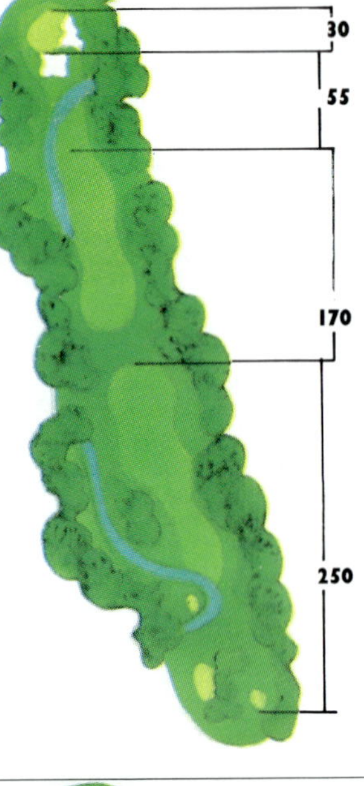

The view from the tee is frightening; trees form a tight fence along the fairway. Players who keep it straight and long can get home in two. The elevated green is fronted by bunkers.

16

Par 3
204 yards

A simple hole with the green set below the tee. The green is large and slopes slightly from right to left. The length usually precludes birdies.

17

Par 4
430 yards

A large bunker along the left side of the fairway dictates a drive to the right. A gully lies just short of the green.

18

Par 4
437 yards

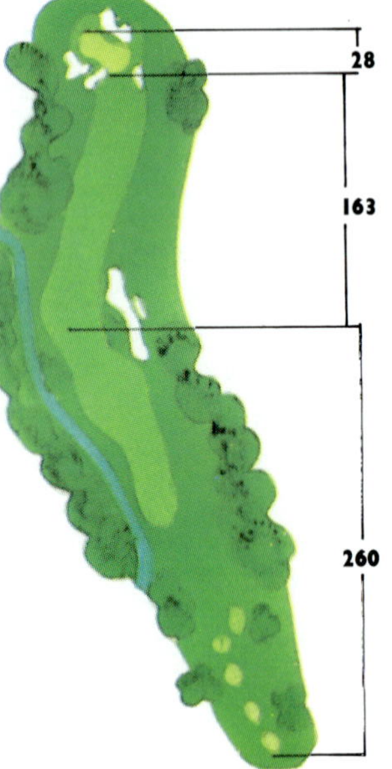

The big finish, Nicklaus style. A well-placed drive needs to fade just around the corner to leave a medium approach. The elevated green is surrounded by bunkers and spectators.

THE COURSE: WESTCHESTER COUNTRY CLUB, RYE, NEW YORK

$\mathcal{T}$his year's Buick Classic is the second of four Buick Motor Division title sponsorships on the PGA TOUR®. Formerly known as the Westchester Classic, the tournament debuted in 1967. Westchester Country Club is consider one of the best-conditioned course on the tour, a fact that the 1990 champion will quickly attest to. After winning the 1990 US Open Championship, Hale Irwin was able to keep his adrenaline going right into the following week and win the Buick Classic. In 1991 Billy Andrade won the Kemper Open the week prior and followed it with a win at the Classic. In 1992 David Frost scored a 268 and won by a record 8 strokes over the field. Lee Jansen won the event in 1994 with a score of 268 and last year Vijay Singh repeated his 1993 victory with a winning score of 268.

Jack Nicklaus won the inaugural Classic in 1967 and repeated the victory in 1972. Other champions include Arnold Palmer (1971), Johnny Miller (1974), Ray Floyd (1981), and Seve Ballesteros who repeated his victory of 1983 in 1988. The Tournament record still belongs to Bob Gilder's 261 in 1982.

Dates:	June 6-9
Network:	USA & CBS
Times:	USA Thur 4:00-6:00 EST
	Fri 4:00-6:00 EST
	CBS Sat 4:30-6:00 EST
	Sun 3:00-6:00 EST
Yardage:	6,779
Par:	71
Slope:	139
Rating:	73.4
1st Prize:	$216,000
1995 Winner:	Vijay Singh
1995 Winning Score:	(278) 70,69,67,72
Principal Charitable Beneficiary:	United Hospital Medical Center
Benefits To Date:	Over $23 million in last 28 year
Ticket Information:	1-800-765-4PGA

1

Par 3
192 yards

The course gets serious right from the start. Players will be using anything from a 2 to 6 iron from the tee, depending on the winds. A two-tiered green makes putting difficult.

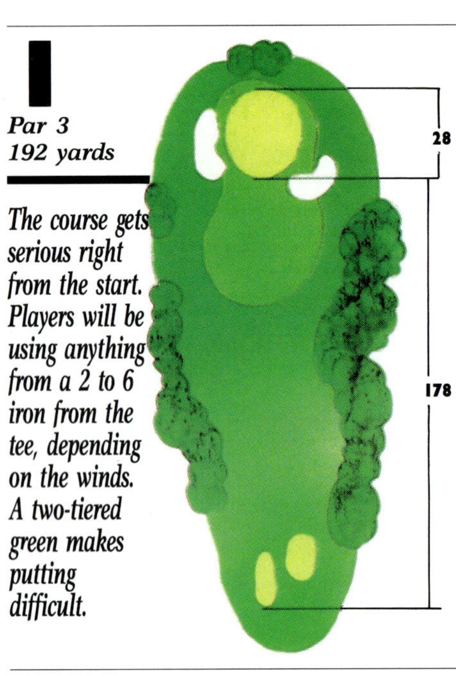

2

Par 4
386 yards

Birdie opportunities present themselves early in the round. By favoring the left side of the fairway, players will have a clear shot to the well-bunkered green.

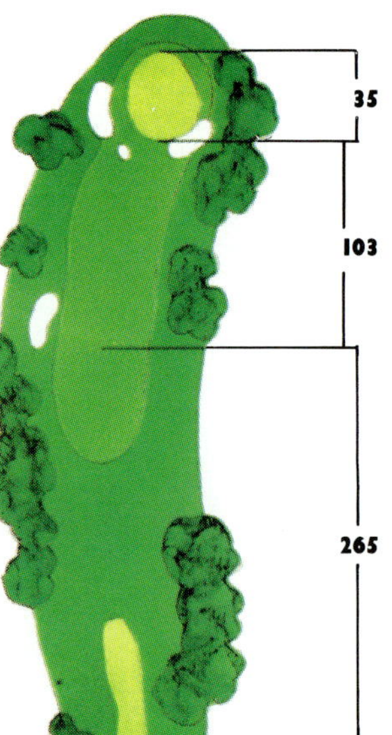

3

Par 4
419 yards

The drive is played from an elevated tee to a deep fairway. The approach ascends back up a hill to a sometimes hidden green. It's a tough shot from the rolling fairway to the raised green.

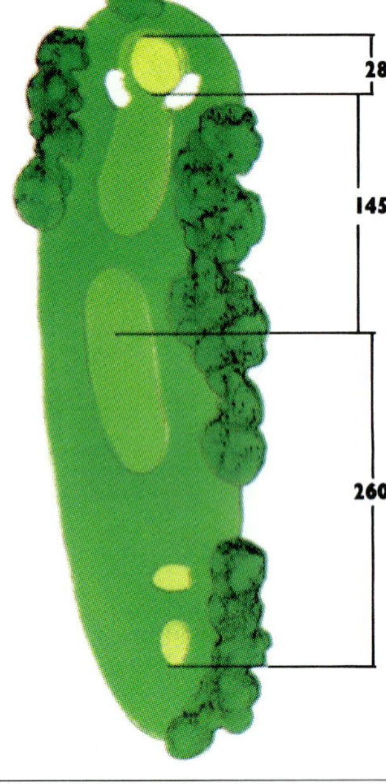

4

Par 4
422 yards

The tee shot is blind on this dogleg left par 4. By favoring the right side of the fairway, players will be able to hit a clear shot to the green. Severe downsloping is beyond the green.

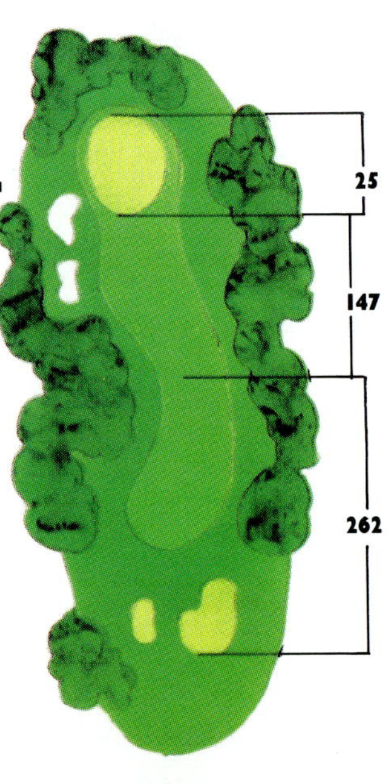

5

Par 5
573 yards

The undulating fairway can present some unfavorable lies. A good second shot will leave no more than 100 yards into the long narrow green.

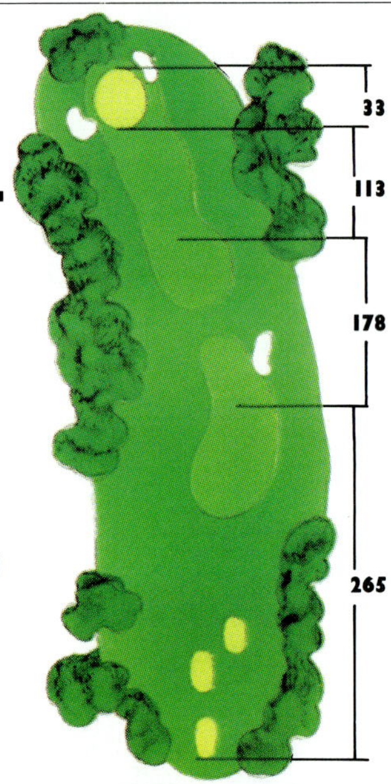

6

Par 3
133 yards

The large green is well protected in front by deep bunkers. The shortness of the hole makes birdies a good possibility.

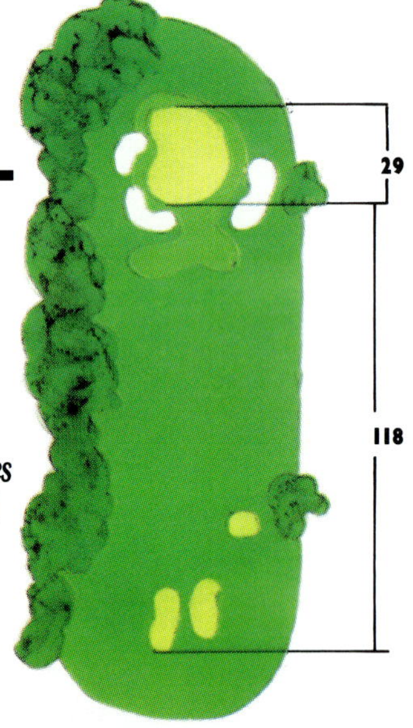

7

Par 4
333 yards

Position off the tee is important for a clear shot to the green. The putting surface is severely undulated making putting tough.

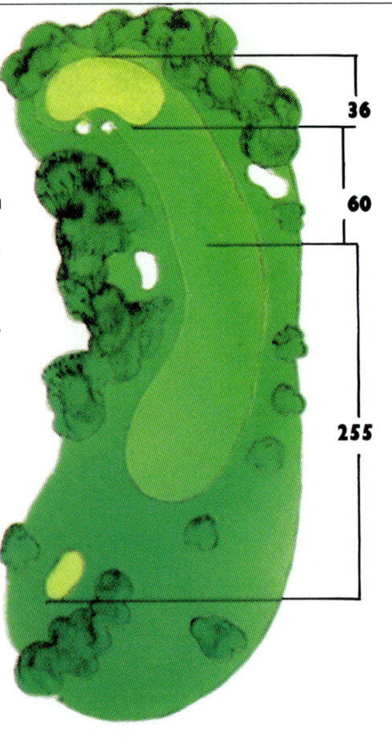

8

Par 4
455 yards

Again, the dogleg bends to the left and and players will be backing off their drives for position. The green is very fast and well protected.

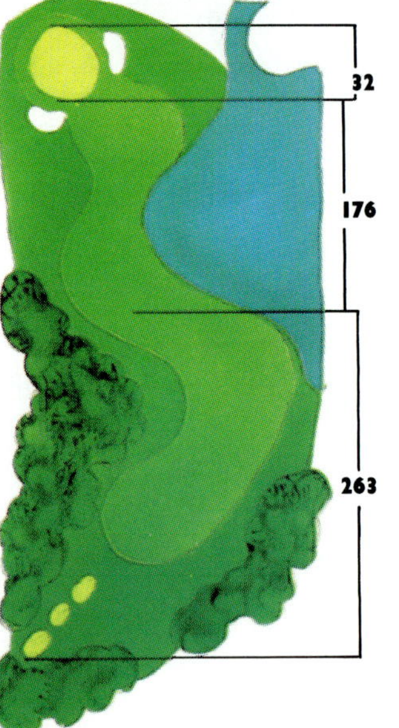

9

Par 5
505 yards

Players reaching for the green in two will have to contend with deep-faced bunkers bordering the green. Players laying up will have a blind third shot.

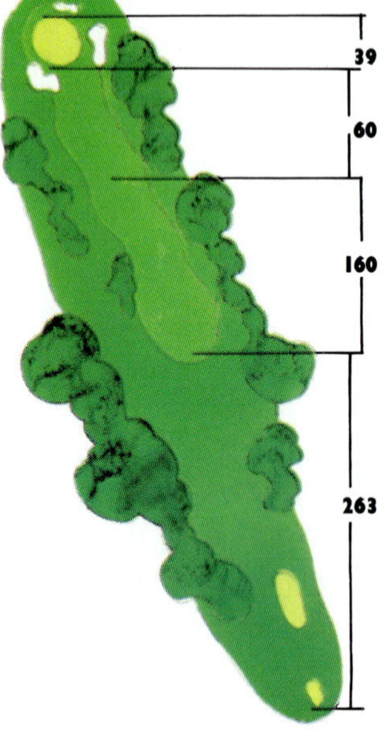

10

Par 4
314 yards

Some long hitters will try to reach this green from the tee. Others will play a conservative fairway wood or long iron off the tee. The approach is to a green sloping from back-to-front.

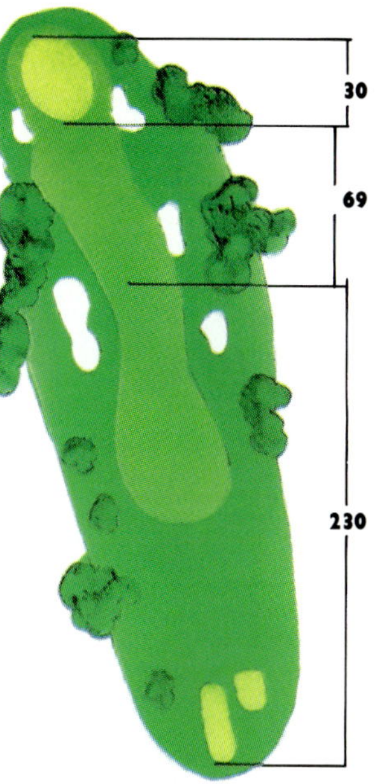

11

Par 4
444 yards

Players will be content with par on this hole. A long drive must be followed with a long iron into the bunkered green.

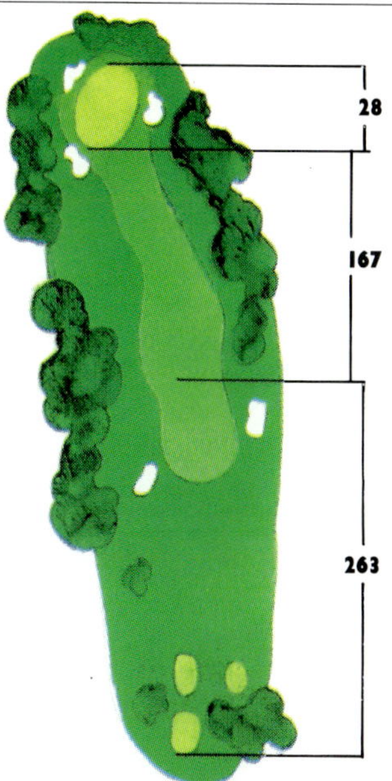

12

Par 4
476 yards

The 12th ranks in the top-5 for toughness on the PGA Tour. The first shot is hit to a deep valley and the second is played to an elevated green.

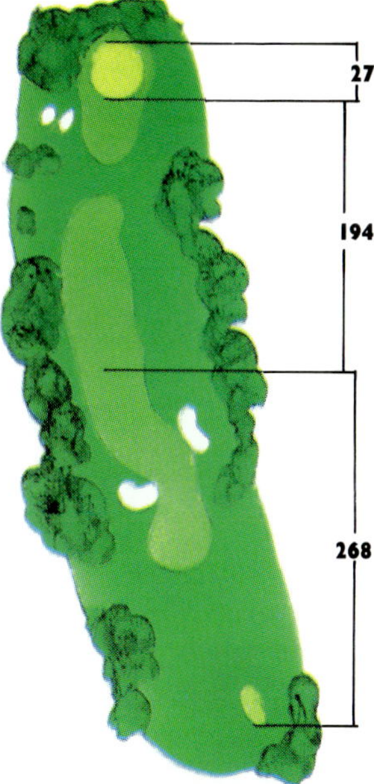

13

Par 4
381 yards

The shot off the tee must carry a small rock formation. The approach shot from the left side of the fairway must be accurately hit to the green to avoid deep rough and bunkers.

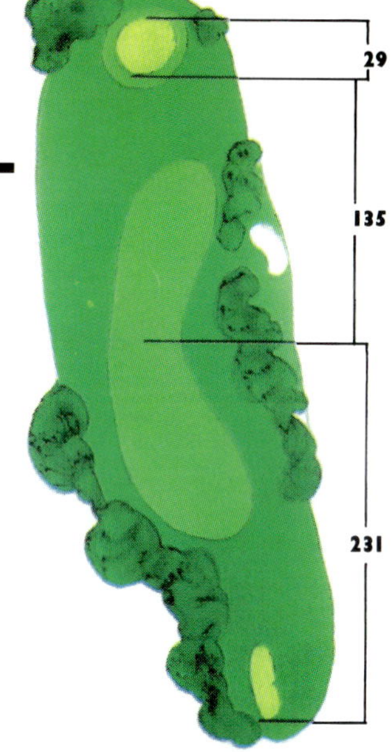

14

Par 3
154 yards

Six hole in-ones have been made on this hole during tournament time. The green is elevated and slopes off severely on the sides.

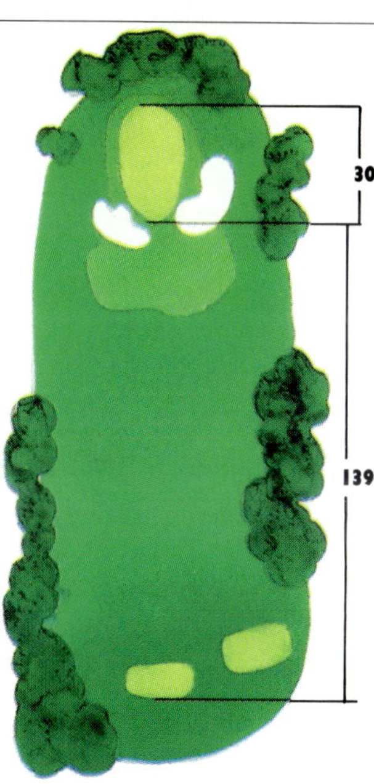

15

Par 4
477 yards

A large, white oak is at the corner of the dogleg. The approach to the slippery green is downhill making it difficult to stop the ball on the surface.

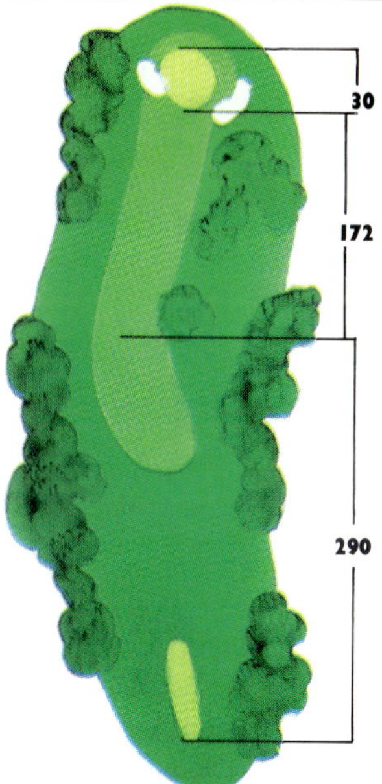

16

Par 3
204 yards

The 16th is the longest and most difficult par 3 on the course. The small green has large bunkers on both sides and deep rough beyond.

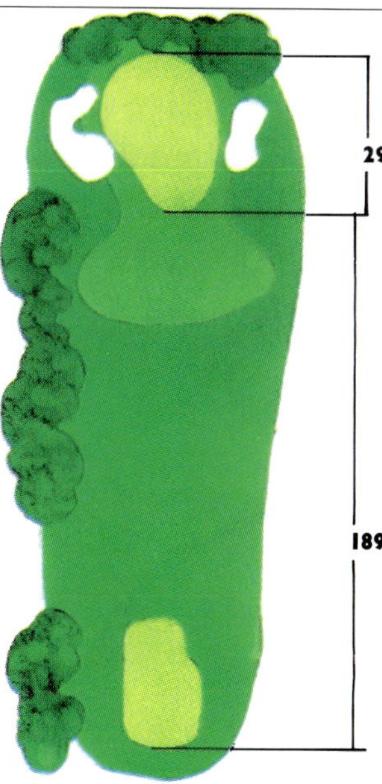

17

Par 4
376 yards

Not a long par 4, but when the pin is placed on either side of the green the approach becomes very difficult.

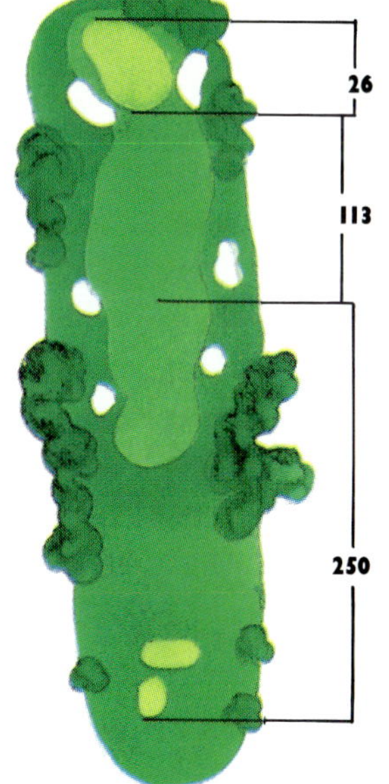

18

Par 5
535 yards

Bob Gilder won the 1982 Classic with a tremendous double-eagle on this 18th. Birdies will be a frequent sight on Sunday.

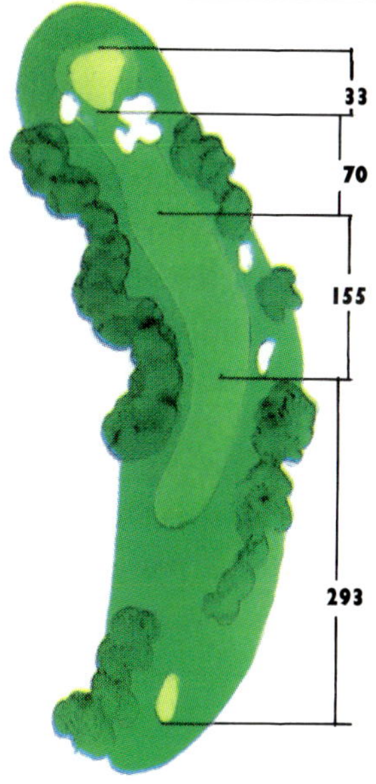

THE COURSE: OAKLAND HILLS COUNTRY CLUB, BIRMINGHAM, MICHIGAN
A USGA Sponsored Event

Oakland Hills is hosting its 6th U.S. Open. From its very beginning in the early 1920s, Oakland Hills began to make its mark in the annals of American golf history. The 1924, 1937, 1951, 1961, and 1985 US Opens, along with the 1972 and 1979 PGA Championships and the 1981 U.S. Senior Open were all held at this proud venue.

Five U.S. Opens and two PGA Championships. A Western Open and a U.S. Women's Amateur. Donald Ross and Robert Trent Jones. Cyril Walker, Mike Brady, Glenna Collett Vare, Ralph Guldahl, Ben Hogan, Gene Littler, Gary Player, David Graham, Arnold Palmer and Andy North.

There you have it, the history of Oakland Hills as a site for major golf championships. It's a bit bare bones, admittedly, but the task of capturing in any thing less than an entire book the tumultuous—and very human—drama that has characterized the events played over the great South Course of the Oakland Hills Country Club is a daunting one indeed.

Dates:	June13-16, 1996
Network:	ESPN & NBC
Times:	TBA
Yardage:	7105
Par:	72
Slope:	143
Rating:	76.5
Total Purse:	$1,950,000
1st Prize:	$350,000
1995 Winner:	Corey Pavin
1995 Winning Score:	280(72,69,71,68)
Ticket Information:	1-800-336-4446

1

Par 4
436 yards

The opening shots of this year's U.S. Open will be hit from an elevated tee to a landing area framed by bunkers left and right. A middle-iron approach will be a tough shot. The green is protected by a swale, or on the tongue to the back-right of the green. The rough guarding the entrance to the green has been cut back for the Championship.

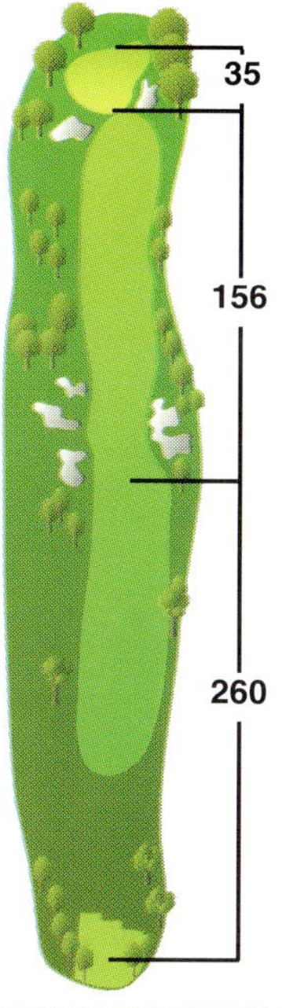

2

Par 5
527 yards

Birdie is possible on this dogleg-left if the drive avoids the fairway bunkers, and sets up a long second shot to the green. Otherwise, players will lay up in front of the four bunkers protecting the front of the green and face a delicate pitch to a two-tiered green, the upper tier of which slopes away from the approach.

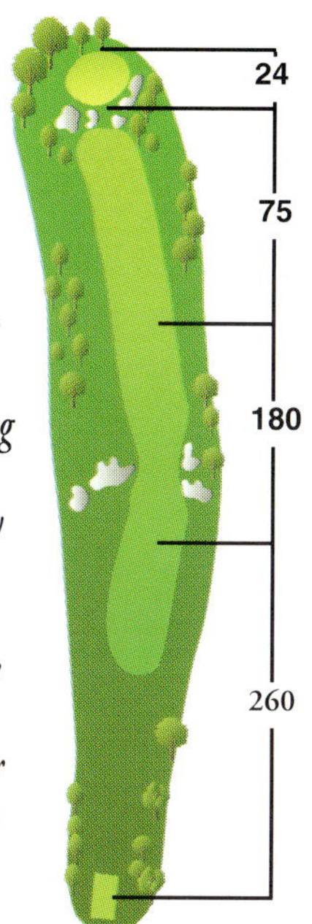

3

Par 3
199 yards

The first par three usually demanding a long iron into the prevailing wind. Two deep bunkers guard the left side. If the pin is cut on the small plateau at the back of the green, par will be a good score.

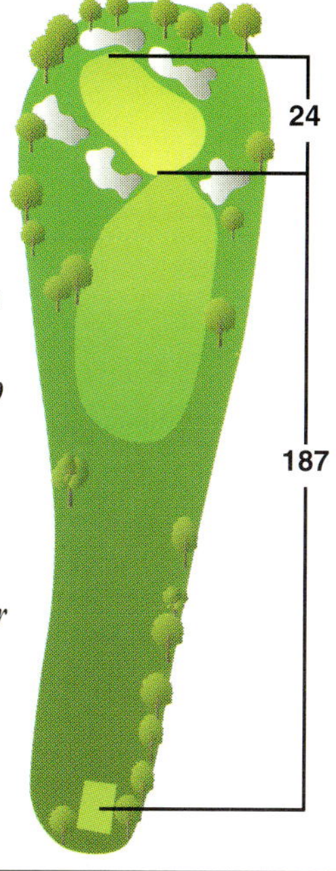

4

Par 4
433 yards

The 24-yard wide landing area is not a huge target. Tee shots hit right of the cluster of bunkers on the inside of the dogleg can catch the slope of the fairway and end up in either of the two bunkers to the right of the landing area. A safe drive leaves an approach that plays shorter than the yardage, as the green lies below the fairway.

5

Par 4
457 yards

This is another tight driving hole with trees guarding the left of the fairway and two bunkers guarding the right. The green is one of the toughest on the golf course. The entrance is protected by deep bunkers left and right while the green itself slopes down from back to front and has severe contours and crowns. Anyone hitting long or to the right is looking at bogey. The creek that crosses the fairway shouldn't come into play.

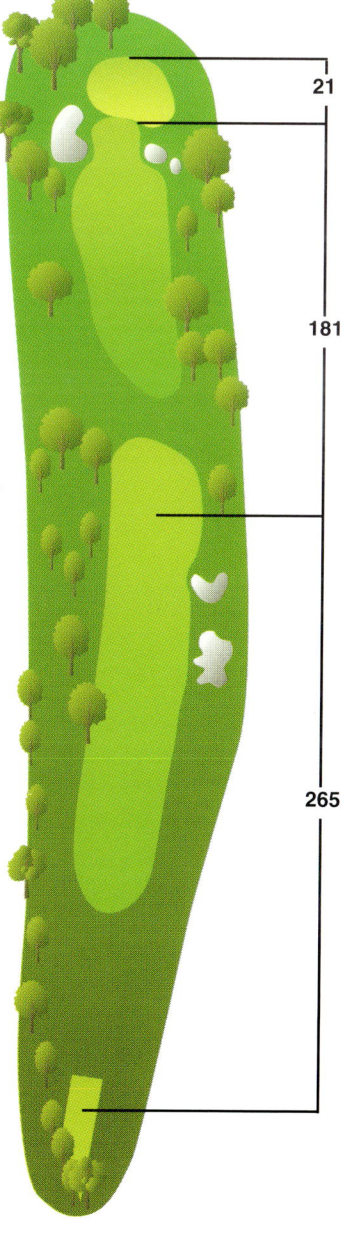

6

Par 4
359 yards

Most players will hit 3-wood from the tee on this, the shortest par four on the course, and take the bunkers to the left of the fairway out of play. Although the sixth also has the deepest green on the course, the putting surface is split into two tiers with the higher portion demanding a tough carry.

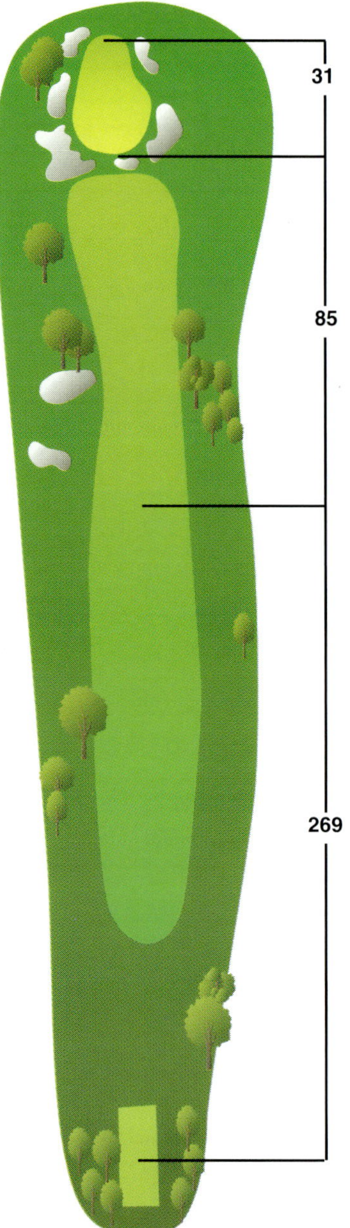

7

Par 4
405 yards

Again players may lay up from the tee to avoid trouble, in this case a trio of bunkers left of the dogleg and a lateral water hazard to the right. The green slopes gently from back to front but is deceptively fast. The players will hit only a short iron in, but when the pin is cut in the left half of the green, the shot will be treacherous because of the deep bunkers protecting that side.

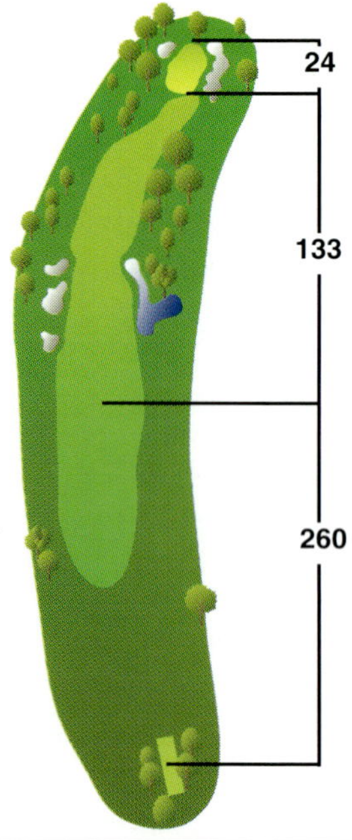

9

Par 3
217 yards

The second of Oakland Hills' excellent par threes requires a long iron or fair way wood to a large undulating green that runs on a diagonal from left to right. With its contours, its small crown in the middle-right and its terrace running along the left of the putting surface, from front to back, this green will likely see numerous three-putts.

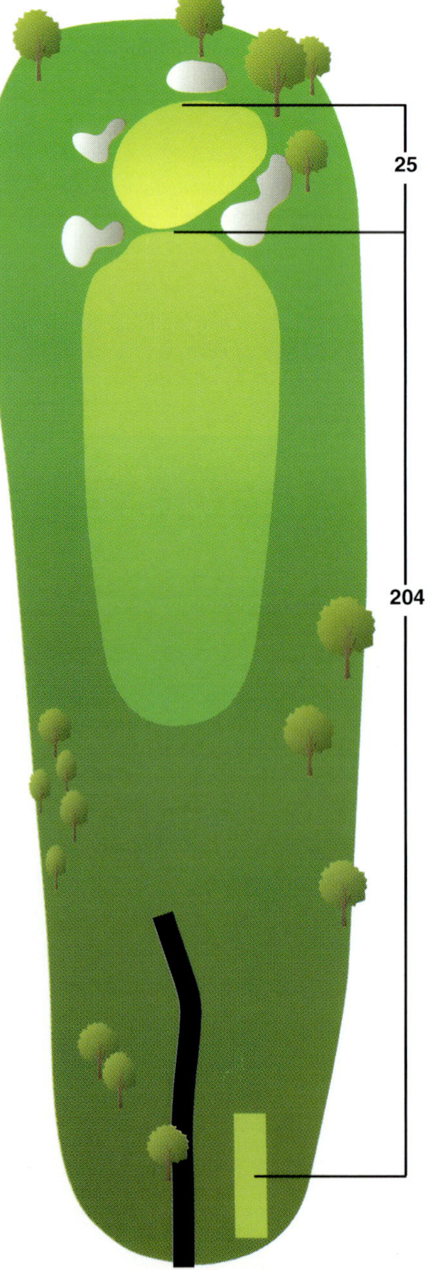

8

Par 4
439 yards

The toughest driving hole on the first nine has pairs of bunkers pinching the fairway on each side of the landing area. The lip of the first bunker on the left is too high to allow anything but a short-iron lay-up while a pitchout is the only recovery possible from the clump of trees farther to the left. The uphill approach demands a fair way wood or long iron to a moderately contoured green guarded by bunkers left and right.

10

Par 4
454 yards

A 3-wood from the elevated 10th tee will avoid not only the three bunkers that line the landing area (one left, two right) but also the steep slope beyond the bunkers. A ball catching the gradient could easily roll into thick rough. The uphill second shot is played to a green with a ridge running through the center. A deep bunker guards the right side while the bunker left of the green is relatively shallow.

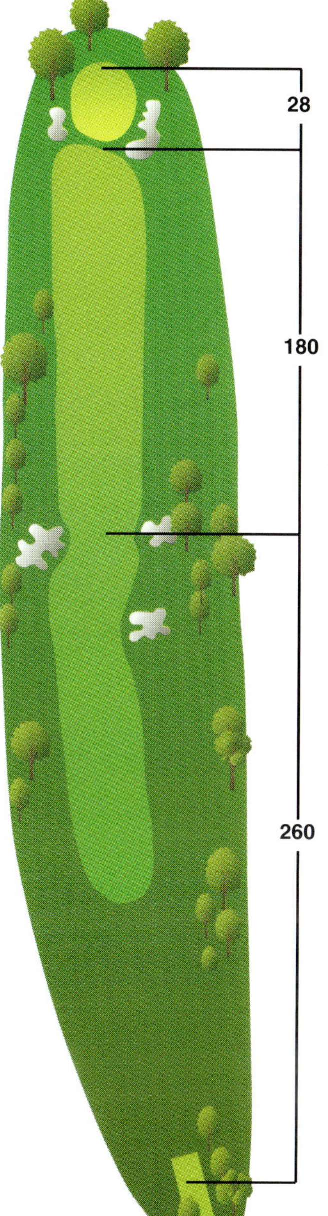

11

Par 4
411 yards

The fairway left of the bunkers guarding the crook of the slight dogleg right is the ideal landing area, which means the tee shot must carry the hill some 230 yards out to leave a short-iron approach. The long, narrow green is flanked on each side by two deep bunkers. Club selection is crucial on the approach as the back tier of the green is four feet higher than the front tier. If the pin is cut front, leaving an uphill putt will be difficult.

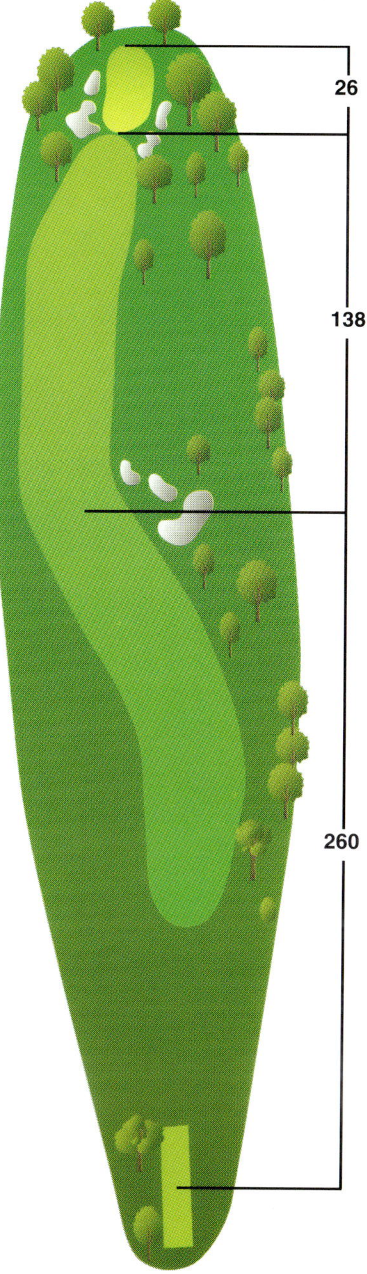

12

Par 5
560 yards

The tee on the South Course's longest hole stands 40 feet above a wide landing area, with a cluster of bunkers left of the fairway. Most players will leave their second shots short of a bunker some 70 yards left of the green and try to get up and down on a green that has a ridge running steeply from front-right to back-left.

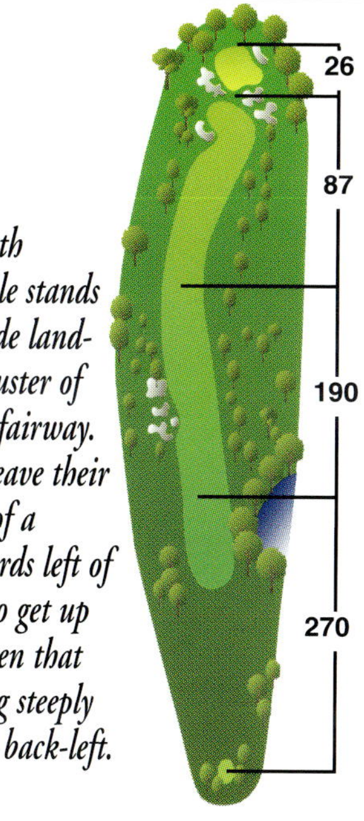

13

Par 3
172 yards

A deep bowl in the front of the green places a premium on club selection to any pin position on the back half of the green. The player has to protect from going over the green because it is very difficult to play the bunker shot and keep the ball on the back terrace.

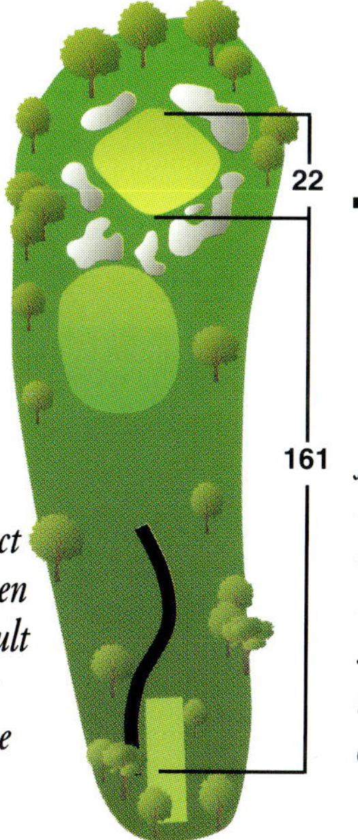

14

Par 4
465 yards

With no fairway bunkers and little movement in this dogleg-right, the first of five tough finishing holes looks innocuous enough. But trees line the entire hole and the second shot is one of the most challenging on the course.

15

Par 4
399 yards

Some may gamble on this hole, especially late in the championship, and try to cut through the gap between the bunker in the heart of the fairway, 240 yards out, and the trees on the inside of the dogleg. Those taking the safer, outside route will face a middle-iron to the green and a tougher line of approach. The saucer-shaped green is rife with crowns and contours and is flanked by bunkers, three to the left and two to the right.

16

Par 4
409 yards

Although Gary Player all but won the 1972 PGA Championship by hitting his second shot stiff from behind a tree in the rough right of the fairway, and over the pond fronting the green, the safest way to play Oakland Hills' signature hole is to hit the fairway and leave a short-iron to a wide, shallow green that has a ridge running from front to back. An approach hit long to take the water out of play will risk catching one of four bunkers.

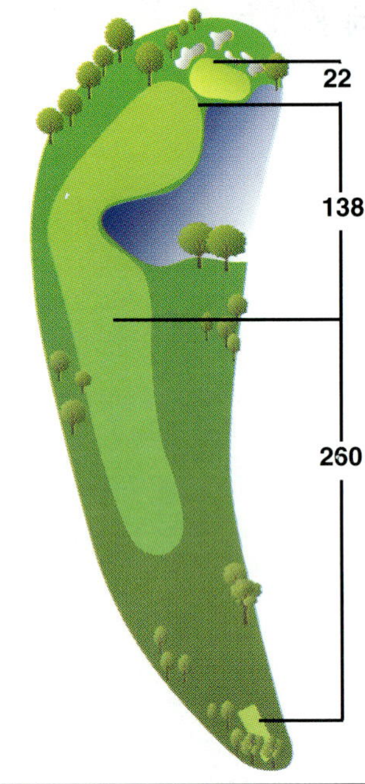

18

Par 4
453 yards

The trouble runs from tee to green on one of the toughest finishing holes in golf. Out of bounds is on the left while three fairway bunkers guard the inside of the dogleg. Another bunker guards the outside of the turn. The long-iron second shot must hold a shallow green originally designed to hold short shots on what members play as a par five. Anything hit to the wrong side of a hump back on the green could well be punished by a three-putt. A great finishing hole.

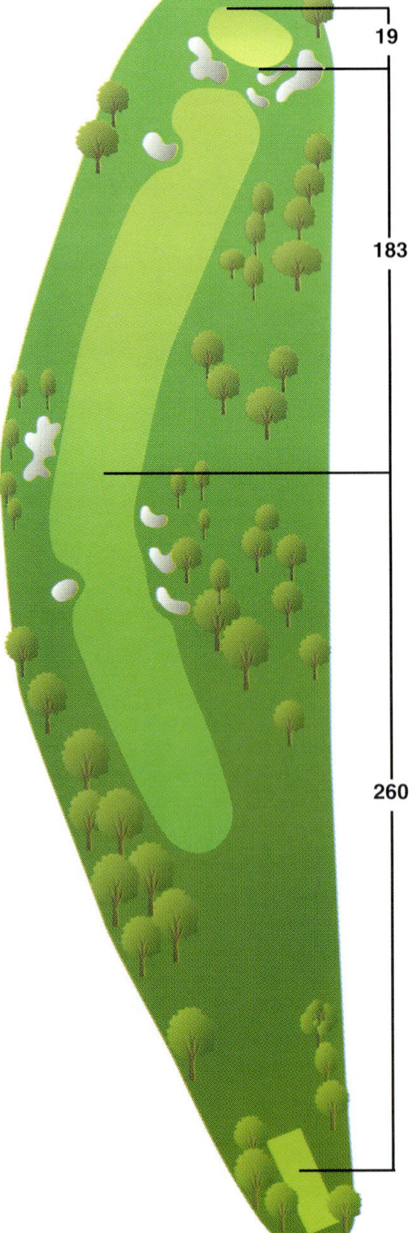

17

Par 3
201 yards

The green sits some 30 feet above the tee and has a ridge running from front right to back-center and a small crown in the front-left. Six bunkers protect the putting surface, demanding a high, accurate tee shot to what is normally a blind pin position.

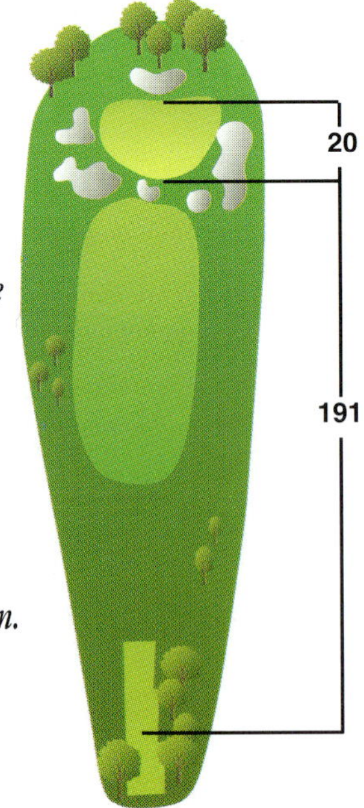

THE COURSE:TPC AT SOUTHWIND,
MEMPHIS, TENNESSEE

*T*he FedEx St. Jude's Classic has endured many spectacular feats since its inception. In 1977, at Colonial Country Club, Al Geiberger scored an unbelievable 59 for the second round competition and went on to win the tournament! That same year, President Gerald Ford-just barely out of office-fired a hole-in-one during the Classic's Pro-Am. Jay Delsing set the course record at the TPC at Southwind with a 10-under-par 61 in 1993's last round.

TPC at Southwind was chosen as the new site for the FedEx St. Jude Classic after 31 years at Colonial Country Club. In 1989, five holes on the Southwind course were listed on the TOUR's list of 100 most difficult holes and the PGA TOUR® announced in its annual report that the TPC network experienced its most successful initiation ever with the unveiling of the Southwind course for the FedEx St. Jude Classic. Clearly the new course was a great addition to the PGA TOUR's® schedule.

Dates:	June 20-23, 1996
Network:	CBS
Times:	TBA
Yardage:	7006
Par:	71
Slope:	135
Rating:	74.8
Total Purse:	$1,250,000
1st Prize:	$225,000
1995 Winner:	Jim Gallagher, Jr.
1995 Winning Score:	267 (65,62,66,72)
Principal Charitable Beneficiary:	St. Jude Children's Research Hospital
Charitable Benefits to Date:	Over $6.6 million in 26 years
Ticket Information:	1-901-748-0534

1

Par 4
426 yards

A great starting hole. The three bunkers along the right provide the target off the tee. A mid-iron to the green must navigate bunkers and a sloping putting surface.

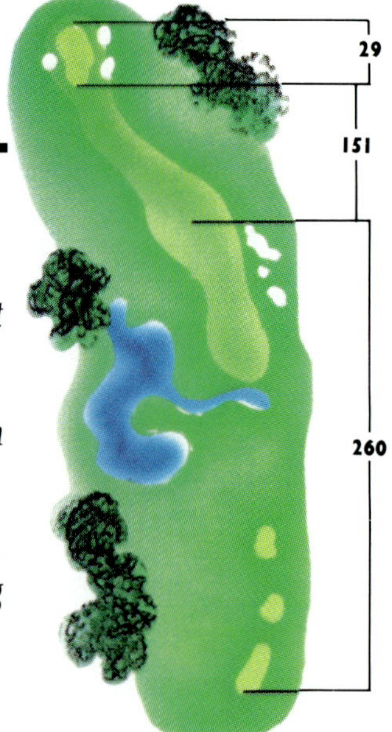

2

Par 4
387 yards

Again the fairway bunkers provide the target line. A large mound is found along the right side of the fairway near the green. Although short, tournament average is usually above par.

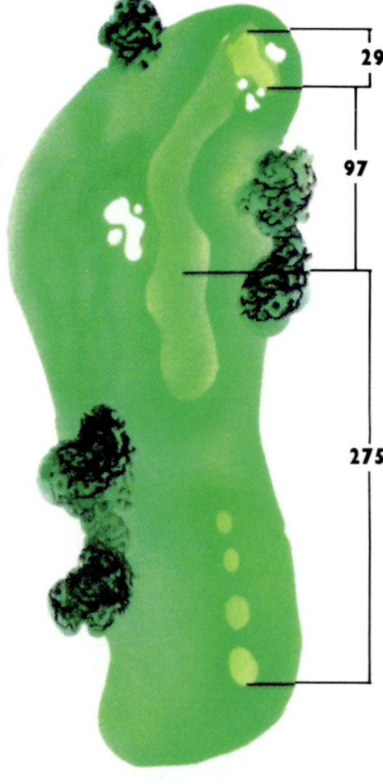

3

Par 5
525 yards

A par 5 that is reachable but risky. Bunkers and water around the green make for difficult saves if green is missed on the approach. Birdies are common.

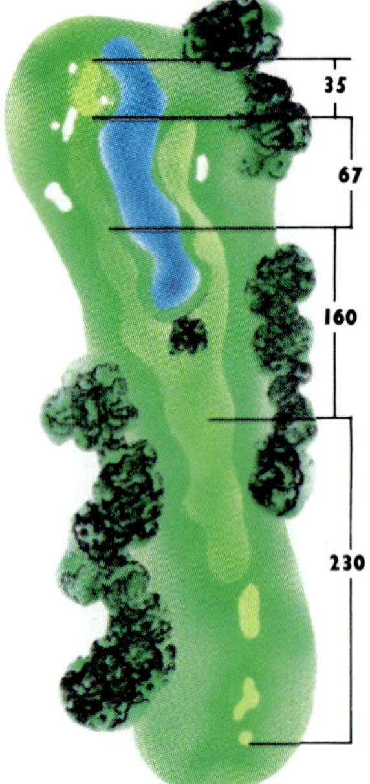

4

Par 3
194 yards

Wind can cause problems on this longer par 3. Three bunkers tightly surround the rolling putting surface. Par on this hole is a good score.

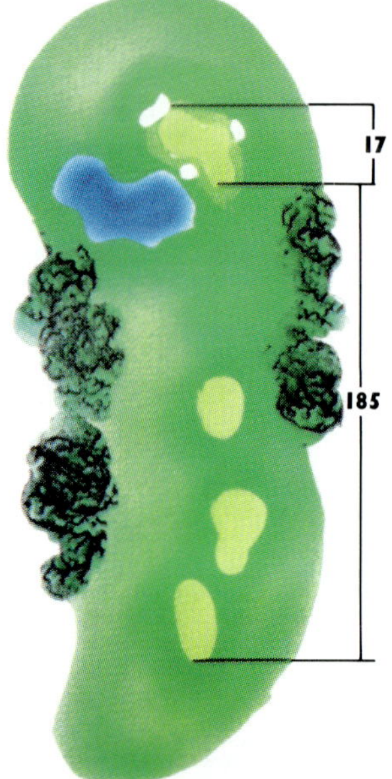

5

Par 5
527 yards

The right side of the fairway will set up a chance for getting home in two. As the easiest hole on the course, you will expect a lot of birdies and, perhaps, a few eagles.

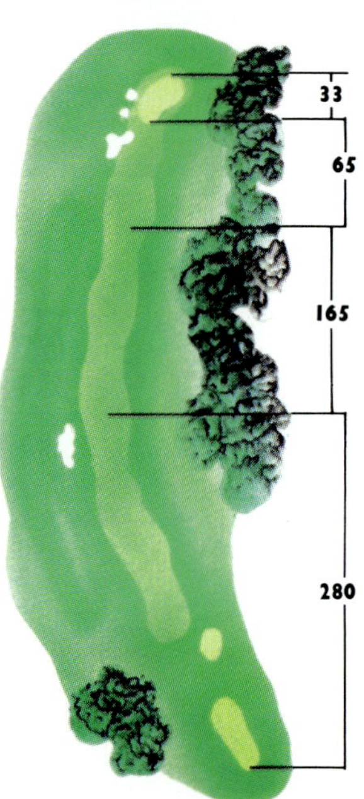

6

Par 4
427 yards

The sixth opens up a bit for a big drive. The second shot must be accurately hit in order to keep from having a long rolling putt.

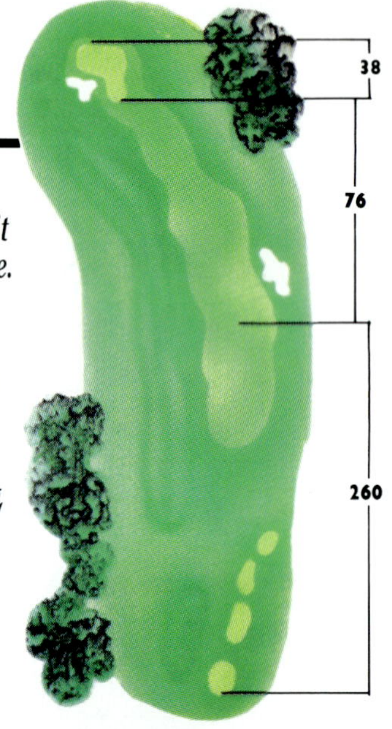

7

Par 4
458 yards

As the longest par 4 on the front side, this 7th will elude the birdie seekers. Two well-hit shots should place the ball in the heart of the green. Two putts, par and on to the next.

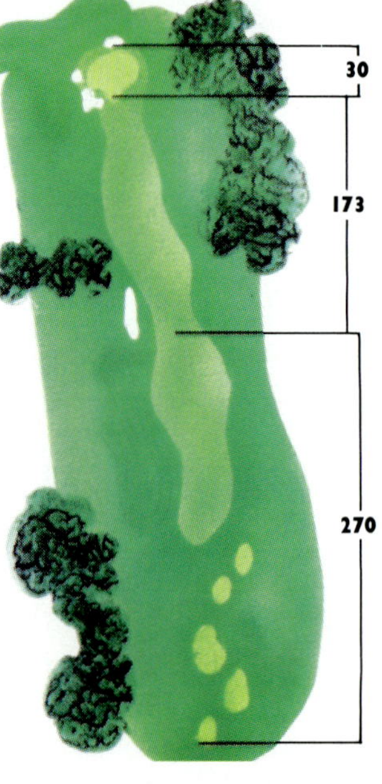

8

Par 3
169 yards

This eighth can be tough against the wind. A cut shot in from the left should place the ball on the putting surface. Players will be very pleased with par.

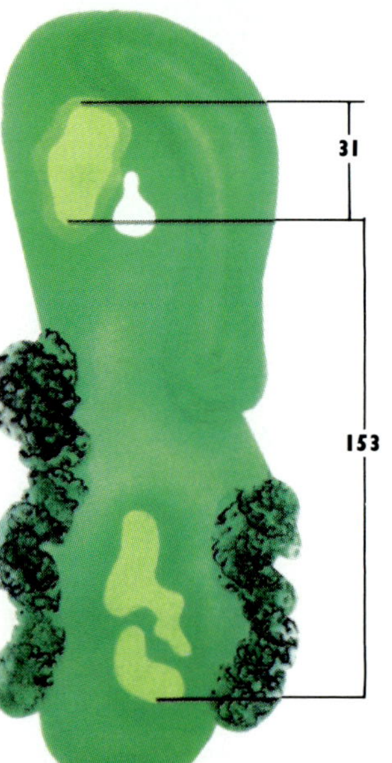

9

Par 4
450 yards

A long finishing hole for the front nine. A birdie on this can start the adrenaline pumping for a big run on the back.

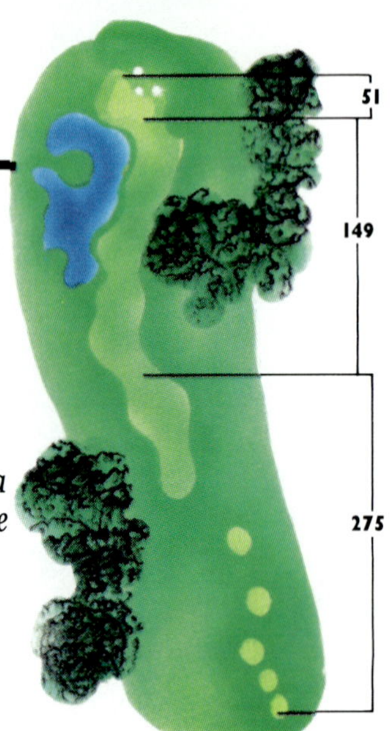

10

Par 4
447 yards

A tough hole to start out the back side. This 10th hole requires an accurate tee shot to find the short grass of the fairway. The large, rolling green is well protected by water and sand.

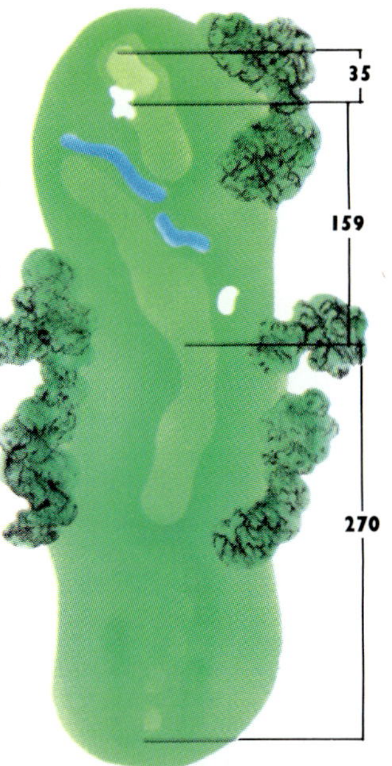

11

Par 3
146 yards

An island-like green is the target from the tee. There is little room for error and the small putting surface makes approaches that much more difficult.

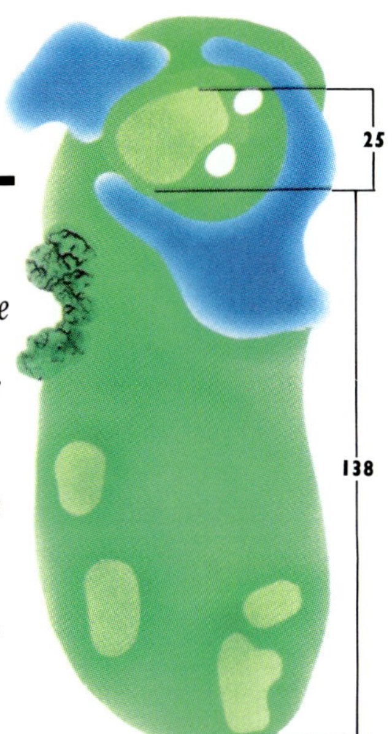

12

Par 4
475 yards

The challenge presents itself in the form of a dogleg. Cutting the corner may yield a shortcut, however, safer play will include an iron off the tee and a mid-iron to the pin.

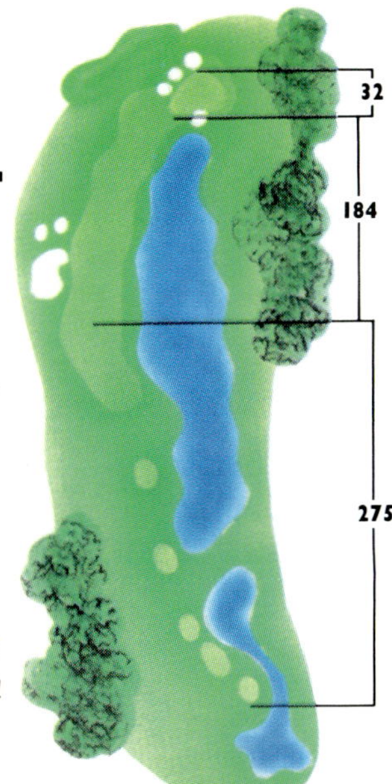

13

Par 4
430 yards

A number of bunkers are scattered in the driving area. Players will be playing a draw over the first three bunkers on the left. The large green is backed by natural stadium seating

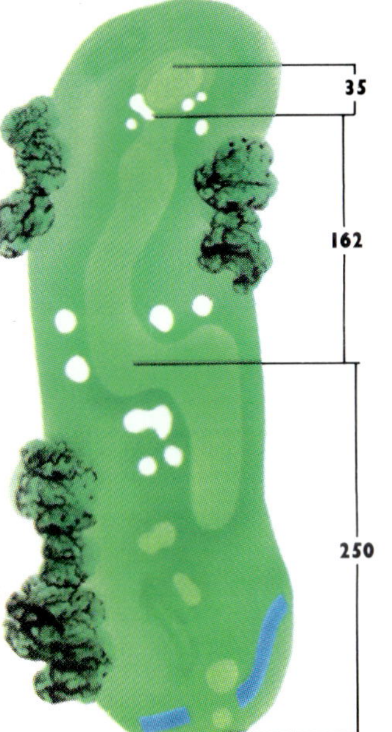

14

Par 3
231 yards

The shapely green can provide for very tricky putts. At 231 yards, accuracy is only a chance. Players will be more than pleased with par.

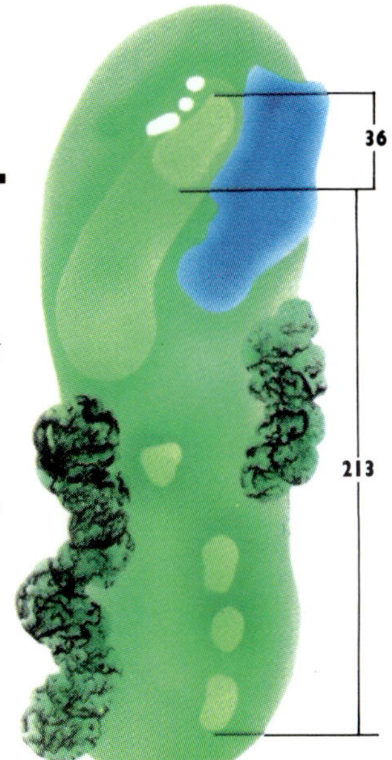

15

Par 4
385 yards

A simple dogleg — short with absolutely no bunkers. In 1989, Hubert Green birdied this hole on his way to a round of 63. He had a chance at matching Geiberger's 59.

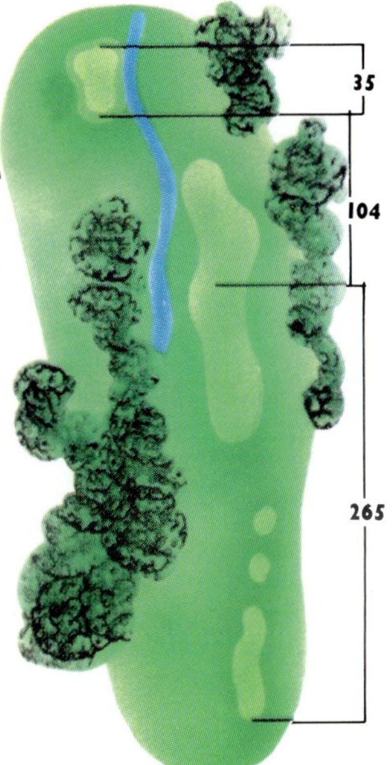

16

Par 5
528 yards

A birdie hole, by definition. The fairway is open to the big drive, thus allowing the chance at getting home in two. Players beware — bunkers are numerous near the green.

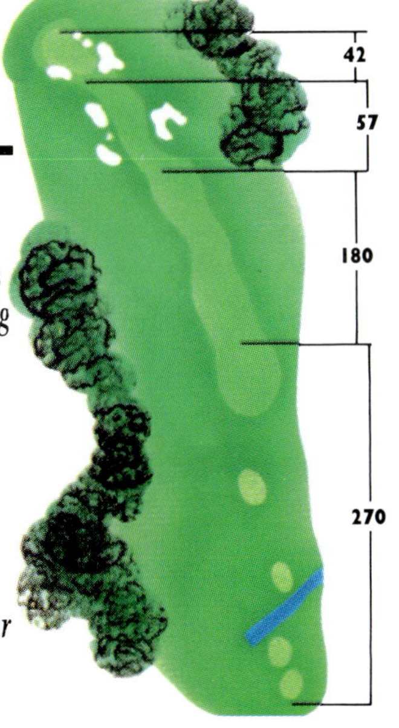

17

Par 4
464 yards

The drive should end up just about 40 yards short of the creek. A mid-iron to the flagstick will yield the birdie — if the putter is working correctly.

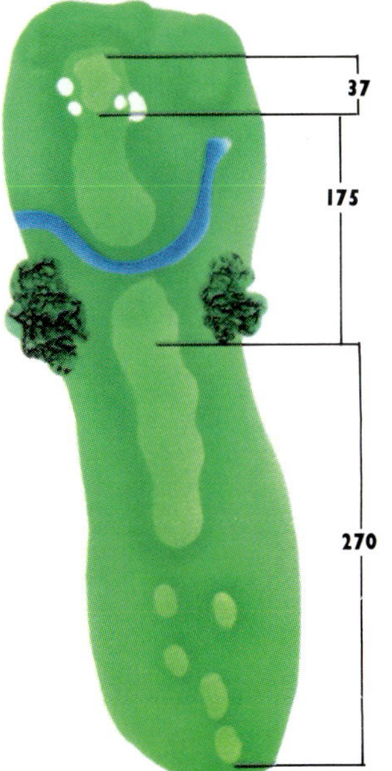

18

Par 4
437 yards

The edge of the lake encroaches in from the left. Some players will try to cut off the corner, however many will find the water. Average score is usually above par.

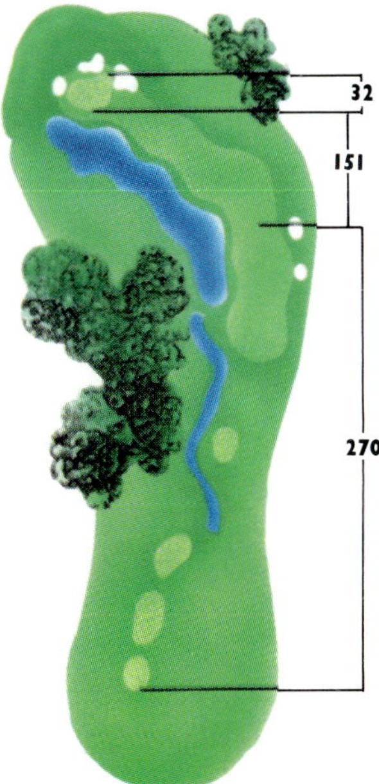

The Bell Atlantic Classic

FOR THE BENEFIT OF
ST. CHRISTOPHER'S
HOSPITAL FOR CHILDREN

THE COURSE: CHESTER VALLEY GOLF CLUB,
MALVERN, PENNSYLVANIA

The Bell Atlantic Classic is a SENIOR PGA TOUR® event benefiting St. Christopher's Hospital for Children. The three-day event, 54-hole tournament is played at Chester Valley Golf Club in Malvern, Pennslyvania and attracts an excellent field each year. The first tournament in 1985 saw Don January capture the $30,000 first place prize of the $200,000 purse. Since then, the purse has grown to $750,000 and the winner takes home in excess of $135,000.

The tournament is now entering its twelfth year and is considered one of the premier charitable events on the SENIOR PGA TOUR® since its inception. The tournament has raised millions for St. Christopher's Hospital for Children in Philadelphia.

Chester Valley Golf Club has been the tournament site ten of eleven years. With its elevated greens and narrow, sloping fairways,Chester Valley Golf Club is considered an extremely difficult course. Although the undulating layout of the course is a detriment to many of the SENIOR PGA TOUR® pros, it provides excellent vantage points for the 100,000 plus spectators who attend the tournament every year.

Dates:	June 21-23, 1996
Network:	ESPN
Times:	Fri 4:00-6:00 EST
	Sat /Sun 2:00-4:00 EST
Yardage:	6,376
Par:	70
Slope:	126
Rating:	68.6
Total Purse:	$750,000
1st Prize:	$135,000
1995 Winner:	Jim Colbert
1995 Winning Score:	207 (68,71,68)
Principal Charitable Beneficiary:	St. Christopher's Hospital for Children, Philadelpia, PA
Ticket Information:	1-610-644-2582

1

*Par 4
368 yards*

On this hole players will use a 2-iron or a 3-or 4-wood off the tee. One must be careful to land their tee shot on the right center of the sloping fairway to avoid trees and the creek that runs along the left side. A short-to medium-iron will reach the green on the second shot.

2

*Par 5
537 yards*

The tee shot is the key to the par-5 second hole. Players will use a driver and must hook the ball into the sloping fairway to avoid a kick to the right that will leave the ball in the rough. Most golfers will lay up on their second shot, leaving a short pitch to the green.

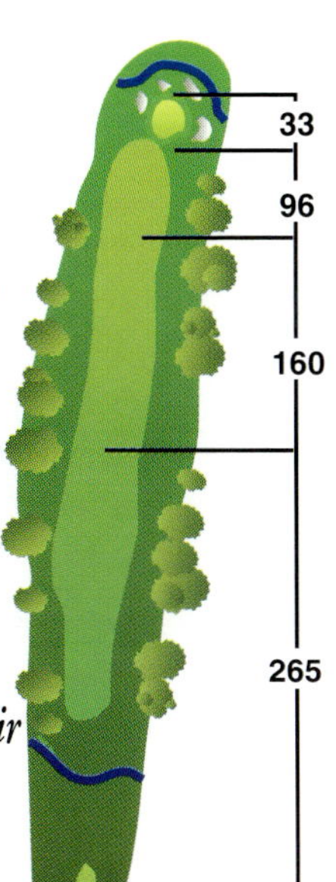

3

*Par 4
338 yards*

Players will leave the driver in the bag and use a 2-or 3-iron off the tee to avoid hitting through the fairway which doglegs to the right. With a tee shot landed safely in the fairway, a 7-,8-or 9-iron is all a player will need for a relatively simple approach shot.

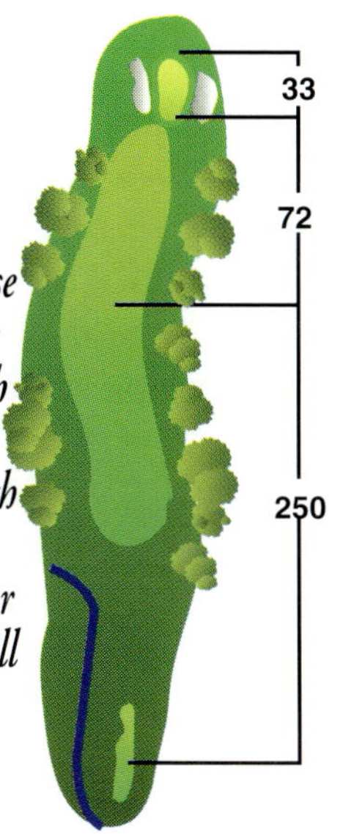

4

*Par 4
378 yards*

Players will use a 3-wood off the tee in order to keep their drive short of the bunker on the left-hand side of the fairway. A drive landed just short of this bunker is ideal and will leave players a 9-iron away from the green. The tee shot must be straight or players will find trouble on either side of the fairway.

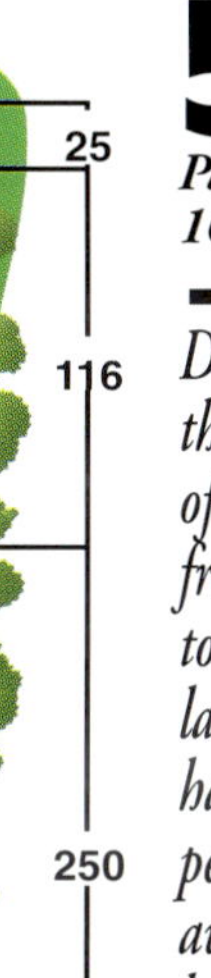

5

*Par 3
162 yards*

Due to its severe green, this short par-3 is one of the hardest holes on the front nine and one of the toughest greens. A tee shot landed on the front, right-hand side of the green is perfect. A player must avoid the upper right-hand portion of the green or risk an extremely challenging first putt.

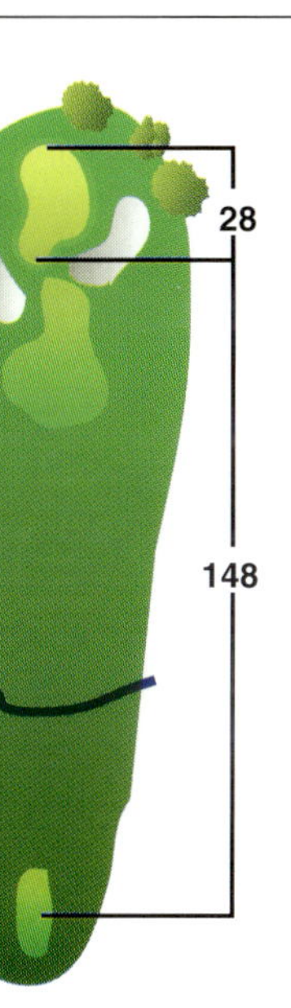

6

*Par 4
411 yards*

Most players will use a 3-wood off the tee and lay up short of the creek. However, players must me careful to hit their first shot long enough to reach the driving area and avoid a downhill lie on their approach to the green.

7

*Par 3
163 yards*

Players will use a 7-or 8-iron from an elevated tee. The water hazard is large, but manageable, with a strong drive from the tee. Sand traps bunker the green's fairly open approach.

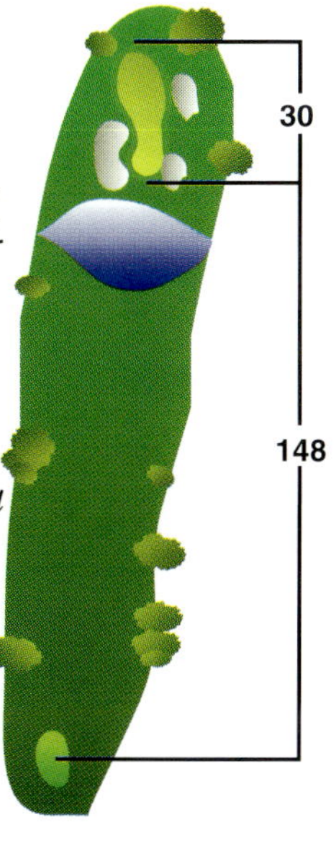

8

*Par 4
385 yards*

This is one of the most difficult holes on the Senior PGA Tour. To set up the second shot, players must reach the driving plateau, a challenge for even the longest hitters. Players are faced with a difficult uphill shot on a sloping fairway.

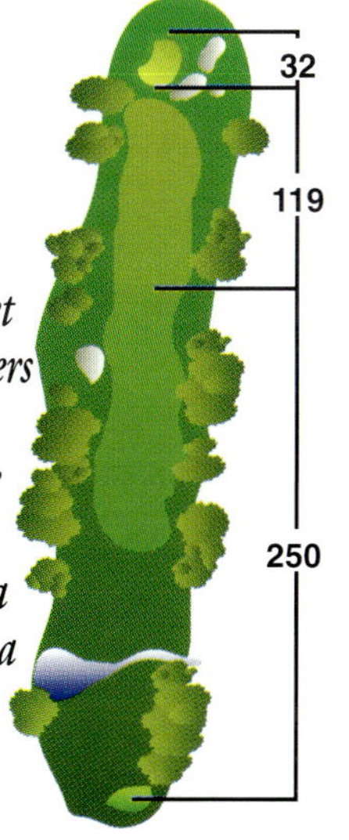

9

*Par 4
470 yards*

Smart players will use a 3-iron to a driver on this short par-4. Some players can almost reach the green with a driver, leaving themselves a very short chip shot to the green. With a straight drive, this hole presents no major obstacles.

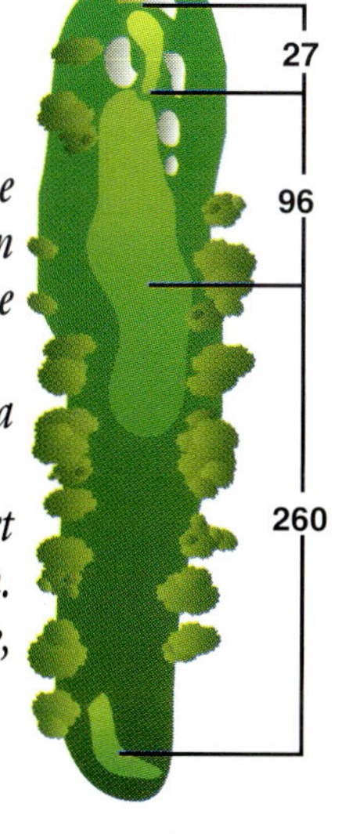

10

Par 3
188 yards

This is an elevated tee shot, across a valley, leading to an elevated and well-bunkered green. To the experienced player it presents nothing particularly unusual.

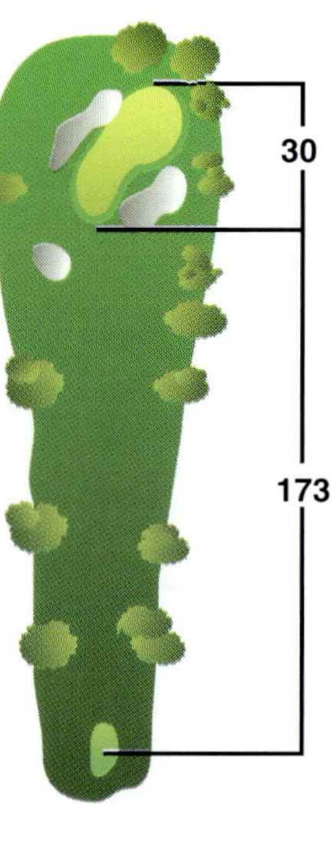

11

Par 4
357 yards

Players will use a 2-, 3- or 4-iron off the tee and must land on the extreme right side of the fairway to set up a second shot. A drive in the middle or left side of the fairway leaves a player blocked by tall trees from the green.

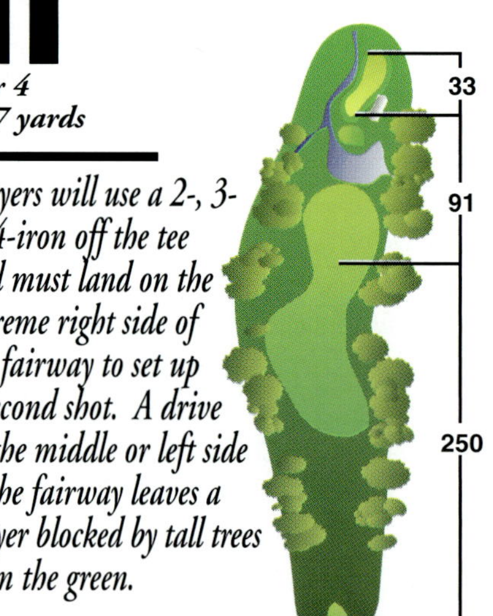

12

Par 4
410 yards

This hole challenges players with a sloping, tree-lined fairway that makes it one of the most difficult driving holes on the course. The green is very severe and is almost as difficult to putt as the fifth hole.

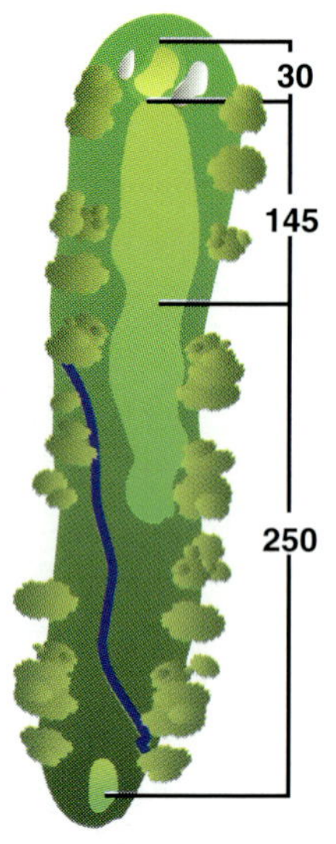

13

Par 4
416 yards

This is the key hole on the back nine. Players will select a 2-iron or a 3- or 4-wood off the tee. With a good tee shot, players are left with a 7-, 8- or 9-iron to the green.

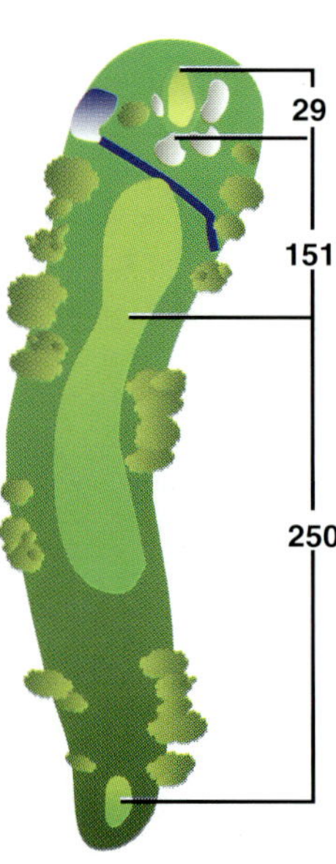

14

Par 5
488 yards

A driver off the tee will carry over the creek for the long-ball hitters. Some players will lay up just short of the creek with a 3-wood and still have a chance of reaching the green in two.

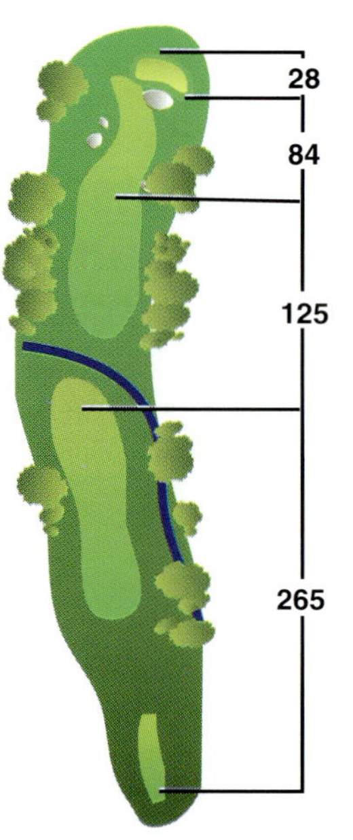

15

Par 3
179 yards

This is the most difficult hole on the course. The tee that angles to the left and a green that slopes to the right create a difficult perception for players. A long iron from the tee must be accurate, since the green is small and surrounded by trees.

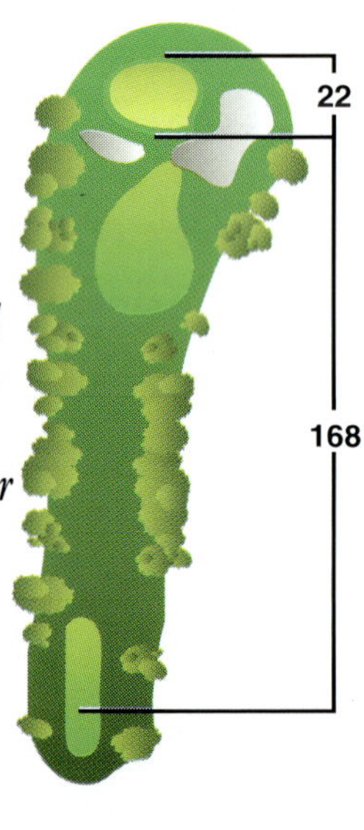

16

Par 4
403 yards

Most players will hit a driver off the tee and fade the ball around a sever dogleg right. Player who keep the ball to the right side of the fairway will leave themselves with an easy second shot and a good chance for a birdie.

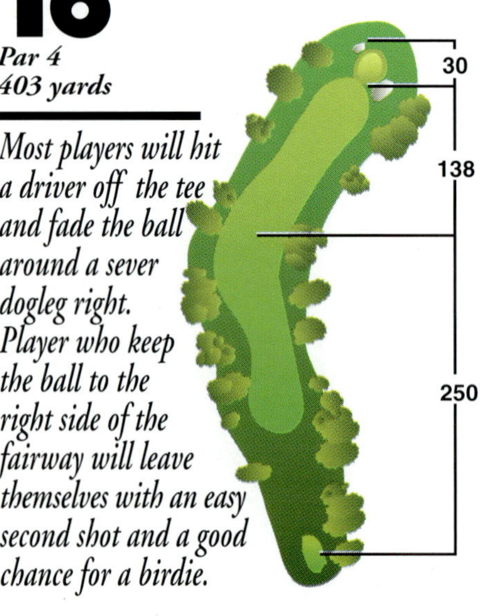

17

Par 4
391 yards

Players must keep their drive to the right center of the fairway and long enough to enable them to see the green on their second shot. Most players will use a 6-,7-or 8-iron on a difficult approach shot to this small forward-tilting green.

18

Par 4
435 yards

Players will use a driver or 3-wood off the tee on this finishing hole. A large bunker on the right side of the fairway, forces players to be more cautious and land their tee shot on the left-center portion of the fairway.

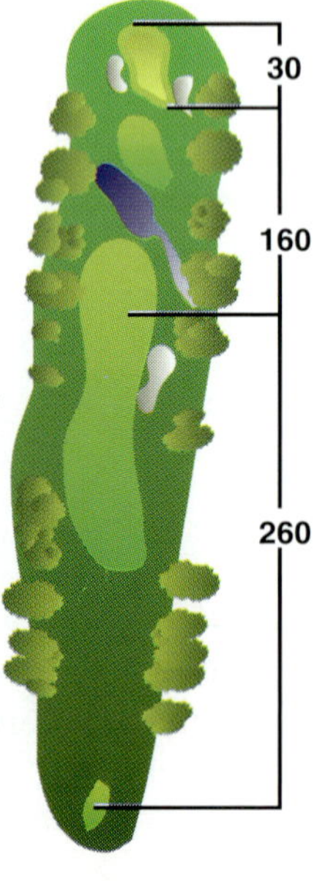

THE COURSE: TPC AT RIVER HIGHLANDS,
CROMWELL, CONETICUT

The Canon Greater Hartford Open was played on a new golf course in 1991 and has quickly become one of the most popular stops on the PGA TOUR®. The TPC at River Highlands was completely re-designed by PGA TOUR® architect Bobby Weed with the assistance from PGA TOUR® player consultants Howard Twitty and Roger Maltbie. The Challenging re-design and breathtaking views overlooking the Connecticut River were met with rave reviews from the players and will surely be a formidable test of golf for this years tournament.

The tournament itself was the brainchild of two enterprising members of the Greater Hartford Jaycees. Ted May and Dr. Philip Sehl created the event in an effort to raise money for charitable beneficiaries. After discovering that the Los Angeles Jaycees and Greensboro Jaycees had established PGA events they thought it was worth the effort. Since its inception, the tournament has been a stable contributor to the community, raising over $ 11,000,000 for various charities.

Dates:	June 27-30, 1996
Network:	CBS
Times:	Sat /Sun 4:00-6:00 EST
Yardage:	6820
Par:	70
Slope:	135
Rating:	72.4
Total Purse:	$1,200,000
1st Prize:	$216,000
1995 Winner:	Greg Norman
1995 Winning Score:	267 (67,64,65,71)
Principal Charitable Beneficiary:	Greater Hartford Jaycees
Ticket Information:	1-203-522-4171

1

Par 4
434 yards

The opening hole begins the tournament easy enough. A big drive down the middle will leave a medium iron to the green. The large putting surface will require accurate shots for birdies.

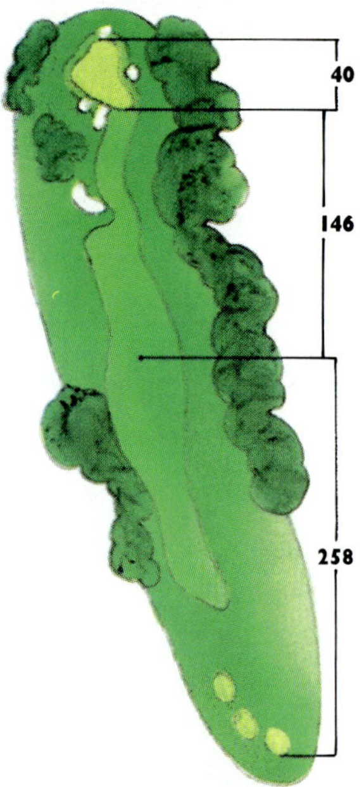

2

Par 4
341 yards

Slight dogleg left, this second hole ascends uphill towards the green. The kidney-shaped green can cause problems for the putter.

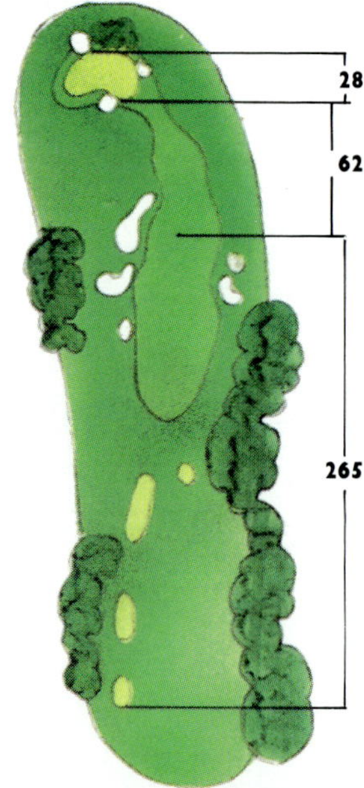

3

Par 4
431 yards

Generally a straight hole, this third still requires precision off the tee. The approach is into a narrow, gently rolling putting surface.

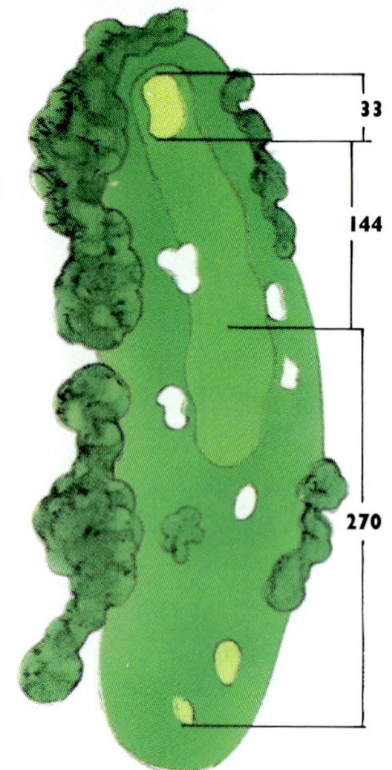

4

Par 4
460 yards

A long par 4 requiring two well hit shots to reach the two-tiered green. Winds can cause problems on the approach.

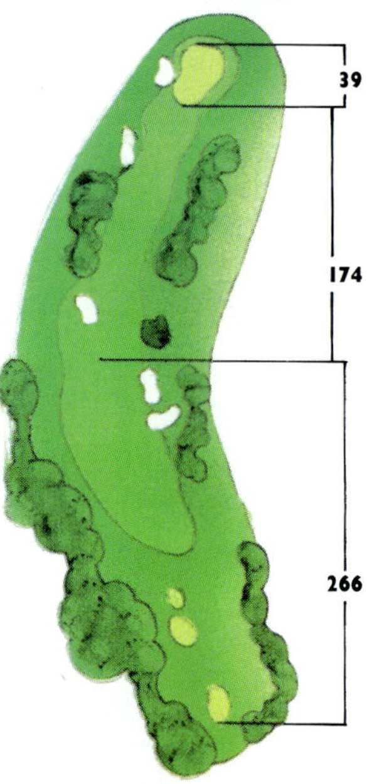

5

Par 3
223 yards

As the longest par 3 on the course, this fifth hole is one that players will be happy to par. The large green is protected by bunkers in front.

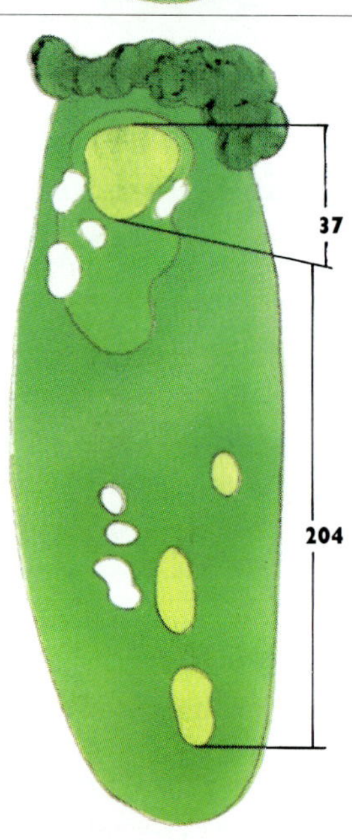

6

Par 5
574 yards

This is the longest hole on the course. The dogleg dictates a drive down the left middle. The second shot will be played with a mid-iron also to the left side. The tight green demands accuracy.

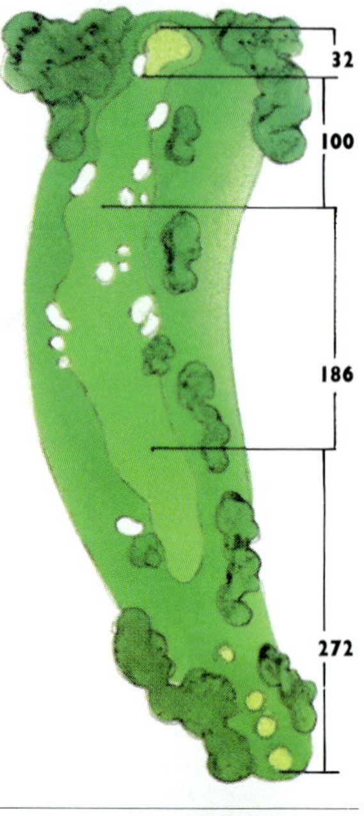

7

Par 4
443 yards

Precision off the tee is a must to place the drive in the short grass of the fairway. Out-of-bounds is to the left and bunkers along the right. The shallow green sits among the trees and bunkers.

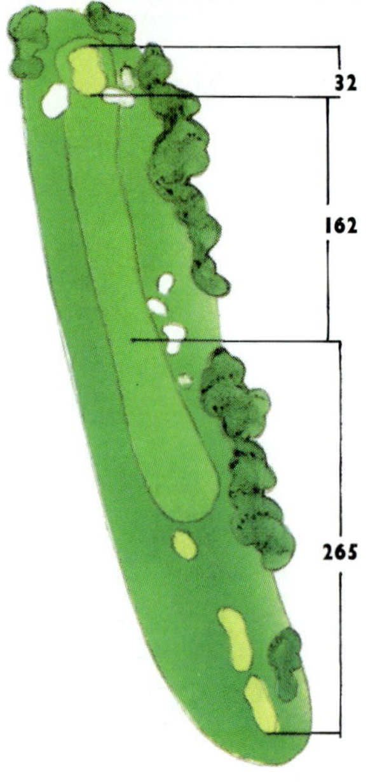

8

Par 3
202 yards

The tee shot must at least carry 180 yards to safely reach the far side of the water. The gently sloping green is tightly guarded by trees on the left.

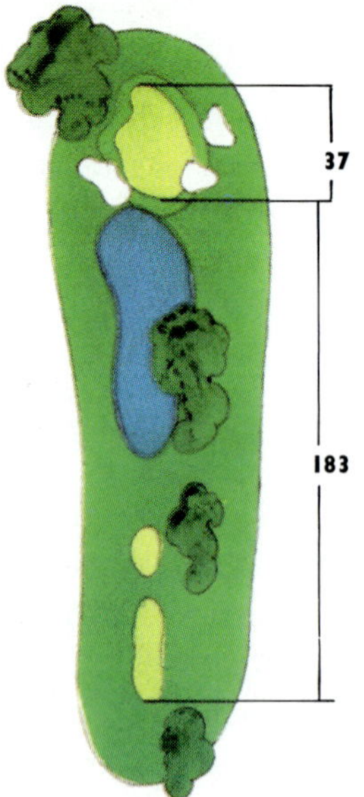

9

Par 4
406 yards

The first bunker to the right should be the target off the tee. The drive over the bunker and to the left middle of the fairway will leave a mid-iron to the flat, spacious green.

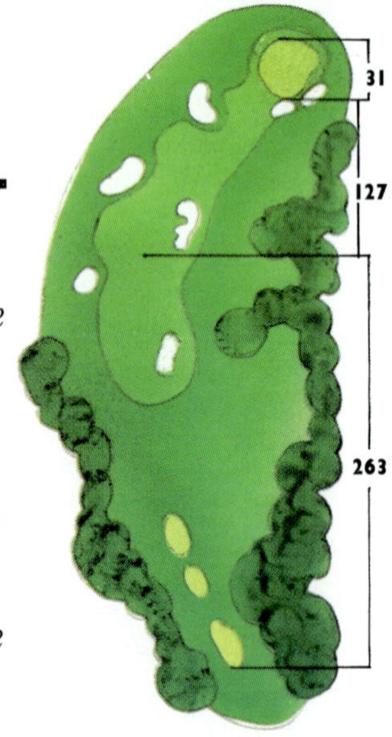

10

Par 4
462 yards

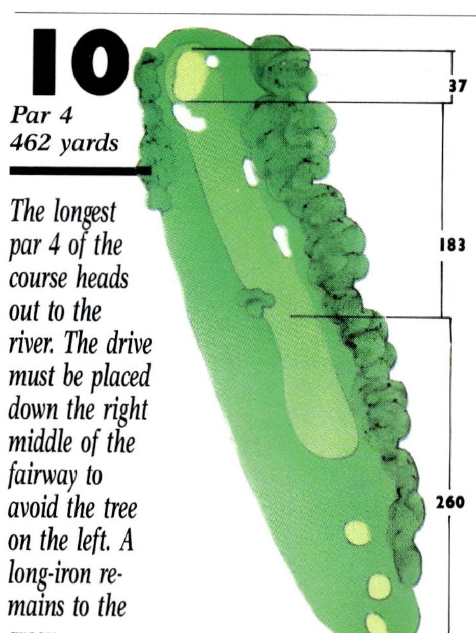

The longest par 4 of the course heads out to the river. The drive must be placed down the right middle of the fairway to avoid the tree on the left. A long-iron re-mains to the green.

11

Par 3
158 yards

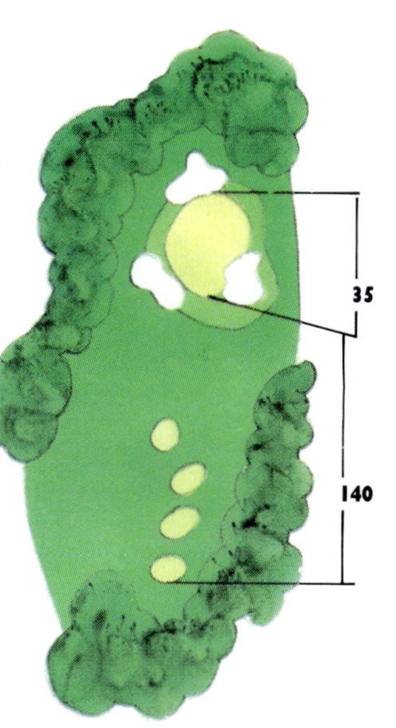

The elevated tee overlooks the Con-necticut River. A short to mid-iron, depending on the wind, must be hit close to the pin to have a makeable putt on the undulating green.

12

Par 4
411 yards

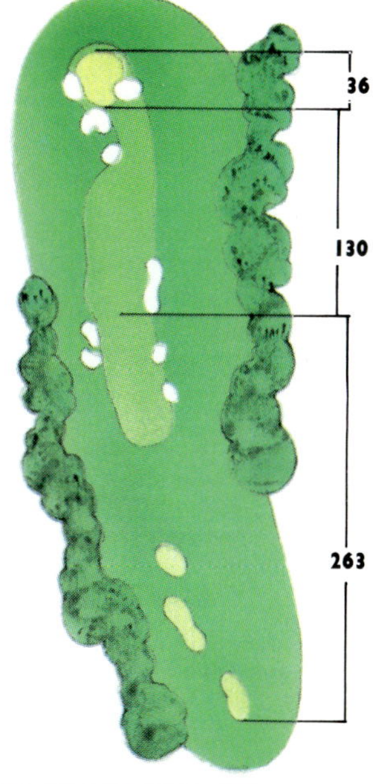

A formidable par 4 that parallels the Connecticut River. Driving precision is a must to avoid the bunkers left and right. The green sits beyond many deep bunkers.

13

Par 5
523 yards

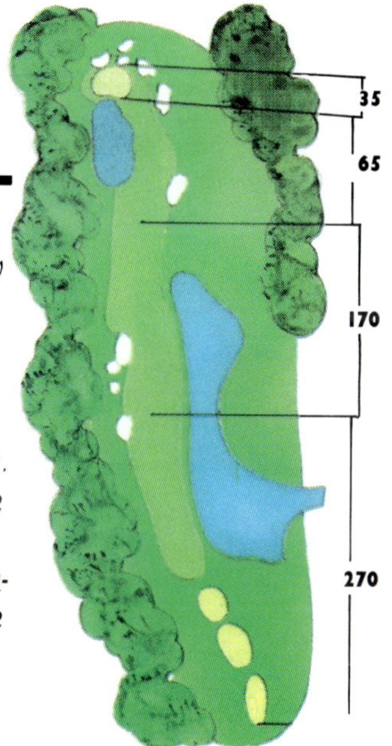

Water can come into play on the first and second shots. Players will favor the left side of the fairway off the tee. The third shot is very im-portant for the the chance at birdie.

14

Par 4
421 yards

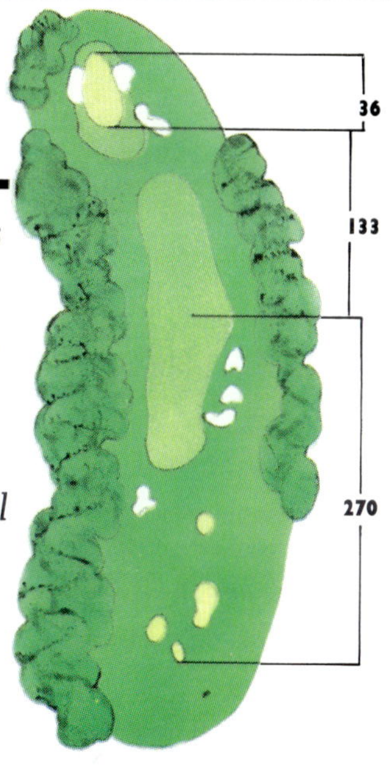

The tee shot is played uphill over a bunker on the left. By favoring the right side of the fairway, the players will be able to open the view to the green.

15

Par 4
296 yards

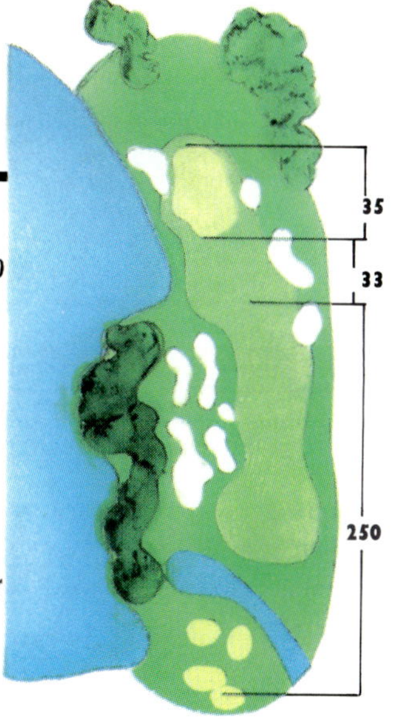

The tee shot may be able to reach the green, but the shot is risky. Birdies should be in abun-dance while players gather momentum for the last three holes.

16

Par 3
171 yards

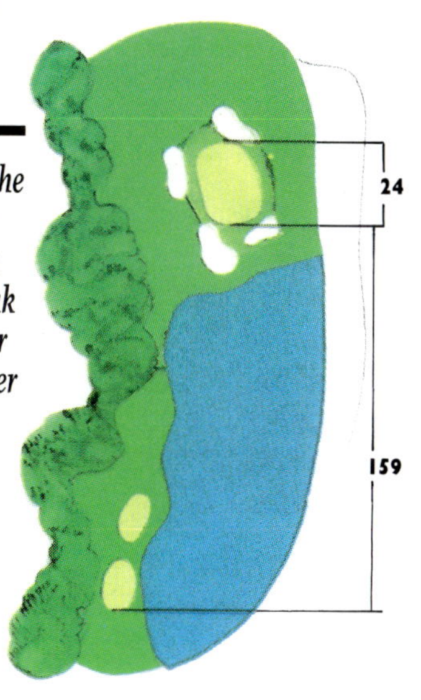

All carry to the green — this sixteenth can make or break a player. Four bunkers corner the green, catching all errant tee shots.

17

Par 4
420 yards

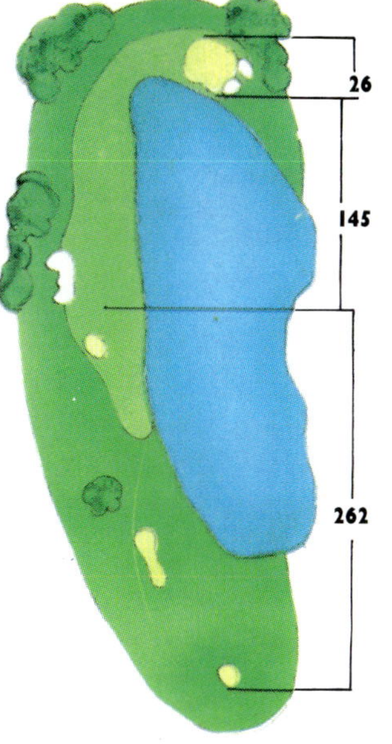

The fairway snaps right nearer the green. The drive must keep left of the water and right of the bunkers. A well hit ap-proach is im-perative to avoid a bogey, or more.

18

Par 4
444 yards

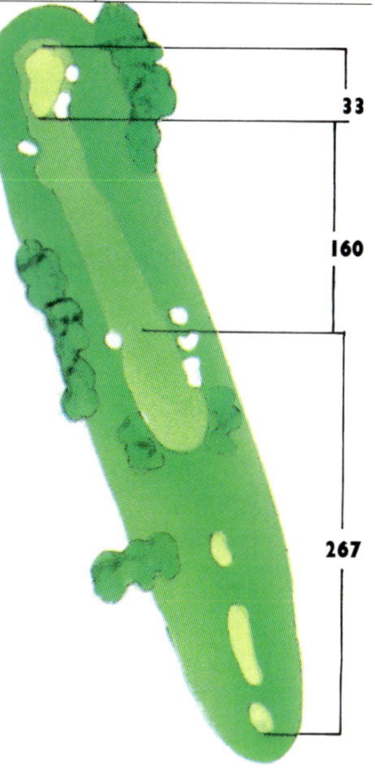

This hole was extended 25 yards during the remodeling. It is a long par 4 to finish the tournament. Long narrow green requires correct club selection in order to have a makeable putt.

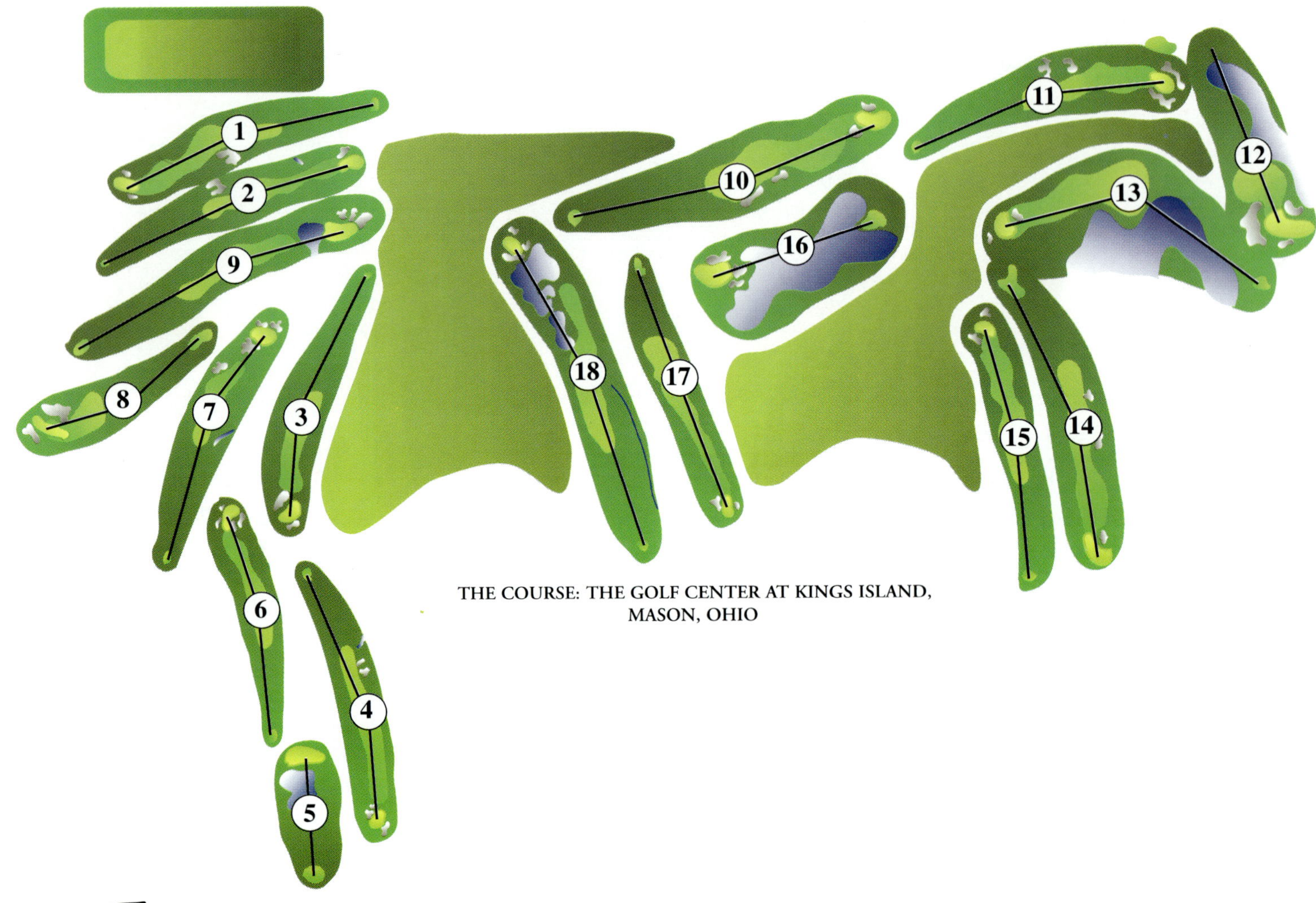

THE COURSE: THE GOLF CENTER AT KINGS ISLAND,
MASON, OHIO

*I*n 1995, Mike Hill won with a record breaking 17 under par (196) at the Kroger Senior Classic. Mike won a first place check of $135,000 of a $900,000 purse. Mike previously won the last Ohio Kings Island Open on the same course when the events played here were PGA tournaments.

The Grizzly course was built and opened in 1972 and has a rich history of past tour events. The Golf Center originally hosted a men's PGA TOUR® event, the Ohio Kings Island Open. Nicklaus won the inaugural event in 1973 when he shot 13 under par 271. Other OKIO winners included Miller Barber (1974), Ben Crehshaw (1976), and Mike Hill (1977). There was no winner in 1975 because there was no Tournament that year as there was a conflict with the Ryder Cup which was being held in the United States.

In 1978 the LPGA Championship was brought to the course with national television coverage and a major sponsor : Mazda Motors of America. The ladies were here until 1990 and it was then that the newest SENIOR PGA TOUR® event was to have a stop in Mason, Ohio.

Dates:	June 28-30
Network:	ESPN
Times:	TBA
Yardage:	6628
Par:	71
Total Purse:	$900,000
1st Prize:	$135,000
1995 Winner:	Mike Hill
1995 Winning Score:	196 (64,66,66)
Principal Charitable Beneficiary:	The Kroger and The Johnny Bench Scholarship Funds
Ticket Information:	1-513-398-5742

1

Par 4
412 yards

A demanding opening hole with a slight dogleg left. Most players will hit a short to medium iron for their second shot into a well-bunkered two tiered green. Another bunker is situated to the left side of the green which will catch most pulled iron shots.

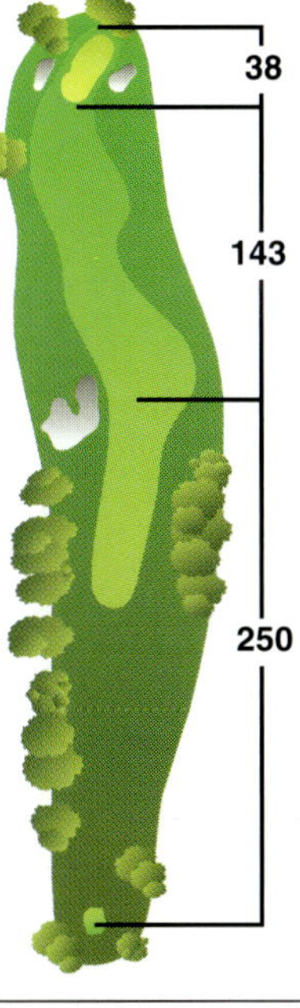

2

Par 4
412 yards

One of the best holes on the course, a bunker on the left of the fairway in the landing area and water on the right. It will demand a strong second shot to a deep green that is double-level, trapped on the left and sloping to the right toward trees and water.

3

Par 4
374 yards

Players will probably hit either a fairway wood or long iron off the tee to insure accuracy. The approach from the left of the green, trapped front right and back, could be blocked by trees. Depth and size of front bunker makes the second shot seem shorter than it really is. Creek runs along right side.

4

Par 5
518 yards

A long tee shot should give the players a chance to reach the green in two. Trees will come into play on the right side of the fairway on the second shot. The green is well protected with bunkers right and left.

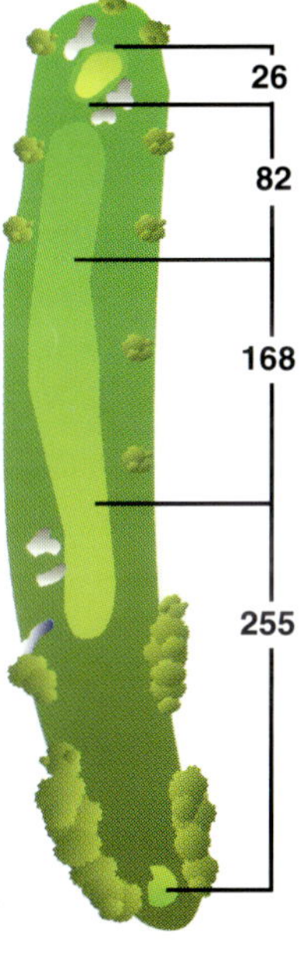

5

Par 3
163 yards

Most players will hit a middle iron into this large green. There is a lake in front of the green to enhance the character of the hole.

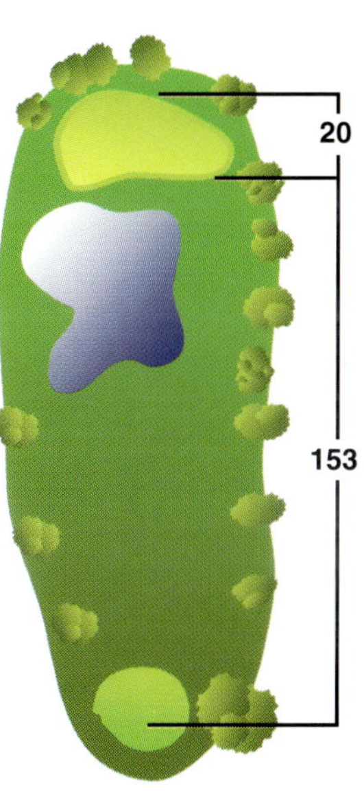

6

Par 4
402 yards

Accuracy off the tee is important to avoid the trees and the long rough on the right side of the fairway. The player will need to work the ball from right to left to avoid the high rough and tree problems. This green, well protected with bunkers front and rear, will be tough to hit and hold.

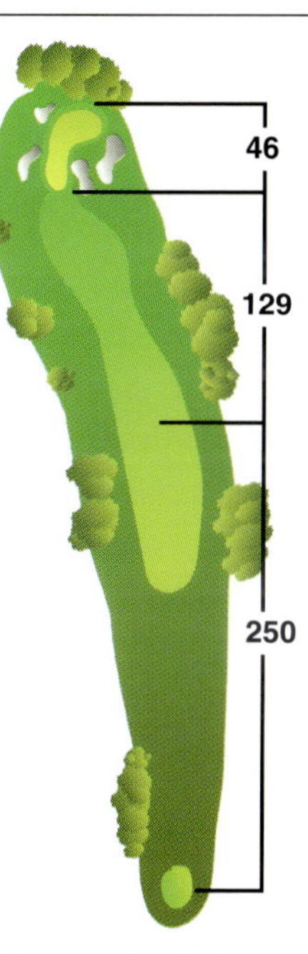

7

Par 4
377 yards

The long hitters may try and drive this green. There is a creek on the right and a bunker guarding the left side of the fairway. Although a short iron is all that is required for the second shot, the green is well protected front and rear by bunkers and trees on the right.

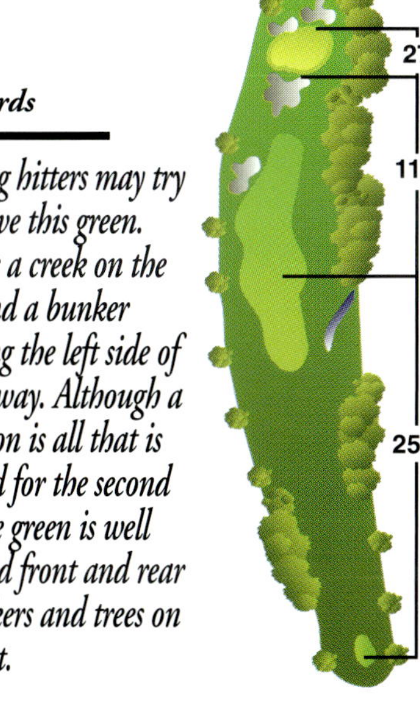

8

Par 3
191 yards

Considered an excellent par three, especially if the wind is a factor. Most players will hit a medium to long iron into a long and narrow green. However, if the pin is placed directly behind the large bunker, the approach will be difficult.

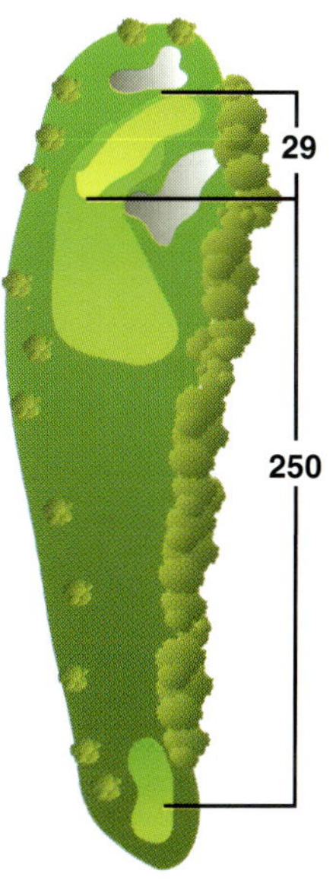

9

Par 5
489 yards

This hole requires an accurate drive and an accurate fairway wood to a long rolling green protected by bunkers on the left. Excellent birdie opportunity.

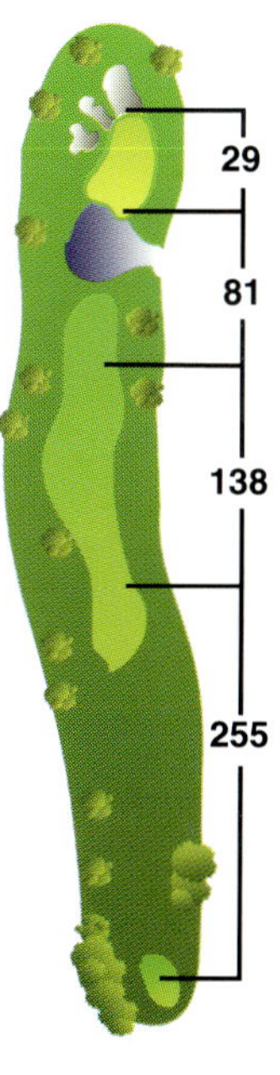

10

Par 4
366 yards

This relatively short hole will be simple for the player who hits a long, straight drive and avoids the rough. There is a bunker on the right in the driving area, one in front of the green and another on the left side of the green.

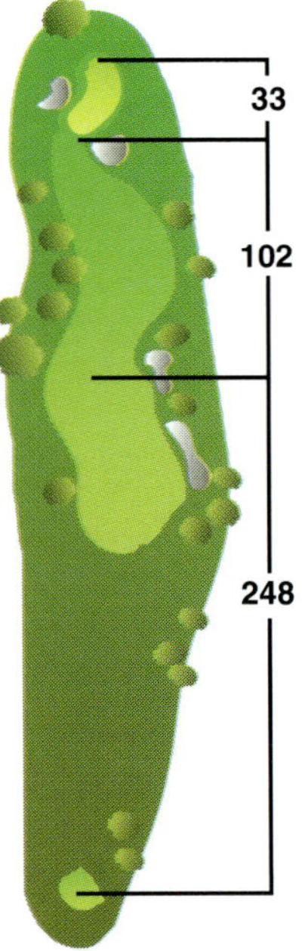

11

Par 4
398 yards

A good drive from an elevated tee will result in birdie possibilities. Players will hit a middle iron into a green guarded by bunkers on the left and right.

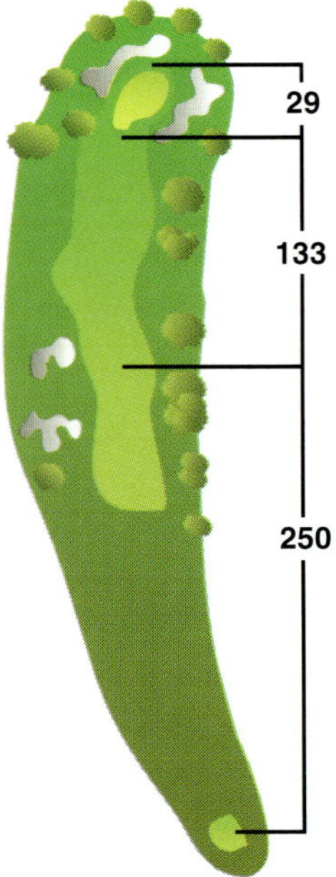

12

Par 3
198 yards

Players hit from a sightly elevated tee over a lake and a front bunker to a large green presenting some putting problems. Most players will hit a long iron. There are also bunkers at the back center of the green and to the right and the back.

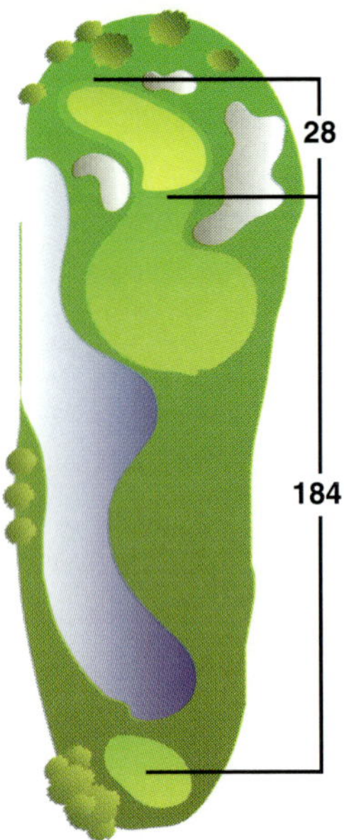

13

Par 4
412 yards

This hole could be one of the most penalizing if the player elects to go over the long end of the lake that cuts into the fairway. The fairway doglegs to the left to a green that is bunkered in front. A bunker is also situated at the back center of the green.

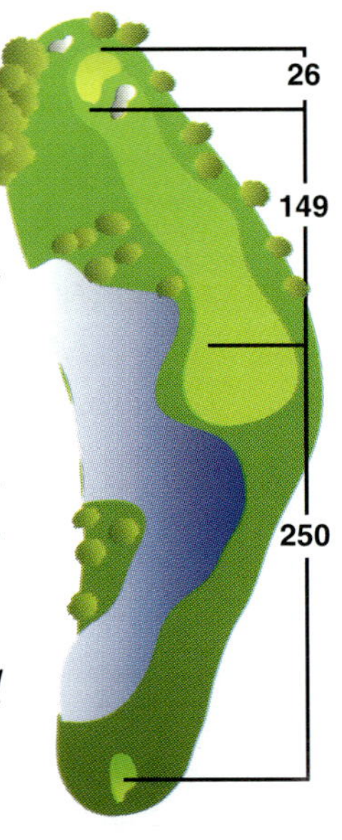

14

Par 4
423 yards

The drive out of a narrow opening of trees must be well placed, working the ball from left to right, as there are out-of-bounds to the left, a fairway bunker some 200 yards out on the left and a small creek running along the right. A long iron or more is needed to reach the green.

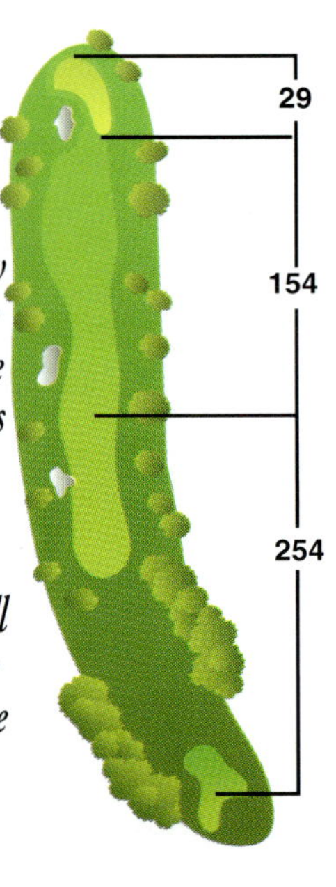

15

Par 4
369 yards

This hole calls for an accurate tee shot having to work the ball from right to left into a narrow fairway that, if long enough, could reward the player with a birdie. Players missing the fairway will find high rough on the left and right, with trees and a creek on the right.

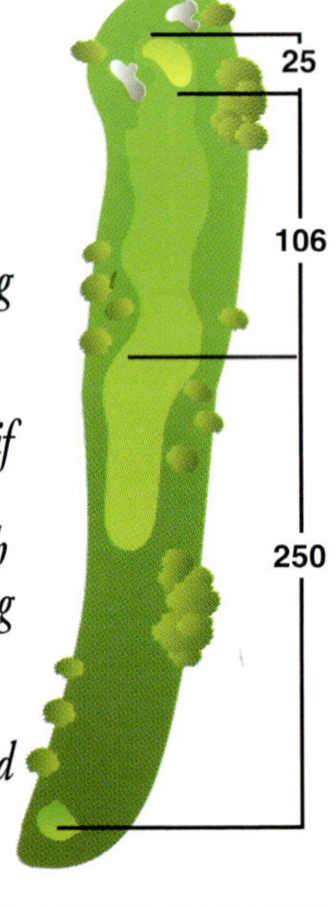

16

Par 3
186 yards

A rough par three. Most players will hit a medium to long iron over the water toward a double-tiered green that is surrounded in front by bunkers. Even players who reach the green with their tee shot will find it difficult to birdie the hole.

17

Par 4
392 yards

The prevailing wind is usually in the face of the player and he will have a long second shot to a green with a narrow opening. With green-side bunkers on the right and left, the uphill second shot will place a premium on accuracy. Like # 16, this long par four will yield few birdies.

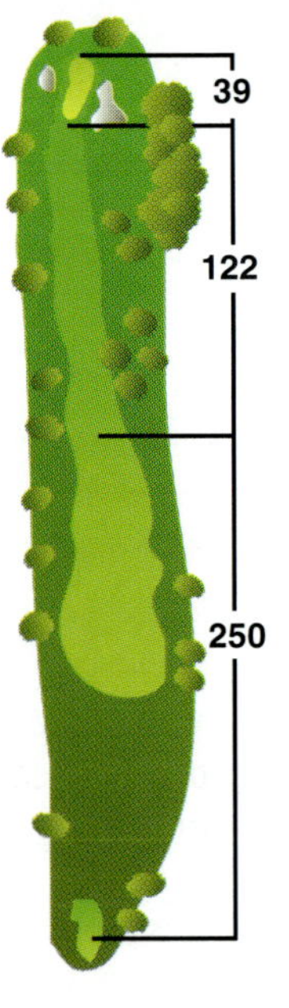

18

Par 5
546 yards

After a long, accurate drive the player may elect to use a fairway wood and gamble on reaching the green in two. The players who elect to play safe will have to accurately play a medium iron short of the lake, leaving them with a short iron to the green, which is guarded by bunkers. Very few will try to reach this green in two shots.

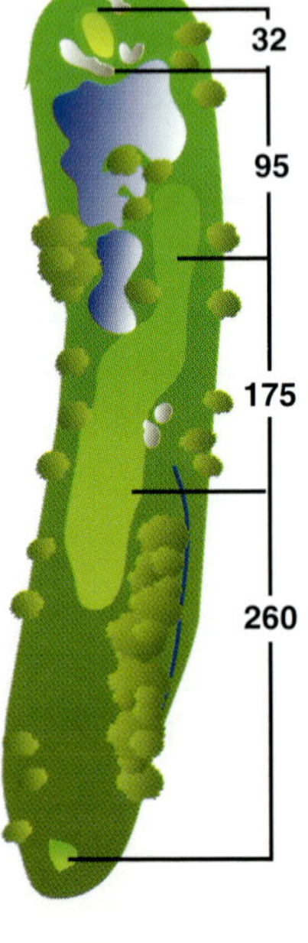

THE COURSE: COG HILL GOLF CLUB, LAMONT, ILLINIOS

When the Jemsek family decided to build the No. 4 course at Cog Hill Country Club, they determined that the layout should be playable to the amateur and worthy of the professional's respect. Since 1964, the public has reaped the benefit of the idea and in 1991 Jemsek Golf realized a dream with their "Dubsdread" course hosting the Western Open.

The Western Golf Association offered a total purse of $300,000 for the very first Western Open, held at Glen View Club in Golf, Illinois in 1899. Golf legend, Walter Hagen won the Open in 1916. His prolific 5-title Western Open Champion record (1916, '21, '26, '27, and '32) has held to date, although Billy Casper's string of four wins in 1965, '66, '69, 'and '73 was the most recent modern-day challenge (Willie Anderson took four Open victories between 1902 and 1909). Tom Watson's 1974, '77, and '84 string is perhaps the closest attempt of the current era to equal "the Haig's " feat.

The Open has played at numerous Chicago area courses since the early 1960s. The event has been played as far west as San Francisco, as far south as Texas and as far east as New York.

Dates:	July 4-7
Network:	CBS & USA
Times:	USA
	Thur 4:00-6:00 EST
	Fri 4:00-6:00 EST
	CBS
	Sat 4:30-6:00 EST
	Sun 3:30-6:00 EST
Yardage:	7040
Par:	72
Slope:	142
Rating	75.6
TotalPurse:	$2,000,000
1st Prize:	$360,000
1995 Winner:	Billy Mayfair
1995 Winning Score:	279 (73,70,69,67)
Principal Charitable Beneficiary:	Evans Scholarship Foundation
Ticket Information:	1-708-724-4600

1

Par 4
408 yards

A great starting hole. The dogleg gets players thinking right from the beginning. Four bunkers lie waiting on the left and one lone bunker will catch drives through the fairway.

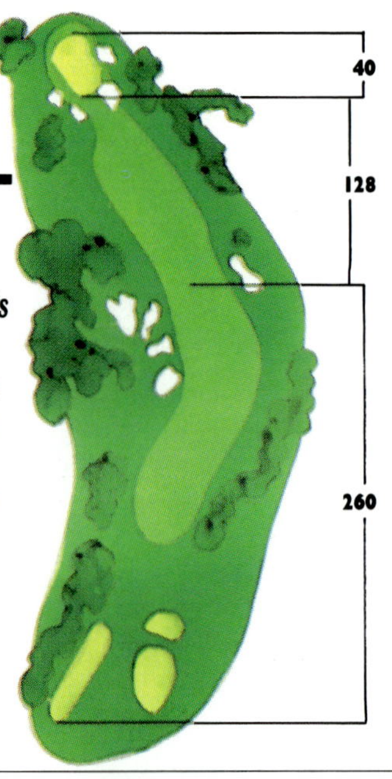

2

Par 3
179 yards

Trees, right and left, narrow the path to the large green. The putting surface ridges in the center and slopes away towards the back. Accurate shots are needed for few putts.

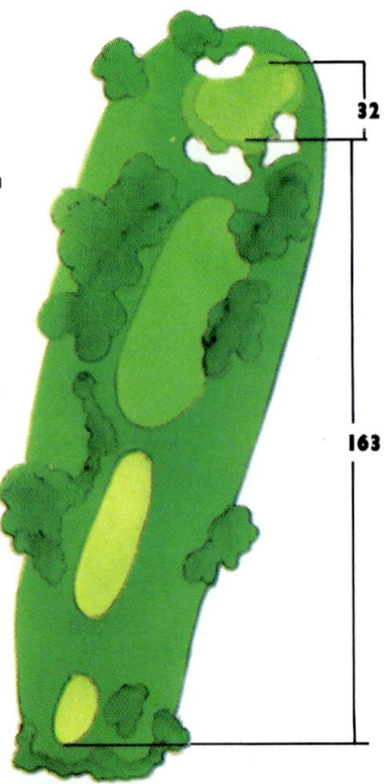

3

Par 4
414 yards

A missed drive to the left or right can easily find the water. The two tiered green is large and flat. Keeping the ball on the correct level is a must for the approach.

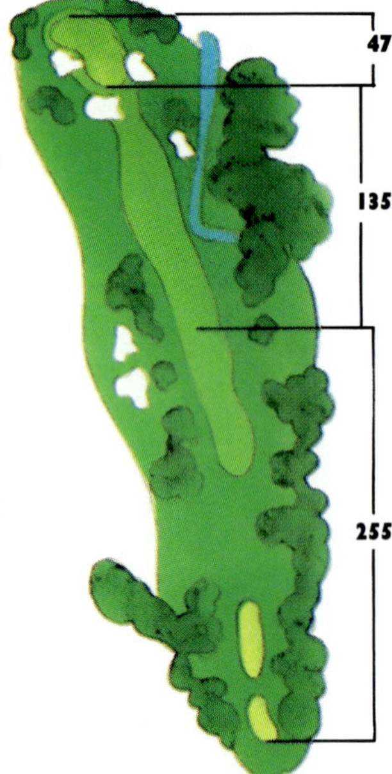

4

Par 4
427 yards

A narrow driving hole — sand and water are present left and right. Players will use a club for control off the tee. The small green is tucked tightly in among bunkers and trees.

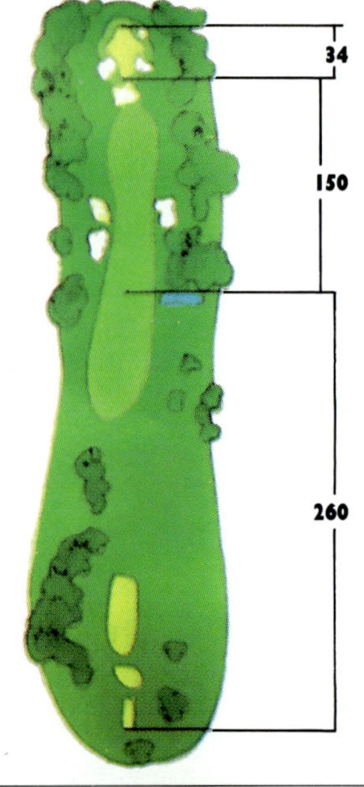

5

Par 5
509 yards

The distance won't be a problem for the players, but many bunkers on the way to the green will cause a few to play conservatively. Birdies will be frequent.

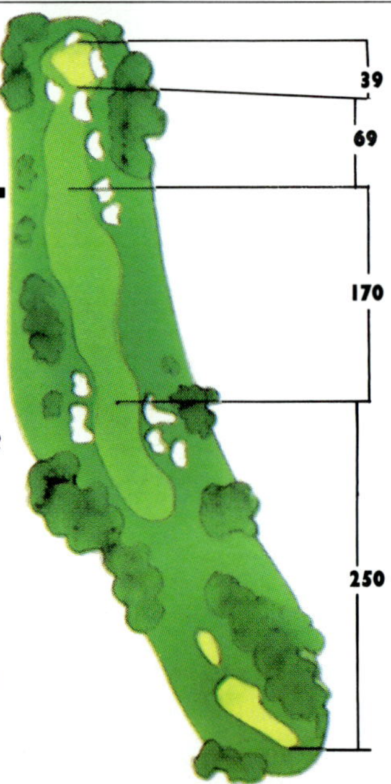

6

Par 3
224 yards

A long "short" hole. The path to the green is downhill and the putting surface is large, sloping towards the front. Pars are a welcome score.

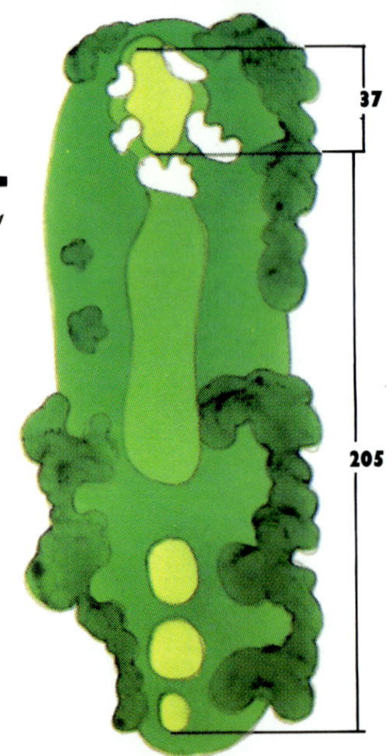

7

Par 4
411 yards

Dogleg right with bunkers on the inside and outside corners. The clover-leaf shaped green makes for some tricky pin placements. Bogeys are common.

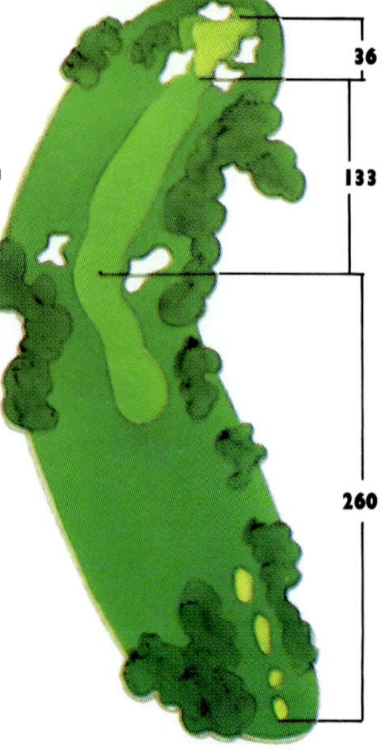

8

Par 4
387 yards

Water to the right will grab the tee shot pushed off to that side. Willows make the landing area very narrow. The approach opens up to a generous green.

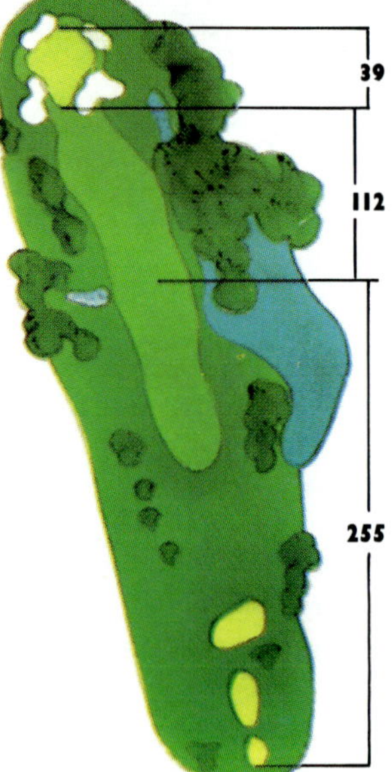

9

Par 5
565 yards

A par 5 requiring control and precision on all three shots to the green. The green is flat and rewards the accurate approaches with easy putts.

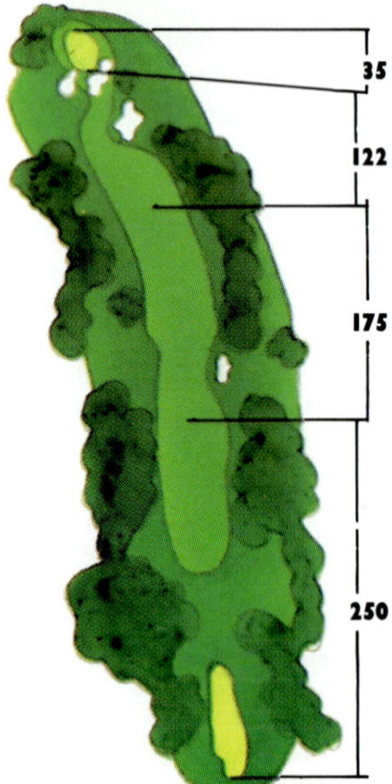

10

Par 4
375 yards

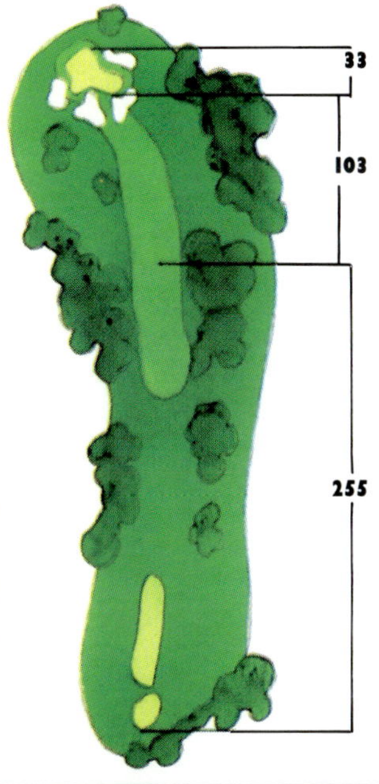

Birdies are in abundance on this opening hole to the back side. The right side of the fairway is favored to keep away from the tree on the left near the green.

11

Par 5
548 yards

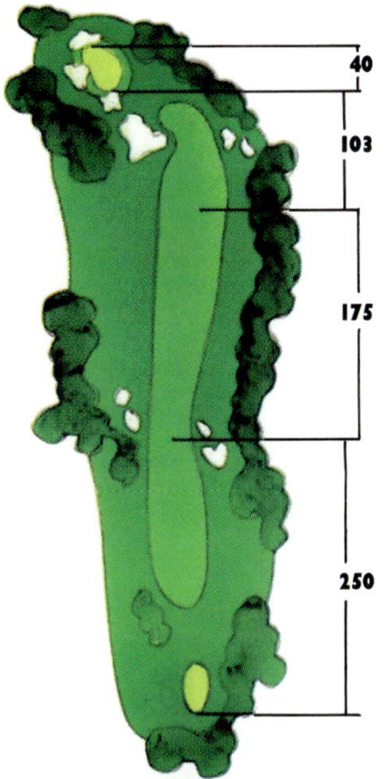

Again, the right side of the fairway is favored but watch out for the out-of-bounds along that side. A long second shot will have to clear a few trees to reach the putting surface.

12

Par 3
197 yards

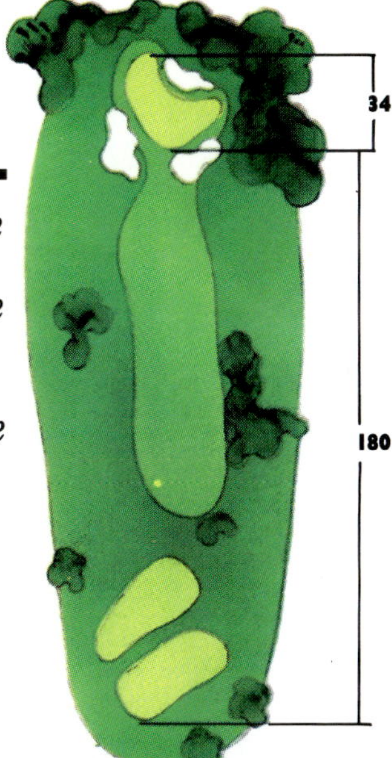

An elevated tee does not help in avoiding the wind. The L-shaped green will leave some players with difficult putts. Par 3 will be achieved by most all players.

13

Par 4
433 yards

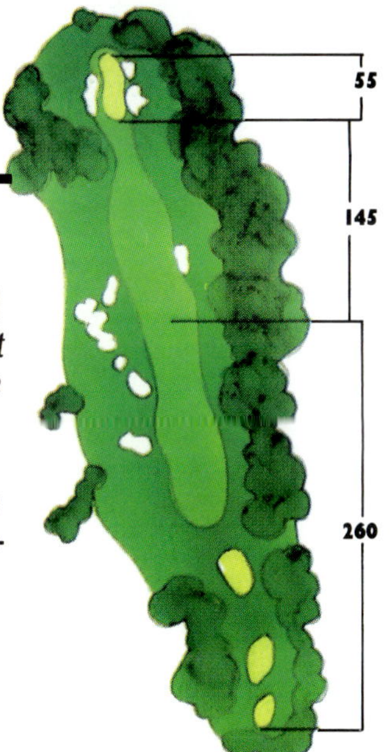

The long straight fairway is defined by bunkers left and OB to the right. A deep gulley crosses in front of the long green. Accuracy on the approach is a must.

14

Par 3
185 yards

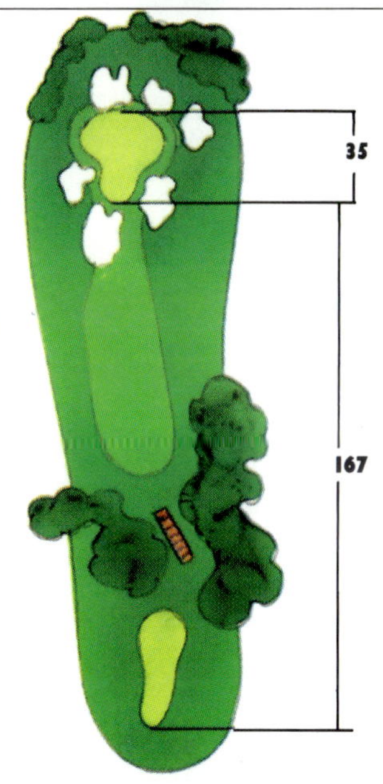

The two-tiered green has levels right and left. A total of six bunkers encircle the putting surface causing all mishit shots to most likely end up in the sand.

15

Par 5
510 yards

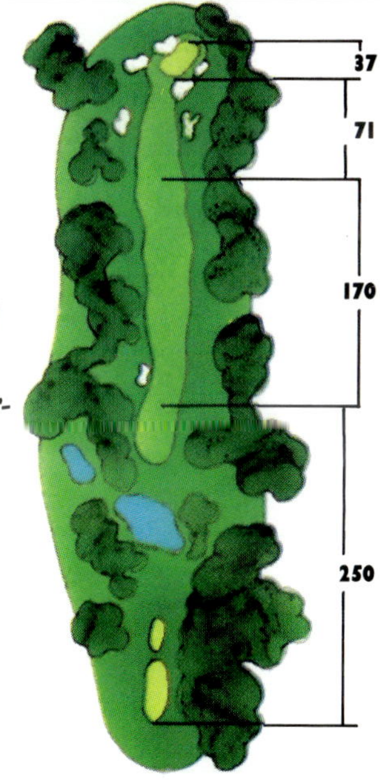

A ravine, just off the tee, is an easy hazard to cross on the drive to the fairway. A lone bunker along the left tightens up the landing area. The easiest hole on the back nine.

16

Par 4
425 yards

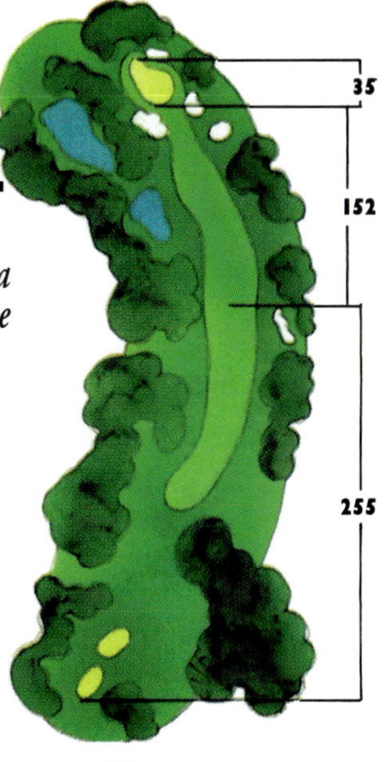

A long dogleg left requiring a drive down the right side of the fairway to open the shot to the green. The left side drops off into lowlands and the green is backed by impressive bunkers.

17

Par 4
413 yards

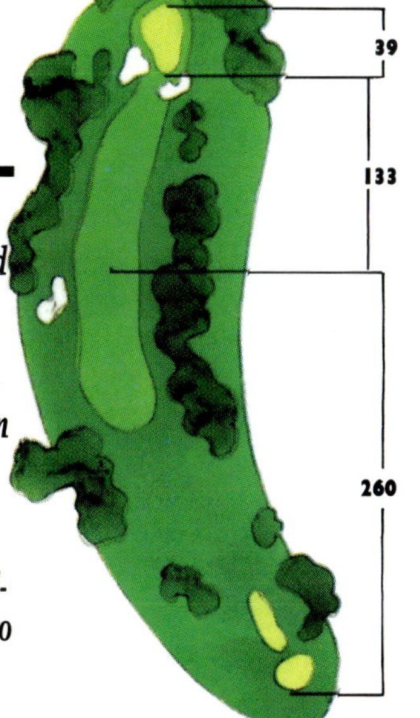

A three-wood or 1-iron faded off the tee should place the ball in excellent position for the approach. The large green slopes gradually from back to front.

18

Par 4
430 yards

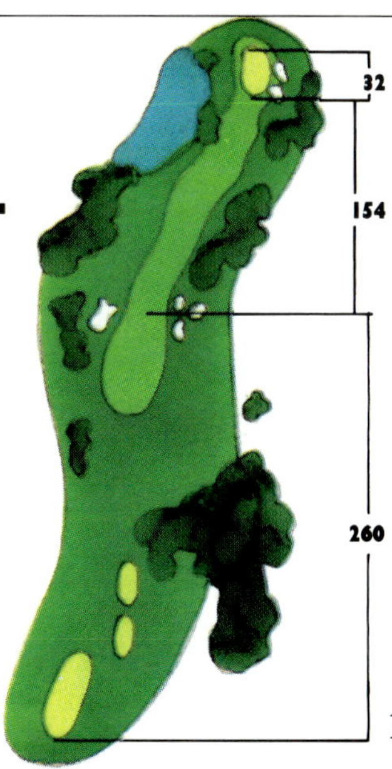

This is where tournaments can be won and lost. The long narrow fairway and water-edge green make the win very tough right to the end.

A USGA Sponsored Event

THE COURSE: CANTERBURY GOLF CLUB, CLEVELAND, OHIO

$\mathcal{D}$ueling close friend and fellow Ohio State alum, Tom Weiskopf edged Jack Nicklaus for his first U.S.G.A. title last year at the 16th U.S. Senior Open at Congressional Country Club. Weiskopf will defend his title at the historic 75-year-old Canterbury Golf Club, just outside of Cleveland in this year's event.

Weiskopf's connections to Canterbury and the northeast Ohio area stem from his childhood. He grew up in near-by Bedford, Ohio, and his mother is a former Canterbury member. His brother, Dan, was the 1979 Canterbury Club Champion. In the 1973 PGA Championship, Weiskopf finished at one under par, six shots behind Nicklaus.

Home to three of the most challenging finishing holes in all of golf, Canterbury will be a true test to the over-50 set. The par-five 16th plays to 608 yards and a level lie for the second and third shots is rare. The 17th is a tough 215-yard three-par with an elevated green that slopes back to front. Number 18 is seven stories up hill from tee to green, with bunkers and out of bounds on the right. Three to five shot swings over these holes was not uncommon on the final day of the 12 previous major championships held at Canterbury since 1932.

The Herbert Strong-designed layout is ranked 50th in the nation and 87th in the world by Golf Magazine. Former champions include the likes of Walter Hagen, Jack Nicklaus, Arnold Palmer, Mark O'Meara, Miller Barber and Chi Chi Rodriguez.

Dates:	July 4-7
Network:	ESPN & NBC
Times:	TBA
Yardage:	6,772
Par:	72
Slope:	138
Rating:	73.9
Total Purse:	$1,000,000 plus
1st Prize:	$175,000
1995 Winner:	Tom Weiskopf
1995 Winning Score:	275 (69,69,69,68)
Principal Charitable Beneficiary:	Cleveland Clinic Foundation Hospice of the Western Reserve Easter Seal Society of Northeast Ohio
Ticket Information:	216-561-2133

1

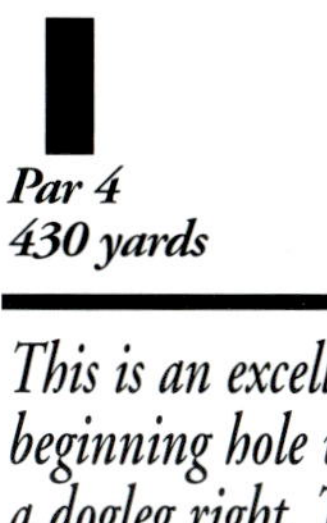

Par 4
430 yards

This is an excellent beginning hole with a dogleg right. They will be hitting into a prevailing wind with a blind tee shot. The players will get home here with a five or six-iron. They'll be hitting into a well bunkered green, which tilts severely from back to front.

2

Par 4
346 yards

Many of the players will use a three wood off the tee to keep the ball in play on this dogleg left fairway. They will be hitting into a hill with two bunkers on the right and trees on the left. Some of the long hitters can cut the corner of the dogleg with a driver and then get home with a wedge.

3

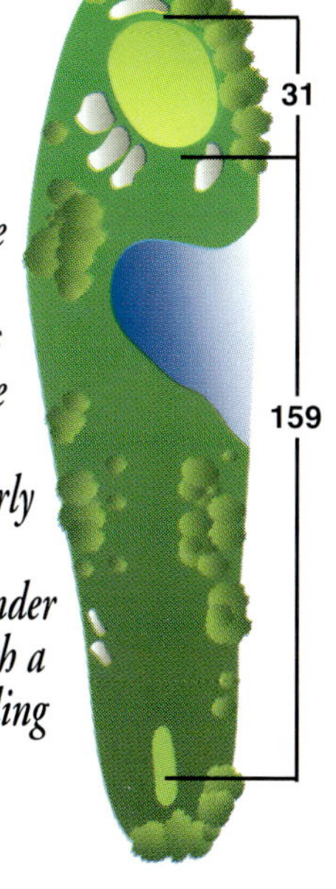

Par 3
165 yards

This is one of the more picturesque holes on the course. The players will be hitting over the water and toward the clubhouse. It has a fairly large flat green which should be reachable under normal conditions with a five or six iron depending on the length and the strength of the hitter.

4

Par 4
418 yards

The players will hit from an elevated tee to a bunkered fairway on the left that is contoured away from the hitter. There is a dogleg left and the fairway is bordered by deep rough on the right and on the left. It is important to put the tee shot in the fairway. The second shot to the green is very deceptive. The pin is visible but not the green.

5

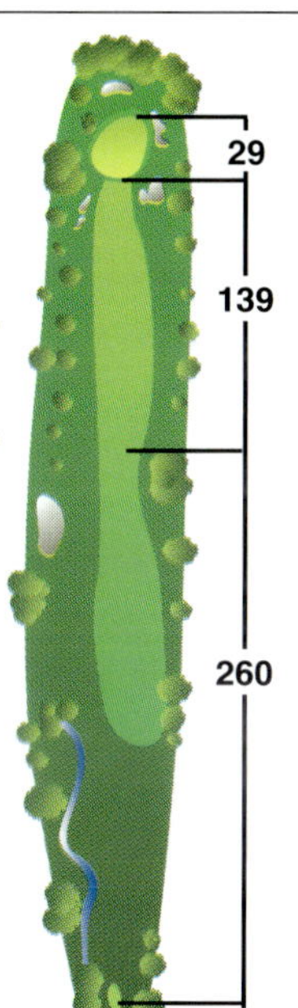

Par 5
382 yards

The players will hit their tee shots from an elevated tee. There is one fairway bunker on the left and a large tree looms treacherously about 170 yards from the green. A six or seven iron is required to get home to the green surrounded by traps. The putting surface slopes severely and the golfer must be careful where he puts his second shot.

6

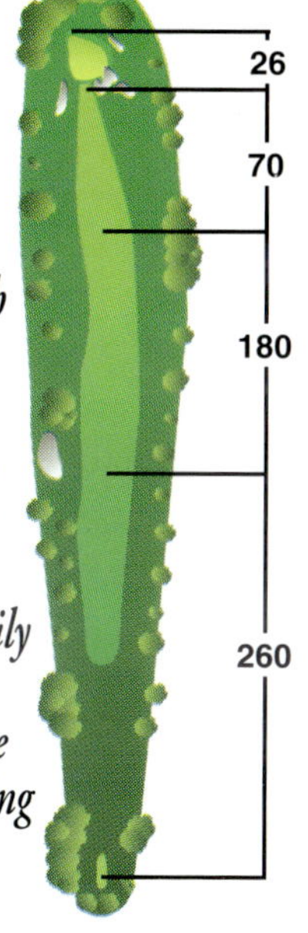

Par 5
500 yards

Long hitters with a good drive will be able to reach the green with either a one or two iron while other players will play up short and come in with a nice little pitch shot. The green is quite small, heavily trapped and just a third of the green is exposed due to a large bunker protecting the front side.

7

Par 3
175 yards

The green is well protected by bunkers and a severe drop off of some 30 feet to the left and large trees to the right off the tee. This hole calls for a little cut shot left to right to avoid the trees and trouble to the left. A four or five iron will be used to reach the large green.

8

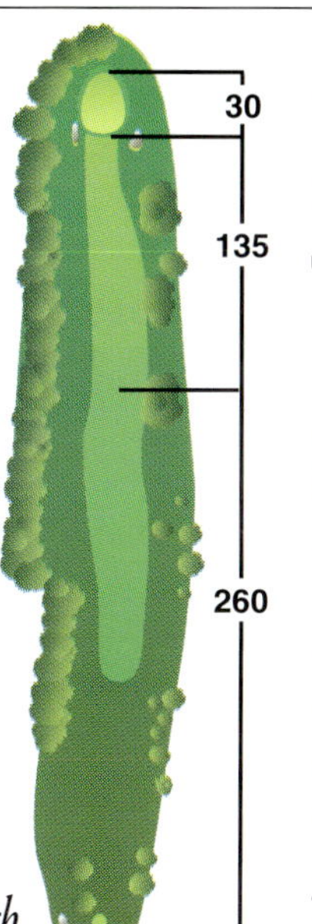

Par 4
382 yards

The golfers can pick up a fairly easy par here or sky to astronomical figures. The eighth is one of the key holes in the golf course to get by with a par. Tee shots will tend to land on a crested ridge. The second shot is critical because the green has trees behind it and a terraced slope to the right going into heavy rough.

9

Par 5
525 yards

This hole goes back toward the clubhouse and is a very difficult hole. There are trees bordering the fairway on both sides with out-of-bounds left. The players will not be able to see the green on their second shots. A wedge will be needed on the third shot to reach the very large, two-terraced green, which is protected by two large bunkers in front.

10

Par 4
360 yards

There is a 40 degree dogleg right. Many of the players will hit off the tee with an iron for position. The second shot to a shallow green should be with a nine iron at most. The pond which guards the front right of the green should not come into play. This is a downhill hole with trees and out of bounds on the right and higher rough on the left.

11

Par 3
165 yards

The tee is elevated and the players will he aiming at a well bunkered green with a five or six iron. The players will hit over a ravine with trees on the left. The green is elevated so missed shots will roll downhill on both sides making a tough chip back to the putting surface.

12

Par 4
372 yards

Some of the players will hit fairway woods or irons for placement purposes while some of the bigger hitters will cut the corner with a driver. The shot to the very small green will be in the short iron range, a seven or eight iron. The green is protected by three bunkers that demand accurate second shots.

13

Par 5
490 yards

The golfers must hit their tee shots to the right center of a hogback fairway. Out of bounds guards the left side with trees on the right. If the tee shot goes off the top of the hogback the green will be visible on the second shot which will be a downhill long iron to the well bunkered green

14

Par 4
385 yards

Trees are on the right with out of bounds very evident on the left side of the fairway. Here's another hole where many of the players will hit either a fairway wood or a long iron off the tee to get good position on the contoured fairway. A six or seven iron should be enough to get home to the elevated green sandwiched by trees on both sides.

15

Par 4
358 yards

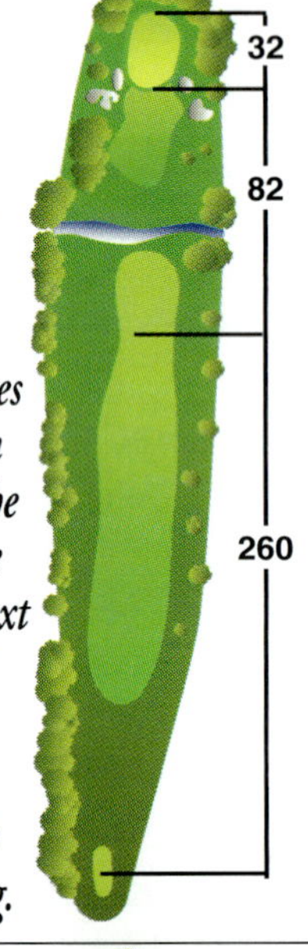

There is a creek out about 250 yards on this straight-away hole and out of bounds on the left with trees and rough on the right. An iron off the tee will keep the ball back far enough so the player can negotiate the next shot. The green is elevated some 30 feet sitting on a high hill. It's well trapped and double terraced which puts a premium on putting.

16

Par 5
605 yards

The players will hit their tee shots out of a shoot to a very uneven fairway, which falls away down a fairly steep embankment. The second shot is very critical as the golfers will he hitting to an elevated plateau. From there the players probably will use a nine iron or wedge to get down to the small flat green.

17

Par 3
232 yards

Both the tee and green are elevated as the players will be shooting over a valley with out of bounds right. If the hitter misses the green, he'll find insurmountable trouble. The putting surface is well bunkered and the terrain slopes off severely on the sides.

18

Par 4
438 yards

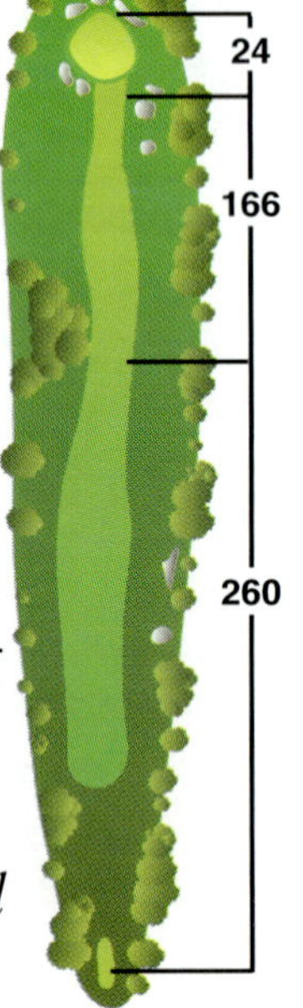

This is the most difficult hole at Canterbury to make par. It's all up hill and the players will hit into an undulating fairway, with bunkers and out of bounds guarding the right side, and trees bordering the fairway on the left. The green is reasonably flat and well trapped. The distance to the putting area on the second shot is deceiving.

THE COURSE AT KINGSMILL GOLF CLUB, WILLIAMSBURG, VIRGINIA

*M*iller Barber took the honors at the 1977 inaugural Anheuser-Busch Golf Classic, previously the Kaiser International at the Silverado Country Club in Napa, California. Tom Watson in 1978 and Ben Crenshaw in 1979 were among the Classic Champions at Silverado before the tournament headed across the country to Williamsburg, Virginia in 1981, where it has been played on the River Course at Kingsmill on the James.

The 19-year-old Pete Dye course is heavily wooded, so much so that colonies of deer are often visible spectators on the 16th hole. The course calls for liberal use of long irons, though a sure putter is also a necessity to conquer tough pin placements and multi-tiered greens.

Kingsmill's resident touring pro and two-time U.S. Open Champion Curtis Strange calls No. 9 the most formidable. "This is the longest par 4 on the course (452yards) and plays even longer...the summer winds come off the James River and are in our faces." Says Strange of No. 17 along the James, "a good 17th hole of a golf tournament...you suck it up here. There's no place to bail out."

Dates:	July 11-14
Network:	ESPN
Times:	TBA
Yardage:	6797
Par:	71
Slope:	137
Rating:	73.3
Total Purse:	$1,100,000
1st Prize:	$ 198,000
1995 Winner:	Ted Tryba
1995 Winning Score:	272 (69,67,68,68)
Principal Charitable Beneficiary:	Lions Charity Foundation
Ticket Information:	1-804-253-3985

1

Par 4
360 yards

A double fair-way allows an alternate route to this green. The left side is favored, open-ing the angle for the ap-proach. Bunkers left and right will catch errant shots.

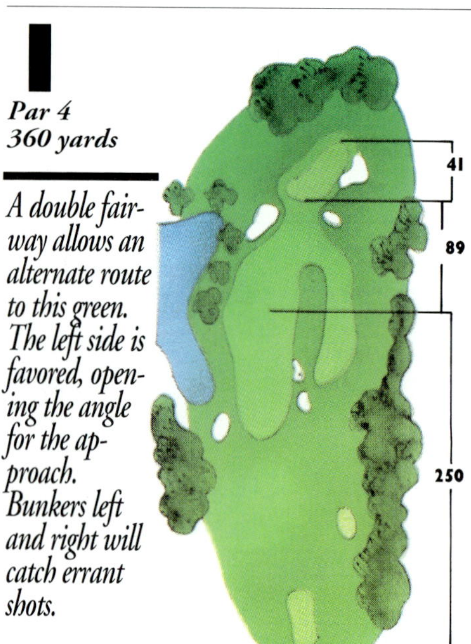

2

Par 3
204 yards

The shape of the green can make for some tough pin placements. Players will be drawing the ball into the putting surface to avoid the bunkers to the left.

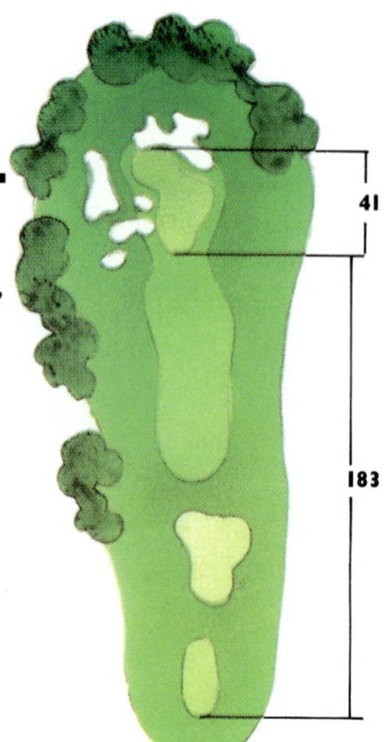

3

Par 5
538 yards

Two fairway bunkers along the right side persuade the drive to the left. Trees sneak in from the left to hinder attempts at reaching the green in two.

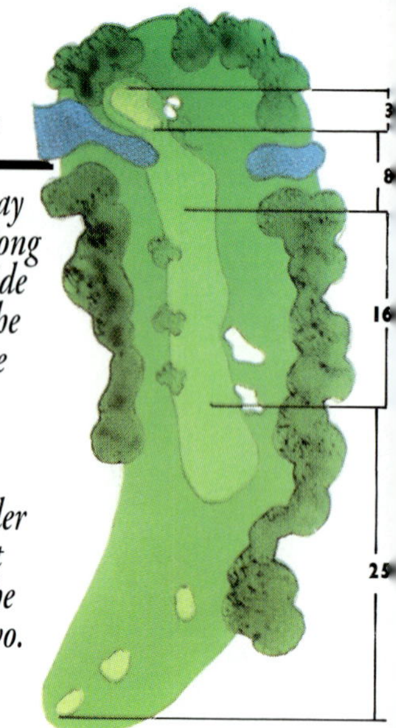

4

Par 4
437 yards

A long, dog-leg left. Water crosses early and continues up to wrap around the green. A big drive down the right side is ideal for the approach into the long, roll-ing putting surface.

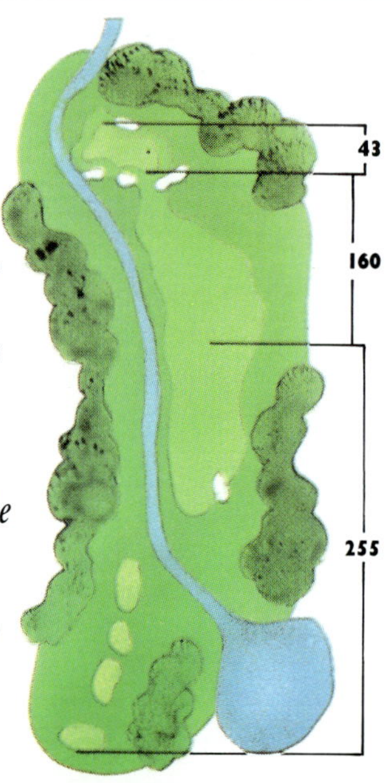

5

Par 3
183 yards

A picturesque hole. The un-dulating green is protected by bunkers on its four corners. With the wind swirling, this can be a difficult 3.

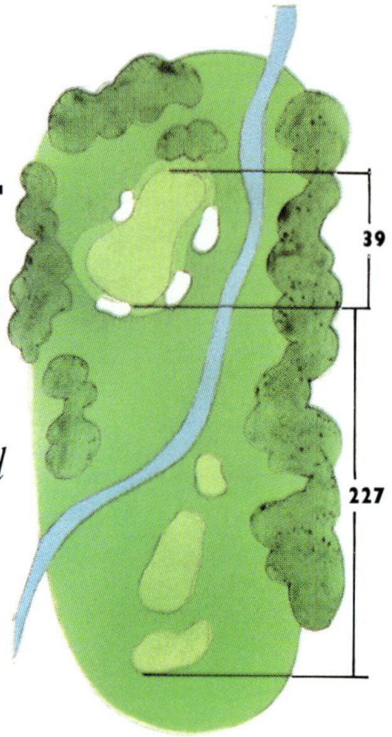

6

Par 4
365 yards

Not long, however the dogleg adds the difficulty. The drive should be fad-ed around the bunker on the right. A short approach need only find the heart of the green to avoid the bunkers.

7

Par 5
516 yards

The rolling fairway may leave the player with a tough lie to get home in two. The elevated green lies with-in a series of bunkers. Bird-ies are a must to keep up with the field.

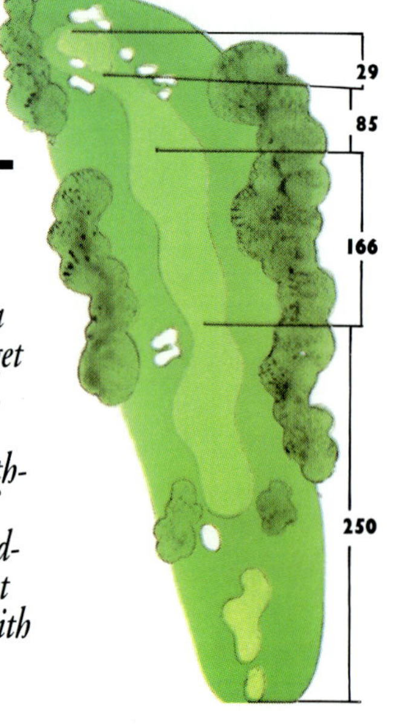

8

Par 4
413 yards

Described as the most dif-ficult hole on the course. Water moves in from the left side, however the ideal drive is to the left. The two-tiered putting surface is surrounded by sand.

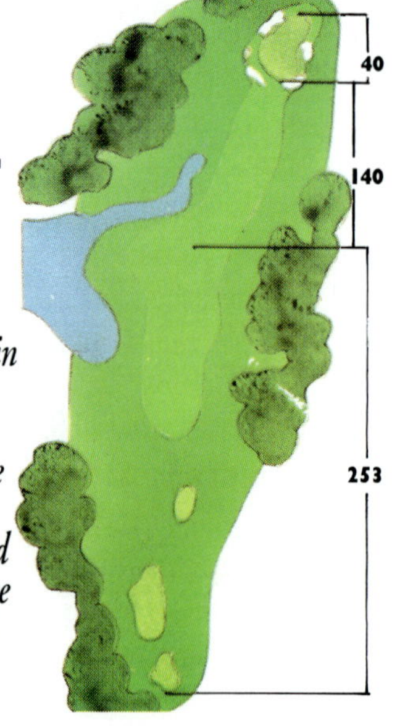

9

Par 4
452 yards

Slight dogleg left with bunkers block-ing the view around the corner. A big drive down the right side still leaves a long-iron for the approach.

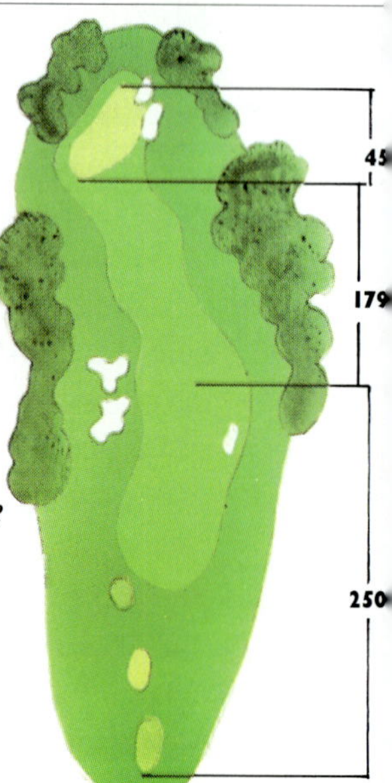

10

Par 4
431 yards

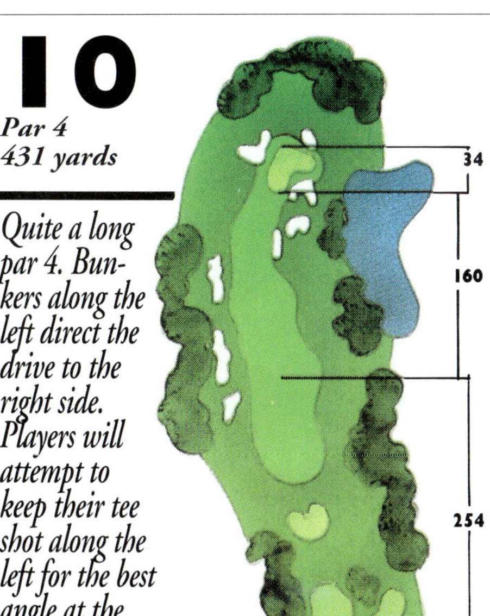

Quite a long par 4. Bunkers along the left direct the drive to the right side. Players will attempt to keep their tee shot along the left for the best angle at the bunkered green.

11

Par 4
396 yards

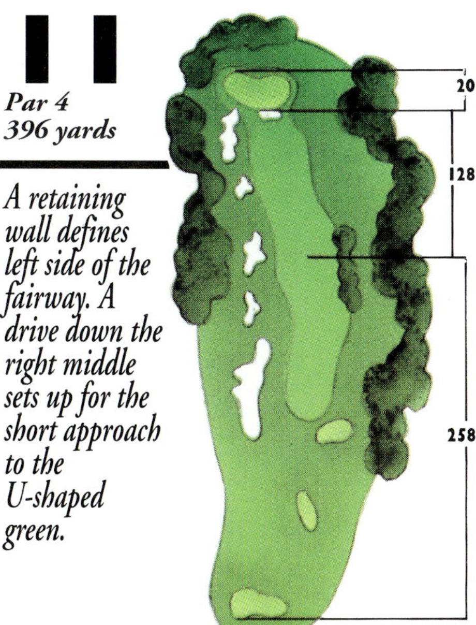

A retaining wall defines left side of the fairway. A drive down the right middle sets up for the short approach to the U-shaped green.

12

Par 4
395 yards

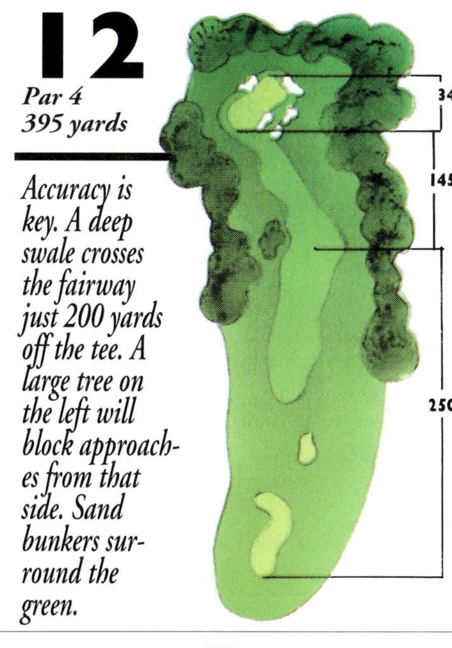

Accuracy is key. A deep swale crosses the fairway just 200 yards off the tee. A large tree on the left will block approaches from that side. Sand bunkers surround the green.

13

Par 3
179 yards

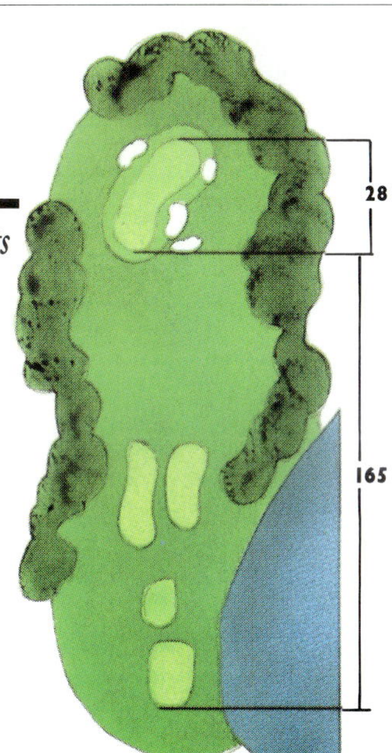

The green sits deep within the trees. Swirling winds add to the difficulty of getting the ball onto the short, wide green.

14

Par 4
383 yards

One

A fairway wood or long iron is the requirement to get into good position for the approach. One lone bunker fronts the short green. Birdies are frequent.

15

Par 5
506 yards

A short but very tough par 5. The tee shot must be aimed to the left to avoid the bunker on the right. A large ravine pulls the fairway down on the right.

16

Par 4
427 yards

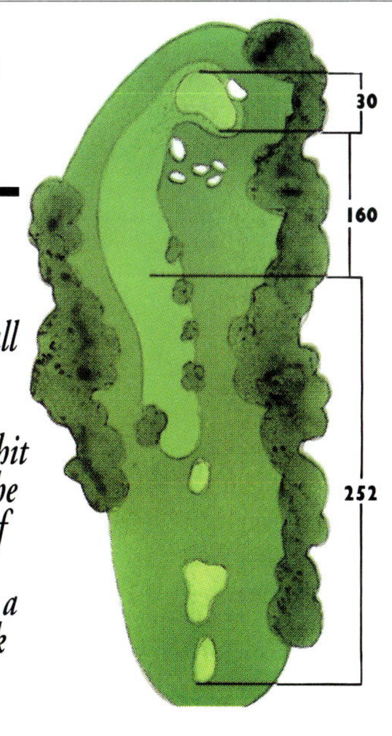

The fairway sweeps off to the right. A retaining wall drops off on the right. Players will hit a driver to the left middle of the fairway and then hit a soft shot back to the green.

17

Par 3
177 yards

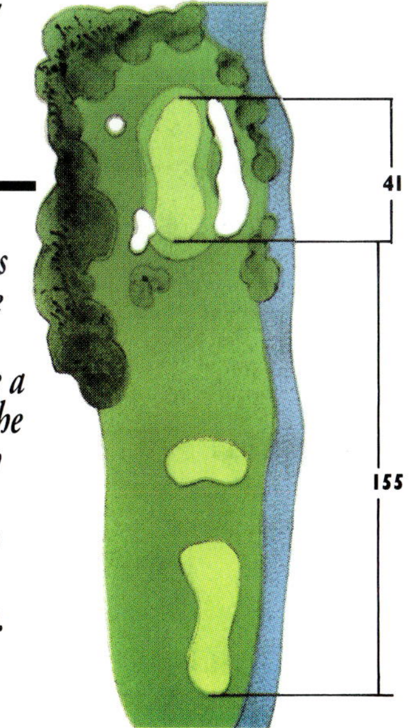

The James River borders the right side of the hole. Wind can be a big factor. The long, narrow green slopes from back to front with a dip half-way.

18

Par 4
435 yards

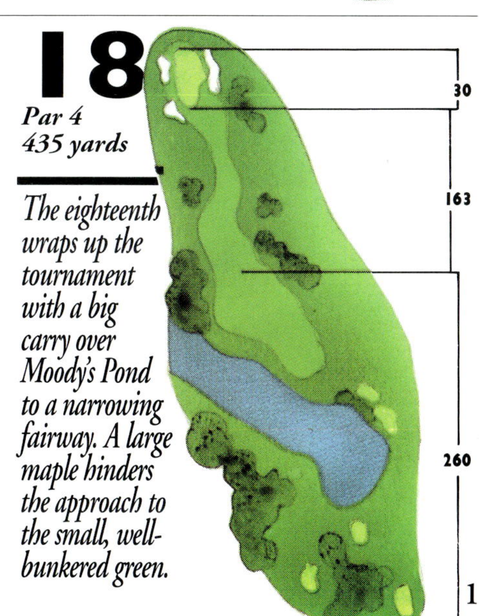

The eighteenth wraps up the tournament with a big carry over Moody's Pond to a narrowing fairway. A large maple hinders the approach to the small, well-bunkered green.

THE COURSE: TPC OF MICHIGAN. DEARBORN, MICHIGAN

*I*t's another year of the renewed partnership, as Ford continues as the title sponsor for the SENIOR PLAYERS Championship.

Among those expected at the SENIOR PGA-TOUR® major are Jack Nicklaus, 1990 money leader Lee Trevino, Legends of Golf Arnold Palmer (the only two-time winner of the event), Gary Player and Chi Chi Rodriguez, and defending champion J.C. Snead.

In 1993 the golfers returned to the Nicklaus designed TPC of Michigan. The course received rave reviews from players and spectators alike who took advantage of the Stadium Golf concept to enjoy a "front-row seat" at every hole.

Dates:	July 11-14
Network:	ABC & ESPN
Times:	ESPN
	Thur/Fri 4:00-6:00 EST
	ABC
	Sat/Sun 3:00-4:30 EST
Yardage:	6876
Par:	72
Slope:	142
Rating:	74.9
Total Purse:	$1,250,000
1st Prize:	$225,000
1995 Winner:	J.C.Snead
1995 Winning Score:	272 (69,68,66,69)
Principal Charitable Beneficiary:	Henry Ford Health System
	William Beaumont Hospital
	Oakwood Hospital Foundation
	Boy Scouts of America-Detroit Council
Ticket Information:	1-800-741-3161

1

Par 4
408 yards

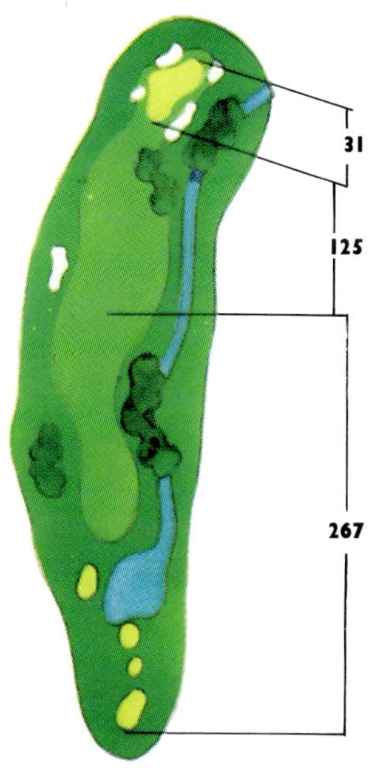

Players will be favoring the left side of the fairway from the tee. Anything to the right will most likely be blocked by a large cottonwood tree. Green is guarded by four bunkers.

2

Par 4
411 yards

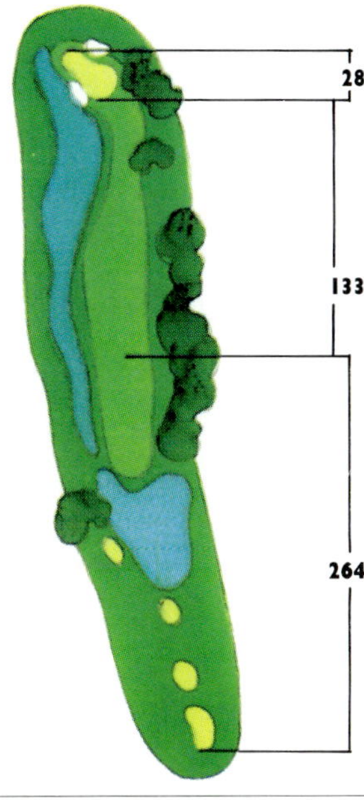

A tough par 4. The drive must carry wetlands to a narrow fairway. Water plays in from the left and continues up to border the green. Difficult putts can be found if the approach is not accurate.

3

Par 5
547 yards

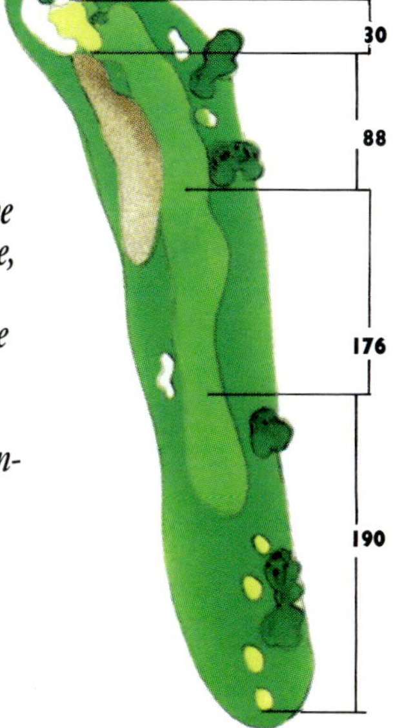

A long, tight par 5. From the chute off the tee, the drive must be placed in the center of the fairway. The second must contend with bunkers right and wetlands left. Birdies are a must.

4

Par 3
210 yards

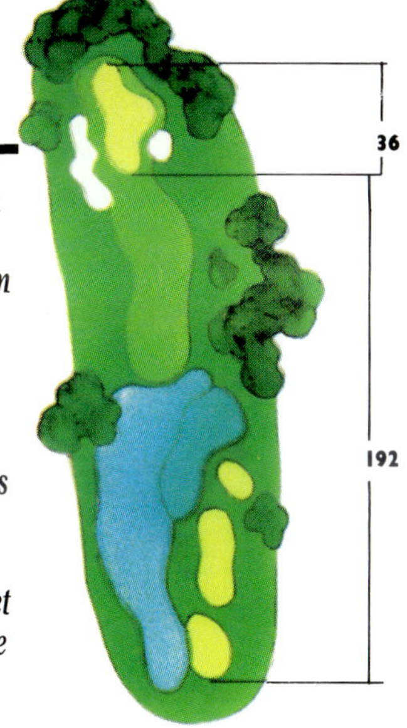

Club selection can be anywhere from a mid-iron to fairway wood, depending on the wind. Green provides many pin-placements. Birdies will get the adrenaline going.

5

Par 4
394 yards

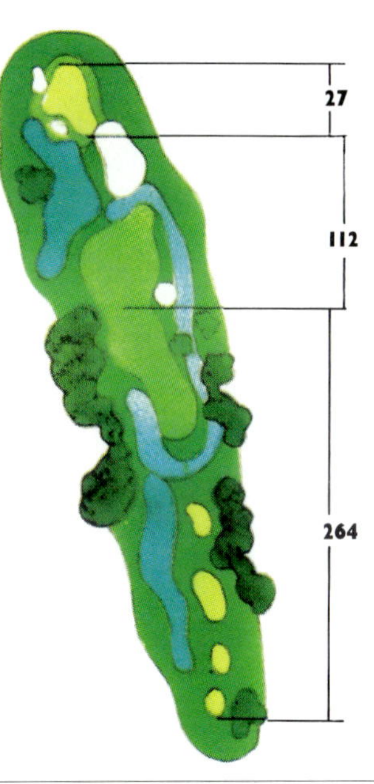

The shot off the tee must simply carry the wetlands, keep clear of the bunker right and more wetlands to the left. The approach follows to a green placed among many hazards.

6

Par 4
340 yards

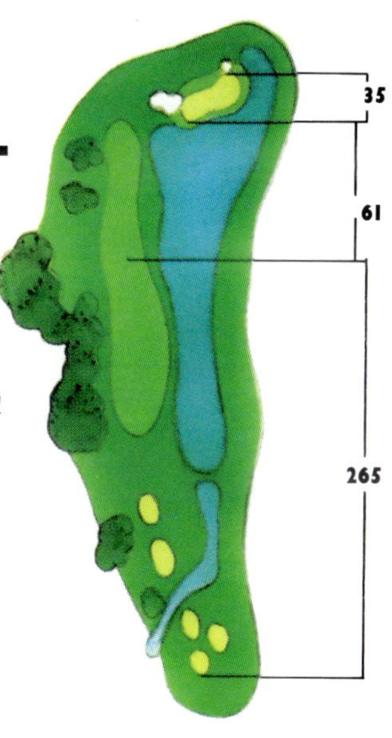

A fairway wood or long-iron from the tee will place the ball in excellent position for the approach. The length dictates for the birdie but the water regulates for the par.

7

Par 5
542 yards

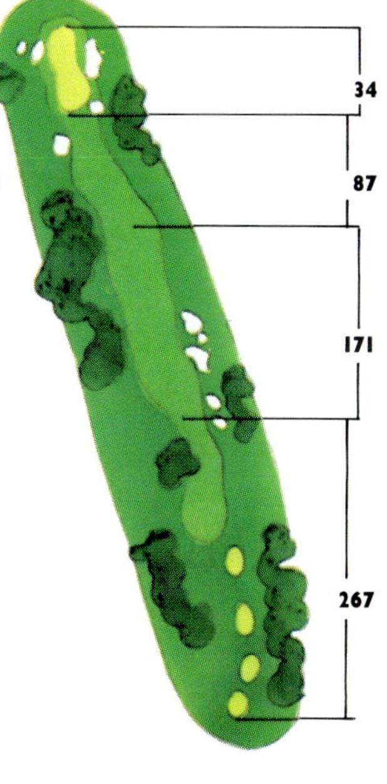

The right side of the fairway will allow for a big second shot to the green. Trees hinder the left while bunkers may come into play on the right. The putting surface is long and narrow.

8

Par 3
182 yards

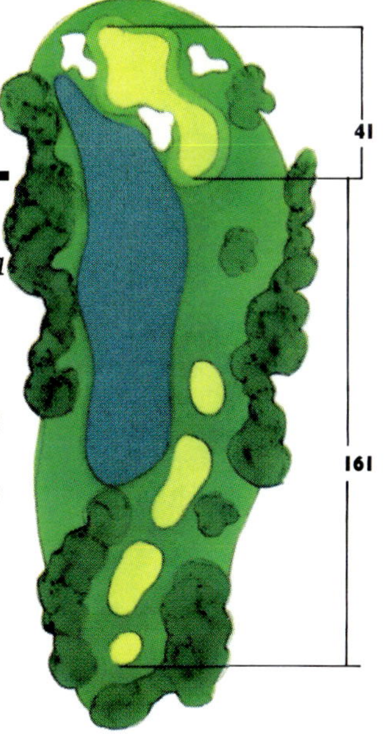

Wetlands define the area from tee to green. The long twisting green can be a place where three putts are found — the right line and length from the tee may relinquish the birdie.

9

Par 4
432 yards

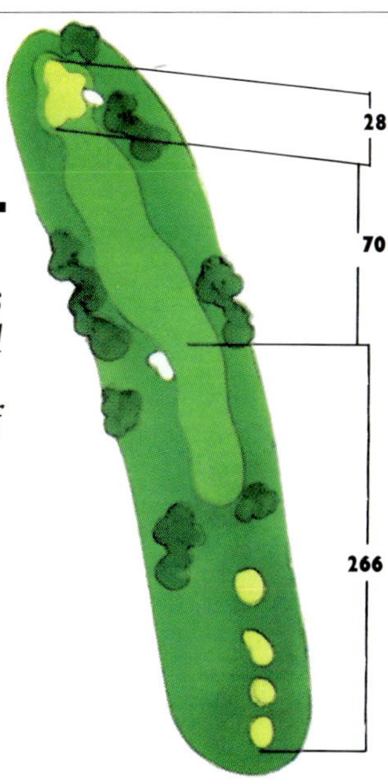

Long and fairly straight, this par 4 is a good hole to birdie. The left side of the fairway allows for a clear shot to the green — cottonwood to the right blocks shots from that side.

10

Par 4
393 yards

Placement off the tee is key. Bunkers and swales along the left and right can deter the approach. The elevated putting surface is guarded in front by a menacing pot-bunker.

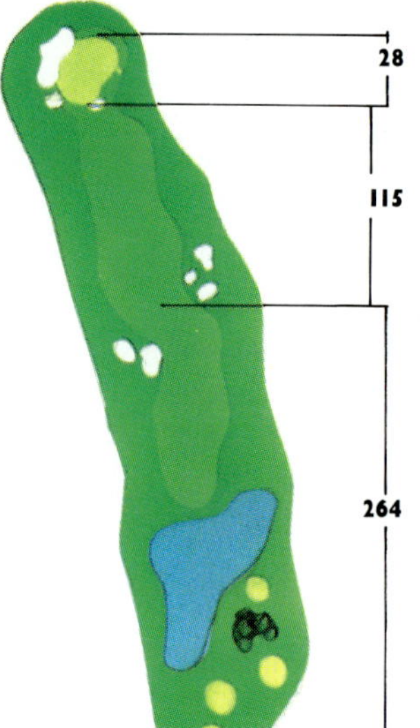

11

Par 4
410 yards

Options are open for the player. Two fairways — the left is easy to hit leaving a long second shot and the right is tough to hit but sets up for a wedge to the green.

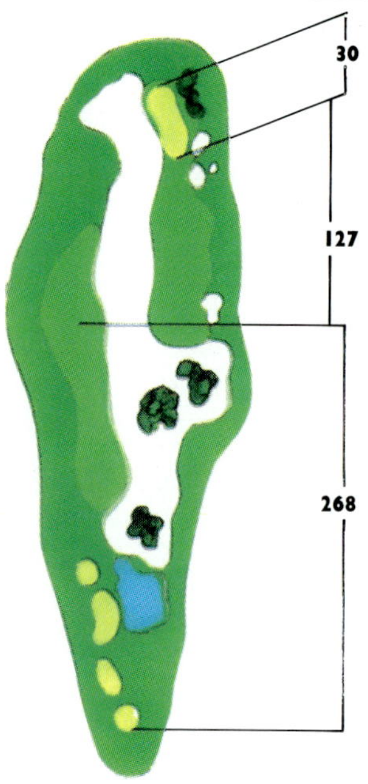

12

Par 3
166 yards

The beautiful view from the elevated tee includes a picturesque green fronted by a waterfall and a rolling putting surface.

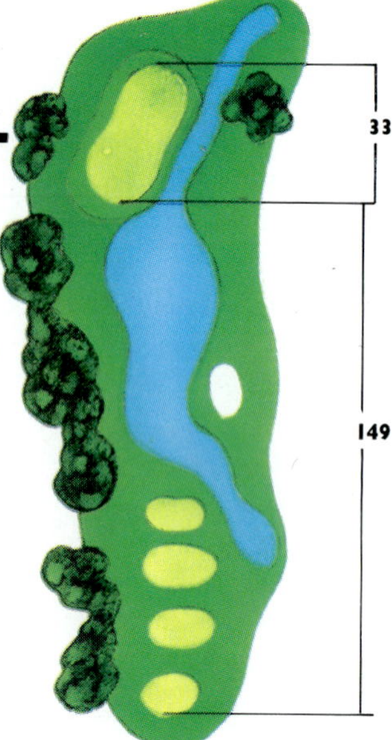

13

Par 5
506 yards

The slight dogleg entices attempts for the green in two. Average score for this hole will be below par — look for many birdies.

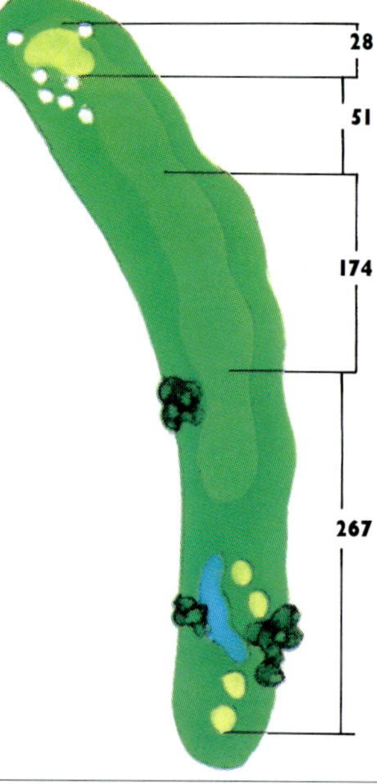

14

Par 4
455 yards

Players will be hitting a big drive down the right side of the elevated fairway. The approach is to the largest green on the course — reachable only by a long carry over wetlands.

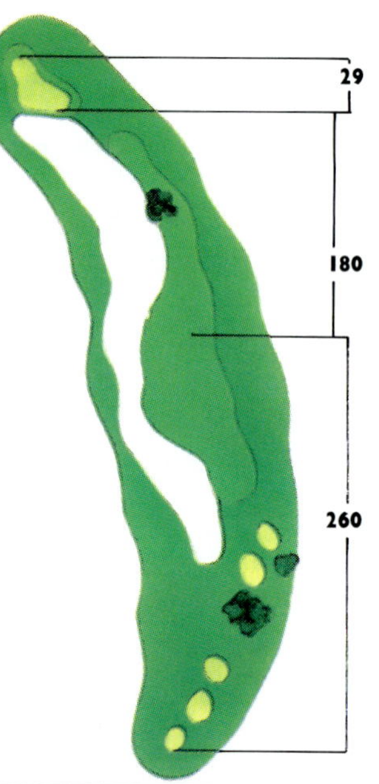

15

Par 3
192 yards

The long angled green is hidden from a large mound in front. An accurate tee shot must find the pin placed on the rolling surface.

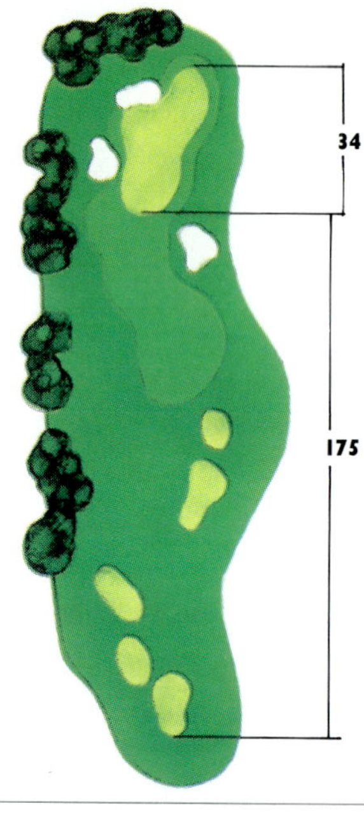

16

Par 4
376 yards

As the second shortest par 4 on the course, players will be using either a fairway wood or long-iron to place the ball in prime position for the approach. Birdies heat up the competition.

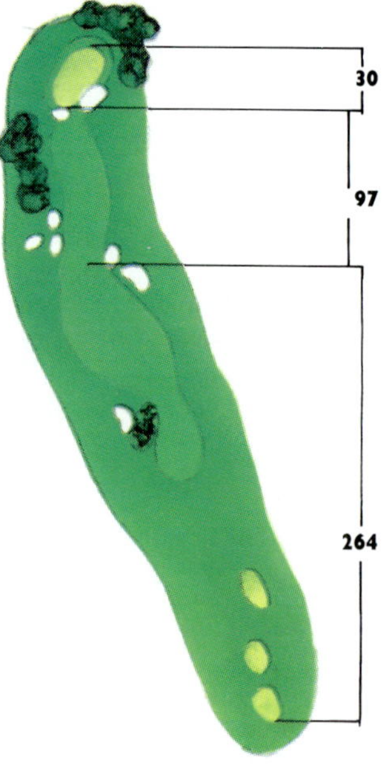

17

Par 5
556 yards

The momentum continues as players hit out of a narrow chute to the tight fairway. Three well played shots set up for the birdie.

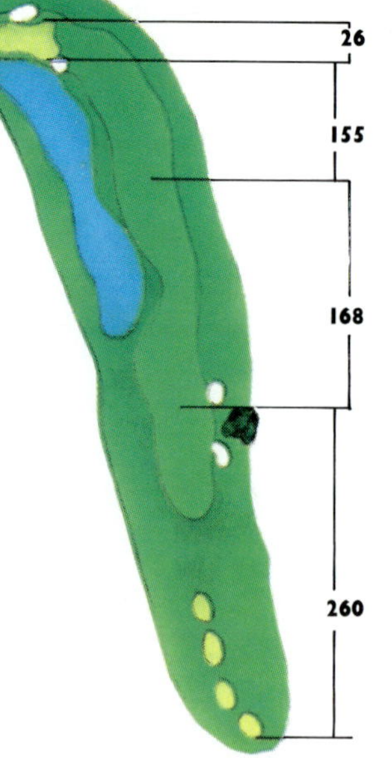

18

Par 4
450 yards

Caution is taken to avoid the wandering creek along the left side of the fairway. From that side of the fairway the players will have a clear shot to the green.

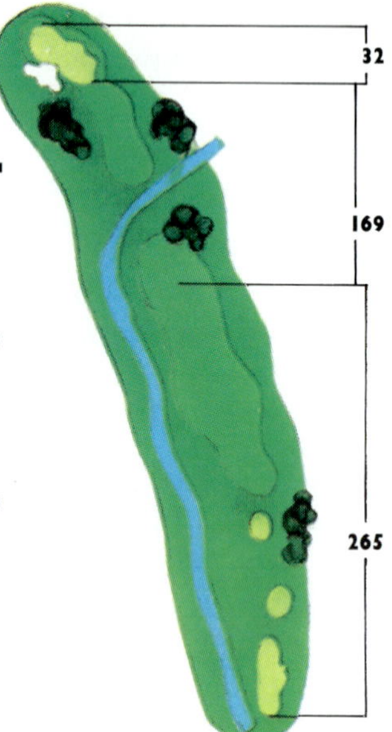

THE COURSE: ROYAL LYTHAM & ST. ANNES GOLF CLUB, LANCASHIRE , ENGLAND
*** A Royal and Ancient Sponsored event.**

*W*hen the R&A took its Open Championship to Royal Lytham for the first time in 1926, Robert Tyre (Bobby) Jones won the first of his three titles. A most memorable shot of that championship is marked by a plaque next to a bunker on the 17th hole, but that monument is the lone indication of U.S. success on this northwest English coast.

U.S. forces made their best challenge at Lytham in 1979 but Seve Ballesteros got it up and down from parking lots and other assorted wayward places and won by three over Jack Nicklaus and Ben Crenshaw. In 1988 the Open was won at Lytham again by Seve in a close battle with Nick Price. The 1995 Open at St. Andrews was won by the U.S.'s John Daly in a play off with Constantino Rocca of Italy.

Dates:	July 15-21
Network:	ABC
Times:	TBA
Yardage:	6857
Par:	71
Total Purse:	$1,107,638
1st Prize:	$199,375
1995 Winner:	John Daly
1995 Winning Score:	282 (67,71,73,71)

1

Par 3
206 yards

A hole that plays longer than it looks. With it being the first hole it is always a good idea to take more club than you think it needs. There is more room left of the green than right.

2

Par 4
437 yards

Drive as close to the out-of-bounds (right) as you dare to get a good second shot. That will give you a clear run-up to the green where you want to stay left as the green slopes right.

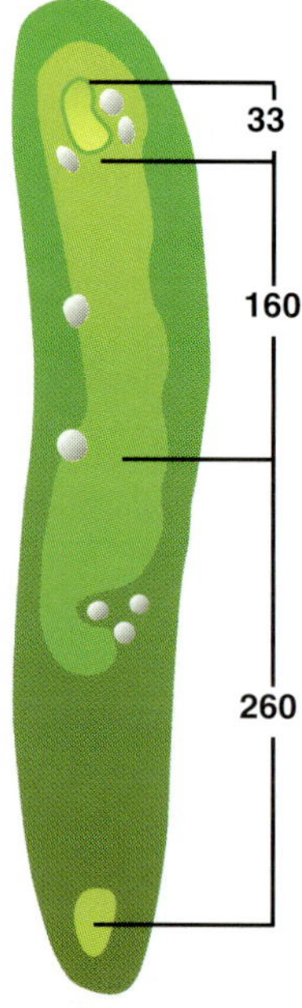

3

Par 4
457 yards

Beware of the second bunker hidden from the tee! Play the approach conservatively as all the trouble is at the back of the green.

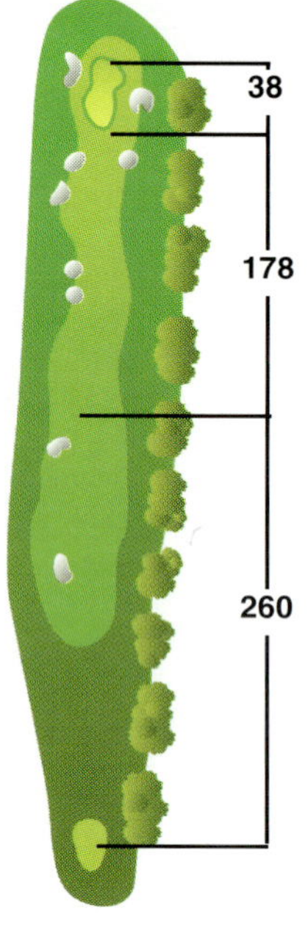

4

Par 4
393 yards

Put the drive slightly right as the left side is blind. The second needs to be long as the bunkers eat into the front of the green.

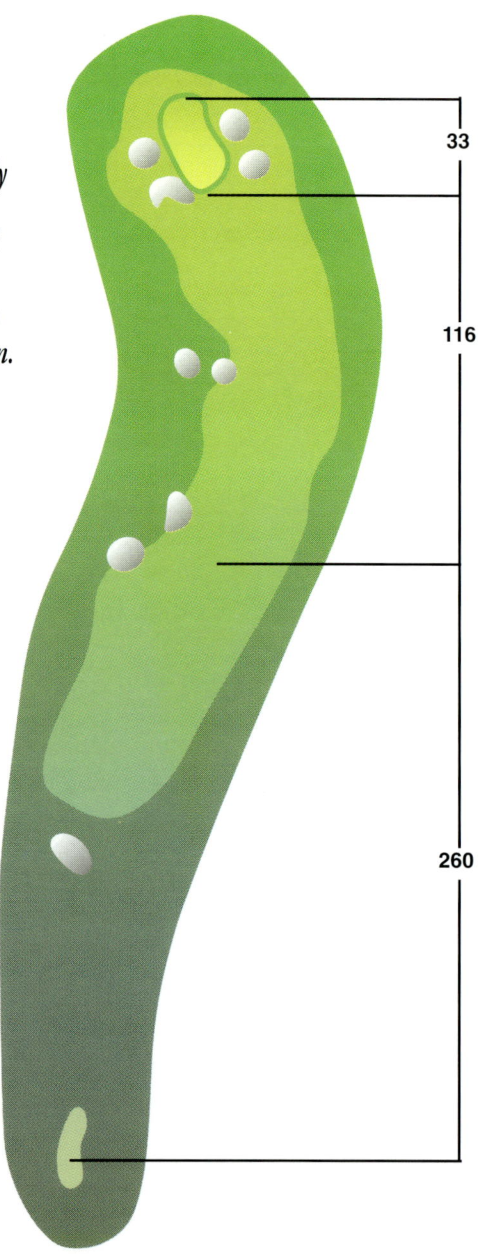

5

Par 3
212 yards

A seemingly flat green but it has a lot of slopes that need a careful putt. If you miss the green it is better to be right. Left is full of danger.

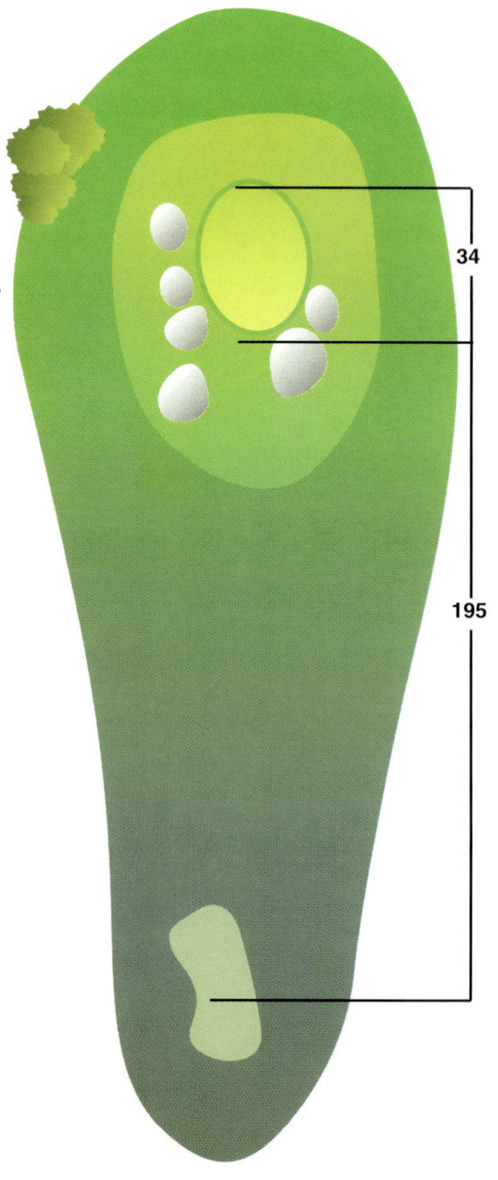

6

Par 5
490 yards

Aim the tee-shot at the distant hospital chimney. The cross bunkers before the green will only be carried by the longest hitters. A sensible lay-up will leave something like an 8 or 9 iron approach.

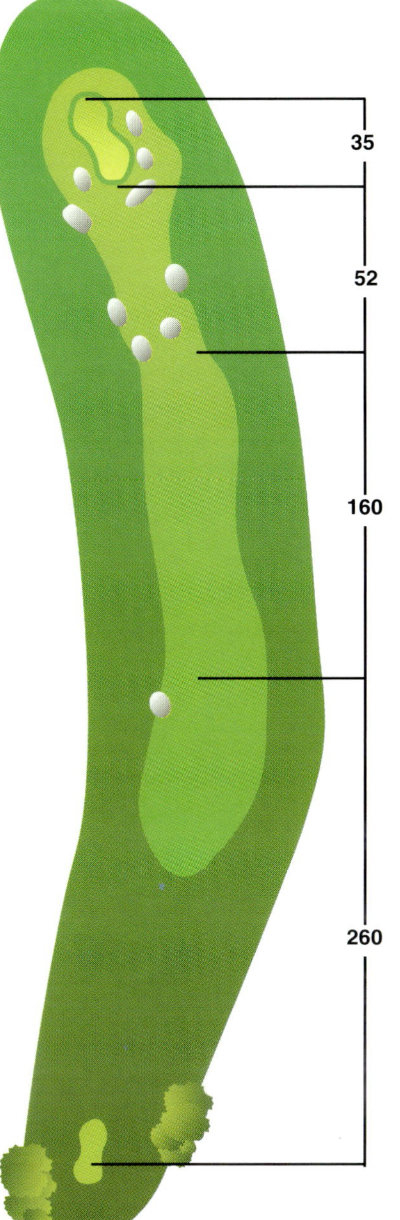

7

Par 5
549 yards

Stay left off the tee, and left down towards the green Anything too far right blocks out a shot to the green and brings new bunker on right into play.

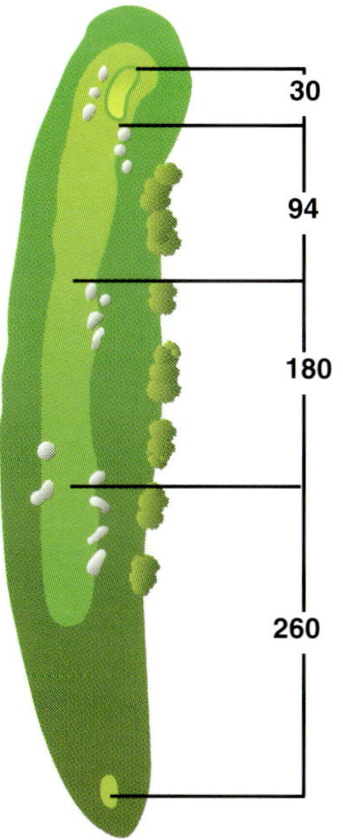

9

Par 3
164 yards

Don't be tricked into aiming for the flag. Go for the middle of the green. Definitely not a hole to attack - play safe!

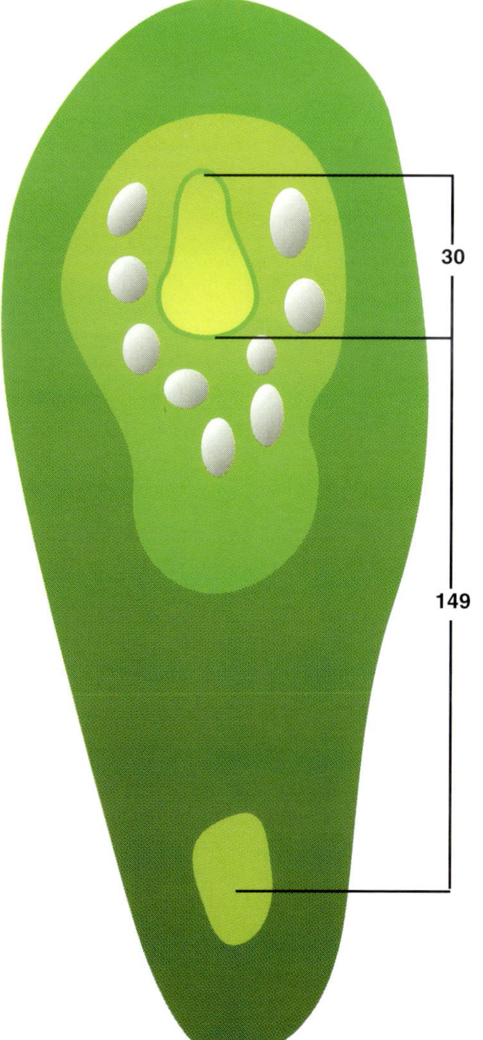

8

Par 4
394 yards

A narrow driving area so a 3-wood or 2-iron is sensible. Play for position. The approach is dagerous with a big valley between the bunkers and the green. You're also playing uphill so take more club - it's longer than you think.

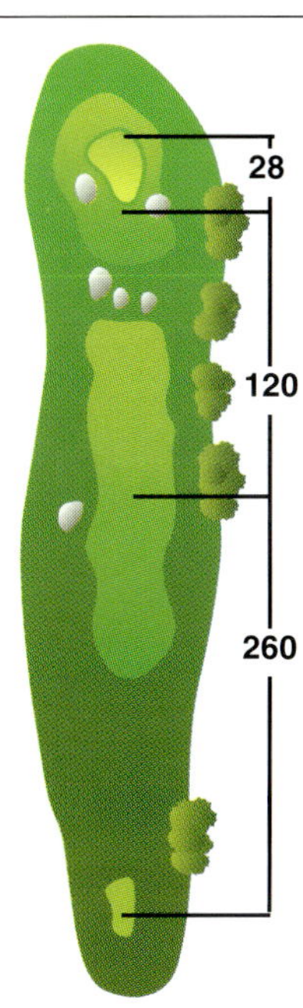

10

Par 4
334 yards

Avoid the bunker on the right off the tee. Shot from the left leaves an open run-up to the green. Off the tee you should aim slightly towards the church spire on the left.

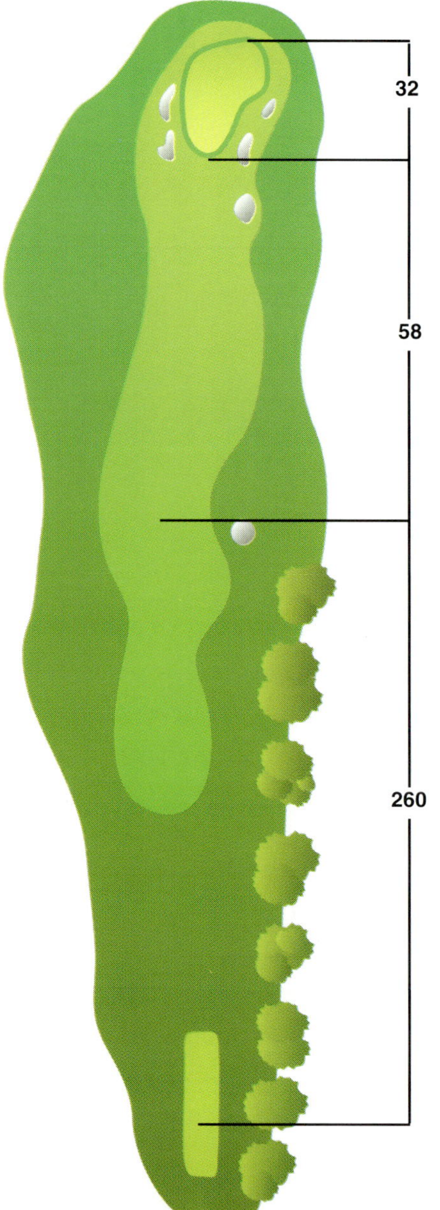

11

Par 5
542 yards

Keep it right off the tee, over or right of the right-hand bunkers - there's plenty of room. Leave the approach short of the bunker protecting the green (62 yards from front), then go for a pitch and putt birdie!

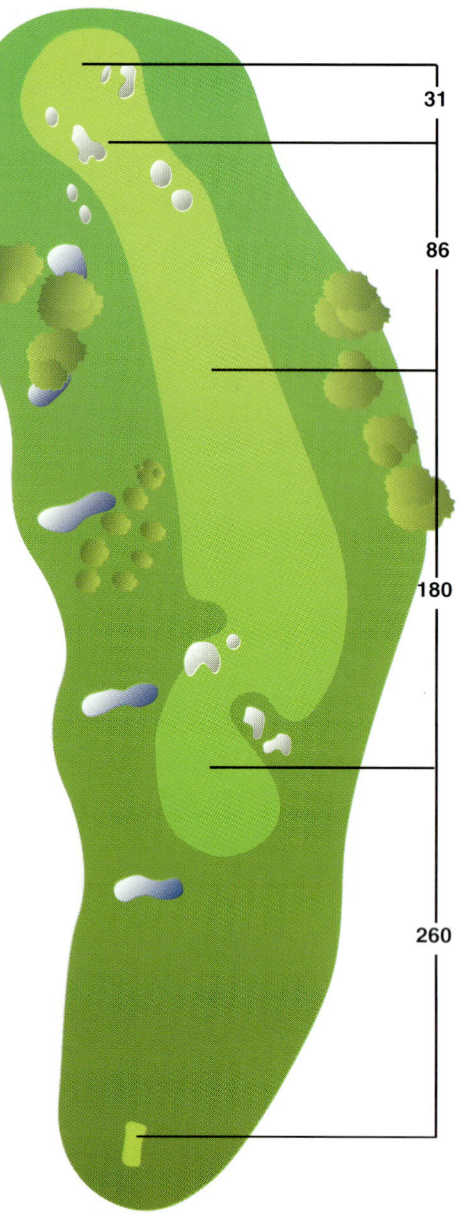

12

Par 3
198 yards

A tough hole, perhaps the most dangerous on the course. It's almost better to underclub and lay-up rather than be over the back. A lay-up would give you another pitch and putt, for par.

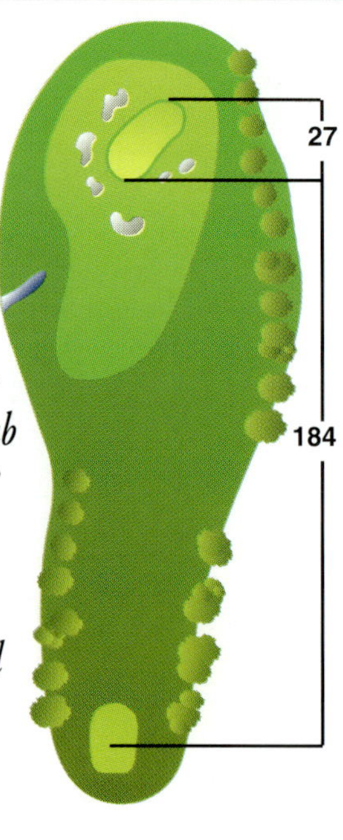

13

Par 4
342 yards

Aim towards the middle bunker on the left, that will hit the middle of the fairway. Any ball right leaves a blind shot to the green. The second to the green is not as long as it looks - choose carefully.

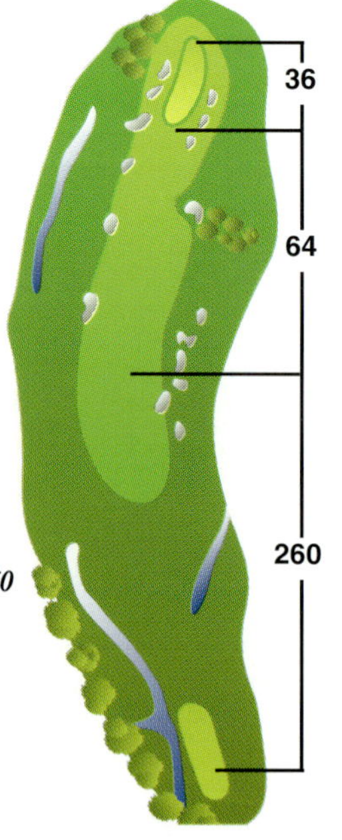

14

Par 4
445 yards

The drive must avoid the bunkers on the right. Then a long second shot (3-wood or 2-iron) could run up to the green, but don't be short as the green slopes front to back, making a putt from the back easier.

15

Par 4
463 yards

Most difficult hole.
The line off the tee is
to the bunker on the
left of the fairway.
Your second shot
should be slightly left
of the green as you
can't see the cross
bunkers guarding
the approach.

16

Par 4
357 yards

Straight over the marker
post will put you in the
left side of the fairway
with the perfect approach
line. From the right you
will have bunkers to cross
and a narrow part of the
green to m for.

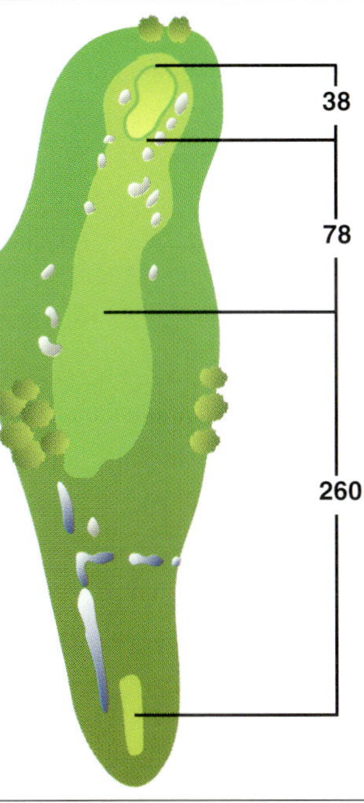

18

Par 4
412 yards

Almost home! You must
stay left off the tee to
avoid the row of bunkers
right. The second shot
then demands a long,
accurate iron. The green
is very long so get it close
to avoid long putt.

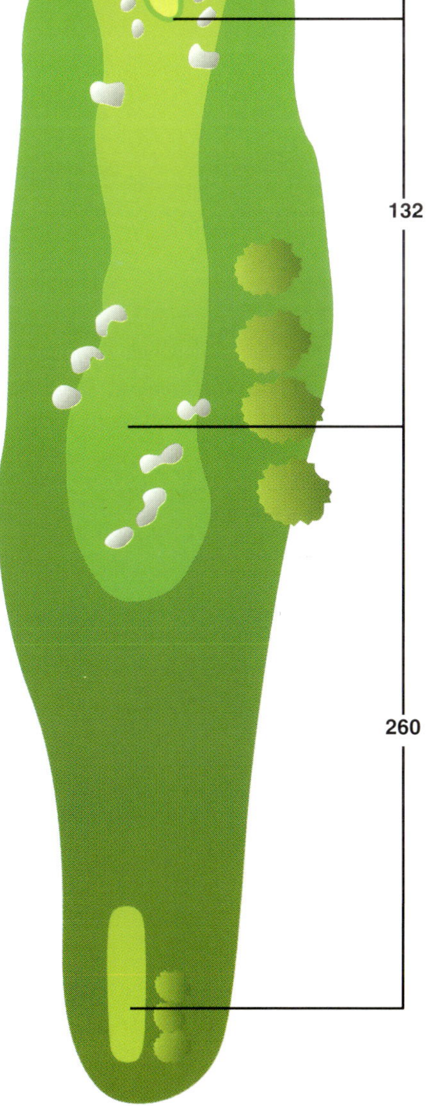

17

Par 4
462 yards

Aim just left of the club
flag-pole. That will put
you in the right side of
the fairway, widening
the dog-leg. Anything
tight left leaves you
blind. Second shot is best
played short and right of
the green, leaving an
easy chip to the green.

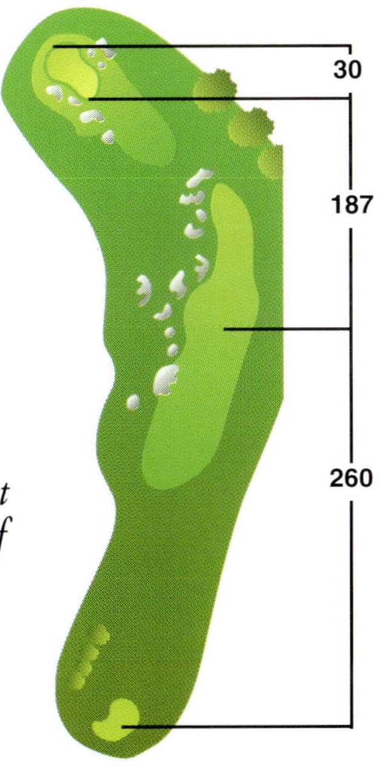

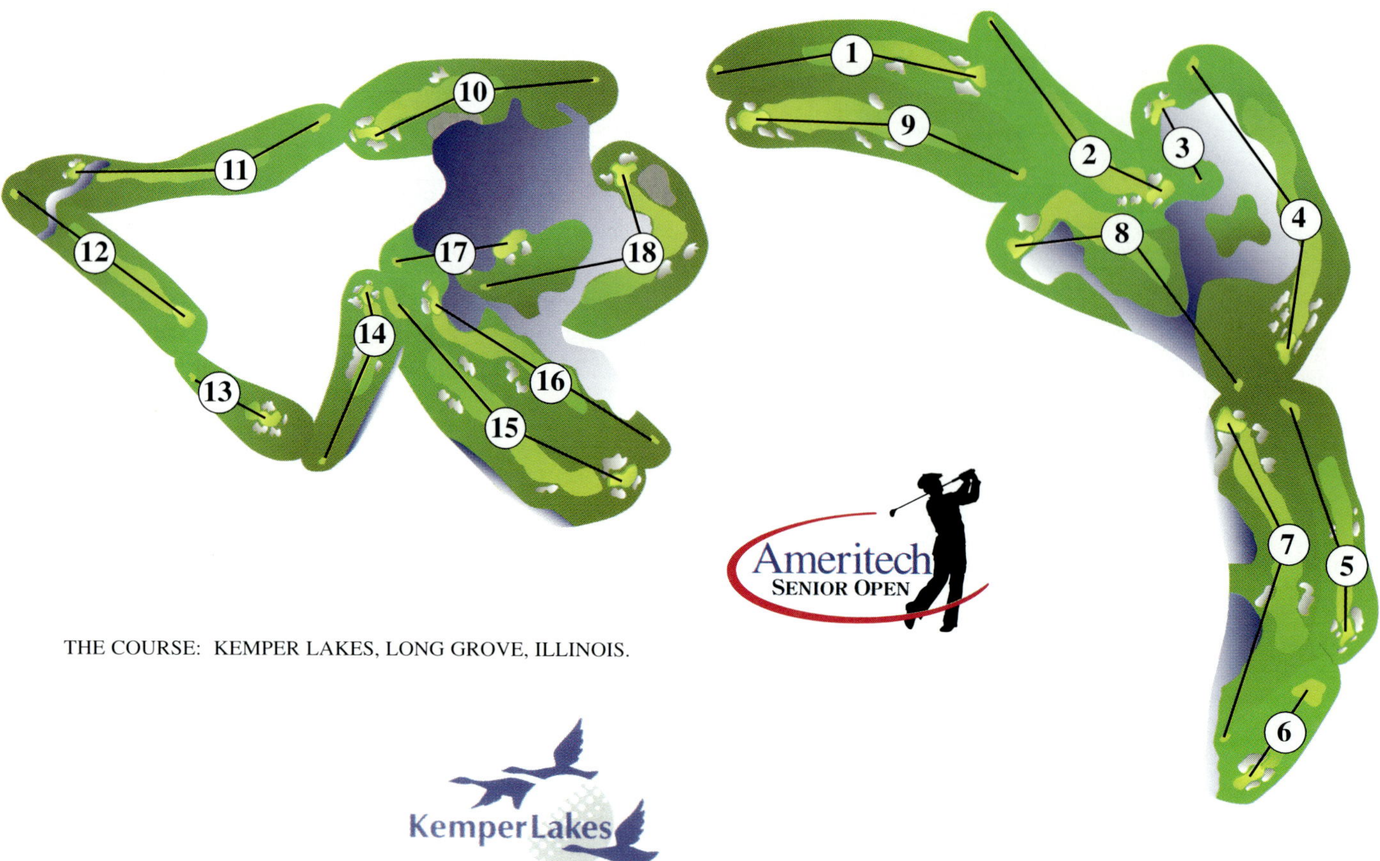

THE COURSE: KEMPER LAKES, LONG GROVE, ILLINOIS.

The Ameritech Senior Open has gained acclaim as one of the top events of the SENIOR PGA TOUR®. In 1989, Bruce Crampton won the inaugural tournament at the legendary Canterbury Golf Club near Cleveland. The 1990 event moved to Grand Traverse, Michigan where Chi Chi Rodriguez won his 15th victory of the year. In 1991, the tournament moved to Stonebridge Country Club where Mike Hill was able to claim victory with a solid 16-under par. In 1992, Dale Douglass pulled away from the pack on the final day to earn a 4-shot victory with a 15-under par total of 201. Dangerous weather forced the cancellation of the final round of the 1993 tournament, and George Archer was declared the winner with 133. In 1994, a unique situation occurred. A sponsor exempted player, John Paul Cain, won the event.

In 1995, Hale Irwin broke a course record with his 21 under par victory. The 1996 Ameritech Senior Open moves to Kemper Lakes, considered one of the finest golf courses in the country.

Dates:	July 22-28
Network:	CBS
Times:	Sat.　　4:30-6:00 EST
	Sun.　　4:30-6:00 EST
Yardage:	6840
Par:	72
Slope:	138
Rating:	73.2
Total Purse:	$850,000
1st Prize:	$150,000
1995 Winner:	Hale Irwin
1995 Winning Score:	195 (66,63,66)
Principal Charitable Beneficiary:	TBD
Charitable Benefits to Date:	More than $400,000 in last 6 years
Ticket Information:	1-800-SENIOR-1

1

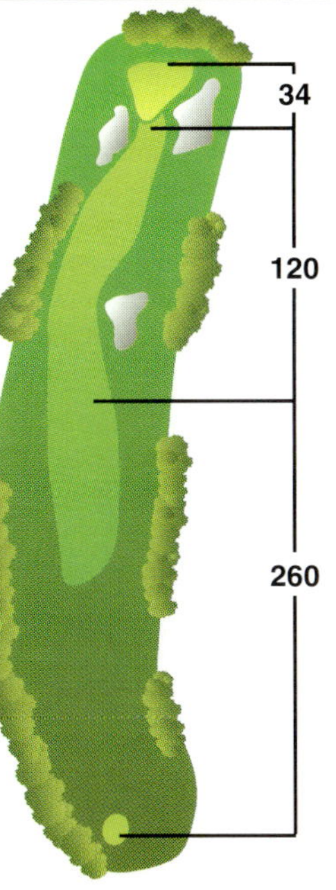

Par 4
406 yards

The drive from an elevated tee on this slight dogleg right hole will land in a valley. Out-of-bounds left and a fairway bunker right makes this a good driving hole. The approach shot is uphill to a large green guarded by deep bunkers on the right and left front.

2

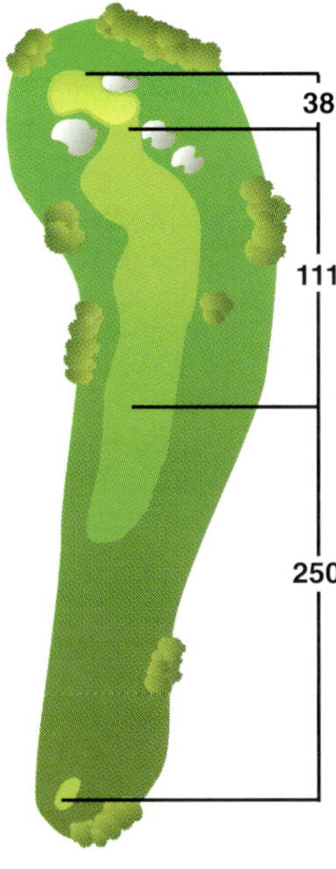

Par 4
380 yards

This hole requires an accurate drive and a pinpoint second shot to a narrow, sloping green. The second shot will usually be played across a huge bunker on the left front of a narrow, contoured green. The back of the green slopes severely to a pond which will catch shots over the green, while a second back bunker awaits long shots to the right.

3

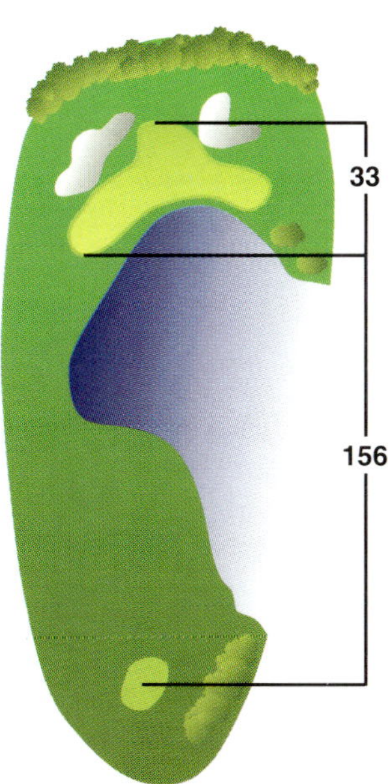

Par 3
173 yards

The tee shot to the bell-shaped green must carry over water. The contoured green is guarded left and right by back bunkers and in front by a retaining wall and water. The green has a large ridge in the back that creates a back shelf for difficult pin placements.

4

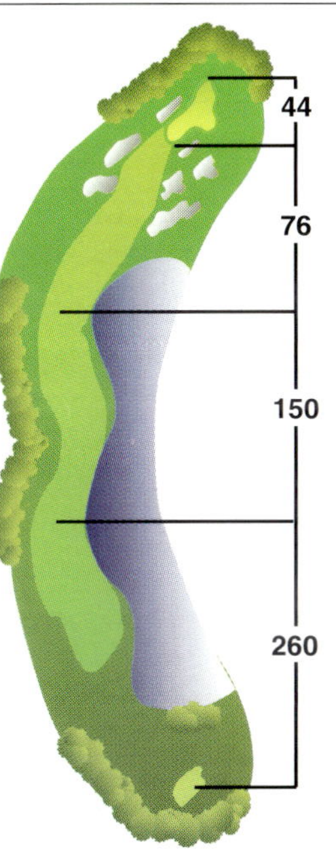

Par 5
508 yards

This first par 5 on the course is reachable with two well-played shots. Water right and out-of-bounds left off the tee make this a demanding driving hole. The player has an option to go for the green or lay up on the left side of the water. The green is guarded by seven bunkers.

5

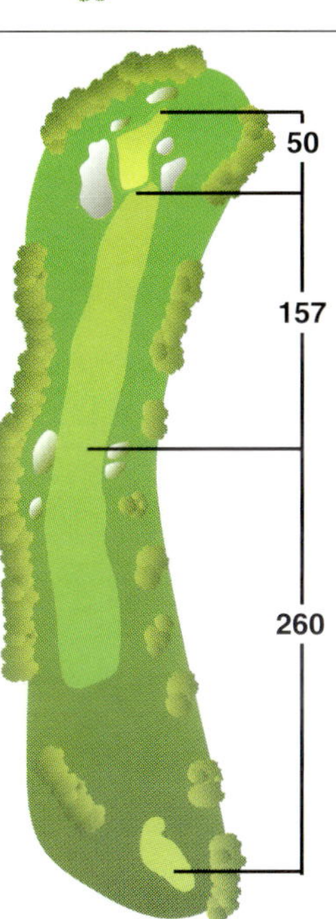

Par 4
442 yards

This long dogleg right usually plays into a prevailing summer wind. Out-of-Bounds left and trees right make this a good driving hole. A long iron - second shot into the large green is guarded by a large bunker left and two small bunkers right. The green is the most contoured on the course.

6

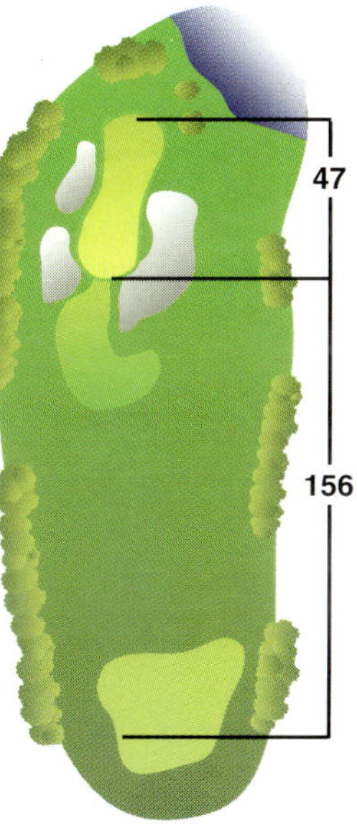

Par 3
180 yards

This par 3 is sneaky hard. The green has a large bunker that wraps around the front and right of the green with two small bunkers front and back left. The narrow angle of the green from the tee requires a tee shot to be the right distance and direction to avoid the bunkers. A pin placed back right brings a lake into play and lengthens the hole considerably.

7

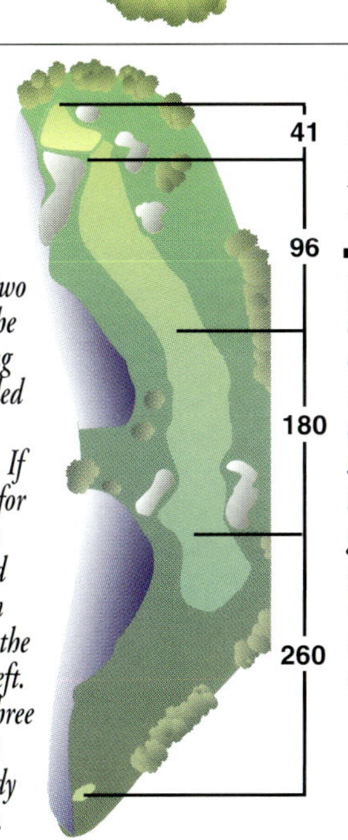

Par 5
557 yards

This hole is reachable in two shots downwind by only the longest hitters. The landing area for the drive is guarded by two large fairway bunkers, one on each side. If the player elects not to go for the green in two shots, the second shot must be played between a large bunker on the right, 100 yards from the green, and a lake on the left. The green is guarded by three large bunkers on the right and a retaining wall, sandy beach and lake on the left.

8

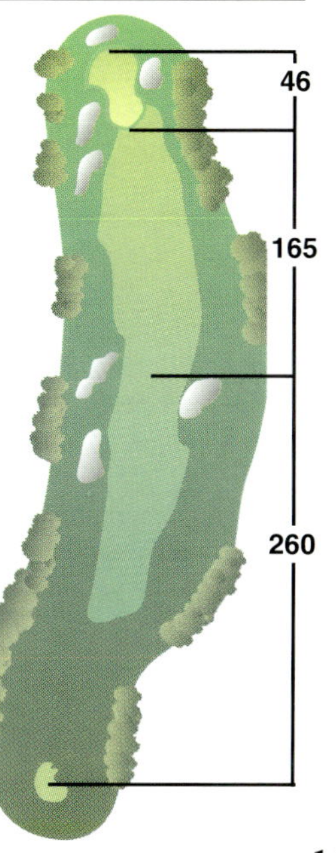

Par 4
421 yards

This par 4 - dogleg left is a lay up hole off the tee, usually requiring a long iron or 3 wood. Your second shot is played to a lightning fast green guarded by a pond to the left and a very large bunker on the right. The two level green is one of the more difficult on the course.

9

Par 4
448 yards

The number one handicapped hole on the course is a long, demanding uphill par 4. The drive must negotiate a deep fairway bunker on the right and two smaller bunkers on the left. The second shot to this long, narrow, hour-glass shaped green is all uphill. The green is protected by two small bunkers on the left and a small bunker on the right. The front of the green is sloped left to right with the back half of the green relatively flat.

10

Par 4
453 yards

This is another long par 4 that requires an accurate drive. A hazard left and a large, deep fairway bunker right make this hole a guaranteed bogey or worse with an errant drive. Second shots to this deep green are protected by a large greenside bunker right and a back-and-front bunker left. The front half of this green is heavily contoured back to front with the back right pin placement the most difficult.

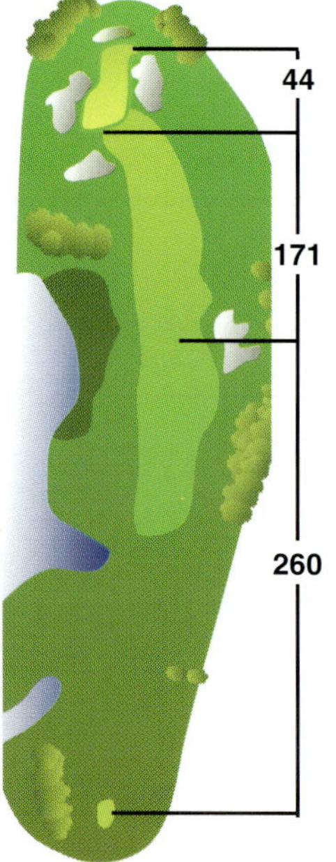

11

Par 5
534 yards

Most long hitters will go for this par 5 green in 2 shots. However, the drive must first avoid large oak trees right and left in the landing area. The downhill second shot to the green is through an avenue of large oaks. The small, narrow green is guarded by a retaining wall and a small pond. A bunker back right and mounds behind the green make a long shot undesirable.

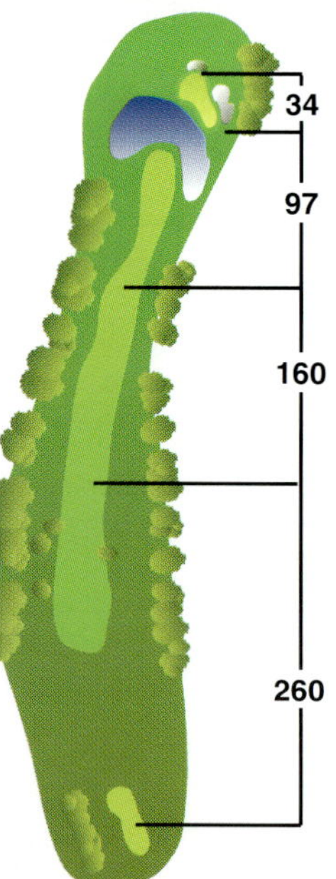

12

Par 4
393 yards

The uphill tee shot must be hit through a narrow opening of large oaks with little margin for error. The green is guarded by large trees that overhang the green on both sides. Second shots often require special draws or fades to get to the pin, unless the drive is perfectly placed. The contoured green has a small shelf on the back third of the green.

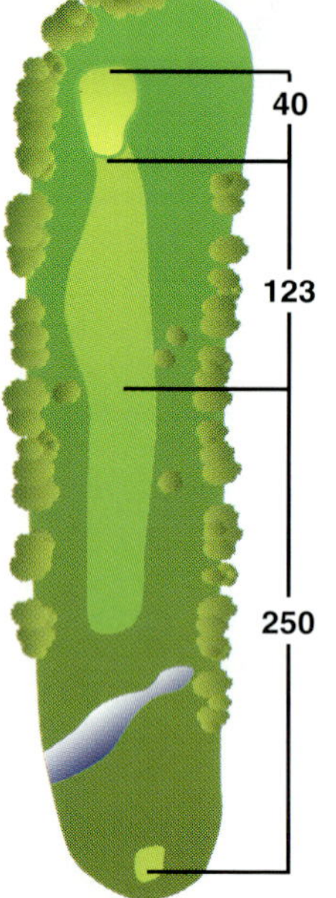

13

Par 3
219 yards

This is the longest par 3 on the course. The narrow, long, three-leveled green is 49 yards front to back, which makes proper club selection crucial. Protected by large bunkers—one left, two right—this is a demanding par 3.

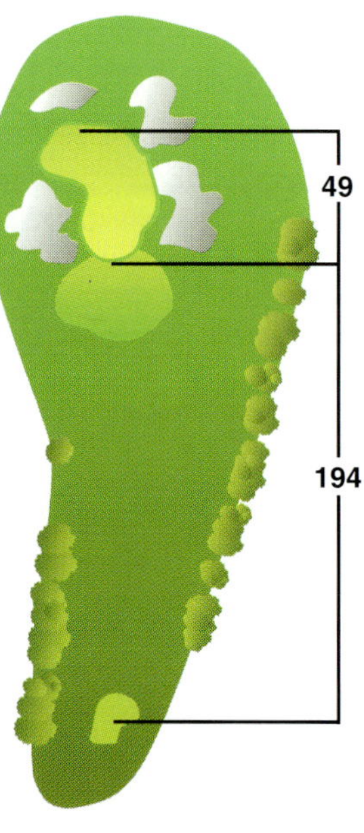

14

Par 4
420 yards

This slighty downhill, par 4 dogleg left has a 100-yard fairway bunker left and large mounds right to define the landing area. The small green is tightly bunkered. This green has numerous pin placements protected by sand, and a large ridge makes the back third of the green 4 feet higher than the other parts of the green.

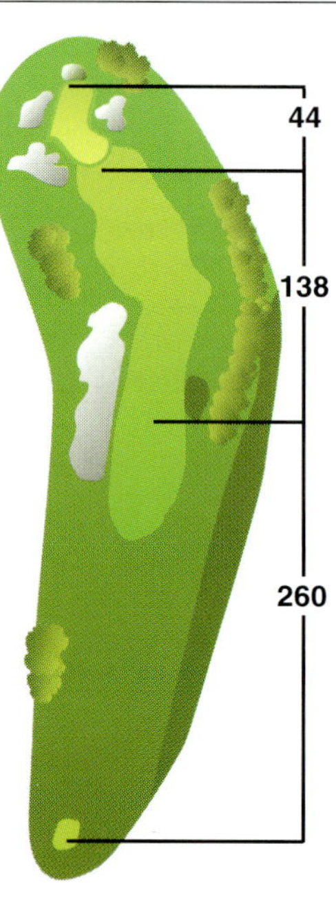

15

Par 5
578 yards

The driving area is protected by two fairway bunkers on the right and one large fairway bunker on the left. The slighty uphill second shot requires a long-iron or wood to a turning point protected by trees on the left and a fairway bunker on the right along with the Out-of-Bounds. The hole then turns sharply left the last 100 yards to a green protected on all sides by greenside sand traps.

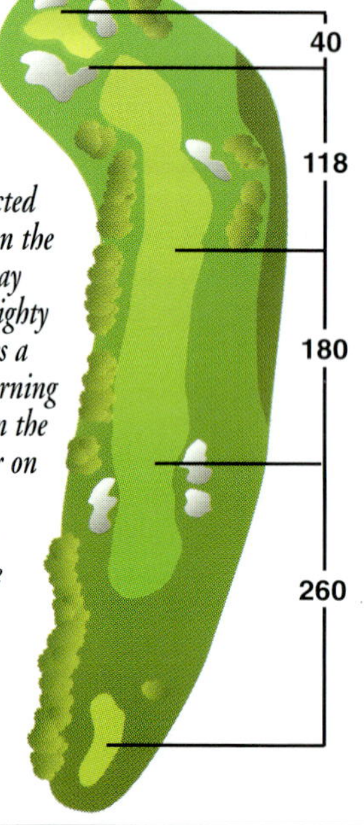

16

Par 4
469 yards

The most demanding par four on the course has water running the entire length of the fairway on the right hand side before forming a pond protecting the front of the green. The landing is guarded by two fairway bunkers on the left and water on the right. The narrow, deep green has a large, deep bunker on the left, behind the green. A ridge through the green makes second shots and putting difficult.

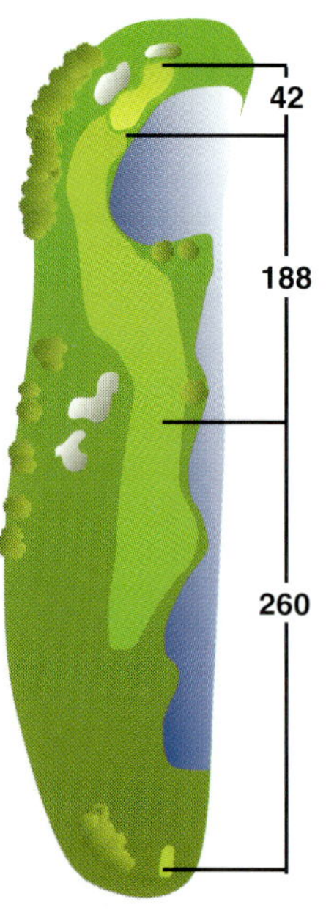

17

Par 3
203 yards

A semi-island green features a wooden retaining wall, protected on three sides by a lake. The right side of the green is guarded by two large, deep bunkers. The 17th also has the longest green on the course, which makes for numerous pin placements. Heavily contoured, the green often produces difficult chipping and putting from all directions.

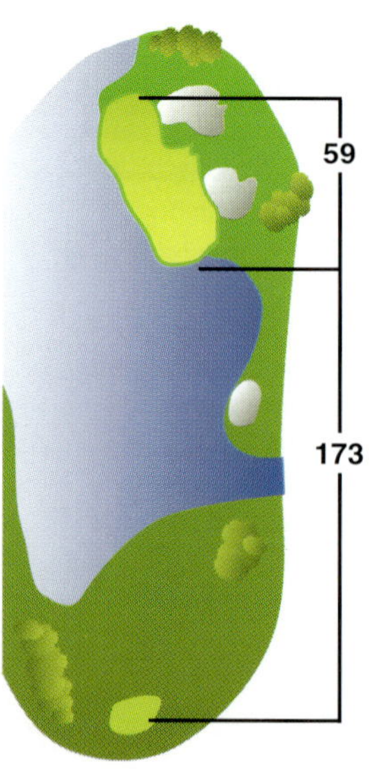

18

Par 4
433 yards

The half-moon shaped, dogleg left fairway is flanked by water on the left from tee to green. The drive must carry 200 yards to clear the lake. Second shot must carry water to a contoured green guarded right and left by water to the right rear by a deep, large bunker. The green has three separate fingers and is heavily contoured .

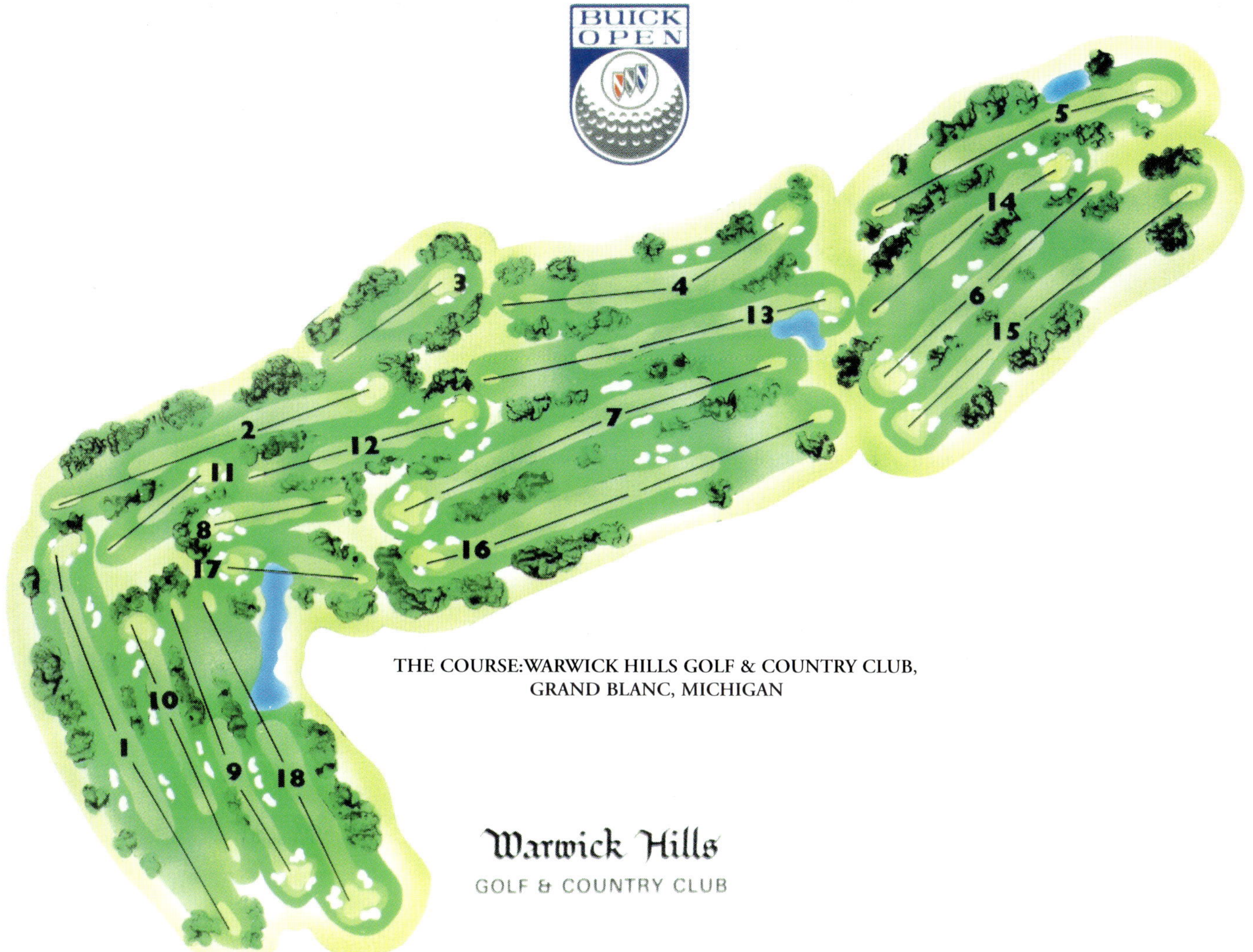

THE COURSE: WARWICK HILLS GOLF & COUNTRY CLUB,
GRAND BLANC, MICHIGAN

*B*uick Motor Division, the long-standing sponsor and corporate partner to major PGA TOUR® events, has brought 27 of 28 Buick Opens to Warwick Hills Golf & Country Club since 1958. As the title sponsor to three other PGA TOUR® tournaments, the General Motors Division is among the PGA TOUR's® leading supporters.

Over the life of the Open, Warwick Hills has been reworked on several occasions: in 1967, architect Joe Lee lowered the original yardage from 7280 to 7014, while raising the challenge with numerous bunker additions and softer greens. 1991 saw the yardage returned to 7104.

Warwick's long, rolling fairways and elevated greens, perennially celebrated as some of the TOUR's best-groomed, were the sight of Chip Beck's amazing come-from-behind victory in the 1990 Open. Eight stokes back of the leader Hale Irwin and thirteen other players after 54 holes, Beck's final round 65 matched the lowest finish ever by an Open winner.

Dates:	August 1-4
Network:	CBS
Times:	Sat. 4:30-6:00 EST
	Sun. 3:30-6:00 EST
Yardage:	7104
Par:	72
Slope:	126
Rating:	73.9
Total Purse:	$1,200,000
1st Prize:	$216,000
1995 Winner:	Woody Austin
1995 Winning Score:	270 (63,68,72,67)
Principal Charitable Beneficiary:	Easter Seals/Red Cross
Charitable Benefits to Date:	$2.5 million in last 13 years
Ticket Information:	1-810-239-9435

1

*Par 5
567 yards*

The opening hole is reachable in two by the longer hitters. The slight dogleg leads to a very large green. Pin placements on the back right corner are tough to get to.

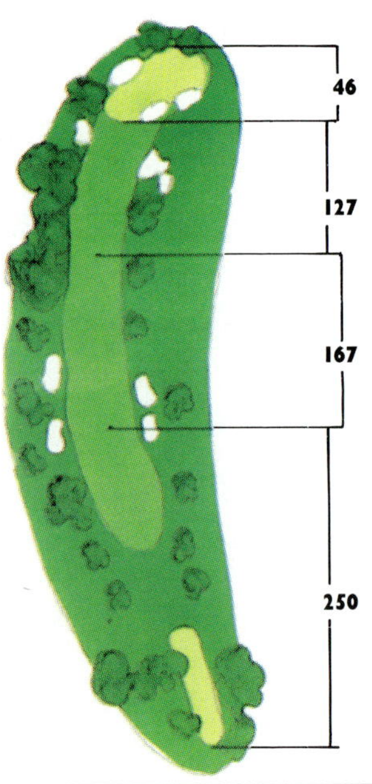

2

*Par 4
431 yards*

Out-of-bounds is to the left, but the more immediate concern is of the narrowing fairway. The putting surface slopes from back to front.

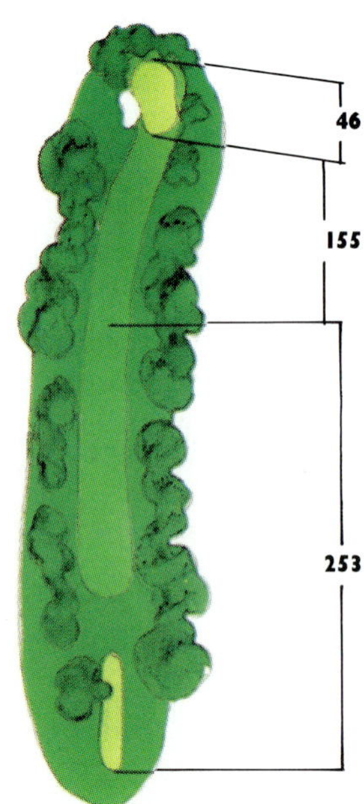

3

*Par 3
187 yards*

The large green slopes right-to-left and provides a good target from the tee. The open green is unprotected from the unpredictable wind.

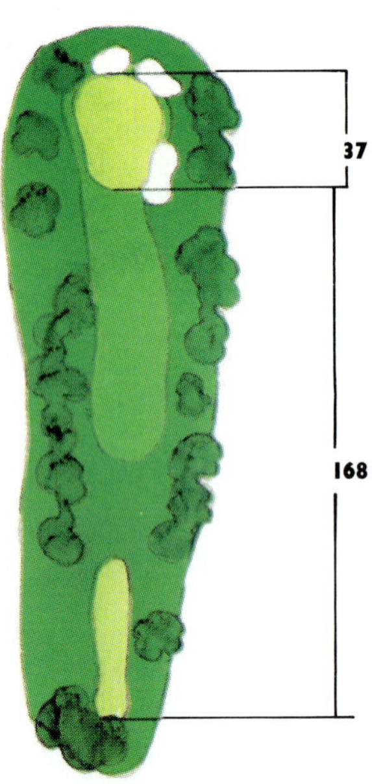

4

*Par 4
401 yards*

The right side of the fairway is favored to keep away from the trees on the left. The green narrows in the front and widens toward the back. Birdies will be frequent.

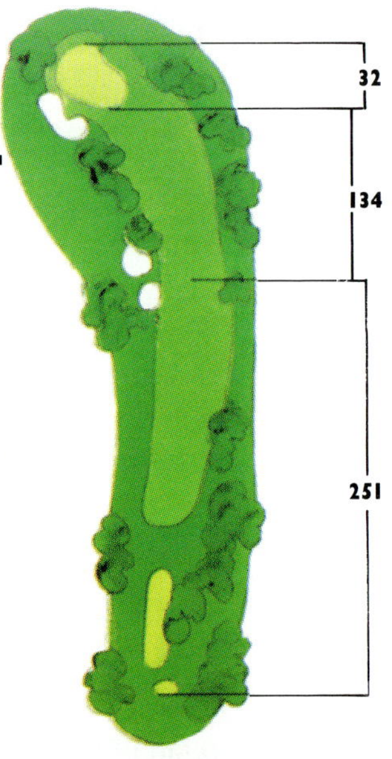

5

*Par 4
437 yards*

Bunkers along the right side of the fairway will catch the errant drives to that side. The spacious green slopes quickly toward the front — putting can be difficult.

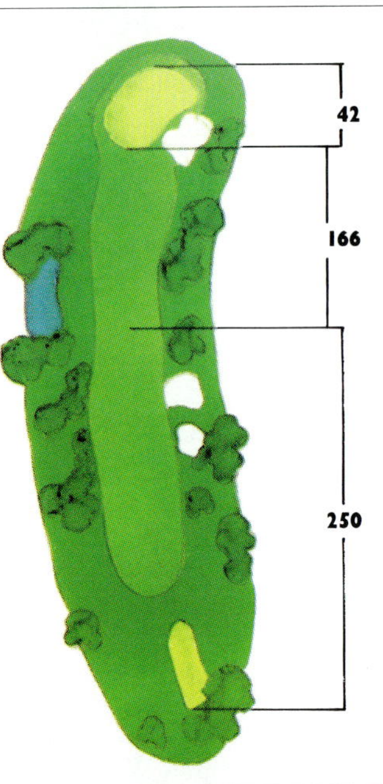

6

*Par 4
421 yards*

Large fairway bunkers are intimidating from the tee. A good drive down the middle of the fairway will leave a medium approach into a very large green.

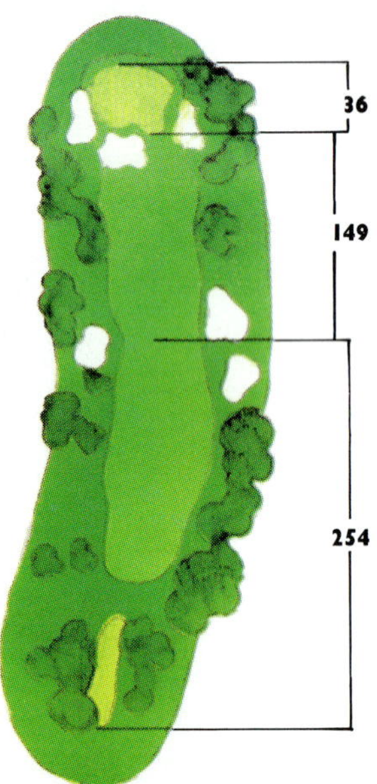

7

*Par 5
584 yards*

Fairway bunkers demand accuracy off the tee. As the longest of Warwick Hills' par 5 holes, this 7th may just be out of reach for those who try to get on in two.

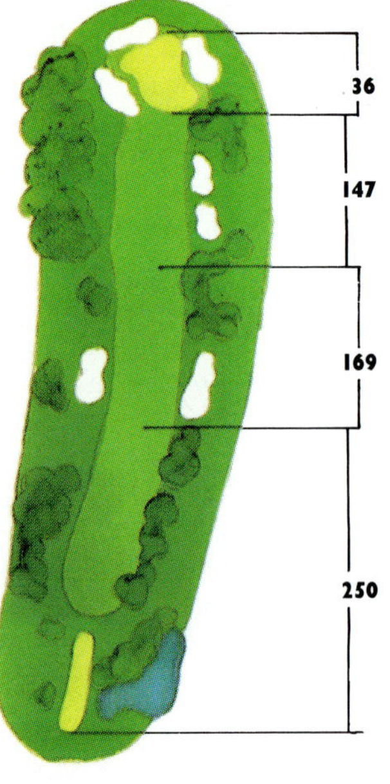

8

*Par 3
197 yards*

The large green is set within the pines. A small hollow forms on the left side of the green and expands to the right side. Pars are respectable here.

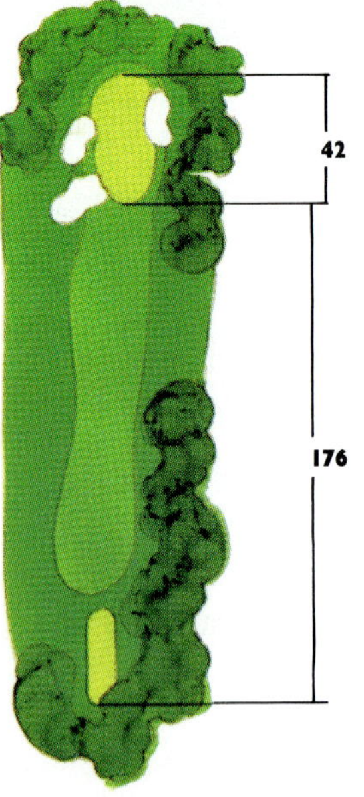

9

*Par 4
337 yards*

Two bunkers on the right side attract many tee shots. This 9th hole is a good finishing hole for the front side. Players making birdie here will get ahead of the rest of the field.

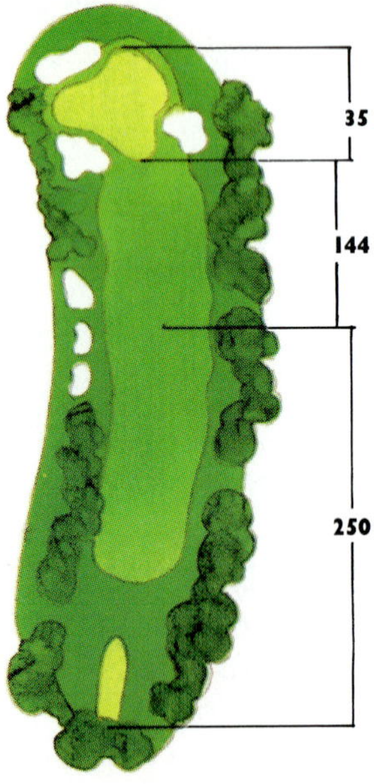

10

Par 4
401 yards

The descending fairway leads to a flat green. The right side of the fairway is favored to get around the fairway bunker on the left. Two large bunkers guard the front half of the green.

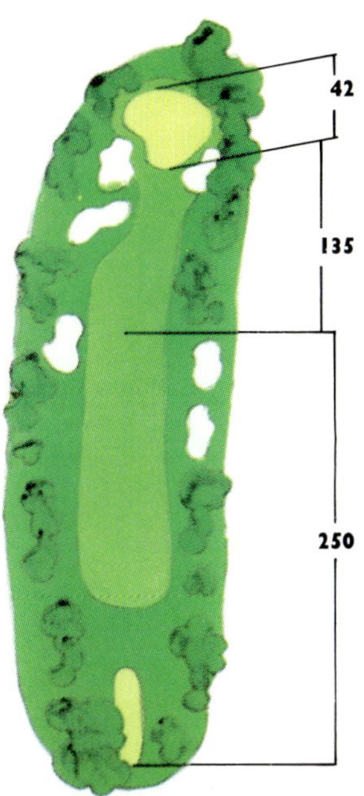

11

Par 3
190 yards

Trees reach in from both sides to make this a tight par 3. The subtle sloping on the green will test the ability of the putter's skills.

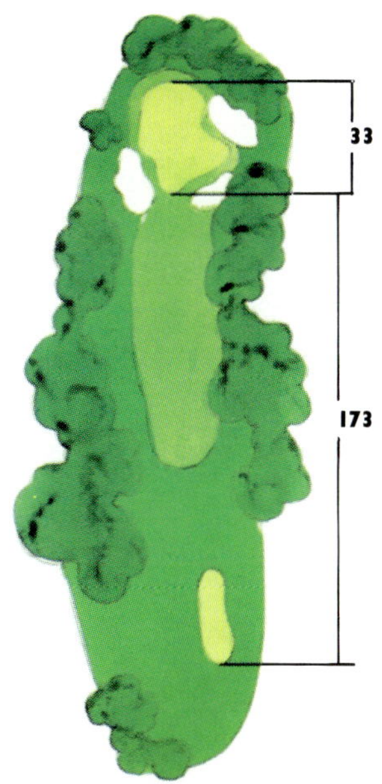

12

Par 4
335 yards

A long iron from the tee will be more than enough club to set up for a short chip to the green. Four bunkers cut into the edges of the putting surface.

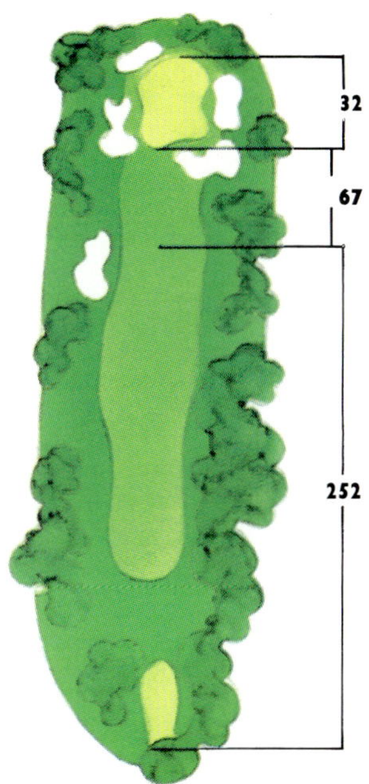

13

Par 5
548 yards

Players will need to birdie this hole to keep up with the rest of the field. A big drive along the left will allow an opportunity for players to reach the green in two. Water encroaches from the right.

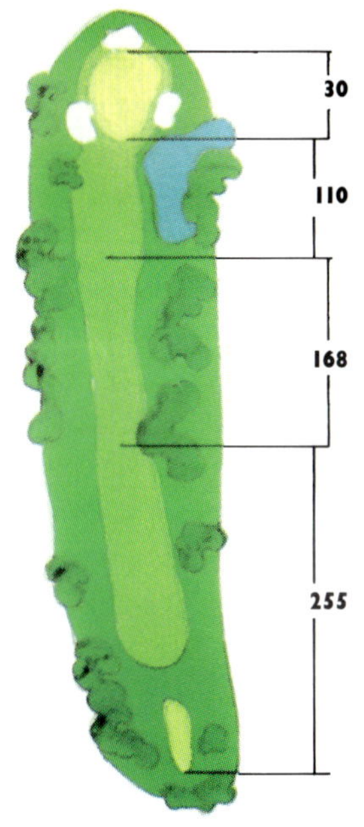

14

Par 4
322 yards

The narrow teeing area leads to a downhill, open fairway. The long hitters may be able to bound their drive up onto the large green. The surface slopes gently toward the front.

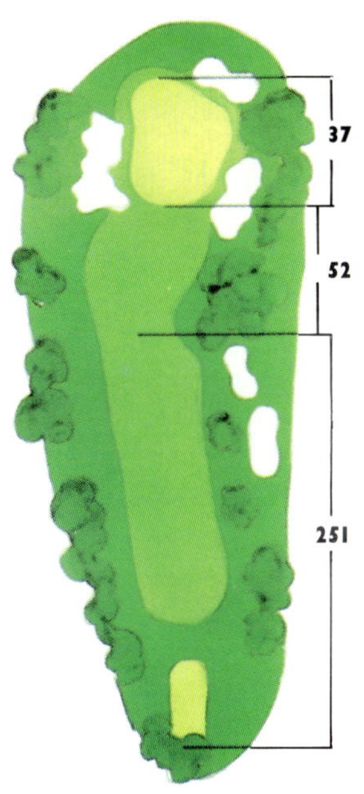

15

Par 4
457 yards

Into the wind, this 15th is the toughest hole on the course. The uphill fairway bends slightly to the left. Players will be very happy with a 4 on this hole.

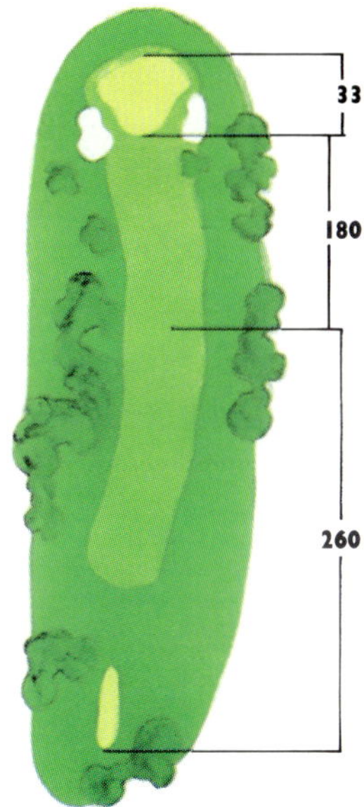

16

Par 5
580 yards

The last charge begins on the 16th. A generous fairway is only marred by a few fairway bunkers. Players should be able to get the ball close to the hole on the third shot.

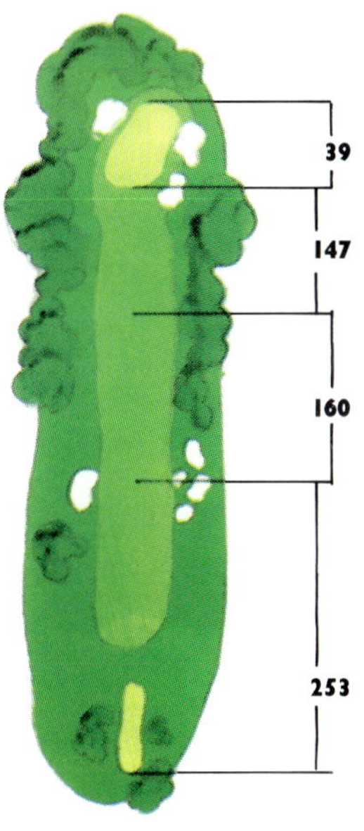

17

Par 3
198 yards

The championship can take a big turn on this formidable par 3. The elevated green slopes from back to front and is well protected by bunkers.

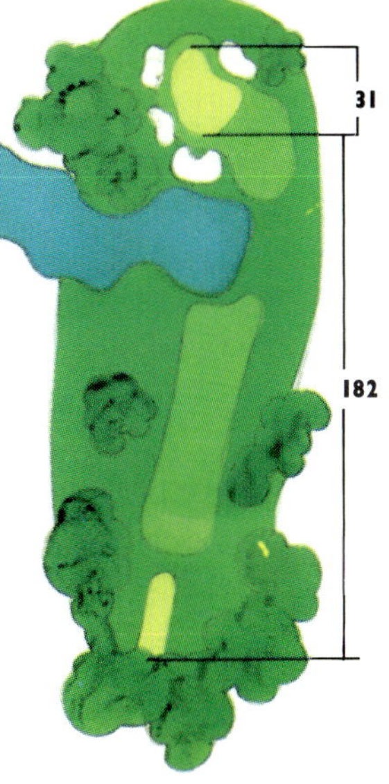

18

Par 4
435 yards

The 18th provides a fantastic finishing hole for the Buick Open. The deceptively sloping green will test the courage and abilities of the finishers. A tough hole to birdie.

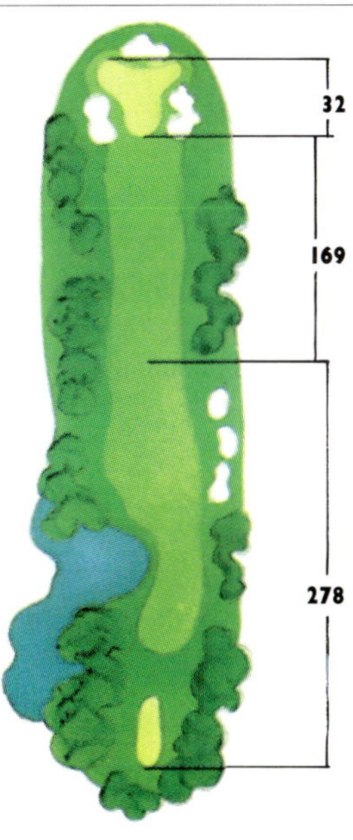

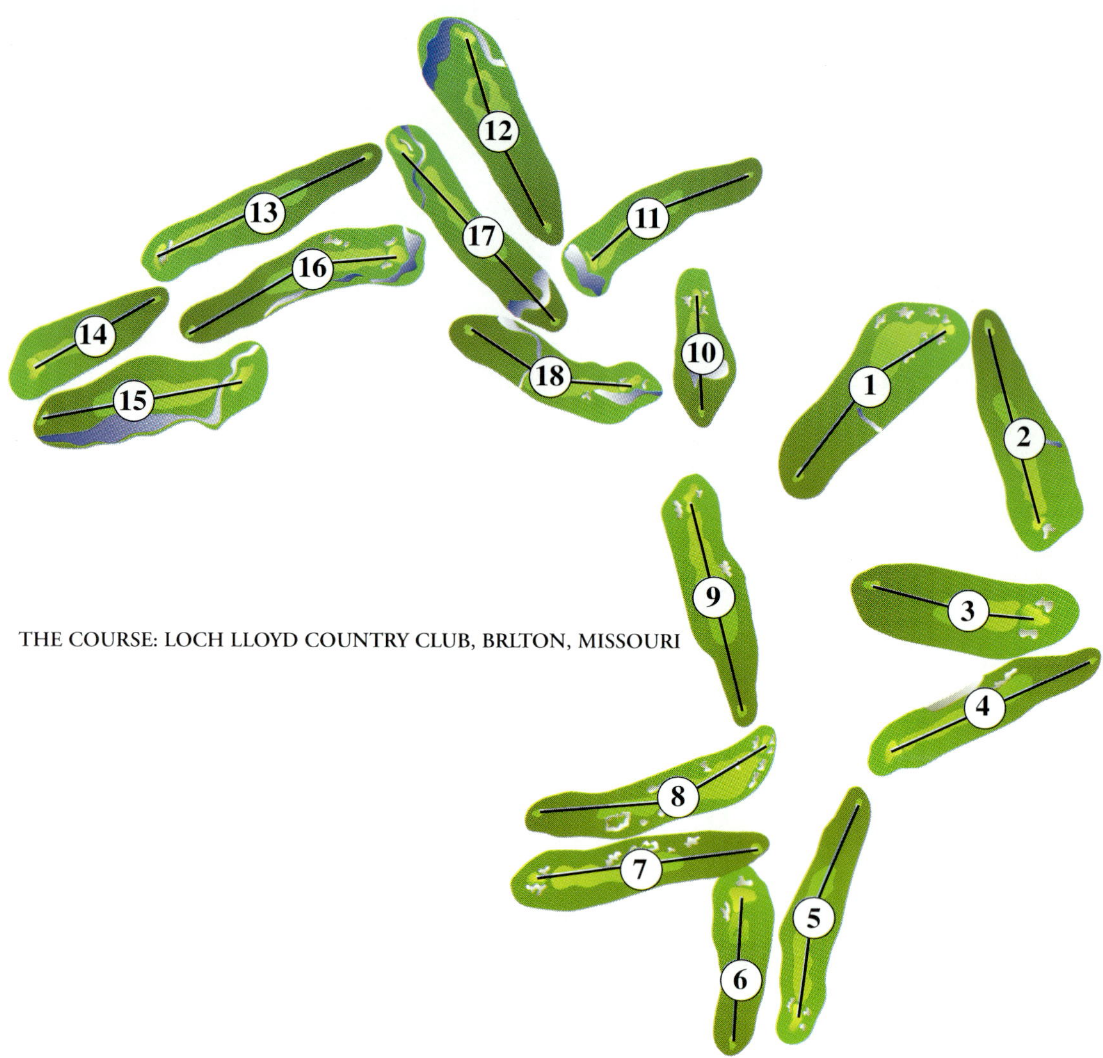

THE COURSE: LOCH LLOYD COUNTRY CLUB, BRLTON, MISSOURI

1996 marks the second year for the VFW Senior Championship. The Veteran's of foreign Wars has become the new title sponsor of the past Southwestern Bell Classic. The tournament will remain at Loch Lloyd Country Club for the sixth consecutive year. Loch Lloyd is one of the most beautiful and challenging courses in the Kansas City area. The wide, in-style layout on the front nine gives way to a tight, hazard-packed back nine that presents the SENIOR TOUR players with almost every kind of golf challenge.

The course features what many of the SENIOR TOUR players have called the best greens on the SENIOR circuit. Bob Murphy is the defending champion. Jim Colbert was the winner of the first event in 1991. Dave Stockton added to his victories in 1993 on his was to Player of the Year. You can bet that who ever wins at Loch Lloyd will have to put well.

This year the tournament has increased the purse from $750,000 to $900,000 and hopes to attract even more of the quality SENIOR TOUR players. Having raised $1.5 million for Crittenton, the charity sponsor and beneficiary, Kansas City is looking forward to another quality event.

Dates:	August 2-4
Network:	ESPN
Times:	TBD
Yardage:	6488
Par:	70
Slope:	131
Rating:	73.2
Total Purse:	$750,000
1st Prize:	$135,000
1995 Winner:	Bob Murphy
1995 Winning Score:	195 (69,63,63)
Principal Charitable Beneficiary:	Crittenton
Ticket Information:	1-816-767-4207

1

Par 4
333 yards

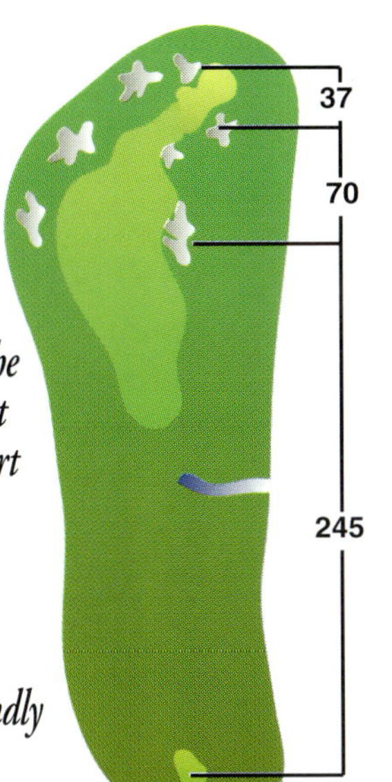

This hole is in no way typical of the rest of the course. The fairway is the widest on the course. A short iron second shot to slightly tiered green should result in the course's best birdie opportunity. A friendly opening hole.

2

Par 4
357 yards

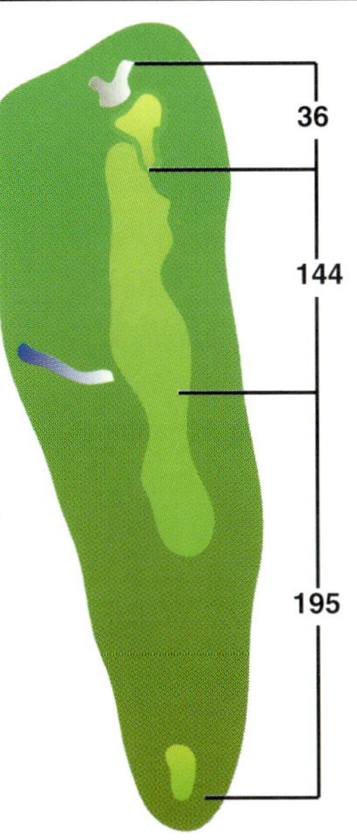

This second consecutive par 4 plays into a prevailing south wind. Left of center off the tee is the prime position because of a big tree on the right. Another short iron onto a subtle green makes this hole a little unpredictable.

3

Par 3
188 yards

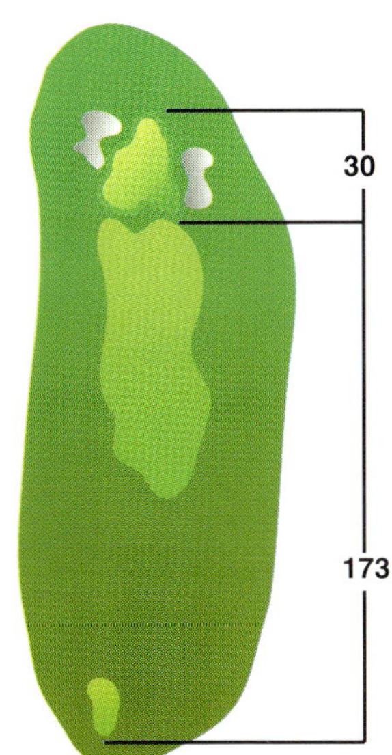

Getting to the green shouldn't be a problem, but a snaking spine running from the front of the green to the back mounds make putting a challenge.

4

Par 4
432 yards

The longest par 4 on the course requires a big shot off the tee. Either a long iron or a wood on the approach gets the player to a low-profile, large green set among native trees. This is one of only five greens devoid of sand bunkers.

5

Par 4
429 yards

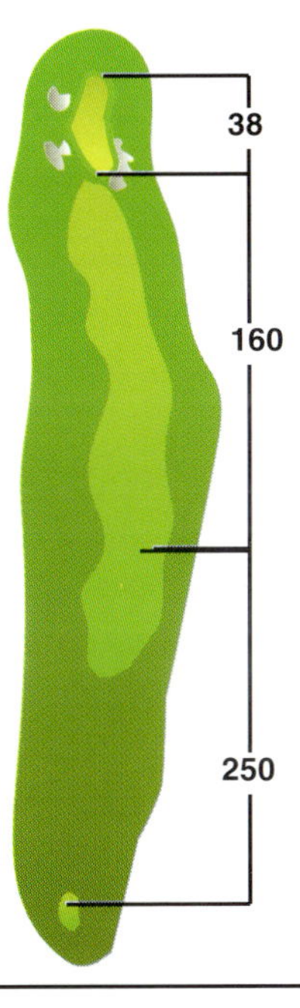

The second consecutive long par 4 goes right into the prevailing wind. Again, a long iron or fairway wood is required for a slightly downhill second shot to a 135-foot-long green, the second longest on the course. Trees guarding the back of the green may cause deception on the second shot.

6

Par 3
184 yards

This par 3 is all uphill to a left-to-right green with a deep valley in the front center. A sand bunker behind the green makes the hole appear shorter and may cause some club-selection difficulty.

7

Par 5
520 yards

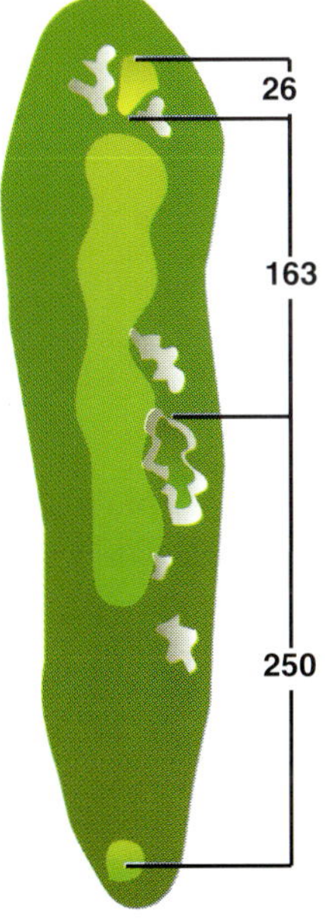

A drive down the middle is necessary to avoid trouble on the right and out-of-bounds on the left. The green has several bunkers that will inevitably come into play. This hole has a links-style appearance.

8

Par 3
164 yards

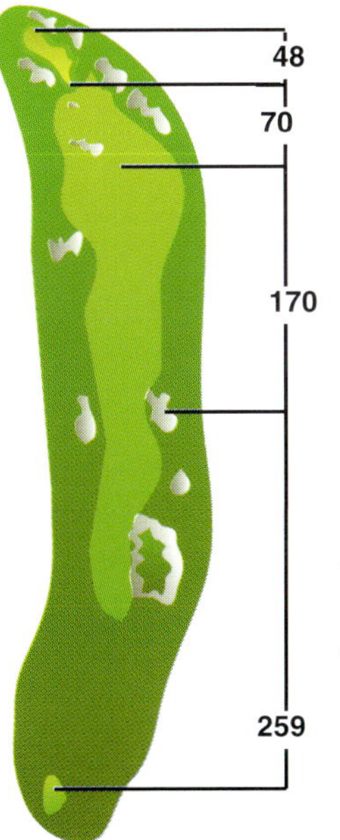

Another links-style hole, No. 8 is the only par 5 on the front nine. It offers the smallest green at Loch Lloyd and 11 sand bunkers, ready to cause havoc. A small pot bunker protects direct entry to the green.

9

Par 4
470 yards

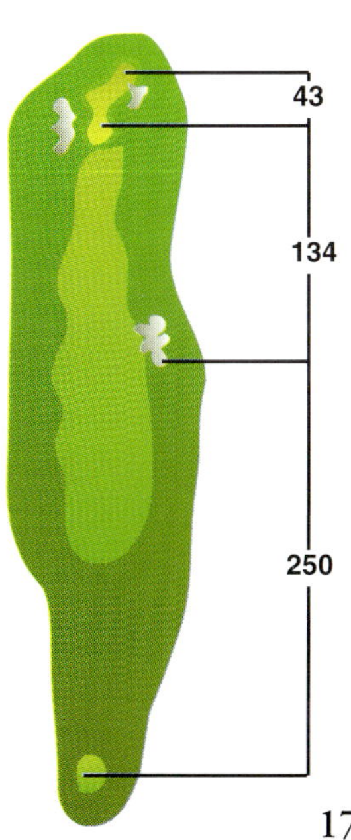

Because this hole plays down wind, it will seldom play to its measured length. After the drive, the second shot will have to be played from a valley to a large hidden green. A big shot off the tee will greatly help matters on this hole.

10

*Par 3
176 yards*

A par 3 to open the back nine. The slightly elevated and narrow green is protected by sand on both sides. Once on the green, putting can be an adventure because of the breaks.

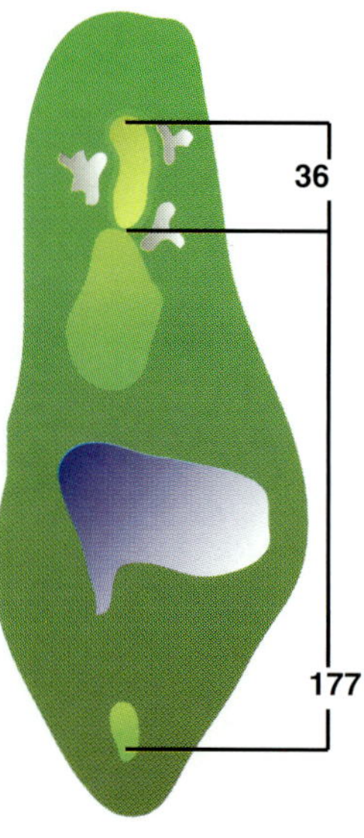

11

*Par 4
390 yards*

The first 10 holes are on high ground, but at this hole, the course drops into a valley. A descending fairway allows for a long run after the drive. A short pitch to the green is difficult because of water guarding the back side.

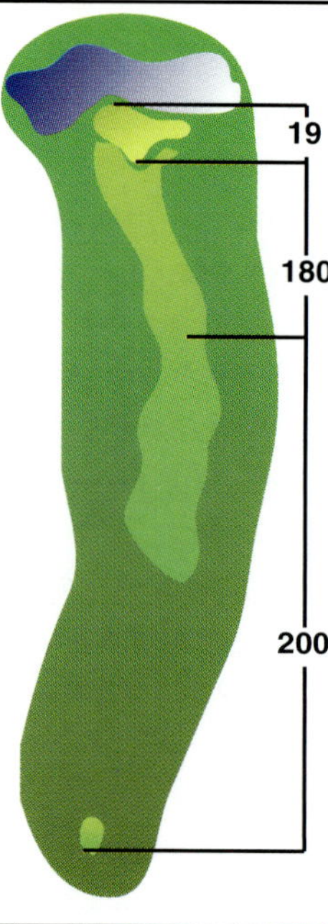

12

*Par 4
399 yards*

High and low sides to this fairway force a decision off the tee. A large tree divides the fairway's two levels at the point where they combine and fall sharply to a green. A tee shot to either level offers a demanding green setting.

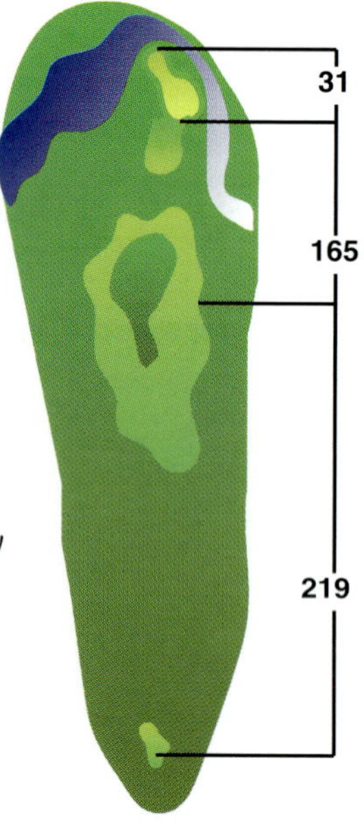

13

*Par 5
488 yards*

This is the last hole without any natural hazards. The huge green is guarded by sand bunkers supported by vertical timbers. The largest green on the course which is designed in three fade-away levels.

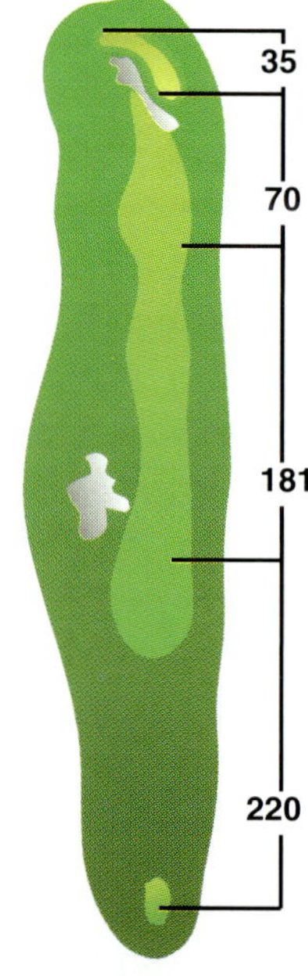

14

*Par 3
222 yards*

This is one of the more difficult holes at Loch Lloyd because of its tremendous length for a par 3. The green is nestled among native trees and the creek that also comes into play on No. 12. There are no sand bunkers on No. 14.

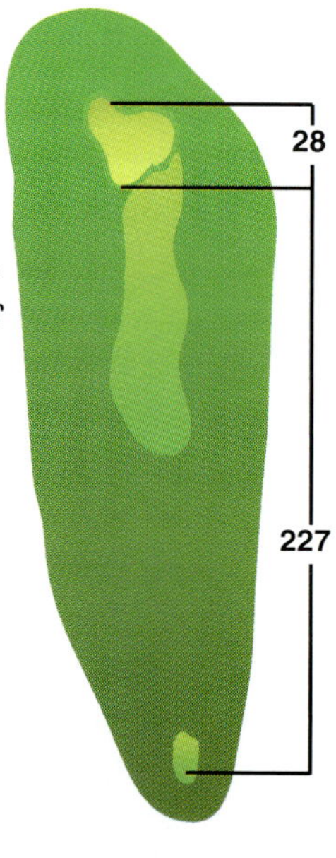

15

*Par 4
370 yards*

The "Moat Hole" has the creek crossing in front of the green. It has been walled in on both sides forming a 20-foot-wide moat. The large green is set low among large hackberry trees. A short-iron second shot must carry the moat.

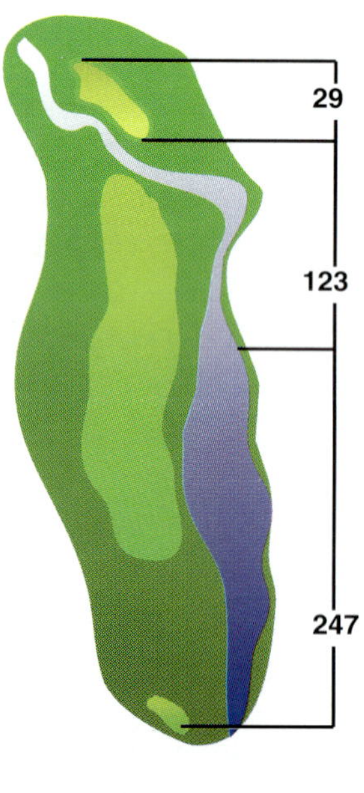

16

*Par 4
370 yards*

The creek borders the right side of the fairway. A drive to the middle is the best position because of a large fairway bunker on the left side. The creek borders the back as well as left and right sides, making accuracy a must.

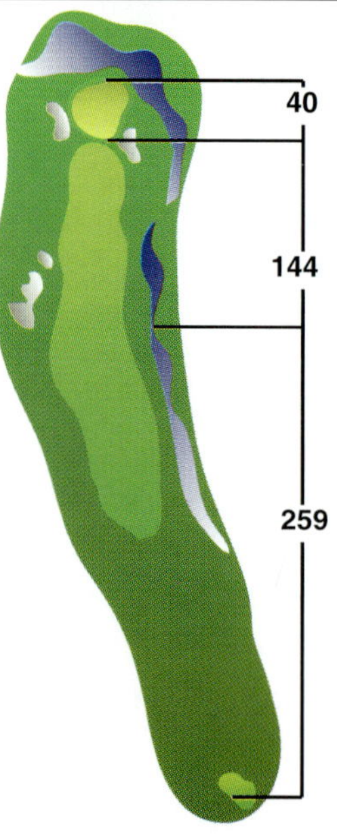

17

*Par 4
383 yards*

A long tee shot is helpful on this hole, which is bordered on the entire left side by the creek that eventually crosses the fairway in front of the green. A waterfall splash pool sits to the right of the green.

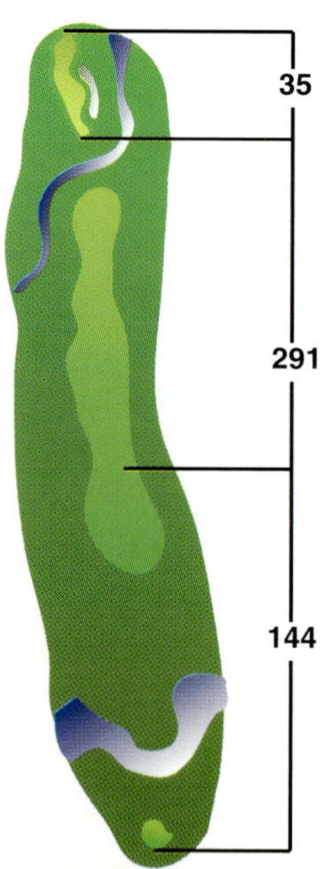

18

*Par 4
382 yards*

No. 18 is not a long hole by closing hole standards. An elevated tee beholds a cascading waterfall behind the green. The ubiquitous creek comes into play left of the fairway. Ponds to the right of the green can also cause trouble.

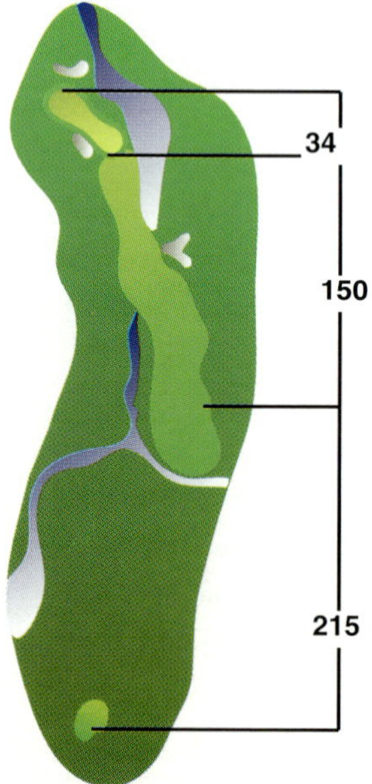

THE COURSE:
VALHALLA GOLF CLUB, LOUISVILLE, KENTUCKY
A PGA of America Sposored Event

$\mathcal{V}$alhalla Golf Club, with its name taken from Norse mythology, is indeed a paradise for golfers and a major challenge to golf's finest players competing in the 78th PGA Championship.

Valhalla was designed by Jack Nicklaus and opened for play in 1986 and quickly became recognized as one of the nation's finest new courses. it is ranked 51st in *Golf Digest's* list of America's 100 Greatest Golf Courses.

According to Norse mythology, Valhalla was a heavenly paradise for ancient Viking heroes. As a leading golf facility, golfers will find their own form of enjoyment in Valhalla's mixture of natural terrain, vegetation and water. Spectators will find some of golf's most spectacular viewing areas in Valhalla's natural amphitheaters.

The scenic par-5 18th hole can accommodate up to 20,000 spectators from its 150-yard marker to the green.

The Rodman Wanamaker Trophy, one of golf's greatest prizes, will go to the player who can master large undulating greens averaging 6,000 square feet, water which comes into play on nine holes and 36 strategically placed bunkers. The 78th PGA Championship is the second major championship to be conducted in the state of Kentucky. The 1952 PGA Championship was hosted by Big Spring Country Club in Louisville.

Dates:	August 8-11
Network:	CBS and TBS
Times:	TBD
Yardage:	7,140
Par:	72
Slope:	142
Rating:	74.9
Total Purse:	A minimum of $2,000,000
1st Prize:	A minimum of $360,000
1995 Winner:	Steve Elkington
1995 Winning Score:	(267) 68,67,68,64
Ticket Information:	Sold Out

1

Par 4
425 yards

A relatively simple dogleg to the left requiring a 3 wood off the tee and a middle iron to a challenging green. There are no bunkers on this hole but a 5 foot swale on the front right and a severe collection area left of the green will attract errant shots.

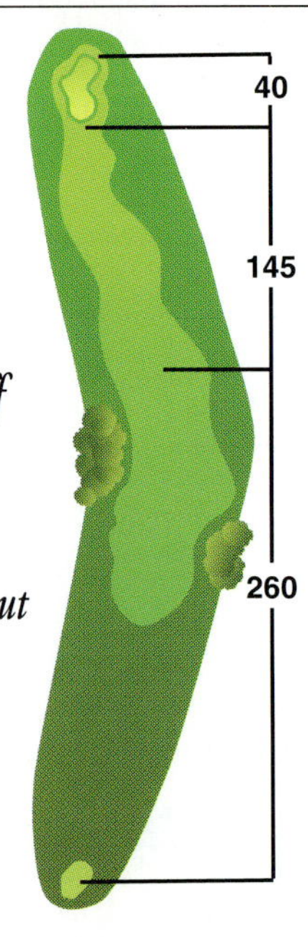

2

Par 5
515 yards

A reachable par 5 that should provide excitement with a few eagles and many birdies. There is some risk though when going for it in two. Probably the easiest hole on the golf course.

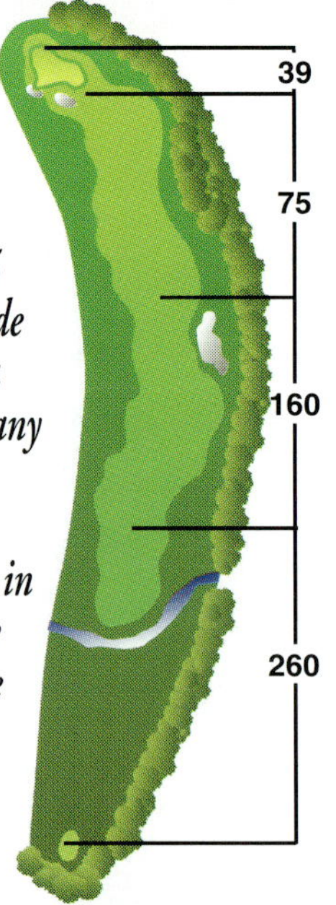

3

Par 3
205 yards

A long iron approach to a green elevated over the main water-way - Floyd's Fork. The hole typically plays into the wind so a par will be considered a good score here.

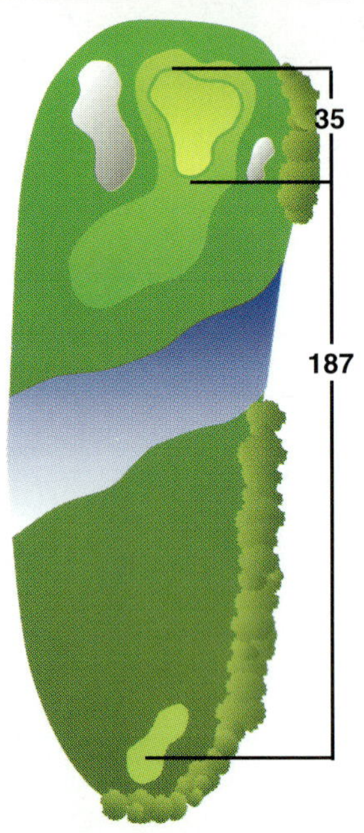

4

Par 4
355 yards

This hole provides a few options for the players. You can risk driving over a deep fairway bunker on the left which would leave a sandwedge shot to the green or you can lay up with an iron which leaves an 8 or 9 iron approach. The green is the most undulating on the course.

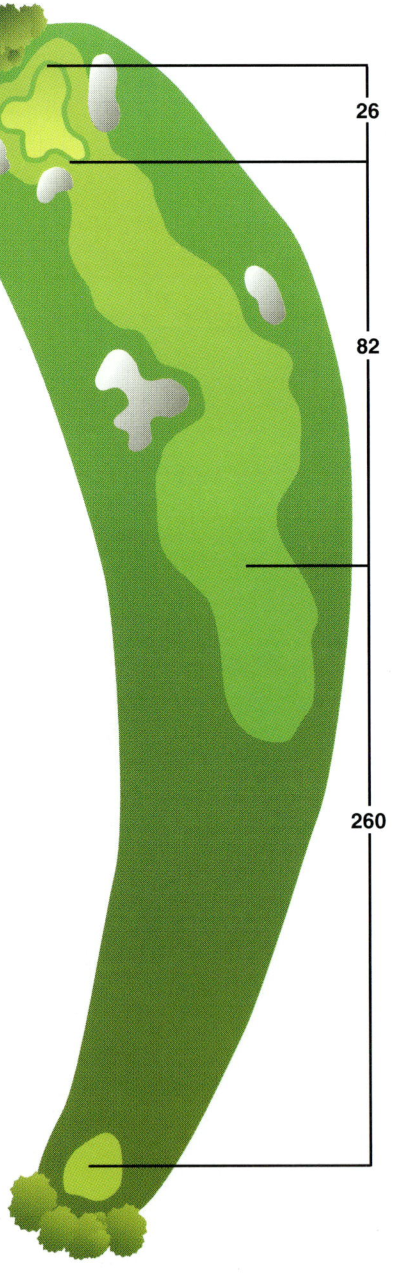

5

Par 4
460 yards

The first of many long par 4 holes at Valhalla. A wide fairway will encourage players to use their drivers leaving a middle iron approach to a relatively flat but well guarded green.

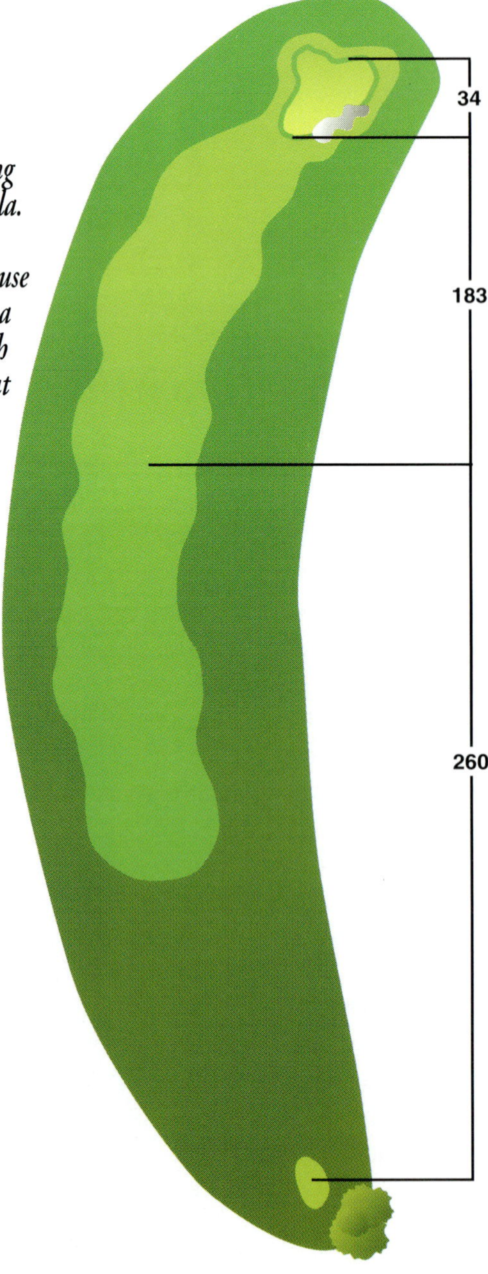

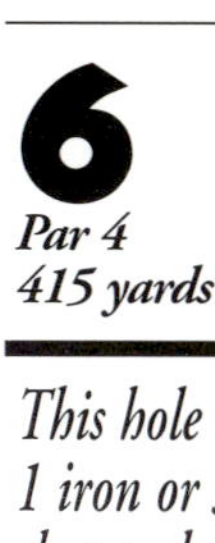

6

Par 4
415 yards

This hole will require as 1 iron or 3 wood tee shot and a mid to short iron approach to a green with little depth. Hitting the approach shot the correct distance is critical on this hole.

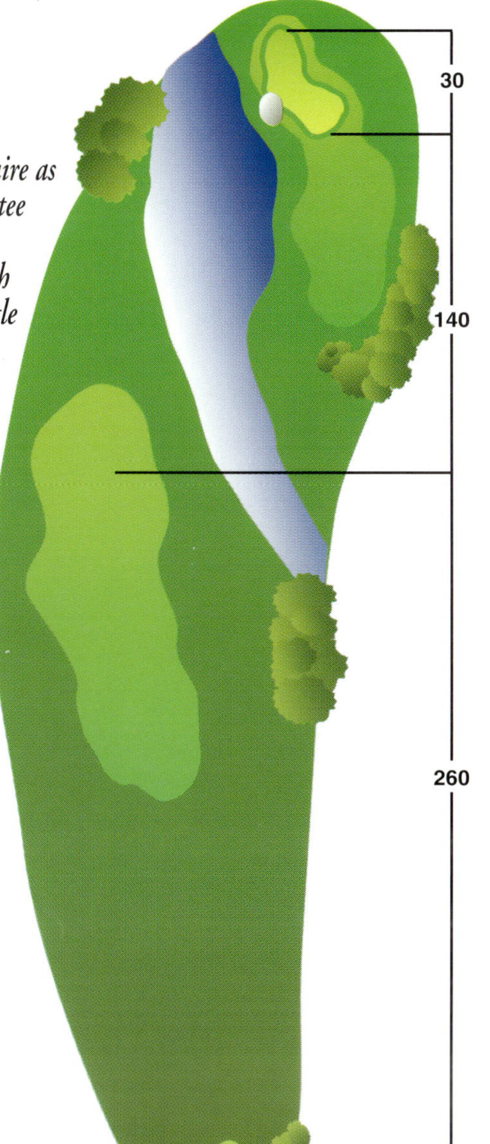

7

Par 5
605 yards

The longest hole on the course is a dogleg left around a quarry-like hazard. It will be difficult to reach in two shots but there will still be numerous birdies on this hole.

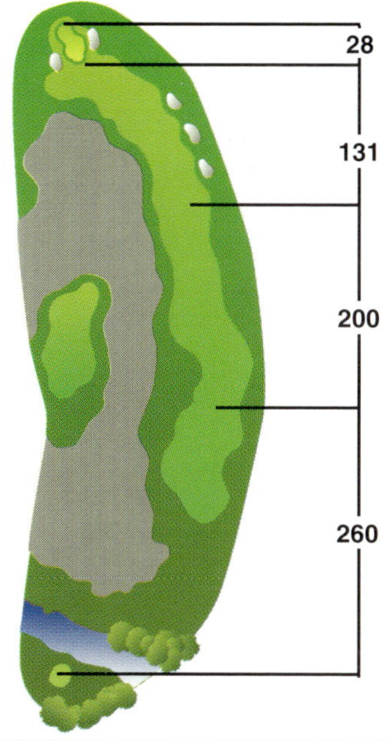

9

Par 4
415 yards

This uphill par 4 plays longer than the listed yardage. A large fairway bunker on the right side will challenge the tee shot. A mid to short iron 2nd shot will be required to this well guarded green. Staying below the hole will be impor-tant as this green slopes severely from back to front.

8

Par 3
165 yards

This par 3 will require a mid to short iron approach depending on the hole location. The front right and back right are protected by bunkers and the left side of the green has a collection area that will attract many shots.

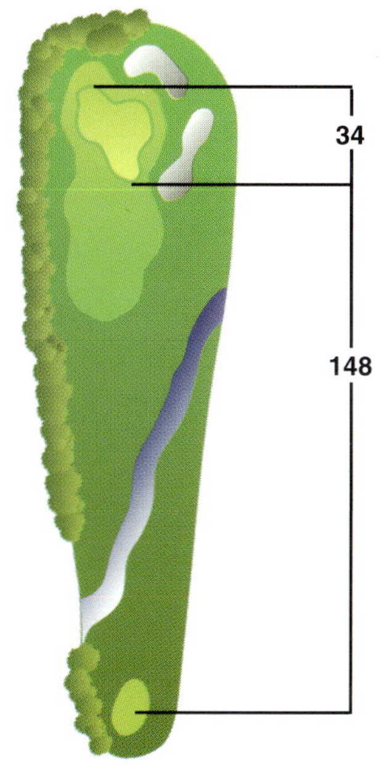

177

10

Par 5
565 yards

A double dogleg par 5 hole where positioning is critical. While some long hitters may be able to reach the green in two, look for most players to lay back and leave a full wedge into the green. The green is guarded in the front with a deep bunker and it slopes away from the players.

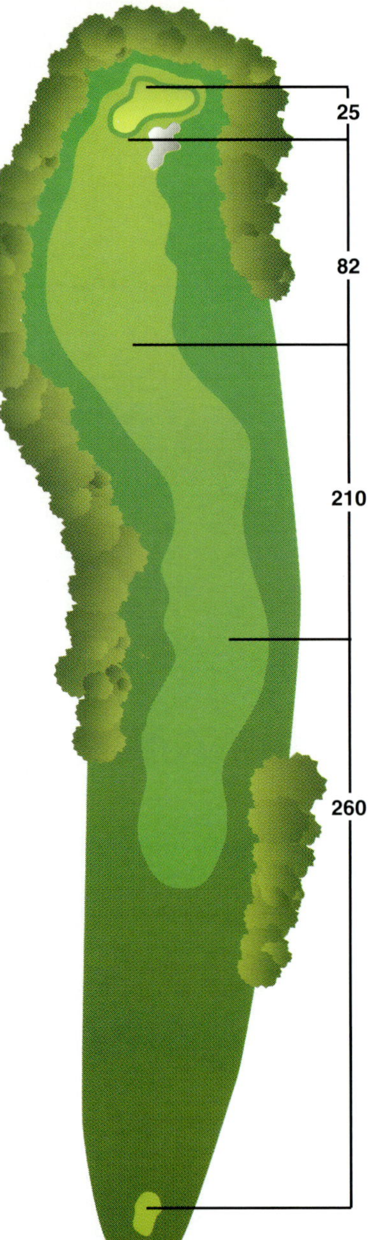

11

Par 3
165 yards

This short par 3 will be difficult if there are gusty winds. The 40 foot length of the green allows pin placements to bring both bunkers into play.

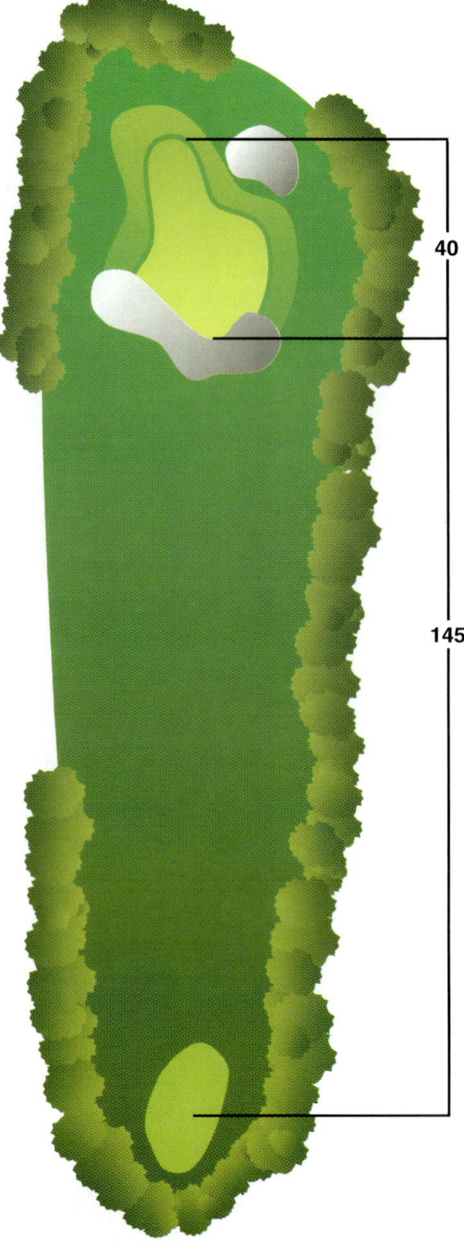

12

Par 4
470 yards

This long par 4 dogleg to the right is one of the most difficult holes on the course. It requires a well placed tee shot and then a long iron to a small undulating green. A par on this hole is a good score.

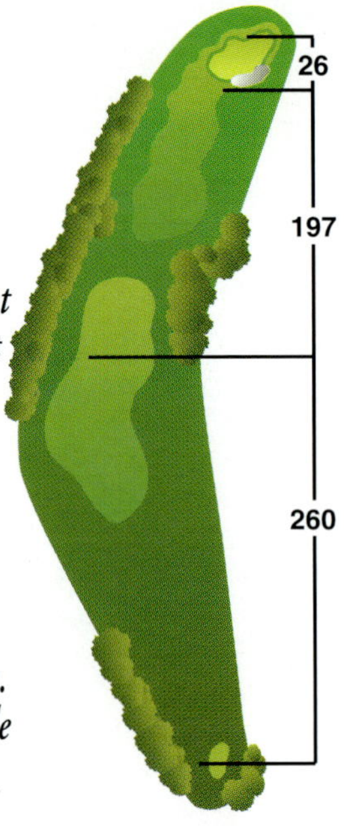

13

Par 4
350 yards

This is the most memorable hole at Valhalla because of the island green. The tee shot will require a fairway wood or long iron leaving a wedge or 9 iron approach. The green is very large but knowing it's surrounded by water makes it a difficult shot.

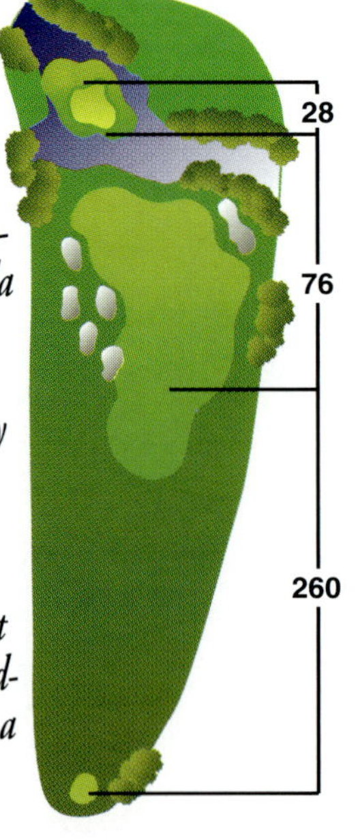

14

Par 3
210 yards

The longest of the par 3 holes plays from and elevated tee to a two level green that slopes severely from left to right. Missing the green to the left is almost a sure bogey and the right is protected by a deep bunker. Depending on the wind conditions this may be one of the most difficult holes.

15

Par 4
410 yards

Considered one of the prettiest holes on the golf course. This par 4 requires a 1 iron or 3 wood tee shot and a mid to short iron approach to an undulating green. The entire right side is guarded by a creek and some trees overhand the left side of the fairway and green.

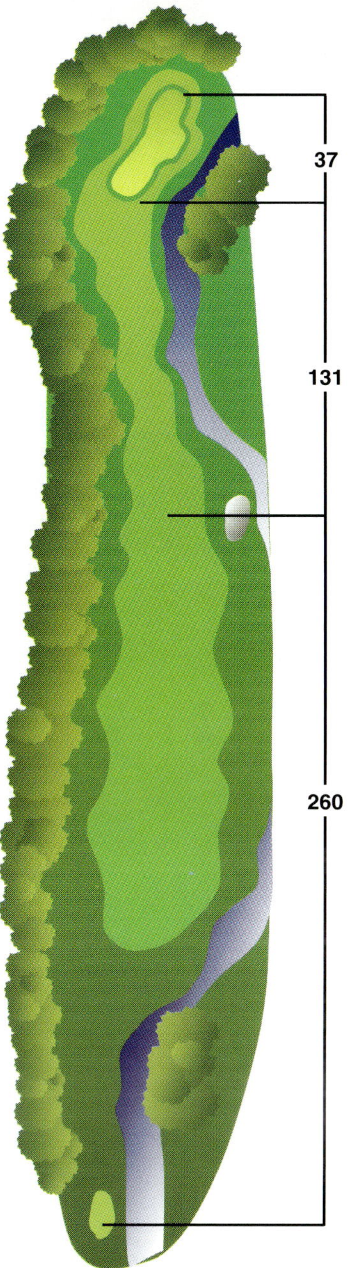

16

Par 4
450 yards

This par 4 like hole #12 is extremely difficult. A creek runs the length of the hole on the right side with wooded areas on the left. A long iron approach will be required to an elevated green. A ball that misses this green will leave the player with a challenging pitch shot.

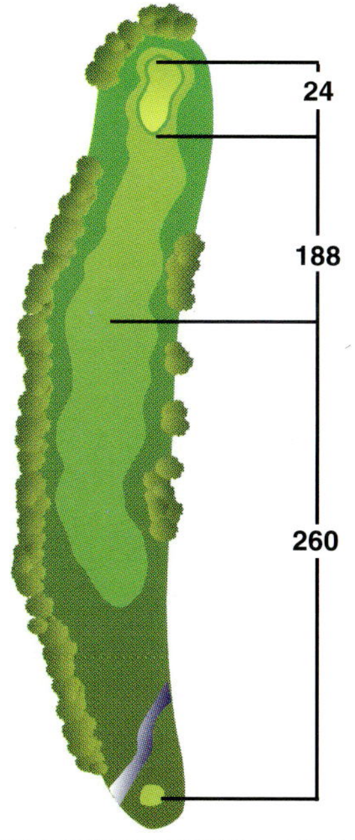

18

Par 5
540 yards

This hole should provide for a dramatic finish to the Championship. The downhill tee shot must be in the fairway for any chance to go for it. Reaching the horseshoe shaped green in two will require a long uphill 2nd shot over a bunker. Going over the green will leave an almost impossible up and down. This is a great hole for a 2 or 3 shot swing.

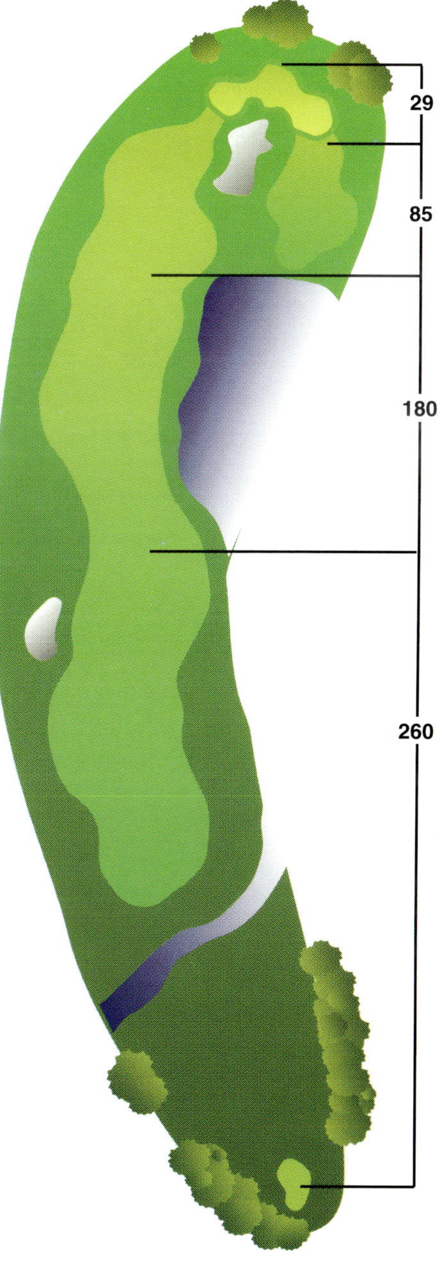

17

Par 4
420 yards

This uphill par 4 requires a well placed tee shot and then a mid to short iron approach to a small green. The green is guarded with bunkers in the front and chipping areas that slope away on the right and back of the green.

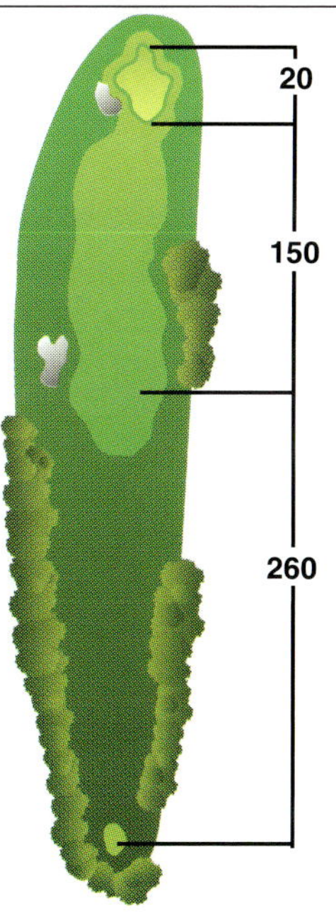

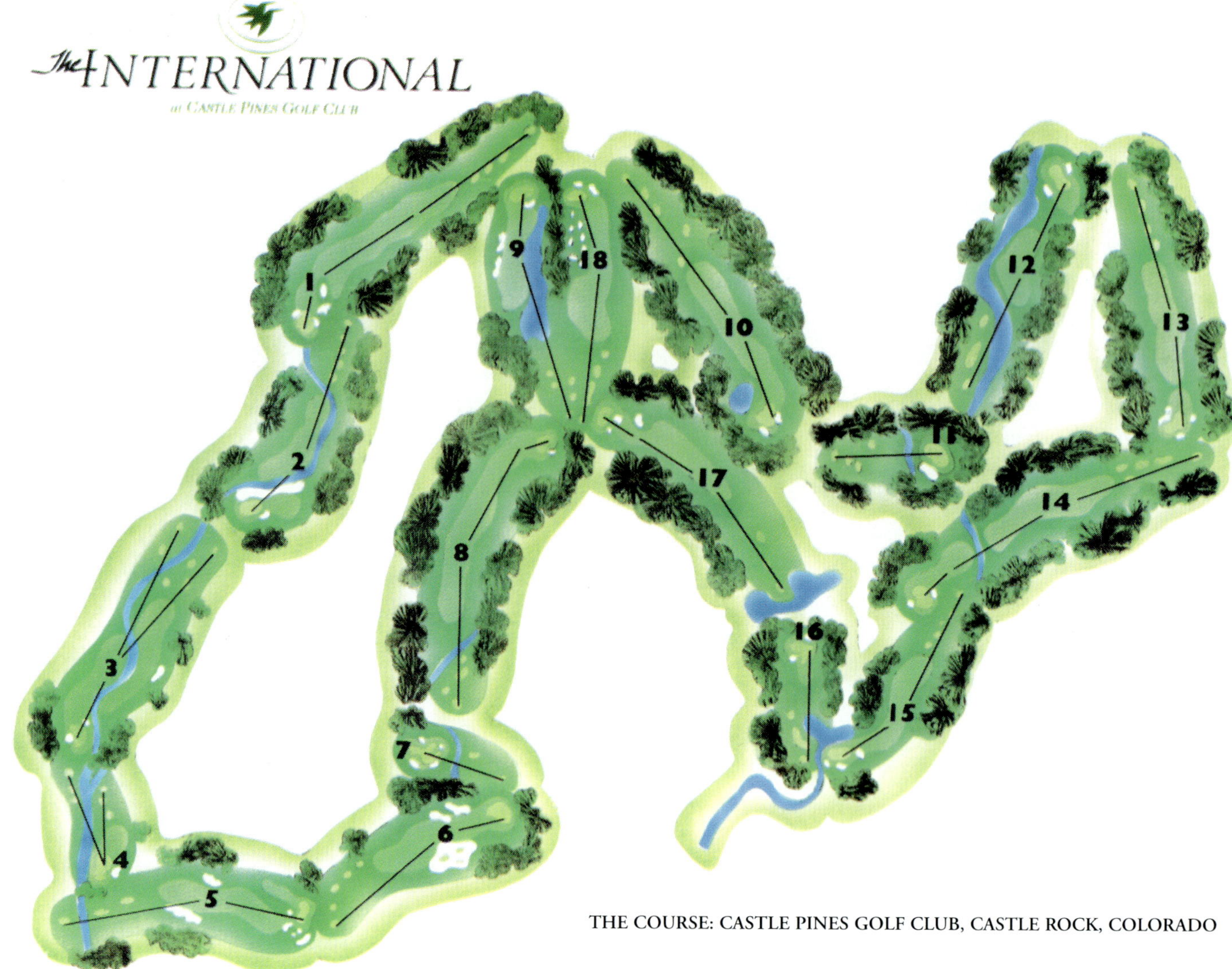

THE COURSE: CASTLE PINES GOLF CLUB, CASTLE ROCK, COLORADO

*L*ee Janzen went home the winner of the 1995 Sprint International. This event uses a modified Stableford Scoring system and the goal is to accumulate points. The tournament play begins on Thursday when all 144 invited players begin competition. By combining the total points accumulated on Thursday and Friday, the cut is selected from the 72 highest scores. On Saturday the 72 players start fresh and battle for the 24 highest scores. The final 24 compete for the overall win on Sunday-starting that morning from scratch. Points are awarded as follows: Double eagle...+8 points; Eagle...+5 points; Birdie...+2 points; Par...0; Bogey...-1; and Double Bogey or more.-3

Jack Vickers' vision to create a formidable golf course on the property where Castle Pines now stands took him a total of ten years with the assistance and design of Jack Nicklaus, and another five years to organize a PGA TOUR® event at the new layout. Ranked in the Top 40 by Golf Digest, the mile-high course is set in the Front Range of the Colorado Rockies. With the thin air at high altitude, players will be able to hit the longer shots of the year.

Dates:	August 15-18, 1996
Network:	CBS & ESPN
Times:	TBD
Yardage:	7559
Par:	72
Slope:	153
Rating:	75.5
Total Purse:	$1,500,000
1st Prize:	$270,000
1995 Winner:	Lee Janzen
1995 Winning Score:	+34
Principal Charitable Beneficiary:	Boys & Girls Clubs of Metro Denver, Inc.
Charitable Benefits to Date:	Over $1.5 million in the last 6 years
Ticket Information:	1-800-755-1986

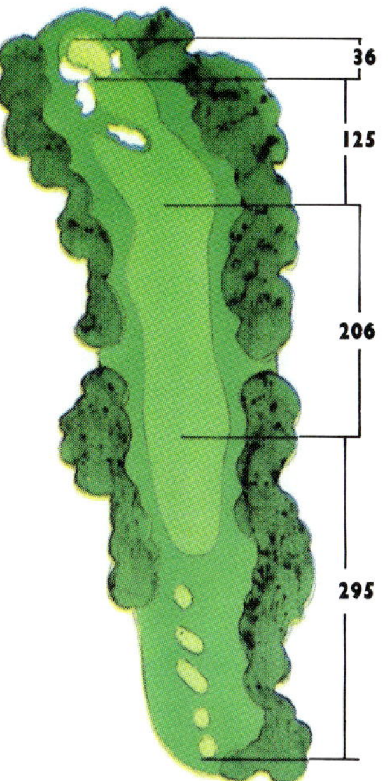

1

*Par 5
644 yards*

The 644 yards may seem like a long way but the thin air and the 120-foot elevation drop will shorten the hole. Many players will start the day with a birdie.

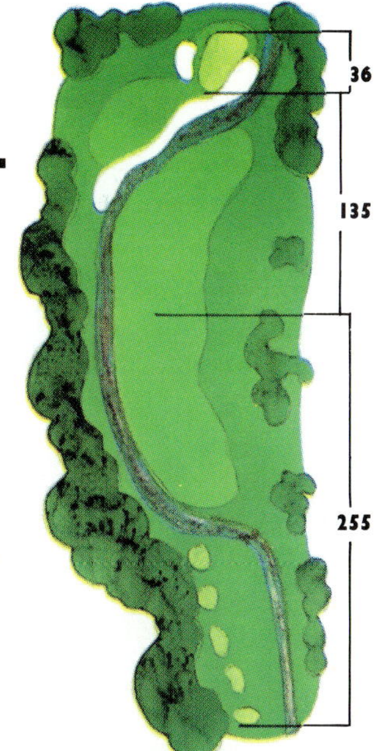

2

*Par 4
408 yards*

A 3-wood or long-iron off the tee will be used to keep the ball short of the creek. The green slopes toward the front and sits well above the guarding bunkers.

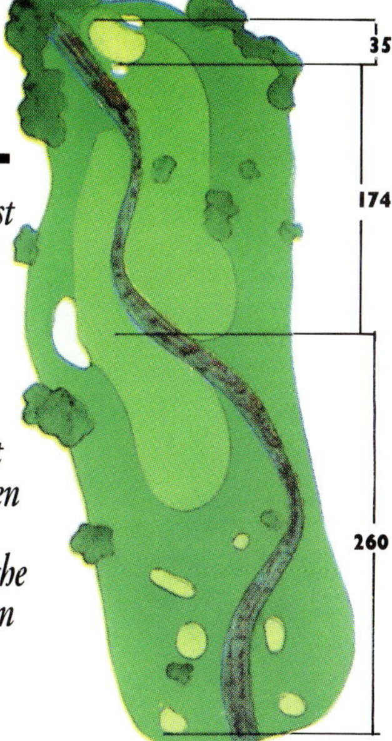

3

*Par 4
462 yards*

The drive must clear Baskins Gulch to set up for a short approach. Players will favor the right side of the green on the second shot to avoid the deep "gulch" on the left.

4

*Par 3
205 yards*

A long carry over Baskins Gulch is a necessity to reach the severely undulating green. Players will need a 4-5 iron to hit the putting surface.

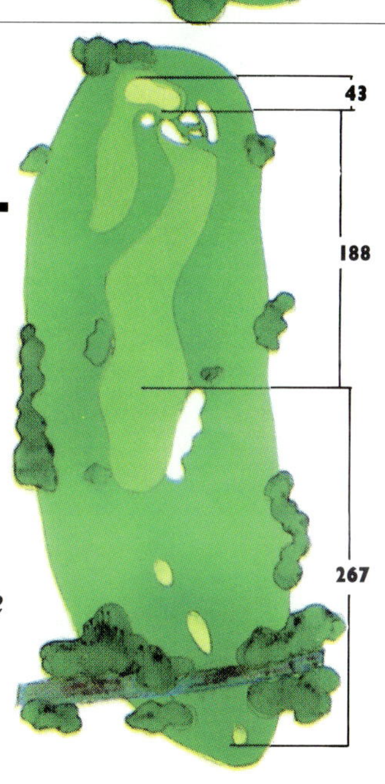

5

*Par 4
477 yards*

The most difficult hole on the course. Uphill all the way to the green. A cluster of bunkers catch all approaches hit short of the elevated green.

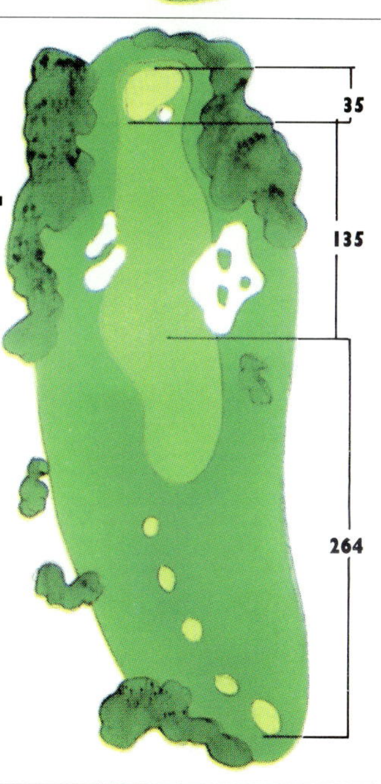

6

*Par 4
417 yards*

The 6th is a tricky driving hole. By favoring the left side, the players will open up the angle to the green. Pin-placements on the back right will be tough to hit.

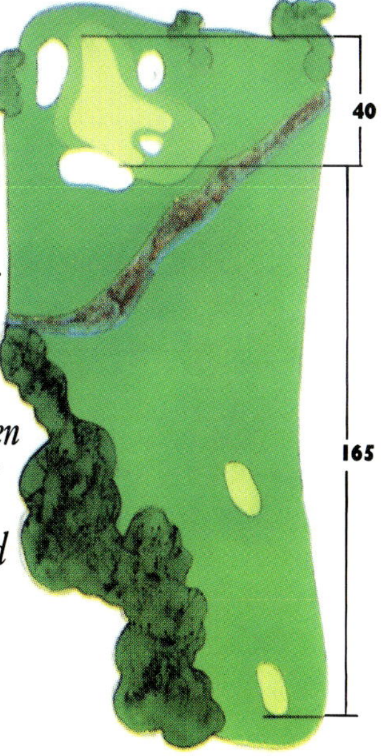

7

*Par 3
185 yards*

The elevated tee is encroached on by trees from the right. The right-to-left sloping green is in a clearing but is fronted by a steep-faced bunker.

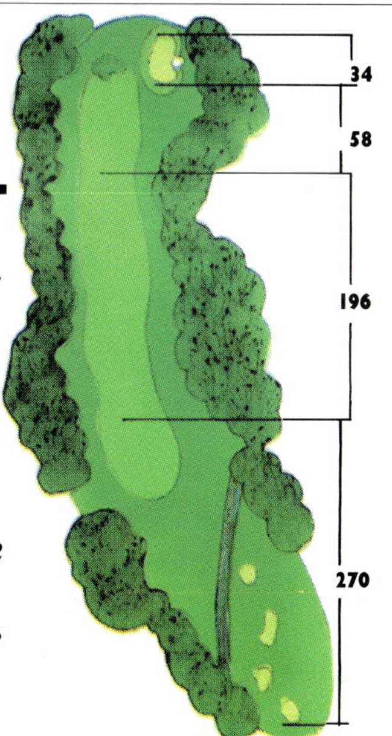

8

*Par 5
535 yards*

This 8th is nearly impossible to reach in two. The fairway and green slope from right-to-left. Two well hit shots will leave a short chip-shot to the pin.

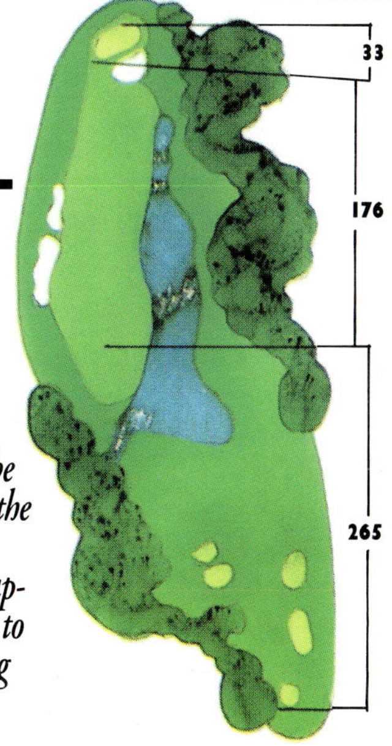

9

*Par 4
458 yards*

A series of ponds and waterfalls border the right side of the hole. The drive should be faced toward the first fairway bunker. The approach shot is to a small sloping green.

10

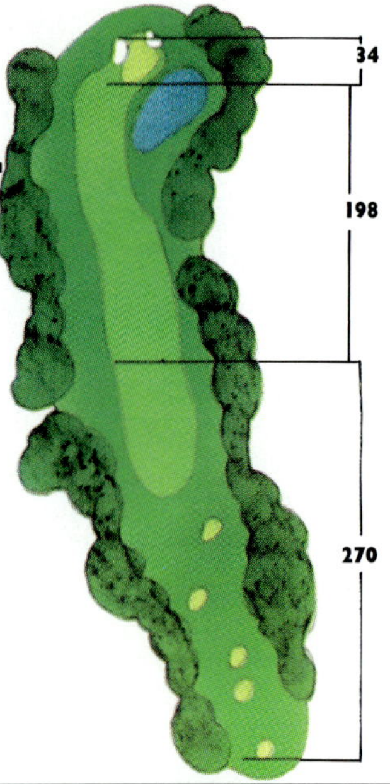

Par 4
485 yards

The players will favor the left side of the descending fairway. The subtly sloping green can then be reached with a 5-6 iron. Pars are the norm, but birdies are not out of the question.

11

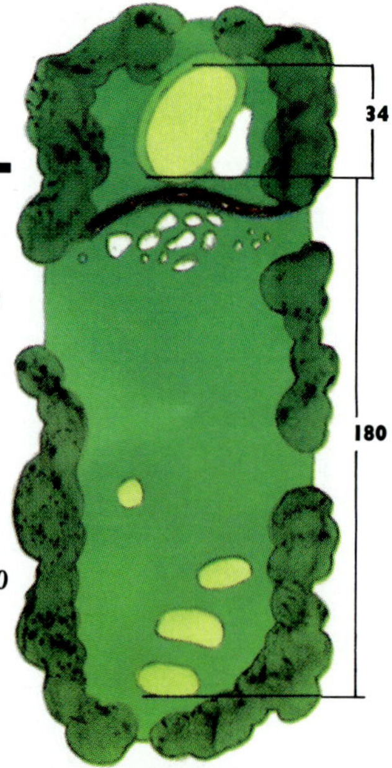

Par 3
197 yards

The green is 75 feet below the tee — club selection will be difficult. Two levels, front and back, make the long putts very difficult to get down in two.

12

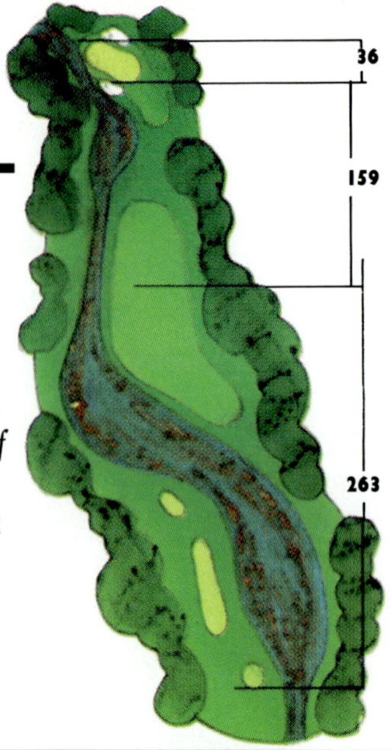

Par 4
440 yards

A birdie here will gain points on the rest of the field. The approach to this green is one of the most difficult shots on the course.

13

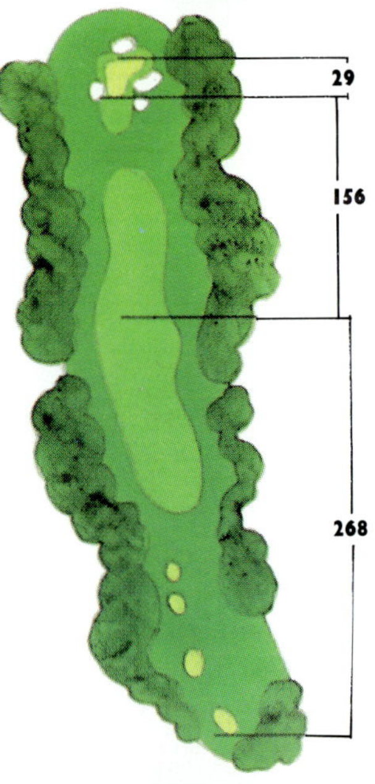

Par 4
439 yards

The fairway ascends for the drive and descends back down to the green. Two levels make up the green, the lower left and upper right.

14

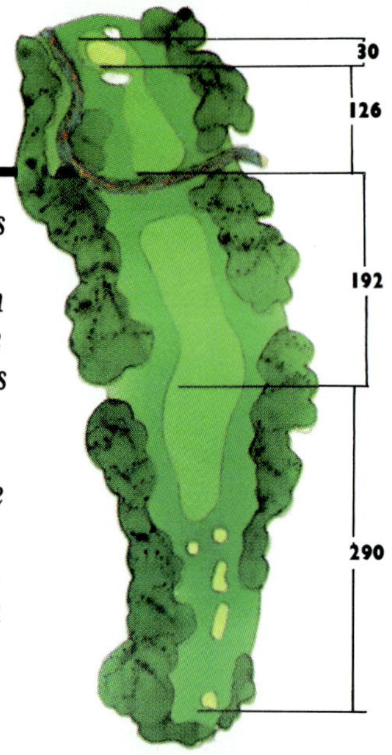

Par 5
623 yards

The 14th plays downhill and is reachable in two shots. The angled green is shallow and flat. Players should be able to hit an iron into the green. Big points can be scored on this hole.

15

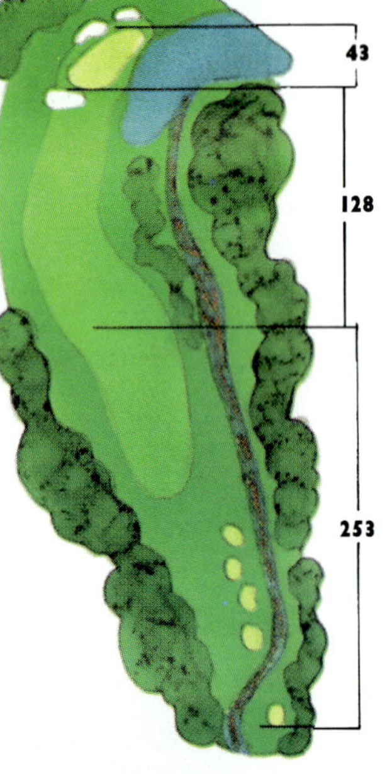

Par 4
403 yards

A fairway wood or long iron down the left side of the fairway will set up for a short approach. Players should be able to hit a wedge shot close to the pin.

16

Par 3
209 yards

When the pin is placed in the back left corner, getting close to the hole will be tough. The narrow green is elevated and unrelenting to those who miss the tee shot.

17

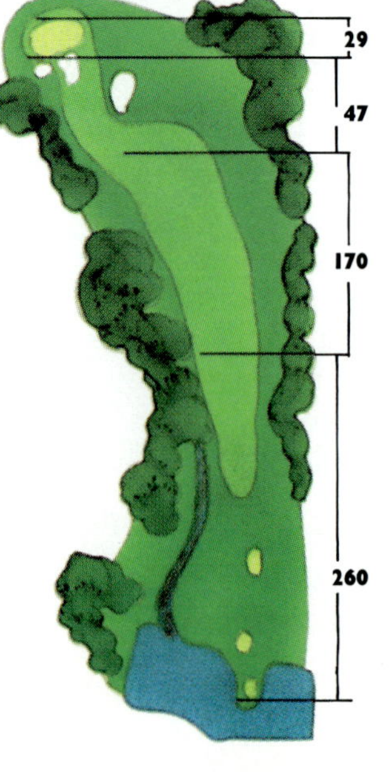

Par 5
492 yards

It's short, but uphill all the way to the green. Even so, players will be able to reach the green in two for the chance at eagle. Birdies are a must.

18

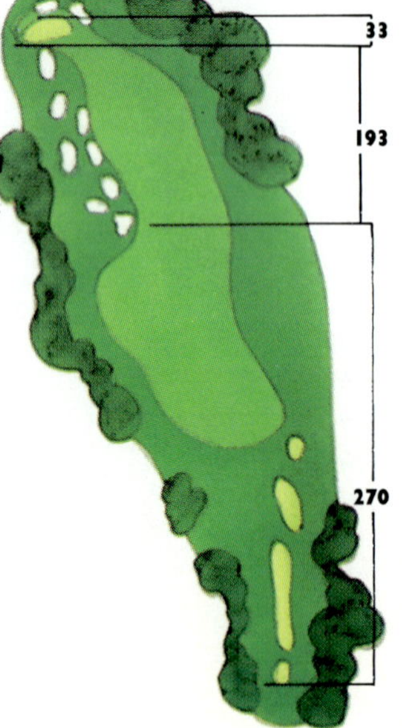

Par 4
480 yards

Players looking for one more point will have to work hard on this finishing hole. Accuracy is a must in order to avoid lengthy putts on the long sloping green.

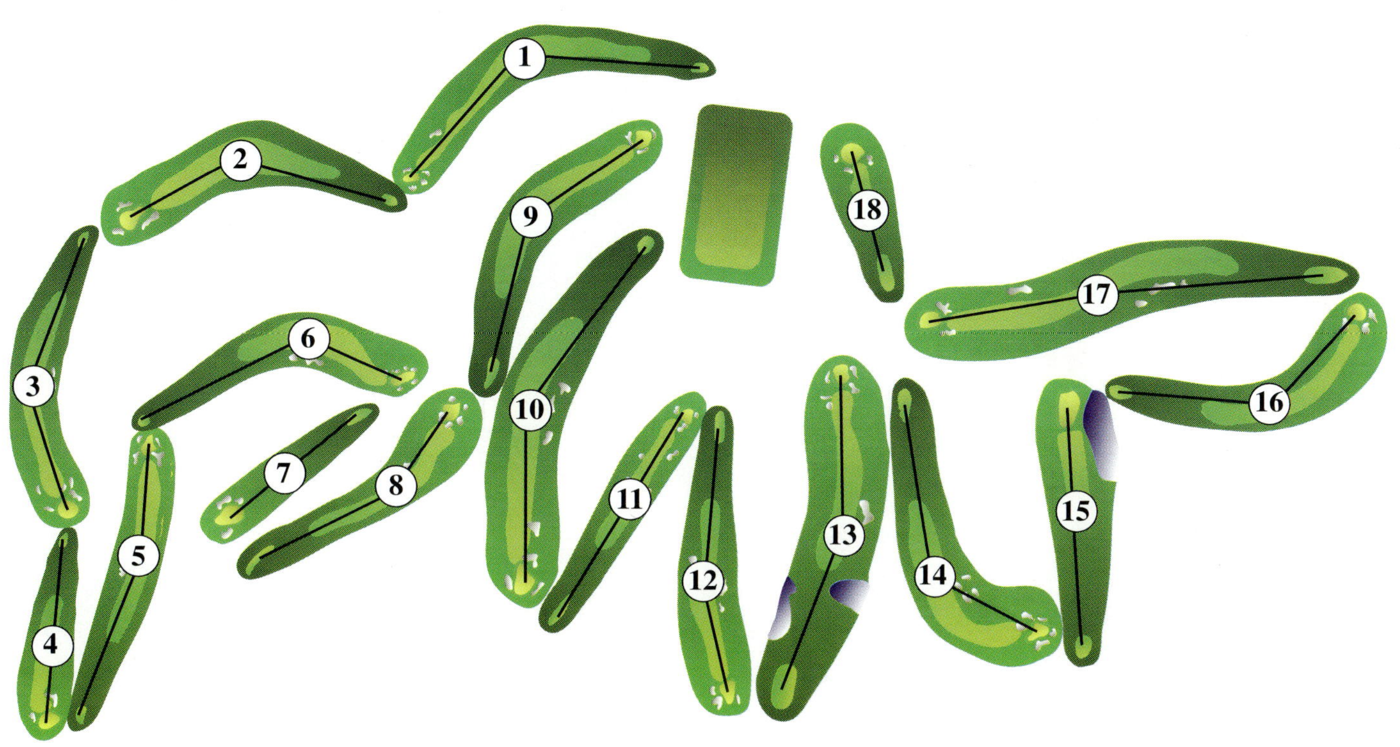

THE COURSE: MEADOW BROOK CLUB, JERICHO, NEW YORK

For more than a century the Meadow Brook Club has represented the finest tradition in American Golf. In 1888, it hosted the first organized golf exhibition on American soil establishing the Club as one of the most historic in the nation and making it the ideal host for Long Island's annual SENIOR PGA TOUR event. In fact, the present Dick Wilson designed course is world renowned for 14 doglegs, huge greens and traditional style. It has been rated as one of their favorite courses by the SENIOR PGA TOUR pros.

The Northville Long Island Classic which began in 1987, as an invitational event was sanctioned by the PGA TOUR® in 1988. The first champion was Gary Player who said. "From the back tees you could play the U.S. Open here." George Archer had an amazing streak in winning three consecutive years, (1990, '91, '92) without a single bogey! 1993 winner, Raymond Floyd says, " It's the golf course that keeps bringing us back." After winning in 1994 with tournament and course records of 200/65, the 1994 champion Lee Trevino said, " I finally whipped this course."

Dates:	August 16-18
Network:	ESPN
Times:	Fri 1:00-3:00 EST
	Sat 5:30-7:00 EST
	Sun 5:30-7:00 EST
Yardage:	6775
Par:	72
Slope:	132
Total Purse:	$800,000
1st Prize:	$120,000
1995 Winner:	Lee Trevino
1995 Winning Score:	202 (67,69,66)
Principal Charitable Beneficiary:	Schneider Children's Hospital of Long Island Jewish Medical Center
Ticket Information:	1-516-674-GOLF

1

Par 5
537 yards

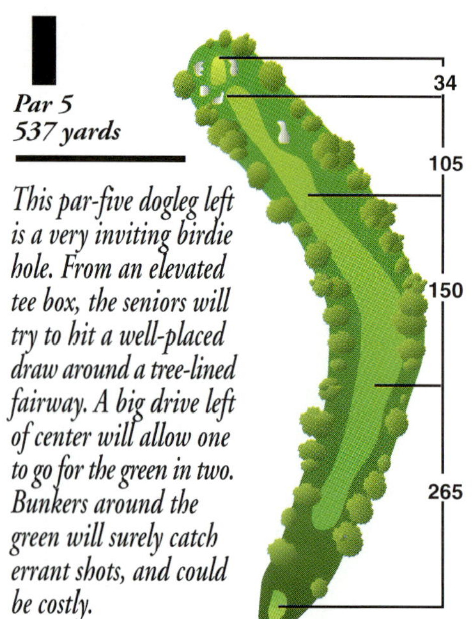

This par-five dogleg left is a very inviting birdie hole. From an elevated tee box, the seniors will try to hit a well-placed draw around a tree-lined fairway. A big drive left of center will allow one to go for the green in two. Bunkers around the green will surely catch errant shots, and could be costly.

2

Par 4
389 yards

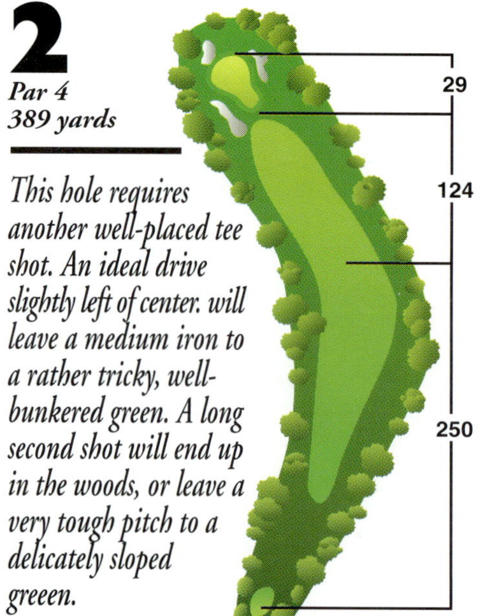

This hole requires another well-placed tee shot. An ideal drive slightly left of center. will leave a medium iron to a rather tricky, well-bunkered green. A long second shot will end up in the woods, or leave a very tough pitch to a delicately sloped greeen.

3

Par 5
478 yards

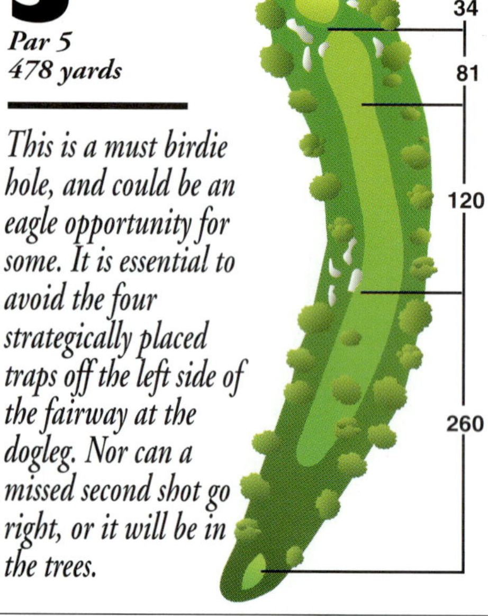

This is a must birdie hole, and could be an eagle opportunity for some. It is essential to avoid the four strategically placed traps off the left side of the fairway at the dogleg. Nor can a missed second shot go right, or it will be in the trees.

4

Par 3
195 yards

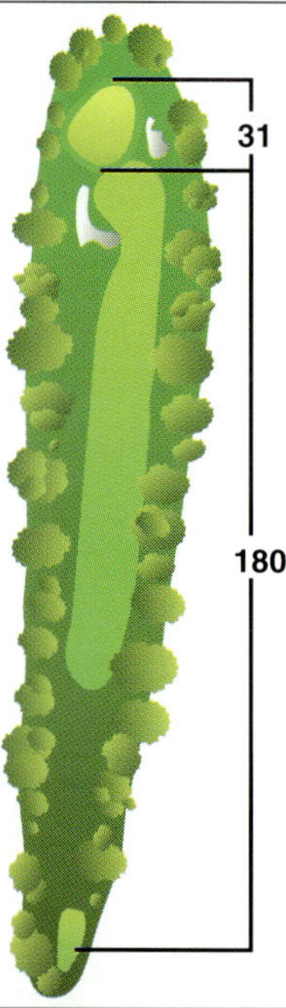

This hole is uphill and usually into the prevailing wind. As such is plays longer than the card. The key here is to take enough club and aim for the right side of a well-bunkered green. Behind and to the left of the green is a severe downslope.

5

Par 4
419 yards

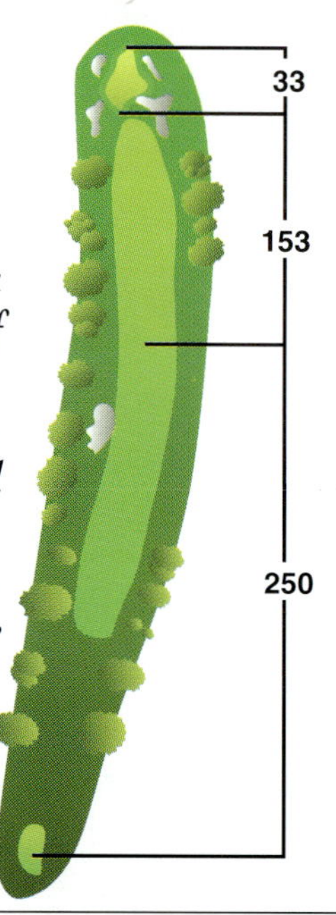

This hole requires a strong drive right of center to the upper level of the fairway. The second shot will be a meduim-to-long iron, to a well-protected but rather large green.

6

Par 4
367 yards

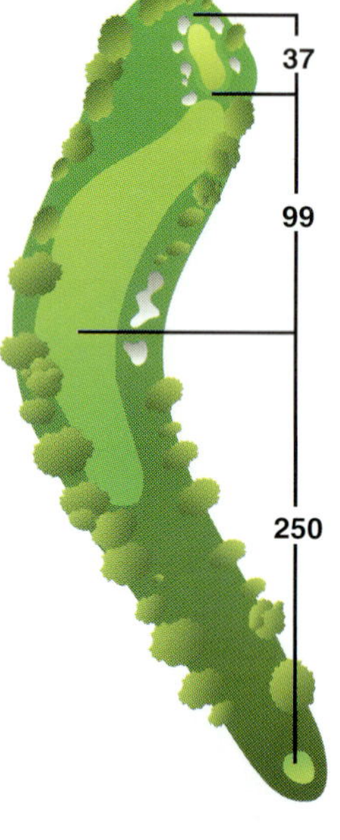

This par four dogleg right is where the pros will look to pick up a stroke. A beautiful tree lined fairway requires a well placed tee shot, followed by a short but accurate iron to a shallow green fronted by some deep bunkers.

7

Par 3
171 yards

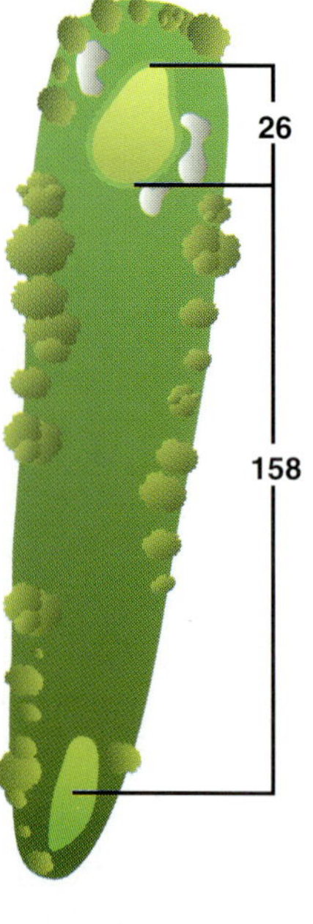

This par-three requires a medium iron to the green. The seniors must guard against tee shots which run off the front left of the green into a waste buinker. A pin position on the right front side, over the bunker, is easier.

8

Par 4
373 yards

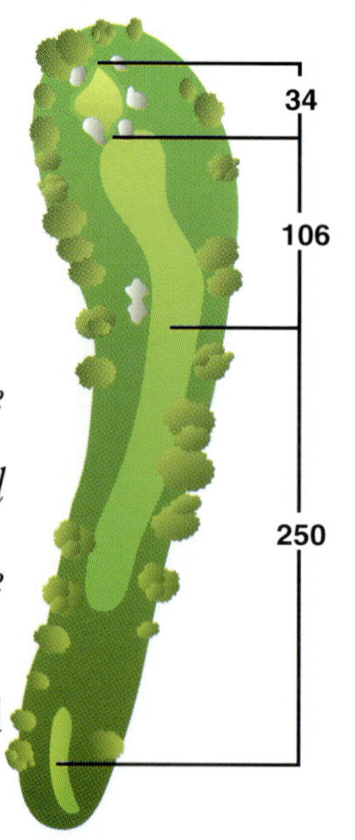

On this hole it's important to set up the approach with a good tee shot down the right center of the fairway. The pros will need to look out for errant drives into the trees on the right, or into the fairway bunkers on the left. A relatively flat, very puttable green.

9

Par 4
417 yards

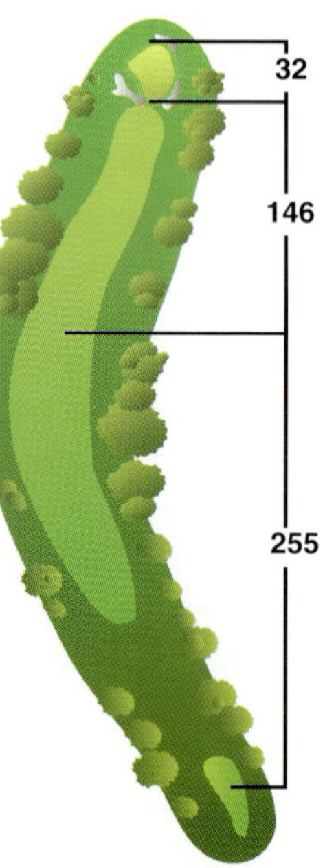

This hole requires a strategically placed drive, setting one up for an uphill, long-iron second shot to a severerly sloped green. Don't be above this hole, as it will be difficult to get down in two. Rated as the10th-toughest hole on the Senior PGA Tour in 1992, with the average score of 4.416.

10

Par 5
506 yards

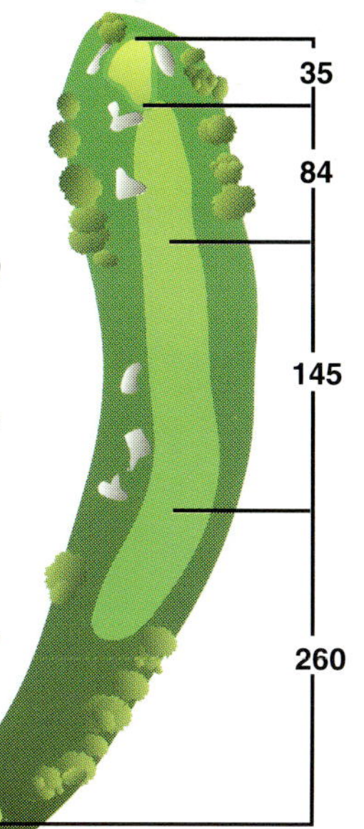

An elevated tee shot to the flat part of the fairway will leave 215-235 yards to the green. The seniors must stay away from bunkers in the left rough on their drives, and also be wary on the well-trapped green on their approach shots.

11

Par 4
389 yards

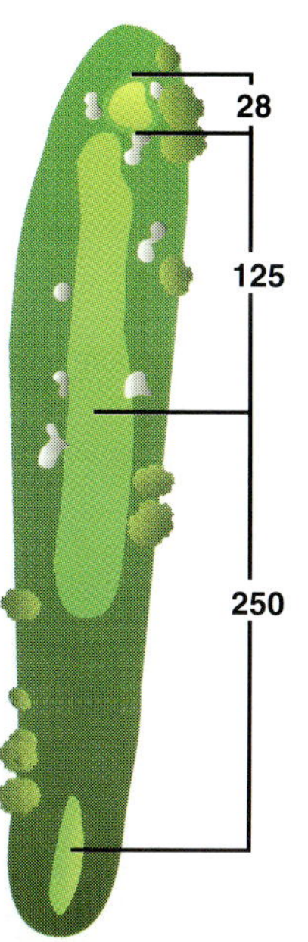

A relatively straight par-four, the 389-yard eleventh calls for a drive up the left side of the fairway, leaving a short iron to he green. A tee shot pushed to the right will cause problems on the approach, as the green is well-bunkered.

12

Par 4
420 yards

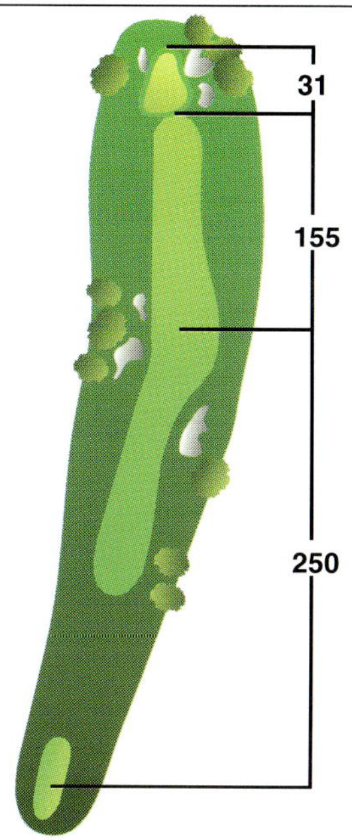

This number-one handicap hole will test any golfer's ability. A straight dogleg left, with bunkers lining both sides of the fairway demands a well-placed drive down the right side of the green.

13

Par 4
412 yards

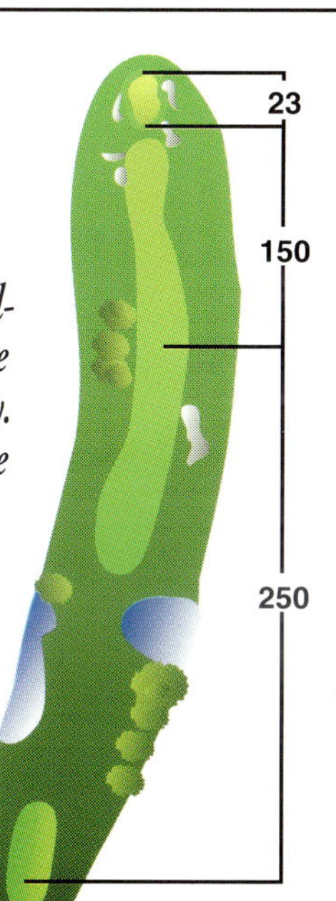

This hole requires a well-placed tee shot down the right side of the fairway. From here, players have a clear approach to the green with a medium iron. Left and right bunkers flank a rather shallow, diagonal green.

14

Par 4
340 yards

This hole requires a pinpoint drive. Four deep bunkers sit in the left rough at the turn, waiting for short tee shots. The green, severely sloped from back to front, is very well bunkered.

15

Par 3
209 yards

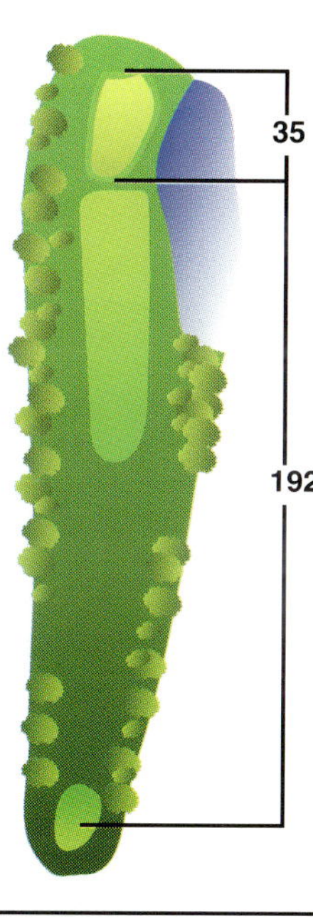

This treacherous-looking par-three measures 209 yards from an elevated tee box. Protecting the right side of the green is a lake, and a tee shot hit left will wind up in the woods. The rather large green slopes left to right, so that a shot landing on the left will feed to a pin position in the back right.

16

Par 4
401 yards

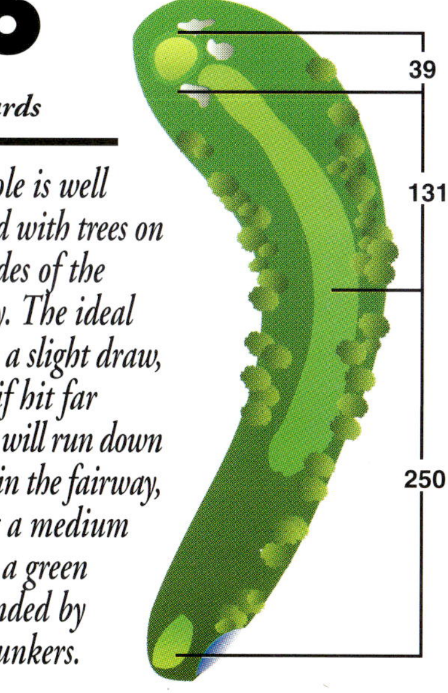

This hole is well guarded with trees on both sides of the fairway. The ideal drive is a slight draw, which if hit far enough will run down a slope in the fairway, leaving a medium iron to a green surrounded by large bunkers.

17

Par 5
585 yards

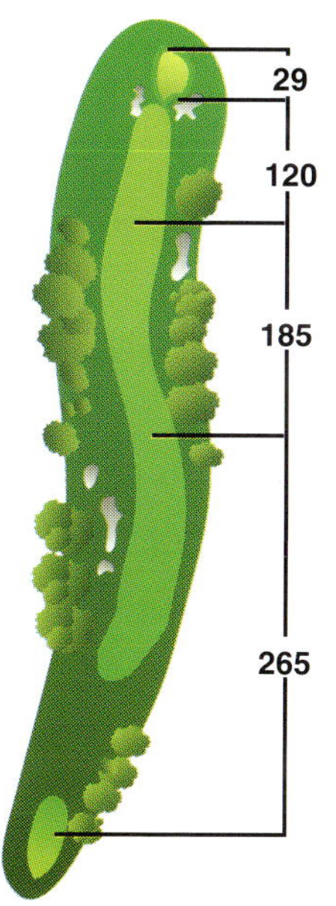

The longest hole at Meadow Brook. A double dogleg, that calls for a good drive down the right side of the fairway, setting up the next shot to the left side of the second turn. Getting home in two will be next to impossible for most seniors. A wedge into the green can set up a very makeable birdie shot.

18

Par 3
167 yards

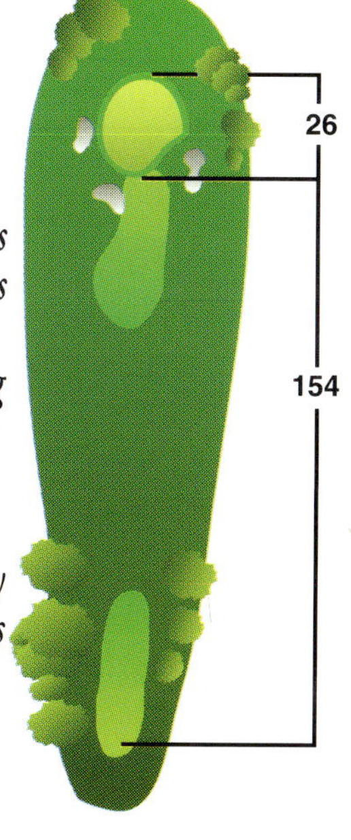

This 18th hole offers spectators a fabulous view and a comfortable seating area. An uphill tee shot to a back-to-front sloping green makes this hole very interesting. Bunkers flank the green on the left and right.

THE COURSE: FIRESTONE COUNTRY CLUB, AKRON, OHIO

Dates:	August 22-25
Network:	CBS & USA
Times:	USA
	Thur /Fri 4:00-6:00 EST
	CBS
	Sat /Sun 4:00-6:00 EST
Yardage:	7149
Par:	70
Slope:	128
Rating:	75.1
Total Purse:	$2,000,000
1st Prize:	$360,000
1995 Winner:	Greg Norman
1995 Winning Score:	278 (73,68,70,67)
Principal Charitable Beneficiary:	Children's Hospital Medical Center of Akron, Akron Regional Development Board, Akron Jaycees Foundation, Beacon Journal Charity Fund
Ticket Information:	1-216-644-2299

*T*he NEC World Series of Golf was first started as a simple match of the winners of the four "majors". As the years passed, however, the field opened to include the champions of about 70 events throughout the year, foreign events included. The larger, more intriguing list of players has given the tournament the unique characteristic of a competition that finds the best of the best of the international and domestic golf TOURS. To be eligible, a player must have won a PGA TOUR® event, one of 24 sanctioned international events, or one of seven specially approved events between last year's NEC World Series of Golf and this year's event.

Ohio native Jack Nicklaus won the 36-hole tournament in 1962 and returned for more WSG titles ('63, '67, '70, and '76). Other NEC winners: Gary Player in 1965, '68, and '72; Tom Watson in 1975 and '80; Lee Trevino in 1974 and Curtis Strange in 1987. Recent winners include Jose Maria Olazabal, Tom Purtzer, Craig Stadler and Fulton Allem.

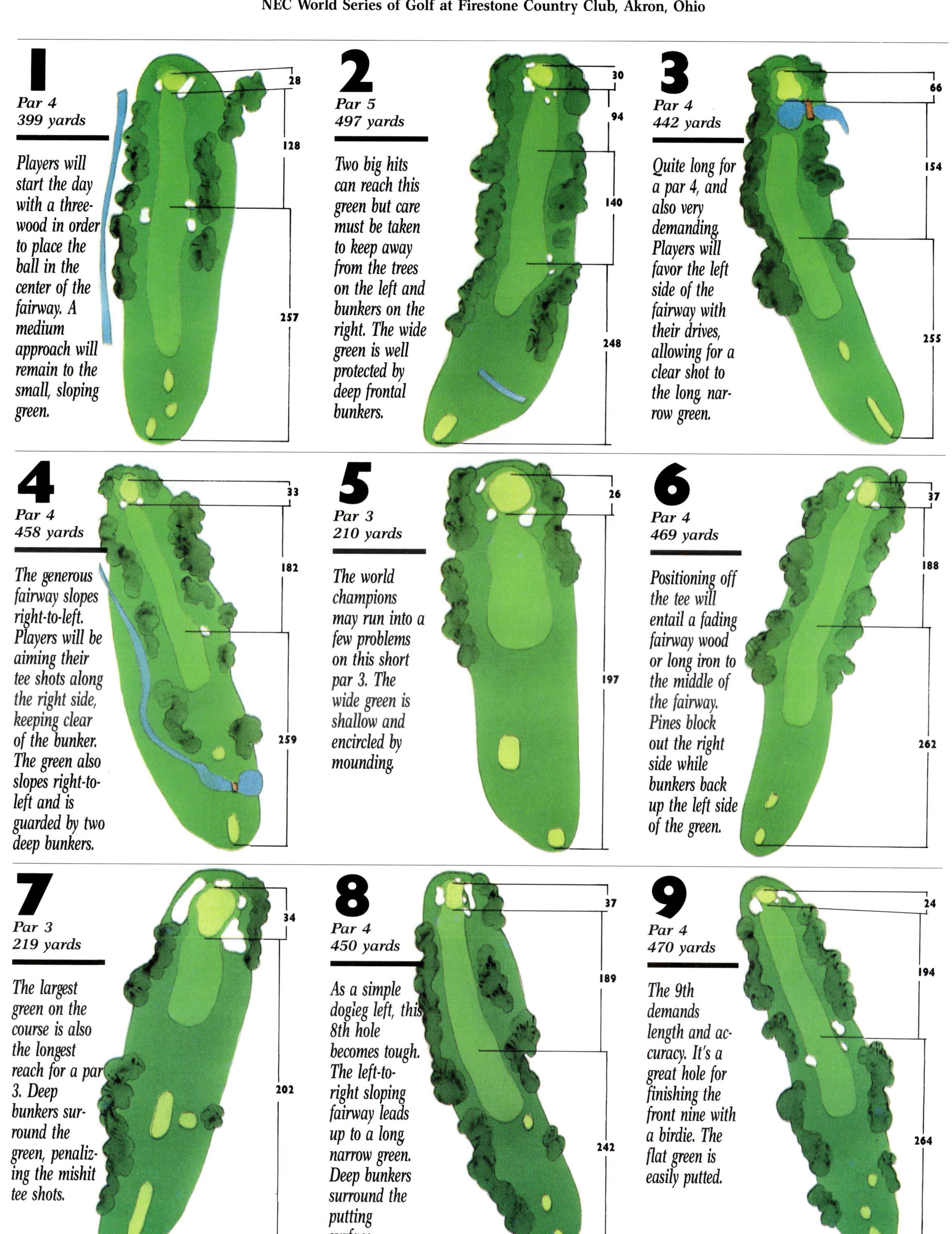
1
Par 4
399 yards

Players will start the day with a three-wood in order to place the ball in the center of the fairway. A medium approach will remain to the small, sloping green.

28
128
257

2
Par 5
497 yards

Two big hits can reach this green but care must be taken to keep away from the trees on the left and bunkers on the right. The wide green is well protected by deep frontal bunkers.

30
94
140
248

3
Par 4
442 yards

Quite long for a par 4, and also very demanding. Players will favor the left side of the fairway with their drives, allowing for a clear shot to the long narrow green.

66
154
255

4
Par 4
458 yards

The generous fairway slopes right-to-left. Players will be aiming their tee shots along the right side, keeping clear of the bunker. The green also slopes right-to-left and is guarded by two deep bunkers.

33
182
259

5
Par 3
210 yards

The world champions may run into a few problems on this short par 3. The wide green is shallow and encircled by mounding.

26
197

6
Par 4
469 yards

Positioning off the tee will entail a fading fairway wood or long iron to the middle of the fairway. Pines block out the right side while bunkers back up the left side of the green.

37
188
262

7
Par 3
219 yards

The largest green on the course is also the longest reach for a par 3. Deep bunkers surround the green, penalizing the mishit tee shots.

34
202

8
Par 4
450 yards

As a simple dogleg left, this 8th hole becomes tough. The left-to-right sloping fairway leads up to a long narrow green. Deep bunkers surround the putting surface.

37
189
242

9
Par 4
470 yards

The 9th demands length and accuracy. It's a great hole for finishing the front nine with a birdie. The flat green is easily putted.

24
194
264

10

Par 4
410 yards

The fairway bunkers define the landing area. A well-hit drive down the left-center will leave a medium approach to the fast, undulating green.

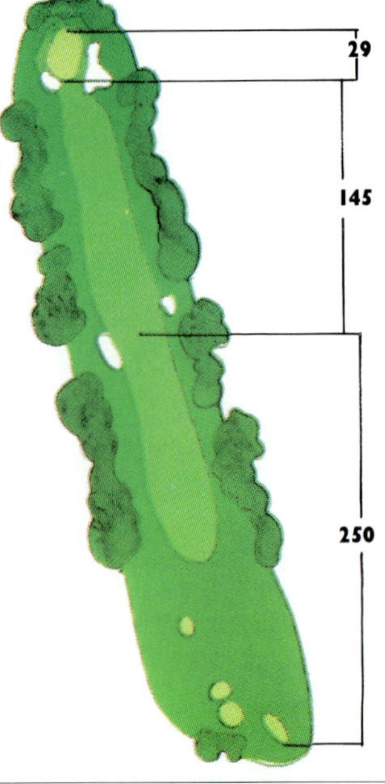

11

Par 4
370 yards

A birdie oppor-tunty that must be taken. It's the shortest par 4 on the course and there are no fairway bunkers. The green is flat and shallow.

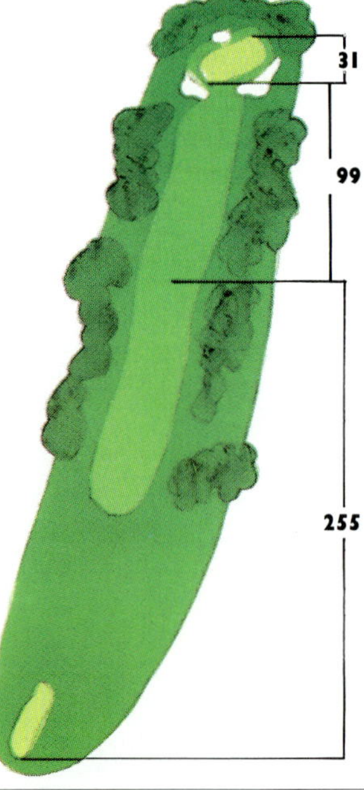

12

Par 3
178 yards

The 12th is the shortest hole on the course. It is slightly uphill and the green sits on a ridge. Deep bunkers sur-round the put-ting surface. Players will be pleased with par.

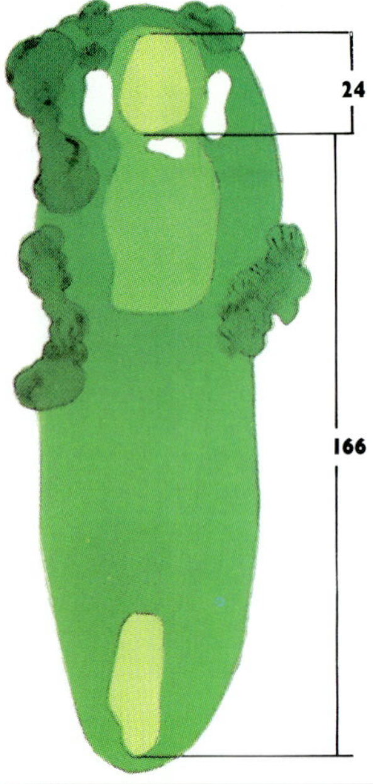

13

Par 4
457 yards

The 13th was originally designed as a par 5. A large oak tree on the right side of the fairway defines the corner of the dogleg. Players will need to hit two good shots to reach the elevated green.

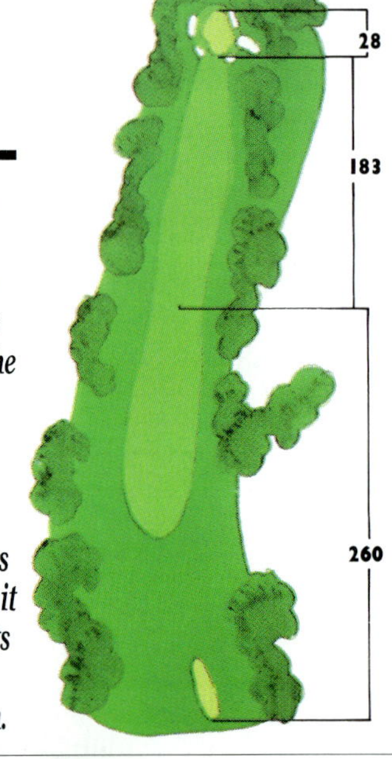

14

Par 4
418 yards

Three fairway bunkers are just within driving distance. A high cut-shot into the green is required to place the ball close to the hole.

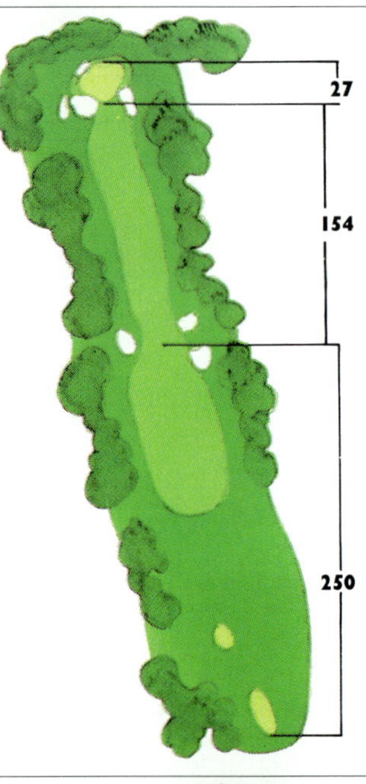

15

Par 3
221 yards

The long nar-row green is flat and fast. Into the wind, the 15th will require as much as a 4-wood to reach the green.

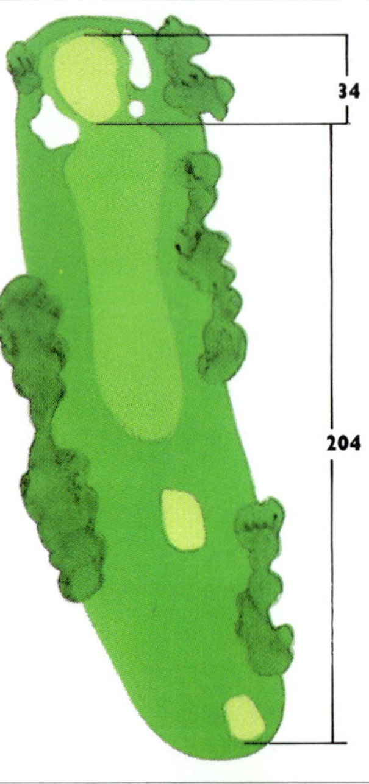

16

Par 5
625 yards

Three well planned shots will be re-quired to get past this hole with no more than par. Laying-up on the second shot will allow players to hit a full wedge into the green.

17

Par 4
392 yards

Four fairway bunkers make the landing area very nar-row. The small, un-dulating put-ting surface is hidden by the deep bunker in front.

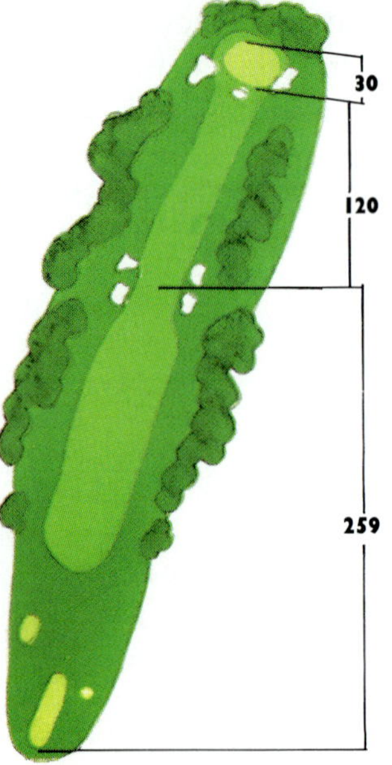

18

Par 4
464 yards

A punishing finale awaits the leading con-tenders. The fairway slopes right-to-left as the hole turns the dogleg. The narrow green is fast and is surrounded by deep bunkers.

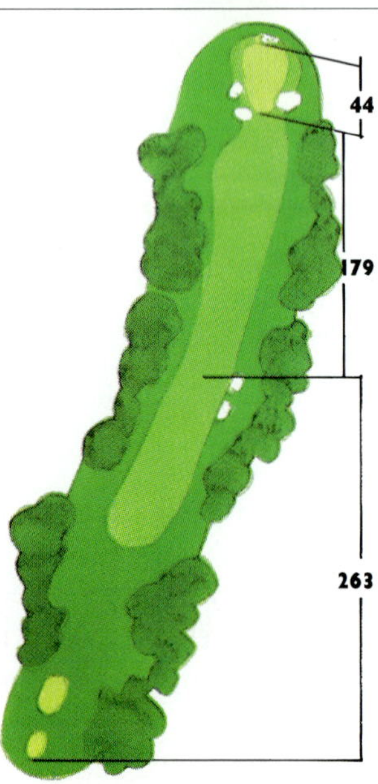

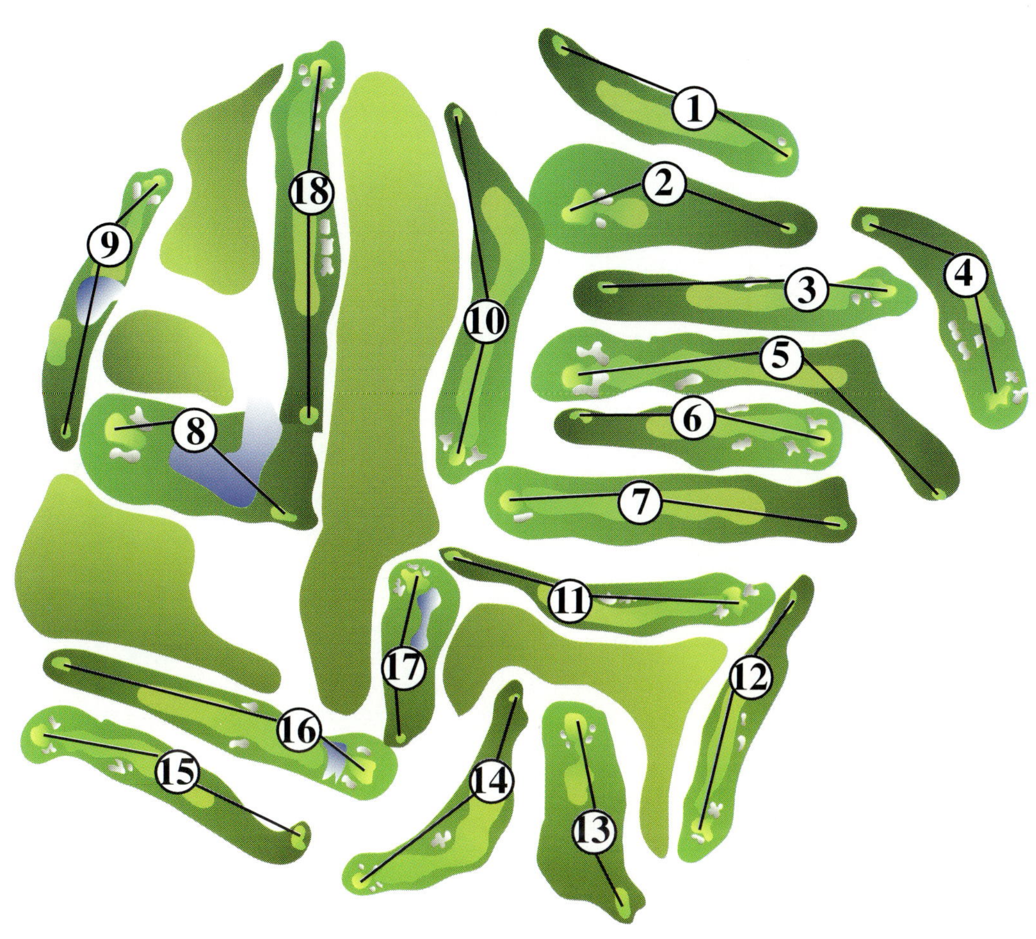

THE COURSE: NASHAWTUC COUNTRY CLUB, CONCORD, MASSACHUSETTS

*N*ashawtuc Country Club, located in historic Concord, Massachusetts, has been proud to host the SENIOR PGA TOUR® since 1984. The course, originally designed by Geoffrey Cornish and undergoing redesign by Brian Silva, has become a favorite among the professionals. Nashawtuc is best known for its meticulously manicured greens, which roll true and allow players to believe they can make any putt if they stroke it properly. However, the subtle breaks on the greens, leave players frustrated as they walk to the next tee more times than not.

Over the years, the Bank of Boston Senior Classic presented by NYNEX had had its share of excitement and memories. One of the oldest events on the SENIOR PGA TOUR®, the tournament has had two playoffs and three repeat champions. Don January and Bob Charles each successfully defended their titles in 1983, '84, and 1989, '90 respectively. In 1988, Chi Chi Rodriguez became the first SENIOR PGA TOUR player to win three consecutive years in 1986 to '88. Jim Albus provided the excitement in 1994 when he held off Sunday charges by playing partners Raymond Floyd and Lee Trevino to take home a check for $112,500. In 1995 the tournament winner was Isao Aoki with a winning score of 204.

Dates:	August 23-25
Network:	ESPN
Times:	Fri 1:00-3:00 EST
	Sat /Sun 5:30-7:00 EST
Yardage:	6740
Par:	72
Slope:	130
Rating:	73.1
Total Purse:	$800,000
1st Prize:	$120,000
1995 Winner:	Isao Aoki
1995 Winning Score:	204 (69,66,69)
Principal Charitable Beneficiary:	Various Charities.
Ticket Information:	1-508-371-0116

1

Par 4
387 yards

This opening hole presents an instant challenge for golfers. The fairway veers slightly from right to left, requiring draw on your drive. The trees at the dogleg have been trimmed back, but a mistake to the left still could make your second shot tough to play.

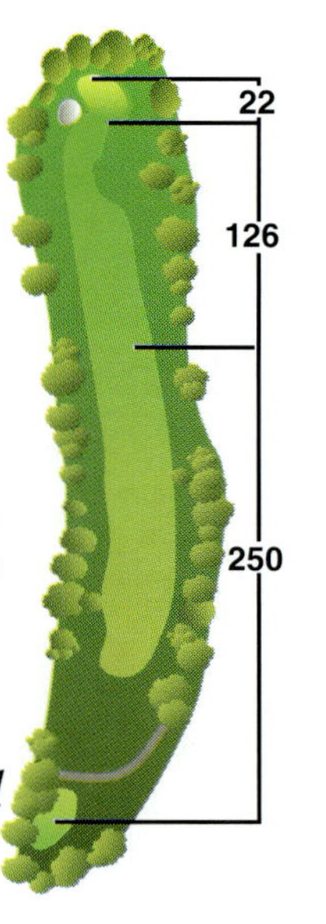

2

Par 3
189 yards

This par 3 hole does not yield many birdies, owing to a sloped green that makes putting a challenge. The sand traps around the green have been rebunkered and moved up tighter to the green.

3

Par 4
372 yards

A little longer this year, thanks to a rebuilt, newly mounted tee. Still, players will need to keep their tee shots to the right side of the fairway, which is sloped and tends to kick everything to the left.

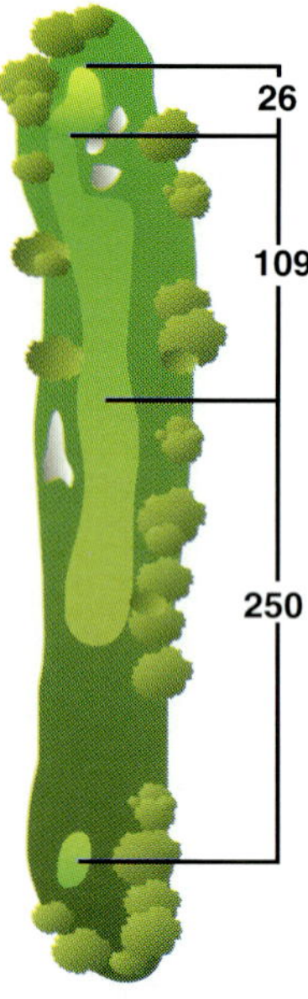

4

Par 4
294 yards

This short hole challenges the golfer to use strategy. The most common tactic is to tee off with a 4 or 5 iron, hitting your ball into the middle of the fairway, setting up a clean approach.

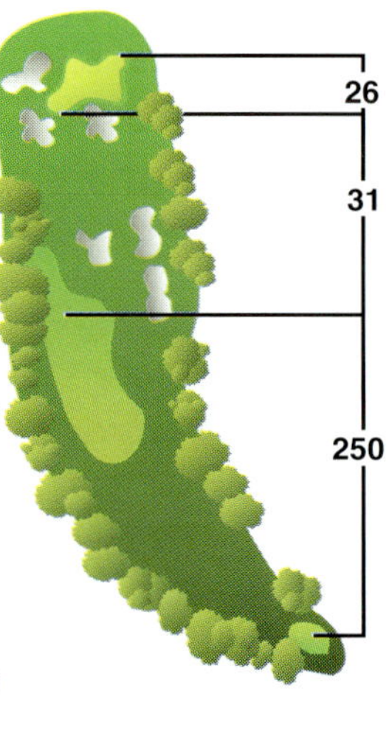

5

Par 5
518 yards

This is the "Rocky Thompson hole". In 1991, Thompson came up with a shortcut: Instead of hitting a long iron or shot wood onto the fairway, which doglegs sharply to the left some 225 yards out, he hit his tee shot over a house.

6

Par 4
365 yards

This flat, straight-ahead par 4 gives pros another possible birdie. In sizing up your tee shot, you're looking at a fairway that's fairly open. Once your on the green you have to deal with the back-to-front slope and its phantom breaks.

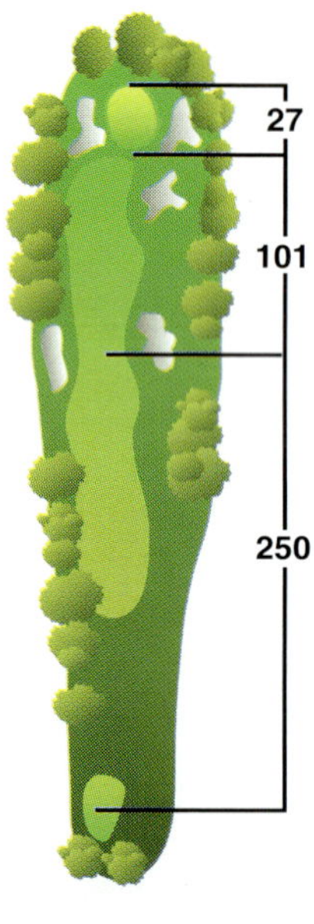

7

Par 4
454 yards

This hole gives you a chance to let loose on you tee shot. The fairway is wide open—but just make sure you land on it because a ball hit on either side could put you in some thick rough. A well-struck drive leaves you a fairway wood or long iron away from the green, which is sloped and very large.

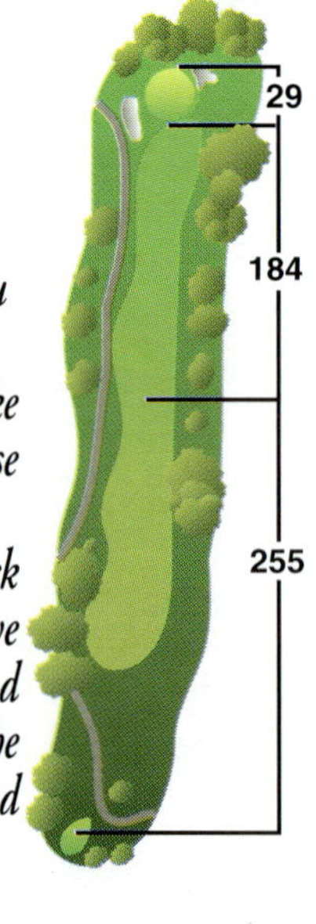

8

Par 3
192 yards

There's more pond than fairway on the hole, but the water shouldn't come into play. More of a problem are the bunkers that guard the green, which demand an on-the-money tee shot.

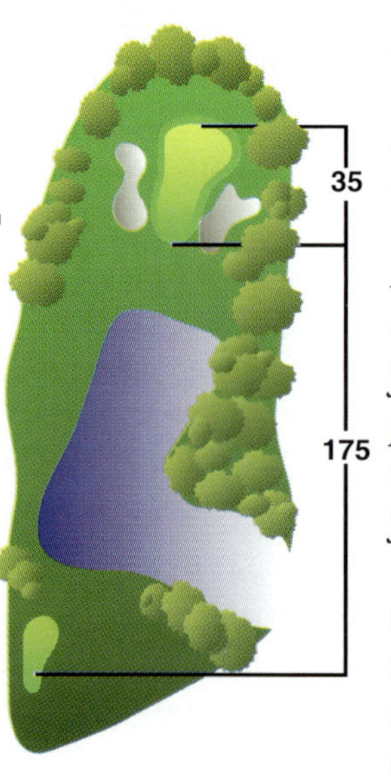

9

Par 5
540 yards

A water hazard protrudes all the way across the fairway. To avoid it, most pros lay up with a 3,4, or 5 wood or a long iron just shot of the ladies' tee. The second shot requires another long iron over the lake, leaving a 100 to 125 yard approach shot to an elevated green.

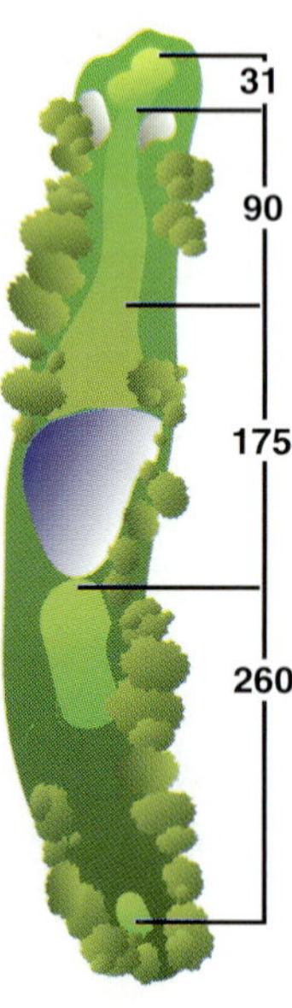

10

Par 5
510 yards

The tee shot on this hole is crucial. Because of the trees along the left, it's best to hit your drive with some fade to it, allowing your ball to follow the dogleg. Either way, you're trying to set up a straight-on second shot.

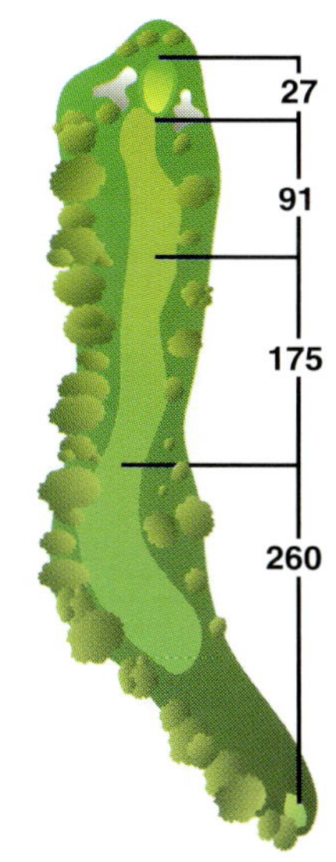

11

Par 4
423 yards

A challenging par 4 where the wind can become a factor. On your drive, you'll want to stay to the right in order to avoid the trees, bunkers, and rough to the left side. The green features harsh ridges, phantom breaks, an tough rolls.

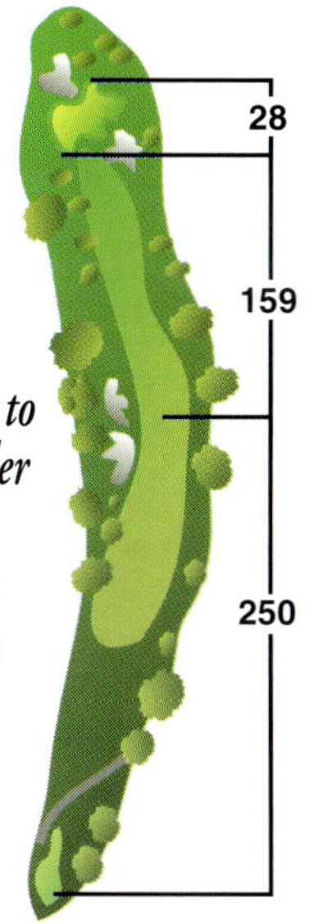

12

Par 4
413 yards

On this hole you'll want your drive to head slightly to the right, not only to avoid the lateral hazard on the left, but because the pronounced fairway slope will kick your ball from right to left. You'll be hitting to a green that's fast and sloped to the right.

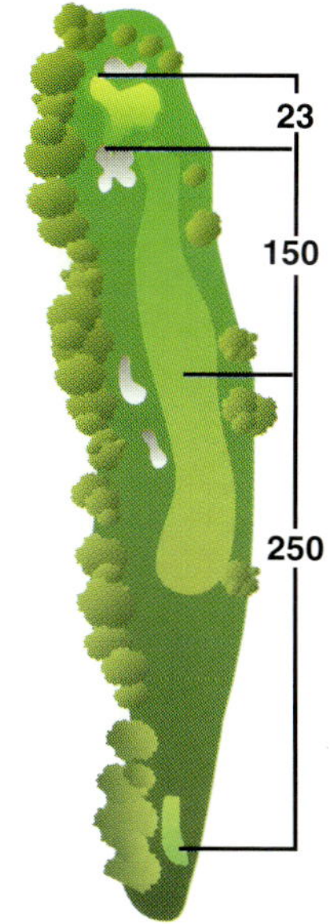

13

Par 3
199 yards

This hole received a makeover last year: a rebuilt tee, repositioned bunkers, and an added bunker. The greater variance will have golfers looking hard at the placement of the front side bunkers.

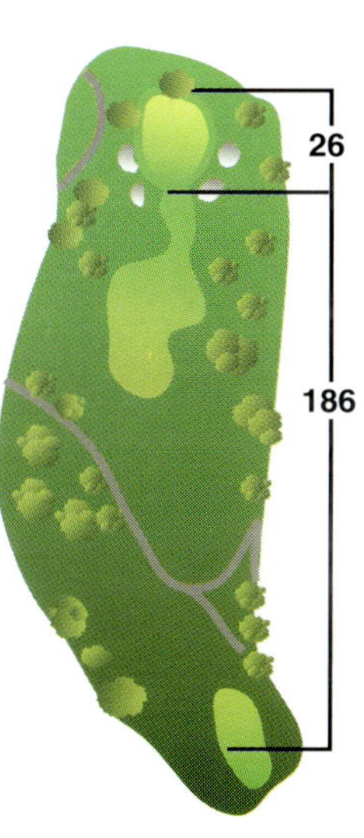

14

Par 4
367 yards

This enigmatic hole features a sharp dogleg right, and a bunker at the crook of the dogleg, and a hazard running up the fairway's left side.

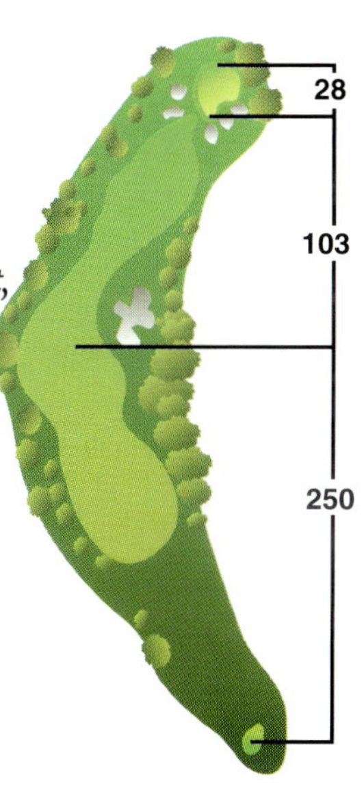

15

Par 4
342 yards

This hole invites birdies if you can hit a straight drive and steer clear of a few danger zones. The biggest hurdle may be the farway's width—it gets tight 220 yards out. Your approach has to be dead-on to the green.

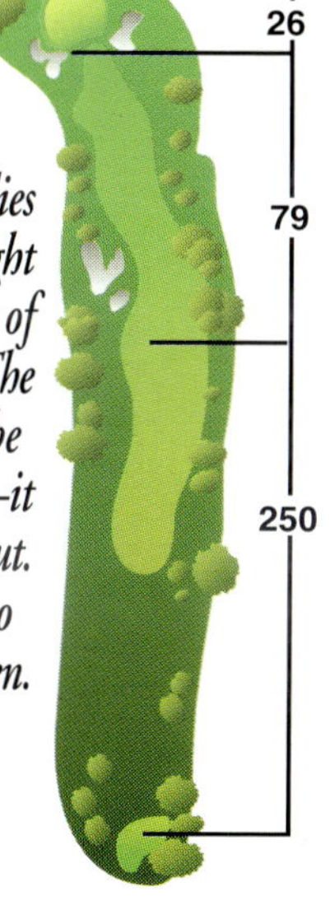

16

Par 4
408 yards

Golfers with straight drives will be rewarded here. But if you hit a severe hook or a slice off the tee, you could end up in sand or in difficult rough. The green is elevated and two-tiered, which can cause putting problems.

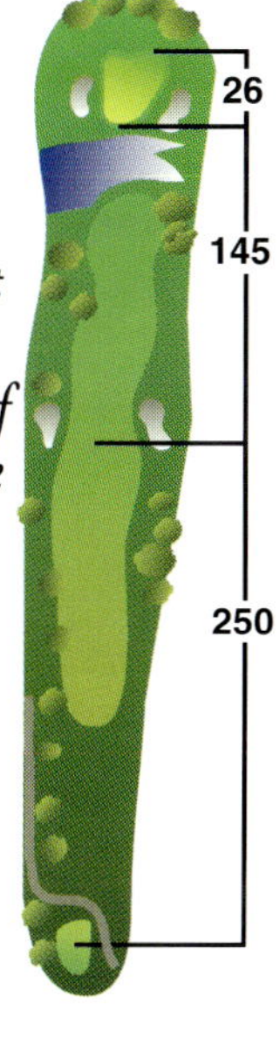

17

Par 3
176 yards

This is not a birdie hole—unless you pull off a spectacular tee shot like Bob Murphy did with his hole-in- one in Round 3 of last years tournament. More realistically, you have to take into account the pin position. If the flag is on the right, the water can become a problem.

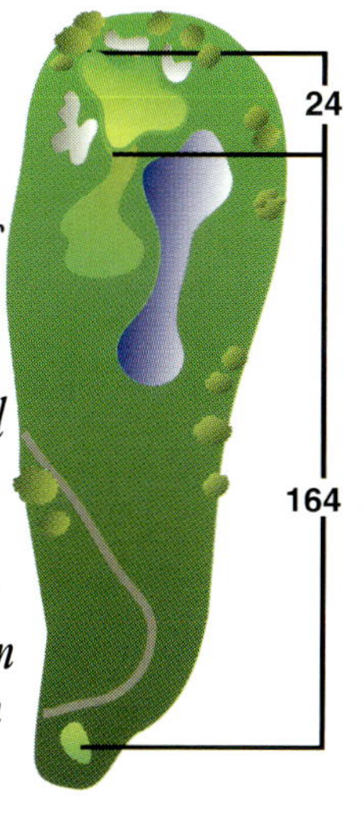

18

Par 5
521 yards

This hole is reachable in two, so you'll see some birdies here, If you don't slice your drive, the trio of bunkers sitting 235 yards from the tee won't be a problem. In fact, it's advisable to keep your drive on the left side of the fairway in order to open up approach shot.

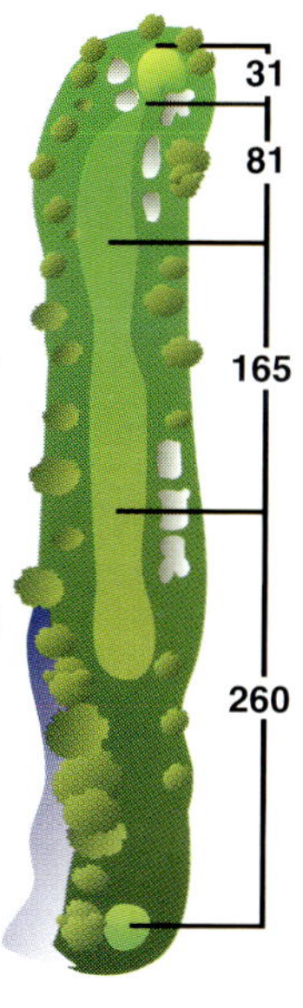

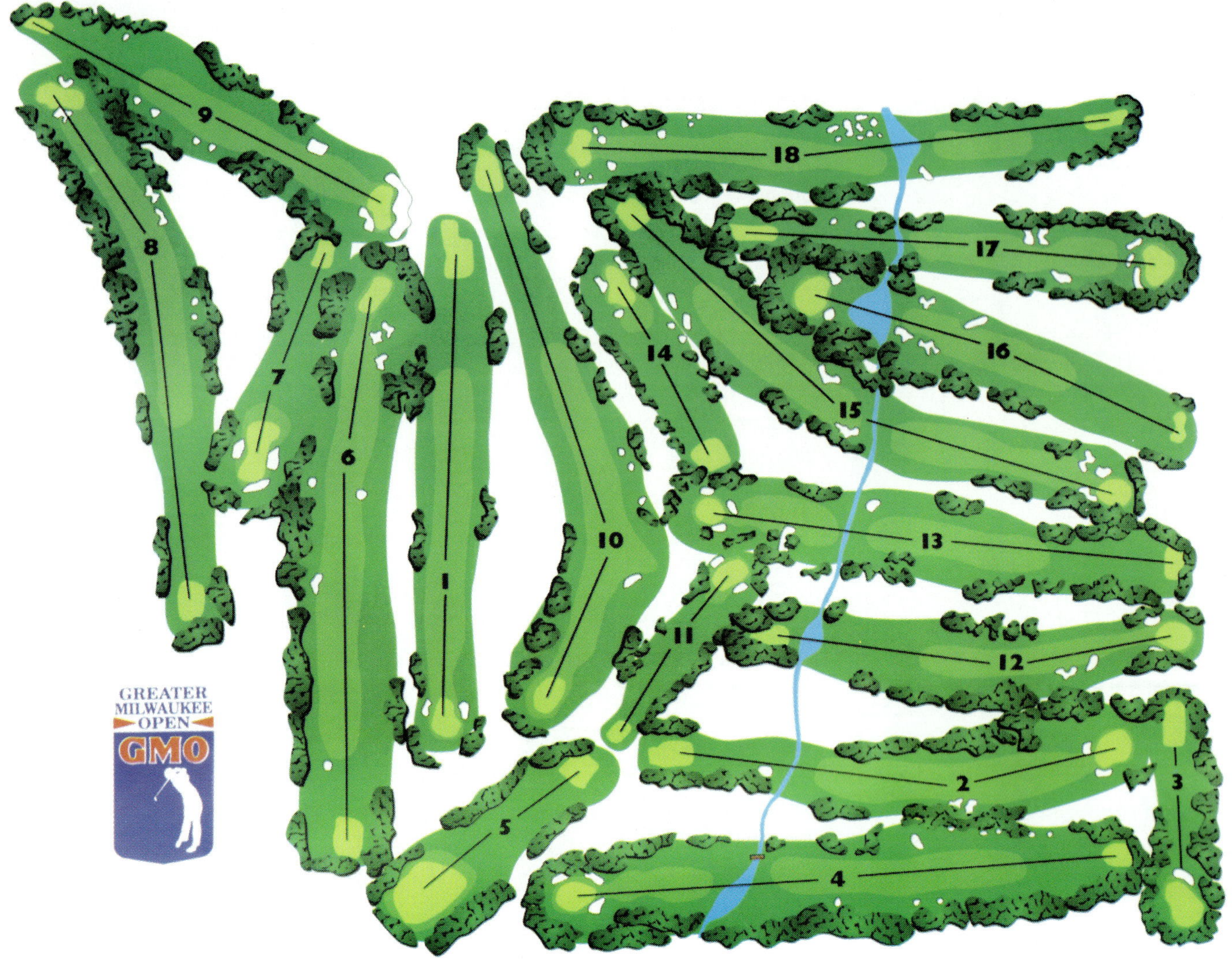

THE COURSE: BROWN DEER PARK, MILWAUKEE, WISCONSIN

*T*he scene of the 28th Greater Milwaukee Open is the Brown Deer Park Golf Course, the jewel of Milwaukee County's sixteen public golf courses. Since 1985, nearly $3 million in renovations have been made to prepare this course for tournament play. Built in 1929, its narrow, tree-lined fairways have hosted three USGA National Public Links Championships (1951, 1966, and 1977).

Dates:	August 29-September 1
Network:	ABC
Times:	Sat 1:30-3:30 EST
	Sun 4:00-6:00 EST
Yardage:	6,739
Par:	71
Slope:	132
Rating:	72.6
Total Purse:	$1,000,000
1st Prize:	$180,000
1995 Winner:	Scott Hoch
1995 Winning Score:	269 (68,71,65,65)
Principal Charitable Beneficiary:	St. Luke's Medical Center of Milwaukee
Charitable Benefits to Date:	Over $2.75 million
Ticket Information:	1-414-365-4GMO

1

Par 4
443 yards

Straightaway par 4 with a narrow landing area. Large green with bunkers on both sides.

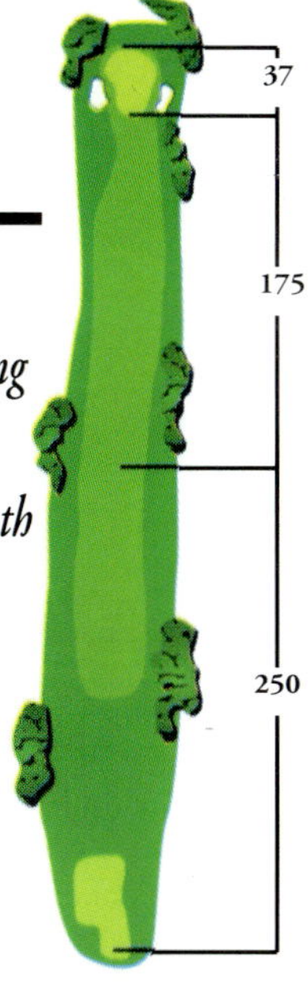

2

Par 4
421 yards

Drive across the creek through narrow opening to elbow of dogleg left. Long, uphill second shot to very undulating green.

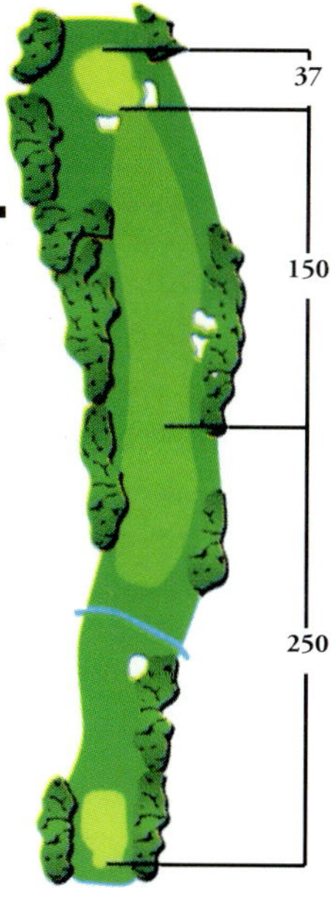

3

Par 3
170 yards

The third hole looks easy, but a narrow opening between trees makes the tee shot difficult. Green slopes severely from back to front and is guarded in front by a large bunker.

4

Par 4
468 yards

This long par 4 plays downhill from the tee to a landing area protected on the left by trees and the right by a bunker. Approach shots to the small green are over a creek and around a large tree in the fairway.

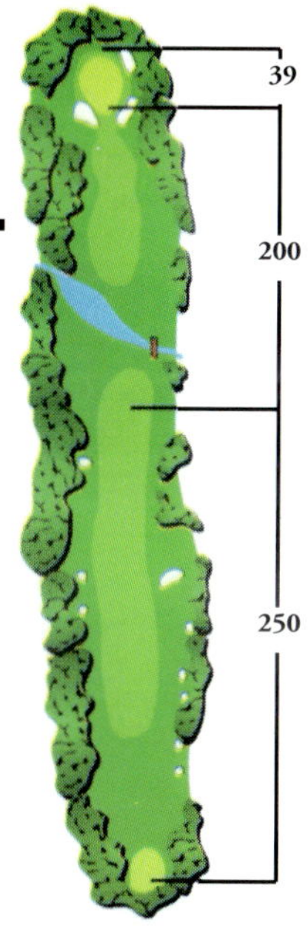

5

Par 3
170 yards

This new hole plays uphill to a small putting surface surrounded by three large bunkers. Wind could be in the player's face on this hole.

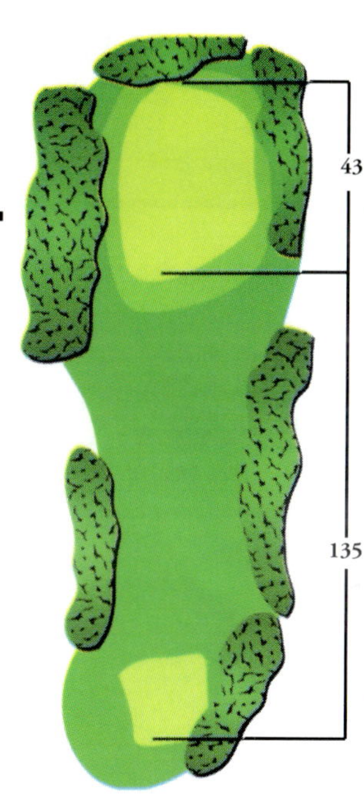

6

Par 5
550 yards

This long par 5 will be reachable only with a strong tail-wind. Drive to a large landing area that narrows with 2 trees in the fairway as you approach the green. Long, narrow putting surface has a ridge through the center.

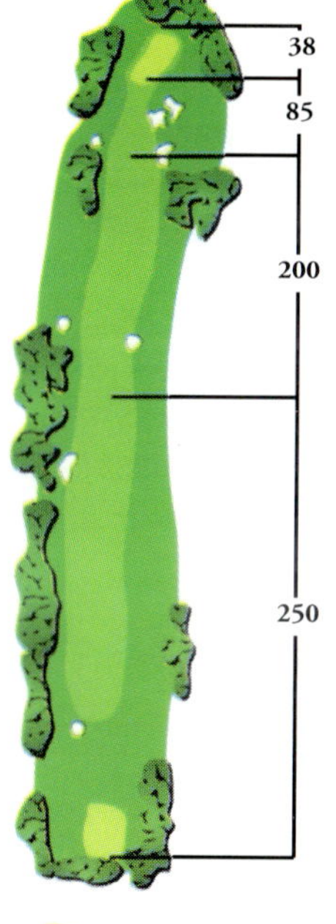

7

Par 3
215 yards

This long par 3 is difficult because of the constant crosswind. The narrow green is bunkered on both sides.

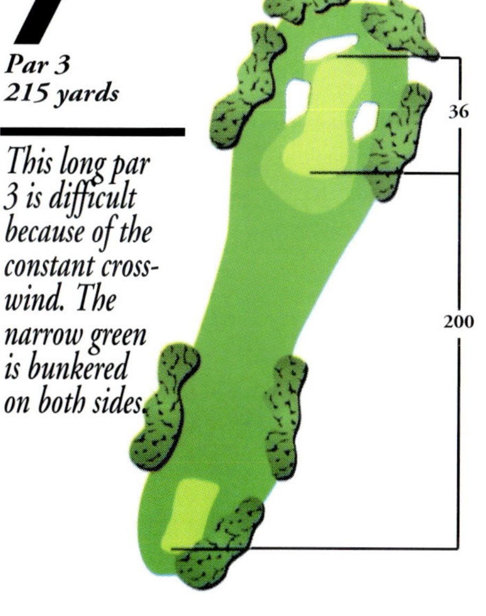

8

Par 4
426 yards

Tee off from back in the woods to the corner of this dogleg left. Trees on left will block your sight of the green if you do not hit drive far enough. Green is heavily trapped, sloping from left to right.

9

Par 4
355 yards

This short par 4 is a break between tough 8 and 10, but do not miss the fairway. Well-bunkered green will be difficult to hit from the deep rough.

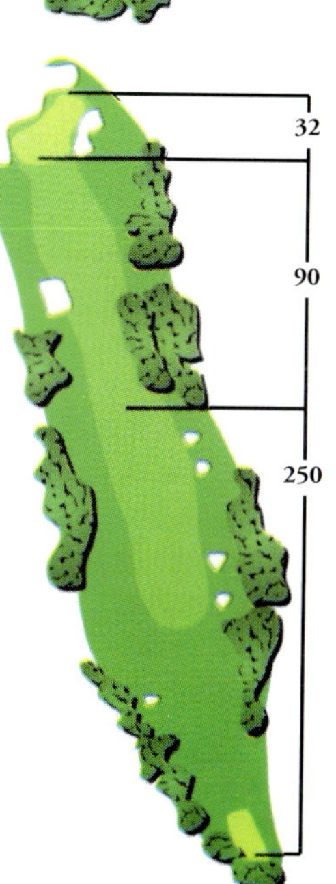

10

Par 4
455 yards

Long par 4 where drive must be left center of fairway to see the whole green. Long second shot to a well bunkered green.

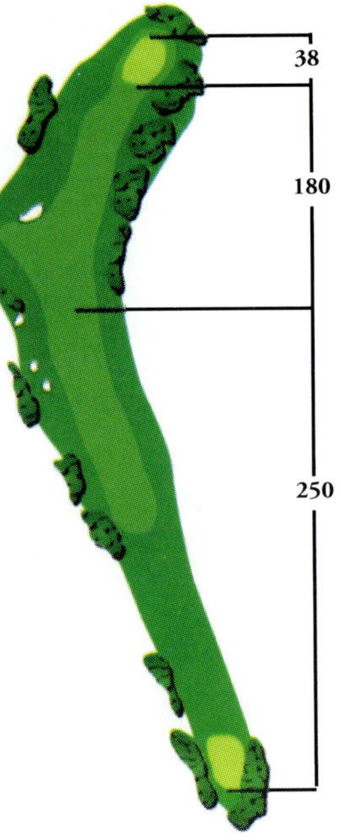

11

Par 3
198 yards

Water and sand on the players left present most of the problems for the players on this hole. Sloping green makes birdies difficult.

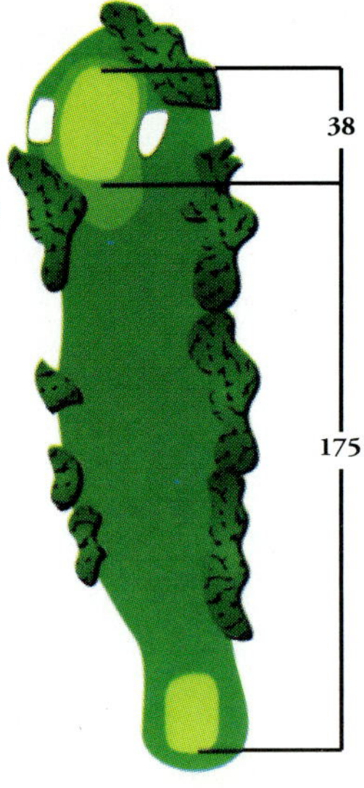

12

Par 4
371 yards

Three wood or iron off this tee will set up an uphill approach to the green. Trees on both sides of the fairway will cause most of the problems here.

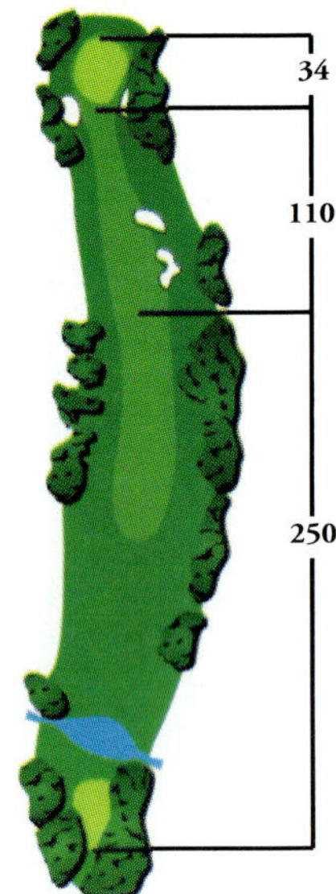

13

Par 4
413 yards

Drive must be short of creek and preferably on right side on this down-hill par 4. Small undulating green will prevent good birdie opportunities.

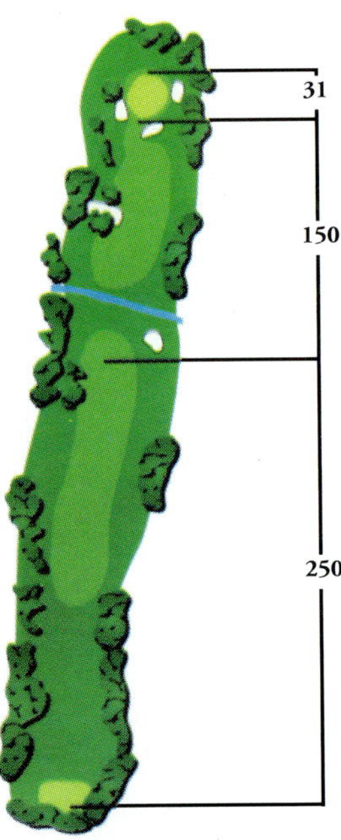

14

Par 3
195 yards

Elevated tee allows players to see wide but short putting surface. Three large bunkers protect pin and trees make accuracy essential.

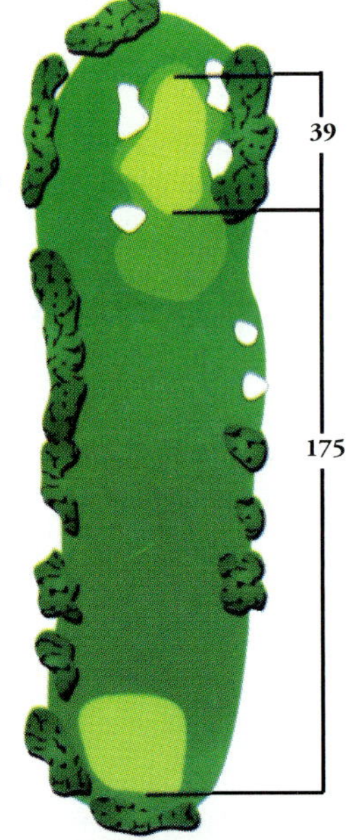

15

Par 5
527 yards

This dogleg left is reachable in 2 with the right tee shot. Wind should assist second shots to this small, sloping green. Watch out for woods on the right and over the green.

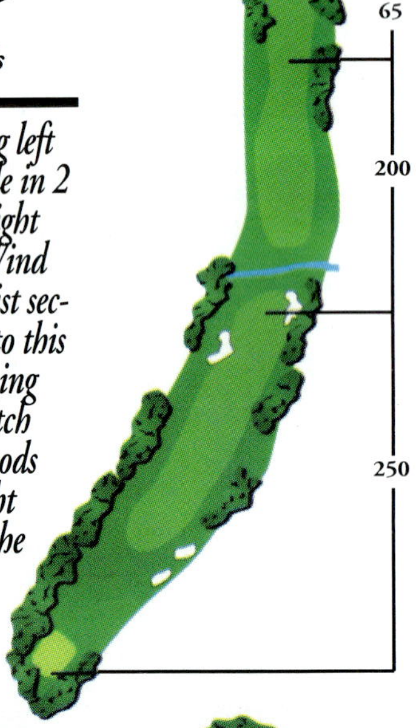

16

Par 4
371 yards

Narrow landing area and tough green are the trademarks of this par 4. Trees on the left and sand on the right make driving difficult. Short iron to green that is guarded in front by the creek.

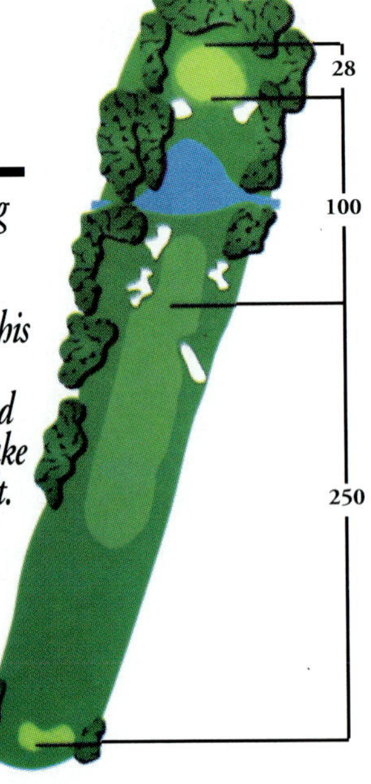

17

Par 4
378 yards

Drive between two large willows to a narrow fairway that is tree-lined. Large green is surrounded by sand creating few birdie chances.

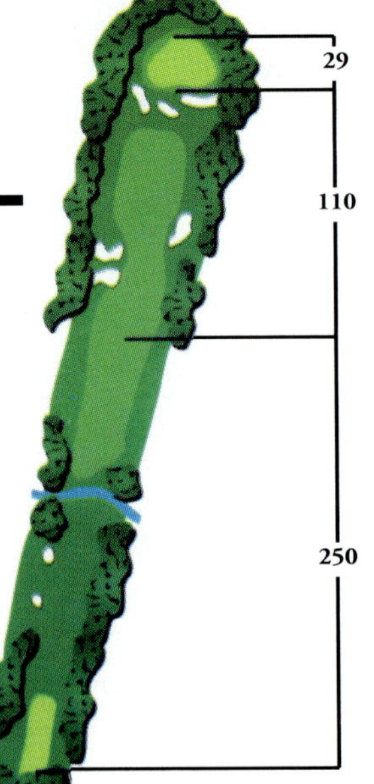

18

Par 5
565 yards

Into the wind, this par 5 may well decide the tournament. A good drive over the creek will decide whether you can go for the green in two or lay up. Green has five bunkers out front to penalize the daring golfer who needs eagle to win.

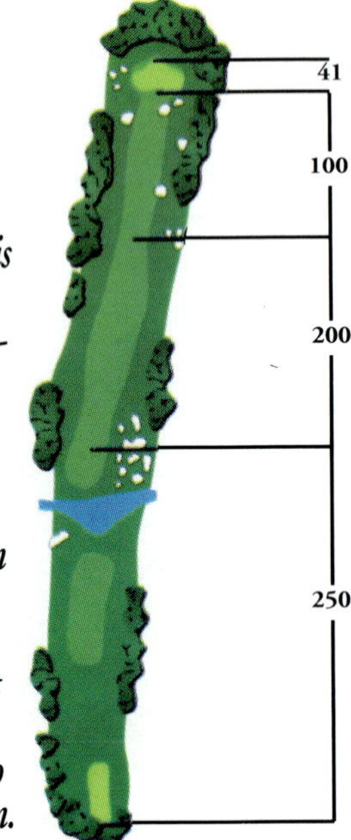

THE COURSE: GLEN ABBEY GOLF CLUB, OAKVILLE, ONTARIO, CANADA

"*Glen Abbey was the first golf course I built myself. It's a reflection in many ways of Muirfield Village. At Glen Abbey, I corrected many of the mistakes I had made at Muirfield.*" So says Glen Abbey Golf Club designer Jack Nicklaus. And the Canadian Open has fared well at the Glen Abbey site in great part due to Nicklaus' superb architecture. Built on a large, country estate, the course has been the site of the Canadian Open for the past fourteen years. Glen Abbey will again be the site in 1996 for the 87th playing of the Bell Canadian Open.

The Royal Canadian Golf Association calls "The Abbey" home for itself and the Canadian Golf Hall of Fame, Museum and Library. Although the Open has been played on a variety of courses since J.H. Oke won the first championship in 1904, Americans Arnold Palmer, Gene Littler, Lee Trevino, Sam Snead, Walter Hagen and Curtis Strange have been among the winners. How has the designer fared on the course? Nicklaus has been bested by the ghost of the Abbey, coming in second place on seven separate outings.

Dates:	September 5-8
Network:	ESPN
Times:	Thur /Fri 4:00-6:00 EST
	Sat /Sun 4:00-6:00 EST
Yardage:	7112
Par:	72
Rating:	72.0
Total Purse:	$1,300,000
1st Prize:	$234,000
1995 Winner:	Mark O'Meara
1995 Winning Score:	274 (72,67,68,67)
Principal Charitable Beneficiary:	Royal Canadian Golf Association, Canadian Golf Foundation
Charitable Benefits to Date:	Over $10 million
Ticket Information:	1-905-849-9700

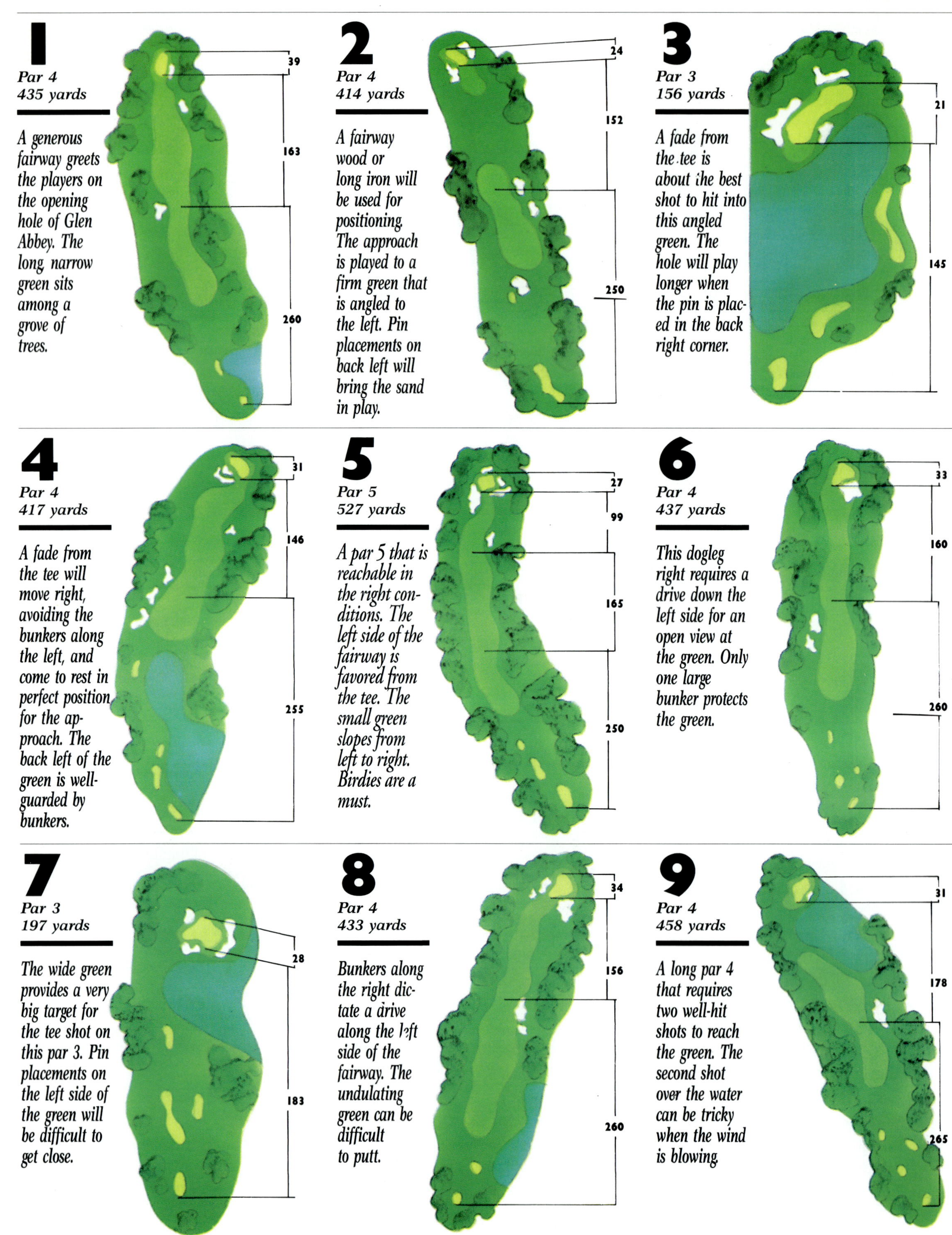

1

Par 4
435 yards

A generous fairway greets the players on the opening hole of Glen Abbey. The long narrow green sits among a grove of trees.

2

Par 4
414 yards

A fairway wood or long iron will be used for positioning. The approach is played to a firm green that is angled to the left. Pin placements on back left will bring the sand in play.

3

Par 3
156 yards

A fade from the tee is about the best shot to hit into this angled green. The hole will play longer when the pin is placed in the back right corner.

4

Par 4
417 yards

A fade from the tee will move right, avoiding the bunkers along the left, and come to rest in perfect position for the approach. The back left of the green is well-guarded by bunkers.

5

Par 5
527 yards

A par 5 that is reachable in the right conditions. The left side of the fairway is favored from the tee. The small green slopes from left to right. Birdies are a must.

6

Par 4
437 yards

This dogleg right requires a drive down the left side for an open view at the green. Only one large bunker protects the green.

7

Par 3
197 yards

The wide green provides a very big target for the tee shot on this par 3. Pin placements on the left side of the green will be difficult to get close.

8

Par 4
433 yards

Bunkers along the right dictate a drive along the left side of the fairway. The undulating green can be difficult to putt.

9

Par 4
458 yards

A long par 4 that requires two well-hit shots to reach the green. The second shot over the water can be tricky when the wind is blowing.

10

Par 4
443 yards

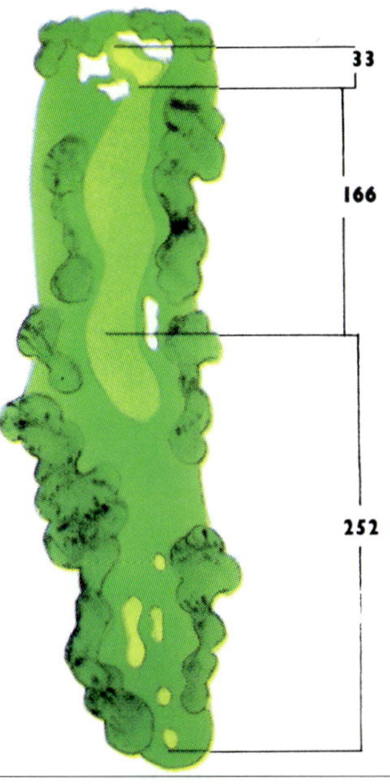

The tee shot is played out of a narrow chute to a fairway that is tight. A fairway bunker along the right dictates players to favor the left. The shallow green can be tough to hold on the second shot.

11

Par 4
452 yards

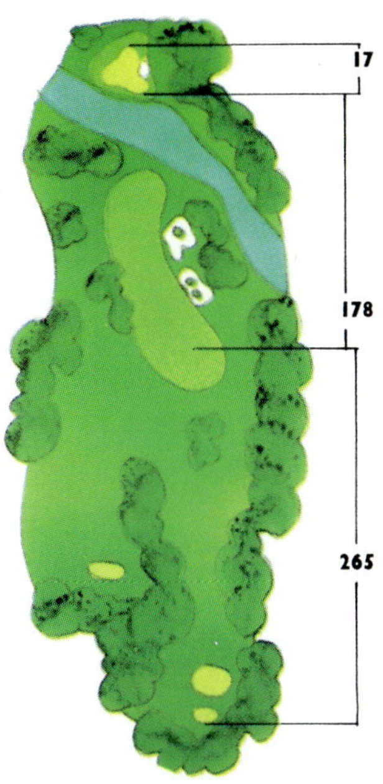

A beautiful hole in its natural beauty. A big drive must be kept clear of the bunkers along the right and the approach must be played over Sixteen Mile Creek to a small green.

12

Par 3
187 yards

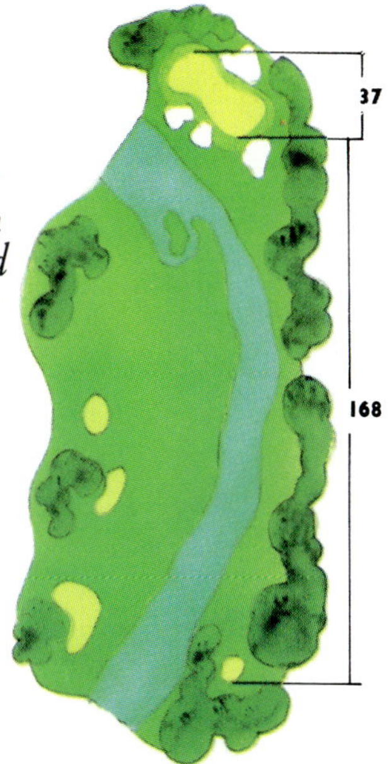

Reconstruction in 1983 moved the teeing area in a position that requires a carry over the creek. An elevated tee affords good visibility of the small green.

13

Par 5
529 yards

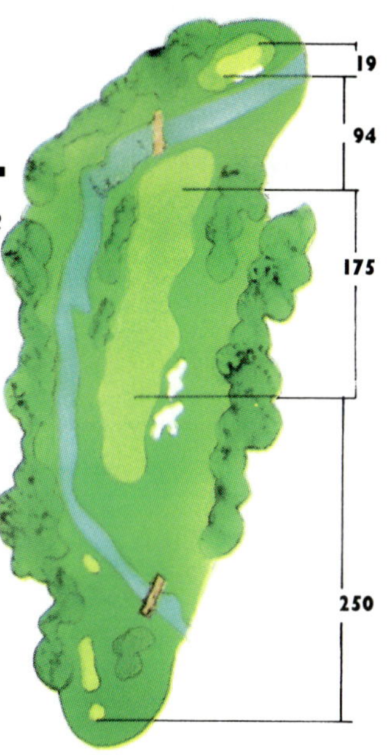

Downwind, the players will be encouraged to go for the green in two. The angle of the green makes the back right corner of the putting surface a difficult place to reach safely.

14

Par 4
426 yards

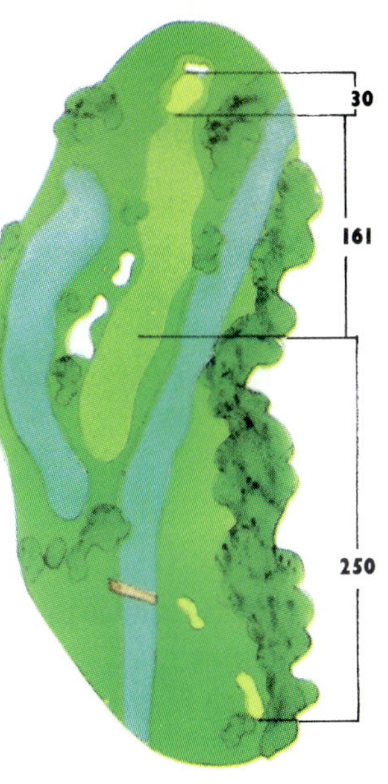

A fade off the tee would play nicely — that's as long as the player starts it down the left. The approach is to a U-shaped green that curves around a mound.

15

Par 3
141 yards

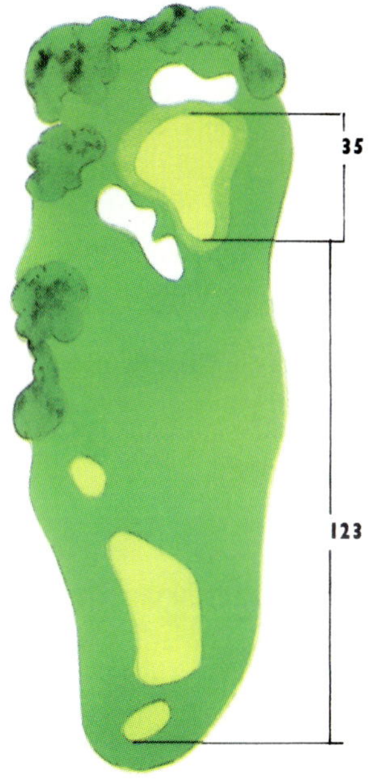

As the shortest hole on the course, this par 3 requires accuracy. Players will attempt to keep their tee shots below the hole for an uphill putt. Too much spin can pull the ball off the green.

16

Par 5
516 yards

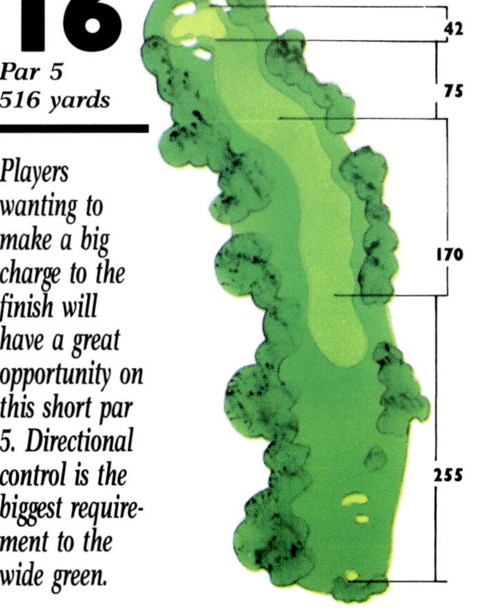

Players wanting to make a big charge to the finish will have a great opportunity on this short par 5. Directional control is the biggest requirement to the wide green.

17

Par 4
436 yards

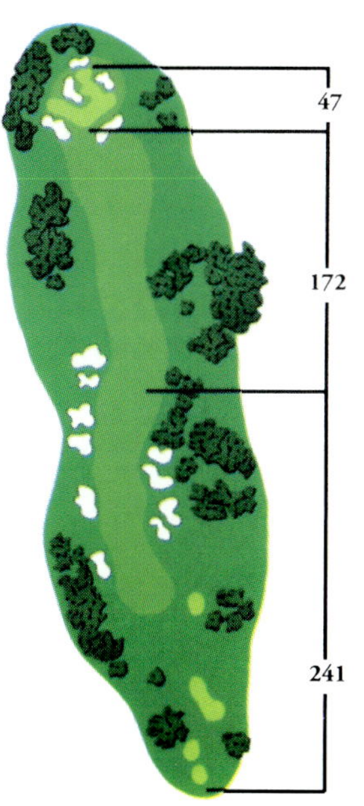

A plethora of bunkers are scattered in the landing area. The left center of the fairway is favored from the tee. The shapely green demands a precise approach.

18

Par 5
508 yards

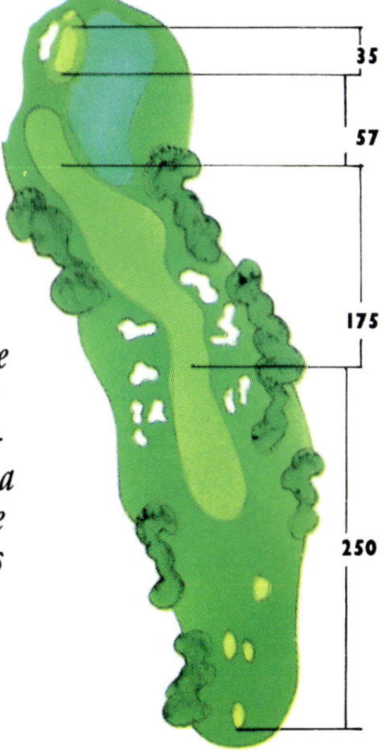

This 18th is also reachable in two, but it is risky. A drive along the right side of the fairway will leave a shot of no more than 230 yards to the green.

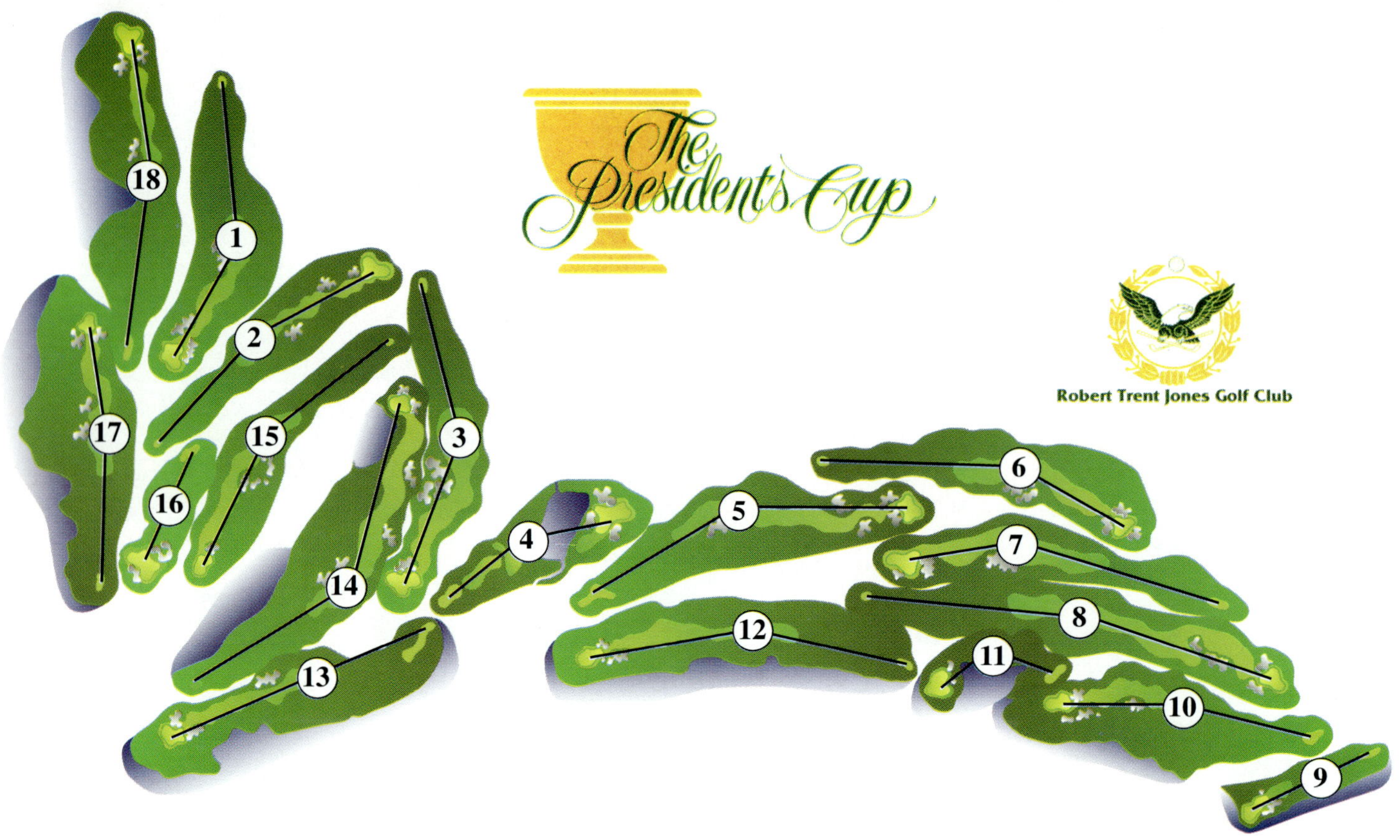

THE COURSE: ROBERT TRENT JONES GOLF CLUB, LAKE MANASSAS, VIRGINIA

*T*he 1996 Presidents Cup will be played September 9-15, with Opening Ceremonies on Thursday, September 12. It will be played again at the Robert Trent Jones Golf Club. In a career that has produced more than 400 golf courses, Jones calls the RTJGC "my masterpiece." The course was built on the largest lake in Northern Virginia, 850-acre Lake Manassas. President George Bush will serve as Honorary Chairman. President Gerald Ford served as Honorary Chairman in 1994.

The Presidents Cup features team match play competition. The competition consists of two teams. 12 players representing the United States and 12 players representing the rest of the world, except Europe. There are 10 matches (five foursomes and five four-ball matches) each of the first two days. Each member of the 12-man teams must play each day. There are 12 singles matches on the final day, all of which are played to conclusion. No singles matches will be halved (tied). If the overall competition is deadlocked at the end of singles play on Sunday, there is a sudden-death playoff between two players—designated in advance by each captain. The United States won the inaugural competition, 20-12.

Unlike other events, the players do not receive prize money based on performance. Instead, 100% of the net proceeds are divided into 26 equal shares for the players and captains to donate to their favorite charities through PGA TOUR Charities, Inc. This concept truly makes the PGA TOUR's charity contributions international in scope. The 1996 Captains are Arnold Palmer for the United States, and David Graham, who returns as Captain of the International Team.

Dates:	September 9-15
Network:	ESPN & CBS Sports
Times:	ESPN Thur TBD
	Fri 8:00-12:00 pm EST
	6:00-6:30 pm EST
	CBS Sat 3:00 - 6:00 pm EST
	Sun 2:00 - 6:00 pm EST
Yardage:	7238
Par:	72
Slope:	136
Rating:	75.9
Total Purse:	Player's compensation donated to myriad charities
1995 Winner:	USA Team defeated International Team
1995 Winning Score:	20-12
Charitable Benefits to Date:	$750,000
Ticket Information:	1-800-668-6875

1

Par 4
407 yards

Try to place tee shot in the fairway left of the large fairway bunker. Player may try to carry the fairway bunker. Green is two-tiered and very severe on the lower level.

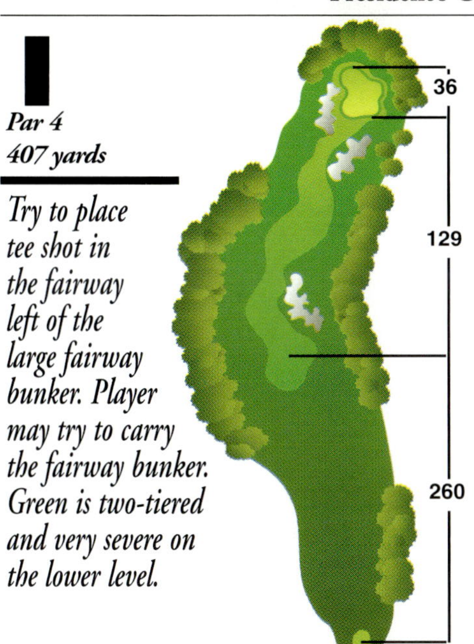

2

Par 4
421 yards

Uphill par four with a plateau in the fairway which is even with the fairway bunker. Elevated green falls off on right side, and a ridge extends through the middle of the green.

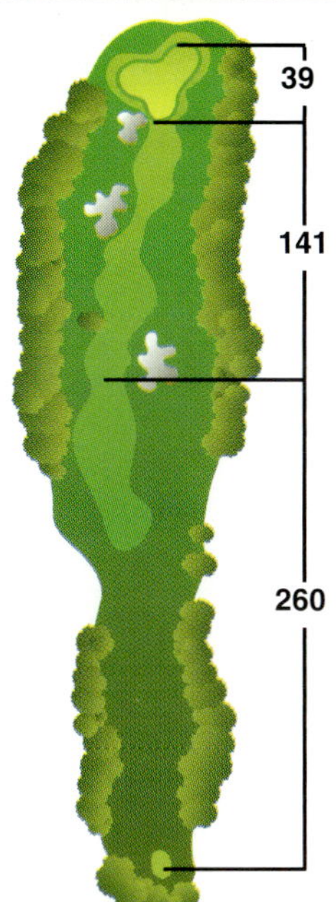

3

Par 4
449 yards

Stay left of bunker complex on right. A long iron or fairway wood may be required for the second shot. The greenside bunker forces the player to carry the ball into the green.

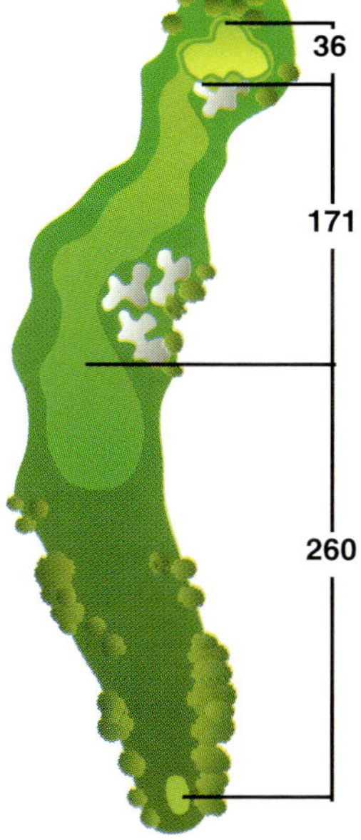

4

Par 3
212 yards

This first par three offers several possible pin placements and an extremely undulating putting green. Lake extends to green side on left side, so proper club selection is important.

5

Par 5
560 yards

This par five is a three shot hole, unless a player is able to carry the fairway bunker at the dogleg. Players who elect to lay up will have a short to mid iron to this elevated green.

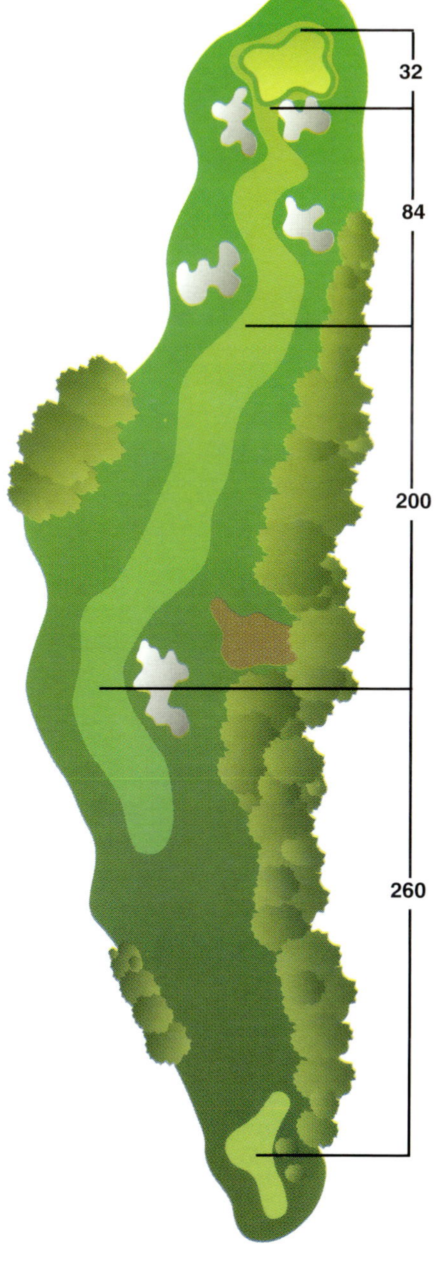

6

Par 4
436 yards

Favor the left side of the fairway, so the green will be completely visible. A large mound in the center of this small green makes this the most difficult green to putt.

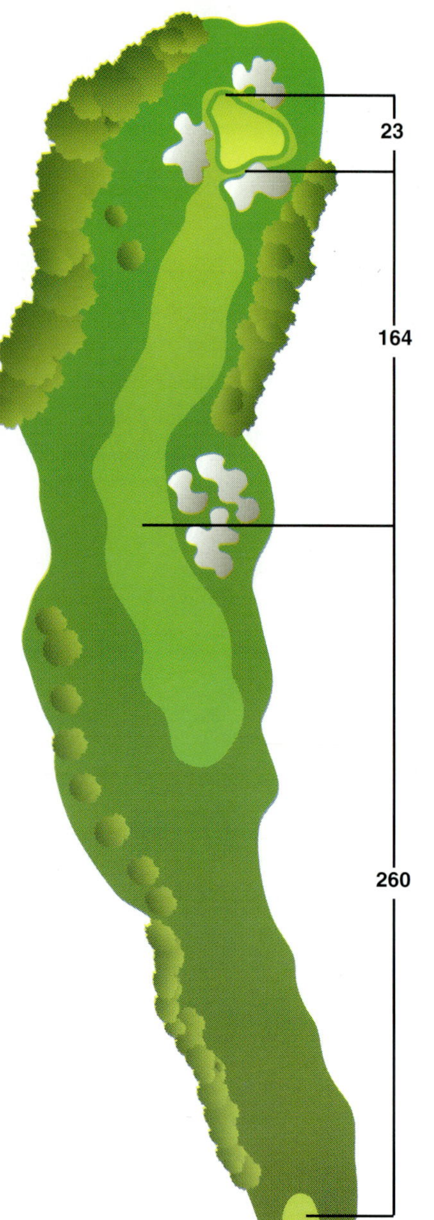

7

Par 4
425 yards

Right side of the fairway should be favored. Ball tends to bounce right to left. Pin placements toward the front of the green are the easiest. Green narrows considerably in the back

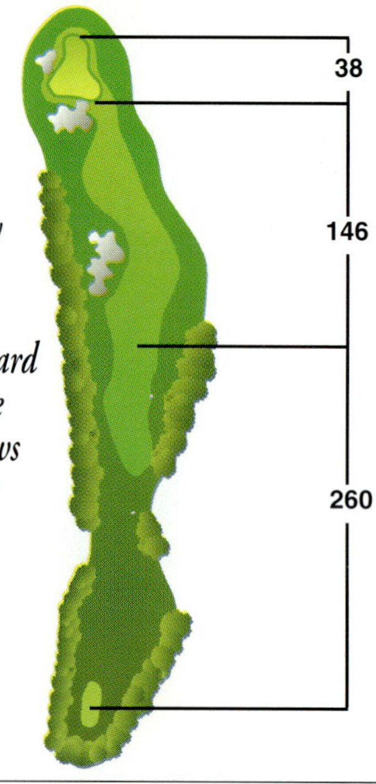

9

Par 3
199 yards

This downhill par three is demanding as well as eye-catching. Green is two-tiered with back pin placements offering a high risk reward factor.

8

Par 5
581 yards

Demanding tee shot. Players may choose to hit a fairway wood to the upper fairway on the second shot in order to leave a short wedge shot to the green or lay up on the lower fairway which leaves an uphill approach shot.

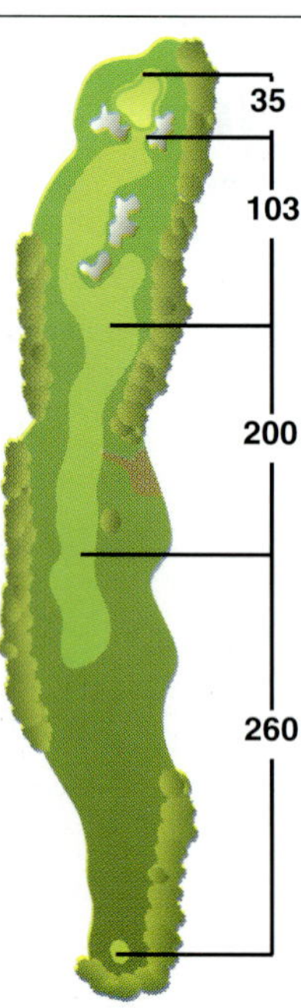

10

Par 4
382 yards

Keep the ball right of the fairway bunker. Ball will kick left off the right hillside. Players will have a short iron to this gently contoured green.

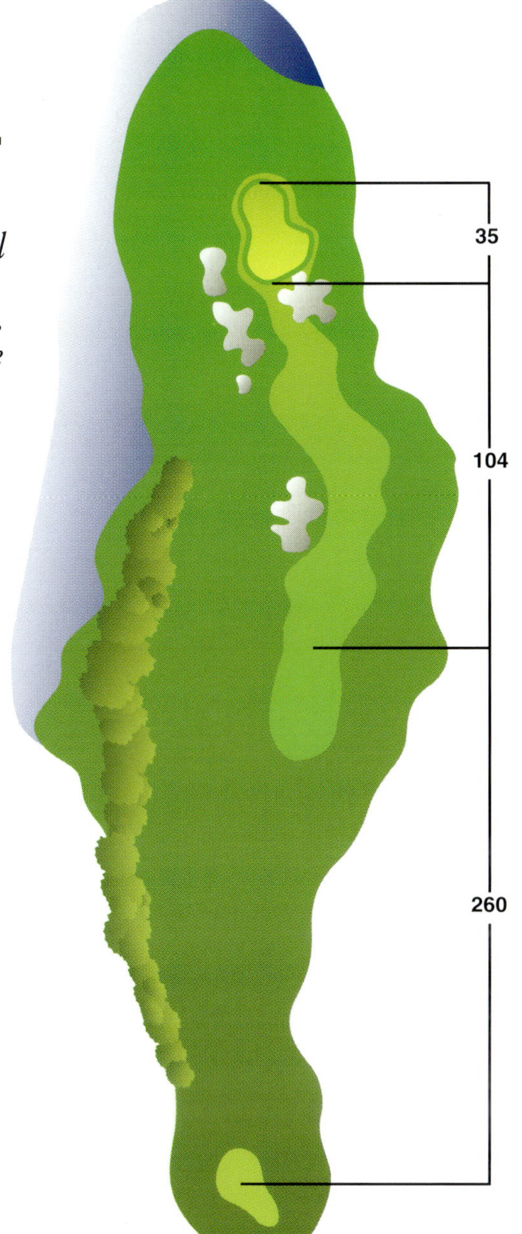

11

Par 3
185 yards

Club selection is critical to this narrow green. A ridge runs through the middle of the green making putts from the opposite side of the ridge challenging.

12

Par 5
507 yards

A reachable par five for the long hitter. The elevated green makes the second or third shots to the green play a little longer than the yardage. Players should avoid going over this green.

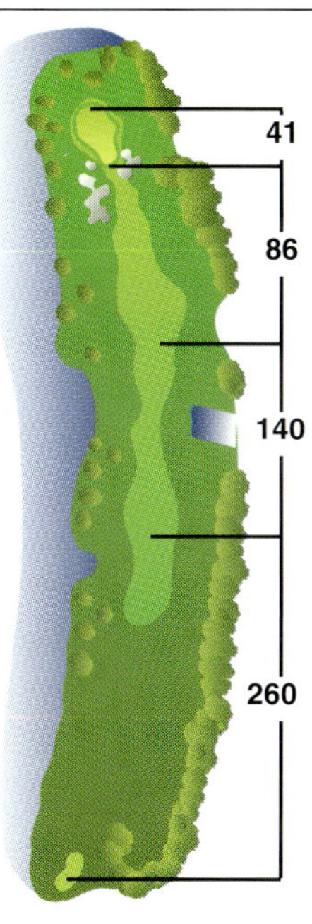

13

Par 4
454 yards

The best line for the tee shot is just inside the right fairway bunker. Long hitters may use a long iron or fairway wood from the tee in order to avoid a downhill lie.

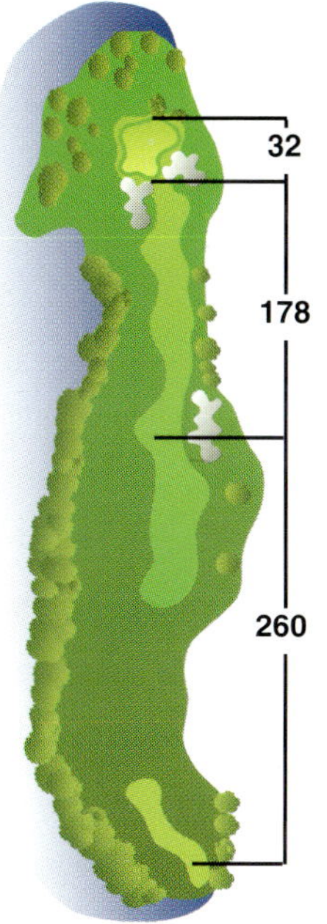

14

Par 5
583 yards

Tee placement determines strategy on this hole. Player may elect to try for green in two shots from the forward tees. approach shot is difficult with the lake guarding the left and front sides.

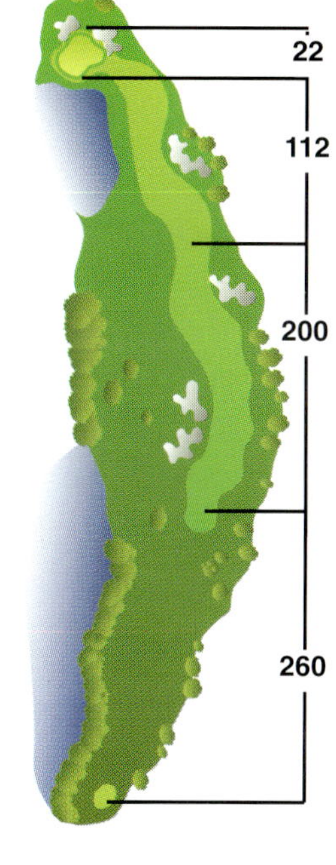

15

Par 4
459 yards

Difficult par four which requires two long shots to reach the green. Players who miss the green will be tested to save par.

16

Par 3
166 yards

Don't let the distance trick you into a false sense of security. Putting and pin placement can make this hole a hard par.

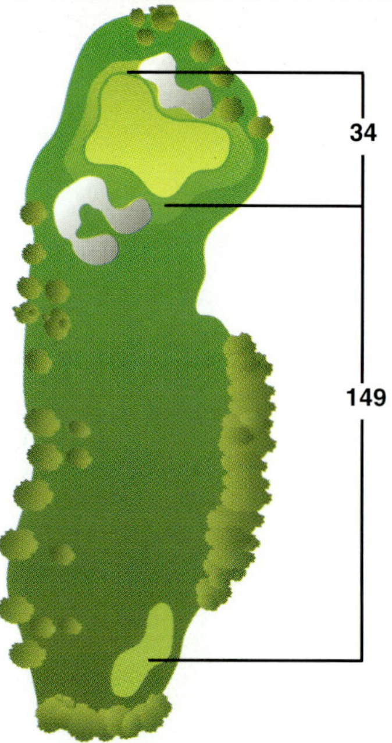

18

Par 4
429 yards

A long carry off the tee is required in order to reach the landing area. The second shot is to a large undulating green which will make your last putts demanding.

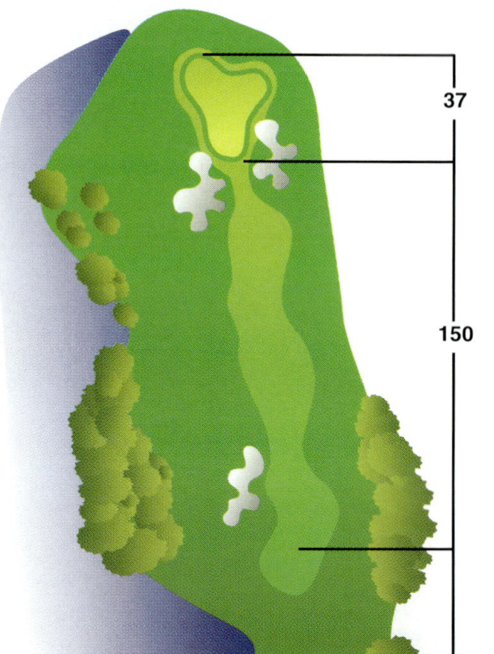

17

Par 4
383 yards

The lone tree is a good target off the tee. A well placed tee shot will set up a much easier approach shot. The uphill second shot can be challenging to this rather small elevated green.

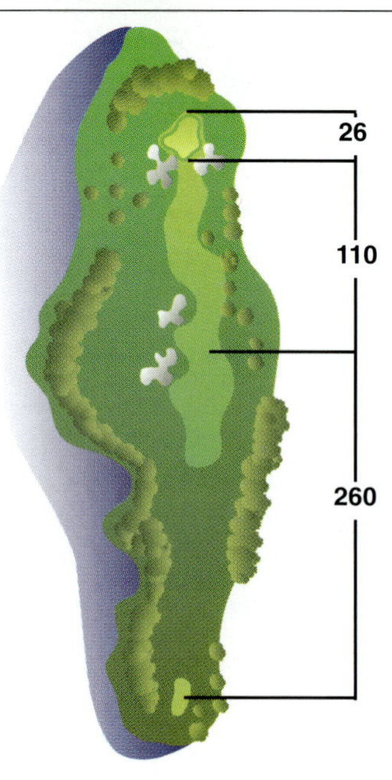
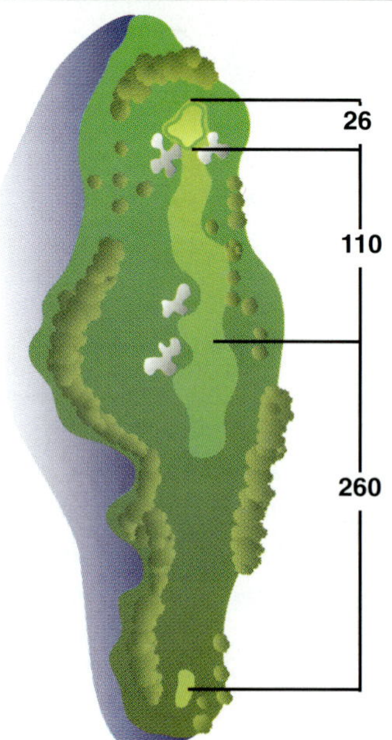

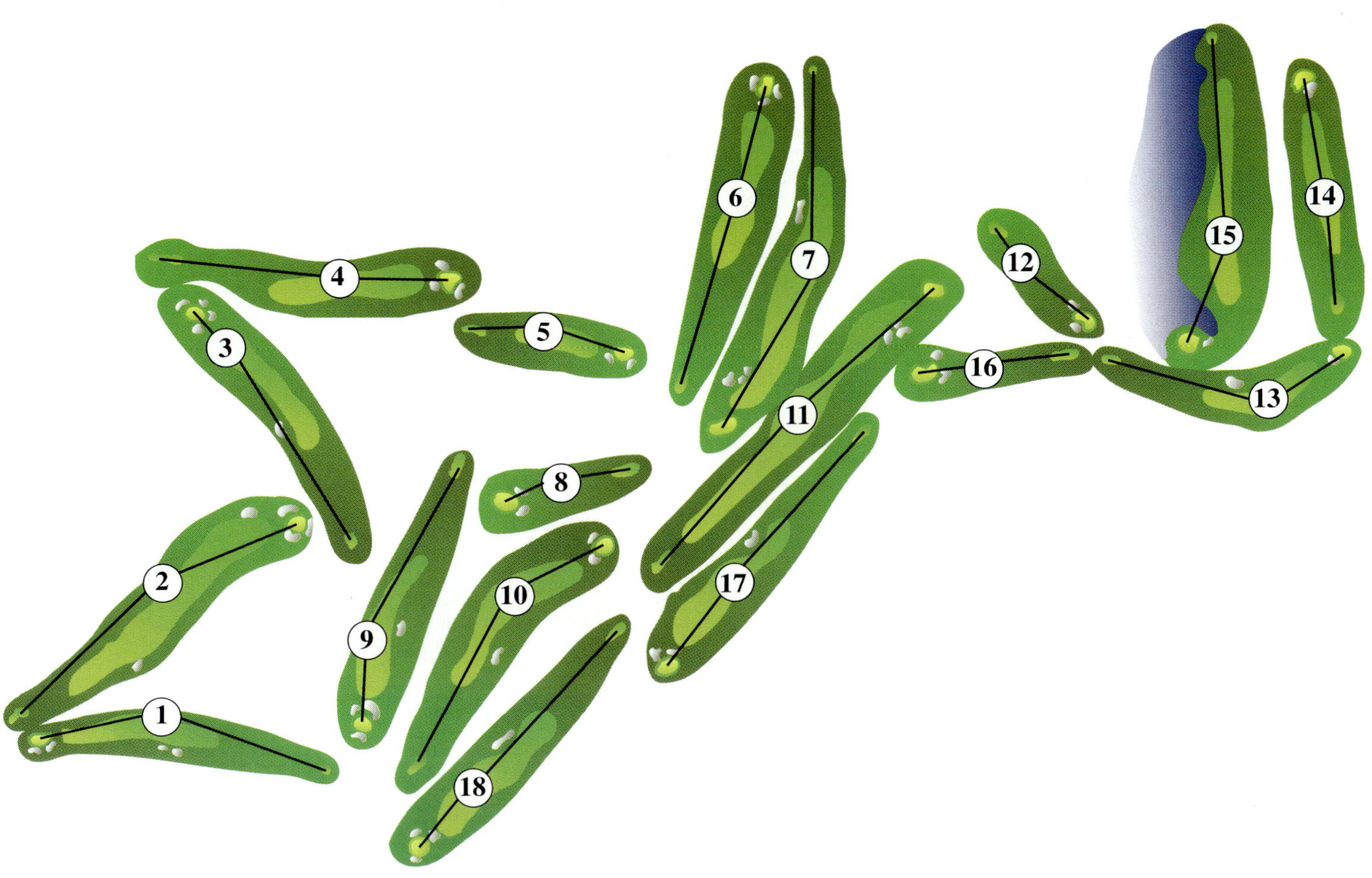

THE COURSE: CALLAWAY GARDENS, PINE MOUNTAIN , GEORGIA

*Y*ou'll find high stakes, familiar faces and fierce competition at the PGA TOUR's Buick Challenge played on Callaway Gardens Mountain View Course. Tight tree-lined fairways are the hallmark of Callaway Garden's challenging course. Architects Dick Wilson and Joe Lee must have had tournament play in mind when they designed this gorgeous par 72 course. The professionals marvel at the famous Number 15, one of the course's most intriguing holes where the threat of water looms over both the tee and approach shots.

The Buick Challenge has seen some of the greatest names in golf competitions during the past 25 years. The tournament originated in Columbus, Georgia and moved to Callaway Gardens six years ago. Today players, their families and fans look forward to the luxurious resort that combines natural beauty, horticulture, and outstanding recreational opportunities for the entire family.

Dates:	September 26-29
Network:	ESPN
Times:	Sat /Sun 4:00-6:00 EST
Yardage:	7057
Par:	72
Slope:	138
Rating:	74.1
Total Purse:	$1,000,000
1st Prize:	$180,000
1995 Winner:	Fred Funk
1995 Winning Score:	272 (69,67,69,67)
Principal Charitable Beneficiary:	Boys Club, West Georgia Youths Council
Ticket Information:	1-706-324-0411

1

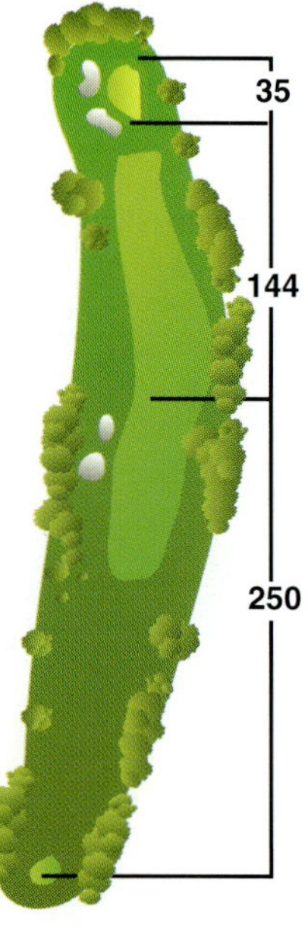

**Par 4
412 yards**

A downhill dogleg to the left requires a slight draw for the second shot from a slightly downhill lie. Two yawning bunkers guard the left side of a two-tiered green.

2

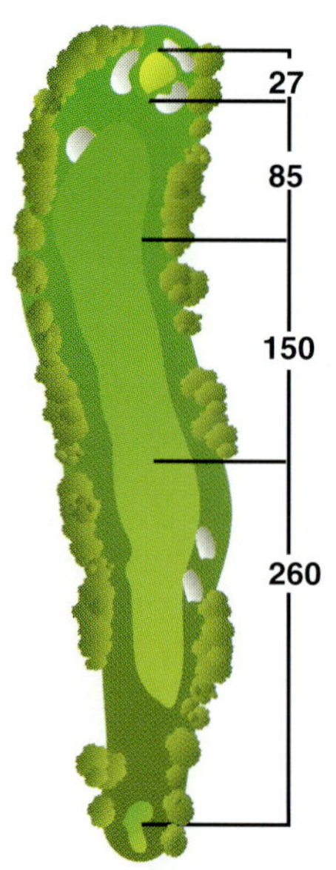

**Par 5
508 yards**

A good birdie hole. The fairway doglegs right around a grove of trees. Stay left for an open approach to the green.

3

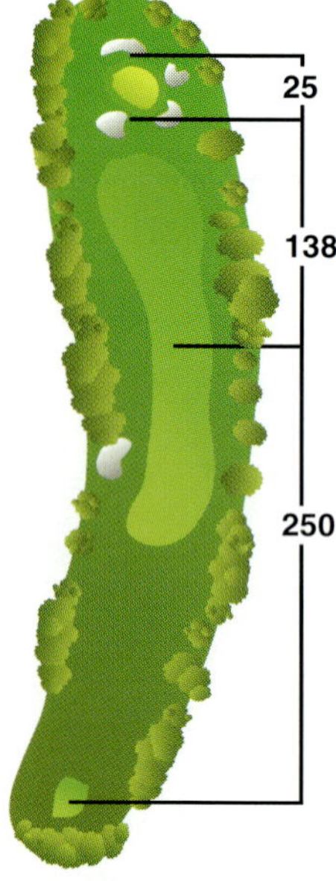

**Par 4
400 yards**

Aim to the right to clear dense trees on left. The golfer must carry his approach shot onto a heavily bunkered green.

4

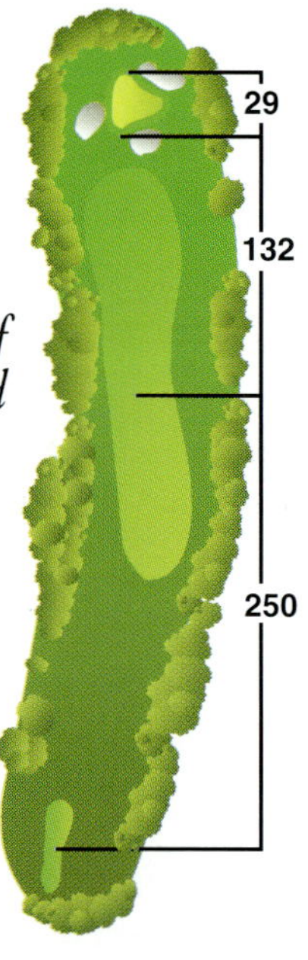

**Par 4
397 yards**

The tee shot must favor, the left side of the fairway to afford an open shot to the green. A downhill slope to the right makes putting difficult.

5

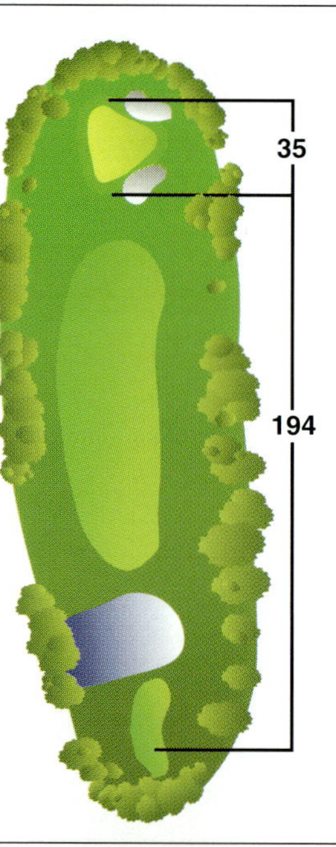

**Par 3
212 yards**

Address the ball off the tee with a long iron or fairway wood. Heavy timber to left of fairway could spell disaster to a straying tee shot.

6

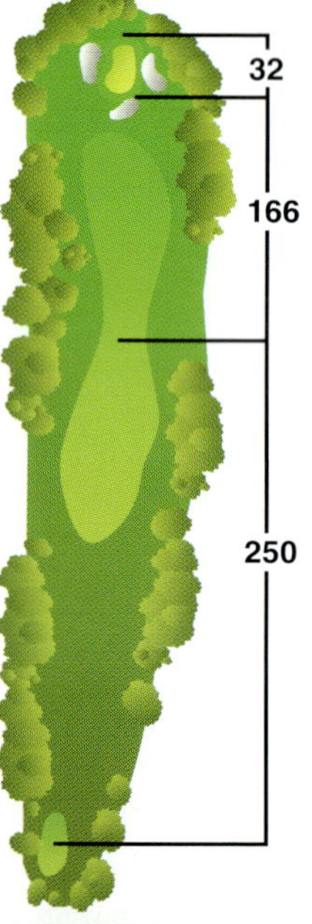

**Par 4
432 yards**

A long uphill hole requiring a straight tee shot, then a long iron to reach the well bunkered green.

7

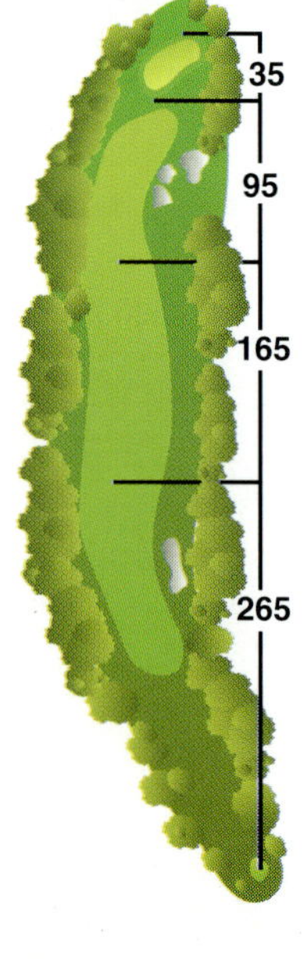

**Par 5
543 yards**

The tee shot, requires a slight fade to enable a green reaching second shot. A hole to pick up a stroke.

8

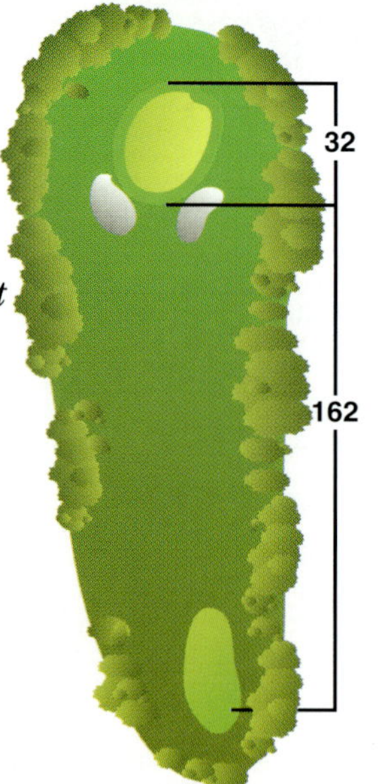

**Par 3
178 yards**

Proper club selection is a must for this deceptive downhill hole.

9

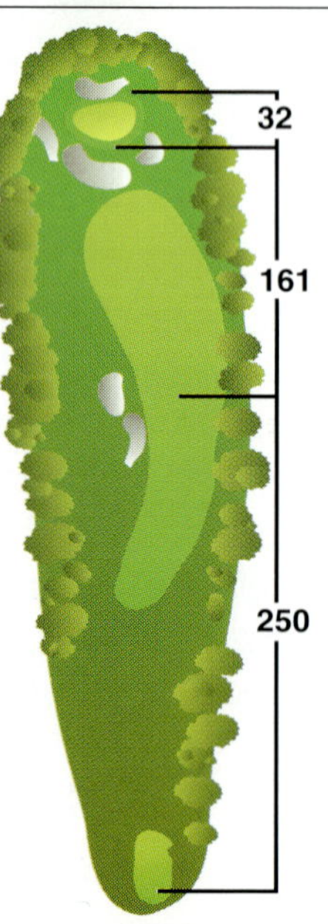

**Par 4
427 yards**

The player must pinpoint his second shot with a meduim iron to clear front or rear bunkers. A difficult putting surface, one of the most demanding on the course.

10

Par 4
431 yards

A slight dogleg to the right, with bunkers guarding right side of the fairway. A medium iron shot to slightly elevated green.

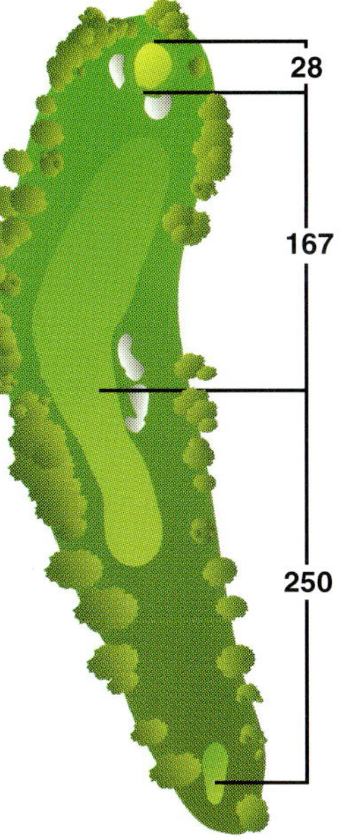

11

Par 5
546 yards

Two large bunkers tighten the second shot on this narrow, straight fairway finesse is required on the approach to the bunkered, rolling green.

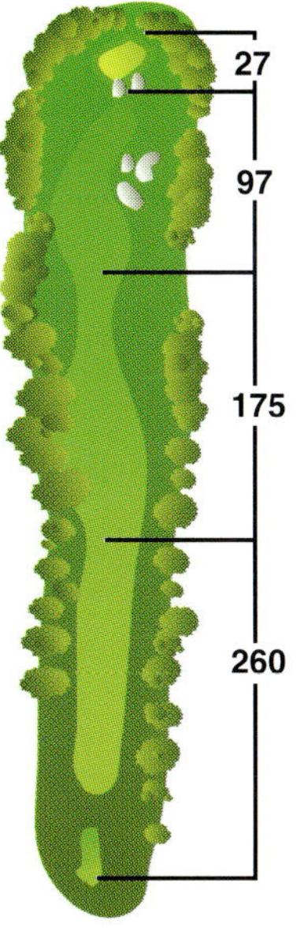

12

Par 3
186 yards

This scenic hole requires a long to medium iron onto the green. Accuracy is needed to stay out of woods to right, water to left.

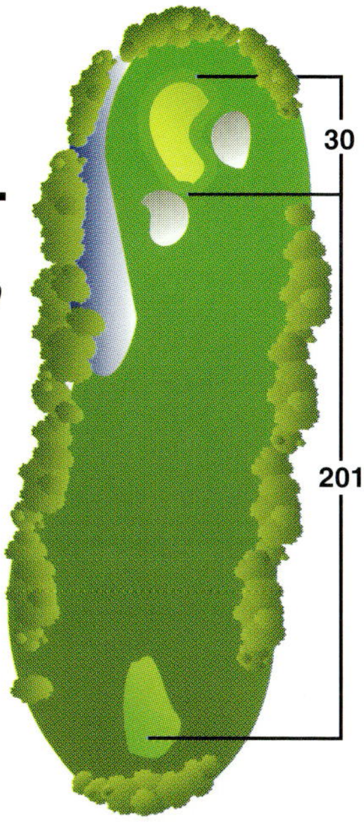

13

Par 4
367 yards

A chance to pick up a shot on par. A sharp dogleg left over a hillside bunder leaves a short approach to the fairly open green.

14

Par 4
421 yards

A long drive will carry the hill, but a medium iron to the green must be accurate. Bunkers at the foot of the green and a sharp decline into a rough over the green spell disaster.

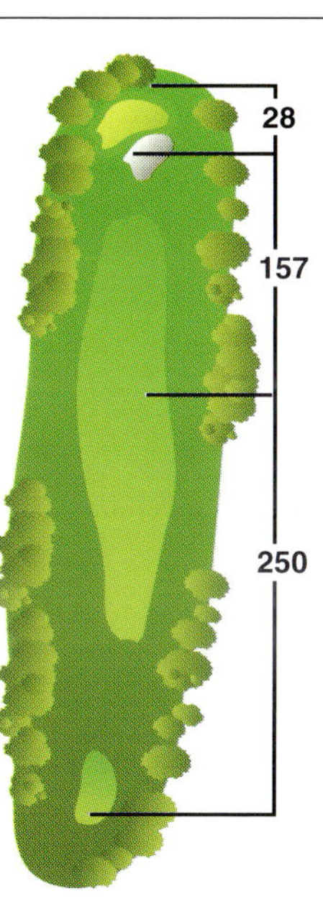

15

Par 5
539 yards

A sloping fairway crossing water twice requires accuracy. The decision rests with the player either to lay up or go over a finger of water to a tempting green.

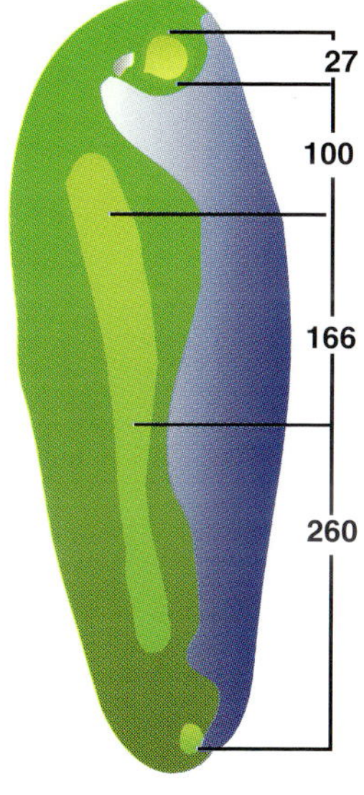

16

Par 3
218 yards

A long-iron or fairway wood will reach this hole. The sloping green, however, makes for a demanding and treacherous putt.

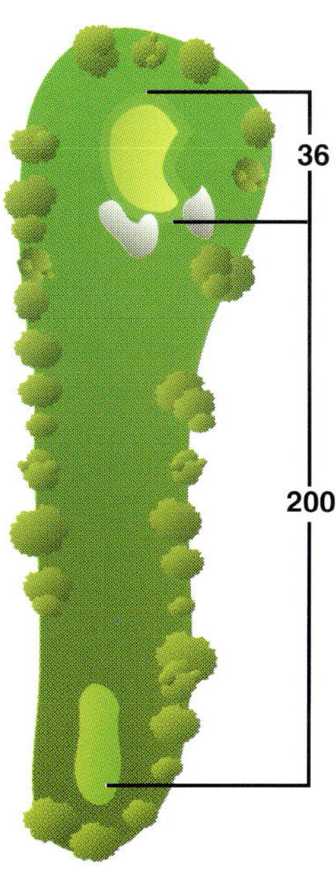

17

Par 4
404 yards

A straight away hole, its oblong shaped green is well bunkered.

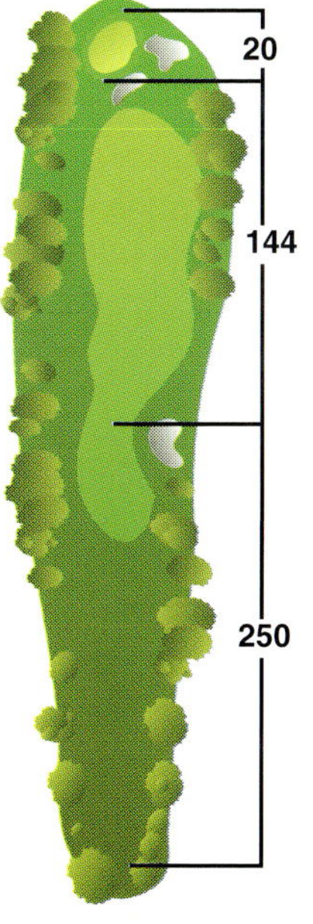

18

Par 4
432 yards

A long tee shot past a bunker on the right. Then a long or medium iron shot onto a huge green protected by two front bunkers.

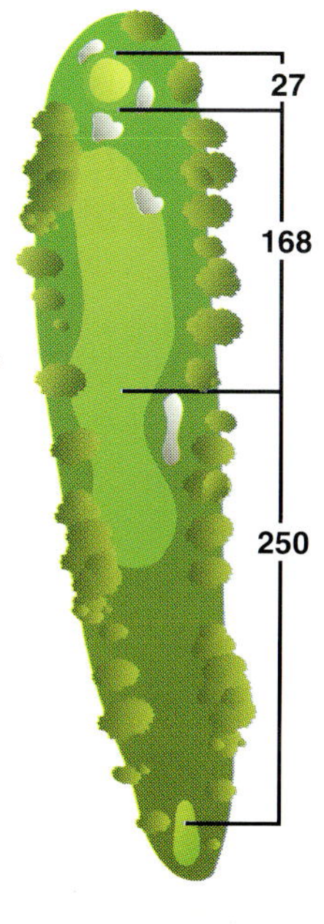

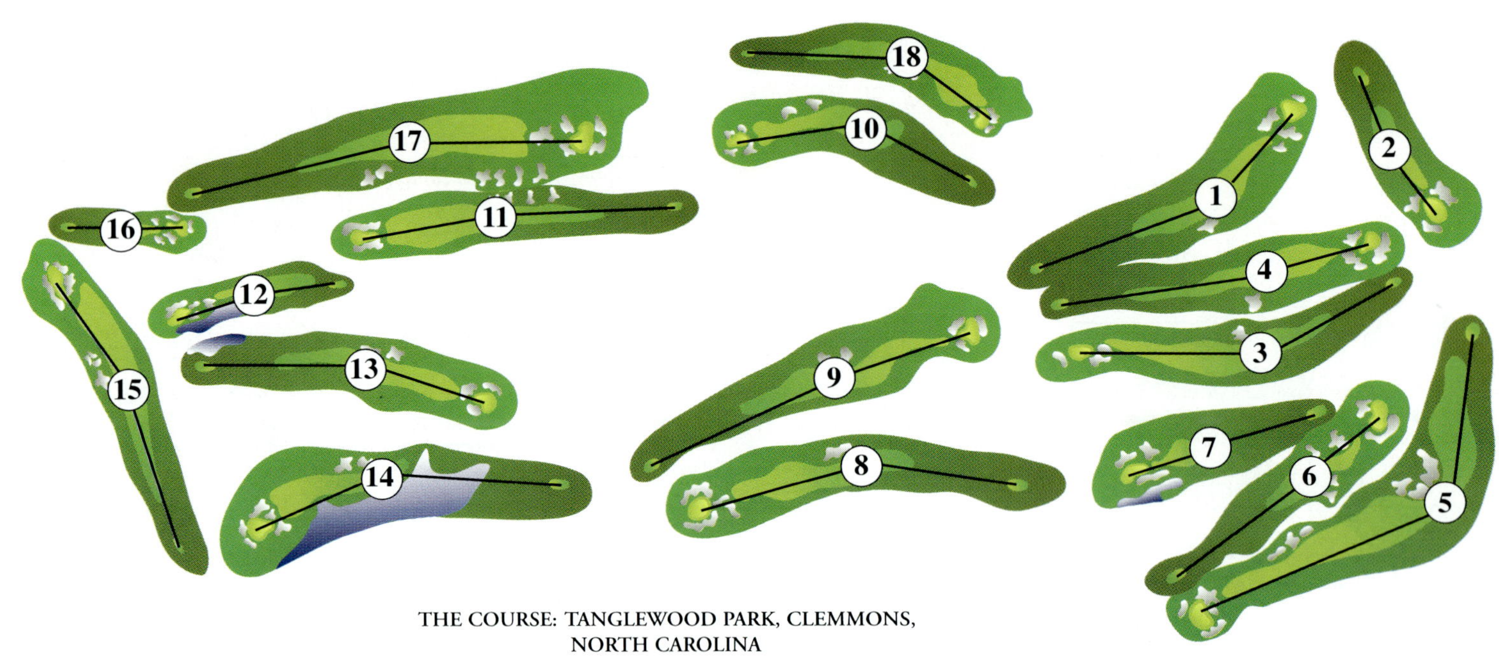

THE COURSE: TANGLEWOOD PARK, CLEMMONS,
NORTH CAROLINA

*I*n 1996 The Vantage Championship will celebrate its 10th season at Tanglewood Park , the site of the 1974 PGA Championship. Twenty-two years after hosting the event, this 1300 acres unveils all its splendor once again. A golfing masterpiece consistently ranked as one of the premier public facilities in the world.

Course designer, Robert Trent Jones, once said this is his finest works, when originally built in 1957. The Championship course already was an excellent test of golf. However, after being selected as the site of the PGA Championship in the early 70's, once again Mr. Jones was called upon to redesign the course with the challenge to make the course not only tough but maintain its beauty as well. Jones increased the course's all around difficulty from 6500 to 7050 yards in length. The chaddition of 45 new sand traps and enlargement of the existing 65 sand traps, adding a new lake and reducing the green size on number 12 from 10,000 to 8,000 square feet; Jones finished work has made Tanglewood one of the most challenging golf courses in the World. Tanglewood will remain the home site of the Vantage Championship long into the future.

Dates:	Septmenber 27-29	
Network:	ESPN	
Times:	Fri	5:00-7:00 EST
	Sat	4:30-6:30 EST
	Sun	4:30-7:00 EST
Yardage:	6706	
Par:	72	
Slope:	135	
Rating:	72.3	
Total Purse:	$1,500,000	
1st Prize:	$225,000	
1995 Winner:	Hale Irwin	
1995 Winning Score:	199 (66,68,65)	
Principal Charitable Beneficiary:	Tanglewood Park and 60 Charities	
Ticket Information:	$16.00 Daily/ $60.00 Season Badge	

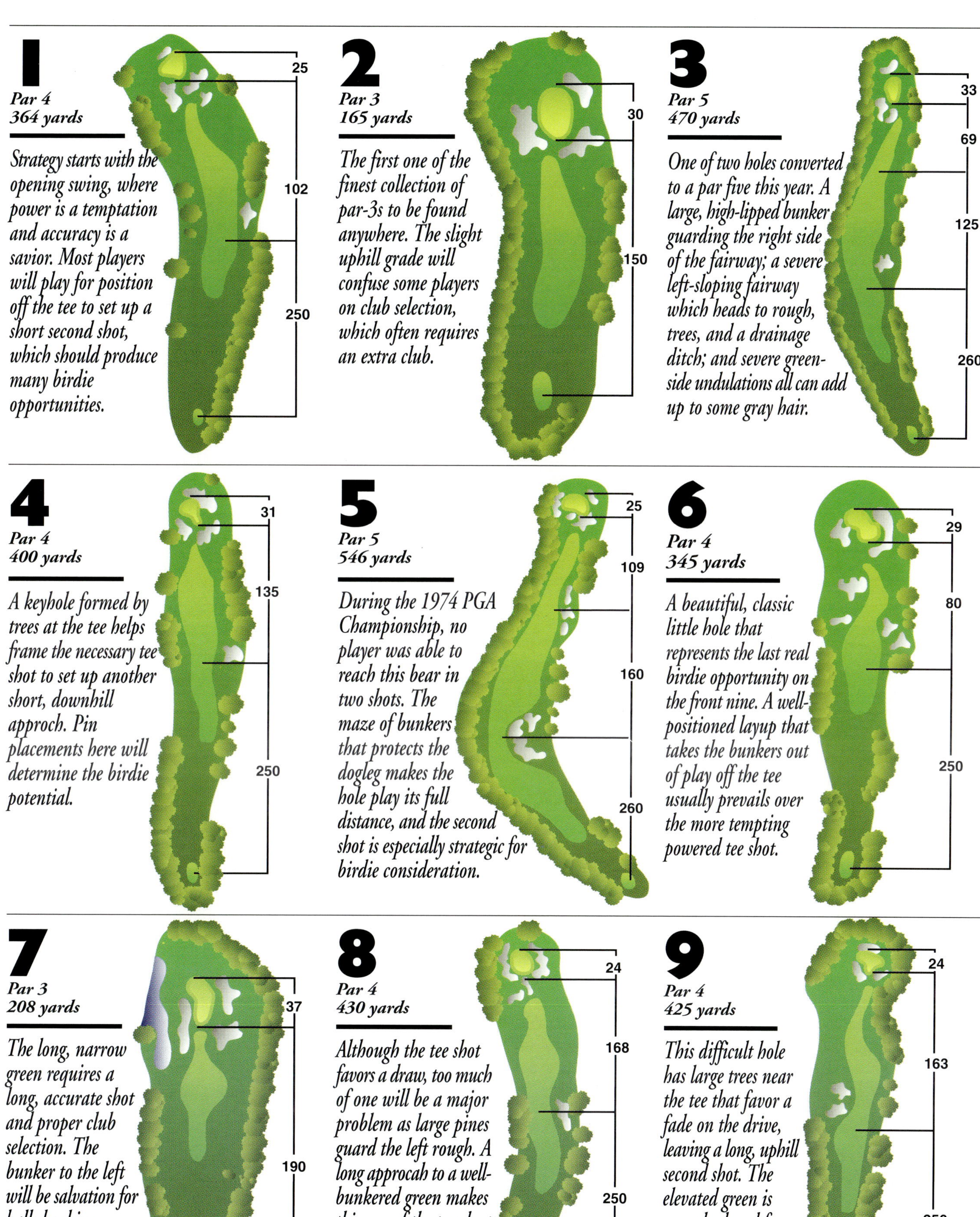
1
Par 4
364 yards

Strategy starts with the
opening swing, where
power is a temptation
and accuracy is a
savior. Most players
will play for position
off the tee to set up a
short second shot,
which should produce
many birdie
opportunities.

25
102
250

2
Par 3
165 yards

The first one of the
finest collection of
par-3s to be found
anywhere. The slight
uphill grade will
confuse some players
on club selection,
which often requires
an extra club.

30
150

3
Par 5
470 yards

One of two holes converted
to a par five this year. A
large, high-lipped bunker
guarding the right side
of the fairway; a severe
left-sloping fairway
which heads to rough,
trees, and a drainage
ditch; and severe green-
side undulations all can add
up to some gray hair.

33
69
125
260

4
Par 4
400 yards

A keyhole formed by
trees at the tee helps
frame the necessary tee
shot to set up another
short, downhill
approch. Pin
placements here will
determine the birdie
potential.

31
135
250

5
Par 5
546 yards

During the 1974 PGA
Championship, no
player was able to
reach this bear in
two shots. The
maze of bunkers
that protects the
dogleg makes the
hole play its full
distance, and the second
shot is especially strategic for
birdie consideration.

25
109
160
260

6
Par 4
345 yards

A beautiful, classic
little hole that
represents the last real
birdie opportunity on
the front nine. A well-
positioned layup that
takes the bunkers out
of play off the tee
usually prevails over
the more tempting
powered tee shot.

29
80
250

7
Par 3
208 yards

The long, narrow
green requires a
long, accurate shot
and proper club
selection. The
bunker to the left
will be salvation for
balls hooking
toward the water.

37
190

8
Par 4
430 yards

Although the tee shot
favors a draw, too much
of one will be a major
problem as large pines
guard the left rough. A
long approch to a well-
bunkered green makes
this one of the toughest
holes on the course.

24
168
250

9
Par 4
425 yards

This difficult hole
has large trees near
the tee that favor a
fade on the drive,
leaving a long, uphill
second shot. The
elevated green is
severely sloped from
back to front,
requiring players to
stay below the hole.

24
163
250

10

Par 4
364 yards

34

97

250

Pines to the left and bunkers to the right will encourage many players to play position shots to set up birdie opportunities on this short hole. However, it is very important to remain below the cup on this sloping green.

11

Par 5
490 yards

40

63

125

255

This hole will reward the accurate hitter with a birdie. A few of the long ball strikers may even be putting for an eagle. The demanding tee shot, which needs to stay along the right hillside of the fairway, and out of the severe bunkers containing lovegrass, will likely determine the outcome of the player.

12

Par 3
182 yards

36

164

Another one of those dandy par-3s. The prevailing wind is usually a factor as it blows across toward the pond on the left. Consequently, the bunkers to the right will catch a lot of balls as players try to

13

Par 4
395 yards

30

130

250

The strategic tee shot favors a fade to a position on top of the hill, but major trouble awaits the player who lets it go too far or too long on the resulting downslope. The green is well-guarded by numerous bunkers. A shot-maker's delight.

14

Par 4
420 yards

26

152

255

Rated by Golf Digest as one of the best 100 holes in America from the championship tees. Trevino played this hole in the PGA Championship by starting his tee shot over the lake to the left. The approach will be particularly difficult from a sidehill lie to an elevated, well trapped green.

15

Par 4
359 yards

32

93

250

A conservative tee shot to the right sets up a short approach and a birdie opportunity. The green runs diagonally across from the player, making pin placement and club selection important.

16

Par 3
183 yards

34

166

All to be seen from the tee of this difficult par-3 are lots of bunkers with a flagstick nestled among their grasp. This severe green produces a tough pin placement from almost anywhere.

17

Par 5
535 yards

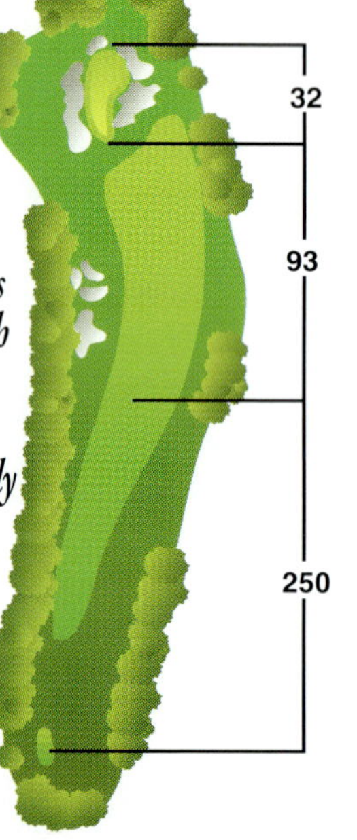

32

99

160

260

Officials have prescribed a severe cut of rough near the green, along with its usual sea of large bunkers to penalize players who unsuccessfully try to hit the green in two shots. A strategically placed second shot, short of all the trouble, should produce a birdie opportunity for the thinking player.

18

Par 4
425 yards

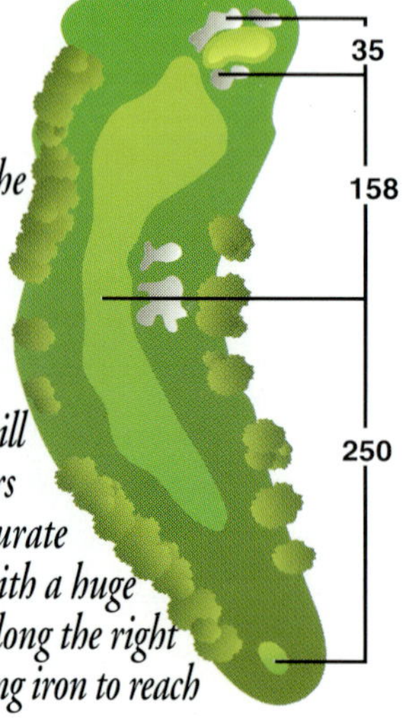

35

158

250

The cemetary to the left of the green offers an omen of what's in store on this very tough finishing hole. Uphill all the way, players Owill need an accurate tee shot, flirting with a huge series of bunkers along the right side, and a good long iron to reach the sloping green.

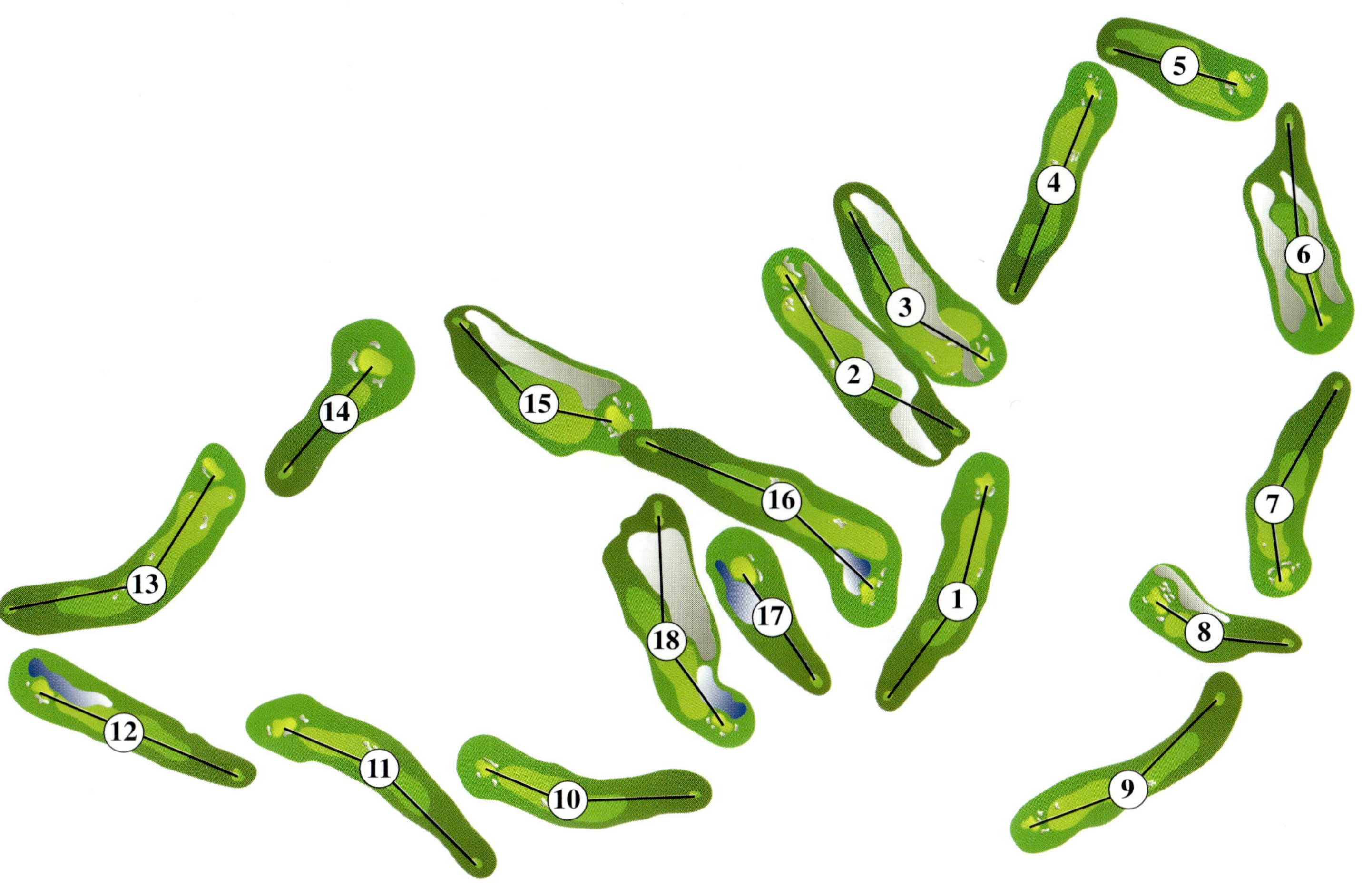

THE COURSE: TPC SUMMERLIN, LAS VEGAS, NEVADA

At the heart of Summerlin's Hills South Village is the Tournament Players Club at Summerlin, Nevada's only stadium course and member of the PGA TOUR's prestigious network of TPC courses. Designed to accommodate spectators with nature amphitheaters and vantage points for unrestricted viewing, the TPC at Summerlin is operated by the PGA TOUR® and began hosting the Las Vegas Invitational in 1992.

An 18-hole championship course designed by architect Bobby Weed and PGA TOUR® professional Fuzzy Zoeller, the TPC at Summerlin has become Nevada's premier private course and was recently ranked by GolfWeek as one of the two top courses in the state.

Dates:	October 3-6, 1996
Network:	ESPN
Times:	Fri 12:00-2:00 / 4:00-6:00 EST
	Sat 3:30-6:00 EST
	Sun 3:30-6:00 EST
Yardage:	6963
Par:	72
Slope:	128
Rating:	71.9
Total Purse:	$1,500,000
1st Prize:	$270,00
1995 Winner:	Jim Furyk
1994 Winning Score:	331 (67,65,65,67,67)
Principal Charitable Beneficiary:	Las Vegas Founders Golf Foundation
Ticket Information:	1-702-382-6616

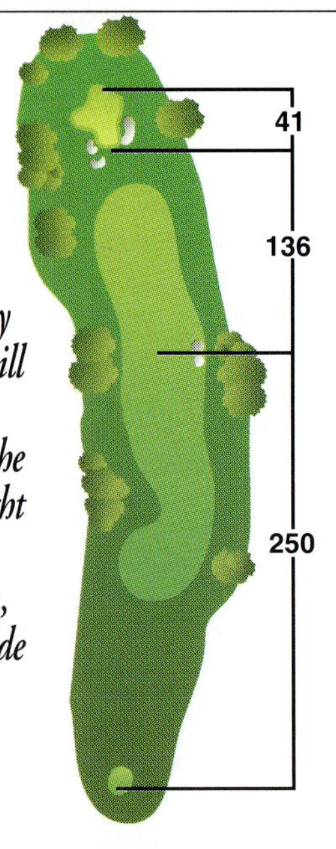

1

Par 4
408 yards

The opening hole plays straight away to a slightly downhill landing area and green. Positioning the tee shot near the right fairway bunker opens up the green, especially the left side pin placements.

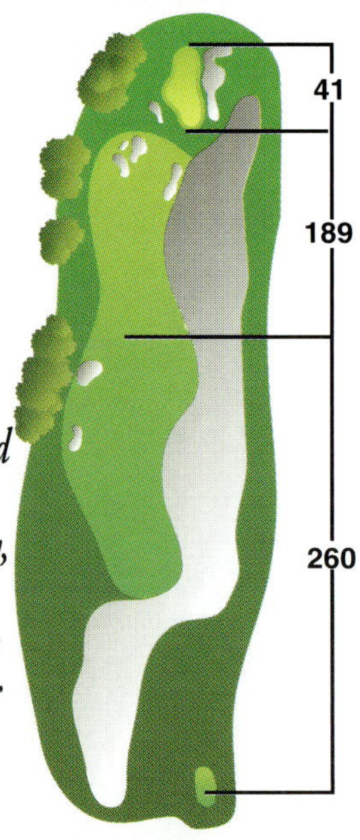

2

Par 4
469 yards

A long, tough, downhill par 4, along an existing wash. The tee shot angle must be figured in ralation to the diagonal wash carry, with bunkers left. The sloping green is large with a bunker bordering the right side.

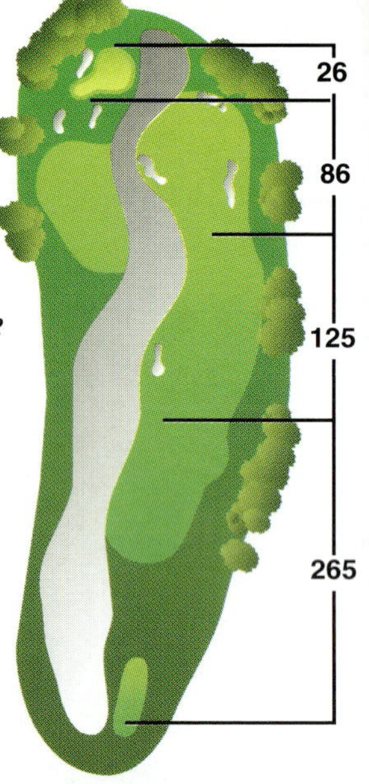

3

Par 5
492 yards

A short reachable par 5 with a double fairway approach. The green is perched above an existng wash, presenting alternate routes for the second shot. Eventually, the wash must be carried. The hole plays slightly buphill and into the prevailing wind.

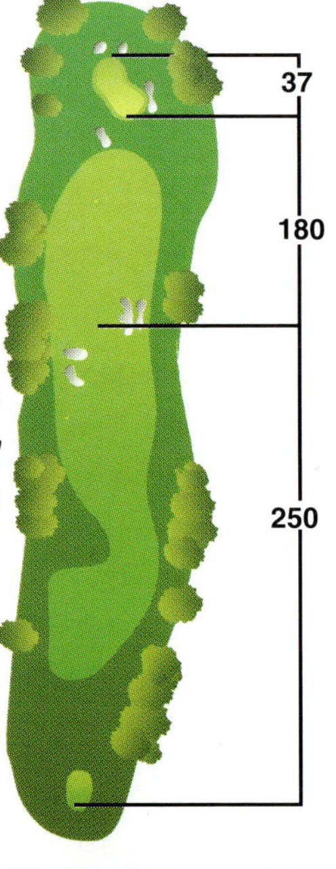

4

Par 4
450 yards

A slightly down hill hole with fairway bunkers left and right. The green sets up slightly right to left with a deep bunker front right.

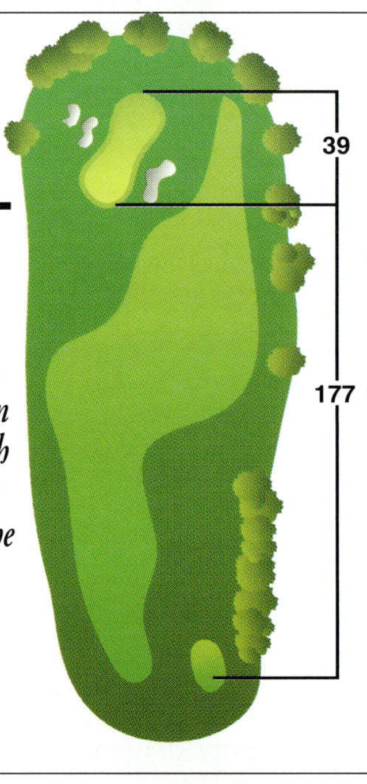

5

Par 3
197 yards

A scenic, demanding downhill par 3 crossing a wash. The green sets in left to right with challenging pin placements to the rear.

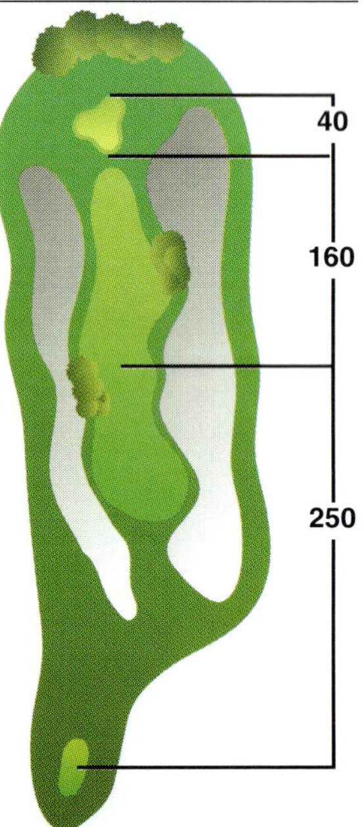

6

Par 4
430 yards

A slightly uphil par 4 with desert flanking each side of the fairway. The green is elevated, and sets in left to right with no bunkers. Choose an extra club for the approach shot.

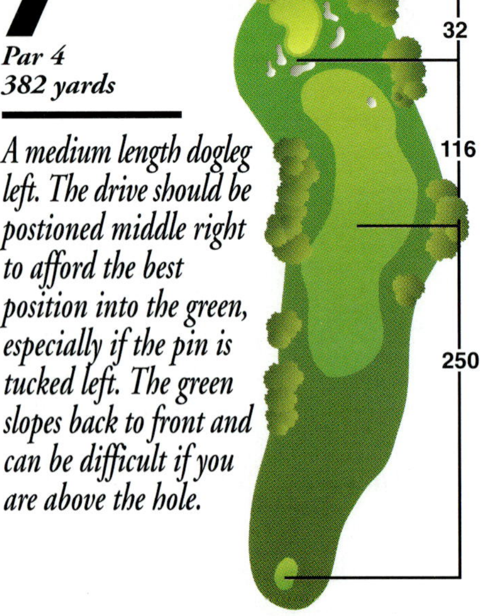

7

Par 4
382 yards

A medium length dogleg left. The drive should be postioned middle right to afford the best position into the green, especially if the pin is tucked left. The green slopes back to front and can be difficult if you are above the hole.

8

Par 3
239 yards

The longest par 3, playing left to right with a wash running down the right side. A large green with bail-out left awaits the tee shot. A good spectator hole with mounds affording views of #8,3,2 and 9.

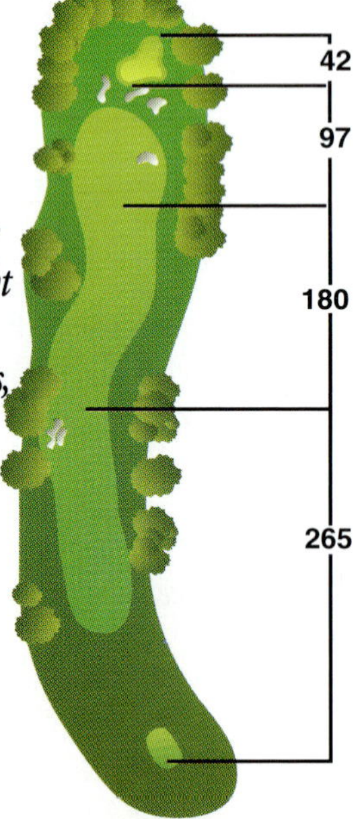

9

Par 5
563 yards

A long downhill par 5, slightly left to right hole. The green is protected by bunkers, both front and left.

10

Par 4
460 yards

A slightly downhill par 4 playing left-to-right with fairway bunkers left. A large deep bunker is positioned front right with the back of the green falling away slightly.

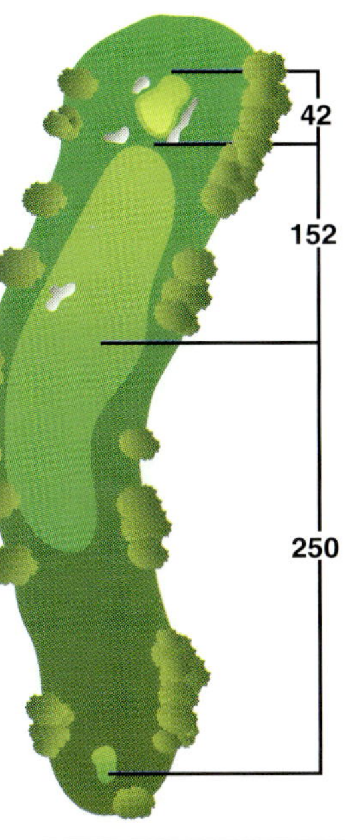

11

Par 4
448 yards

A right-to-left tee shot with fairway bunkers challenging the player on the left side. The approach is to a green making any pin placement along the right side of the green a challenge. Good viewing from the mounds on the right

12

Par 3
182 yards

This slightly down hill hole has a lake just beyond the landing area in the right, which extends along side the green making and pin placement along the right side of the green a challenge. Good viewing from the mounds on the right.

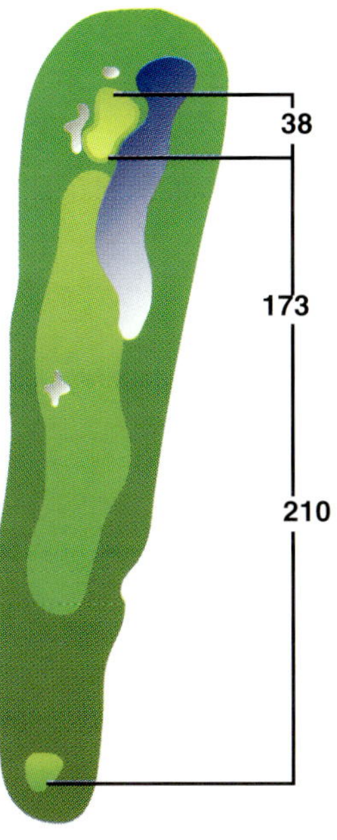

13

Par 5
606 yards

Typically, a 3-shot hole demanding 2 strategic shots to set up the approach. The hole sets up right-to-left off the tee with a cluster of bunkers on the left. A fairway bunker short of the green emphasizes placement for the apprach to the split level green. Don't be long.

14

Par 3
156 yards

The shortest par 3 with a right-to-left orientation. The green is wide, but somewaht shallow in depth with bunkers left and right.

15

Par 4
341 yards

The desert runs the length of the hole on the left with bunkers separating the 2-level fairway. Golfers have alternate routes to play the hole. The green is long and narrow and elevated, with bunkers surrounding it.

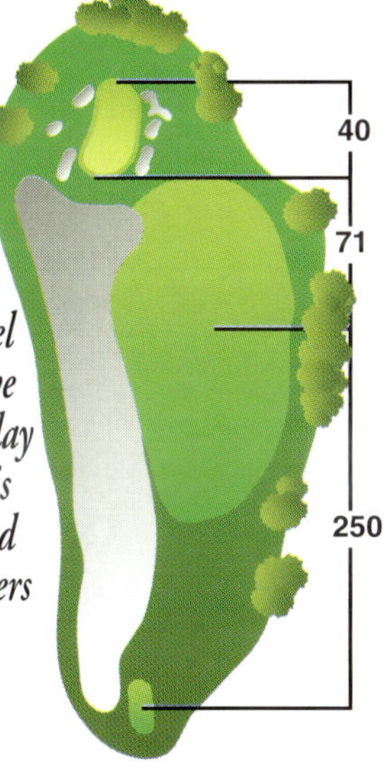

16

Par 5
560 yards

This slightly uphill tee shot presents a gamble opportunity for players going for the green in two. A lake guards the front of the green with bunkers behind.

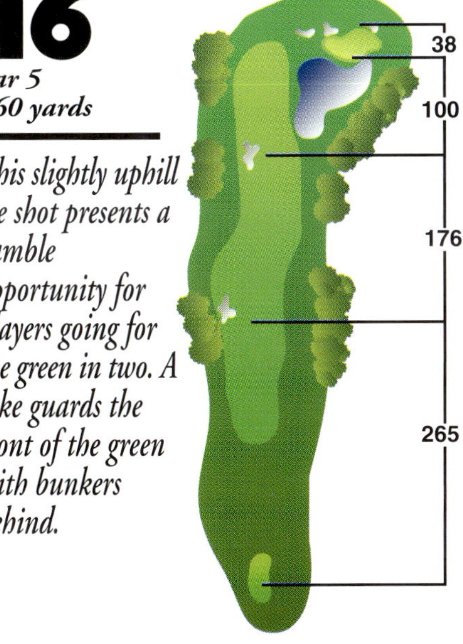

17

Par 3
196 yards

A medium length downhill hole with water protecting the left side. A long green with bunkers on the right to catch the bail-out shot. A great spectaator hole.

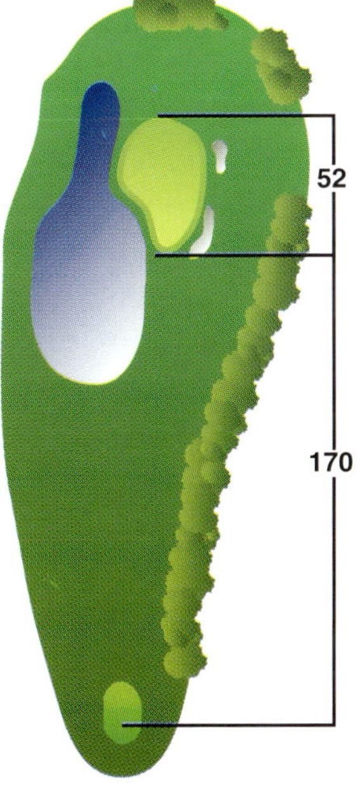

18

Par 4
444 yards

A long, slightly uphill hole requiring the tee shot to diagonally across a desert wash. The approach is to a deep green protected by a small lake on the left. A challenging finish with great spectator viewing.

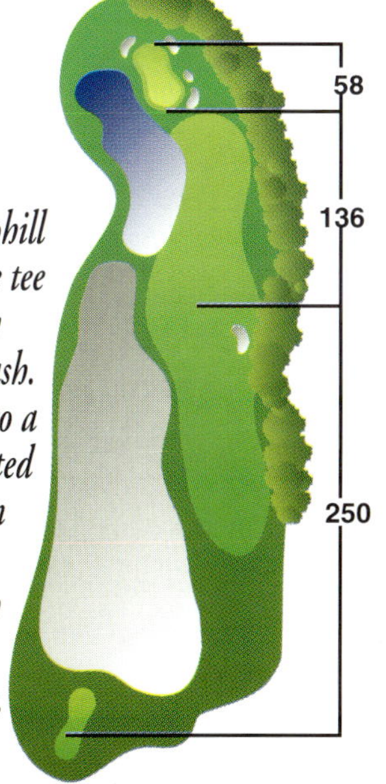

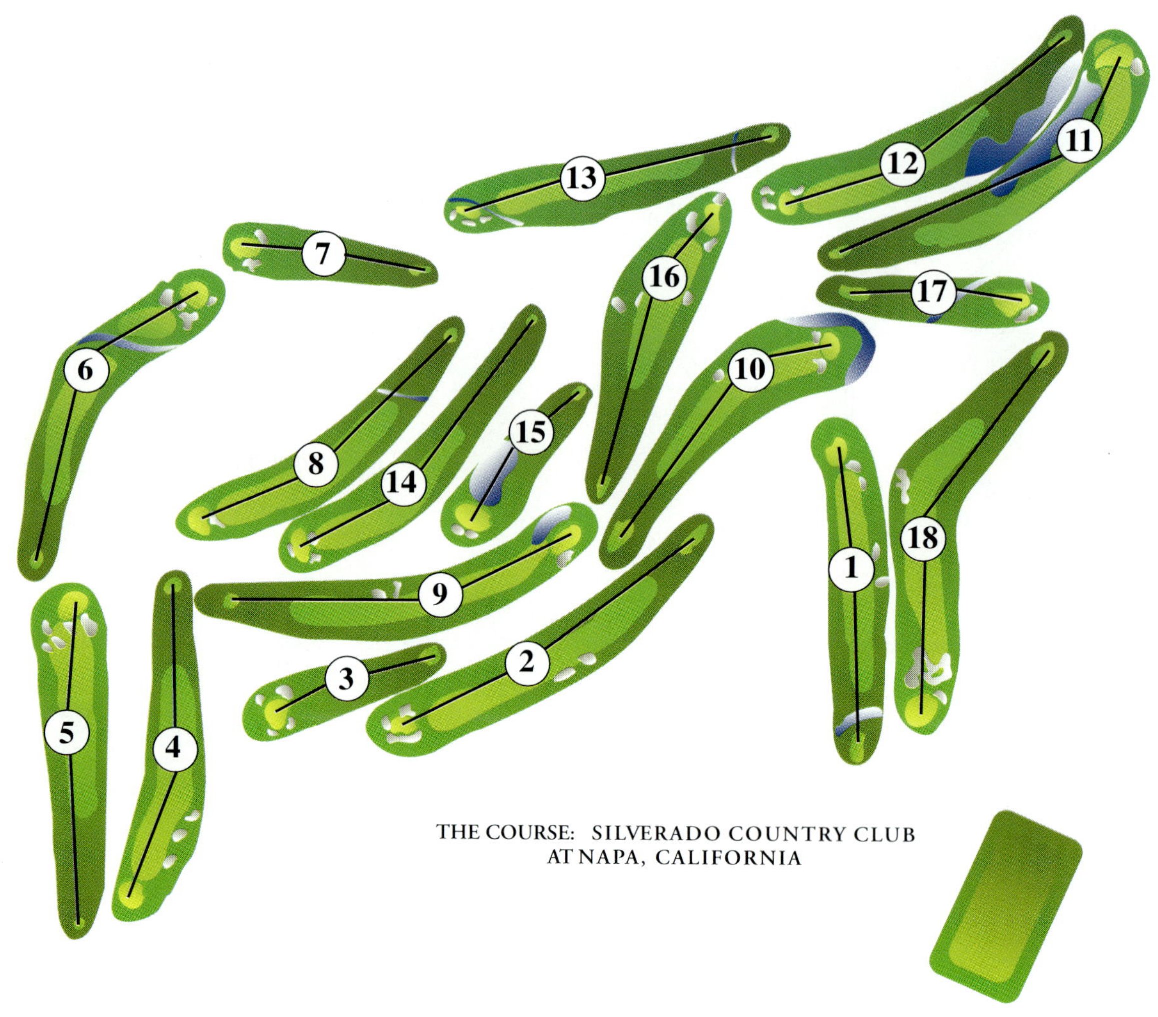

THE COURSE: SILVERADO COUNTRY CLUB
AT NAPA, CALIFORNIA

*L*ocated in the picturesque, rolling hills of Napa Valley, Silverado Country Club is one of the most prestigious golf clubs in northern California. With a colonial mansion serving as the backdrop and heart of the scenic resort, Silverado was opened in 1955 and has been recognized as one of America's "Best Resort Courses" by Golf Digest.

Silverado hosted its first professional tournament in 1968, the Kaiser International Open Invitational, which was won by Kermit Zarley. Between 1977 and 1980, the tournament became the Anheuser Busch Golf Classic. Twenty-six years later winning in Napa, in 1994, Zarley again found himself in the winner's circle at Silverado when he carded his first title on the Senior PGA TOUR with a playoff victory over Isao Aoski.

During its illustrious history, Siverado Country Club has witnessed many of the greatest names in professional golf record victories over its peaceful, oak-line fairways: Jack Nicklaus (Kaiser International, 1968); Johnny Miller (Kaiser International, 1974;75); Tom Watson (Anheuser-Busch Classic, 1978); Lee Travino (The Transamerica, 1990); Bob Charles (The Transamerica, 1992); and Dave Stockton (The Transamerica, 1993).

DATES:	October 11-13
NETWORKS:	ESPN
TIMES:	Fri 3:30-6:30 EST
	Sat. 1:30-3:30 EST
	Sun. 3:00-6:00 EST
PRINCIPAL CHARITABLE BENEFICIARY:	Queen of the Valley Hospital Foundation Boys & Girls Club.
Yardage:	6,685
Par:	72
Slope:	129
Rating:	72.4
Total Purse:	$112,500
1st Prize:	$625,000
1995 Winner:	Lee Trevino
1995 Winning Score:	201 (66,69,66)
Ticket Information:	(707) 252-8687

1

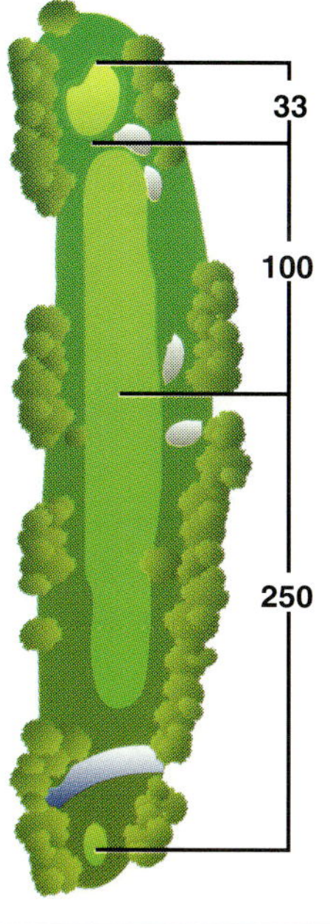

Par 4
366 yards

A sneaky, yet good starting hole. It has a creek in front of the tee, fairway bunkers on the right, and a giant oak tree guarding the left side of the green. If you don't drive the ball in the right center of the fairway, you don't have a clear shot to the green.

2

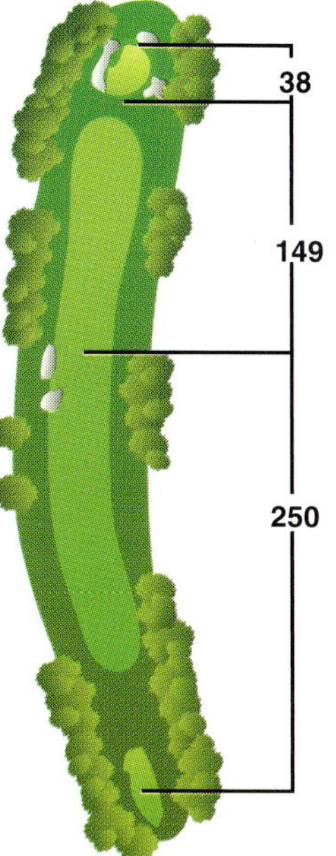

Par 4
418 yards

A dogleg right with fairway bunkers left, it requires two good shots-probably a driver, four iron-to a slightly elevated, well-bunkered green.

3

Par 3
197 yards

All uphill to another well-bunkered hole, it plays about a minimum of 10 yards farther due to the elevation. This hole has quite a bit of undulation on the green with several different tiers on it depending upon pin placement.

4

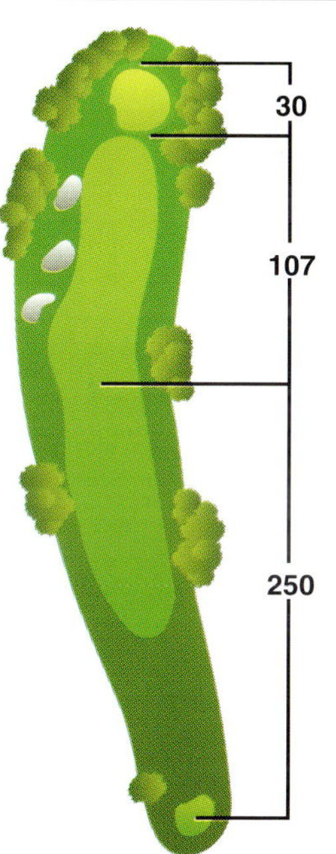

Par 4
372 yards

A "birdie hole." This slight dogleg right travels downhill with fairway bunkers left. Golfers will find a "sneaky" green with big undulation in the center.

5

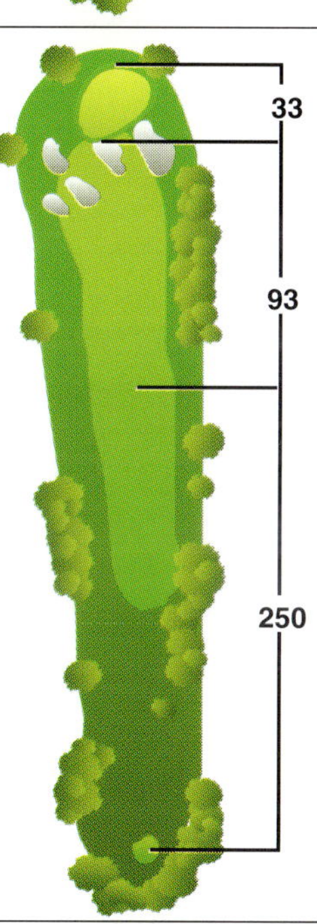

Par 4
359 yards

A premium is placed on the tee shot since out of bounds is left and trees right. A tee shot in the middle of the fairway will leave you with a short iron to an elevated, well-bunkered green that also has undulation.

6

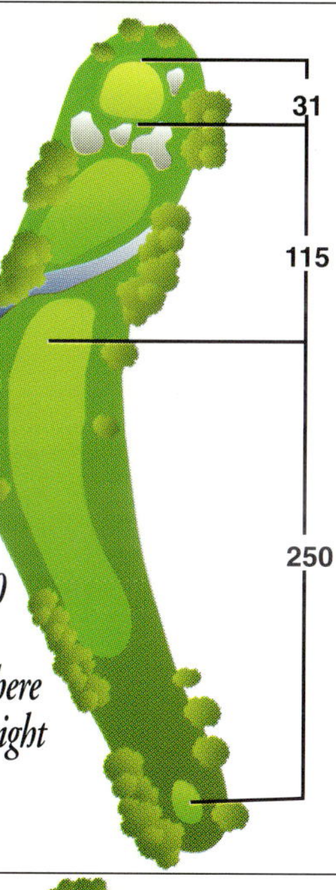

Par 4
380 yards

This severe dogleg right starts off downhill guarded by bunkers. This green offers more undulation than any at the 36-hole golfing facility. A creek located about 120 yards from the green, comes into play, and there is out of bounds both right and left.

7

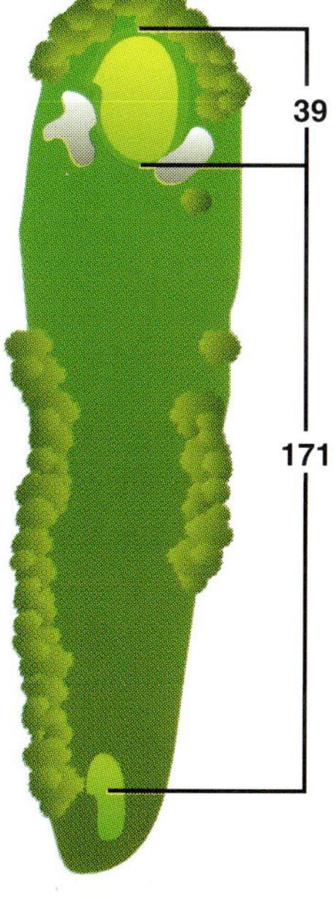

Par 3
191 yards

There's more to this all-downhill hole, which has bunkers left and right of the green. There's also out of bounds left and right.

8

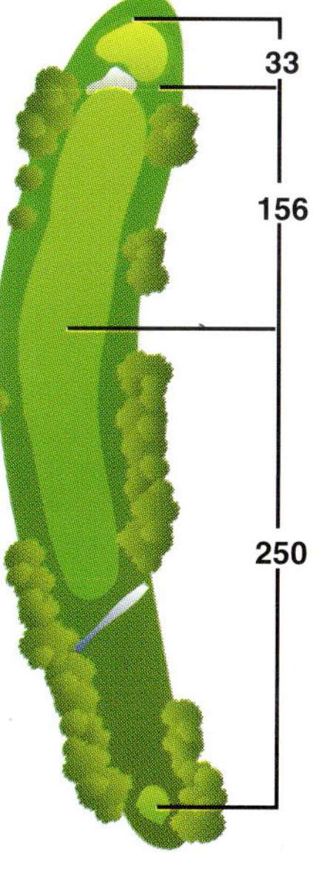

Par 4
422 yards

This dogleg right has a hill in the middle of the fairway and a huge bunker left of the green. The No. 1 handicap hole on the South Course. This hole requires a long tee shot in order to carry the crest of the hill, leaving a player with a mid to long iron onto the green.

9

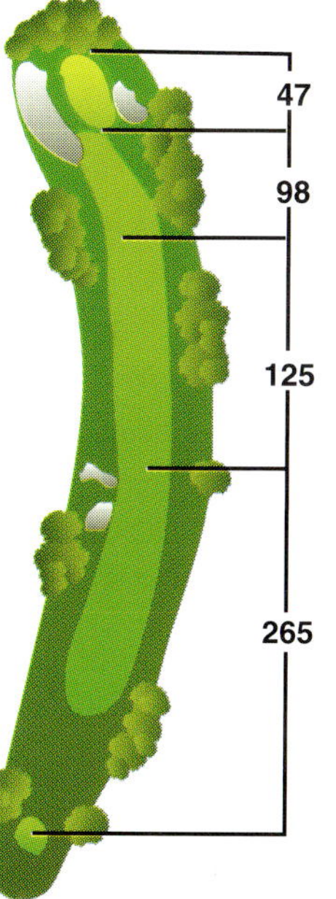

Par 5
512 yards

The only par-5 on the front side, it starts off from an elevated tee and doglegs left with two fairway bunkers left and a pond coming into play near the front of the green. It is easily reachable for the pros in two with a driver to the right-center of the fairway.

10

Par 4
361 yards

This dogleg right, with only one fairway bunker coming into play, finishes on an elevated green that has bunkers left and right. A short hole that rewards players with birdies, it requires left-to-right action off the tee.

11

Par 5
569 yards

This dogleg left is the first of three par-5s on the back nine. There is out of bounds right and water left the length of the hole, may even tougher with a prevailing wind in the player's face that makes the hole play even longer than the actual 569 yards.

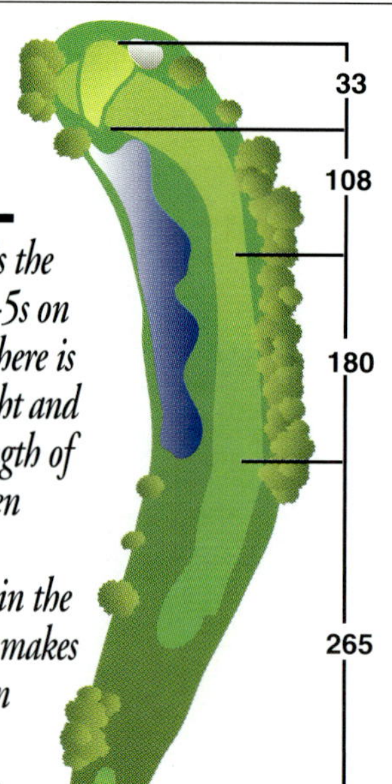

12

Par 4
428 yards

With water left and out of bounds right, this dogleg generally plays downwind. The pros will probably hit driver, four iron onto a green that has bunkers in front and back. An oak tree that overhangs the right side of the green presents problems.

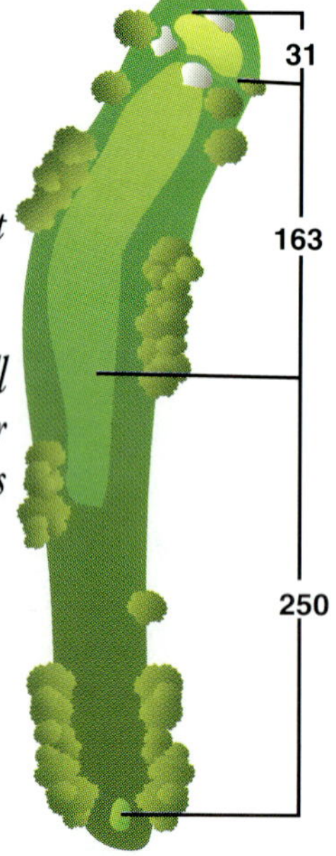

13

Par 5
495 yards

Making this hole more difficult than previous years is a lake that was added to the front of the green. For the most part straightaway, it is sort of a roller coaster with hills coming into play. It's certainly reachable in two.

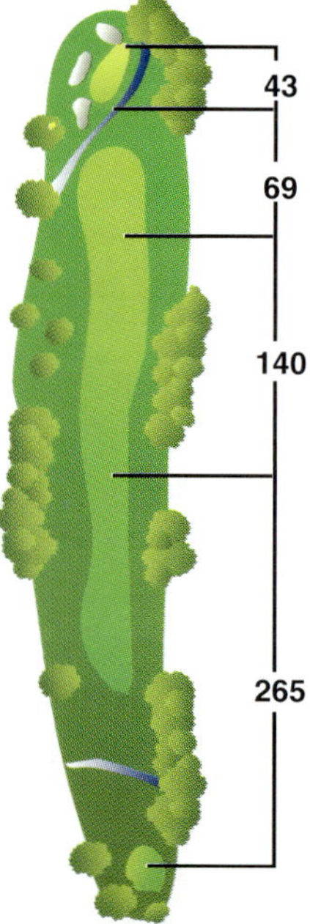

14

Par 4
382 yards

This dogleg right presents a crest in the middle of the fairway bunkers left and right, and bunkers center, left, and right, and very narrow green in depth. Although it's not that long of a hole, a player's second shot must have exact distance or the ball could find a bunker.

15

Par 3
185 yards

A very good par-3. The green is guarded by water to the right and bunkers behind it. There is out of bounds left of the green where it used to be woods. It requires a three or four iron onto the green.

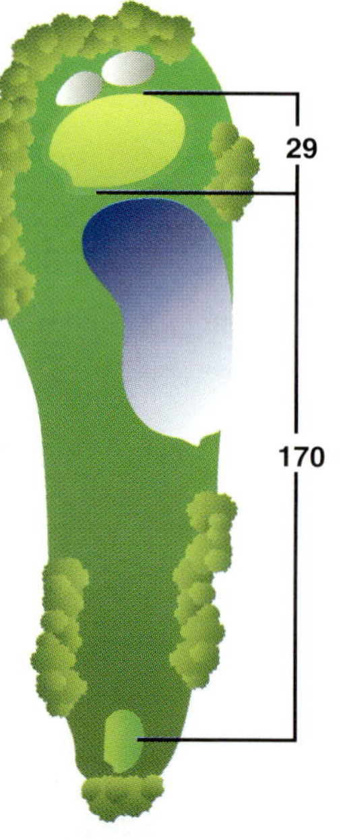

16

Par 4
330 yards

A drive will leave just a sand wedge to the hole. There's an optimum in accuracy off the tee here. Fairway bunkers are located left and right.

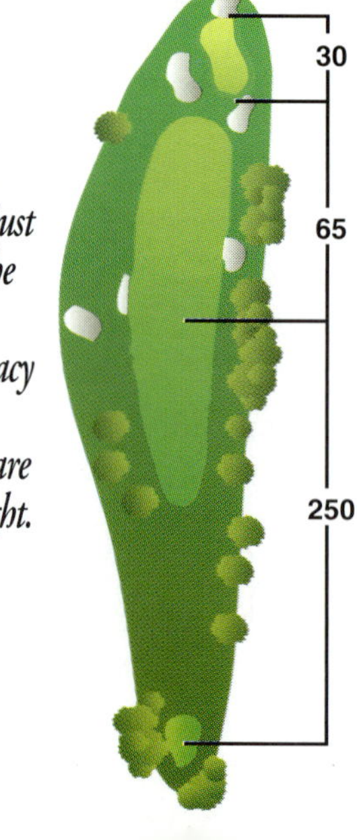

17

Par 3
165 yards

This straightaway hole doesn't appear to be too difficult. But upon further examination, there are bunkers left and right of the green, as well as a hazard in front and left of the green, and several willow trees on the left. Depending on pin placement, the hole plays a variety of different distances.

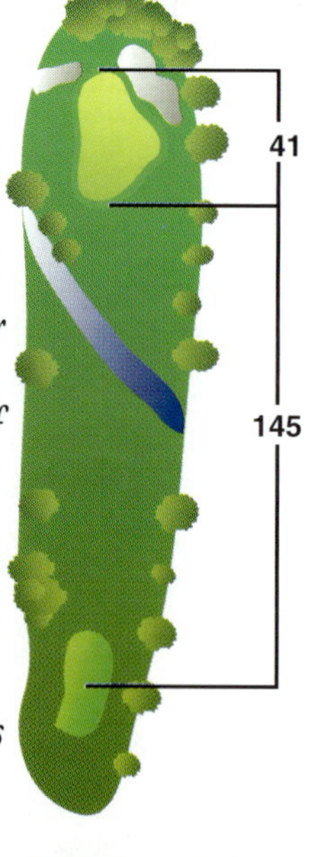

18

Par 5
500 yards

One of the prettiest holes in golf with the Silverado mansion overlooking an extremely big green that has huge fairway bunkers in front, it also presents players with the opportunity of arriving in two and making birdie. It's a severe dogleg left with out of bounds left and trees right.

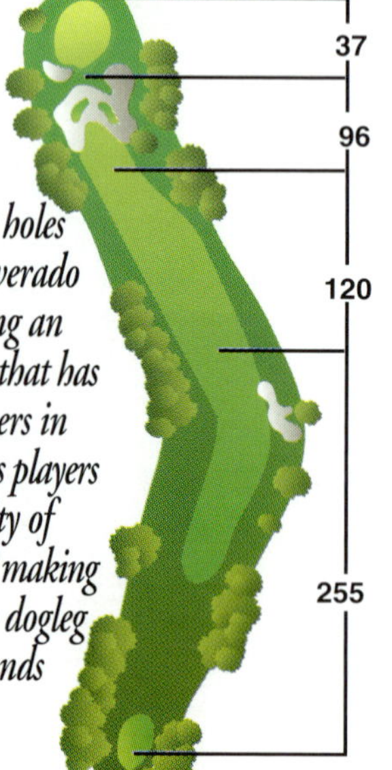

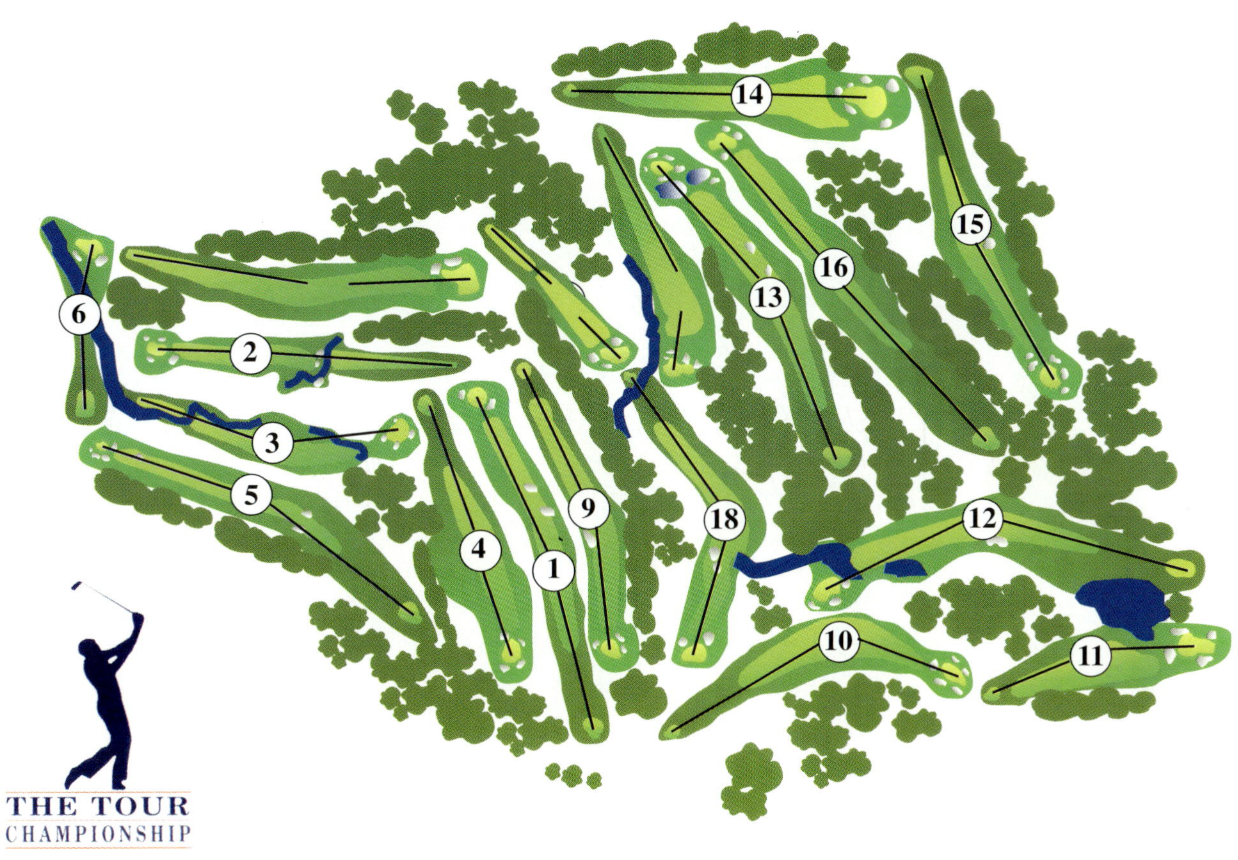

THE COURSES: SOUTHERN HILLS COUNTRY CLUB AT TULSA, OKLAHOMA

The Southern Hills Country Club course, dating from 1935, is now in its prime and has justifiably been rated among the 10 best courses in the country.

The Club is unique in that it came into being during the Depression when other clubs were falling by the wayside. But it was a complex wanted by its farsighted founders, and it is that same desire and pride which has evolved over the years which prompts Southern Hills not only to continue to offer its facilities for major championships, but also to see that each event is staged in the most professional manner possible.

This Championship represents the sixth major golf event hosted by Southern Hills. It has previously hosted the '70, '82, '94 PGA Championships, 1995 PGA TOUR Championship and the '58 U.S. Open as well as the '65 U.S. Amateur.

The original 18-hole championship course was designed by Perry Maxwell. Ben Crenshaw recently completed a new nine holes, "The West Nine," which opened for play October, 1992.

Dates:	October 24-27
Network:	ESPN & ABC
Times:	ESPN Thur 3:00-6:00 EST
	ESPN Fri 3:30-6:30 EST
	ABC Sat. 1:30-3:30 EST
	ABC Sun. 3:00-6:00 EST
Yardage:	6,834
Par:	70
Slope:	136
Rating:	74
Total Purse:	3,000,000
1st Prize:	$540,000
1995 Winner:	Billy Mayfair
1995 Winning Score:	(280)68,70,69,73
Ticket Information:	918-497-4653
	1-800-868-7565

1

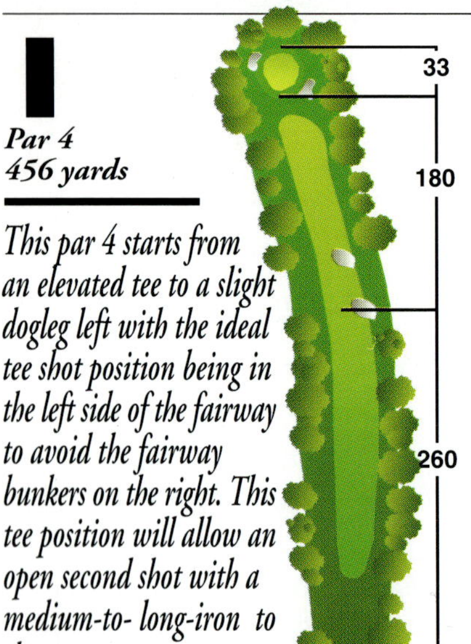

Par 4
456 yards

This par 4 starts from an elevated tee to a slight dogleg left with the ideal tee shot position being in the left side of the fairway to avoid the fairway bunkers on the right. This tee position will allow an open second shot with a medium-to- long-iron to the green.

2

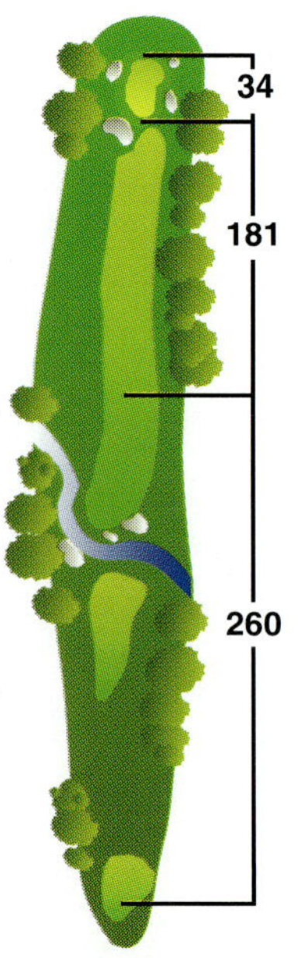

Par 4
458 yards

This is perhaps the most demanding driving hole on the course with a 225 yard carry over the bunkers and a winding creek that runs through the fairway. A long-iron second shot is required to reach this well bunkered green.

3

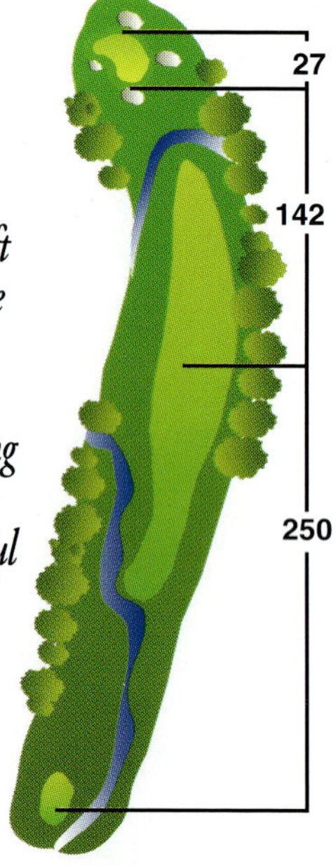

Par 4
405 yards

A sharp dogleg left requires a long tee shot in the right center of the fairway. Bunkering and pin positions will demand skillful short-iron second shots on this deceiving hole.

4

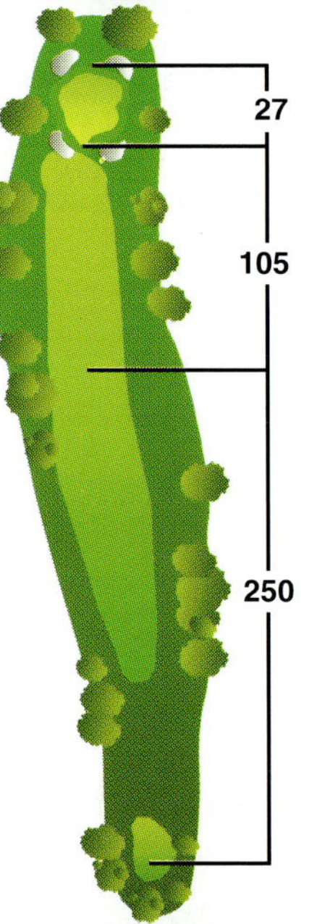

Par 4
368 yards

This picturesque shot par-4 features a rolling fairway leading to the heavily bunkered , elevated green.

5

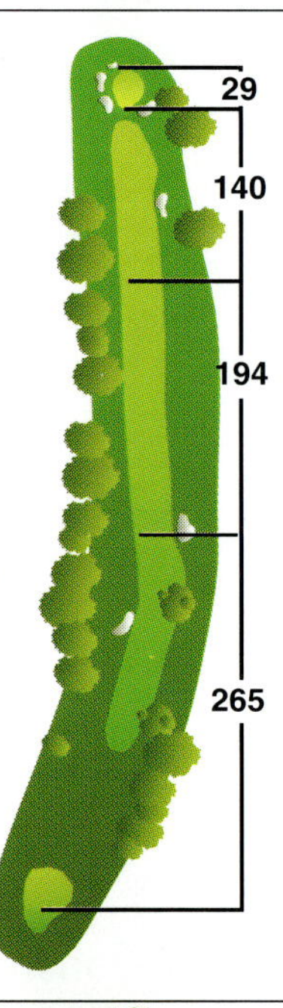

Par 5
614 yards

This par-5 doglegs slightly and is the longest, hole on the course. Due to fairway bunkers, a narrow landing area on the tee shot will cause problems, but the hole does present a birdie opportunity to the straight hitter.

6

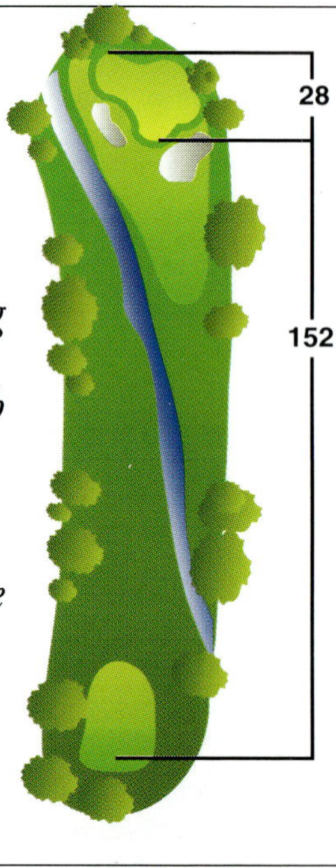

Par 3
175 yards

Although this is a short par-3, shifting winds will cause problems with club selections. A creek on the left side of the green will penalize hooked tee shots and out of bounds is close behind the green.

7

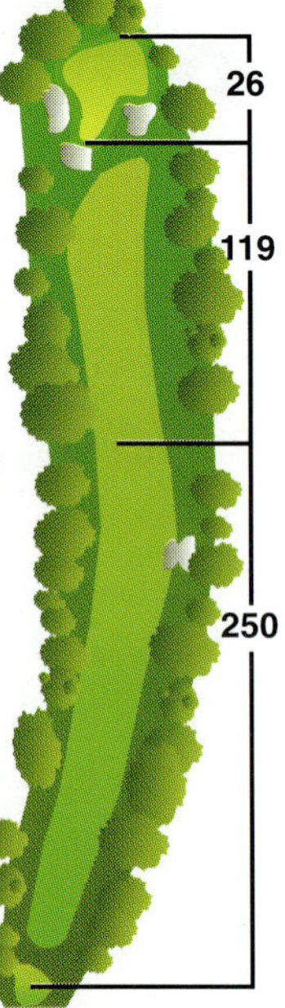

Par 4
382 yards

A blind tee shot to the crest of a hill reveals a narrow situated green bunkered front and left. A steep band guards the right posing a difficult uphill pitch from heavy rough. Most players will drive with a 3-wood to the top of the hill in the left center of the fairway and use a short-iron second shot to the

8

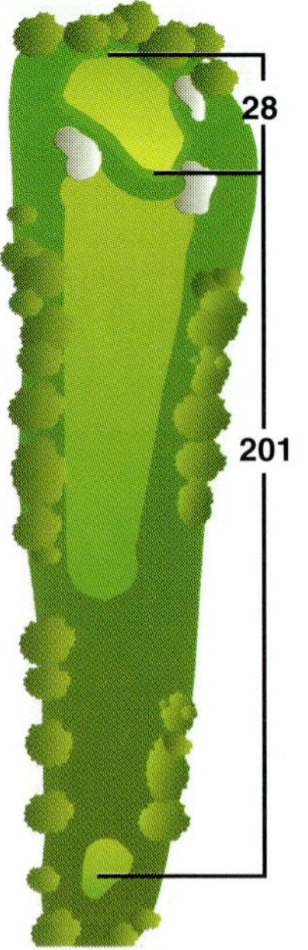

Par 3
215 yards

A demanding par-3 with some tough pin placements. Long irons or possibly a 3-wood will be used here, but it is better to be short than over the embankment at the back and into the creek.

9

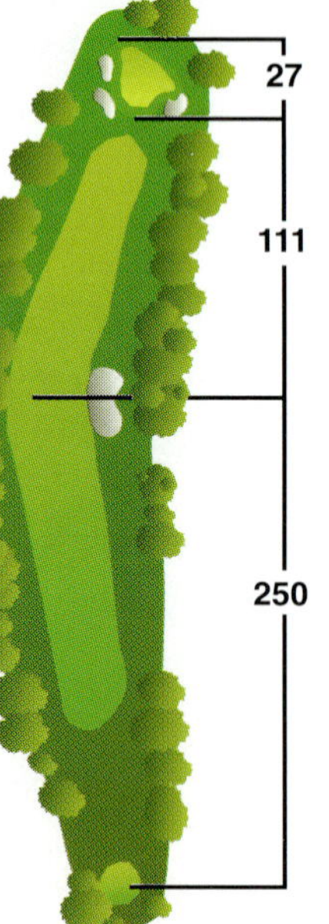

Par 4
374 yards

A dogleg right with a fairway bunker guarding the corner requires a well positioned tee shot. The wind and an elevated green make this hole play longer than its yardage. A severe slope from the back to the front of the green makes this one of the most difficult greens to putt.

10

Par 4
376 yards

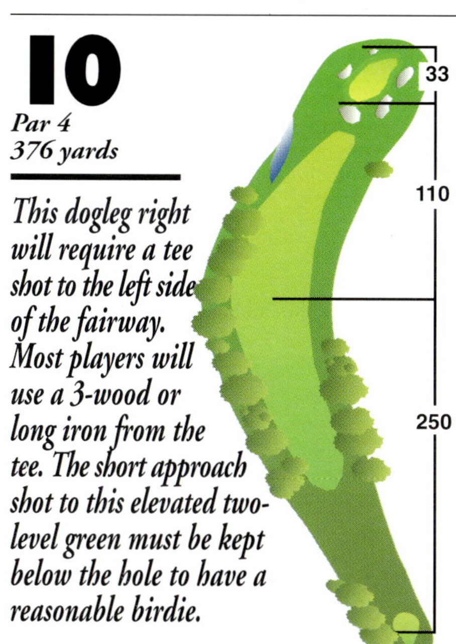
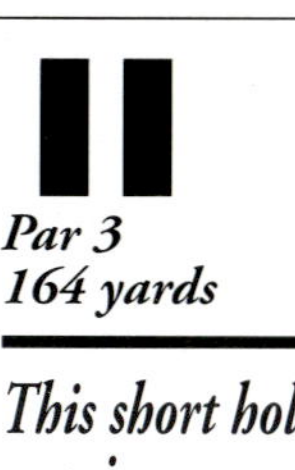

This dogleg right will require a tee shot to the left side of the fairway. Most players will use a 3-wood or long iron from the tee. The short approach shot to this elevated two-level green must be kept below the hole to have a reasonable birdie.

11

Par 3
164 yards

This short hole requires a pinpoint accuracy because this small green is surrounded by four bunkers.

12

Par 4
448 yards

Singled out by Ben Hogen and Arnold Palmer as one of American's greatest par 4-holes. This hole calls for a precision long drive to a blind landing area take full advantage of the right-to-left slope of the fairway. The second sho use a long, to middle-iron, to a well-bunkered green.

13

Par 5
537 yards

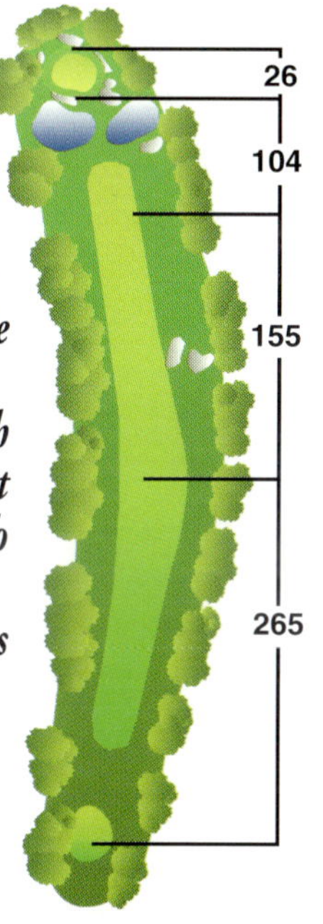

A big drive on the slight dogleg left hole will leave an opportunity to reach the green in two, but not without risk. To reach the green in two, the player faces a blind shot to a small green, well protected by sand and water.

14

Par 3
207 yards

A great par-3 that has length, six bunkers and out-of- bounds on the left. It will require a wood or long-iron firmly struck to negate the prevailing wind. A three here will be well earned.

15

Par 4
405 yards

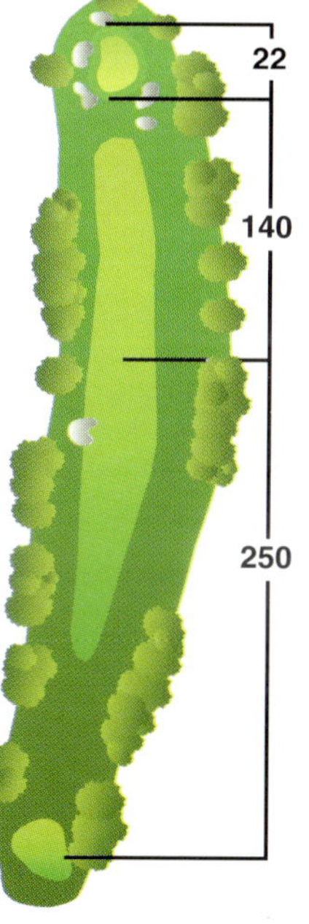

A dogleg left with a bunker guarding the corner requires a well-positioned drive to a very narrow landing area. The second shot, a medium-to-short-iron, must avoid bunkers surrounding the green.

16

Par 4
468 yards

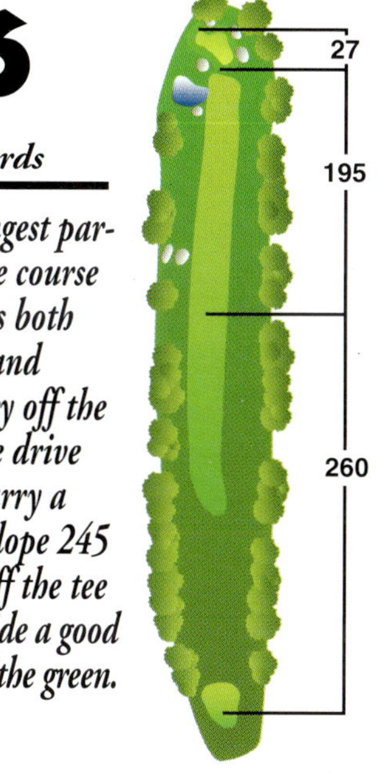

The longest par-4 on the course requires both length and accuracy off the tee. The drive must carry a gentle slope 245 yards off the tee to provide a good view of the green.

17

Par 4
352 yards

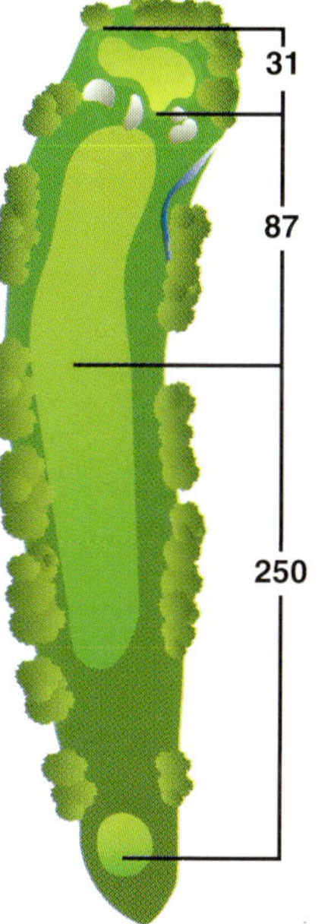

On this short par-4 most players will endeavor to place the tee shot on the left side of the fairway with a wood or long-iron. An accurate short-iron on the second shot is needed to reach the shallow, level green.

18

Par 4
430 yards

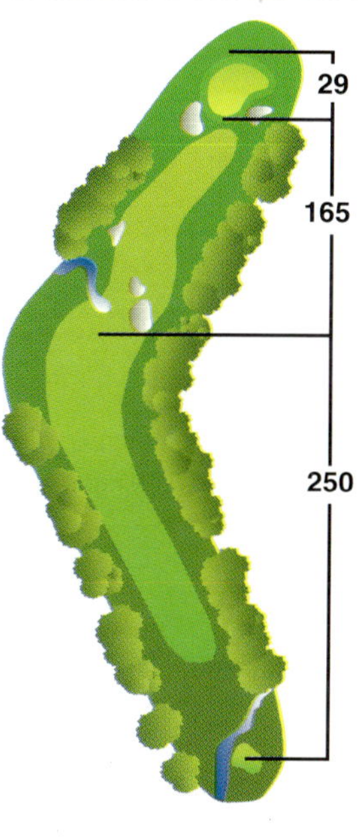

This dogleg right requires a drive to a plateau on the left side of the fairway 200 yards from the elevated green. A long-iron or fairway wood second shot must carry to the severely sloping green.

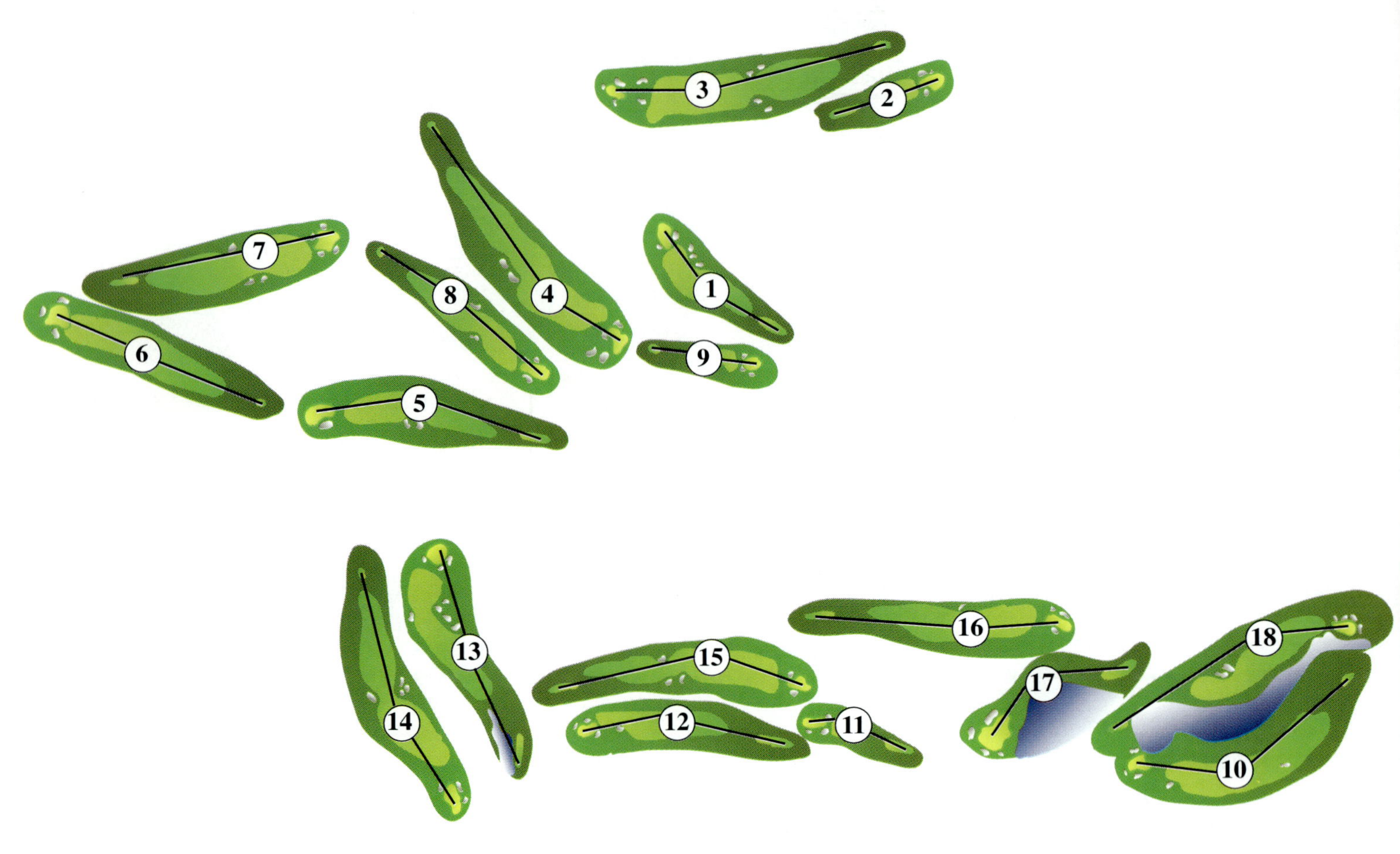

THE COURSE:KAANAPALI BEACH RESORT,
MAUI, HAWAII

*T*o play the course of Kaanapali is to follow in the footsteps of some of the best-known names and greatest players the game has produced.

Bing Crosby was among the guests on opening day in 1962 and just two years later the course was the scene of the World Cup, (then the Canadian Cup). Arnold Palmer and Jack Nicklaus, representing the United States, won the 34-nation competition with Nicklaus winning the individual honors.

Dates:	October 25-27, 1996
Network:	ESPN
Times:	Fri 2:00-4:00 EST
	Sat 4:40-7:00 EST
	Sun 5:30-7:00 EST
Yardage:	6994
Par:	72
Slope:	134
Rating:	72.8
Total Purse:	$600,000
1st Prize:	$90,000
1995 Winner:	Bob Charles
1995 Winning Score:	204 (69,67,68)
Principal Charitable Beneficiary:	Hale Makua
Charitable Benefits to Date:	Over $275,000 since 1987
Ticket Information:	1-808-667-2234

1

Par 4
349 yards

Short dog-leg right, par 4. Three-level green. O.B. left and right.

2

Par 3
219 yards

Straight-away par 3, but be carful of bunkers around green.

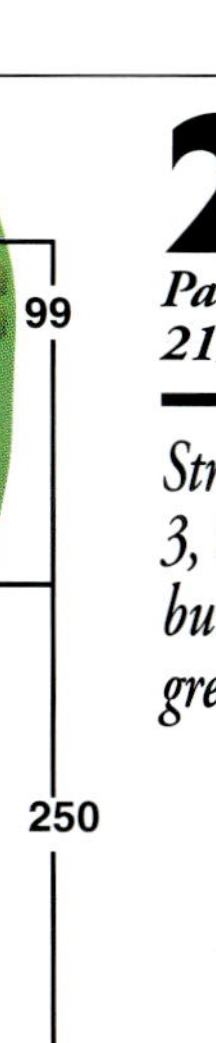

3

Par 5
502 yards

Slight dog-leg right, par 5. Be carful of left-hand fairway bunker in second shot. O.B. left and right.

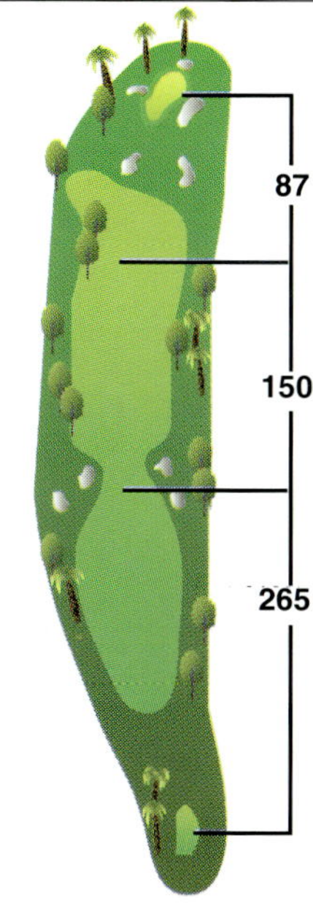

4

Par 4
460 yards

Long downhill par 4. Dog-leg left. O.B. left and right.Be carful of bunkers left of green.

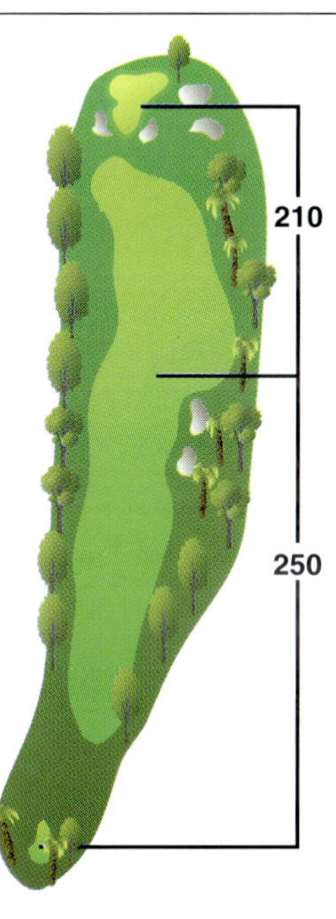

5

Par 4
433 yards

Play tee shot right of center and be careful of left hand bunker. Fairway slopes left. O.B. left.

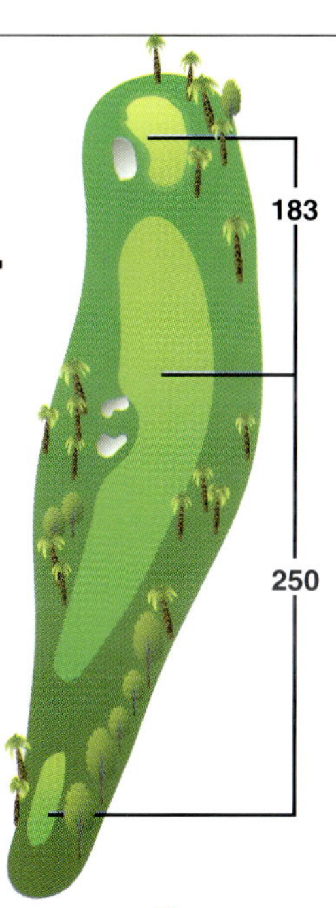

6

Par 5
561 yards

Straight-away par 4. Favor right center on drive. Fairway slopes left and O.B. left.

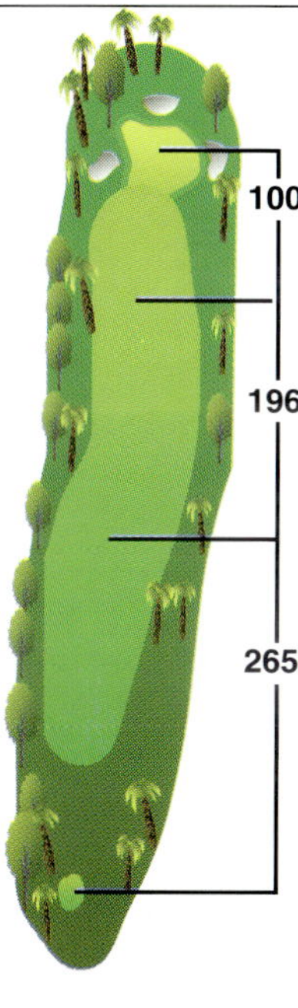

7

Par 4
412 yards

Straight-away par 4. O.B. left and right. Play left center of fairway.

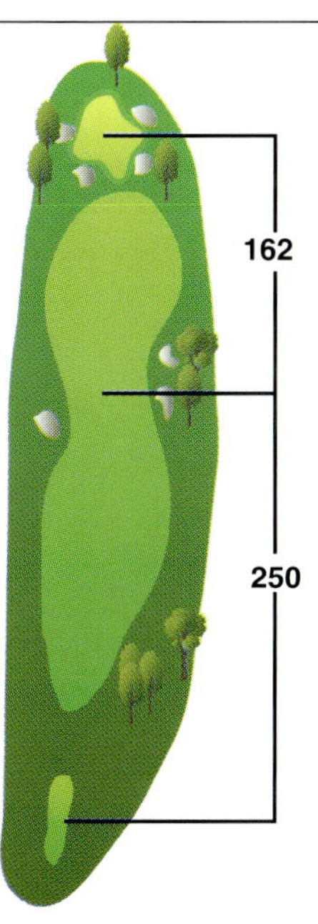

8

Par 4
422 yards

Downhill par 4 Aim for the middle of the green. Guard against right-hand bunker.

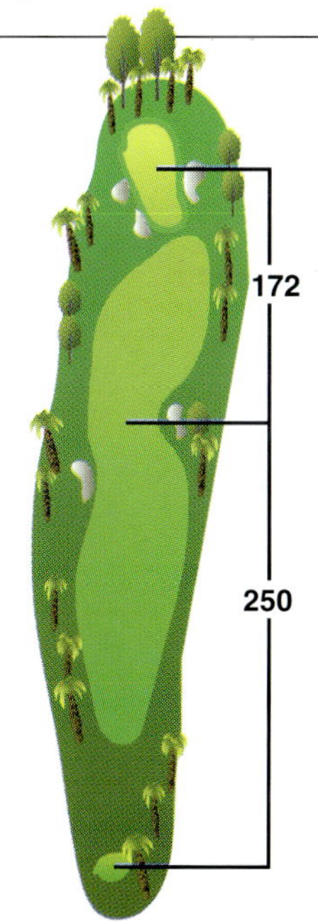

9

Par 3
218 yards

Straight-away par 3. Be carful of well gaurded geen.

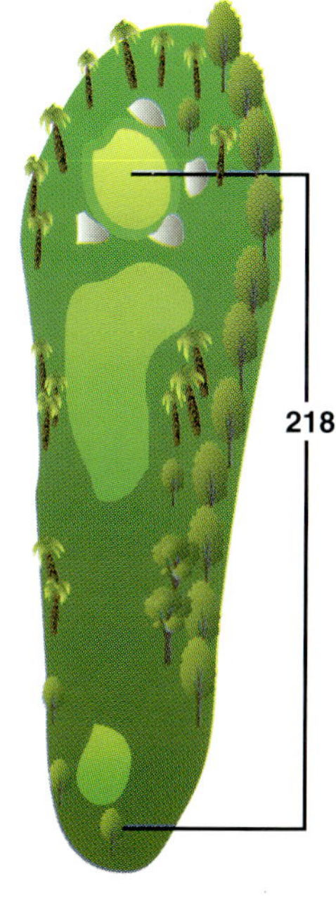

10

Par 5
541 yards

Dog-leg par 5. Water hazard right and in front of green. O.B. left of fairway. Lagoon to be played as lateral water hazard. Drop ball at point of entry.

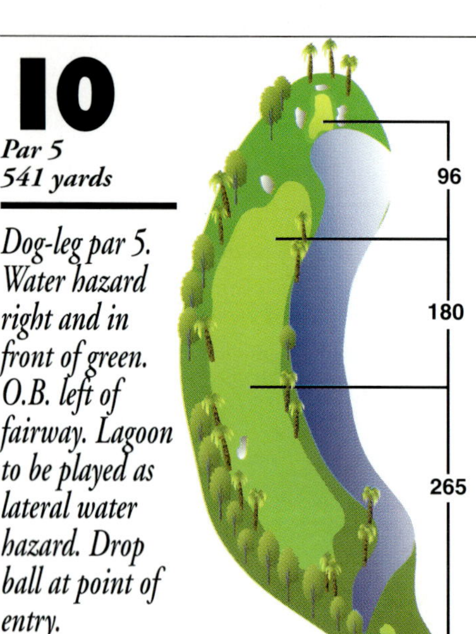
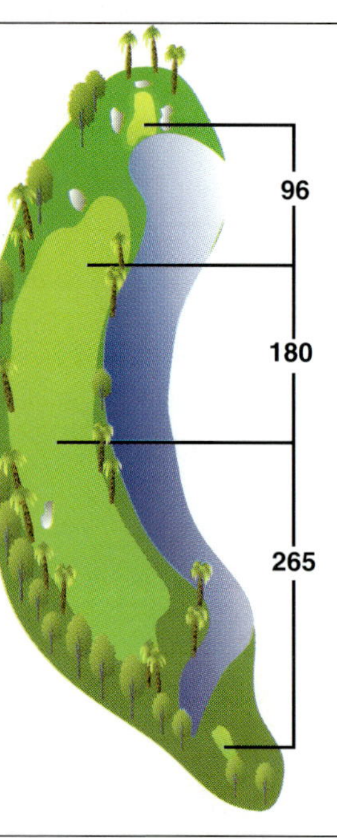

11

Par 3
203 yards

Uphill par 3. Guard against going left.

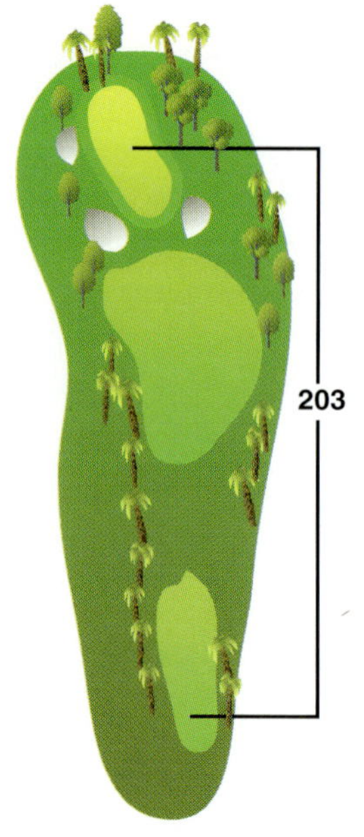

12

Par 4
427 yards

Dog-leg left. Play tee shot right center O.B. left.

13

Par 4
412 yards

Uphill par 4. Guard against right-hand bunker. O.B. right Two-level green. Lagoon to be played as lateral water hazard. Drop ball at pont of entry.

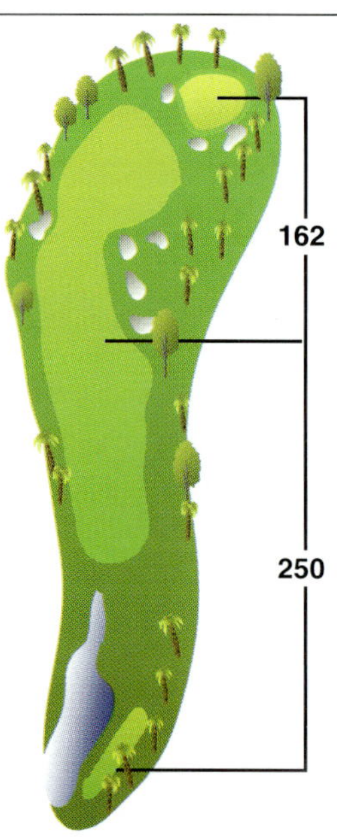

14

Par 4
473 yards

Long par 4, dog-leg left. Water left; O.B. right. Lagoon to be played as lateral water hazard. Ball crossing cart path on right side of fairway is O.B. Ball leading to and around green is O.B.

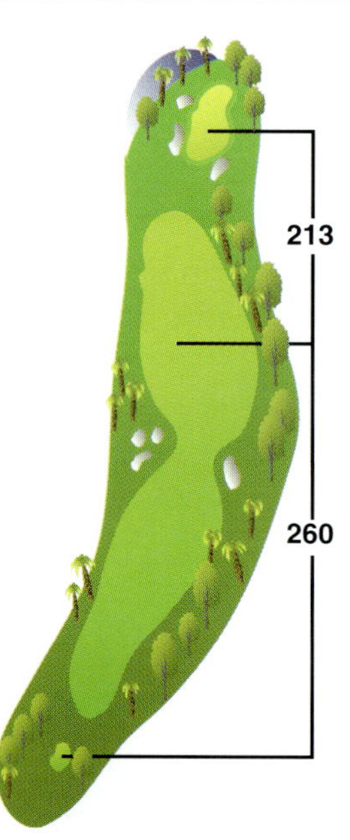

15

Par 5
480 yards

Short par 5. Be carful of bunkers on right.

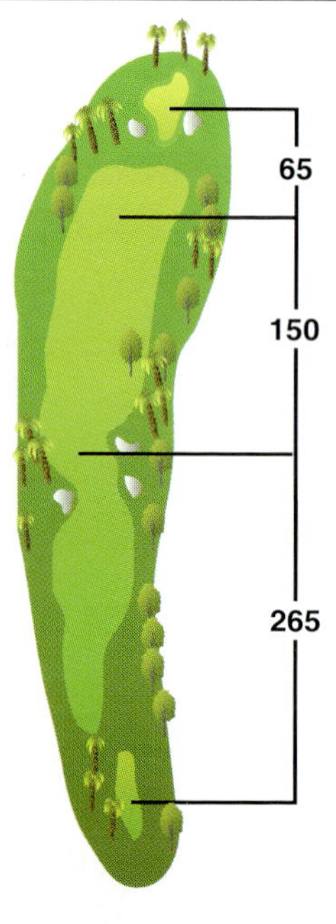

16

Par 4
466 yards

Downhill par4. O.B. left.

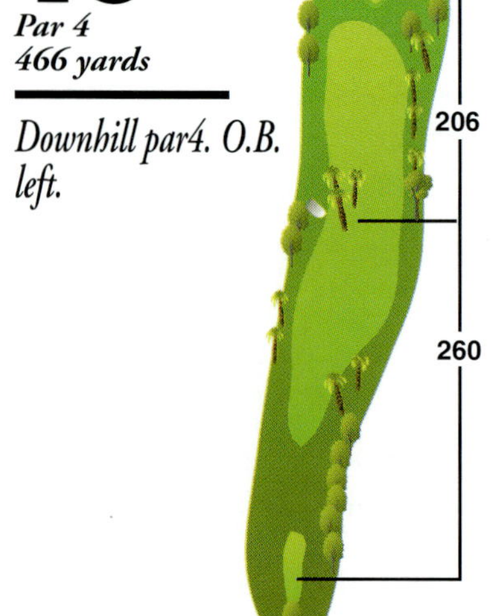

17

Par 3
169 yards

Short par 3. Carry over water. Be careful of right-hand bunker.

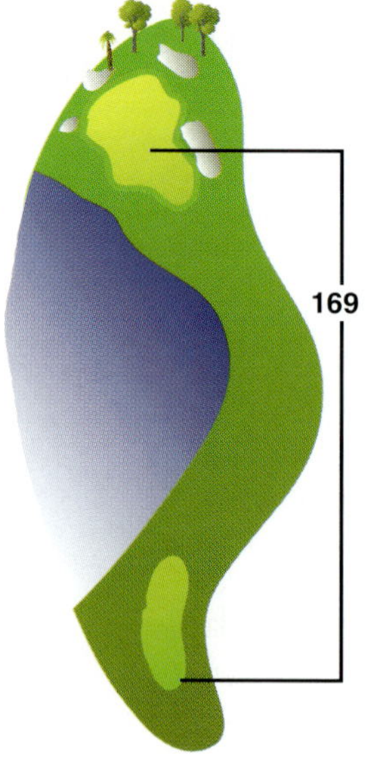

18

Par 4
438 yards

Play tee shot right of left hand bunker. Water hazard right; O.B. left. Be careful on second shot. Lagoon to be played as lateral water hazard. Drop ball at point of entry.

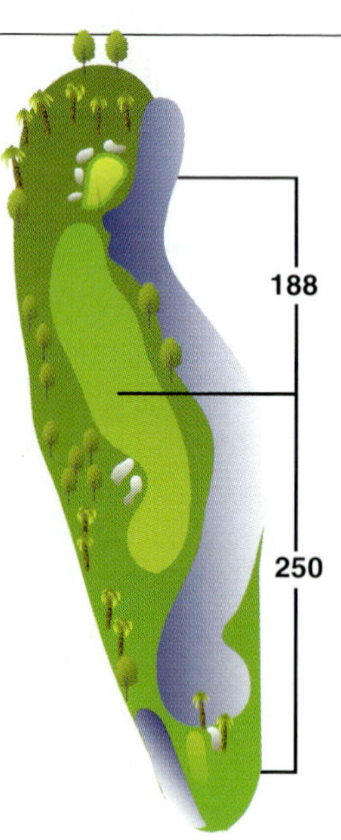

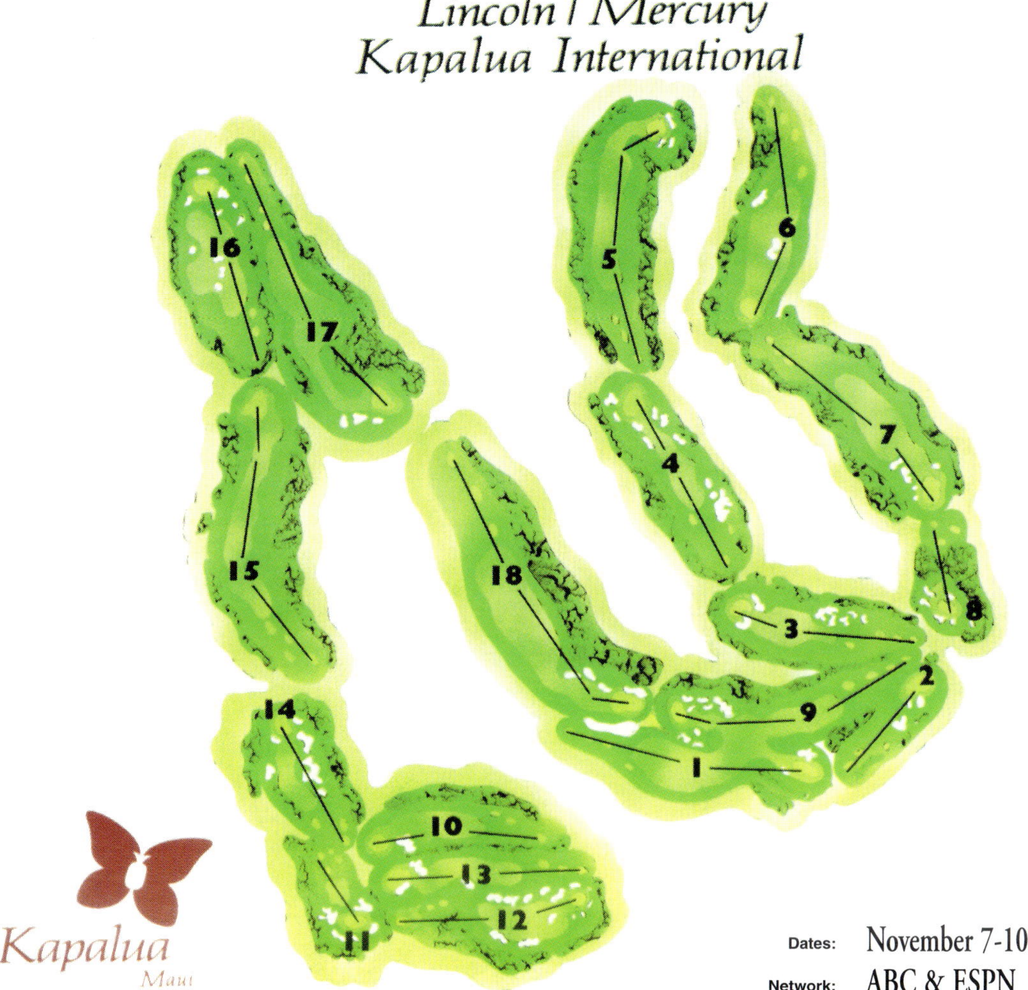

THE COURSE: THE PLANTATION COURSE AT KAPALUA , MAUI, HAWAII

The Lincoln-Mercury Kapalua International will be in its fifteenth year in 1996. The exciting Hawaiian tournament not only offers a glimpse at the beautiful weather of the Islands, but also is the source of a great golf championship. David Ishii won the first event in 1982. Greg Norman won in 1983, Sandy Lyle in 1984, Mark O'Meara in 1985, Andy Bean won back-to-back in 1986 and 1987, Bob Gilder in 1988, Peter Jacobsen in 1989 and David Peoples in 1990. Perhaps the most spectacular winner was in 1991 when a struggling Mike Hulbert claimed the $150,000 winners check after a sudden death play-off with Davis Love III.

A total of 52 professionals are invited to play in the 72-hole championship. Each professional plays with a 3-man amateur team for the first two rounds-pros only for the last two rounds. A great Pro-Am, followed by an exciting championship.

Dates:	November 7-10
Network:	ABC & ESPN
	ESPN
Times:	Thur /Fri 4:00-7:00 EST
	ABC
	Sat 1:30-3:30 EST
	Sun 4:00-6:00 EST
Yardage:	7263
Par:	73
Slope:	135
Rating:	74.6
Total Purse:	$1,000,000
1st Prize:	$180,000
1995 Winner:	Jim Furyk
1995 Winning Score:	271 (65, 65, 71, 70)
Principal Charitable Beneficiary:	J Walter Cameron Center including over 20 Maui Charities
Charitable Benefits to Date:	over $5 million since 1982
Ticket Information:	1-808-669-0244 Admission Free

1

Par 4
473 yards

A long 473 yards starts the day. Fortunately, the hole is downhill and often downwind. The left side of the fairway is favored to shorten the distance to the putting surface.

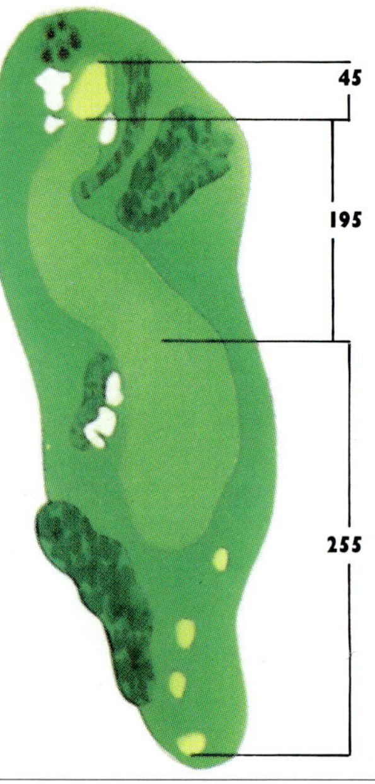

2

Par 3
218 yards

The high lofted shot into the green is the ideal, however the putting surface allows for the run-on shot. The three bunkers short right are mostly out of play.

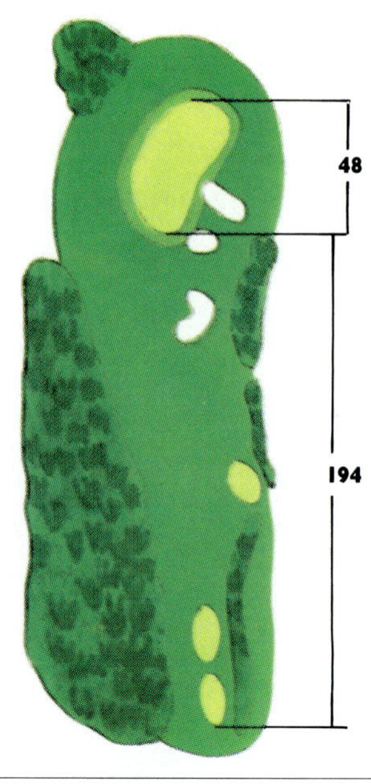

3

Par 4
380 yards

Distance is not the concern here. The generous fairway allows for a little looseness on the tee shot. Strong gusting winds make for a tough approach to the small green.

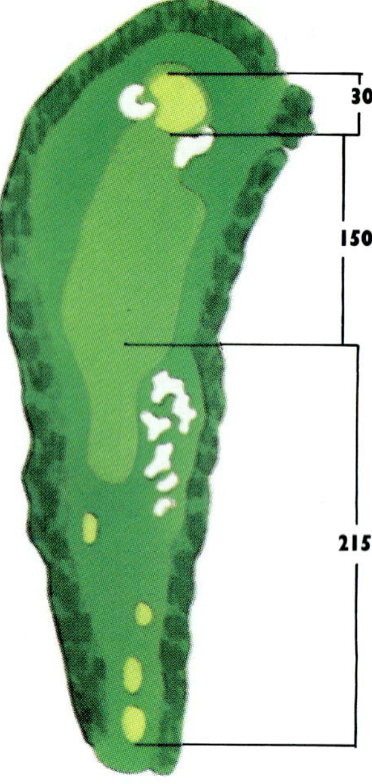

4

Par 4
382 yards

The drive must clear a ridge to reach the rolling fairway. Sloping to the left, the green is an elusive target–especially when the winds are blowing.

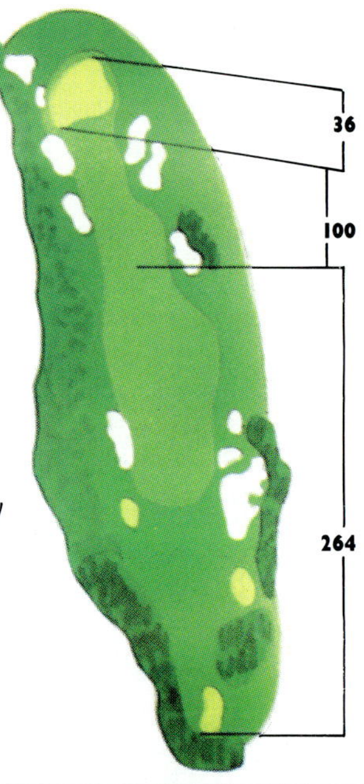

5

Par 5
532 yards

No hazards from tee to green. Conservative players will keep their ball down the left to get the easy birdie. The big hitters may be able to reach the green in two.

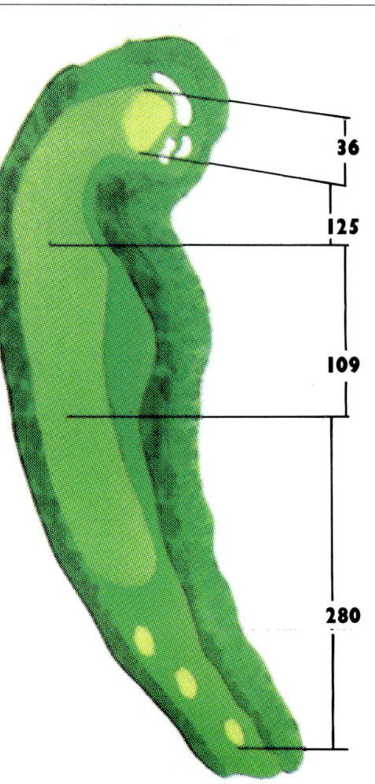

6

Par 4
398 yards

A lone bunker in the middle of the fairway is an obstacle that players will most likely choose to go to the right of. Although the green has no bunkers a cliff drops on the right side.

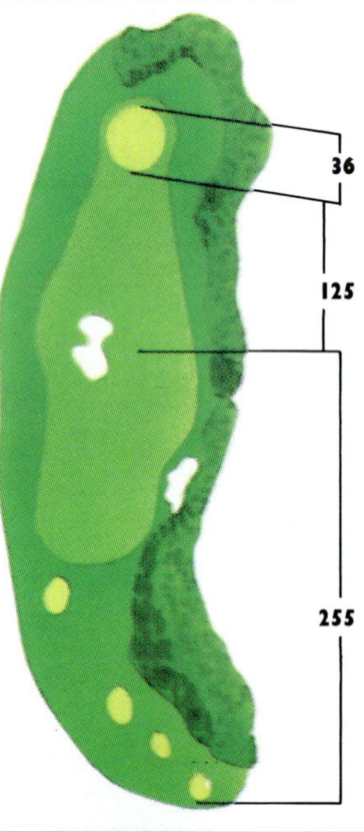

7

Par 4
484 yards

A long par 4 that plays downhill. The wide fairway allows for the big drive. Approaches are made to a long narrow green.

8

Par 3
203 yards

A long carry over a ravine. Once over, the task is to avoid the several bunkers and find the sloping green. Players will be more than satisfied with par.

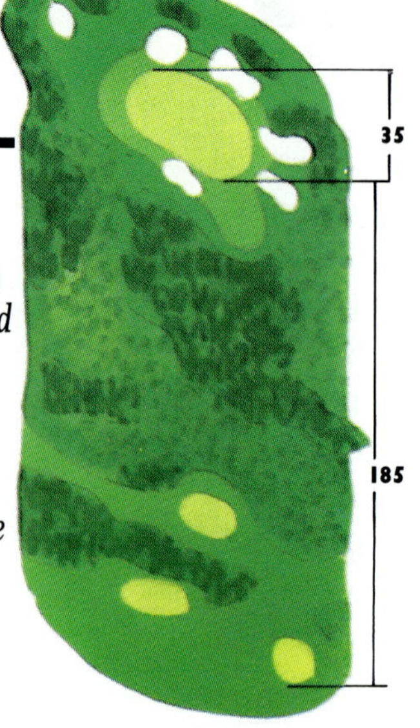

9

Par 5
521 yards

Drives will come to rest just short of a valley that crosses the fairway. The second shot must be placed accurately in position for the third.

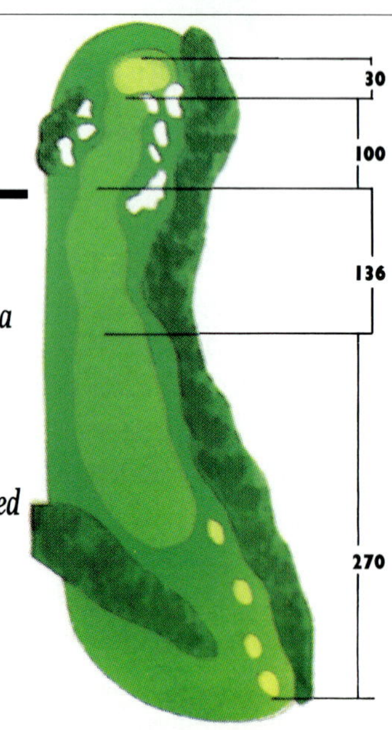

10

Par 4
354 yards

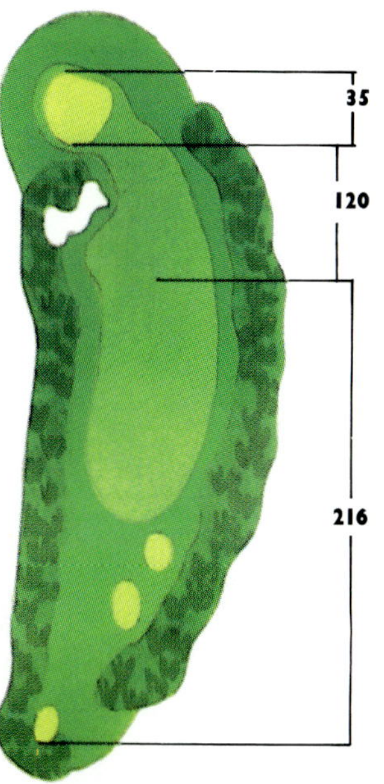

An uphill short par 4. Fairway slopes severely from right to left. The right side of the fairway is obviously favored. The approach is to a plateaued green.

11

Par 3
164 yards

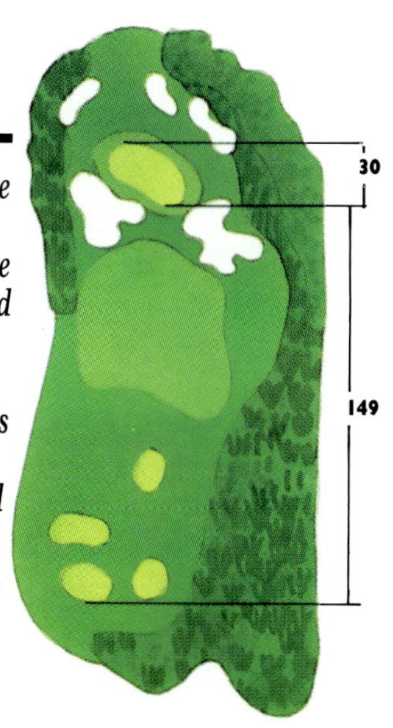

The 11th is the last par 3 of the course. The prevailing wind blows from right to left. Pin placements in the back left corner will be very difficult to hit.

12

Par 4
373 yards

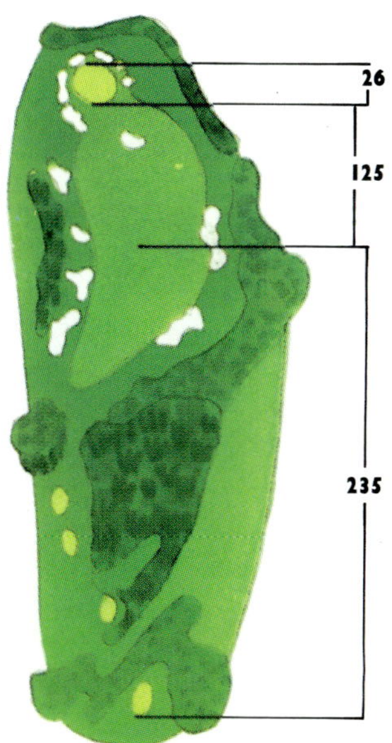

The drive must ascend up to the raised fair-way. A short approach is to a concave green that slopes in from the sides. Bunkers beyond act as a safety net for long shots.

13

Par 4
407 yards

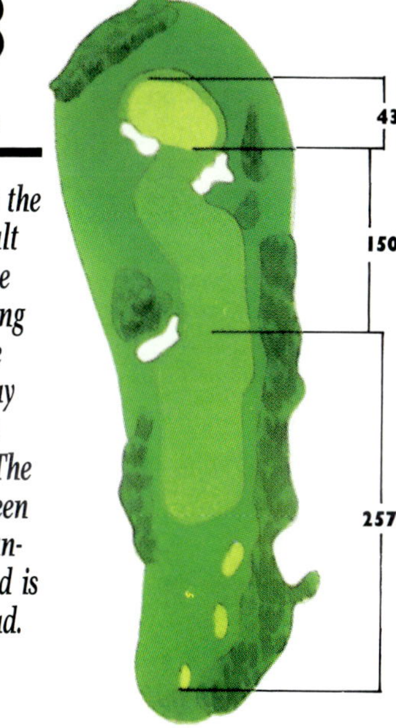

The 13th is the most difficult par 4 on the course. Strong winds make the hole play longer than published. The spacious green is severely un-dulating and is tough to read.

14

Par 4
305 yards

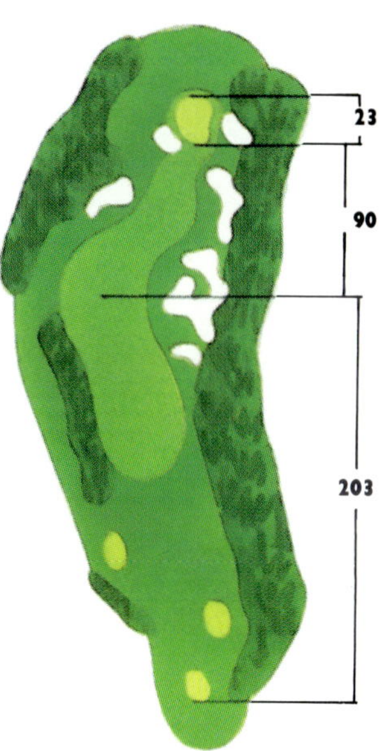

The fairway sits on a plateau above the fairway. Likewise, the course's smallest green is elevated from the fair-way. The prevailing strong wind is from the left.

15

Par 5
555 yards

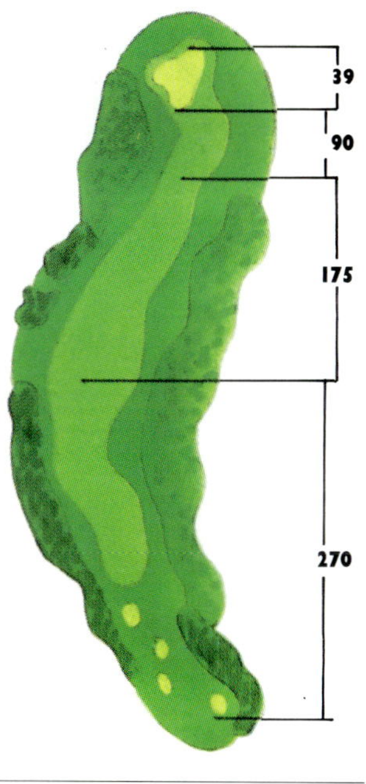

The double-dogleg fairway rolls and pitches through the green. Three shots will be needed to reach the large green. Note the absence of bunkers.

16

Par 4
365 yards

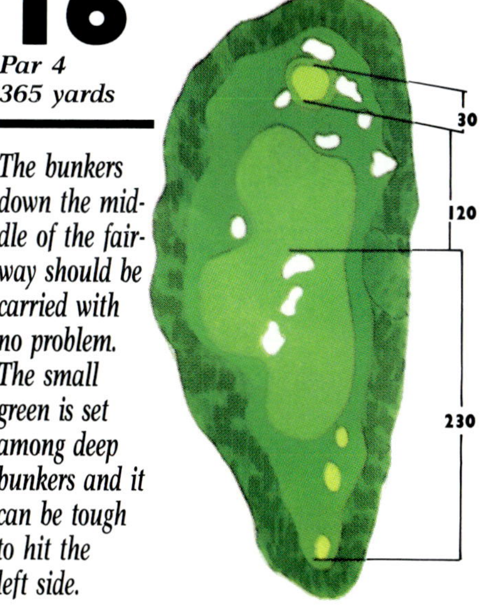

The bunkers down the mid-dle of the fair-way should be carried with no problem. The small green is set among deep bunkers and it can be tough to hit the left side.

17

Par 4
486 yards

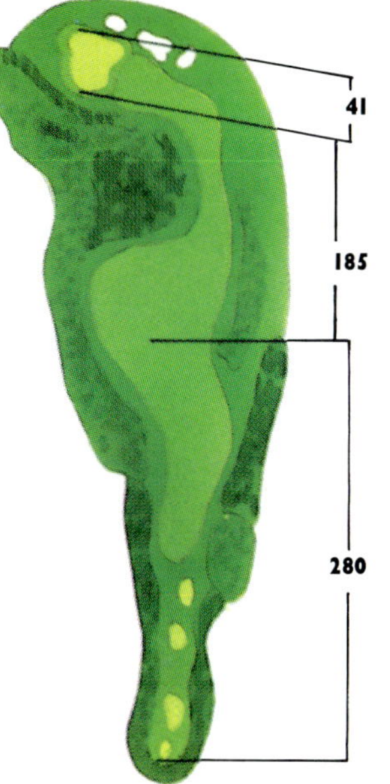

The elevation drops 150 feet from tee to green. The big drive down the left will lead to an approach that must carry a small valley.

18

Par 5
663 yards

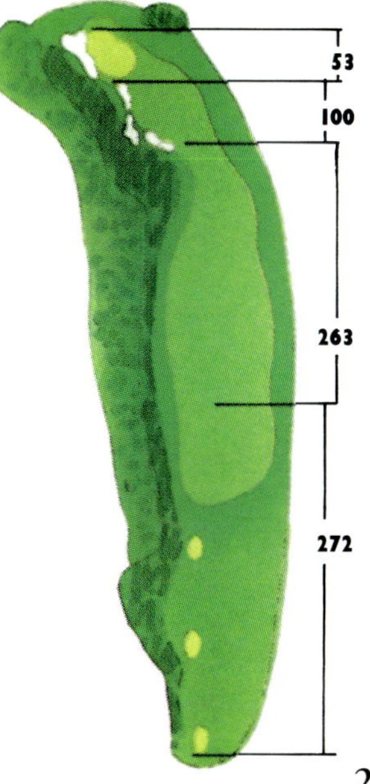

663 yards is a long way to travel. With a prevailing tail-wind and a descending fairway, players are able to reach this green in two! This is how champion-ships are won.

THE COURSE: THE DUNES GOLF AND BEACH CLUB, MYRTLE BEACH, SOUTH CAROLINA

*N*ow in its seventh year, The Energizer SENIOR TOUR® Championship features 31 of the best SENIOR TOUR® players facing off for a purse of $1,500,000, one of the richest on the SENIOR TOUR®, in a dramatic season-ending showdown.

To play the Dunes, Seniors will have to tee it high and let it fly. The course plays 7,015 yards from the tips, but there's more to the Dunes than length. There are plenty of long, tough tracks around the World, but only a few have the charm and character of the Dunes. This is a golf course with all the intangibles, a perfect flow and balance of holes, each of them with the splendid natural setting provided by the Swash, the noble old live oaks, and proximity of the sea. Add to this the breezes and the salt air, and you have one awe-inspiring golf course.

Dates:	November 7-10
Network:	ESPN
Times:	Thu 2:00-4:00 EST
	Fri 3:00-5:00 EST
	Sat 5:30-7:00 EST
	Sun 5:00-7:00 EST
Yardage:	6815
Par:	72
Slope:	132
Rating:	72.1
Total Purse:	$1.5 Million
1st Prize:	$265,000
1995 Winner:	Jim Colbert
1995 Winning Score:	(282)68,69,71,74
Principal Charitable Beneficiary:	Various
Ticket Information:	1-800-741-3161

1

Par 4
425 yards

This par 4 can be played straight away from the tee to green. The tee shot landing area is narrow with encroaching trees on the left and the fairway bunker 249 yards out. If the pin is positioned on the right, the left side of the fairway gives you the best approach to the hole.

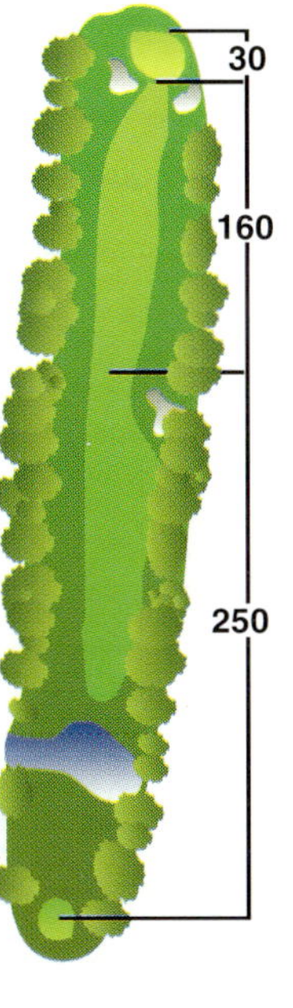

2

Par 4
425 yards

This is a severe dogleg left with a fairway bunker straight out, and a high stand of trees on the left. The drive must be hit over the trees or drawn around the corner. The bunker on the right at the corner tightens the landing area for the tee shot. Deep bunkers guard the green on both sides.

3

Par 4
435 yards

This is a straightaway hole with a fairway that runs uphill to the last trap on the left. There is a high mound on the right side of the fairway and a swale on the left so the best position for the tee shot is on the left side of the fairway.

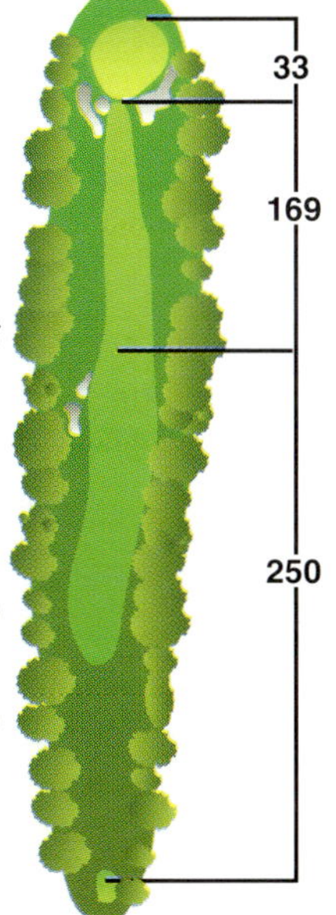

4

Par 5
505 yards

This par 5 tempts the long hitters to try to carry the green in two. The pitch shot for those that lay up still demands a nerveless pitch. The drive must carry a cluster of bunkers placed at the corner of the dogleg left. The green is shallow and falls away at the back.

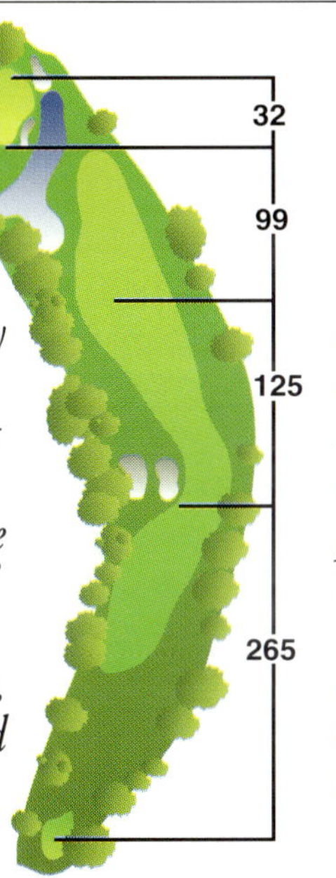

5

Par 3
205 yards

The first par 3 of the course is a very tough hole. It's usually a long iron to an elevated green protected by deep bunkers left and right. The green narrowly opens in the front before sloping away back and to the left.

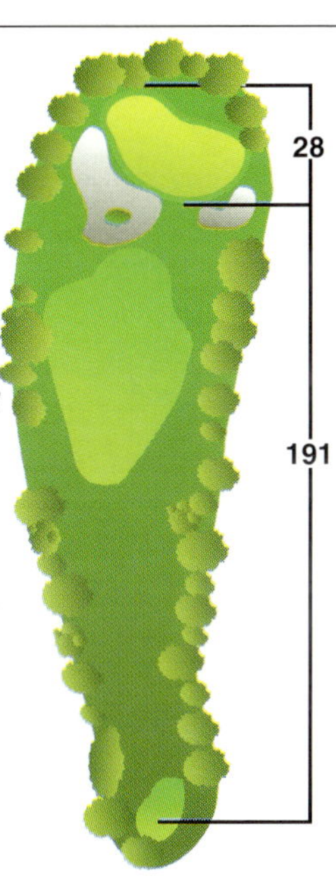

6

Par 4
435 yards

The tee shot is into a gentle rise which tends to shorten the drive and requires the long hitters to land at the top of it without landing in one of the two fairway bunkers to the left, or a good size lake to the right. Be careful of the huge bunker to the right side of the green.

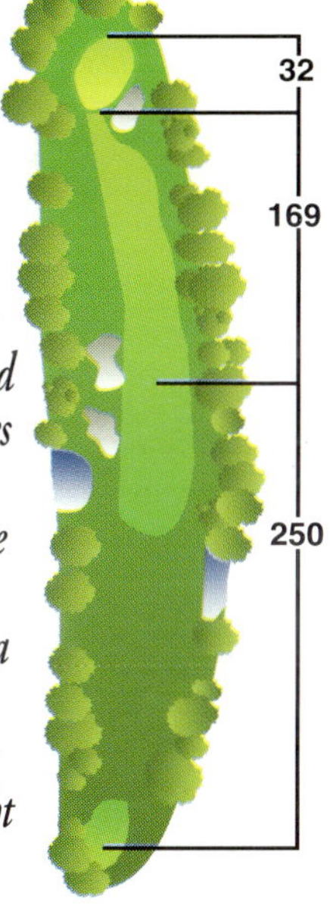

7

Par 4
400 yards

It is basically a straight away hole, trees lining each side of the fairway, a large bunker on the left about 155 yards to the green, and a gentle rise to the fairway. There is a devilishly deep bunker in front of the green.

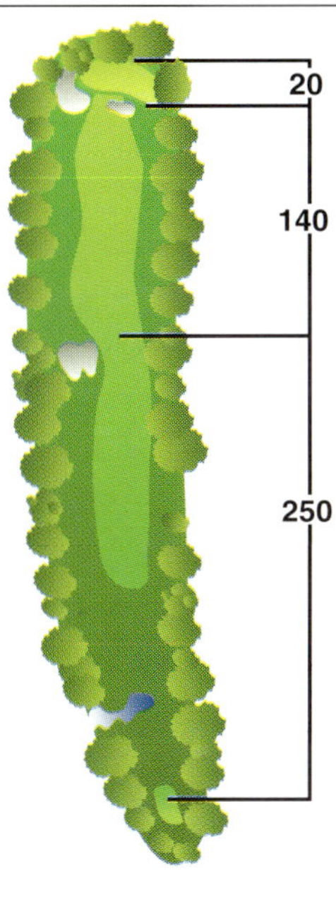

8

Par 5
525 yards

This is a fairly straight par 5. There are two fairway bunkers out on the left, and about 90 yards from the green there are three bunkers on the left and one to the right. There are also three bunkers guarding the elevated green.

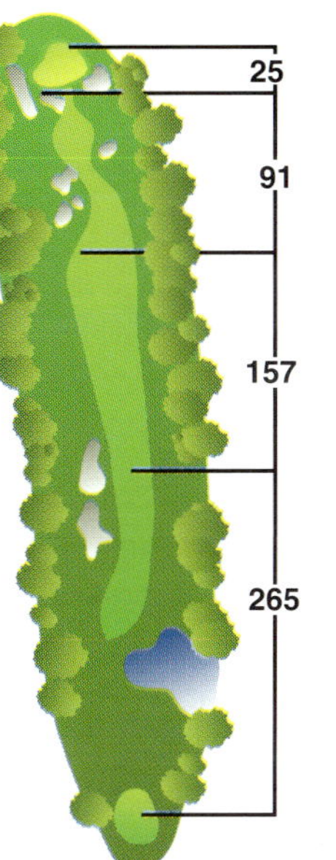

9

Par 3
200 yards

A beautiful par 3 that provides a scenic view of the Atlantic ocean. The breeze is generally off the ocean so club selection can very. The large green is heavily guarded by bunkers and is quite elevated.

10

Par 4
380 yards

This is a unique golf hole. The tee boxes, which are elevated, are just short of a small lake which can catch topped or otherwise short drives. The fairway is expansive and falls away from the tee. The green is quite elevated from the hitting area for the approach shot.

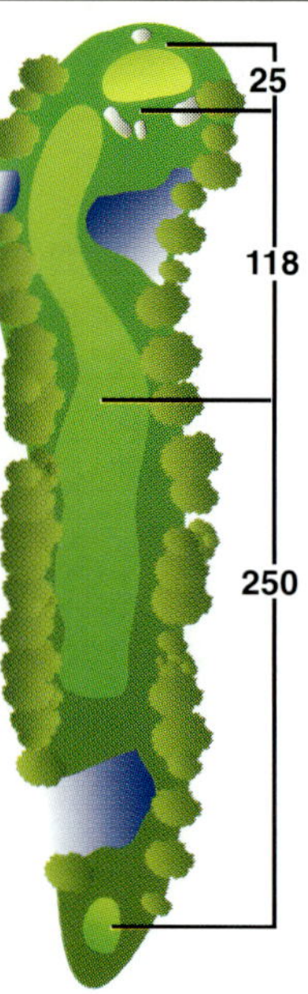

11

Par 4
430 yards

This hole is one of the best par 4's because it does what a good hole is supposed to do. It rewards the well played shot and penalizes one that is loosely played. The drive has to carry the marsh because it guards the right side of the fairway. Playing close to the bunker gives you a better shot into the narrow green.

12

Par 3
245 yards

This par 3 only measures 150 yards from the regular tees, but the green is fairly shallow and sits on a diagonal. It slopes from back to front and right to left and it is protected by a huge bunker on the left and bunkers front, right, and rear.

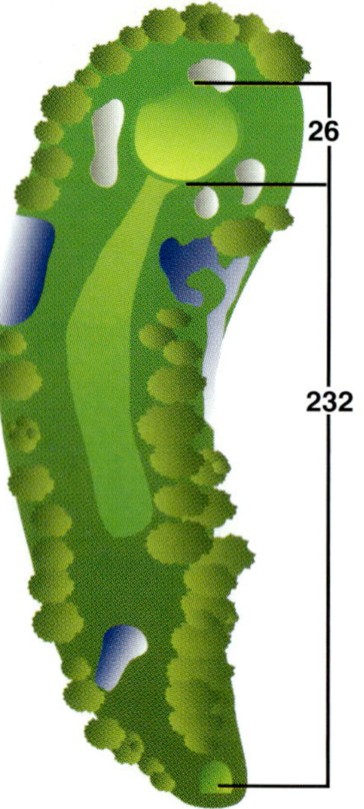

13

Par 5
590 yards

This is the signature hole- the most outstanding hole on the course. It doglegs so severely around Singleton Lake that the golfer feels he is going back on his tracks. The approach to the green is between two well flanking green side traps supported by another bunker in the rear.

14

Par 4
450 yards

The hardest par on the backside. The fairway rises gently from the tee to a mound and then descends gradually to a valley before the green. There are large bunkers on the left side of the fairway. Trees line the right side of the fairway to a well guarded elevated green.

15

Par 5
535 yards

Trees line both sides of the fairway. The green, which is the smallest on the course, is elevated and has a huge bunker front right. The sides of the green fall sharply down from the putting surface.

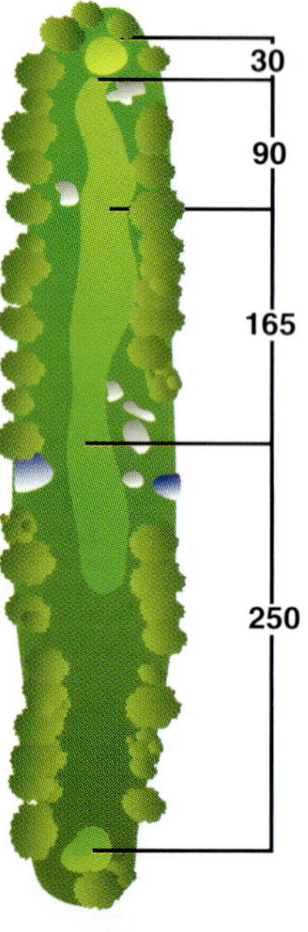

16

Par 4
365 yards

This is one of the more deceptive holes on the course. It appears a great deal easier than it plays. The green is considerably lower than from where an approach shot is made, making the hole appear closer.

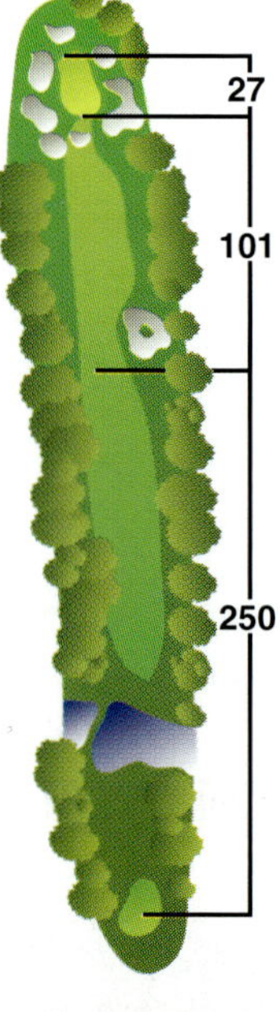

17

Par 3
185 yards

This is supposed to be the easiest hole on the course, but don't be fooled because it plays longer than it seems. The deep bunker guards the good size green, slightly elevated, with another bunker front left and one to the back.

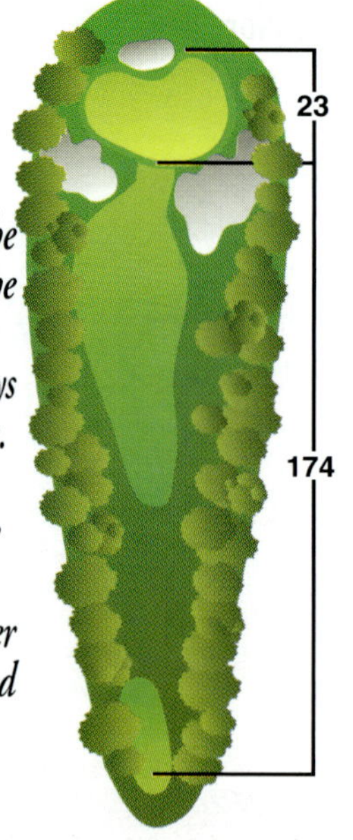

18

Par 4
430 yards

The hole plays much longer because the drive is directly into a fairway sharp rise. To get home in two, the tee shot must get close to the top of the rise. The green is protected by two bunkers in front and one in back.

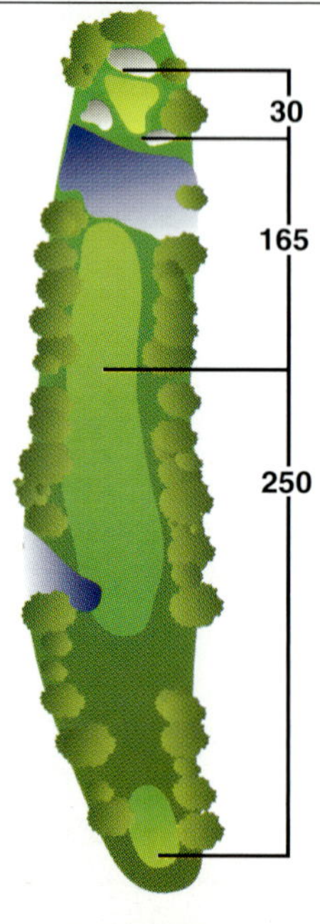

THE COURSE: SHERWOOD COUNTRY CLUB, THOUSAND OAKS, CALIFORNIA

At the close of the 1989 inaugural Franklin Templeton Shark Shootout hosted by Greg Norman at Sherwood Country Club, Tom Weiskopf described the new Jack Nicklaus design as "absolutely spectacular" and "very dramatic".

Each year Greg Norman gathers together twenty elite tour Professionals and pairs them into two-men teams. The format is a 54-hole medal play with best ball on Friday, alternate shot Saturday and scramble on Sunday. A $1.1 million purse is at stake.

DATES:	November 14-17
NETWORK:	CBS & ESPN
TIMES:	ESPEN Fri 4:00-6:00 EST
	CBS Sat 4:00-6:00 EST
	Sun 3:00-6:00 EST
DATE ORGANIZED:	1989
TICKET INFORMATION:	805-379-2664
YARDAGE:	**7,068**
PAR:	72
SLOPE:	146
RATING:	75.6
TOTAL PURSE:	$1,000,000
1995 WINNER:	Mark Calcavecchiat/ Steve Elkingiton
WIN SCORE:	184 (64, 61, 58)
PRINCIPAL CHARITABLE BENEFICIARY:	Children's Charities
BENEFIT TO DATE:	$3.5 Million
TICKET INFORMATION:	1-805-379-2664

1

**Par 4
341 yards**

The long hitters can take a chance and try to reach this hole from the tee. Two well hit conservative shots should be able to achieve birdie.

2

**Par 5
531 yards**

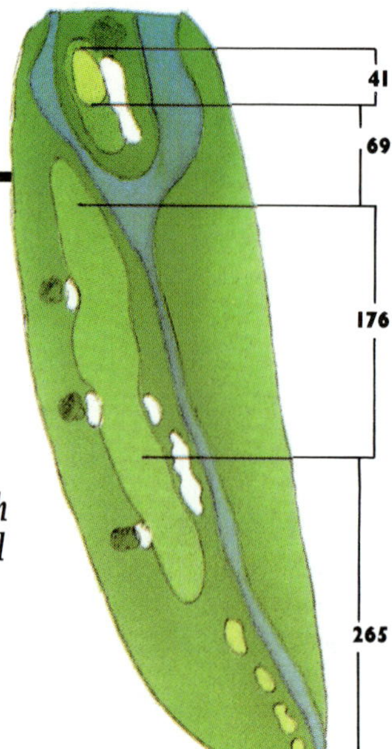

The right-center of the fairway is favored for both the tee shot and the second shot. Laying up with the second will leave a short chip-shot to the island green.

3

**Par 3
202 yards**

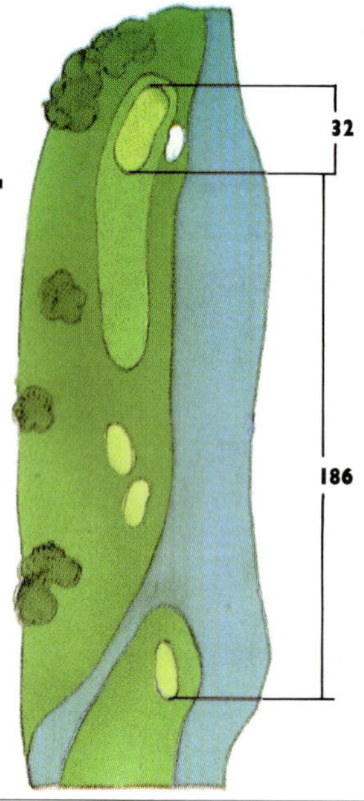

The hole plays the most difficult with the pin placed on the back right corner of the green. Strong winds will make club selection difficult.

4

**Par 4
459 yards**

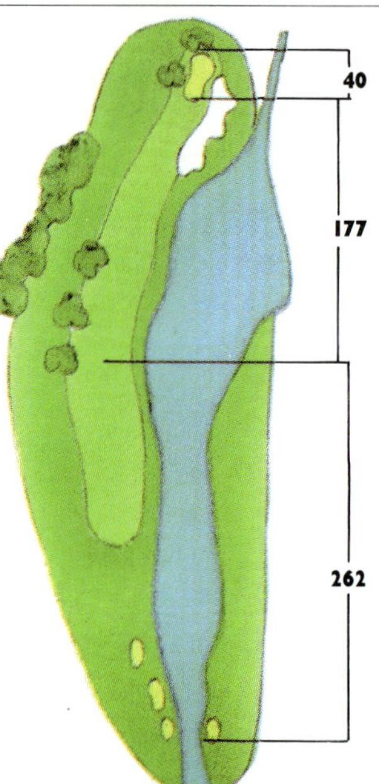

The length of the hole is increased with prevailing headwind. A big drive must be followed with a long shot into a small green set in among a grove of sycamore trees.

5

**Par 5
534 yards**

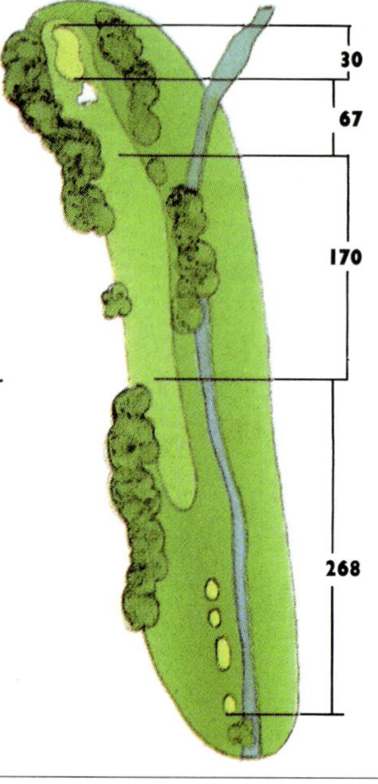

Three well played shots are the only way to reach this green. The putting surface is elevated and fronted by large bunkers.

6

**Par 4
425 yards**

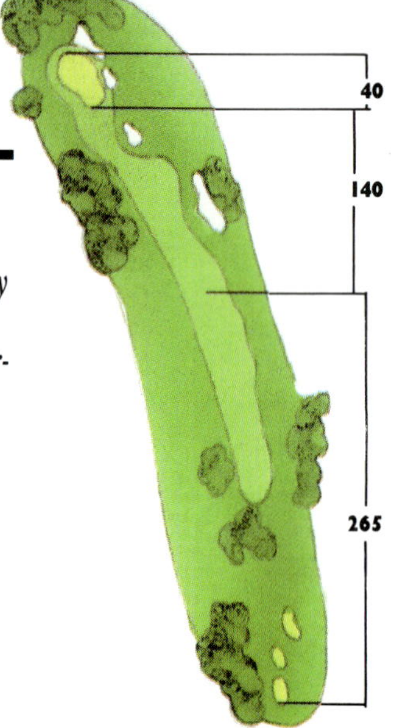

The 6th plays uphill and is well defined by trees on both sides. By favoring the right side of the fairway, the players will have an open shot to the green.

7

**Par 4
449 yards**

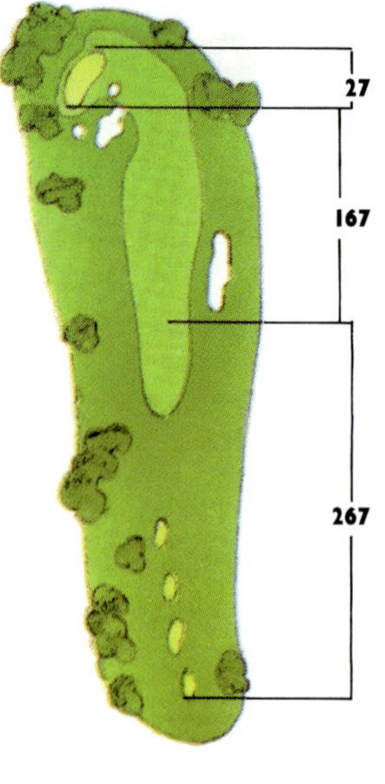

Rock out-croppings divide the fairway. Pin placement determines which fairway to play. Rugged terrain lies along the left side of the fairway and beyond the green.

8

**Par 3
232 yards**

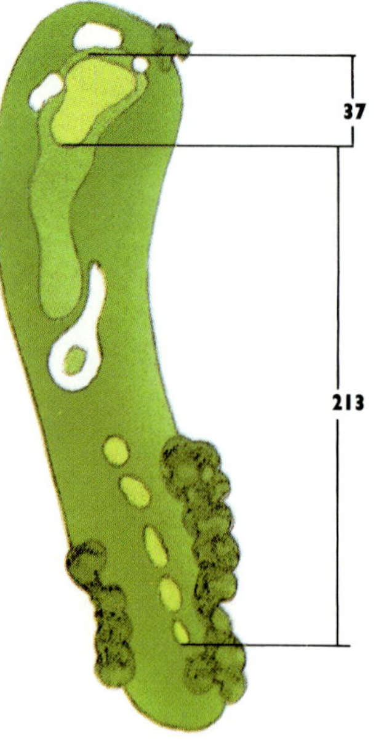

Players will be content with par on this long par 3. The tee sits well above the hillside green. The terrain slopes from left to right.

9

**Par 4
424 yards**

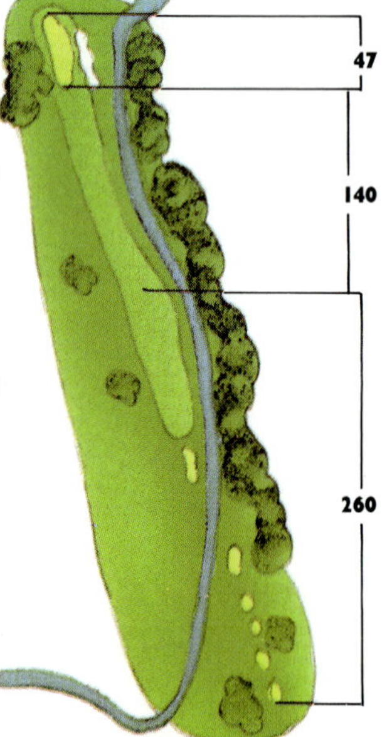

The creek along the right side of the fairway will catch any shots played too closely to that side. A short iron into the long narrow green will have to be tight for the birdie.

10

Par 4
385 yards

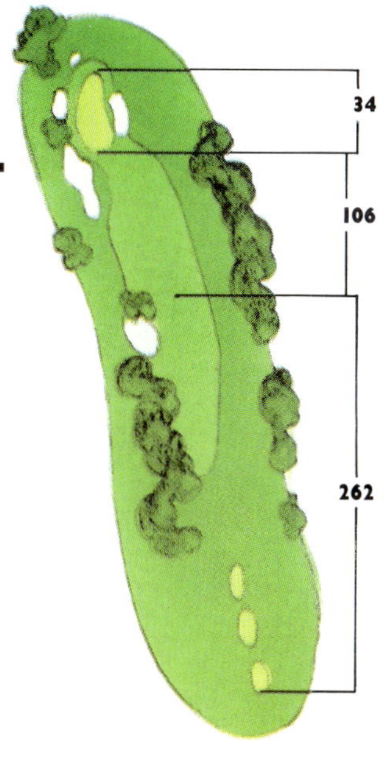

The bunker along the left is the only obstacle from the tee. Pin placements on the back right of the green will be hard to get close to because of the bunker in front.

11

Par 5
522 yards

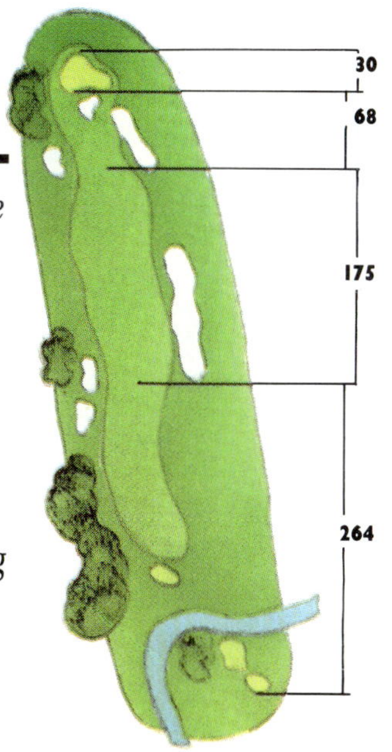

An elevated tee allows players to hit a big drive on the 11th. Bunkers that lie well short of the green protect against attempts at going for the green in two. Birdies are frequent.

12

Par 3
188 yards

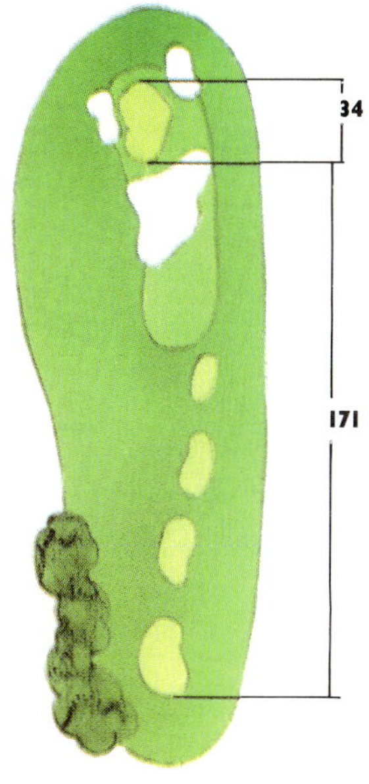

A massive bunker lies short of the green. Usually into the wind, players will be using one club more for the tee shot.

13

Par 5
541 yards

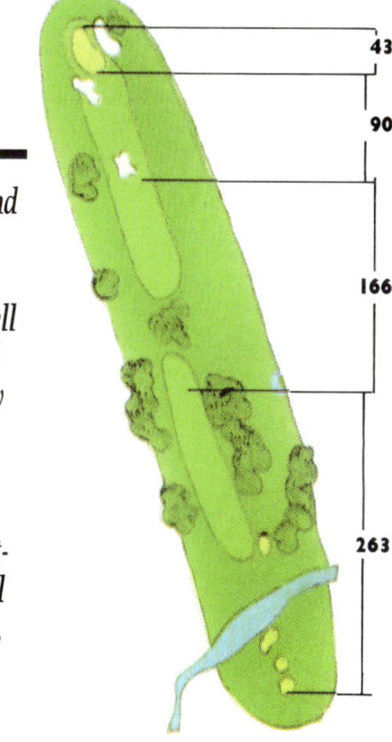

Waterfalls and ponds lie in front of the tee. Three well hit shots will be a necessity to reach the green. It's a spectacular hole for sight-seeing as well as for birdies.

14

Par 4
457 yards

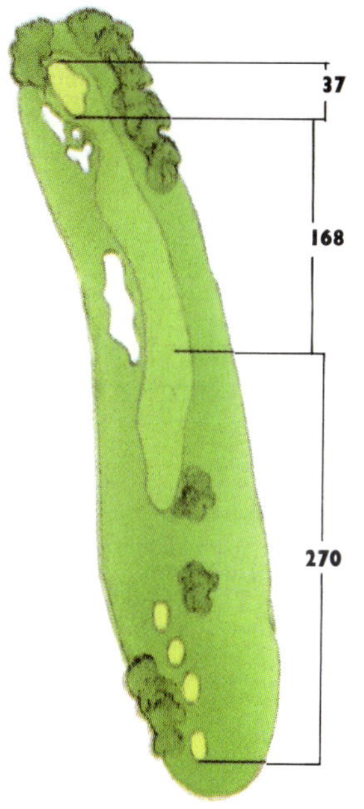

The drive must be played down the right side of the fairway for an open shot to the green. The undulating green will relinquish few putts.

15

Par 3
186 yards

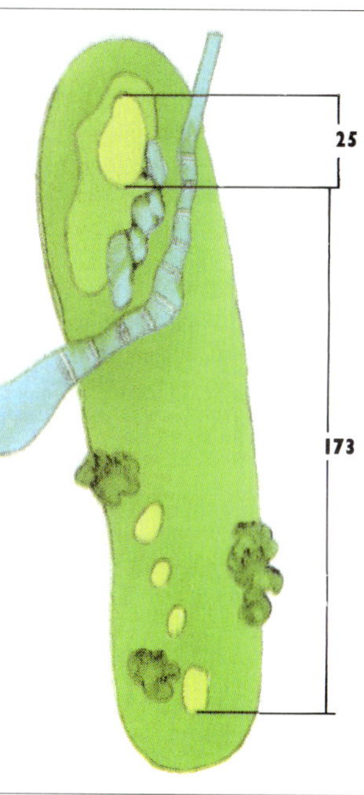

The view from the tee is majestic — seven pools and 14 water-falls gurgle in front of the green and a mountain-side wall looms beyond. The green can be very tough to hit.

16

Par 5
537 yards

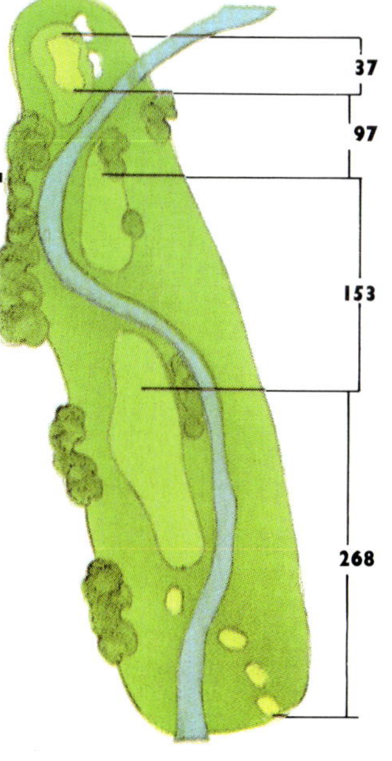

The stream must be crossed three times on the way to the green. Many players will be attempting to get the second shot as close to the green as possible.

17

Par 3
166 yards

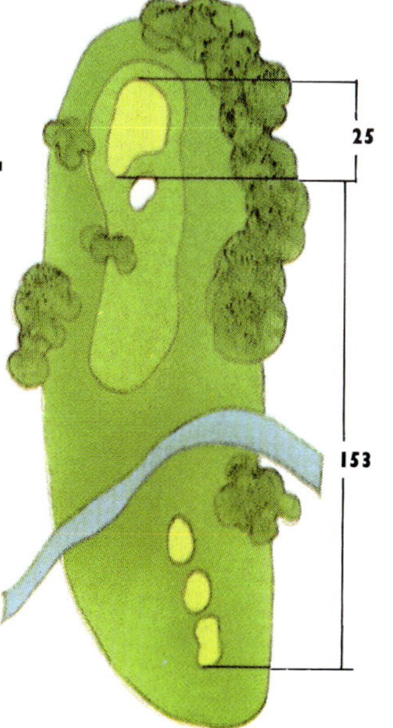

The 17th is an easy birdie hole. The elevated tee plays to the smallest green on the course. However, the banks around the green direct balls on-to the putting surface.

18

Par 4
446 yards

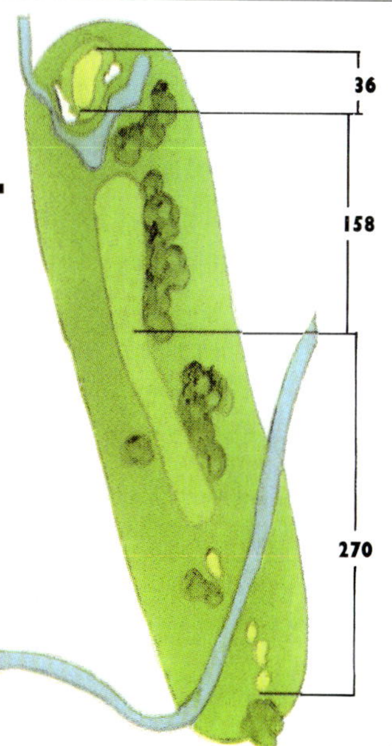

A fantastic finishing hole. The fairway slopes left-to-right. A drive down the left will bound to the center of the fairway, leaving a long approach into the protected green.

THE COURSE: RANCHO LA QUINTA C.C., LA QUINTA, CA

1996 marked the first year for THE SKINS GAME to be held at Rancho LaQuinta Country Club, Rancho LaQuinta, CA. The $540,000 event is one of the top rated television golf events of the year.

Rancho LaQuinta is the fifth home for THE SKINS GAME, which began in 1983 at Desert Highlands in Scottsdale, Arizona. After two years, Bear Creek Golf Club in Murrieta, California became its second home in 1985. The PGA West TPC Stadium Course in La Quinta, California had hosted THE SKINS GAME from 1986 to 1991 when it moved to BIGHORN Golf Club.

Rancho LaQuinta features a Robert Trent Jones, Jr. designed golf course covering 7,068 yards from the championship tees and par is 72.

Dates:	November 30-December 1
Network:	ABC
Times:	Sat /Sun 3:30-6:00 EST
Yardage:	7,068
Par:	72
Slope:	132
Rating:	73.5
Total Purse:	$540,000
1st prize:	270,000
1995 Winner:	Fred Couples
Winning Score:	7 skins
Ticket Information:	1-619-777-7799

1

Par 4
403 yards

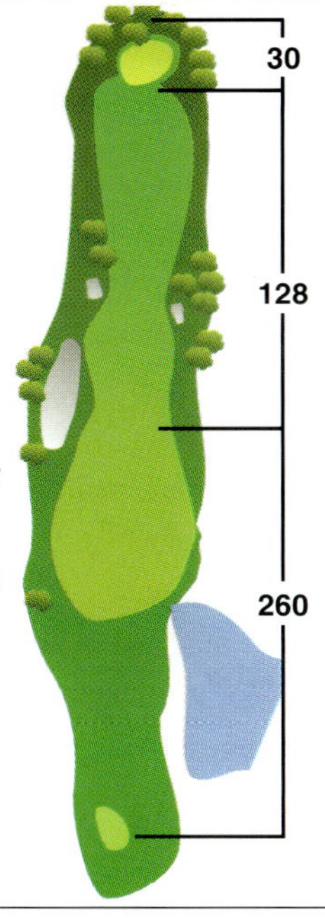

Your round begins with a straightaway par 4 that contains a series of bunkers and large mounds carefully positioned to narrow the fairway. The green is bunkerless yet well guarded by rough, swales and grassy hollows.

2

Par 3
108 yards

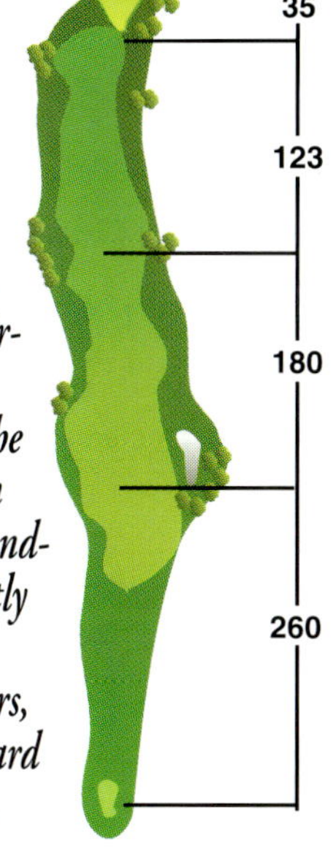

A large water hazard hugs the right side of the green on this medium length par 3. A bunker and some swales will capture missed shots to the left and long. Any pin position on the right side of the green forces golfers to flirt with the water hazard, if they desire to be aggressive.

3

Par 5
576 yards

This straightaway par 5 has no real surprises. The contours of the fairway create interesting lies. The approach to the green would come from the left of the second landing area, playing directly down the length of the putting surface. Bunkers, mounds and swales guard the long, slender green.

4

Par 3
212 yards

A small runway allows golfers to hit short and bounce onto the putting surface. The bunker right, swales and mounds left will make recovery a chore. Par will be an achievement here.

5

Par 4
443 yards

Negotiating this long hole means following a fairway that narrows in spots and is hugged by a series of bunkers along the left side. The approach will require a long iron to a deep green protected by swales left and right and a bunker left. A par will gin found in most cases here.

6

Par 4
352 yards

Water along the majority of the left side and bunkers lining the right side demand an accurate tee shot. Golfers are left with a short iron approach to a long, narrow green which is protected by water on the left side and a swale on the right. Strategy and accuracy are a must on this hole.

7

Par 4
431 yards

From the seventh tee you face a dogleg left with a series of bunkers that squeeze the driving area. Those wanting to avoid the bunkers can play safe to a landing area on the right, leaving themselves a considerably longer approach shot. The second shot calls for a middle iron to an elevated green with a large bunker on the left side.

8

Par 5
584 yards

Number eight calls for a tee shot down the left side to give golfers a view of what remains to the hole. The second shot demands a long carry over bunkers or a lay up to the lower portion of the fairway. The large green is tightly guarded by bunkers on all sides. This hole should produce a few birdies.

9

Par 4
446 yards

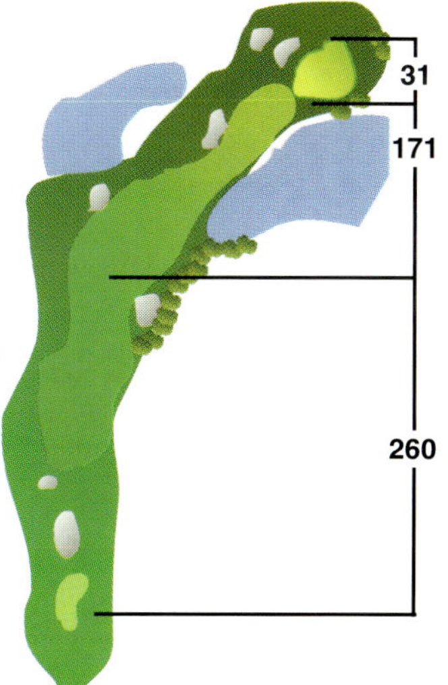

This dogleg bends around a bunker and lake that guards the green and last 120 yards of fairway. Pin placements on the right of the green will require precision for a birdie opportunity.

231

10

Par 5
538 yards

Providing a fast start on the back nine, the prevailing wind on this hole will assist golfers to reach the green in two. Large bunkers are well positioned and the green contains notice-able contours. Birdies and pars will be plen-tiful here.

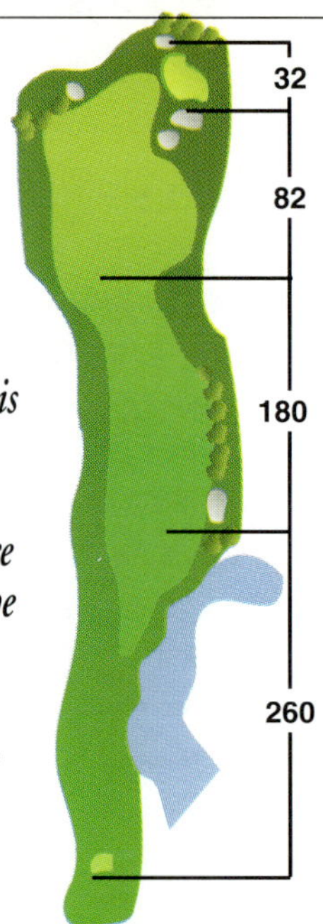

11

Par 4
403 yards

A perfect tee shot is required on this long par 4. Golfers are left with a long second shot to a large green sur-rounded by bunkers, swales and grassy hollows. Par is a good score here.

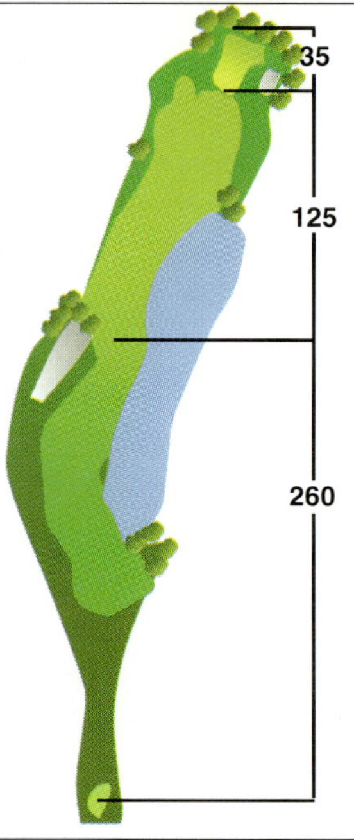

12

Par 3
149 yards

Neatly tucked in a grove of citrus trees, this short par 3 offers a precise challenge. The small green mountains slopes and contours and is well defended by bunkers and hollows.

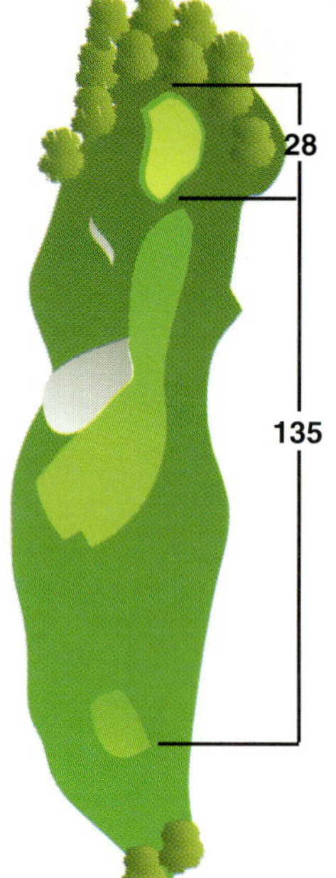

13

Par 4
360 yards

Golfers should not let their guard down on this short par 4. A large bunker right of the fairway comes into play off the tee. The small elevated green adds to the challenge, as it is severely sloped on all sides. Pay attention here from the start.

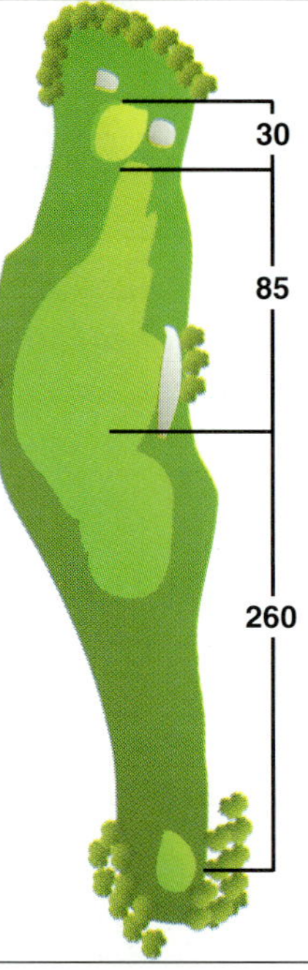

14

Par 5
549 yards

This par 5 features a landing area guarded by a huge bunker down the right side on the tee shot. Long hitters may gamble for the chance of hitting the green in two.

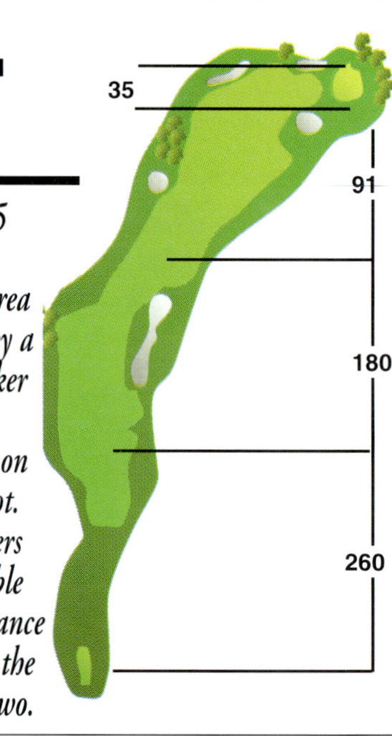

15

Par 3
219 yards

This hole will require a fairway wood for most players. The large, receptive green gives golfers the opportunity to reach in regulation. Golfers playing at the pin placed on the right side of the green will be facing a large bunker to carry. Par would be acceptable all day long here.

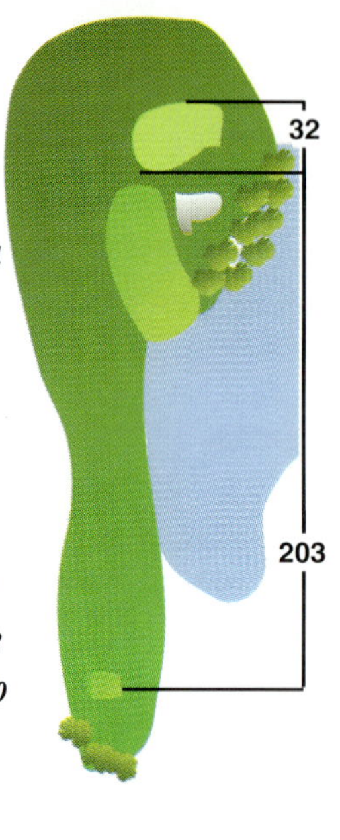

16

Par 4
424 yards

The tee shot must avoid a large lake and fairway bunker left and a lone bunker right. A mid-dle to long iron is required to an elevat-ed sloping green. The sixteenth is an excel-lent beginning of the homestretch.

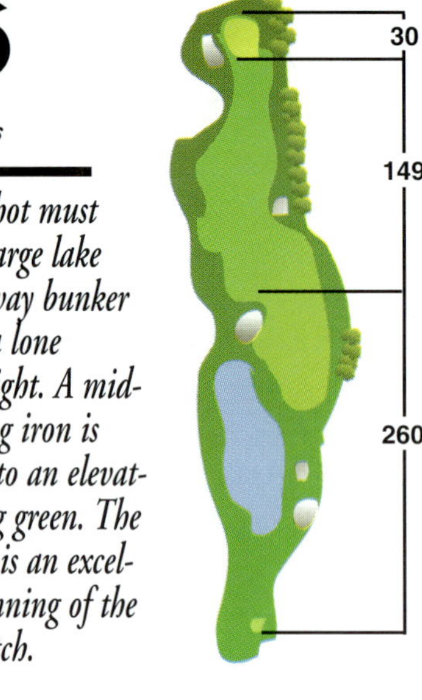

17

Par 3
187 yards

Playing downhill across a lake to a small green, seventeen is a dramatic and chal-lenging hole. Wind will be a factor in club selection. The green surface has noticeable contours lending itself to interesting breaks. Well positioned tee shots may lead to a birdie opportunity.

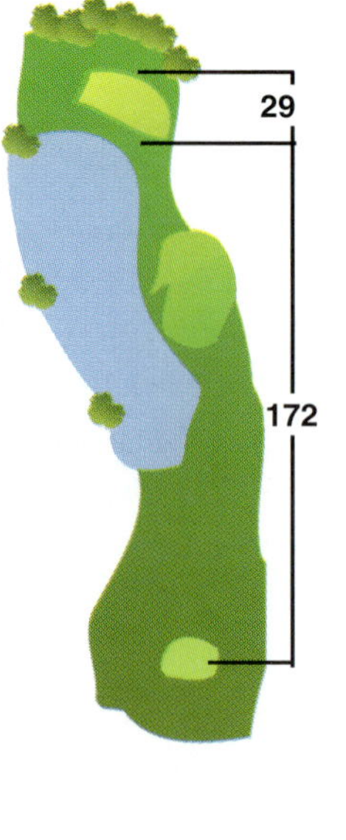

18

Par 5
561 yards

Long hitters will be pleased to find an absence of fairway bunkers on the drive, only to encounter the lake in front guarding the green. Those hitting the green in tow will be rewarded, but missed shots will find tragedy. Most golfers will play safely down the left side and onto the green in three. This hole will certainly make or break a good round.

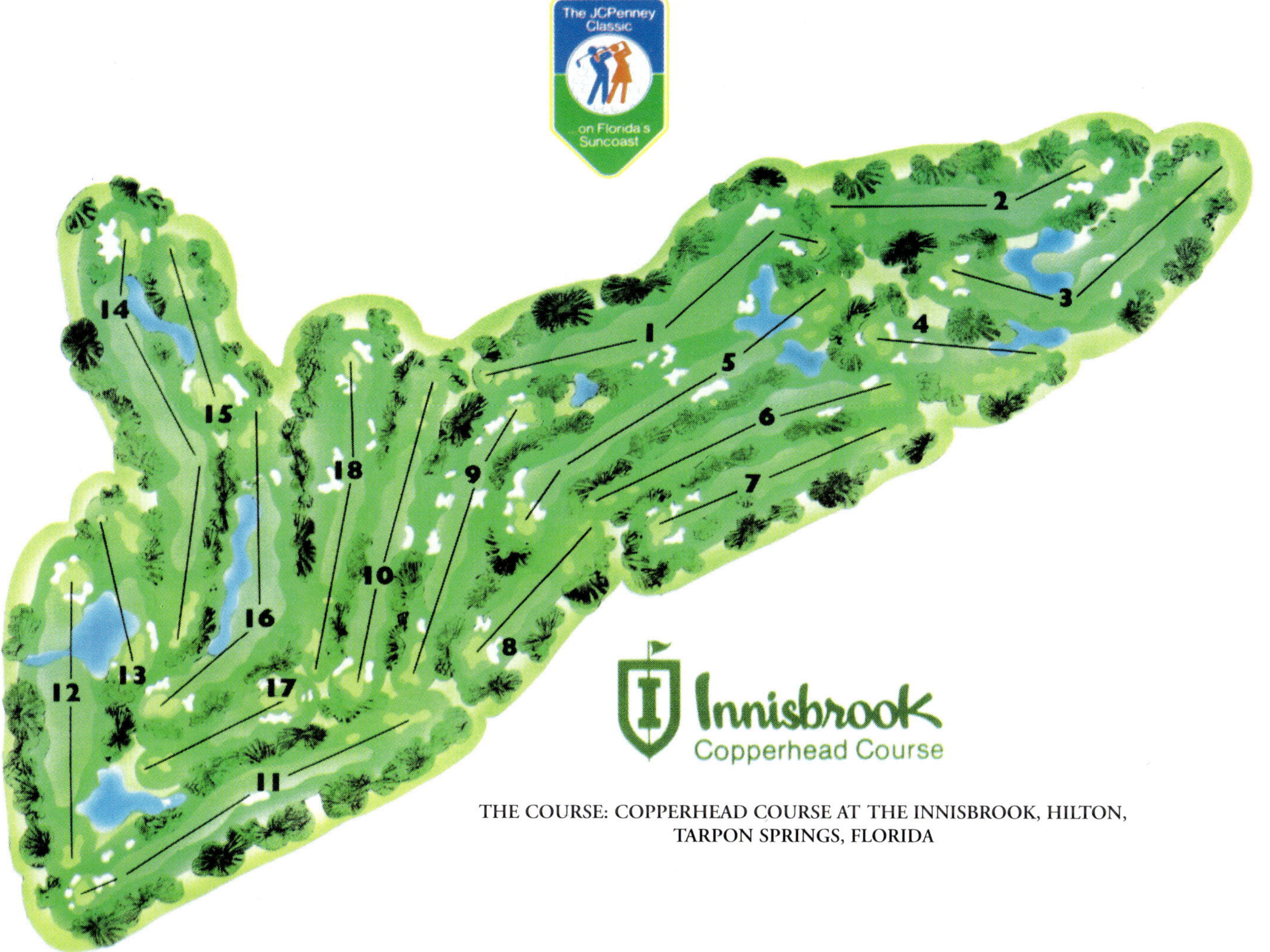

THE COURSE: COPPERHEAD COURSE AT THE INNISBROOK, HILTON, TARPON SPRINGS, FLORIDA

Golf Week has rated Innisbrook's Copperhead Golf Course as one of Florida's greatest courses; Golf Digest ranked Copperhead one of "America;s Greatest" gold courses. For the Fifth year running, Innisbrook has been the home of the JC Penney mixed team format golf tournament. Formerly held at Bardmoor Country Club in Largo, Florida (1977 Through 1989), the event pairs together players from both the PGA TOUR® and LPGA TOUR® to compete on the lush, tree-lined fairways of Copperhead. Large sugar-sand bunkers are generously placed throughout the course, which also features several 80-foot elevations and costly water hazzards.

The unique format of the tournament is a year-end highlight for both TOURS. The Pinehurst format dictates the rules of play: Each memeber of the team hits off the tee and plays his or her partner's ball on the second shot. From the second shot, they decided which ball is in better position and then alternate shots for the remainder of the hole with that one ball. The winning strategy will take best advantage of each other's talents,

Dates:	December 5-8, 1995
Network:	ABC & ESPN
Times:	TBA
Yardage:	7,054
Par:	71
Slope:	135
Rating:	73.5
Total Purse:	$900,000
1st Prize:	$162,500 each
1995 Winner:	TBD, Davis Love III /Bety Danial
1995 Winning Score:	TBD, R57 (66,65,63,63)
Principal Charitable Beneficiary:	JCPenney Classic Charities
Charitable Benefits to Date:	Over $8.4 million in 18 years
Ticket Information:	1-813-942-5566
Resort Information:	1-813-942-2000

1

Par 5
540 yards

A double dogleg par 5 for the opening hole. The teeing area sits deep within the trees. A generous fairway eases the pressure of the first drive.

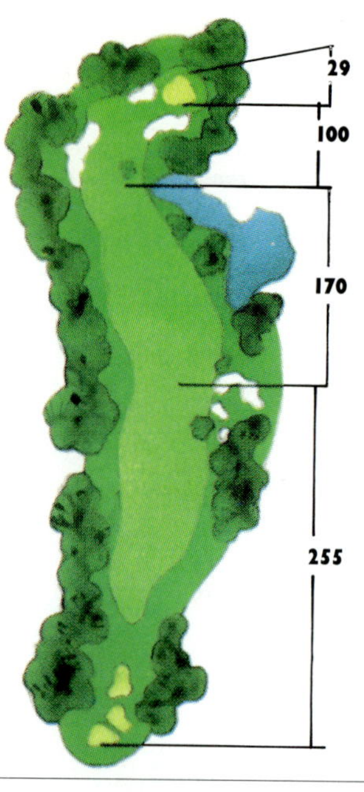

2

Par 4
403 yards

Players will be playing their drives down the right side. The elevated green is narrow and protected by bunkers on the right.

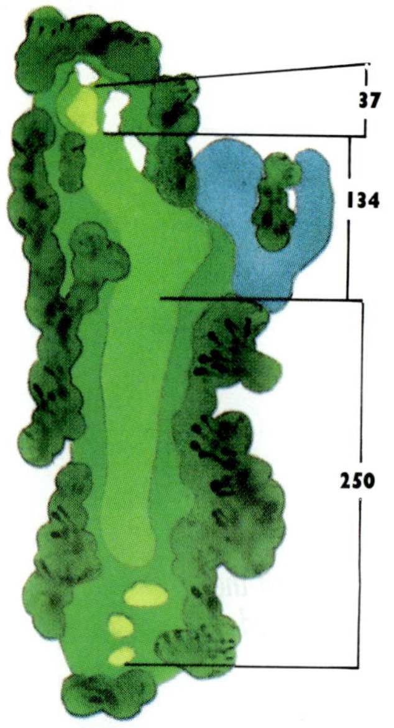

3

Par 4
436 yards

A long hole that can be slightly shortened at the dogleg. But care must be taken to avoid the water. The rolling putting surface is set tightly within trees and bunkers.

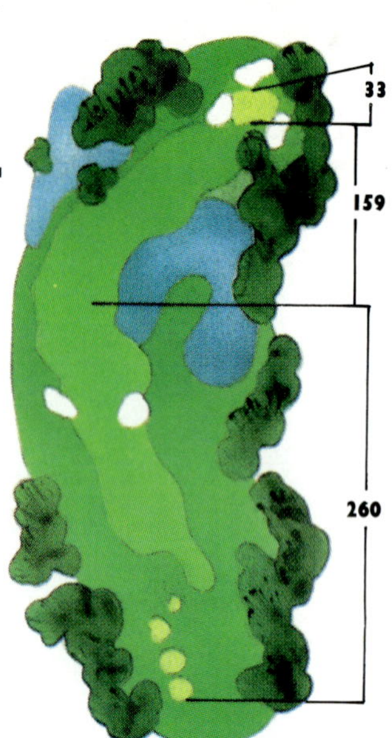

4

Par 3
165 yards

The view from the tee shows bunkers abound around the green. Club selection is important in order to get the ball close to the hole.

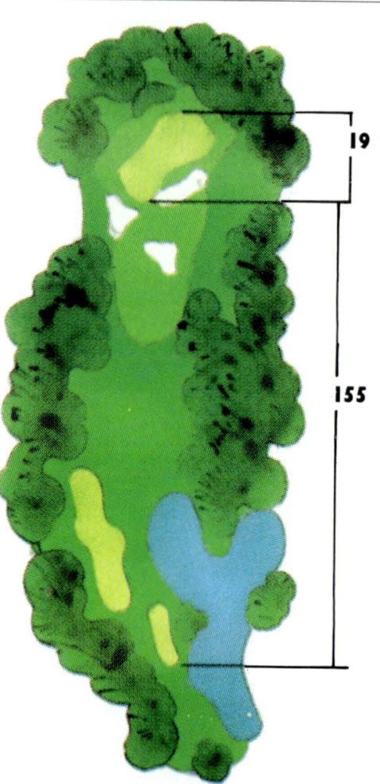

5

Par 5
539 yards

Uphill and narrow the entire way to the green. The players will be aiming their drives to the right center of the fairway. The second shot must be clear of the pine for the approach.

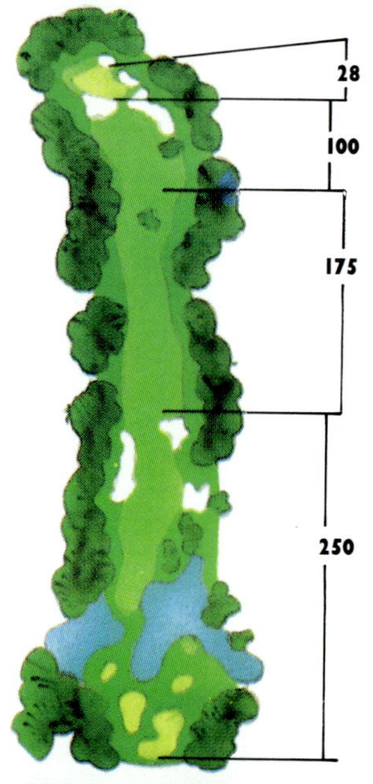

6

Par 4
459 yards

The longest and most difficult par 4 on the course. A long drive is necessary to be able to reach the large, elevated green.

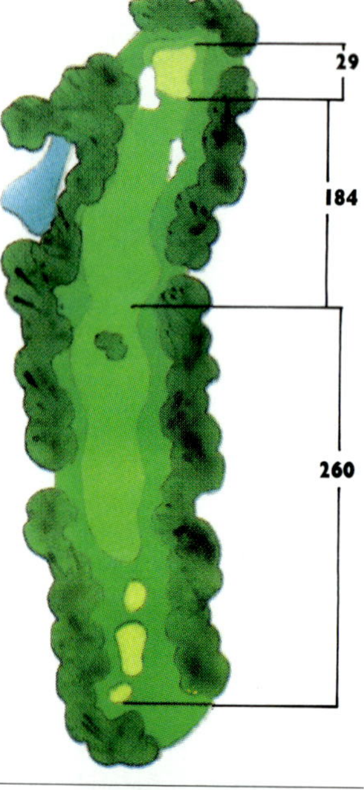

7

Par 4
385 yards

The right side of the fairway is favored for the best angle on the approach. Trees and bunkers on both sides tighten up the requirements for the second shot.

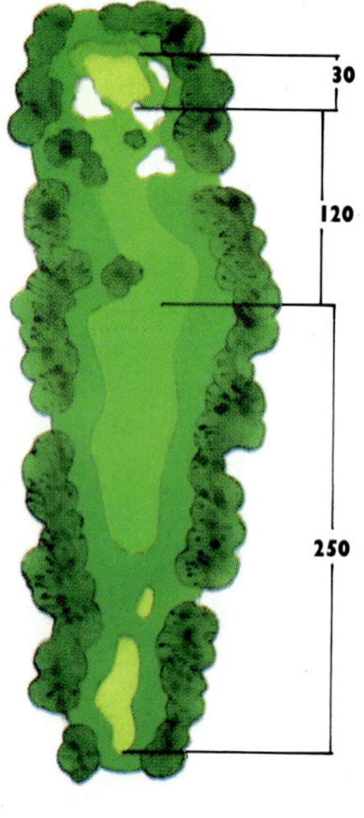

8

Par 3
235 yards

A fairway wood or long iron may be necessary to reach this big par 3. The pines reach in from the right. Club selection is important in order to avoid long putts.

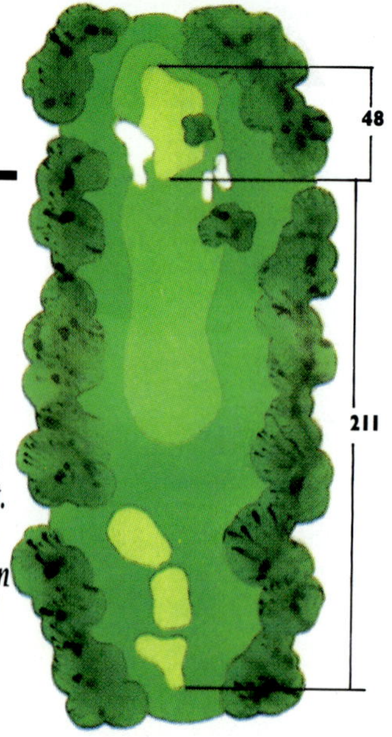

9

Par 4
426 yards

It's long, uphill and well bunkered. Besides that, this par 4 is simple. Players will favor the right side and hit a high, soft approach.

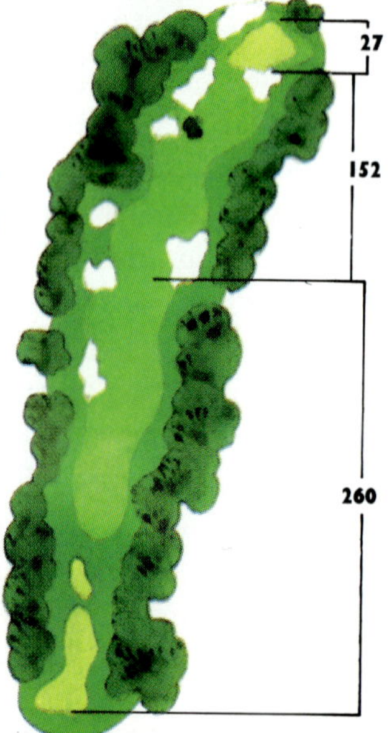

10

Par 4
451 yards

The fairway bunker and the two trees can hinder the approach if the drive is not hit past them. Approach shots are best left short of the hole to leave an uphill putt.

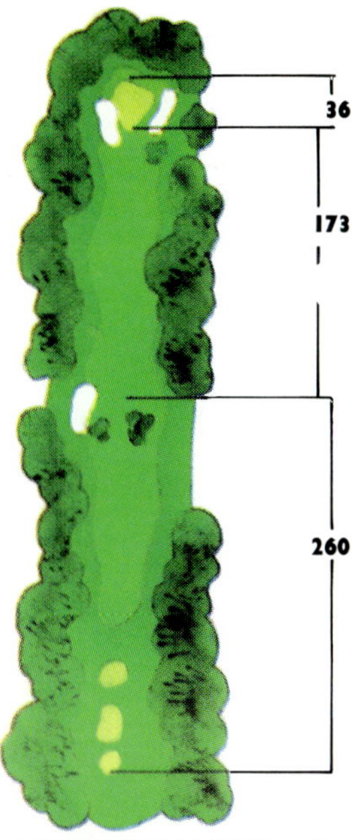

11

Par 5
552 yards

The fairway bends slightly to the left creating an urge for players to keep the ball to that side. Three shots are needed to reach the green with the third played over a large bunker.

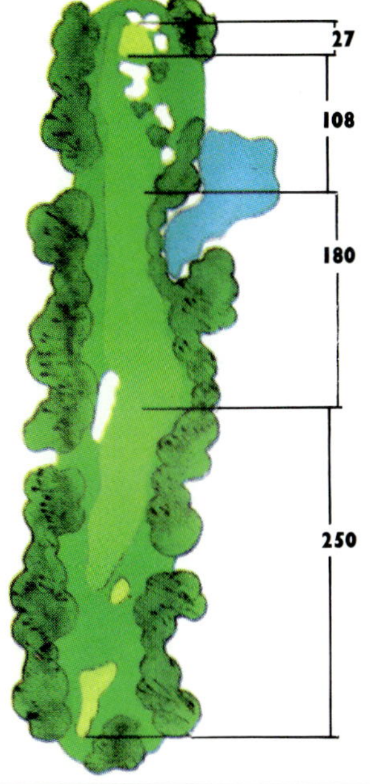

12

Par 4
382 yards

Players will be backing off their drives in order to keep short of the pond. The second shot must be played over the water to a well bunkered, undulating green.

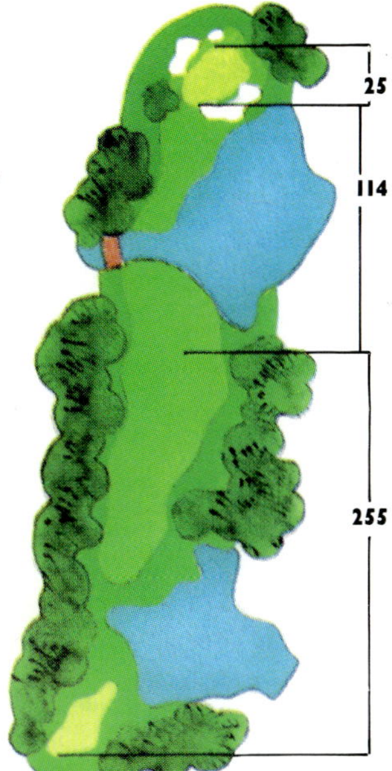

13

Par 3
175 yards

A fade from the left side will help to keep the ball from getting wet. The short, two-tiered green requires accuracy.

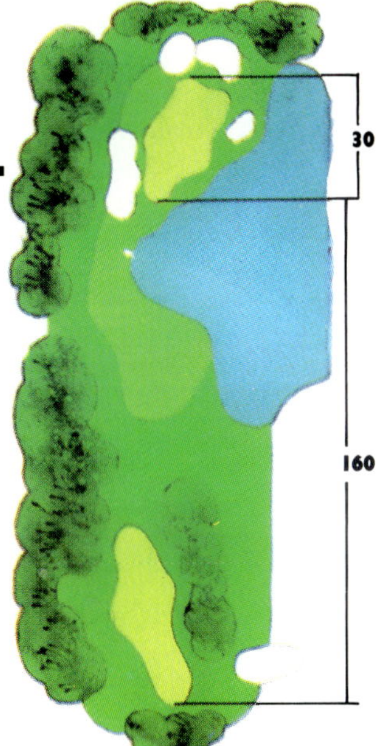

14

Par 5
571 yards

The double dogleg demands three well-placed shots to get to the green — only a few will get home in two. Water and the largest bunker on the course protect the undulated green.

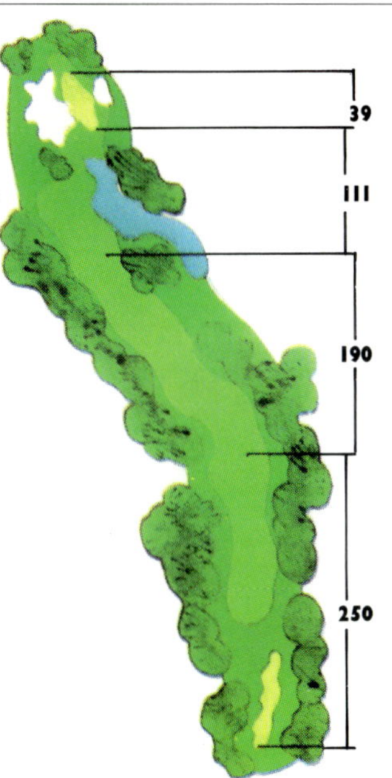

15

Par 3
212 yards

The tee sits above the putting surface. At 212 yards, the tee shot must be hit accurately to avoid the surrounding bunkers.

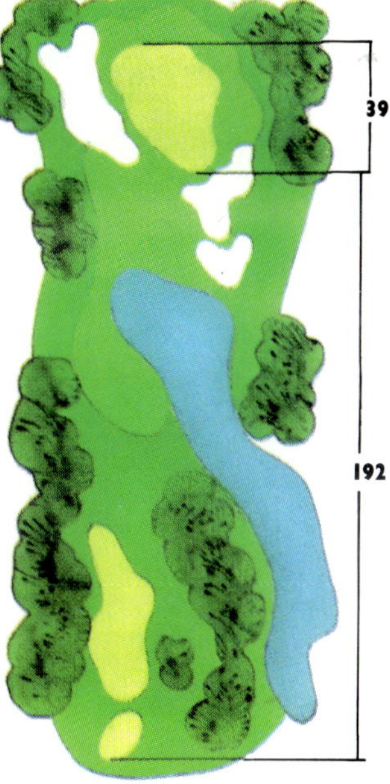

16

Par 4
465 yards

Control off the tee is very important to keep from finding the water or trees. The small green is set among the pines with protecting bunkers.

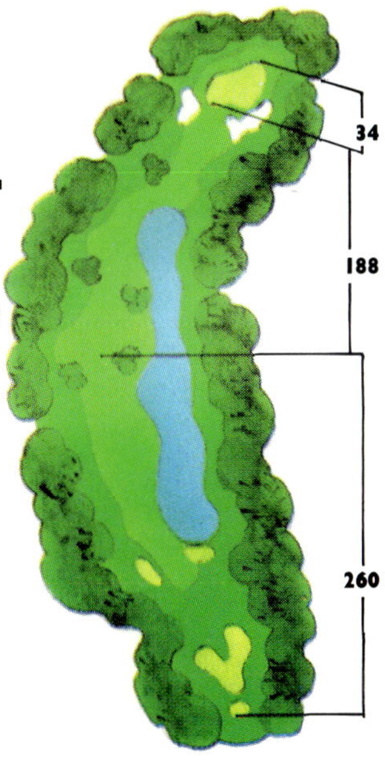

17

Par 3
211 yards

Pin placements can make this an exceptionally tough hole. Players will be concerned with the winds that are stronger above the tree-tops.

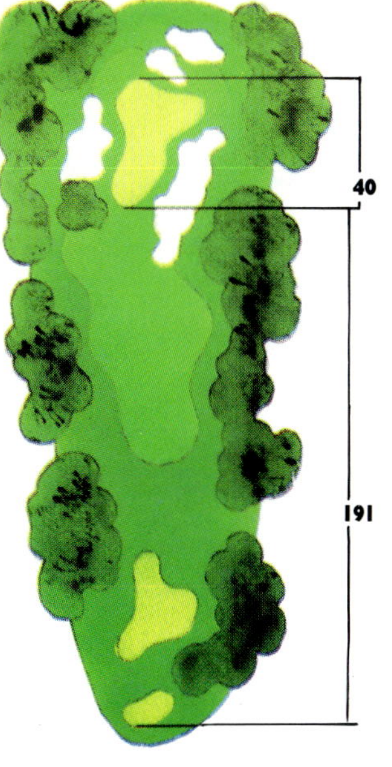

18

Par 4
424 yards

A formidable finishing hole. Narrow fairway dictates directional control on both the drive and the approach. The large, forward sloping green can produce difficult putting.

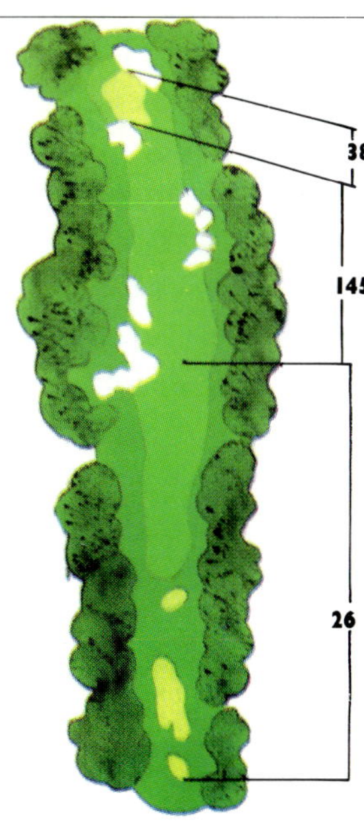

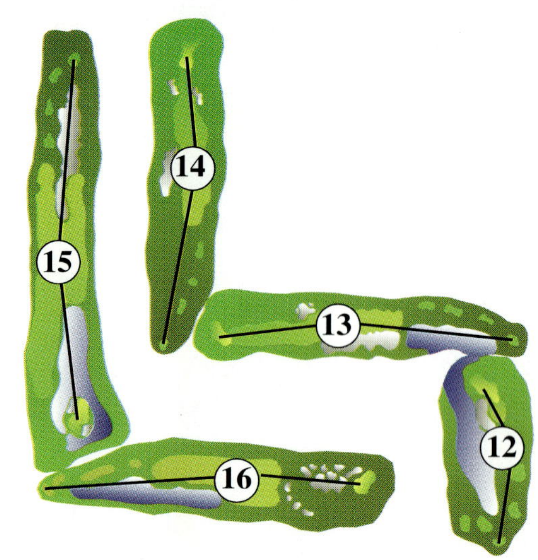

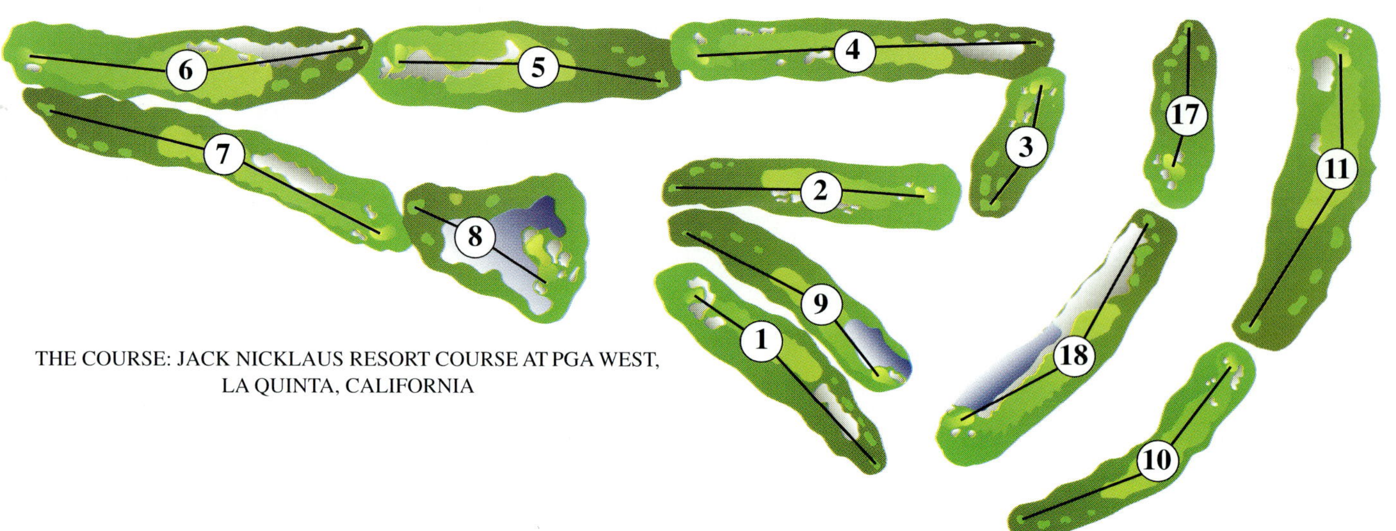

THE COURSE: JACK NICKLAUS RESORT COURSE AT PGA WEST,
LA QUINTA, CALIFORNIA

*T*he Diners Club Matches is in its third year as the season-ending team match play championship for each of golf's three major professional tours. Held at PGA WEST for the first two years, the Diner Club Matches gathers the PGA TOUR, Senior PGA TOUR and LPGA Tour at one site for a unique two-person team competition for three separate titles.

Sixteen teams each for the senior PGA TOUR and LPGA Tour title. The first member on each team will qualify based on winning a current major championship, significant predetermined tournaments, sponsor exemptions, or the money standings. That player will then select a partner not otherwise qualified.

The Diners Club Matches helps benefit the VIVA Foundation, a non-profit organization founded by KSL recreation Corporation. KSL is one of the largest owner operators of golf facilities including PGA WEST.

Dates:	December 12-15
Network:	ABC & ESPN
Times:	TBA
Yardage:	7,126 (PGA TOUR)
	6,884 (Senior PGA TOUR)
	72
Par:	$1.8 million
1995 Winner:	PGA TOUR:
	Jeff Maggert, Tim McGovern
	Senior PGA TOUR:
	Dave Eichelberger, Ray Floyd
Team Prizes:	$250,000 each
Principal Charitable	
Beneficiary:	VIVA Foundation
Ticket Information:	1-800-307-6444

1

Par 4
401 yards

This hole requires an accurate second shot to the green avoiding the bunkers which almost completely surround the green. You need to have Jacks or better for this opener.

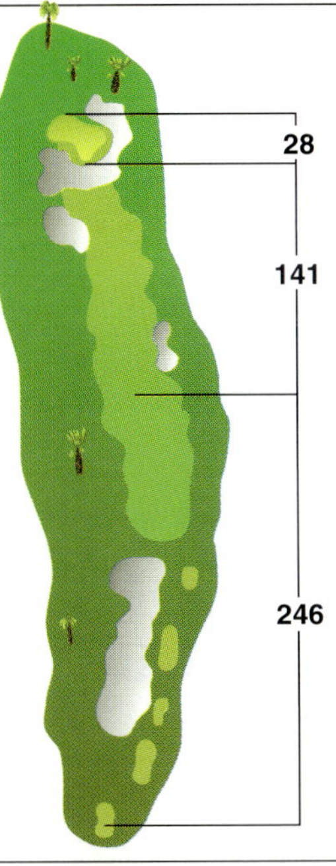

2

Par 4
440 yards

On this straight away hole length is important off the tee to an elevated fairway leaving a middle to long iron to the green. Keep the drive to the left on top with plenty of gun.

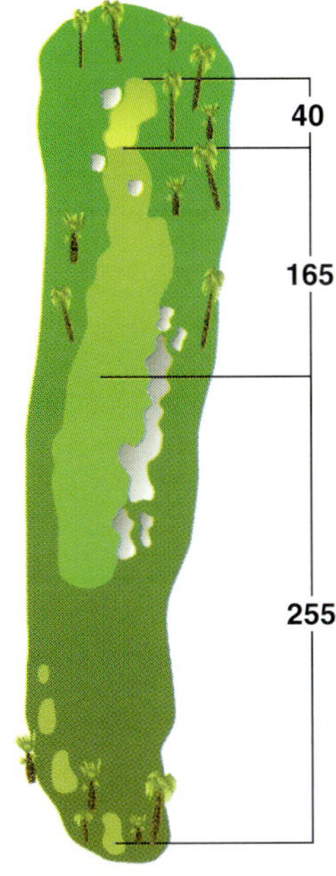

3

Par 3
187 yards

This hole calls for a middle to long iron shot. A player should aim for the pyramid mound behind the green.

4

Par 5
542 yards

This hole tempts a long hitter to go for it in two. Keep the drive up on the ridge and let it run. If you do go for it, don't try to run it up. Placement may be key, not distance.

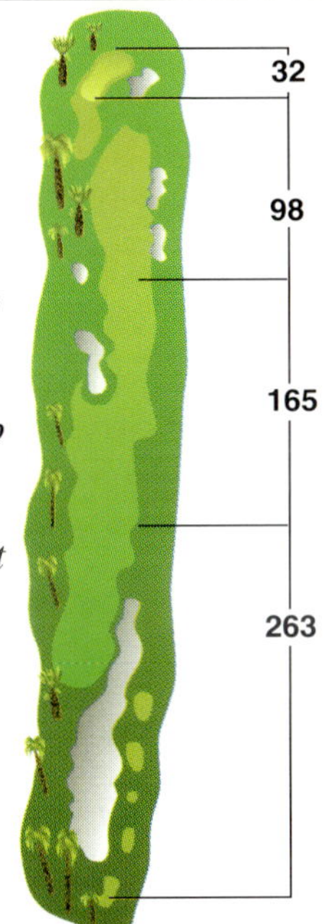

5

Par 4
357 yards

This hole is most deserving of its name with a split fairway to the left and to the right. An accurate second shot is a must with deep bunkers surrounding the green.

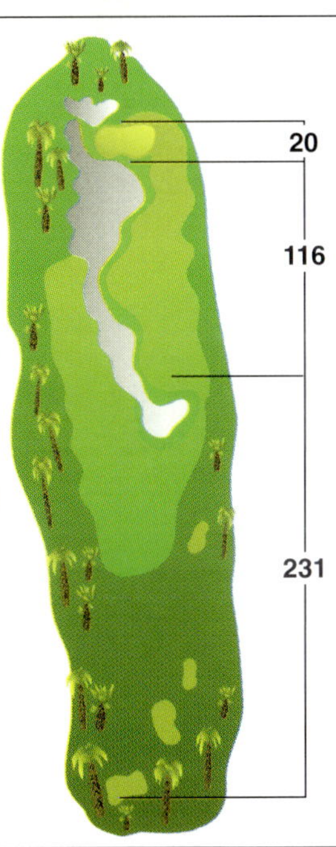

6

Par 4
457 yards

On this hole, length is important. Keep the drive to the left of the bunkers on the right leaving a middle to long iron shot to the green but stay left avoiding the jagged edge.

7

Par 5
520 yards

This short but scenic hole requires a slight fade off the tee. The second shot must be long and staight. This is an easy bridie hole but don't fall asleep or you might end up in Desert Valley on the left.

8

Par 3
164 yards

This medium to short iron hole requires a very accurate tee shot to set yourself up for birdie. The green is heavily guarded by water on three sides and a large bunker in the back. You better be sure to hit enough club or you might end up in the lilly pads.

9

Par 4
470 yards

A very long and deadly accurate tee shot is required to play the longest par 4 hole. After a long drive the player is left with a medium to long iron to the green. The player must choose to either play it safe out to the right or live dangerously over the water. Either way Jack will get his revenge.

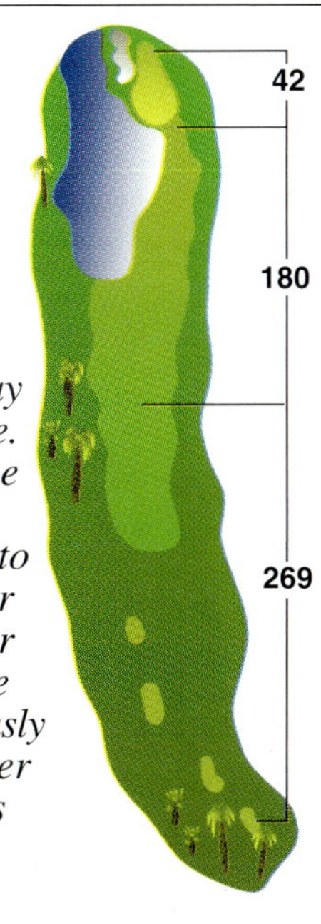

10
Par 4
364 yards

This hole requires an accurate shot with either a driver or 3 wood leaving yourself with a short iron to a very generous green. It is most important to make sure your drive stays on the plateau.

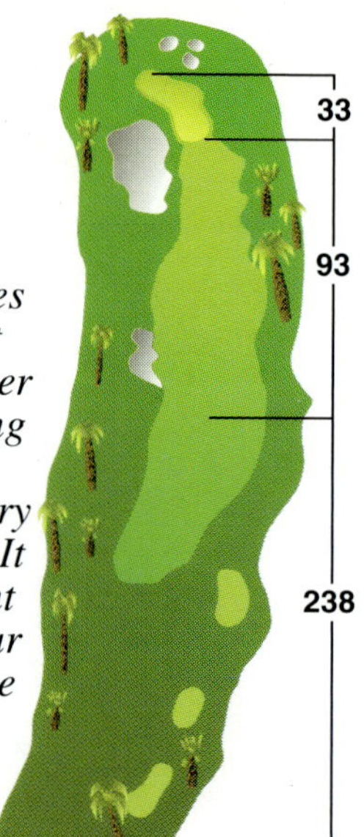

11
Par 5
525 yards

Leave nothing in the bag on your tee shot. Long and straight leaves you with an open shot to a well bunkered and contoured green. Anything left and you must face the moguls.

12
Par 3
182 yards

This hole calls for a middle iron shot. Aim for the middle of the green. There is room short and right if you must. Do not let the water lure you for it is truly a fatal attraction.

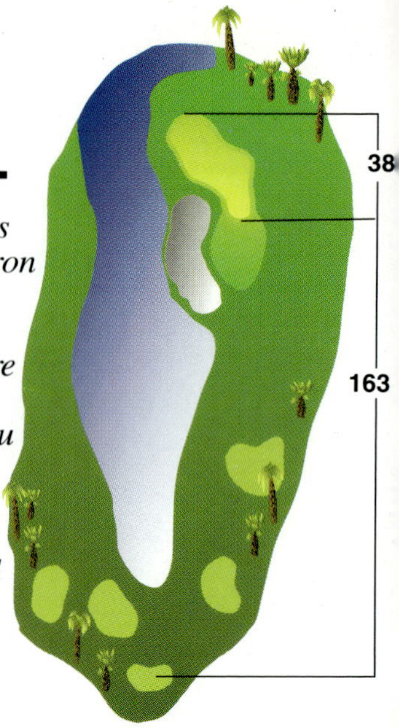

13
Par 4
417 yards

A well defined fairway bordered on the left by sand. Keep your drive down the middle. Be sure to have the right club to this elevated green surrounded by deep grass bunkers.

14
Par 4
435 yards

This hole demands a tee shot down the right hand side of the fairway avoiding the fairway bunkers left. This leaves you with a long to middle iron to a deceptively deep bowl shaped green.

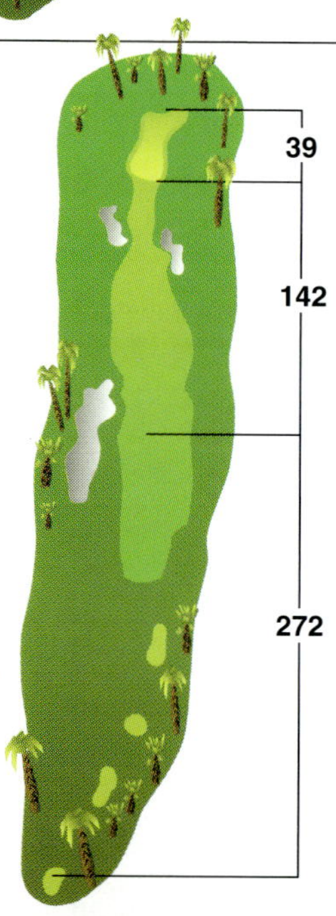

15
Par 5
561 yards

The longest hole on the course requires a tee shot to one side of the fairway bunker. A cautious lay up is required leaving you with a short iron to the long Island green.

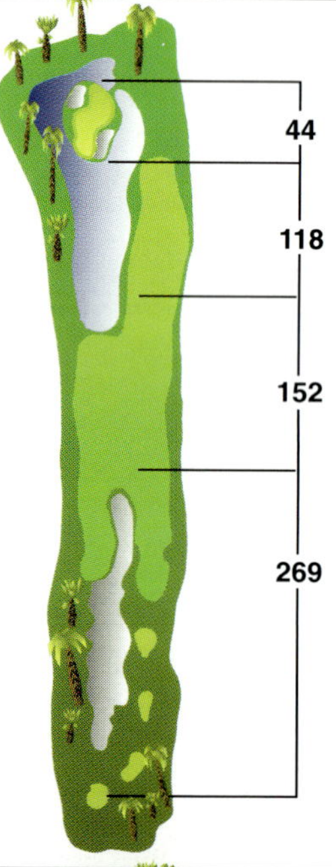

16
Par 4
436 yards

A tee shot to the left center is safest leaving you with a middle to long iron to a green guarded by sand and grass bunkers. Long hitters may go over the water shortening the hole but be sure you get past the cattails.

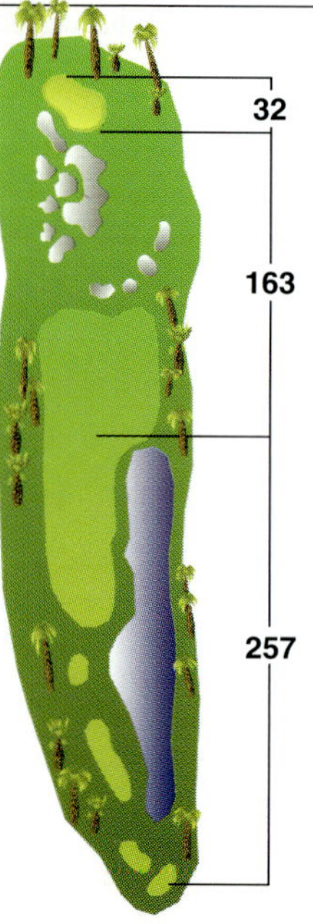

17
Par 3
210 yards

This picturesque hole demands the right club selection. Aim for the middle of the green. Bunkers front and rear combine for a fantastic mountain view.

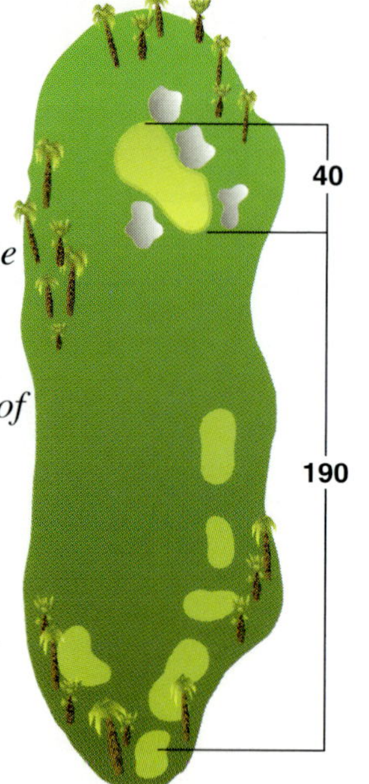

18
Par 4
458 yards

This hole requires length off the tee. Position the drive down the left center for the best angle into this double tiered gr e mounds on the left are tough but the bear trap on the right may be too much.

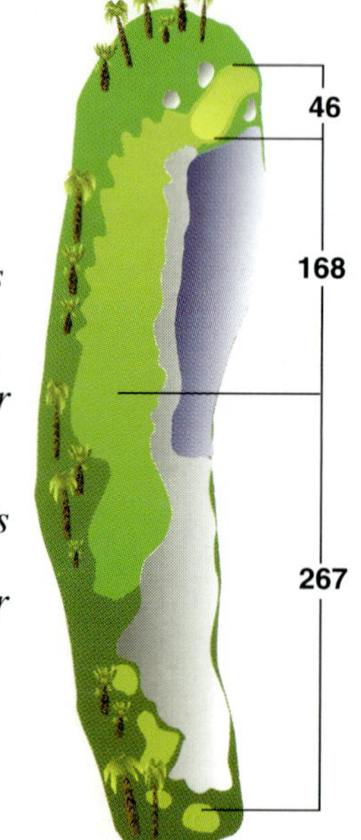

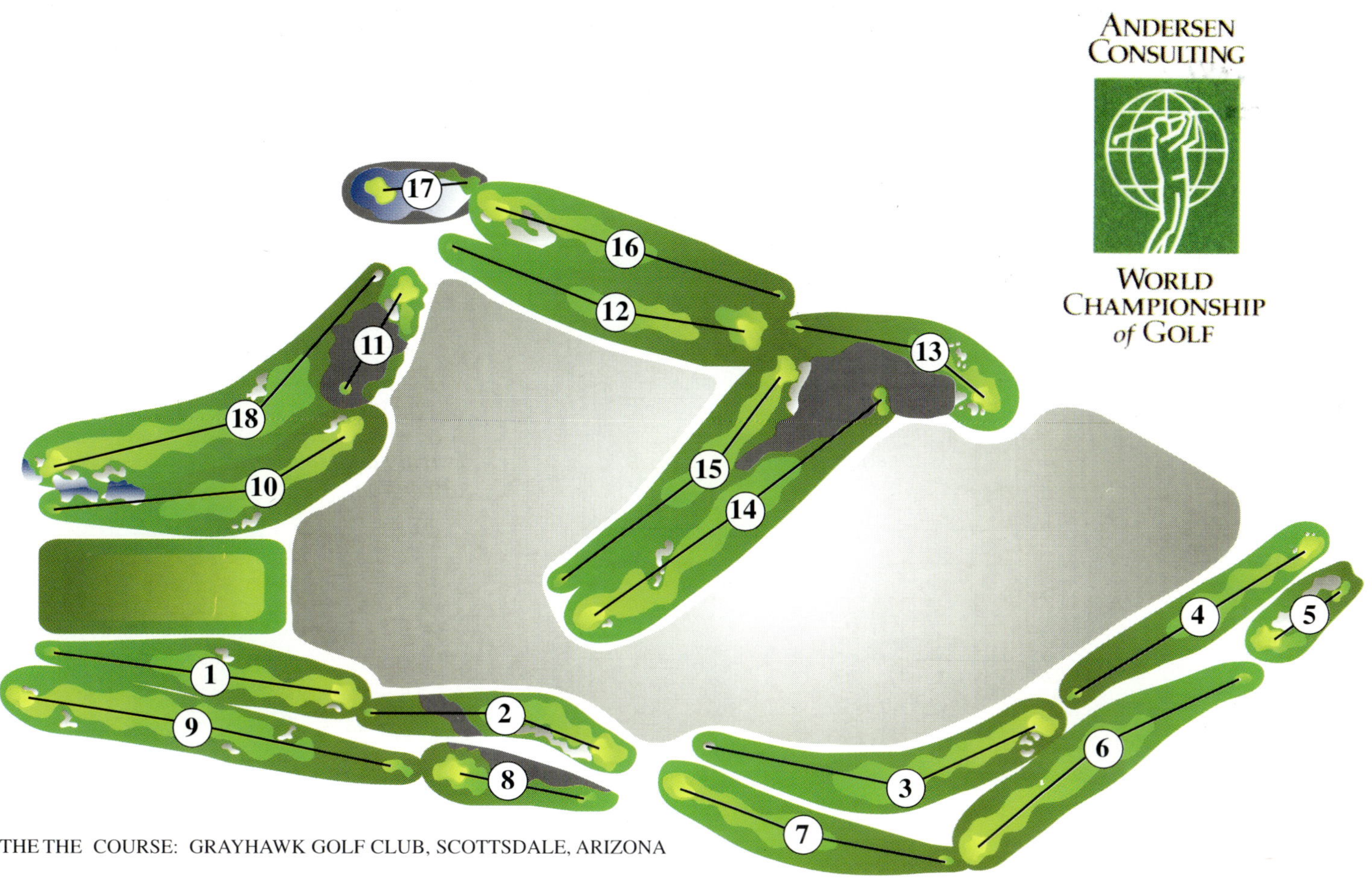

THE THE COURSE: GRAYHAWK GOLF CLUB, SCOTTSDALE, ARIZONA

The Andersen Consulting World Championship of Golf heralds a new era and spirit in international competition and cooperation among the five major professional golf Tours of the world.

Thirty-two Or the world's greatest golfers will compete in single-elimination match play at six sites in four countries and on three continents between February and December 1995 to crown a true world champion. Much will be on the line including the richest purse in golf. $3.65 million.

Four regions supply eigh players each to comprise the 32-player field. The regions are The United States. Europe. Japan and the Rest of the World. which takes in South Africa, South America, Australia, New Zealand and Fiji. Seven of the eight players for each region are invited from the final 1994 Sony Ranking, with each region receiving one sponsor's ezemption.

ANDERSEN CONSULTING
WORLD CHAMPIONSHIP OF GOLF
EVENT SCHEDULE

Japan Championship — March 2-3
Golden Palm Country Club, Kagoshima, Japan

U.S. Championship — April 22-23
Renynolds Plantation/Great Waters Course,
Lake Oconee, Georgia USA

European Championship — May 20-21
London, England

International Championship — July 29-30
Blackwolf Run/River Course, Kohler, Wisconsin, USA

World Championship — January 4-5
Grayhawk Golf Club/Talon Course, Scottsdale, Arizona, USA

10
Par 4
450 yards

The tee shot is to a split level fairway guarded on the right by two sand bunkers. A drive to the right side of the fairway will set up the best view off the green.

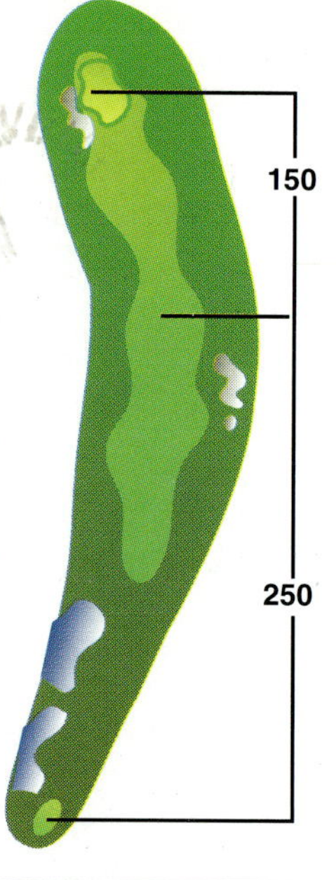

11
Par 3
168 yards

From the island tee the shot is over a dramatic canyon to a very heavily guarded green. This magnificent par three will test the nerves of all who play.

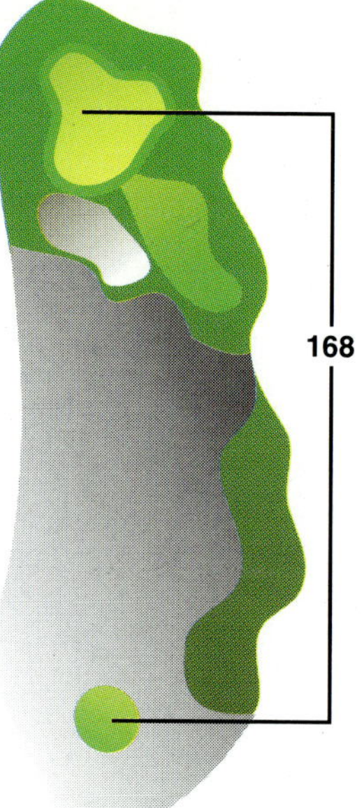

12
Par 4
445 yards

Two strong shots are required on this long par four as it will play into the predominant wind across a natural wash. Three large Ironwood trees enframe the driving area.

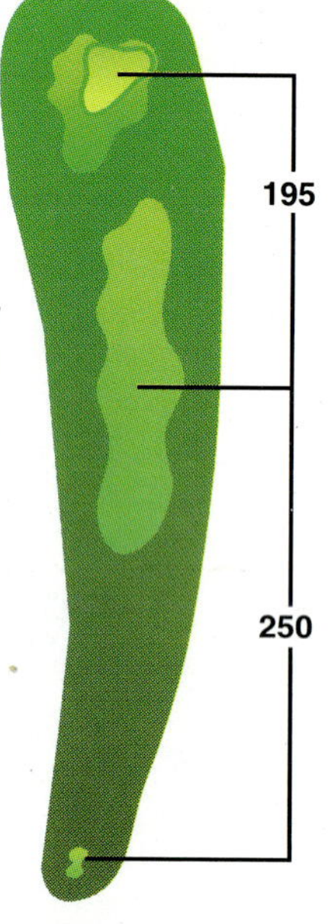

13
Par 4
305 yards

The long hitters will go for this green hoping for eagle. Most players will hit a long iron or fairway wood off the tee to the heavily bunkered landing area, setting up a shot iron the green.

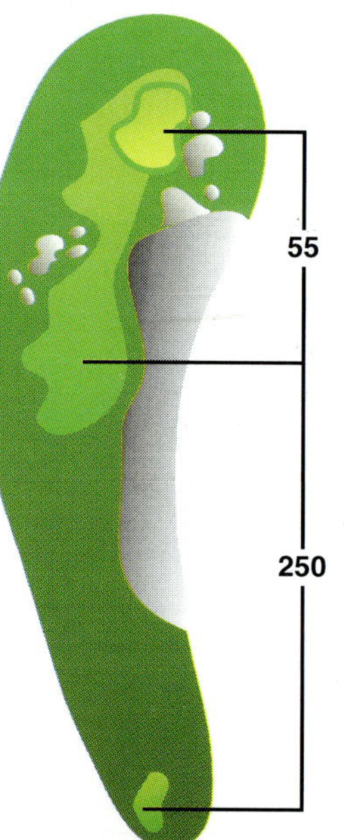

14
Par 5
525 yards

Birdies are a must on this medium length par 5. The second shot will require a decision to clear the cross bunkers, or lay up, setting up a short iron for the approach.

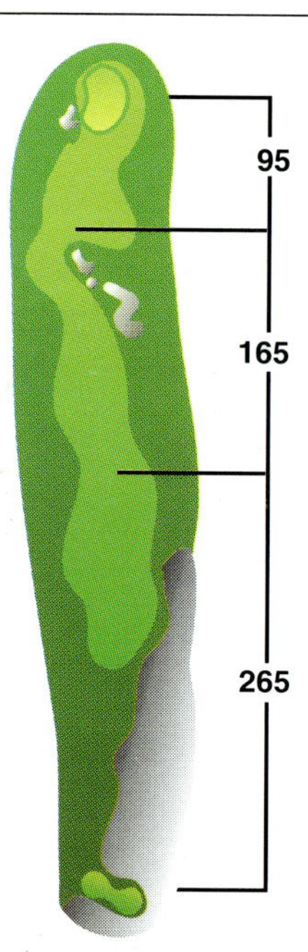

15
Par 4
451 yards

This partially blind tee shot should be played to the left side of the fairway to have the best angle to avoid the right greenside bunker for your approach.

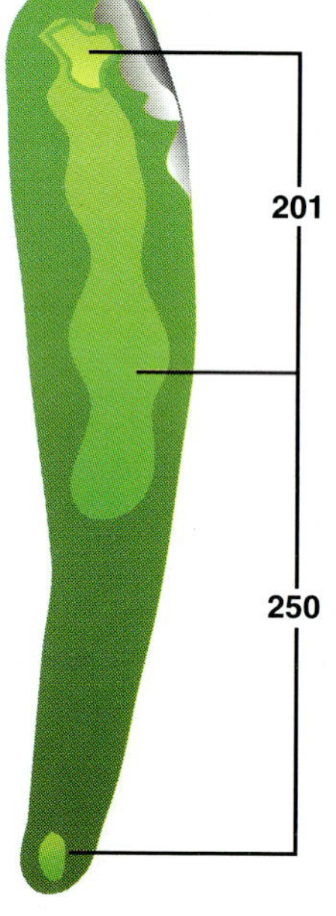

16
Par 4
420 yards

The 16th hole rises gently from tee to green with Pinnacle Peak in the back ground. The advantage of the wide driving area will set up your approach for a birdie opportunity.

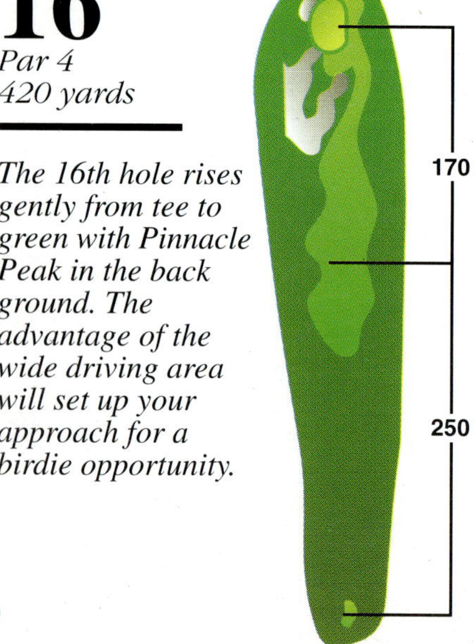

17
Par 3
130 yards

Accuracy is a must to the island green, Too much spin could bring the ball to a watery grave.

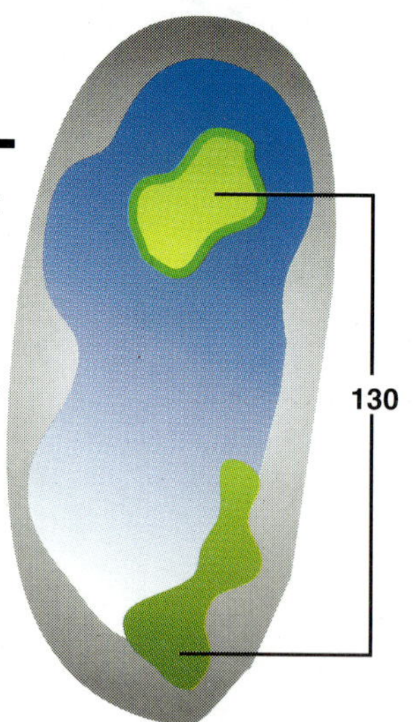

18
Par 5
575 yards

The drive needs to be close to the right side of the fairway bunker to shorten the hole. An approach shot pulled left will find one of the five waterfalls.

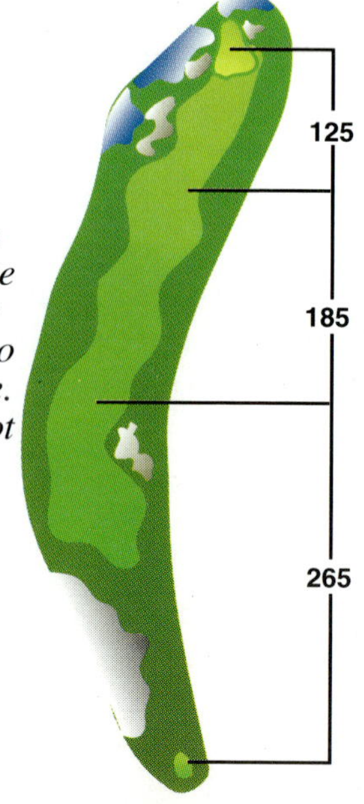